Catherine McAuley and the Tradition of Mercy

Catherine McAuley and the Tradition of Mercy

Mary C. Sullivan, RSM

UNIVERSITY OF NOTRE DAME PRESS
Notre Dame, Indiana

FOUR COURTS PRESS
Dublin, Ireland

This book was first published in the United States in 1995 by
UNIVERSITY OF NOTRE DAME PRESS
Notre Dame, Indiana 46556

Published in paperback in 2000
ISBN 0-268-02259-3 (Notre Dame)

and in Ireland by
FOUR COURTS PRESS LTD
Fumbally Lane, Dublin 8, Ireland

ISBN 1-85182-558-4 (Four Courts Press)

The paper used in this publication meets the minimum requirements of the American National Standard for Information Sciences – Permanence of paper for Printed Library Materials, ANSI Z39.48-1984.

No known portrait of Catherine McAuley was executed during her lifetime. The frontispiece is a portrait done from memory after her death. The painter and the photographer are unknown.

Library of Congress Cataloging-in-Publication Data

Sullivan, Mary C.
Catherine McAuley and the Tradition of Mercy / Mary C. Sullivan.
p. cm.
Includes bibliographical references and index.
ISBN 0-268-02259-3 (alk. paper)
1.McAuley, Catherine, 1778–1841. 2.Nuns—Ireland—Biography
3.Sisters of Mercy—History—19th century. I.Title
BX4483.8.S85 1995
271'.9202—dc20
[B] 95–12283
CIP

Printed in Great Britain by
MPG Books, Bodmin, Cornwall.

Preface

Let us be grateful for the benefits
God has conferred, and profit by
the great example which is still
fresh before our minds.

Michael Blake
Bishop of Dromore, 1833–1860

Writing on November 13, 1841, two days after the death of Catherine McAuley, Michael Blake was filled with gratitude for "the dear departed friend whom I ever esteemed and reverenced, and whose memory I shall ever esteem and reverence."

As I conclude this book, which contains manuscripts by and about Catherine McAuley (1778–1841) and commentaries on the significance of these manuscripts for a detailed understanding of her thought and activity, I am grateful to all those whose work has preceded mine and made it possible. No one assembles a book of this sort alone; rather, she is supported by all those people, known and unknown, who have contributed to the preservation and analysis of the materials she is using.

Someone like Catherine McAuley, the Irishwoman who founded the Sisters of Mercy in Dublin in 1831, will be remembered long after her death only if her contemporaries have carried on the work she created, told stories about her, and committed some of those stories to writing, and only if those who come after that generation have preserved these written materials, and engaged in active dialogue with them. Therefore, I wish, in the first place, to acknowledge the lasting gift to research about Catherine McAuley of all those women and men who wrote biographical accounts of Catherine's life in the twenty-five years immediately following her death. I wish to thank especially the early Mercy annalists and archivists who took the time to record events and who had, over the years, the good sense to preserve so many old documents, despite all the usual temptations to clean house. I am grateful as well to the many present-day archivists and others in the first Mercy communities who have shared with me not only the manuscripts and other documents in their archives, but also their time and their intimate, on-the-spot knowledge of these materials: Mary Magdalena Frisby (Dublin), Mary Celestine Stokes (Tullamore), Mary Paschal Murray (Derry), Mary Albeus Russell and Mary Dymphna Culhane (Charleville), Nessa Cullen (Carlow), Mary Pierre O'Connor (Limerick), Mary Laurentia Faherty (Athlone), Mercedes McCarthy, Mary Imelda Keena and Teresa Green (Bermondsey, London), Maíre de Barra and Mary Ignatius McCarthy (Birr),

Mary Malachy Slavin and Mary Augustine Cahill (Birmingham), and Norah Boland (Brisbane). To the current and former major superiors of the communities in Dublin, Tullamore, Charleville, Carlow, Limerick, Bermondsey, Derry, and Brisbane, who have given me permission to publish the manuscripts, annals, and autograph letters presented in this book, I am deeply grateful: without their generous collaboration this book would not have been possible. And to the communities in all the Irish and English convents I visited over the last four years, who gave me such open-handed, encouraging hospitality—including door keys, good tea, access to photocopying, and last-minute rides to the train or bus—I offer my heartfelt thanks.

The scholars who have written on Catherine McAuley over the last century and a half have contributed immensely to our knowledge of Catherine and her associates. When one prepares a book like the present one, one realizes even more the debt that is owed to those—all but one are Sisters of Mercy—who have published books on Catherine McAuley in the past: the biographers, Mary Vincent Harnett, Mary Austin Carroll, Roland Burke Savage SJ, Mary Bertrand Degnan, Mary Angela Bolster, Joanna Regan and Isabelle Keiss, and Mary Carmel Bourke; and the editors of Catherine McAuley's letters, Mary Ignatia Neumann and Mary Angela Bolster. I also wish to note those who have published books on other early Sisters of Mercy. These include, first and foremost, Mary Austin Carroll, to whom we are permanently indebted for her research, not only on Catherine McAuley, but on all the women included in her four-volume *Leaves from the Annals of the Sisters of Mercy,* completed in 1895. Other biographers of early Sisters of Mercy include Mary Catherine Garety and Kathleen Healy, on Frances Warde; Frances (formerly Mary Xaverius) O'Donoghue, on Mary Vincent Whitty; and Mary Hermenia Muldrey, on Mary Austin Carroll. To this list of acknowledgements must be added the name of Mary Dominick Foster, the Dublin Sister of Mercy who earlier in this century initiated the assembling of primary sources about Catherine McAuley; and John MacErlean SJ, who did extensive research on Catherine, her family, and her early associates, and who began the work of identifying the biographical manuscripts and autograph letters by and about her.

In this preface—as a mark of my personal gratitude—I especially wish to note three Sisters of Mercy whose published research on Catherine McAuley is indispensable to scholarship on her: Mary Bertrand Degnan (1900–1974), of the Albany, New York community; Mary Ignatia Neumann, of the Baltimore community; and Mary Angela Bolster, of the Cork community. Readers of the present volume will find numerous references to their published work. Where I may have occasion to offer slightly different data or interpretations from theirs, I do so with great respect for their research.

Mary Bertrand Degnan's scholarly biography of Catherine McAuley (1957) followed the biographies written by Harnett, Carroll, and Burke Savage. Her extensive archival research and the new information presented in her text and endnotes have added immeasurably to precise knowledge of Catherine's life and that of her contemporaries. One has only to imagine the huge task that lay before her to realize how much McAuley scholarship has been enriched by her painstaking investigations, accomplished before Catherine McAuley's letters were published.

To Mary Ignatia Neumann, the editor of *The Letters of Catherine McAuley, 1827–1841,* all scholarly work on Catherine owes a permanent debt of gratitude. It is not possible to do authentic research on Catherine's life, thought, and activity without consulting her letters, the direct expressions of her mind and heart. The autographs of these letters are not in one repository but spread throughout many archives in Ireland and elsewhere. It was Mary Ignatia Neumann who undertook the work of locating, transcribing, and publishing them for the first time (1969). All references to Catherine's letters in the present volume are to her edition, unless otherwise noted. I wish to thank her publicly.

Careful examination of the two-volume *Documentary Study for the Canonization Process of the Servant of God Catherine McAuley*, privately published in Rome in 1985, reveals the monumental gift Mary Angela Bolster has given to our knowledge of Catherine McAuley. The sheer size of this *Documentary Study* (over 1200 pages) testifies to her lifelong commitment to research on Catherine McAuley and the early Sisters of Mercy, as well as to her extensive knowledge of the primary sources. She has devoted enormous energy to furthering contemporary understanding of Catherine McAuley's spirit and life, and it is incumbent on any present-day researcher to study her work, especially *The Correspondence of Catherine McAuley, 1827–1841* (1989) and the *Documentary Study.* For all this help as well as for her friendship, I am deeply grateful to her.

Rochester Institute of Technology has contributed generously to my research for this book, by awarding me a sabbatical leave, travel funds on several occasions, and research grants to cover most of the expense of typing the manuscript. I particularly thank my division chair in the College of Liberal Arts, Joseph Nassar, and my dean, William Daniels, for graciously supporting this project. The Sisters of Mercy of Rochester, New York have also been, of course, wonderfully encouraging: they have borne the rest of the expense of this research; our leaders have always appreciated and aided this endeavor; and the community with whom I live have been a steady help—understanding my clutter of boxed notes, relieving me of chores, and, most of all, showing constant interest and support. My aunt, Kathryn Holyer, and my brothers, Walter, Jim, and Joe, have also helped the book, and me, by their friendship and love.

I wish to thank Linda Henderberg, the most skilled professional typist one could hope to have, and all those who have read and commented on various parts of the manuscript: my colleague at the university, Anne Coon; five Sisters of Mercy: Mary Magdalena Frisby (Dublin), Teresa Green (Bermondsey), Mary Hermenia Muldrey (New Orleans), Mary Celeste Rouleau (Burlingame), and Marilyn Williams (Rochester); and two priest friends and scholars: William H. Shannon, Professor Emeritus of Religious Studies, Nazareth College of Rochester, and, especially, Ernan McMullin, Professor Emeritus of Philosophy,

University of Notre Dame, for his unfailingly wise suggestions and thoughtful critique throughout the whole process of this research.

In a work of this sort the possibilities for error are great indeed. One can misread, misinterpret, and misrecord—as well as inadvertently neglect relevant data. For all these positive errors and omissions—wherever they may be now lurking—I apologize to the readers, trusting that one day others will correct and refine what I have presented.

Contents

Introduction

My research for this book began in September 1987 when I went to the Dublin archives of the Sisters of Mercy for two weeks. There I saw for the first time the original manuscript of the Rule and Constitutions of the Sisters of Mercy, handwritten by Catherine McAuley herself in the mid-1830s. I realized that this manuscript had never been critically edited or published, although a limited facsimile edition of it had once been privately distributed in the United States. The copies of the Rule which were published following its confirmation in Rome in 1841 represented several layers of alteration of Catherine's original text. While the Italian text was the official, approved version of the Rule, a fully detailed account of its genesis and of Catherine's original intentions and preferences, as revealed in the structure and wording of her own manuscript, had not been published—even though this manuscript is the most important of Catherine's writings and a foundational text of the Sisters of Mercy world-wide (presently numbering about 15,000 members on six continents).

A key aspect of my earlier research on Catherine's transcriptions of the "Spirit of the Institute" essay and her "Act of Consecration" had been the realization that a reader-writer's mind is remarkably revealed in the editorial choices she makes in the course of an inexact transcription: that is, in the intellectual and, in this case, spiritual sensitivities and preferences which are exposed in what the writer selects, omits, and alters as she both appropriates and transforms the thought and diction of another text.[1] Although it has been known for over 150 years that Catherine's manuscript of the Rule was composed on the basis of the form and content of the previously approved Rule of another Irish religious order of women, the Presentation Sisters, its exact sentence-by-sentence relation to the Presentation Rule and its many significant departures from that Rule had not been completely documented in an accessible format. Here again, as I have since discovered, the mind of Catherine McAuley would be strikingly revealed in her transformation of the structure, content, and language of a pre-existing text, but in this case, because of the avowedly serious, public, and enduring nature of the Rule of any religious order, her editorial choices would provide even more profound insights into her convictions and values.

In September 1987, in the same Dublin archives, I also discovered typed transcriptions of eyewitness memoirs about Catherine McAuley written by her contemporaries. Some of these had been quoted before, but I had never seen the complete texts. For example, I saw transcriptions of five letters written from London in 1844–1845 by Clare Moore, one of Catherine's earliest and most trusted associates. These letters, begun three years after Catherine's death, are addressed to Clare's sister in Dublin and present, in a reflective way, what Clare knew and remembered about Catherine McAuley. There were in the Dublin archives other typed transcriptions of eyewitness memoirs, but I had no time just then to search for the original manuscripts.

Finally, during Summer 1990 and again in November 1992, I went to ten archives of the Sisters of Mercy in Ireland and England to find, and (where possible) photocopy, the original autographs of these biographical manuscripts about Catherine McAuley. What I found was beyond my most hopeful anticipations—not only the manuscripts I was looking for, and information about their authors, but autograph letters and other original biographical manuscripts I did not know existed, as well as entries in the Annals of various early Mercy communities that provide still further information about her contemporaries' perceptions of her and about the 1868 compilation of her *Sayings.* During these years I also corresponded with Norah Boland RSM, archivist of the Sisters of Mercy, Brisbane, Australia, who sent me excellent photocopies of Mary Vincent Whitty's five autograph letters written in November 1841.

The present book is not, in any modern or critical sense, a biography of Catherine McAuley, though its contents are in fact biographical and may be useful not only to her future biographers but also to those writing analyses of a theological, historical, or literary nature. Certainly a fully analytical and critical biography of Catherine McAuley should one day be written, drawing not only on the biographical data but also on wide historical evidence of the social, economic, political, and ecclesiastical contexts in which Catherine lived and worked. The present volume is intended as a preliminary but necessary contribution to that end. Its purposes are threefold: first, to provide a detailed but fairly succinct chronology of Catherine's life to assist readers in placing the contents of the rest of the book; secondly, to present in their entirety (or, in the case of Annals, by means of substantial excerpts) the texts of ten manuscripts (or collections of autograph letters) written about her by her close associates in the Sisters of Mercy, and the complete text of the original Rule of the Sisters of Mercy as composed by Catherine McAuley and revised by Daniel Murray, with introductory chapters to these source documents; and thirdly, to provide, as a preface to each of the biographical manuscripts, information about the women who were the authors or principal sources of these manuscripts—women who were among Catherine's "first born", as she called them, and on whom so much of the successful founding of the Sisters of Mercy as well as the fruitful development of the Catholic Church in Ireland, England, Australia, and the United States depended. I conclude the book with a brief epilogue.

A few comments about the names I use may be helpful. In this book, which involves references to dozens upon dozens of Sisters of Mercy, priests, and bishops, I have generally chosen not to use the ecclesiastical title, "Sister", "Father", or "Reverend", unless I am transcribing or quoting other sources, or unless such a title is needed for clarity. Moreover, in manuscripts of the early nineteenth-century in Ireland, such as those presented here, professed sisters are often referred to as "Mrs." and priests are often given the title "Mr." or "Dr." In naming each individual Sister of Mercy I have tried, initially, to give both her baptismal name and her name received on reception into the community; thus, Georgiana Moore, who received the name "Mary Clare" at reception, is initially referred to as "Mary Clare (Georgiana) Moore", and later, as "Mary Clare Moore", or simply "Clare Moore". All Sisters of Mercy except some lay sisters received the name "Mary" at reception. Readers will also note the problems associated with the correct spelling of certain baptismal names, surnames, and names in religion; I have attempted to resolve some of these problems, in the notes which accompany various chapters. In terms of style, I have generally tried not to use only surnames in referring to the men discussed—unless it appeared cumbersome to do otherwise or is standard practice for certain names—because it would have been confusing to refer to certain women in this way: we do not have a tradition of talking about "McAuley" or "Warde" or "Whitty". However, I have generally thought it appropriate to refer to published scholars, including Sisters of Mercy, by their surnames. Finally, I have used the place names in use in the 1830s and 1840s, but have indicated the current names as well; this is particularly pertinent to those cities, towns, and counties in Ireland which have now recovered their original Irish names.

At this point it is reasonable to ask: Why would general readers as well as historians, theologians, and church ministers be interested in a book of manuscripts by or about Catherine McAuley and her contemporaries?

First, there are ecclesial, and strikingly human, reasons. On April 9, 1990, Catherine McAuley was declared Venerable by John Paul II. He publicly confirmed what historians and theologians selected to examine her life had found: namely, that Catherine had, with constancy and to a heroic degree, lived in fidelity to her God-given capacities for faith, hope, and love, and that she had done so with prudence, justice, temperance, and fortitude.[2] Catherine is thought to be the first woman in Ireland to be so recognized by the Church, under norms for the veneration of saints established by the Council of Trent and procedures operative since the 18th century. (Earlier Irish women saints, such as Brigid, Attracta, Ita, and Lelia, had been recognized by acclamation of the local churches.) Thus the example of Catherine's life—her human way of loving God and of following the example of Jesus in merciful love of her neighbor—is now offered to the ecclesial community for its private guidance, support, and solace.

Not only do Sisters of Mercy and their associates have a great affection for Catherine McAuley, but when they come to know her, men and women of today, the world over, quite plainly love her, and say that they are inspired and animated by her. The Sisters of Mercy were extraordinarily favored to have been founded in 1831 by a woman whose personality remains attractive to so wide a following, and whose character is so engaging and encouraging: a free, creative, forthright, affectionate, intelligent, courageous, humorous, original, and originating woman who dared to take a fresh look at her own milieu. She made a commitment to outgoing, merciful service to the poor, sick, homeless, dying, and uneducated of her day which added a new depth and tenderness to church ministry, and her vision, still relevant and flexible today, continues to inspire not only Sisters of Mercy but thousands of other church people.

Yet how do we acquire knowledge of such a woman? How do we, or can we, interpret the thinking of a historical person, who lived a past historical life? Where are the most telling clues to her character? Is Catherine McAuley, for example, to be found in what she read, or what she wrote, or what she did, or in all three, and if so, in what order of priority? Is the contour of her life revealed in her most characteristic themes, actions, and vocabulary? And, how do we define "characteristic"? Is she what her close associates said she was? are they reliable narrators? to what extent? Is she what present-day commentators say she is? Is she best revealed in certain gestures which seem to have the suggestive power of symbols? What role does Catherine's temperament play in concealing or revealing her character to observers?—for example, her preference for what is practical, her emphasis on example over verbal explanation, her personal reserve about her own interior religious experience? To use Leon Edel's phrase, how do we find "the figure under the carpet, the evidence on the reverse of the tapestry, the life-myth of a given mask" (162)? Perhaps the manuscripts presented in this book can help us approach some of these questions.

But there are also historical and theological reasons for interest in Catherine McAuley. Some of these could arise from the following questions: What was the complex of positive and negative forces—of which Catherine McAuley's own personal talent was a part—which led to her founding an enduring movement? What were the liturgical, devotional, and other spiritual influences on her life? What was the effect on her thinking of the penal era in Ireland and its aftermath? Who, beyond the Sisters of Mercy, were her friends? Why, given the magnitude of her achievement and that of her early associates, are she and they so strangely neglected in many historical studies of nineteenth-century Ireland, and of the evolution of the Catholic Church both there and elsewhere? Why has she not been considered more influential in the formation of theologies of religious education and of ministry to the poor and to the sick? Why is her ground-breaking contribution to re-designing the structures and mission of religious orders of women not more frequently mentioned in histories of religious life? Why is she, whose heroic virtue is recognized, not yet publicly declared a Saint by the Church?

It is easy to suggest quick and—so far as they go—accurate answers to some of these questions: she was a Catholic, she was a member of a religious order, she was a woman, she lived in the nineteenth century, she did not figure directly in Irish episcopal careers in that century, and the Sisters of Mercy, whose documentary resources are in geographically scattered archives, have not over the years found sufficient means to make her more widely known. Perhaps the numerous details provided in the manuscripts presented in this book can encourage fresh responses to these questions and motivate further scholarly attention to Catherine's life and work.

Where the Irish Catholic Church is concerned, the innovative, revolutionary half of the nineteenth century was probably not that presided over by Paul Cullen, Archbishop of Dublin from 1852 to 1878, but the first half of the century, that nurtured by the leadership of the more pastorally creative Daniel Murray, coadjutor and then Archbishop of Dublin, from 1809 to 1852. In reading the early biographical manuscripts about Catherine McAuley one will discover the precise nature of her contribution to this development: her founding and leading a women's community-movement of direct uncloistered advocacy and service of the "poor, sick, and ignorant". This movement was desperately needed in the Dublin of her day, with its cholera, typhoid fever, unemployment, homelessness, widespread poverty, masses of orphans, and disregard for unskilled young girls and women; and it is, I believe, still needed in the wider world of our own day, with its illiteracy, hunger, disease, school drop-out rates, teenage motherhood, widespread urban and rural poverty, street violence, neglect of children, homelessness, racism, third- and first-world oppressions, and policies of marginalization.

Over the 150 years since her death in 1841, Catherine McAuley has been respected and even admired in the Church—as a religious founder. But the work she did and the values she stood for have not enjoyed the wider historical recognition and influence that would have required, obviously not just in her case, a substantial revision of the various taxonomies on which historians and theologians as well as the Church herself often rely. In another sphere, and on another level, it is worth recalling that Catherine of Siena (1347–1380) and Teresa of Avila (1515–1582), two great teachers in the Christian Church, were not designated Doctors of the Church (a title that publicly acknowledges lasting theological contribution and influence) until 1970, and they are the only two women so recognized. It is not unreasonable to hope that the universal Church might one day recognize, for example, some of the saintly Nurses of the Church and School Teachers of the Church and might turn to their biographies and writings for theological understanding and direction.

New theories of history and new approaches to social criticism will undoubtedly affect the self-evaluation of the Catholic Church in the next centuries and will produce new ways of recognizing and being influenced by the contributions of the full range of Christian lives and vocations. This in turn will involve a new evaluation of many historical persons and groups, among whom will be people like Catherine McAuley. An indirect aim of my research is to assist this development, by providing reliable texts of source documents which can help to reshape historical and ecclesial perceptions of the significance of all those who contribute to the mission of the Church and who engage in all kinds of specifically Christian labor.

In her Rule, Catherine said:

> The sisters shall feel convinced that no work of charity is more productive of good to society, or more conducive to the happiness of the poor than the careful instruction of women, since whatever the station they are destined to fill, their example and advice will always possess influence, and where ever a religious woman presides, peace and good order are generally to be found. (Rule 2.5)

She was here referring not to members of religious orders but to servant girls and poor women empowered by Christian knowledge. She wished for them in their future roles all the guidance and strength which could come from knowing God's consoling love of them.

May Catherine McAuley be this sort of resource to men and women who value the consolation of God and who seek to find it and share it with others, in scholarly ways and in the ordinary ways of daily life. And may this book contribute in some ancillary way to that end.

A Portrait of Catherine McAuley

A very few days after [her brother-in-law's] death [in January 1829] I saw our foundress for the first time. My brother took me to introduce me. She was sitting in the little parlor on the right side of the hall as you enter. She was then upwards of 40* but looked at least 10 years younger. She was very fair with a brilliant color on her cheeks, still not too red. Her face was a short oval but the contour was perfect. Her lips were thin and her mouth rather wide, yet there was so much play and expression about it that I remarked it as the next agreeable feature in [her] face. Her eyes were light blue and remarkably round with the brows and lashes colorless but they spoke. In repose they had a melancholy beseeching look; then it would light up expressive of really hearty fun, or if she disapproved of anything they could tell that too. Sometimes they had that strange expression of reading your thoughts, which made you feel that even your mind was in her power, and that you could not hide anything from her. Her nose was straight but thick. She wore bands made from her own back hair which were so well managed as to be quite free from the disagreeable look bands of the kind usually give. The color was pale golden not in the least sandy, very fine and silky. She was dressed in black British merino which according to the fashion of the time fitted tight to her shape. She was remarkably well made, round but not in the least heavy. She had a good carriage, her hands were remarkably white but very clumsy, very large with broad square tips to the fingers and short square nails.

Mary Clare Augustine Moore (1808–1880)

*Probably fifty or forty-seven.

A Chronology of Catherine McAuley's Life 1778–1841

Readers who may be unfamiliar with details of the life of Catherine McAuley may find this chronology a relatively succinct, and perhaps helpful, overview.[1] Those who are already familiar with Catherine's life-story may also find it useful, as an abbreviated outline of some of the major events and personal relationships in her life. Since the present volume is not a biography of Catherine McAuley, as such, understanding the chapters and texts which follow may be assisted by reference to this chronology. At least that is the hope of the author.

A biographical chronology is, almost by definition, a rather cold arrangement of a person's life: it does not explicitly reflect the underlying thoughts, feelings, and motivations informing that life, nor does it describe the historical contexts surrounding it; it may suggest but it certainly does not state the suffering or joy, the worry or hope, inherent in the events it records. As an abbreviated sketch, it is therefore severely limited in presenting the full reality of that life. But if it is as accurate as possible, it may be useful as a summary inviting thoughtful amplification and analysis.

In 1841 Catherine wrote: "Let us take one day only in hands, at a time, merely making a resolve for tomorrow; thus we may hope to get on taking short careful steps, not great strides" (310).[2] This chronology presents only a few of the days in her life, only a few of the short steps she took. However, viewed together they can perhaps intimate her "great strides"—the qualities and accomplishments of which she was herself very likely unaware, but for which she is now widely remembered and admired.

*c.*1723	Birth of Catherine's father, James McGauley, in or near Dublin.
*c.*1753	Birth of Catherine's mother, Elinor Conway, in Dublin. (The Limerick Manuscript says her name was "Eleanor".)
*c.*1777	James McGauley and Elinor Conway are married.[3]
September 17 or 29, 1778 or 1781	Birth of Catherine Elizabeth McAuley at Stormanstown House, Dublin. Though the exact date of Catherine's birth cannot be verified, it has become general practice to use the date, September 29, 1778. However, there is some evidence for the year 1781. Catherine's sister, Mary, whose birthdate is not known, may have been older or younger than Catherine.[4]
April 26, 1783	Birth of Catherine's brother, James William.
July 18, 1783	Her father, James McGauley, makes his will. His death occurs shortly afterwards.

August 2, 1783	James McGauley's will is probated.
June 24, 1784	Catherine's mother, Elinor Conway McAuley (McGauley), leases a house in Glasnevin, Dublin, which she subsequently sells on June 20, 1787.
June 6, 1787	She leases part of a house at 52 Queen Street, Dublin; the rest of the house is occupied by her friend, Mrs. George.
August 13, 1796	She sells the house on Queen Street, and, about this time, moves with her family, or at least with Catherine, into the home of her brother, Surgeon Owen Conway, at 28 East Arran Street, Dublin.
October 21, 1798	Death of Catherine's mother.
*c.*1801	Catherine moves into the home of William Armstrong, a relative, on Mary Street, where her sister Mary and brother James already live.
*c.*1803	She moves into the home of William and Catherine Callaghan at 31 Mary Street, Dublin, as a companion to Mrs. Callaghan. The Callaghans are childless. Shortly afterwards, she moves with the Callaghans to Coolock House, a twenty-two acre estate in northeast Dublin.[5]
August 18, 1804	Marriage of Mary McAuley, Catherine's sister, to Dr. William Montgomery Macauley, an apothecary and later a surgeon.[6]
October 3, 1819	Death of Catherine Callaghan.
1821	Catherine's brother, Dr. James McAuley, marries Frances Ridgeway.
January 27, 1822	William Callaghan signs his last will and testament, and a codicil designating Catherine as his sole residuary legatee.
August 9, 1822	Death of Anne Conway Byrn, Catherine's cousin. She leaves four children: Catherine, James, Anne, and the baby Teresa. Catherine McAuley adopts the ten-year-old Catherine Byrn at this time. She had adopted her godchild Teresa in 1821.[7]
November 10, 1822	Death of William Callaghan. He had been received into the Catholic Church on November 9, 1822.[8]
May 11, 1823	Daniel Murray becomes Archbishop of Dublin. He had been parish priest of Saint Andrew's, Townsend Street, and coadjutor since 1809 to the late Archbishop John Troy.
*c.*1823–1824	William Callaghan's will, which had been contested, is finally settled and Catherine becomes the sole residuary legatee of the Callaghan estate. Her inheritance includes about £25,000, Coolock House itself, and the furniture and plate.
June 22, 1824	Catherine leases from the Earl of Pembroke property at the corner of Baggot Street and Herbert Street in southeast Dublin, at a cost of £4,000 and an annual rent of £60, for the purpose of building a large house for various kinds of religious, educational, and social service of poor women and children.
July 1824	Michael Blake, parish priest of Saints Michael and John's

	and Catherine's friend, lays the first stone for the new building on Baggot Street.
August 17, 1824	Dr. Blake goes to Rome to re-establish the Irish College.
December 14, 1824	Catherine signs a Deed of Agreement for construction of the House on Baggot Street: John B. Keane, architect; Denis Lenehan, builder; and John Curran, carpenter. Rev. Edward Armstrong and Rev. Michael Doyle are designated as her agents. (The Deed may have originally designated Rev. Joseph Nugent as the second agent but may have been revised upon his death.) As the building progresses Catherine's brother James calls it "Kitty's Folly".
May 30, 1825	Joseph Nugent, then a curate at Saints Michael and John's, dies of typhoid fever. Catherine nurses her friend before his death.
1827	Catherine makes Dr. William Macauley's home on Military Road near the Royal Hospital her principal residence during her sister Mary's illness, but she makes regular trips to Coolock House and, after September 24, daily trips to the House on Baggot Street.
August 11, 1827	Burial of Mary McAuley Macauley, Catherine's sister. She leaves five children: Mary, James, Robert, Catherine, and William, ages sixteen to five.
September 24, 1827	Feast of Our Lady of Mercy: opening of the House on Baggot Street, as a school for the education of poor young girls and as a residence for homeless girls and women. Anna Maria Doyle and Catherine Byrn, Catherine's first co-workers, move in on that day and begin these works of mercy.
May 15, 1828	Death of Edward Armstrong, parish priest of St. Michan's and Catherine's close friend and spiritual director in relation to the Baggot Street project. Catherine nurses him before his death.
May or June 1828	Catherine moves into Baggot Street with Teresa Byrn, age seven, and begins negotiations for the sale of Coolock House. However, she frequently visits at the home of her brother-in-law and his children. Her nieces Mary and Catherine Macauley evidently also live regularly, if not full time, with her at Baggot Street.
September 10, 1828	Catherine writes to Rev. Francis L'Estrange ODC, Prior of the Discalced Carmelites, St. Teresa Church, Clarendon Street, Dublin. She explains that the house on Baggot Street is devoted to "the daily education of hundreds of poor female children and the instruction of young women who sleep in the house", and she invites co-workers: women "who prefer a conventual life, and are prevented embracing it from the nature of property or connections, may retire to this house. It is expected a gratuity will be given and an annual pension paid sufficient to meet the expense a lady must incur" (69).

Mid-September 1828	Catherine sells Coolock House.
September 24, 1828	Archbishop Murray gives permission for the House on Baggot Street to be called "of our Lady of Mercy".
October 13, 1828	Georgiana Moore joins the Baggot Street community as a resident co-worker, serving at first as governess for Catherine's younger niece, Catherine Macauley, and her godchild, Teresa Byrn.
November 1828	Frances Warde becomes a resident member of the Baggot Street community, having become associated with the work of the House on June 22, 1828.
November 22, 1828	At Baggot Street Archbishop Murray receives Mary Macauley, Catherine's niece, into the Catholic Church, and gives the community permission to visit the sick in their homes and in hospitals, as Catherine had requested.
January 21, 1829	Anne O'Grady joins the community on Baggot Street.
January 25, 1829	Death of Catherine's brother-in-law, Dr. William Macauley, after a very brief illness. Each of his five children, now ranging in age from seventeen to seven, chooses Catherine as his or her legal guardian. She is now the adoptive mother of nine children, having custody also of two of the Byrn children, Catherine and Teresa, and at least two other children: Ellen Corrigan and Ann Rice.
March 2, 1829	Catherine registers her nephews—James, Robert, and William Macauley—in the lay boarding school at Carlow College. They are listed as "McAuley" in the school records.
April 8, 1829	Catherine establishes the four-member Baggot Street Trust, which in effect assigns the House of Mercy to Archbishop Murray should she and her two associates named in the Trust, Anna Maria Doyle and Catherine Byrn, cease to fulfill the stated purposes of the House.
June 4, 1829	Dedication of the chapel in the House on Baggot Street. Archbishop Murray presides and Michael Blake, having returned from Rome, preaches the sermon. The Archbishop recommends that the chapel be opened to the public and that the money from Sunday collections be used to support the women and girls sheltered in the House. He assigns Daniel Burke OSF, as chaplain, and Redmond O'Hanlon ODC, as confessor.
July 15, 1829	Marcella Flynn becomes a resident member of the community.
September 8, 1829	Margaret Dunne joins the community.
November 22, 1829	Catherine's older niece, Mary Macauley, becomes a member of the community.
November 30, 1829	Elizabeth Harley joins the community.
1829 or early 1830	Rev. Matthias Kelly, administrator of St. Andrew's Parish, Townsend Street, visits Baggot Street and says, though without authorization to do so, that the House of Mercy is to be given to the Sisters of Charity, but that Catherine and

	her associates may retain apartments. Catherine contacts Archbishop Murray who comes himself to Baggot Street to say that this is not his wish or plan. However, in the course of their conversation he admits that "the idea of a convent starting up of itself in this manner" never entered his mind. In the midst of much clerical and lay criticism of their way of life, Catherine begins the long deliberation at the end of which she and her associates will agree, against her earlier judgment, to found a new religious congregation of women dedicated to the service of the poor.
June 10, 1830	Georgiana Moore, having left the House for one year, returns as a resident member of the community.
June 18, 1830	Caroline Murphy joins the community.
July 12, 1830	Mary Anne Delany joins.[9] There are now twelve members in the Baggot Street community.
September 8, 1830	As formal preparation for founding the Sisters of Mercy, Catherine McAuley, Anna Maria Doyle, and Elizabeth Harley enter the convent of the Presentation Sisters on George's Hill, Dublin, and begin their novitiate there on December 9, 1830.
May 26, 1831	Mary Jones joins the community on Baggot Street.
June 28, 1831	Death of Caroline Murphy at Baggot Street. She is buried in the vault of the Carmelite Priory at Saint Teresa's Church, Clarendon Street, the first of thirteen Dublin Sisters of Mercy who will be buried there over the next decade.[10]
July 24, 1831	Anna Carroll joins the community.
December 12, 1831	At George's Hill, Catherine McAuley and her two associates—now called, in religion, Mary Ann Doyle and Mary Elizabeth Harley—each "vow perpetual poverty, chastity and obedience, and to persevere until the end of my life in the Congregation called the Sisters of Mercy, established for the visitation of the sick poor, and charitable instruction of poor females." Thus Catherine and they found the new Institute of the Sisters of Mercy.
December 13, 1831	Archbishop Murray appoints Catherine the superior of the Sisters of Mercy.
December 1831	Michael Blake becomes parish priest of Saint Andrew's, succeeding Matthias Kelly.
January 23, 1832	Seven of the remaining ten women who had been living and working at Baggot Street during Catherine's absence are formally received into the Sisters of Mercy at the first reception ceremony on Baggot Street: Mary Josephine (Catherine) Byrn, Mary Frances Teresa (Frances) Warde, Mary Angela (Margaret) Dunne, Mary Joseph Teresa (Mary) Macauley,[11] Mary Clare (Georgiana) Moore, Mary Magdalen de Pazzi (Mary Anne) Delany, and Mary Agnes (Anna) Carroll. Mary Aloysius (Anne) O'Grady is also

	received on her deathbed. Mary Jones and Marcella Flynn will receive the habit and the names, Mary Gertrude and Mary Magdalen, on October 8, 1832.
Late January 1832	Anna Carroll leaves to enter the Presentation Convent on George's Hill.
February 8, 1832	Death of Mary Aloysius (Anne) O'Grady.
April 25, 1832	Death of Mary Elizabeth Harley.
March–December 1832	Cholera epidemic in Dublin. At the Board of Health's request, and after Archbishop Murray gives permission on April 26, Catherine and other sisters work for several months, in shifts from 9:00 a.m. to 8:00 p.m., in a cholera hospital set up on Townsend Street.
June 10, 1832	Anne Moore enters the community. She will receive the habit and the name, Mary Elizabeth, on October 8, 1832.
December 1, 1832	Mary Josephine (Catherine) Byrn leaves to enter the Dominican Convent in Cabra.
January 24, 1833	Four women profess their vows at the first profession ceremony on Baggot Street: Mary Frances Warde, Mary Angela Dunne, Mary Clare Moore, and Mary de Pazzi Delany.
March 17, 1833	Michael Blake is consecrated Bishop of Dromore. He will reside in Newry until his death in 1860. Walter Meyler succeeds him as parish priest of St. Andrew's.
May 2, 1833	Amelia White enters the community. She will receive the habit and the name, Mary Teresa, on December 4, 1833.
November 3, 1833	Mary Teresa Macauley, who had thought about transferring to a Carmelite monastery but who is now dying, professes her vows as a Sister of Mercy in a private ceremony.
November 12, 1833	Death of Mary Teresa Macauley, just after midnight.
December 8, 1833	With the assistance of Rev. John Rice OSA—the brother of Edmund Rice, founder of the Irish Christian Brothers—Catherine sends to Rome two original chapters of what will eventually become the new Rule and Constitutions of the Sisters of Mercy. These two chapters—on the Visitation of the Sick and the Protection of Distressed Women—having been approved by Archbishop Murray, are accompanied by a formal petition for approbation of the Sisters of Mercy and a copy of Catherine's Act of Profession. The chapters are understood at this time to be additions to the Rule and Constitutions of the Presentation Sisters, which Catherine had not yet fully revised for the Sisters of Mercy.
January 5, 1834	Mary Marmion enters the community. She will receive the habit and the name, Mary Cecilia, on July 3, 1834.
January 28, 1834	Catherine's niece, Catherine Macauley, who had lived at Baggot Street since 1828–1829, enters the community there. She will receive the habit and the name, Mary Anne Agnes, on July 3, 1834.[12]
February 11, 1834	Mary Gertrude Jones and Mary Magdalen Flynn profess their vows.

July 2, 1834	Clara Frayne enters the community. She will receive the habit and the name, Mary Ursula, on January 20, 1835.
July 13, 1834	Catherine applies to the Commissioners of National Education for recognition of the school at Baggot Street as a National School.
September 4, 1834	Mary Carton enters the community, intending to be a lay sister. She will receive the habit and the name, Teresa, on July 1, 1835, and will profess her vows on July 1, 1837.[13]
September 17, 1834	Myles Gaffney, curate at Saint Andrew's and the priest whom Archbishop Murray had asked to assist Catherine in composing the Rule and Constitutions, becomes Senior Dean of Maynooth College.
October 8, 1834	Mary Elizabeth Moore professes her vows.
October 21, 1834	Bishop Blake responds to Catherine's letter about Dr. Meyler's recent decision to close the convent chapel to the public. This decision cuts off a needed source of funds for the House of Mercy. A series of disagreements with Dr. Meyler, parish priest of St. Andrew's, thus begins.
March 24, 1835	Catherine opens a branch house on Sussex Place in Kingstown, just south of Dublin. While she intends the house primarily as a place of convalescence for sick sisters at Baggot Street, she decides early on to give "the coach house, stable and part of our garden" to create a school for the poor young girls she had seen "loitering about the roads in a most neglected state" (87). (In 1921 the name of this town is changed back to Dún Laoghaire.)
March 24, 1835	After examining the two chapters of the Rule sent to Rome in late 1833, the Holy See sends Archbishop Murray a letter of praise, which indicates that Pope Gregory XVI "has not only approved the establishment of that society [i.e., "a society of ladies, called of Mercy"], but has declared that it is truly worthy of his paternal benevolence and Apostolic Benediction" (Bolster, ed. 17).
May 3, 1835	Archbishop Murray, having received the above letter, communicates its content to Catherine. This day is thereafter regarded as the date of receiving papal approval to proceed toward final papal confirmation. (Some biographers give the date, May 23, but the early biographical manuscripts give "the third of May".)
August 15, 1835	Elizabeth Scott enters the community. She will receive the habit and the name, Mary Aloysius, on February 29, 1836.
December 9, 1835	Having served in this role herself for four years, Catherine now appoints Mary de Pazzi Delany as Mistress of Novices. Apparently Frances Warde served, at least informally, as Bursar. Mary Ann Doyle, whom Catherine had earlier appointed as her Assistant, now served for a time at the house in Kingstown. On this day, also, Mary Teresa (Amelia) White professes her vows.

April 21, 1836	Catherine founds St. Joseph's Convent of Mercy in Tullamore, Ireland. Mary Ann Doyle is appointed superior.
October 22, 1836	Catherine's niece, Mary Anne Agnes (Catherine) Macauley, and Mary Cecilia Marmion profess their vows.[14]
October 29, 1836	Catherine founds St. Joseph's Convent of Mercy in Charleville (Rath Luirc), Ireland. Mary Angela Dunne is appointed superior.
1837	Five deaths occur at Baggot Street during this year: Mary Veronica Corrigan (February 9), Mary Rose Lubé (March 11), Mary Aloysius Thorpe (June 30), Mary Anne Agnes Macauley (August 7), and Mary de Chantal McCann (October 27). During the preceding two years two other sisters had also died: Mary Mechtildis (Bridget) Gaffney, the sister of Myles Gaffney (June 14, 1835), and Mary Agnes Marmion (February 10, 1836).
January 25, 1837	Mary Ursula (Clara) Frayne professes her vows at Baggot Street. In 1842 she will accompany Mary Francis (Marianne) Creedon to make a foundation of Sisters of Mercy in St. John's, Newfoundland; in 1845 she will leave Dublin to found a convent of Sisters of Mercy in Perth, Australia.
February 5, 1837	Anna Maria Harnett enters the community on Baggot Street. She will receive the habit and the name, Mary Vincent, on July 1, 1837.
April 11, 1837	Catherine founds St. Leo's Convent of Mercy in Carlow, Ireland. Mary Frances Warde is appointed superior.
June 20, 1837	Catherine writes to Charles Cavanagh, her solicitor, outlining the property, materials, and money she had earlier contributed towards the construction of the school for poor girls adjacent to the convent in Kingstown (Dún Laoghaire). Because she had donated £50, she is now charged with the entire cost of renovating the coach house and stable for the school (about £450), even though she had clearly understood that the parish priest would be answerable to the builder and would apply to the National Board of Education for a grant. The Kingstown controversy ensues. In January 1838 law proceedings are started and attempts are made to serve Catherine a summons. Later that year the sisters will withdraw from Kingstown.
July 6, 1837	Catherine founds a Convent of Mercy on Rutland Street in the city of Cork. Mary Clare Moore is appointed superior.
August 7, 1837	Catherine's niece, Mary Anne Agnes (Catherine) Macauley, dies of consumption.[15]
August 8, 1837	Mary Clare Moore, the older sister of Mary Clare (Georgiana) Moore, enters the community on Baggot Street. She will receive the habit and the name, Mary Clare Augustine, on February 21, 1838.
August 15, 1837	Catherine's godchild, Teresa Byrn, who had been living in Baggot Street, enters the community. She will receive the habit and the name, Mary Camillus, on February 21, 1838.

Autumn 1837	Daniel Burke OSF, chaplain at Baggot Street since 1829, is reassigned to accompany to southern Africa the newly appointed Vicar Apostolic of the Cape of Good Hope, Patrick Griffith.
October 3, 1837	Catherine is already in serious disagreement with Walter Meyler, parish priest of St. Andrew's, Westland Row, over arrangements for a new chaplain to serve the community and the women and girls sheltered in the House of Mercy on Baggot Street: she wishes him to assign a single chaplain to whom she would pay a modest salary; he wishes the parish curates to take turns serving, and demands a greater salary than the community can afford. The chaplaincy crisis worsens and is not resolved until early 1839. Dr. Meyler then agrees to assign one curate, and Catherine agrees to increase the salary and to keep the convent chapel closed to the public.
November 1837	In Kingstown Catherine falls on the stairs, going from the community room to the chapel, and breaks her left wrist. In the previous July she had fallen down a flight of stairs at Baggot Street.
December 19, 1837	She appeals again to John Hamilton, archdeacon of the Dublin diocese, who has been trying to help in the chaplaincy affair. She says she received so disturbing a letter from Dr. Meyler that, after reading a few lines, "I read no more and put it out of my power ever to do so by burning the letter" (Bolster, ed. 43–4).
February 14, 1838	Death of Kate Coffey, a postulant in the Carlow community.
February 21, 1838	Mary Aloysius Scott professes her vows at Baggot Street.
July 3, 1838	Catherine writes that having received a legacy of £1,000 she has engaged Mr. Mullins to build a commercial laundry at Baggot Street, as a source of income for maintaining the women and girls sheltered in the House of Mercy. His bid is the lowest by far; however, as it will turn out, he has agreed to provide only a bare room, without laundry fixtures.
July 26, 1838	Catherine opens a branch house, St. Anne's Convent, in Booterstown, to the south of Dublin. She intends the house as a replacement for the Kingstown convent if they have to withdraw from that parish.
August 23, 1838	She writes to Frances Warde: "I have been tortured with my unfortunate mouth, only just getting a little better" (132). She suffers frequently from severe inflammation of the mouth and gums.
September 24, 1838	She founds St. Mary's Convent of Mercy in Limerick. Mary Elizabeth Moore is appointed superior.
October 24, 1838	Mary Vincent Harnett, a founding member of the Limerick community, professes her vows there.
November 1838	The community withdraws from Kingstown.

December 1838	According to his letter of October 28, 1903, Catherine's nephew, William (Willie) Macauley, aged seventeen, goes to sea for the second time, sailing from England.[16] He does not come to see his aunt before this departure, and because she loses all contact with him, she later presumes that he has died at sea. William eventually settles in Australia. A few years after Catherine's death, he re-establishes contact with the Sisters of Mercy at Baggot Street and with his cousin, Mary Camillus (Teresa) Byrn.
*c.*1838	In a meeting with Rev. Richard Baptist O'Brien who is preparing to become the President of St. Mary's College, Halifax, Nova Scotia, Catherine evidently indicates that she is willing, if permitted, to serve herself in a foundation in Nova Scotia. He later reports that she said: "The institute requires me not at home; it has young, intelligent, and devoted children. We ought to provide for the instruction of the poor and the relief of the sick in the colonies" (Harnett xxix–xxx, 205).
January 15, 1839	Ellen Whitty enters the community on Baggot Street. She will receive the habit and the name, Mary Vincent, on July 24, 1839.
May 9, 1839	Mary Gertrude Jones dies at Baggot Street, and is buried in the Carmelite vault in St. Teresa's Church, where the eleven Dublin sisters who died before her are buried.
September 24, 1839	Frances Warde and the Carlow community found St. Mary's Convent of Mercy in Naas, County Kildare. Mary Josephine Trennor is appointed superior.
November 18, 1839	Catherine, Mary Clare Moore, and the two English sisters who had made their novitiate in Cork and professed their vows there on August 19, as well as others in the founding party, depart from Dublin for Bermondsey, London. They sail from Kingstown to Liverpool and then proceed by train to London, arriving on the night of November 19.
November 21, 1839	The new Convent of Mercy designed by Augustus Welby Pugin and erected adjacent to Holy Trinity Church in Bermondsey is blessed, and Mary Clare Moore is appointed temporary superior.
December 12, 1839	In Bermondsey, Catherine assists Clare Moore at a ceremony in which six English women who had been preparing for the community's arrival receive the habit of the Sisters of Mercy.
Late December 1839–early January 1840	From London, through Bishop Thomas Griffiths, Vicar Apostolic of the London District, Catherine sends to Rome for final approval and papal confirmation the completed text of the Rule and Constitutions of the Sisters of Mercy and a petition for its approval signed by the superiors of all the autonomous houses, together with letters of endorsement from Archbishop Murray and all the bishops in whose dioceses Convents of Mercy are situated.

January 4, 1840	Catherine's nephew, Robert Macauley, age twenty-one, dies while she is in London.
January 13–14, 1840	Catherine returns to Dublin. She had been ill in London, and is now "chiefly confined to bed"—with a stomach ailment and "my old mouth complaint . . . which has kept me on infant's diet more than 10 days" (195).
February 26, 1840	She writes to Charles Cavanagh, her solicitor, about the builder of the public laundry, who plans to charge extra to put in the water pipes. She calls Mr. Mullins's interpretation of the contract—as providing only for bare space—"an unkind, unjust transaction".
February 27, 1840	Mary Clare Augustine Moore professes her vows at Baggot Street.
March 3, 1840	In Rome, Paul Gavino Secchi-Murro, consultor for the Congregation for the Propagation of the Faith, submits a positive report on his examination of the proposed Rule and Constitutions of the Sisters of Mercy.
March 6, 1840	Catherine appoints Mary de Pazzi Delany, Assistant; Mary Cecilia Marmion, Mistress of Novices; and Mary Aloysius Scott, Bursar.
March 8, 1840	Mary Francis Mahony dies in the convent in Cork.
March 10, 1840	Mary Francis Marmion dies at Baggot Street.
March 20, 1840	Mary Teresa Vincent (Ellen) Potter dies in the convent in Limerick. Catherine had frequently exchanged letters in verse with this "sweet little poet".
April 1840	Catherine re-opens the house in Kingstown at the request of Archbishop Murray.
May 6, 1840	She founds St. Vincent's Convent of Mercy in Galway. Mary Teresa (Amelia) White is appointed temporary superior, with the intention that Mary Catherine Leahy will assume this role in six months. (However, Teresa White will remain superior in Galway until 1855; she will then found a convent in Clifden. Catherine may have initially intended that Teresa remain a member of the Baggot Street community, so as to be available to be elected to succeed her as superior. She evidently once said of Teresa: "Of all the sisters, Sr. M. Teresa has most of my spirit, and I trust more to her guiding the Institute as I wish than to any other Sister.")[17]
June 10, 1840	Mary Bourke, a postulant, dies of typhus in Galway, while Catherine is there.
July 20, 1840	In Rome, the Congregation for the Propagation of the Faith unanimously votes in favor of approving the Rule and Constitutions of the Sisters of Mercy and subsequently forwards its recommendation to Pope Gregory XVI for eventual papal approval and confirmation.
July 27, 1840	In a letter to Teresa White, Catherine speaks of Bishop Michael Fleming, Vicar Apostolic of Newfoundland, as "my Bishop". She is planning to establish a foundation in

	Newfoundland and perhaps, at least at first, to go there herself. (The foundation in St. John's, Newfoundland, will be made in June 1842, seven months after Catherine's death.)
July 29, 1840	Catherine hears indirectly—through a visit from Rev. Richard Colgan OCC, on his return to Dublin, and later through a conversation of Rev. James Maher with his nephew Rev. Paul Cullen, also home from Rome—that the Rule and Constitutions has been reviewed positively by the Congregation for the Propagation of the Faith, but she will wait another year for papal confirmation.
October 1840	Responding to the temperance movement of Rev. Theobald Mathew, Catherine takes the pledge of total abstinence, in Galway, as a support and encouragement to others.
October 14, 1840	She writes to Cardinal Fransoni, Prefect of the Congregation for the Propagation of the Faith, soliciting his aid in obtaining for the Rule "the full approbation of the Holy See" and noting that "one hundred and forty-two Sisters are now devoted to God and His poor in this order" (238).
November 1 and 5,1840	In Bermondsey, Mary Ursula O'Connor and Mary Scholastica Burroughs die of typhoid fever.
December 8, 1840	Frances Warde and the Carlow community found a Convent of Mercy in Wexford. Mary Teresa Kelly is appointed superior.
December 27, 1840	In an effort to heal the Crottyite schism in the parish, Catherine founds a Convent of Mercy in Birr, although she has initially no assurance of revenue. Mary Aloysius Scott is appointed superior.
January 4, 1841	Catherine is exhilarated by the work to be done among the poor of Birr, and writes: "All my wardrobe is washing. I came home yesterday with at least half yard deep of mud, melted snow, and I have not a cold in my head—I was out 5 hours. Hurra for foundations, makes the old young and the young merry" (289).
February 5, 1841	Still in Birr, she writes: "I feel the frost most acutely in my right side from my hip to my ankle. I have put on a great flannel bandage with camphorated spirit, and trust in God it will, like a dear good old acquaintance, carry me safe back" (305).
March 1841	She writes from Baggot Street to Frances Warde: "My rather new visitant, a cough, has been with me very constantly since the first Sunday after my return. To please my kind tormentors I took one large bottle of medicine and put on a small blister, from which I (for want of faith perhaps) did not receive any benefit. I am now doctoring myself . . . and I think, *Mr. Time* taken into account, I am doing very well. I do think that the cough has made a resting place with me, and will be no unusual visitor in future. I am now

	going to hide from the Doctor who is gone up to four influenza patients" (Bolster, ed. 204–5). Although she had made earlier remarks about having an "old man's" cough, her more explicit references to this "constant" cough—a symptom of her pulmonary tuberculosis—begin in early 1841.
March 1841	While Mary Cecilia Marmion is in Birr for her health, Catherine temporarily assumes the duties of Mistress of Novices at Baggot Street, until the end of May. She writes of the novices: "It is my greatest happiness to be with them" (326).
March 31, 1841	She complains about conditions in the South Dublin workhouse set up under the Poor Relief Act of 1838: "the reduced, moral, orderly person cannot bear to go [there]" (324). Fifty-two women and girls are crowded into the House of Mercy on Baggot Street at this time.
April 12, 1841	She writes: "My old cough is tormenting me, some stings in my chest. I believe I must go to Birr" (329).
April 29, 1841	James Macauley, Catherine's eldest nephew, dies at age twenty-five.
May 4, 1841	Catherine humorously anticipates a reception and profession ceremony at Baggot Street: "Not one prepared voice for the choir—add to this my blunders and Mother de Pazzi's over zeal and excitement and you will have a picture of a charming ceremony. God will help us through it" (330). Among those professed is Mary Camillus (Teresa) Byrn, Catherine's godchild.
May 16, 1841	Frances Gibson enters the Baggot Street community for an eventual foundation in Liverpool (July 1843). In July 1841 Catherine will try to arrange that the foundation be made from Carlow (since Frances Warde is prepared to make it more quickly), but Bishop George Brown of Liverpool will prefer that the foundation come from Baggot Street.
May 24, 1841	Catherine returns to Dublin from Birr through Tullamore. The last nineteen miles of the coach journey take over five hours: "a cross driver, slow horses and broken harness" (340).
June 6, 1841	Gregory XVI confirms the Rule and Constitutions of the Sisters of Mercy, but it will be some time before Catherine receives official notice of this.
June 14, 1841	Clare Moore returns to Baggot Street from Bermondsey, and then goes to Cork to resume the role of superior. (However, on December 10, she will return permanently to Bermondsey, Mary Clare Agnew, the superior there since June, having been removed from office.)
June 30, 1841	Bishop John England of Charleston, South Carolina, visits Baggot Street seeking a foundation in his diocese. Catherine has to refuse, having already promised foundations in Birmingham, Newfoundland, and Liverpool.

July 5, 1841	The papal decree of approval and confirmation of the Rule is promulgated in Rome. Cardinal Fransoni will communicate this in a letter addressed to Archbishop Murray on July 31, posted together with printed copies of the approved text in Italian. This packet will reach Dublin sometime after August 19.
Late July 1841	Catherine writes to Frances Warde: "Having heard from a priest some unfavorable reports of Bermondsey, I wrote to Mr. Butler [the parish priest] begging him to tell me the real state. I this moment received the enclosed. Read it and send it again to me when you are writing. . . . Sr. Agnew is fond of extremes in piety—that is her greatest error" (354). However, on August 3, she will write, "Most satisfactory letters from London, all going on remarkably well" (358).
August 4, 1841	She declines an invitation to go to Carlow for retreat: those left behind at Baggot Street "would feel it very much indeed. It is quite impossible for any one in my situation to think of pleasing themselves. My pleasure must be in endeavouring to please all" (360).
August 16, 1841	She writes: "I was aware the confirmation of the Rule was granted but I have not received it yet. Probably his Grace may bring it on Thursday to the Ceremony" (362).
August 19, 1841	Four of the six young women destined for the Birmingham, England foundation profess their vows in a ceremony at Baggot Street. Mary Vincent (Ellen) Whitty also professes her vows on this day, as does Mary Justina Fleming, the sickly niece of the Bishop of Newfoundland. She will die of consumption on December 10, 1841. After the ceremony, Catherine writes: "Dr. Murphy of Cork received an account of the confirmation of our Rule. Dr. Murray has not yet, and is much surprised" (363).
August 20, 1841	Catherine signs her will. In the evening she, the six sisters for Birmingham, Mary Cecilia Marmion, Mary Liguori (Frances) Gibson (now a novice), Myles Gaffney, and Redmond O'Hanlon sail from Kingstown to Liverpool and then travel by railway to Birmingham, arriving about noon on August 21.
August 21, 1841	Catherine founds St. Etheldreda's Convent of Mercy in Handsworth, Birmingham. Bishop Nicholas Wiseman, coadjutor to Bishop Thomas Walsh, receives the founding party at the new convent designed by Augustus Welby Pugin. (In 1842 the name of the convent will be changed to St. Mary's.)
September 6, 1841	Mary Juliana (Juliana) Hardman, who had professed her vows at Baggot Street on August 19, is appointed superior of the Birmingham community. Mary Cecilia Marmion will, however, remain in Birmingham for several months to assist her.
September 6, 1841	Catherine is severely ill in Birmingham. She sends detailed

	instructions to Teresa Carton at Baggot Street about preparing a low bed and a quiet sleeping space for her when she returns: "Move your Bed to where Sister M. Clare's is and clear out your corner for mine, where I will not hear the noise of the street. I will want a fire. . . . You are not to leave the room—a little coughing [i.e., Teresa's] will never disturb me . . . . It is strange to me, my Dear Sr. Teresa, to write so much about myself—and give such trouble. My best love to all" (Autograph, Archives of Sisters of Mercy, Dublin; Bolster, ed. 257).
September 17, 1841	She writes from Birmingham: "I have been very weak and sick for the last 12 or 14 days . . . . I cannot leave the one aired [i.e., dried] room without coughing violently" (373–4).
September 20, 1841	She leaves Birmingham, arriving in Dublin on September 21.
September 24, 1841	She asks Mary Ann Doyle in Tullamore to care for Mary Justina Fleming who is severely ill and needs a change of air. In the same letter she reassures Mary Ann, "I am going to propose myself as Deputy to Dr. O'Rafferty in the guardianship of your convent", evidently not aware that she is suffering her own last illness (376).
September 25, 1841	She writes to Frances Warde about the "weary passage from Liverpool" earlier in the week, the "comfortable tea" in Kingstown on their arrival, and the decision of Bishop Brown that the English sisters for the Liverpool foundation should be "prepared in the Mother House" (377–8). She does not mention her health.
September 26, 1841	She writes to Mary Aloysius Scott in Birr. Since her return from Birmingham she has seen Dr. William Stokes twice. His opinion is that "My right lung was diseased." However, she says, "I do not think my lung is affected . . . if my lung is actually engaged, the progress will not be checked, and the fact of no debility, not half so much as I have had when my gums were inflamed, shews that it cannot be . . . I here humbly confess that my chief motive just now is to shew that one of the most distinguished amongst our medical professors may be mistaken and that we should not immediately take up their opinions" (Autograph, Archives of the Sisters of Mercy, Birr).[18]
October 12, 1841	Writing to Frances Warde, she says she mentioned to Rev. Tobias Kirby, Vice Rector of the Irish College in Rome, "some evident mistakes in the copy of our Rule" (which she has by now received), and "he told me to select them and forward the document to him, with Dr. Murray's signature, and said we would without any more trouble obtain permission to rectify the evident mistakes." On a more personal note, she writes, "I have felt the last bad change in the weather very much. Father O'H[anlon]

brought your affectionate note. I humbly hope I am done with travelling for some time. If ever any poor sinner got a surfeit of it I have." She then adds: "I was cautioned not to speak of any mistake in the R[ule]" (Photocopy of autograph, Archives of the Institute of the Sisters of Mercy of the Americas, Silver Spring, Maryland).

October 15, 1841 — Catherine responds to a letter written on October 13 by a supplier of "timber and slates" for the Booterstown convent, who claims that £130 is still owed to him "for the last 4 years" and that if the debt is not paid "we will be obliged (very much against our inclination) to issue an execution and attach the Convent where our property is." Catherine does not offer to pay the debt, but writes, in part: "Twenty guineas a year left by Mrs. Verschoyle [the deceased Booterstown benefactor] is the only fund to meet extra expenses which every distinct establishment must incur. It is small but not so to us . . . . As to any legal proceedings there is no occasion to have recourse to them. The Sisters can return here [to Baggot Street] and whoever has a just claim may take possession of the house until their demand is satisfied, if there is no other means of providing for it" (383).[19]

October 18, 1841 — She writes to Charles Cavanagh, Esq., asking him to secure the twenty pound legacy bequeathed to her by Mrs. Ryan, a widow who had lived at the Shelbourne Hotel.

October 26, 1841 — Unaware that the bequest has now been received, she again writes to Mr. Cavanagh, asking that he secure the £20. This is apparently her last extant letter.

c. October 29—November 1, 1841 — Catherine becomes bedridden. On Tuesday, November 16, Mary Vincent Whitty will write: "Thursday [i.e., November 18] 3 weeks [i.e., October 29] was her first day in bed." Catherine is suffering from pulmonary tuberculosis complicated by an empyema (abscess).

November 8, 1841 — She is anointed on Monday by Redmond O'Hanlon.

November 10, 1841 — Mary Ursula Frayne writes from Baggot Street to the superiors of the various foundations to say that "our very dear and much beloved Revd. Mother is considered to be past hope of recovery." She adds: "May Almighty God in His Infinite Mercy prepare us all for the heavy affliction that awaits us."

November 11, 1841 — During the very early morning Catherine wraps up her shoes and instruments of penance in paper and twine, and asks Mary Vincent Whitty to burn the parcel without looking at its contents. Later Thursday morning, she converses individually with each sister present in the house, and then Mass is celebrated in her room. During the day, she signs the codicil to her will, adding to the names of the sisters previously listed in her bequest the names of all the other professed members of the house. She is visited by her brother James, his wife Frances, and their daughters; by several priests, including Redmond O'Hanlon, Myles Gaffney, Walter Meyler, and William Walsh, curate in Kingstown; and by Dr. William Stokes. She asks Teresa Carton: "'Will you tell the Sisters to get a good cup of tea—I think the Community Room would be a good place—when I am gone, and to comfort one another, but God will comfort them'" (Letter of Mary Vincent Whitty to Mary Cecilia Marmion, November 12, 1841).

Catherine McAuley dies, about ten minutes to eight in the evening.

November 12, 1841 — Mary Ursula Frayne writes to the superiors of all the convents: "Our dear and much beloved Revd. Mother is gone to receive the rewards of her good works. She departed this life after receiving the last Sacraments between the hours of 7 and 8 yesterday evening. May Almighty God strengthen us all, and enable us to submit with calm resignation to this heavy affliction."[20]

November 14, 1841 — The new cemetery in the garden of the Baggot Street convent is consecrated on Sunday by Bishop William Kinsella of Ossory.

November 15, 1841 — After the Solemn Office and Requiem Mass, the body of Catherine McAuley is buried in the earth, like the poor, as she had wished.

2

A General Introduction to the Early Biographical Manuscripts

I. ORAL TRADITIONS

The young Carlow annalist for 1843 depicts a scene which must have been frequently repeated in Irish and English convents of Sisters of Mercy in the years following Catherine McAuley's death in 1841:

> Our evening recreations were most cheerfully sustained. . . . On Sundays it was left to our choice: either to do some trifling work at our desks or gather round Rev. Mother [Frances Warde] on the sofa, and listen to the oft told early history of the Order. The subject was ever most pleasing to dear Rev. Mother, awakening as it did so many bright happy holy recollections of her first days in Baggot Street. . . .

At the heart of the oral traditions which developed about Catherine McAuley were the vivid memories of her earliest associates, especially the women who had joined her efforts in the years 1827 to 1830: Mary Ann Doyle, Frances Warde, Clare Moore, Magdalen Flynn, Mary Angela Dunne, and Mary de Pazzi Delany; to these voices were added those of women who came to Baggot Street during the next decade: Elizabeth Moore, Teresa White, Mary Josephine Warde, Mary Aloysius Scott, Mary Clare Augustine Moore, Mary de Sales White, Mary Vincent Harnett, Mary Juliana Hardman, Mary Agnes O'Connor, Mary Ursula Frayne, Mary Francis Creedon, Mary Vincent Whitty, and Mary Liguori Gibson. Among these women were the superiors of the nine autonomous foundations Catherine herself had established outside Dublin; the superior who succeeded her at Baggot Street;[1] the superiors of convents in Newfoundland and Liverpool, which she had planned but which she did not live to found herself; and the superiors of foundations made in Perth and New York within five years of her death.[2]

As the Tullamore Annals testifies, Catherine's death had been a great, and unexpected, human loss to the, by then, well over 150 living Sisters of Mercy:

> No tongue can describe the grief of the entire Community for what did they not lose in losing her? And the account came so unexpectedly. True, they heard she was ailing, breaking down fast, but it would appear as if they never contemplated death in reference to her at all. They almost thought she could not, would not die so soon and leave the Institute still in its infancy and, as it were, but rudely formed.
>
> The death of any one to whom the survivor has been united is a bereavement—it is hard to look the thought full in the face that we shall never see such a one again. But when that one has been light to one's feet, the stay and encouragement of

> one's very soul in the everyday difficulties and perplexities of life—the removal of such a one is a foretaste of death to those who remain behind. No wonder then that the poor sisters felt the blow keenly and required all the grace they could get to reconcile them to the loss of their sainted mother.

The Bermondsey Annals speaks of "our holy Foundress"; the Carlow Annals, of "our revered" and "venerated Foundress"; and the Tullamore Annals, of "our Venerated Foundress". The Annals of other foundations use the same or comparable adjectives. Such language was not simply conventional. Although they remembered her poor singing voice, her worn-out underclothing, and her occasional "frets", the first Sisters of Mercy believed with Michael Blake, her long-time friend, that Catherine McAuley was "holy, and eminently holy". Consequently, the cherished stories of her words and actions—and of what they knew of her inner life and thought—became all the more widespread after her death as, at first orally and then in writing, they shared their memories,

The Christian concept of "tradition" embraces all those formal and informal means by which living faith in the God revealed in Jesus of Nazareth is handed on through history, by and to members of the human community under the guidance of God's Spirit. Among these monuments of tradition, these humanly accessible modes of transmission, is the example of the lives of holy men and women. Here, as Yves Congar points out, the "means of communication are the attraction that one life exercises on another by the radiation of its inner dynamism." For, as Congar explains, a person "can act on another . . . interiorly, either by generation or by teaching . . . in one or other of its forms" (371). And since "all teaching aims to reach the 'heart' of those receiving it, . . . the teaching that does so in the most perfect way is that which has its origin in a direct, personal, and living communication between one morally mature or wise person and another" (372).[3]

Such was the radiant effect of Catherine McAuley on those who knew her, and especially on those who lived with her. And this effect was itself generative, producing other attractive lives, and other works of mercy—and the vivid oral traditions which led to the composition of the biographical manuscripts presented in the following chapters.

II. WRITTEN COMPOSITIONS

Some of the early biographical documents presented in this volume were written hurriedly under the pressure of other more immediate obligations. All of them were written by Sisters of Mercy whose primary work was not the writing of memoirs or annals. What is remarkable, therefore, is how much about Catherine McAuley these women in fact committed to writing, under circumstances that did not foster the sort of leisure such recollections would normally seem to require.

As the superior of the Bermondsey community, Clare Moore, for example, lived in the midst of one of the poorest areas of London, on the south side of the

Thames at Dockhead. Besides making constant visits to the sick in their homes and in local hospitals, the community ran a school for hundreds of poor children and fed the hungry who came to their door. It is therefore understandable that, in her five letters, Clare often apologizes "for the confused medley I send" and laments that "my memory fails me". Mary Vincent Whitty, on the other hand, wrote under the distracting emotional burden of the imminent death of Catherine McAuley whom she was helping to nurse; she did so out of loyalty to Mary Cecilia Marmion who was unavoidably absent. Similarly, all the other authors of these manuscripts were engaged in the daily demands of the works of mercy. Why then, in the two decades after Catherine's death, did so many of them take the time, deliberately, to remember her and to commit their memories to writing?

Catherine once commented on the powerful influence a single person can exert. She was speaking of the pro-temperance crusade of Theobald Mathew whom she admired and whose cause she supported, having seen the dire effects of alcohol abuse among the Irish poor. She wrote of Mathew: "What an agent he has been in the hands of God" (322). Yet Catherine was herself just such "an agent" for the women whose writings are here presented. They were among her "first-born", as she called them: the women—nearly all of them thirty years younger than she—to whom she entrusted the future of the Sisters of Mercy, and whom, as Mary Vincent Whitty notes, she remembered by name as she lay dying: "I asked her to bless the Mothers with their foundations and she went over every name saying, oh, I remember them all—May God bless them." It was these women, varied in their perspectives and in their firsthand knowledge, who were the first biographers of Catherine McAuley. When they realized that her oral instructions to them, and the oral stories about her which they treasured, needed to be expressed in a more enduring and widely available form, they began to commit their memories to writing.

Thus, on September 1, 1844, not quite three years after Catherine McAuley's death, Clare Moore wrote from London to her sister Clare Augustine Moore, then in Dublin:

> Besides what I mentioned of the affairs of Baggot St. previous to dearest Revd. Mother's going to George's Hill, there are still some little matters which I will write down at once, and then you can, if you like, set about compiling your grand work up to that period, without fear of being interrupted by any fresh "reminiscences" of mine.

This long letter was the third of five letters Clare wrote to her sister over a year's time, all for the purpose of assisting her to compose her "grand work", a memoir on the life of Catherine McAuley. In 1844 Clare Augustine had also solicited three letters of reminiscences about Catherine from Mary Ann Doyle, then living in Kells. After Mary Ann moved to Derry in 1848, the Derry Large Manuscript, for which she was probably the principal source, may have been completed, though it was probably begun before 1847. Similarly, in 1849–1850 or shortly thereafter, the Bermondsey community annalist copied into their Annals the long entry for 1841, on the life and death of Catherine McAuley.

Meanwhile, according to Limerick records, Mary Vincent Harnett, with the help of Frances Warde's, Mary Ann Doyle's, and Elizabeth Moore's recollections, had begun to compile the document known as the Limerick Manuscript, the longest of the biographical narratives about Catherine's life. The numerous verbal correspondences between certain long portions of the Limerick Manuscript and both the Derry Large Manuscript and the Bermondsey narrative—even to verbatim passages of the Derry and Bermondsey documents in the Limerick account—suggest that there was some sharing of copies of manuscripts prior to completion of the first draft of the Limerick Manuscript sometime in the early 1850s. These correspondences and especially the fact that passages from the presumably earlier documents are woven into the much longer Limerick text suggest further that the Bermondsey and Derry biographies are original narratives, inspired by the recollections of Clare Moore and Mary Ann Doyle, two of Catherine's earliest associates, and that the Limerick Manuscript is, as Mary Vincent Harnett acknowledges, a compilation, not only of original material provided by Frances Warde, Mary Ann Doyle, Elizabeth Moore, and herself, but also of material contained in the Derry and Bermondsey, and perhaps other, manuscripts. In chapter one of *The Life of Rev. Mother Catherine McAuley,* Harnett's published biography (1864) based on the Limerick Manuscript, she says: "The following memoir, compiled from the writer's personal knowledge, as well as the narrations of others, has been in manuscript several years, and would have so continued many years more but for the recommendation of a venerable Passionist Father who recommended its publication" (1).[4] Thus the family relationship among some of the early biographical manuscripts begins to emerge. Interestingly, the Derry Small Manuscript, the Dundalk Manuscript, and, apparently, the Liverpool Manuscript and Cork Manuscript 2—documents not included in the present volume—are nearly identical to the life of Catherine McAuley presented in the Bermondsey Annals.[5] This fact further illustrates the widespread copying and sharing of manuscripts that preserved the memory of Catherine McAuley.

Some manuscripts presented in this volume were created in a less complicated way. For example, the various letters written about Catherine were simply composed extemporaneously as the writer took pen to paper: Mary Ann Doyle's three letters, over a period of several months; Clare Moore's five letters, over a year; and Mary Vincent Whitty's five letters, over ten days. The entries in the Tullamore and Carlow Annals, on the other hand, were written as each annalist found time to write, often considerably after the events described, and sometimes, it is presumed, drawing on the oral or written memories of other members of the respective communities.

III. THE QUALITIES OF THE NARRATIVES

The "fields and broad palaces of memory" are, according to Saint Augustine, that uniquely personal interior space where one's images of past experiences in the external world are lodged: images which the mind once formed of what was outward, not grasping the outward realities in themselves but only perceptions of them. These images wait in the vast inner chamber of memory to be re-collected and thought, when there is need or desire (*Confessions* 10.8).

Catherine's contemporaries and her first biographers had stored in their memories their own personal images of her, such that, while there is considerable commonality of remembered perception, noticed after the fact, each of these writers speaks in her own voice, out of the particularity of what she had grasped of Catherine. Their narratives are, then, individual realizations of the one, never completely accessible, historical character and plot. Each narrator gives us the only Catherine she can give us: her version of her, as it were: the Catherine she perceived, treasured, and remembered.[6]

This variety of experience, memory, and recollection results, in turn, in a variety of narrative problems, perspectives, and tonalities. First, since each narrator is fallible, as well as limited in the range of her firsthand experience, numerous textual problems are discovered when the manuscripts are compared with one another and with other historical documents. Chief among these are the following: misidentification of names (for example, "Kelly" where it should be "Gaffney"), variant spellings of names (for example, "Byrn" and "Byrne", "Mary Ann" and "Mary Anne"), errors of fact (for example, that Catherine McAuley was born in 1786 or 1787), and variant sequences of events and transcriptions of quoted material. Some of these problems can be easily resolved in the reader's mind; others take more extensive investigation; and still others are presently unsolvable. However, all of them are testimony to the individuality of the narrators.

What is most vivid about the manuscripts is the difference in perspective and tone which the authors exhibit. Each narrator had her own angle of vision, her own window of time and circumstance through which she viewed Catherine. Each narrative point of view is thus framed by the author's age, her personality, her time at Baggot Street, her needs, her talents, and her feelings toward Catherine. In addition, each narrative is shaped by the personal discretion of the narrator, her command of language, her emotions at the time of writing, her ignorance or knowledge of certain events or situations, the extent to which she had or had not absorbed a somewhat hagiographical style, her fatigue or forgetfulness, and her consciousness of an intended audience.

For example, Mary Vincent Whitty, to whom we owe the earliest biographical narrative—her sequence of firsthand accounts of Catherine's last illness, death, and burial—wrote, in profound grief and haste, to one person (the absent Mistress of Novices, Mary Cecilia Marmion), certainly never dreaming that her letters would one day be published. As she said to Mary Cecilia: "I hope I am not doing wrong in letting such a careless note as this is leave me, for I know you will excuse it." Clare Augustine Moore, on the other hand, was aiming, over the twenty years of her writing, to produce a comprehensive work. She writes calmly, with an artist's eye for detail, and a straightforward affection for

Catherine, while maintaining certain critical judgments about her. Similarly, the style of Clare Moore's five letters, written only for her sister, is different from that of the Life in the Bermondsey Annals, by definition meant for posterity. In the former, she narrates in the first person, with numerous disavowals of knowledge; in the latter, she writes in the third person, and what she knows only imperfectly is left out. Clare's reverence for Catherine McAuley and for her teachings is evident, but she is also fair and circumspect in the way she portrays other people and events. Her sister, on the other hand, is often downright indignant at the difficulties Catherine had to endure.

Sometimes the authors of these manuscripts make an overt effort to set an incorrect record straight (for example, "Revd. Mother never was a Protestant, as has been said"); at other times, they remain discreetly silent about an event or situation which is known, from other sources, to have occurred (for example, the harmfully eccentric behavior of Mary Clare Agnew while she was superior of Bermondsey from June to December 1841). Moreover, only Clare Augustine Moore's Memoir, even though it condemns the disclosure, mentions the burning of Catherine's instruments of penance the night before she died. Mary Vincent Whitty cannot speak of this in her letters, because she was not supposed to have even seen what was in the bundle she burned; and the other authors cannot, because they could have been aware of the full contents of the burned parcel only years later, when Mary Vincent was urged by Vincent Grotti, a Passionist priest, to speak of what she saw.

Within the documents, and among them, there are numerous narrative gaps and repetitions: the failure to mention something because the narrator does not realize (or wish to report) that she knows something that others do not know, or will not know in the future unless she tells them; and the repetition, in manuscript after manuscript, not only of key events, but of emphasis on certain values. For example, much may be permanently lost because Mary Ann Doyle says casually of their time at George's Hill: "I don't think there was any thing occurred during our Noviciate which would be worth mentioning"; and because Clare Moore says rather apologetically:

> Many things come into my mind but having often related them at Recreation I get puzzled and think, Oh, I wrote that to her long ago, and sometimes also I make foolish repetitions, but you would excuse if you knew how little time I have.

On the other hand, the cumulative effect of repeated descriptions, within and among the manuscripts—of Catherine's humility, for example, or of her abiding concern for mutual charity and companionship with the poor—serves to ground such interpretations of her character in a wide range of individual perceptions.

Like all historical evidence these biographical manuscripts have strengths and limitations. As contributions to the historical record about Catherine McAuley they provide the best contemporary evidence available: they are extended, firsthand accounts written by people who knew Catherine McAuley well, lived with her, and enjoyed her confidence. No other comparably well-informed testimonies are extant. The letter of Michael Blake and the articles attributed to Myles Gaffney are important reflections on Catherine's life, but they are much less detailed than the biographical manuscripts written by her associates in the Sisters of Mercy. (Dr. Blake's letter is included in two of the manuscripts presented in this volume, and where the full articles attributed to Myles Gaffney present information different from that in the excerpts of these articles included in the biographical manuscripts in this volume the relevant passages are provided in the notes accompanying the excerpts.) The extant letters of Catherine's nephew William Macauley, written many years after her death, and the extant letters of her god-child and her cousin, Teresa Byrn and Catherine Byrn, are also important sources of information, particularly about Catherine McAuley's life prior to 1827, and as such should be published. But none of these statements fundamentally contradicts the portrait presented in the biographical manuscripts in this volume—except insofar as Willie's memory of Catherine's blonde ringlets (". . . my aunt's front of ringlets, her own hair cut off when it began to turn gray. That was pride for you!") may emphasize her all too human concern for her appearance; or his lifelong questions about the whereabouts of his supposed inheritance from his father or older brothers may insinuate that Catherine or the Sisters of Mercy had retained, or had disposed of, money or property actually belonging to him, a natural enough query of a youngest, orphaned son.[7]

If fondness for one's biographical subject constitutes a limitation on one's reliability as a biographer, a possible weakness of the biographical manuscripts presented in this volume may be the fact that they were written by women who loved and revered Catherine McAuley, and were members of the Institute she founded. In this respect they were, admittedly, devoted followers of her teachings. Certainly their sentiments of affection and admiration are obvious as one reads the manuscripts. But equally obvious are the authors' attempts to name and portray whatever flaws in Catherine's thinking or behavior they judged worth mentioning. Nonetheless the manuscripts are to some extent hagiographical: I use this descriptive term in its strict, non-pejorative sense. These women clearly regarded Catherine as a saint, and in this they were probably not mistaken. Hence if they were faithful both to their subject and to their estimate of her, their manuscripts will present not only her life-story, but also all those aspects of her life which appeared to them to be holy. The writer who has least presented Catherine McAuley in this way is Catherine herself, in her own letters, where her weaknesses and shortcomings are freely displayed and acknowledged.

IV. CATHERINE'S "SAYINGS"

A striking feature of some of the manuscripts is their contribution to the written tradition of the "sayings" of Catherine McAuley. The Bermondsey Life, in particular, quotes her maxims a number of times; the Limerick Manuscript repeats these quotations and adds others; and Mary Vincent Whitty's letters record still other sayings, expressed during the last five days of Catherine's life. A predominant aspect of Catherine's relationship to the first Sisters of Mercy was her role as a teacher and practical guide in their spiritual development. Consequently, they treasured her memorable statements, even before her death; after her death, these became one of her most tangible legacies to them.

However, it was not until 1868 that Catherine's sayings were first collected in a separate publication, on the initiative of Clare Moore in Bermondsey. The Bermondsey Annals for 1868 records this event—in Clare Moore's own handwriting:

> One of the resolutions of good which followed the August Retreat this year was a determination to collect even a few of the maxims and practical sayings of our revered Foundress. The design was submitted to the Bishop [Thomas Grant] who approved of it and when he saw the Manuscript he advised to communicate the project to the Community at Baggot Street Dublin, the Parent House of our Institute, as suggestions or additions might be made which would prove useful. The little collection was sent, and returned with expressions of satisfaction; nothing was remembered additional, except the wish which our revered Foundress had expressed, that those who came on business, or even visitors to the Convent and the poor, should not be kept waiting either at the door or in the Convent longer than necessary, as she had noticed negligence on that point in some of the Communities. The Bishop recommended to have the Maxims classified under different heads: —Humility—Charity—etc. with references to the Chapters of our Rule which they served to illustrate. It was intended that each Sister should write a copy for her own use, but on consideration this plan seemed troublesome and the cost of MS. [manuscript] books almost as expensive as printing.

The Annals then describes the printing, and the distribution on December 12, 1868, of copies of *A Little Book of Practical Sayings . . . of Our Revered Foundress*, as well as of photographs of Catherine's handwriting: "Five hundred copies were printed, and some were sent to the different Convents of our Institute with which this Community had intercourse." The Annals notes that "Some of the Rev. Mothers, who had had the happiness of hearing the instructions of our revered Foundress, bore testimony to the fidelity with which her words had been recorded." For example, Mary Ursula Frayne wrote from Melbourne, Australia: "How exactly dear Reverend Mother's words are noted down, I could almost fancy myself listening to her once more."[8] The twenty-seven years since Catherine's death had not dulled the memory of her voice.

Of course Catherine's sayings may have undergone the same diverse range of transmission as the sayings of other revered persons in history. For example, as in the particularly striking case of Jesus of Nazareth, a person's sayings may retain a remarkable degree of verbal agreement across various written documents, or they may be shifted to different contexts and undergo different interpretations, or they may be consciously altered for the purpose of underscoring a different sense, or they may be ascribed to one person when they are in fact the utterance of another.[9] In a living tradition which looks back to one stellar exemplar of all that a community cherishes, there is, in addition to the desire to preserve the actual words he or she once spoke, the assumed freedom to interpret and adapt, and even to attempt to speak the mind of the person as he or she might now speak it.

V. THE TEXTS OF THE MANUSCRIPTS

To varying degrees some of the manuscripts presented in this volume have been quoted in the past, in published biographies of Catherine McAuley, as well as in other published work. Beginning with Mary Vincent Harnett's *Life of Rev. Mother Catherine McAuley* (1864) and Mary Austin Carroll's *Life of Catherine McAuley* (1866), biographers have depended on material in these manuscripts to provide details about Catherine's life and the lives of her contemporaries.[10] In this century Roland Burke Savage, Mary Bertrand Degnan, Mary Ignatia Neumann, Mary Angela Bolster, Mary Carmel Bourke, and Joanna Regan and Isabelle Keiss—in addition to Kathleen Healy, Mary Hermenia Muldrey, and Frances (formerly, Mary Xaverius) O'Donoghue (the modern biographers of Frances Warde, Mary Austin Carroll, and Mary Vincent Whitty respectively)—have all recognized the irreplaceable value of these manuscripts.

But scholarship on Catherine McAuley and the Sisters of Mercy has now reached the point where published quotations from these documents, no matter how numerous or lengthy, are not enough. Historians, theologians, biographers, and other scholars, as well as general readers, now need the full texts so that they can formulate their own interpretations and correlations.[11] Although each of these manuscripts has been available for well over a century, access to the various archives requires travel which, in some cases, may be prohibitively expensive or otherwise difficult. Moreover, some of the manuscripts are now in a very fragile state, and others are very difficult to read. For these reasons, it has seemed essential that the manuscripts should be published here in full. Except for Cork Manuscript 1 and the preface to Cork Manuscript 3, neither of which is included here,[12] the manuscripts presented in this volume comprise *all* of the original biographical manuscripts on Catherine McAuley which were written by her contemporaries in the Sisters of Mercy and are still extant.

Each of the manuscripts presented below is preceded by a brief introduction to the author, or to the person assumed to be a principal source of the content of the document. The story of each of these women is well known and revered in the particular Mercy foundations with which she was affiliated, but beyond that, even in international Mercy circles, her life, personality, skills, and accomplishments have not been well known—despite Mary Austin Carroll's early efforts to present portraits of many of these women in her *Leaves from the Annals of the Sisters of Mercy*. Books and articles have been written on a few of them, but some of these have not enjoyed wide distribution. In addition to her important contributions to our knowledge of Catherine McAuley's life, each of these women was, in her own right, a very significant contributor to the historical development of the Catholic Church in the nineteenth century and to the social and ecclesial enrichment of the people in Ireland, England, Australia, or the United States. The respective introductions in this volume are, therefore, an attempt to make these women better known as historical figures and to portray the flesh-and-blood lives behind the manuscripts attributed to them.

Before studying the texts, it is helpful to recall the circumstances under which many of them were written. As Clare Moore says in one of her letters:

> I put down what comes into my mind for if I stopped to select and place things in order you might wait long enough for any information. I send this in scraps also, lest if I kept it back to write it out fair—to revise and correct—you might never see it at all.

To all the women who have allowed us to "see it at all"—who wrote or provided information for these manuscripts about Catherine McAuley—church history, in the fullest sense, owes an enormous debt of gratitude. These little known writers speak for important aspects of the underside of that history: the plight of the poor, the sick, and the neglected; and the lives and works of women and men who relieved their human misery and addressed its causes. The history of the church in the nineteenth century is, as everyone acknowledges, more than the record of episcopal consecrations, synods, and correspondence with Rome; it is also, among other precious realities, the record of its food and shelter shared, its deaths hidden in hovels and convents, and its consolations extended to those who were considered to be "the least".

The manuscripts presented in this volume are not, of course, either singly or together, the complete story of Catherine McAuley. No historical documents can be that. Rather they are partial interpretations of a woman whose life, like that of any historical personage, can never be fully retrieved, that is, completely and purely presented, by any historical writer. But having once lived and died, Catherine now lives on in our world in the recorded memories of her contemporaries, and in the interpretations of those who, standing in a new time, in the midst of new questions and new historical realities, seek to engage in honest dialogue with representations of her feelings, intentions, and values, as these were perceived by her contemporaries, in their own context.

While historical knowledge is, admittedly, partial and subjective, still, as Philip Sheldrake has pointed out, "an orientation towards the present and the future demands a sense of the past" (29). Stories, such as these about Catherine, are essential to the full wisdom of any era and culture, "because without storytelling we put ourselves out of contact with the basic realities in our world. In other words, it is only through stories that we can situate and understand our existence in time" (29). To encounter the earliest stories about Catherine McAuley's life and work, and to engage with the Catherine presented in these stories, may be to uncover what Sheldrake calls "a story within a story": the universal human calling to be authentic, reverent, merciful human beings.

Editorial Note:

Every effort has been made to present each text exactly as it is found in manuscript form. Hence, the wording, spelling, capitalization, and paragraphing follow the original as closely as possible, consistent with clarity, even when the wording or spelling appears inaccurate, according to present knowledge or the standards of the time. Where the greatest difficulty arises is in punctuation. It is sometimes nearly impossible, when reading a manuscript, to identify commas, periods, and dashes correctly. Moreover, in some manuscripts dashes are used for the various kinds of pauses that commas, semicolons, and periods now represent. I have done my best to follow the original where I could figure it out, rather than risk inserting misleading full stops, but I have also sometimes deleted commas and dashes or inserted commas, semicolons, and periods where this seemed necessary for the sake of clarity. If the manuscripts are inconsistent in capitalization I have left the inconsistencies. But since it is often hard to decide whether a word begins with a small capital letter or a large lower case letter, I may have misinterpreted some of these letters. Where I add wording to a text for the sake of explanation or correction, I enclose it in square brackets after the exact wording of the text. However, many seeming inaccuracies are left without bracketed insertions when I am not confident of a correct insertion. The use of "[*sic*]" is generally kept to a minimum on the ground that readers will trust that the original texts are exactly presented, although "[*sic*]" is occasionally inserted after certain antique spellings and misspellings, lest the readers' confidence in the accuracy of a text be unnecessarily shaken. In the few instances where I have altered paragraphing or an abbreviation in a text, the alteration and my reason for it are given in a note. Except in Mary Vincent Whitty's letters, I have usually changed ampersands to "and".

My aim has been to present printed texts which are as faithful to the originals as it is humanly possible to make them. But, of course, and regrettably, here and there I may have erred, though the task of going through the manuscripts again is not one I would wish on anyone. I believe that the texts presented here provide reliable readings of the originals; they are the result of careful re-readings as well as repeated proofreadings. Where informational notes appear necessary for more fully understanding the texts, these are provided.

3

Mary Ann (Anna Maria) Doyle, 1809?–1866

Anna Maria Doyle, the daughter of James Doyle and Catherine Tynan of Church Street in Saint Andrew's Parish, Dublin, was born in 1809 or 1800.[1] On September 24, 1827, she and Catherine McAuley's young cousin, Catherine Byrn, took up residence in the newly built House on Baggot Street, and under Catherine's supervision began the poor schools and shelter there.[2] She was thus Catherine's first associate who became a professed Sister of Mercy, Catherine Byrn later transferring as a novice to the Dominican Sisters in Cabra, a northern suburb of Dublin.[3]

Anna Maria's brother, Michael Doyle, a priest of Dublin, served as curate at Saints Michael and John's on Exchange Street at this time. In the Deed of Agreement for the construction of the House on Baggot Street, Michael Doyle and Edward Armstrong are designated to act on Catherine's behalf in negotiations with the builders and to supervise the execution of the building contract. Perhaps Anna Maria heard of Catherine's intended work on Baggot Street from her older brother, though she does not refer to him in her letters to Clare Augustine Moore or in the Derry Large Manuscript. However, the Bermondsey Annals identifies her as "Miss Anna Maria Doyle, sister to one of the priests of St. Michael's and St. John's Chapel".[4]

In the first of her three letters of reminiscences about Catherine, written to Clare Augustine Moore in 1844, Mary Ann (Anna Maria) Doyle explains the origin of her affiliation with the House on Baggot Street:[5]

> The Convent was then nearly finished. During the time of its being built, I sometimes walked near it, and felt a great attraction to it. I once asked the man who had care of it to allow me to see it, and was so delighted that I fixed my heart on it. I was introduced to Revd. Mother. We were much pleased with each other. At the time I was about entering a Presentation convent, but being the then only child of aged parents, I felt much, and the prospect of being able to visit them determined them, and myself, in the choice of uniting with Revd. Mother in the formation of the new establishment.

In the Derry Large Manuscript, of which Mary Ann Doyle was evidently the principal source—since it contains, more than any other early manuscript, extensive information about the years 1823 to 1832—she describes her moving into Baggot Street in 1827, though here she does so in the third person:

> When early in the Autumn the building was in some degree habitable it was determined that she should enter at once though she was to have but one associate, Miss Catherine Byrne, then very young. Miss McAuley herself could not then make the institution her residence on account of the recent death of her sister, her niece being quite too young to undertake the management of her Father's household.

> However, as it was determined that the house should be opened, Miss McAuley wrote to Miss Doyle saying that as all needful preparations would soon be completed she might enter if she pleased on the 23rd or 24th of the current month which was September. Miss Doyle . . . though she did not then know of the feast, fixed on the 24th, but in another note remarked that she should be particularly rejoiced to begin her labours on that day as it was dedicated to our Lady of Mercy, suggesting at the same time that House of Mercy would be a good name for the institution. . . . The schools therefore were opened on the appointed feast, and some young women admitted to the dormitories of whom two sisters of the name of Fay were the first.

Anna Maria Doyle was at Baggot Street for the following three years, and then went to the Presentation Convent on George's Hill, Dublin, with Catherine McAuley and Elizabeth Harley, on September 8, 1830. She received the Presentation habit on December 9, 1830, and on December 12, 1831 professed her vows as one of the first three Sisters of Mercy, taking the name, Sister Mary Ann Teresa Doyle.[6]

In April 1836 she and Mary Teresa Purcell were selected for the first autonomous foundation outside of Dublin—in Tullamore, established on April 21. As the Tullamore Annals explains, "These two were judged sufficient as two young ladies were awaiting the arrival of the Sisters to join them and others were expected." The temporary convent (used for over five years) was small and poor, but as the Annals reports:

> Mother M. Anne, whose ideas of spaciousness in convents nearly coincided with those of S[t]. Peter of Alcantara, was well pleased with the straitness of the cells and parlor. Our V[enerated] Foundress notices this in a pleasant letter she wrote at the time to Baggot St., thus—"Mother M. Anne has met with her 'beau-ideal' of a conventual building at last, for our rooms are so small that two cats could scarcely dance in them. The rest of us however would have no objection to larger ones."

This was not the only source of laughter. As the Annals notes, among the many presents given to the new community was Rev. Walter Murtagh's "offering of a cow":

> This created great amusement, and was regarded as a great favor, it being the first *live-stock* of the Order, but the Community not possessing even a blade of grass at the time, the poor animal had to be sent to the country to graze. In the early correspondence our Ven. Foundress often mentions this famous cow, desiring her best wishes to "*Madame La Vache*".

It was in Tullamore also that Catherine McAuley planned to set up a week-long "Nonsensical Club" when she returned for a reception ceremony in late July 1836. As she wrote to Mary Delamere, a Tullamore postulant: "I will be president, you vice-president, and Catherine [probably Catherine McAuley's niece Catherine, who was to accompany her on this visit] can give lectures as professor of folly" (78–80). Catherine called this letter "a preparatory meditation"!

Mary Ann Doyle, whom Catherine playfully called the "Divine Mother", was at first a timid, cautious superior. Yet she conducted the annual August retreat for her community, whenever a Jesuit priest from Tullabeg College was not available, and she instituted the yearly practice of preparing children, often in very large numbers, to receive their first Communion on the feast of Our Lady of Mercy (September 24), after which "they came in procession to the convent where they breakfasted".

Catherine McAuley once mildly complained that the new foundation in Birr should have been made from nearby Tullamore, noting that "it is quite a shame to be such creepmouses in such a cause" (272). However, Catherine did not live long enough to see Tullamore catch fire in this respect. On February 9, 1844 Mary Ann herself, with one other sister initially, founded a community in Kells, the first foundation from Tullamore. She served three years as superior, and then, in 1848, having returned to Tullamore, she went to Derry as part of a small group of Tullamore sisters who founded the first community of Sisters of Mercy in the northern part of Ireland.

Although Mary Ann did not at first have Catherine's boldness in responding quickly to perceived needs, she evidently had a certain good sense about what was possible. As the Tullamore Annals explains:

> Mother M. Anne might have been too cautious; however she erred on the safe side. Her zeal led her rather to perfect the sisters entrusted to her, before she sent them out to spread the new Institute . . . and when she could not spare her more experienced subjects, she knew it would not advance the glory of God to form foundations of half-trained inexperienced members.

One of Mary Ann's experiments in eagerness turned into an embarrassment: in 1840 she invited Theobald Mathew, the acclaimed Apostle of Temperance, to preach at a reception ceremony in Tullamore, apparently not adverting to the fact that the town was (as it still is) the heart of the Irish distillery business. When the Bishop of Meath, John Cantwell, "heard of it", according to the Annals, "he thought it most imprudent just then and ordered M. M. Anne to write immediately and decline [Mathew's] proffered services." As it turned out, the "principal Benefactor of the Convent was a Distiller & many influential persons in the King's Co. also." Mary Ann was "dreadfully frustrated", but Mathew was "not in the least degree offended, and sympathised cordially with her."[7]

Though Catherine McAuley was more lively—at least by her own estimate—than Mary Ann Doyle, her junior by many years, she had enduring affection for and confidence in her first companion. Mary Ann was one of the four members of the Baggot Street Trust established in 1829; she was Catherine's Assistant from 1831 or 1832 to 1836; she supervised the Kingstown branch house for a year; she was chosen in 1836 as the superior of the first foundation outside of Dublin; and in late September 1841, when Catherine was severely ill, she turned to Mary Ann for help, asking her to receive and care for Mary Justina Fleming, a newly professed sister who was dying at Baggot Street (Neumann, ed. 376). Although there are only three published letters from Catherine to Mary Ann, it is not possible that this was the extent of Catherine's correspondence with her.[8]

One of the poignant personal losses entailed in Catherine's early death, in relation to the ongoing life of the Institute, is that she did not live to see her young companions come to the maturity she herself already enjoyed in the 1830s. Mary Ann Doyle was a young woman when she went to Tullamore. She lived thirty more years, dying in Derry on September 11, 1866.[9] She is buried there, in the vault of the Long Tower Church, not far from the ancient site within the walls of Derry where Saint Columba (521–597) founded his monastery and built his church in the years 546 to 563, before he sailed to Iona.

When Derry was founded in 1848, Mary Catherine Locke was named superior. Mary Ann Doyle served as assistant and mistress of novices. However, in 1854 she asked to be relieved of these responsibilities. The Bermondsey Annals for 1866 includes Catherine Locke's account of Mary Ann's remaining years in Derry. (Catherine was then superior of the convent in Dundee, Scotland which she had founded in 1859.) She says of the older Mary Ann Doyle: "she lived so sequestered and retired . . . that little can be said except that her life was hidden with Christ in God. She was a model of the hidden life; always occupied in her cell writing, or reading, or working scapulars for the poor, for her health was too weak to admit of her being employed in the more laborious functions. She was particularly fond of translating French works on the religious state, of which I am sure she must have left many manuscripts" (2:[95]–[96]).

Timid though she may have been in her earlier years, and sickly in her later years, one can still see in Mary Ann Doyle something of the courageous missionary spirit of Saint Columba. One of the touching manuscripts in her handwriting in the Derry archives of the Sisters of Mercy is a prayer "For a person under sentence" of death. The existence of this manuscript suggests that early on Mary Ann herself may have visited the Derry (or Tullamore or Kells) jail and consoled prisoners about to be executed. She would have prayed with each one of them: "O God, Thy will be done. . . . . Give me courage patiently to suffer . . . be with me and help me in this my last hour. Deal with me not according to my sins, nor reward me according to my iniquities. But according to the multitude of thy tender mercies have compassion on me . . . shelter me now under the shadow of Thy wings and stand by me in the day of tribulation."[10]

To Mary Ann Doyle we are indebted for at least three important sources of information about Catherine McAuley: her three letters of reminiscences about Catherine, written to Clare Augustine Moore in 1844; the content of the Derry Large Manuscript, a long and original manuscript dealing ostensibly with the years "1823" to "1832", but having many important flashbacks to earlier years in Catherine's life; and the Tullamore Annals for the years 1836 through 1841, many passages of which speak of Catherine. These texts are all presented below.

As Catherine wrote to Elizabeth Moore on January 13, 1839: "It commenced with 2, Sister Doyle and I" and "it evidently was to go on" (154–5). Catherine was a firm believer in beginning well, and the history of the Sisters of Mercy owes a great deal to Mary Ann Doyle—for her early and long sustained work as a co-founder of the Institute.

THE LETTERS OF MARY ANN DOYLE, KELLS, TO MARY CLARE AUGUSTINE MOORE, BAGGOT STREET, DUBLIN, 1844

My dear Sister,[1]

I frequently heard our dear Revd. Mother M. Catherine speak of her earnest desire to have it in her power to afford safe lodging to poor females who would be working out all day. She appeared well acquainted with the dangers to which they were exposed in the lodgings to which they had to return at night; before God gave her the means of erecting the House of Mercy she wished that she were able to take two rooms for the purpose, no religious establishment then affording such protection. She was also much devoted to schools, and while in the world visited them as much as she could. Many Protestant relations to whom she was much attached and whose conversion she ardently desired induced her to think of forming a society of ladies who would devote themselves to the practice of the works of Mercy without making vows that they might be at liberty to visit their relations and remain with them in sickness and affliction.[2]

I think the building of the convent commenced immediately after the death of Mr. Calla[g]han.[3] Revd. Dr. Blake, I believe, chose the situation and laid the first stone about the time that he was going to Rome to establish the College, I think in the year [18]23.[4]

It was about four years until the house was finished. During this time Revd. Mother's only sister was in a very bad state of health which engaged her time and attention very much, she being a Protestant, her husband a most bigoted character, five children whom he endeavoured to bring up in the same sentiments. The eldest child (our beloved Sister Mary Teresa) was much attached to her Aunt and anxious to become a Catholic. The poor sister was a long time dying; dear Revd. Mother never left her. They then had a house at Dundrum, their own residence was the Royal Hospital. About three weeks before her death she was attended by a priest (Revd. Mr. McCormick); her husband did not know of it for long after her death. Revd. Mother was then obliged to remain with the children.

The convent was then nearly finished. During the time of its being built, I sometimes walked near it, and felt a great attraction to it. I once asked the man who had care of it to allow me to see it, and was so delighted that I fixed my heart on it. I was introduced to Revd. Mother. We were much pleased with each other. At the time I was about entering a Presentation Convent, but being the then only child of aged parents,[5] I felt much, and the prospect of being able to visit them determined them, and myself, in the choice of uniting with Revd. Mother in the formation of the new establishment. On the 24th of September 1827, the day I selected for commencing, not ever knowing that it would [be] the Order of Mercy, the school opened,[6] and some poor young women were admitted. A cousin of Revd. Mother's (Sister M. Josephine, then very young—now a Dominican nun)[7] assisted me. Revd. Mother came almost every day, and her niece, but did not enter the house entirely for nine months. During this time her old and beloved friend, Very Revd. Edward Armstrong, under whose advice she had acted for years died.[8] She attended him constantly during his illness and received much instruction from him.

Immediately after his death she came to remain in the convent, and brought with her [her] two nieces. The eldest[9] was received into the Church in a few months (on St. Cecelia's day) by the Most Revd. Dr. Murray. On that day his Grace granted permission for us to visit the sick. Sr. M. Frances was then with us. (The younger niece[10] was received into the Church a few months after, by Very Revd. R. O'Hanlon—Sister M. Ann Agnes).

The January following Mr. Maccauley [Macauley], the father of these children, Revd. Mother's brother-in-law, died of a few days illness. She attended him but did not succeed in converting him. She was then appointed Guardian to her three nephews;[11] they were received into the Church the year following by the Chaplain, Revd. D. Burke, in the convent chapel. The eldest niece then became one of the Sisters. Before this time Dr. Blake returned from Rome, and took the greatest interest in the establishment.[12] Through his interest the convent chapel was opened after much difficulty and opposition. It was dedicated on the Octave of the Ascension 1829 by the Most Revd. Dr. Murray—a Pontifical High Mass and sermon from Dr. Blake in which he spoke in highest terms of Revd. Mother. She was much affected on that day and would not be present at the ceremonies but remained in prayer in the convent. At this time and long after she had much to feel from disapprobation expressed by many priests and others. Much jealousy existed regarding the Sisters of Charity.[13]

We had much consolation in the support and kindness which the Revd. gentlemen of St. Teresa's Church always evinced for the establishment, particularly the Very Revd. R. O'Hanlon. The House was still getting on wonderfully—school, House of Mercy, and the poor sick all well attended to, sisters increasing. It was then considered things could not be permanently settled unless some served a regular noviciate. The obstacles to Revd. Mother's becoming a religious were now removed. Application was made to Rome for permission to serve a Noviceship in an enclosed order, which was granted and thought to be a great favour. We had then 12 sisters.

Application was made to George's Hill. They kindly consented to receive us. On the 8th of September 1830 we left Baggot St. The Sister chosen to come with [us] was a saintly creature.[14] Revd. Mother went though her noviciate in a most edifying manner; her cheerfulness was the admiration of all, tho' she had much care on her mind, still directing Baggot St., and suffered much from a disease of the gums during the time. For some time she was treated with indulgence and respect, but a change of Superiors taking place, she was put under a young and very strict Mistress of Novices. She then went through every humble duty with pleasure, assisted me in the sacristy, swept, served in refectory, and every other humble office. Our Noviceship was severe, being only one year. Our holy Mistress left nothing undone for our spiritual improvement. My dear companion,

Sr. M. Elizabeth, was not sufficiently strong, besides being very scrupulous, so that her health was broken down. She died about four months after her profession,[15] which was a great trial to us, particularly to me. There was some difficulty regarding our profession as our vows could not be the same as these[16] made by the community. They submitted the difficulty to Most Revd. Dr. Murray, who removed it by the form of vow which he proposed. He came himself some time before our profession and examined us, particularly on our profession in the new order, "we are about to erect called *of the Sisters of Mercy.*"

The profession took place on the 12th of December 1831. The reception and profession should have been on the feast of the Conception, but being the feast day of the Church of the Conception, his Grace could not attend.[17] Soon after the ceremony we returned to Baggot St. accompanied by Revd. Dr. Blake who said as we were coming that the Order of Mercy should be dated from that day. Before we left the convent he in presence of the Superioress congratulated us on the manner in which we spent our noviciate, what edification we had given, and hoped we would infuse the same spirit to those to whom we were returning.

My dear Sister,[18]

From this time, I am sure Mother M. de Pazzi[19] could inform you of every thing interesting. The cholera[20] raged immediately after, our dear Revd. Mother's exertions then, all that was done for the poor. She brought home an infant from the Hospital in her arms, whose mother died.

She received comfort and advice from Revd. Dr. Gaffney who was much interested for the establishment and who gave the first retreat. I am not aware of Revd. Mother having had any intention of uniting with the Sisters of Charity. Her property was too considerable not to form a new establishment for the poor. I was told that the old gentleman[21] would have left his property for public charities but being well aware of the use she would make of it.

I cannot say much of Revd. Mother's life in the world. I know she had much to contend with regarding religion, being constantly with Protestants and Quakers.[22] Her parents died when she was very young. I believe Mr. and Mrs. Calla[g]han adopted her. Mrs. C. was bedridden for three years during which time Revd. Mother attended with affection. She died a Catholic, some time before her husband.[23]

Revd. Mother never was a Protestant, as has been said.[24] She told me that in some doubt she had recourse to the celebrated Dr. Beatie [Thomas Betagh] who quite convinced her. At another time she sought instruction from Most Revd. Dr. Murray, then a curate in the old chapel in Liffey St.

While we were in George's Hill Sr. M. Josephine[25] was cured of a long illness, which was considered miraculous. I heard Dr. Blake say at the time it should be recorded in the annals of the house.

I heard Revd. Mother express doubts of it. Mother M. de Pazzi knows the particulars.

My dear Sister, I hope you will be able to make some sense of this. You will make every allowance for me under present circumstances. If any thing should occur to you that I could give information on you have only to write to me and I will promise an answer by return of post.[26]

*

Convent of Mercy, St. Columbkill's

My dear Sister,

I lose no time in sending an exact copy of my vow.[27] The name of the Superioress when we commenced our Noviciate was Mary Clare Angela Doyle; at our profession, Mary Francis de Sales Knowd.

I don't think there was any thing occurred during our Noviciate which would be worth mentioning.[28]

I will not forget dear Revd. Mother's intentions the next month. I hope to have our two postulants received about the 24th. I beg prayers for them, and for myself if it be the Holy Will of God to restore my health which continues very poorly.

I will not forget you on your great Saint's day.[29] I suppose dear Revd. Mother has heard that Miss Agnew is gone to Rome with another lady who left a convent, to get changes made in the Rule.[30] She was most pressing to get it from me, but I would not give it. I heard lately from Mother M. Clare. She was well.

Present my best love to dear Revd. Mother,[31] Mother de Pazzi, Mother Vincent,[32] Sr. M. Magdellen [Magdalen] and all the Sisters.

I remain, my dear Sister,
Yours affectionately in C[hrist]
Sister M. A. Doyle

Aug. 21st.

*

Convent of Mercy, Kells Nov. 17

My dear Sister,

I cannot tell exactly the time of the appointment. I know it was in January immediately after Sister Ursula's reception.[33] The first Chapter, I may say, was held before Sister M. Gertrude's (Jones) profession. I left Dublin before they were regularly held.[34] Mother M. Clare I am sure recollects, if Mother M. de Pazzi does not. She also could inform you as to the drawing up of our holy Rule as she assisted dear Revd. Mother.

With love to Revd. M[other], Mother de Pazzi, M. Vincent, Sr. Magdellen [Magdalen], and Sr. Genevieve.[35]

I remain, my dear Sister,
Yours affectionately in C[hrist]
Sister M. A. Doyle

THE DERRY LARGE MANUSCRIPT[1] "NOTES ON THE LIFE OF MOTHER CATHERINE McAULEY BY ONE OF THE FIRST SISTERS OF MERCY"[2]

1823

. . . [From this time she took][3] great delight in projecting means of affording shelter to unprotected young women. She had then no expectation of the large fortune that afterwards was hers, but her benefactor[4] had once spoken of leaving her a thousand pounds, and she thought, if she had that or even a few hundreds, she would hire a couple of rooms and work for and with her protegees. The idea haunted her very dreams. Night after night she would see herself in some very large place where a number of young women were employed as laundresses or at plain-work, while she herself would be surrounded by a crowd of ragged children which she was washing and dressing very busily. The premises[5] therefore were planned to contain dormitories for young women who for want of proper protection might be exposed to danger, a female poor school, and apartments for ladies who might choose, for any definite or indefinite time, to devote themselves to the service of the poor, without the restriction of vows, and remaining at liberty to visit their relatives or even to remain with them for a time in case of affliction or sickness.[6]

While the building was carried on Miss McAuley resided chiefly at Coolock House, still keeping her intentions with regard to the proposed Institution a secret, as she had reason to know that her family would resent it extremely. They rather wished or affected to wish that she should marry, and she had some advantageous proposals, for tho' no longer young she still wore the appearance of youth, and in person and manners was very engaging. At that time she lived in what is usually called good style, that is, she kept a carriage, dressed well, went into society and sometimes gave parties at her own house; but employed the greater part of her time in works of piety and charity, especially in the instruction of poor children in the female schools of St. Mary's Parish, Abbey St. She was also very regular in the performance of every duty of religion, fasted rigorously, and during Lent never tasted wine. She rose very early, prayed much, and was most assiduous in her attendance at Sermons and at the public Offices of the Church.

1824, 25, 26

The building[7] during these three years proceeded slowly enough, the foundress meanwhile endeavouring by all means in her power to acquire such information as would be useful to her in the execution of her charitable design. She visited the Kildare St. schools where, on account of her Protestant connexion, she was supposed to be a Protestant and was initiated into their method of inducing Catholic children to attend under the idea that there should be no interference with their religion, while at the same time the work of proselytism was slowly, silently, but successfully carried on. At the same time she learned the names and residence of a great number of the children and in many instances succeeded in her efforts to have them removed. The solicitation of some friends induced her to visit the Convent of the Sisters of Charity, Stanhope St., it being supposed that their cooperation might be of use to her in directing the proposed institution. But to herself it was evident that this could not be, and the more information she acquired concerning the government and general management of the House of Refuge the more she became convinced that the principles on which it was conducted were utterly incompatible with her design. The only consequence of these visits was therefore to confirm her in her resolution never to admit the interference of a non-resident committee, and never to close the doors of the institution against anyone because they had experienced its protection before. Reports were afterwards circulated that she proposed to these religious that they should take the Establishment under their protection, but this she never did and never wished to do.

On the 30th of May 1825 she had the affliction to lose her good friend the Revd. Joseph Nugent, after fifteen days of severe suffering, during which she attended him day and night. Soon after she began to suffer greatly from an apprehension that her charitable projects could never be realised on account of the expenses they would necessarily entail; but she was encouraged by the exhortations of the Revd. Mr. Armstrong who then suggested among other and higher motives of consolation, that a good subscription for the purpose might be easily raised, as the institution was situated in such a fashionable neighbourhood. This trial afterwards frequently recurred tho' at intervals, and she had need of all her fortitude to bear up against it; yet putting her trust in God, whose aid she continually implored by fervent prayer she resolved to continue what she had begun—and leave the issue to Him. It was about this time that she took charge of a little orphan that she saw cast into the street from a celler [*sic*] that her parents had occupied.[8] As there were doubts as to the fact of her being baptised Miss McAuley procured conditional Baptism to be administered and henceforward the protection of orphans was added to the plan of this institution.

1827

During the early part of this year the building was carried on slowly indeed but still it was sufficiently advanced to excite a good deal of attention and while the greater number wondered what that huge fabric was intended for, others were found to publish their conjectures as authentic information though in general these conjectures were not very far from the truth. The foundress however continued to decline any determinate explanation, wishing to avoid all altercation with her family and therefore only answered the usual enquiry by saying she was building the house for the poor. Among others who received this vague intimation of her design was her elder sister. This lady though she had early forsaken the Catholic faith and was married to a very biggotted [*sic*] Presbyterian, Dr. William Macaulay of the Royal Military Hospital, was far from participating in the disapprobation with which her husband and brother regarded the matter.

She[9] had indeed no precise idea of the nature of the benefits her excellent sister prepared to confer on the poor yet she would frequently speak of the delight she hoped to experience in seeing the poor enjoying the comforts of that great house; but she did not live so long. Her health which had long been precarious now hopelessly declined and every possible dilligence [*sic*] being used to prevent her Catholic friends from endeavouring to recall her to her first faith she prepared herself to die receiving Communion according to the Anglican Rite. Yet notwithstanding her husband's vigilence [*sic*] the words of Truth eventually reached her; for as hers was a lingering disease our dear foundress from time to time found means of seeing her alone, when she would strongly represent the errors of the Protestant faith, with the consolation, peace and security which our holy Church affords to those who die in her bosom. The dying sufferer listened and believed; but as it was impossible to see a priest in her own house she, by her sister's advice, affected to desire a change of air, and was brought to Dundrum where Dr. Macauley's professional duties would not admit of his being constantly resident. But even there it was not without much difficulty and danger that a Catholic Priest, the Revd. Mr. McCormac,[10] curate of the parish, was introduced to administer the Sacraments. She died three weeks after in great sentiments of devotion, having informed her daughter concerning her faith which she exhorted her also to embrace; though at the same time requiring that the most profound secrecy should be observed in everything relative to the matter as she dreaded the consequences which might befall her sister. Her death occurred in the month of August. When her husband after some time discovered that she had died a Catholic, Miss McAuley was obliged to save her life by running out of the house at night, and in her dressing gown. The servant who had warned her of her danger securing the door prevented her being pursued, and she thus ran down the Military road to Dr. Cusack's lodgings in the Royal Hospital where she found shelter for the night. The next morning a reconciliation was effected and she returned to the house of her brother-in-law which for some time before her sister's death had been her usual residence.

It was there that in the Spring of this year [1827], Miss Anna Maria Doyle was introduced to her. When out walking this lady had remarked the building with a feeling of indescribable attraction; she eagerly watched its progress and at length asked the person in care of the premises to allow her to enter. She was delighted both with the place and its destination, in so much that she resolved to become a member of the projected society. Her intention had been to enter a Convent of the Presentation Order, but as she was the only child then left to her aged parents, the hope of being permitted to visit them, joined to a strong interior impulse made her prefer uniting in Miss McAuley's design. Her parents were of course desirous to confirm her in this decision, and having procured an introduction she offered herself to the foundress to share in her good work; and when early in the Autumn the building was in some degree habitable it was determined that she should enter at once though she was to have but one associate, Miss Catherine Byrne, then very young. Miss McAuley herself could not then make the institution her residence on account of the recent death of her sister, her niece being quite too young to undertake the management of her Father's household.

However, as it was determined that the house should be opened, Miss McAuley wrote to Miss Doyle saying that as all needful preparations would soon be completed she might enter if she pleased on the 23rd or 24th of the current month which was September. Miss Doyle though, though[11] she did not then know of the feast, fixed on the 24th but in another note remarked that she should be particularly rejoiced to begin her labours on that day as it was dedicated to our Lady of Mercy, suggesting at the same time that House of Mercy would be a good name for the institution. Nor can we think it was without a special providence of God that a day was chosen which in an especial manner placed the house and subsequently our holy Order under the protection of His immaculate Mother and caused them to be named from the most amiable of her attributes by which she most resembles Him whose mercies are above all His works. The schools therefore were opened on the appointed feast, and some young women admitted to the dormitories of whom two sisters of the name of Fay were the first. The costume adopted for the resident members, was a wide round dress of black valentia made in one from the throat to the ground with full wide sleeves confined at the wrist; plain lace caps, with black muslin lining, having a very high caul and an open quilling round the face. Miss McAuley visited the establishment almost daily, accompanied by her eldest niece, and took an active part in the school, in which some secular ladies also assisted to teach. On Christmas day [footnote on manuscript: "first Mass celebrated"] a plentiful dinner of roast beef and plumb [*sic*] pudding was provided for the children that attended the school.

1828

Miss Doyle and Miss Byrne continued for many months of this year to be the only resident members. In May the Revd. Edward Armstrong who had some time before been appointed Parish Priest of St. Michan's, North Anne St., fell ill and died in the course of the ensuing month. He had been an early friend and benefactor of our dear foundress, he had interested himself greatly in her charitable projects especially in the foundation of this house, he moreover possessed great influence with the Archbishop whose confessor he was, and she felt his loss most severely. It occurred too at a time when his advice and approbation would have been a great consolation to her for many had begun to murmur at her proposed institution. Of this he had been aware and did all in his power to promote the interests of the establishment. He wrote to His Grace urging every motive likely to secure his protection and also applied to others whom he hoped would, and whom he knew were able to serve her; yet when he told her of this and of the favorable assurances he had received, he emphatically repeated again and again: "Do not put your trust in any human being but place all your confidence in God." This precept she certainly observed. Revd. Mr. Armstrong furnished the first dormitory opened in the house and at his [death] bequeathed £50 to Miss McAuley who had attended him during his last sickness.

After his death Coolock House was sold as also the library, pictures, and a great part of the furniture, retaining only such as might be useful in the establishment at Baggot St., whither the foundress now removed, in the month of June, bringing with her her little godchild and her deceased sister's two daughters,[12] both of whom were supposed to be Protestants. On the 22nd of June Miss Frances Warde was associated to the pious labors of the institute, though rather as an amateur in good works than as one meant to give up the world for the service of God's poor; for though she resided pretty constantly at Baggot St. yet she did not assume the black dress and plain cap of the resident members, but went out to drive and visit her friends 'till the following November. The house was still quite unfinished. The sitting room and oratory was the room fronting Herbert St. between the great Hall and private staircase, and was both plainly and scantily furnished, having in it but one chair, some priedieux, with a few forms and tables. Every morning prayers were read from F[r]. Gahan's *Catholic Piety,* after which there was meditation. Night prayers were also read from the same excellent work and were followed by a lecture from the *Elevation of the Soul.* In the morning exercise the young women protected by the institution joined, and in the evening not only they but the young girls of the neighbourhood were admitted. The community said the Rosary of the Blessed Virgin walking together up and down the room and also on Monday the Rosary for the Dead, on Wednesday that of St. Joseph, on Friday that of the Sacred Heart. There was likewise an oratory neatly fitted up in a room on the great corridor. They went to confession every Saturday to the Discalced Carmelite Friars in Clarendon St. and every Sunday heard Mass in their Church. Recreation was held on the great corridor, where during the winter months a fire was lighted.

In the meantime, Miss Mary Macauley, the elder of our dear foundress's nieces, who was devotedly attached to her and had for some time been greatly averse to the practices of the Anglican Church became a Catholic. On the feast of St. Cecelia she formally renounced the heresy in which she was born and received conditional Baptism from His Grace the Archbishop but this was of course kept secret from her father. She was then in her sixteenth year. That same day, November the 22nd, the Archbishop gave permission for the visitation of the sick which Miss McAuley requested at the suggestion of Miss Doyle. The community then adopted an outdoor costume: for winter a coarse grey Cloak with a hood, a black silk bonnet and muslin veil; in summer the Cloak was replaced by a black rock-spun shawl. The visitation began on the 30th of November. Our dear foundress, Miss Doyle, Miss Byrne and Miss Warde who had become a member in the preceding month, went in the carriage to Sir Patrick Dunne's Hospital[13] where the Physicians knowing Miss McAuley's family and friends to be all Protestants and probably supposing she and her companions were of that persuasion not only allowed them to speak to the patients, but also gave a general order for their admission in future.

The Christmas dinner this year attracted much attention. It was laid out in the long room on the first floor which runs from the front of the building to the private staircase of the east wing and was then used as a school room. Several charitable persons had sent in contributions of beef, fruit, etc. Protestants as well as Catholics of the best fashion came in great numbers to see the children at dinner and Daniel O'Connell Esq., then Member for Clare, who has ever been a benefactor to our institution, carved. On St. Stephen's day a lottery of fancy work, etc., was drawn, which was considered productive.

1829

In the beginning of this year a circumstance occurred which strongly demonstrated the benefit which the institution was calculated to produce. Late one evening in answer to a violent ringing, the door, secured by the chain, was cautiously opened and admitted the flushed face of a very young girl, who implored a shelter for the night saying she had travelled on foot from Killarney and knew no one in Dublin. The wild glare of her large dark eyes, the disorder of her hair and dress naturally excited unfavorable suspicions, but as she was evidently in great distress our dear charitable foundress would not refuse her relief, so she was brought into the hall and had some bread and milk given her. She then, though very incoherently, for she was stupefied with fatigue, hunger and terror, told her name and how on account of a quarrel with her severe step-mother she had run out of her father's house; when not knowing in what manner to retrieve this imprudence she had proceeded on to Dublin, where she had no friends and no resources. In the Country she had heard of the Sisters of Charity, and conceiving that the very fact of her necessities would be a sufficient recommendation, she got herself directed to Stanhope St., where of course she was denied admission, but as some consolation was told, that in Baggot St. a Miss McAuley had a great house where every sort of people were let in; for thus did even the pious and charitable speak of our poor institution then. She was not exactly taken into the house that night but a safe lodging was procured for her in Little James's St. and Miss Doyle having recognised her father's name as that of a professional gentleman who had married a second time to one that was accused of much harshness towards his elder children it was resolved to admit her next day and make due enquiry as to her identity. This having been satisfactorily proved as well as the truth of her story in other particulars, she was protected 'till a situation was procured for her a few months after; but though she conducted herself well in it she did not remain long, for her father forgave her and brought her home.

The premises were still in an unfinished state, and a serious error in the plan was now observed. It had been proposed that the ceiling of the Chapel should be on a level with that of the rooms on the first floor; but as these rooms as well as the parlors are lofty, when the chapel was ceiled it was found to be of such disproportionate height that a second ceiling had to be put up some feet lower. Speaking of the Chapel it may be here remarked that our dear foundress, having reason to expect the requisite permission, had designed it for public accommodation, and the room adjoining was to be fitted up as a sort of pew for herself and associates. The architect erected a regular convent grate at which she was rather annoyed; the idea of a grate where there was to be no nunnery seeming to her laughably inappropriate, so little did she foresee what God designed to work by her means.

On the first feast of St. Agnes, January 21st 1829, Miss Anne O'Grady entered. In February Dr. William Macauley died of ulcerated sore throat attended with fever, having been not quite three days ill. His pious sister-in-law made every effort to induce him to become a Catholic but could not prevail; though in his will, which excited much surprise, he left it at the option of his children whether they would place themselves under her guardianship or under that of her brother, Dr. James McAuley, a rigid Protestant. They all preferred the former arrangement to their uncle's great astonishment and indignation which he expressed in no very measured terms. The daughters therefore continued to reside here and their three brothers who soon after became Catholics were sent for their education to Carlow College.

The Very Revd. Dr. Blake having brought several fine paintings from Italy, gave Miss McAuley a Madonna and Child which though rather small for the purpose she preferred to all the rest. But if she found comfort and encouragement in the kindness of her friends she had to endure much unkindness and contradiction from many who had no cause to act as opponents. Our Saviour says that a man's enemies are those of his own household and her present trial arose chiefly from the misconceptions of Catholics whose piety and benevolence engaged them in similar pursuits. It was a galling thing to many that one who had been born their inferior in rank and fortune should now occupy a more influential position than rank or wealth had procured for them. Others who patronised the institutions under the care of Sisters of Charity, dreaded lest this new establishment should divert the public attention from those objects in which they took an interest. Several of the clergy made no secret of their opposition though obliged to confess that it was grounded not on any mismanagement or misconduct which had come to their knowledge, but on an opinion that hereafter evil consequences would ensue from certain arrangements which were not such as they thought advisable. The Revd. Mat[t]hias Kelly, administrator of St. Andrew's parish, came here one day and having led the foundress through the house told her to choose one or two rooms for herself, as the Archbishop wished to place the establishment under the direction of the Sisters of Charity, though she could have a private entrance and some priveleges [*sic*], etc., etc. She believed him and meekly answered that, "Dr. Murray could do as he pleased with the house for it was his." When the revd. gentleman took his leave she immediately wrote to his Grace to say, that if such were his determination she should acquiesce in it; but the next day he came to the institution and assured her with great warmth that so far from having authorized such a communication he had never entertained the idea of depriving her of her property or putting any obstacle to her benevolent exertions which he was most desirous she s[houl]d continue.

These contradictions though very painful to our venerated foundress had nevertheless an effect that proved most beneficial to the institution, namely that the distrust with which so many truly pious persons regarded it under its present form, induced her to think of associating or at least assimilating it to some Religious Order. This was the advice of the vicar general[14] and therefore having been duly authorized she sent to several convents in and near Dublin requesting each to lend a copy of their Rule, which she received from all but Loretto [Loreto] and the Sisters of Charity. These rules she carefully reviewed and read aloud to those who were to form her Community, when the Rule of the Presentation Order was unanimously preferred; though the Poor Clares of Harold's Cross offered to affiliate the House to theirs, while the same proposal was made by the Carmelite nuns and urged by the Discalced friars of that Order who had been most kind from the beginning. The Augustinian Rule of the Presentation, however, seemed more adapted to the purposes of the institution, in which opinion the Archbishop as well as the vicar general coincided; and though the affair proceeded no farther for some time it was considered as decided that our little community should be modelled into a religious Order and all future arrangements were made with reference to this intention.

In Lent this year dinner was each day provided for the young women protected in the house of whom a few only had hitherto been maintained, the rest having to work at their several employments. To meet the additional expence [*sic*] a collection was begun by means of notes written to the wealthy of every creed throughout the city and though the replies were often insulting in the extreme, yet on the whole the scheme was very beneficial to the institution. The receipts of the first month amounted just to £2[.] 10, but the charity became better known and excited more interest. Indeed, it frequently happened that they who on the first application seemed to think the most overbearing insolence too mild an expression of their indignation at being thus importuned, seeing that they roused no angry feelings, but that all was endured meekly and cheerfully, grew ashamed and have often proved our best benefactors. The notes were written in the name of C. McAuley.

On account of some acts of petty pilfering and other indiscretions it was now found necessary to put an end to the indiscriminate admission of strangers to prayer in the work-room which in the beginning had been attended with no inconvenience. The first article missed was the chair on which Miss McAuley usually sat and it was taken one day that she had been congratulating with her companions on the honesty of their poor visitors, and that though they had so long kept open house nothing had been stolen. She boasted a day too soon. In Easter week there was a bazaar for the benefit of the institution at Morrison's

Hotel, Dawson St., the proceeds of which amounted to £280. The rooms were lent gratis.

Miss Knaresborough of Kilkenny now proposed to join the community. She was rather delicate indeed but not so much so as to preclude her from being an efficient in the labours of the institution had she entered on them. The time appointed for her coming had elapsed and she was anxiously expected but she did not arrive in Dublin for many days after, when instead of presenting herself here she went to consult Surgeon Collis [Colles] on the propriety of so doing. This gentleman who though very much inclined to promote works of mercy was not considered very steady even in the vital principles of Christianity decided in the negative of course; so she returned home and soon after married a person of advanced age but very rich.

On the Octave of the Ascension of our Lord the Chapel was dedicated by the Archbishop under the invocation of our Lady of Mercy. A pontifical High Mass was sung on the occasion and the Very Revd. Doctor Blake preached a sermon in which he highly eulogized our dear foundress who was not present at the ceremony, having remained in prayer within the house. At the dejeune [*sic*] which had been prepared for the Clergymen and strangers present some unpleasant feelings were manifested. Miss McAuley was personally acquainted with few Catholics and many inquiries were made of the different inmates of the establishment and even of herself concerning "this very extraordinary person Dr. Blake mentioned". Among others to whom this question was addressed was one of the clergymen who had officiated at the High Mass but his answer indicated anything rather than a concurrence with the sentiments of the preacher; in fact he said a great deal that shewed he neither liked the foundress nor the institution. At last however he paused when the Revd. Wm. Young, P.P. of Baldoyle, turning to Sister Frances Warde who stood near him and listened in the greatest surprise and confusion to this angry oration, asked her if she were not a member of the community. She of course replied in the affirmative. "Then my dear" said he "have the goodness to assure Miss McAuley of my respect for her and my good wishes for the prosperity of the institution. I am but a poor priest yet I will contribute my mite; I wish I could do more." He gave her a sovereign. There was no more said on the subject just then but a day or two after came an anonymous note directed to C. McAuley Esq. which contained the most mortifying, the most insulting strictures on Miss McAuley's proceedings. She knew the handwriting as that of the priest who had spoken so harshly on the day of the dedication[15] and so did Dr. Blake to whom she shewed it and who expressed himself very strongly on the subject saying that God would scourge the writer of the vile production. He spoke truly: that clergyman who then stood high in the estimation of the public met with some severe reverses and is said to have died without the Sacraments.

Another evidence of displeasure excited this day was very convenient to the establishment and rather amusing. The trustees of the House of Refuge[16] had previously refused to permit that the party wall which divides their premises from ours should be raised though Miss McAuley offered to bear the expenses and it was extremely low. The consequence was that the ceremonial of the dedication having required that His Grace should pass down the walk beside that party wall, the young Protestant women protected in that asylum could not be prevented from looking on; which circumstance joined to the horror excited by a large quantity of holy water that he purposely threw over their low boundary, forced our unaccommodating neighbours to set about raising it themselves the very next morning.

Before he left the house on the day of the dedication of the Chapel the Archbishop gave permission to have it opened to the public and recommended that a gallery should be erected, saying that the collection would pay the expense and help to maintain the young women. On the following Saturday the Revd. Mr. [Francis] L'Estrange said Mass which Mr. [Daniel] O'Connell served and at which he communicated. From this time there was one Mass said on ferias and two on Sundays and festivals, there being music at last Mass on these days. The Revd. Daniell [*sic*] Burk[e] OSF was appointed chaplain and the Revd. R. J. O'Hanlon confessor, so that from this time the community did not go out except to visit the sick. Some alteration was also made in their daily spiritual exercises which were now performed apart from the young women of the House of Mercy. They all rose at the same hour which was earlier than had before been usual with the greater number; at 6 o'clock assembled in the chapel within the grate for morning prayer which consisted chiefly of the Act of Oblation from the larger edition of *Devotion[s] to the Sacred Heart of Jesus* followed by a meditation from the *Journal*[17] 'till 7. Mass was at half past seven. They had breakfast at about a quarter past eight after which, while they still remained in the refectory Miss McAuley read from the *Lives of the Saints* or from *The Sinner's Guide,* neither did they again meet in the chapel 'till they went to examen a little before four. After dinner they made a visit to the B[lesse]d Sacrament which was read from St. Luigori's [Liguori's], and in the evening said the rosary, made a private lecture and prayed.

The confraternity of the Sacred Heart of Jesus was erected in our Chapel on the feast this year. A second dormitory was furnished for poor young women; the community went into separate cells and greater regularity began to be observed in every department. The general Communions which had hitherto taken place on Sundays only were soon after fixed for Sundays, Tuesdays, Thursdays, and Fridays. July the 15th Miss Marcella Flinn [Flynn] entered, as did Miss Margaret Dunne on the feast of our Lady's Nativity. Miss Mary Macauley who had previously resided in the house for more than a year now joined herself to the community; and on the 9th of December Miss Elizabeth Harley entered, so that at the close of this year there were nine Sisters.

1830

From Lent in the foregoing year the custom of giving dinner to the young women in the House of Mercy had been continued and soon after a few had breakfast,

'till this too became general and the greater number remained in the institution all day. Easter week the annual bazaar was held in the round room of the Rotunda and was very productive though chiefly patronized by Protestants.

Every thing was going on prosperously. The schools were crowded. The House of Mercy had proved an asylum for many young persons of great respectability and created universal interest. The protection and recommendation of servants was a measure of which the utility was duly appreciated. The visitation of the sick had had the most beneficial results. Still it was evident that both the prosperity and the permanency of the institution must necessarily be insecure if the community whose labours should uphold it were to continue merely an association of seculars bound together by no bond save their mutual regard and an abstract love of doing good; whose fervor or caprice might find sanctuary in a convent or solace in the enjoyment of the world. Therefore Miss McAuley began once more to reflect on the propriety of forming a religious community in the House of Mercy, a project which Dr. Blake strongly advocated and which was very agreeable to the wishes of her companions. Yet there were great difficulties to be overcome before it could be put in execution; for she did not choose to affiliate as a house of the third order either of St. Francis or Mt. Carmel, not conceiving that their rules were adapted to the purposes of the institution and the Rule she preferred enforced a vow of enclosure which was yet more incompatible with her designs. The Archbishop knowing that it would be a source of much inconvenience if she must leave the infant establishment with great kindness and consideration proposed to spare her the restraints of a noviciate among strangers by sending hither two professed religious of any order to the rule of which she might choose to assimilate ours, that so she and as many of the Sisters as she thought fit might serve a noviciate under them, while the remainder with the management of our temporal affairs should be directed by her. In this however she perceived many causes of objection so that eventually it was decided that if permission could be obtained from the Superiors of the Presentation Convent George's Hill, she and two of our little community should serve a noviciate there.

The Revd. W. J. Whelan OCD being in Rome procured for this Community a grant of indulgences. A translation both of the petition and the grant is here subjoined:

> Most Holy Father, Mrs. McAuley of Dublin with most profound respect informs your Holiness that in the year 182[3][18] with the permission and under the protection of the Most Revd. Dr. Murray the Archbishop, she, at her own expence founded a pious house as a convent, in which with others her companions in pursuance of her resolution she and they occupy themselves in the following charitable works, viz.—they engage and employ themselves etc. . . . [19]

Here follows the petition and grant for the indulgences of 2 days in the month, 2 for the recital of the Litany of the Blessed Virgin, etc.

This Spring a school for young ladies was opened in the refectory; but it proved a signal failure and the very few pupils it ever contained dropped off within the year.[20]

Four young persons named Catherine Hazlitt, Eliza McMahon, M[ary] Davis and Hanagh Fulham were admitted with the intention of becoming lay sisters. They were placed much on the same footing as those destined for choir nuns, eat [or: "sat"] at the same time and table, passed the time of recreation with them, etc. This, it was soon found, would not answer, and as the two first though well conducted did not seem to have a true vocation they were otherwise provided for. Mary Davis was dismissed for some reprehensible levities. On the 10th of June Miss Georgiana Moore entered, as did Miss Caroline Murphy on the 18th of the same month, and Miss Mary Anne Delaney on the 12th of July. There were now twelve in Community, besides Hanagh Fulham. In July this year Miss McAuley was directed to visit Miss Marianne Redmond, suffering from white swelling on the knee. Though wealthy this young lady was peculiarly unprovided for; for she had no friends in Dublin whither she had come accompanied only by a young inexperienced girl, her cousin, and an old country nurse, her parents being both dead. The most eminent Surgeons and Physicians attended her but with so little success that amputation was soon judged necessary; and therefore Doctor Blake pitying her lonely situation entreated that she might be permitted to pass some time in our establishment in order that the operation might be performed here. This being acceded to, she was accommodated with a large room in the centre of the house which was afterwards divided into the noviceship and infirmary. Sisters A[nna] M[aria] Doyle and Margaret Dunne remained with her during the amputation, and with the rest of the community tended her day and night for more than a month; after which time she removed a little way into the Country where she lingered for some time in great agony, and died. She bequeathed certain legacies for charitable purposes but most unaccountably forgot the Institution of Mercy, so that the Sisters reaped no temporal reward for this good work which included in its performance the exercise of a great many virtues.

Meanwhile permission had been obtained for Miss McAuley with two companions to serve a noviciate in the convent she had selected and every necessary preparation was made for her departure. The Sisters chosen to accompany her were Sr. Anna Maria Doyle and Sr. Elizabeth Harley; Sr. Mary Anne Delaney was appointed to preside at the spiritual exercises, and though without title of superiority was in fact superior; while Sr. Frances Warde had charge of the household affairs. Some other arrangements were also made for the sake of greater regularity during her absence. The assistance of secular ladies in the school was henceforth to be declined and except in particular cases strangers were not to be shewn through the house; the windows also that looked on Baggot St. were entirely white muffing. It was moreover arranged that she should be informed of all that passed in the house and that all business of moment should be referred to her decision. Then after many exhortations to act always with charity, humility, fervor and prudence she took leave of her little community in the House of Mercy, and on the feast of our Blessed Lady's Nativity, entered the Presentation Convent George's Hill, Mother Mary Clare Angela Doyle being then Superioress of that house, and Mother M. Teresa Higgins, Mistress of Novices.

During her absence the Sisters who were left in the Institution experienced the most charitable attentions from the Discalced Carmelite Friars of Clarendon St. These gentlemen had been among our first friends and they continued to give effectual proofs of their good will in every possible way. For a long time they supplied us from their own sacristy with vestments and every other requisite for the Altar; besides which they for these three years gave all the Altar breads, incense, and charcoal used in our chapel. The Right Revd. Dr. Murphy, bishop of Cork, was also a good friend and constant visitor; he presented us with a handsome copy of the Missal.

In the beginning of the winter the Superiors of the Convent at George's Hill required that the Sisters in Baggot St. should no longer sleep on straw pal[l]iasses as they had hitherto done. This change though intended to promote their health and comfort proved a source of much real discomfort; for an offer to supply the requisite number of mattrasses [*sic*] at a very cheap rate having been accepted, the contractor instead of the usual quantity of horse hair stuffed them with hair of some other description which for several weeks yeilded [*sic*] a most offensive smell and eventually became almost as hard as the pal[l]iasse though not so even. At the same time the Sisters were ordered to use beer at dinner instead of water. Though some of the community fell into ill health every duty of the Institute was performed with the greatest regularity for the love of God and in the spirit of mutual charity. On the 11th of December the Sisters who had gone to George's Hill received the holy habit in that convent.[21]

At this time the Sisters were rather overworked. There were a great number of sick poor on the list for visitation besides which Sir P. Dunne's [Dun's] Hospital, the Hospital of Incurables at Don[n]ybrook and the Coombe Lying-in Hospital were attended, and the school in which the system of mutual instruction had not yet been adopted was most unnecessarily laborious. This told severely on their health; yet they suffered perhaps more through their own imprudent fervor. Left without a guide and mistaking the real nature of Religious Mortification some addicted themselves to fasts of supererogation, others wore haircloth, used the discipline and remained in prayer during whole hours of the time appointed for rest, not considering that the fatigues attendant on the functions of the institute were a species of mortification which necessarily excluded all corporal austerities, and that by their want of spiritual discretion in thus undertaking more than was recommended they effectually incapacitated themselves for the performance of that which was obligatory. Several of the Sisters fell sick though it pleased God that most of them should recover.

[1831][22]

Sister Catherine Byrne was the first whose illness appeared serious. Sir James

Murray and another physician who attended her said it was spinal disease and that her recovery was almost hopeless though she might probably linger for a long time. When this opinion was reported at George's Hill the Presentation Nuns proposed that a relic of Father Tharesborough which they possess should be applied to our suffering Sister, trusting that God would glorify His servant in her recovery. Accordingly on the feast of the blessed St. Joseph, to whom the patient had always a special devotion, the Revd. Mr. de Luynes said Mass, and the relic having been applied to her back, she, who for a long time had not been able to leave her cell, came down to the Chapel for Benediction and continued in good health so as to be capable of exercising all the functions of the Institute. Nevertheless the same physicians who had so lately pronounced her disease spinal, now maintained that it was on the nerves and that there was nothing supernatural in her sudden recovery.

The Revd. Mr. de Luynes who said Mass this day was a native of France, very pious and very spiritual. Having been introduced to our dear foundress at George's Hill, he at her request visited this house and held some general as well as many private conferrences [*sic*] with the Sisters who were desired to communicate with him concerning their interior. He soon after left Ireland on an American Mission.

The usual bazaar at Easter was not held this year. Soon after the celebration of this great festival Hanagh Fulham, the only lay Sister left in Baggot St., was dismissed under very painful circumstances. This young woman was gifted by God with a remarkably fine voice and great musical talent, which joined to an agreeable person and a very fascinating address would have made her a desirable subject had the qualities of her mind and heart corresponded with her exterior. Though distrusted by several of the Sisters no specific charge could be urged against her 'till she was detected in an attempt to purloin some articles of plate, when the matter was of course reported to Sr. M. Catherine at George's Hill. The fact was undeniable, yet the culprit managed to interest some of the most influential members of the community[23] in her behalf; but notwithstanding their entreaties to have her retained Sister Mary Catherine was inflexible and orders were sent for her immediate dismissal. Still she would not resign all hope, and resolved on a stratagem which she thought could not fail of success. She appeared the next morning with her head quite shorn which she declared was done by supernatural agency, and though no credit was given to this assertion yet the manner, time and place of her doing so herself was a mystery of difficult solution, for not a lock of her very beautiful hair could be found, nor could any one conceive where she had been concealed while she cut it off so completely. However a clue was discovered. One of the Sisters who had lent her a pair of scissors having got it back found a little hair under the rivet and a very little more was after a very diligent search found in the music choir directly over the sacristy; whereupon with a great deal of trouble she was brought to confess that there she had herself executed that which she wished should be considered as a declaration of God's will in favor of her vocation. She was forthwith expelled but gained so far on the mercy of the community as to procure a recommendation to a family resident at Blackrock where she soon shewed that her evil propensity was not yet corrected.

On the 26th of May a postulant, Miss Mary Jones, entered, and on the 28th of the next month Sister Caroline Murphy, whose health had latterly been declining, died the death of the Just. She was a native of Killarney, very beautiful and engaging in the eyes of the world, but still more lovely and precious in the sight of Him whom by a private vow she even in her childhood had chosen for her spouse. She was always pious, patient, modest and charitable beyond her years and bore herself without reproof under many severe trials. During the short time she lived after her entrance into our Institution she gave a great deal of edification, obeying each and all with cheerful alacrity, always rejoicing in labours and humiliations. Nor is it a mere form of words to say that she loved the meanest offices; for she exercised them in preference to all others, taking pleasure in appearing before seculars with her hands all black, the more so if she perceived that it made them consider her as a menial to the Community. She suffered with the utmost sweetness, patience and resignation, and having received the last Sacraments from our confessor, the Revd. R. J. O'Hanlon OCD, expired while he was praying at her side. As we had then neither habit nor cemetry [*sic*] she was buried in the brown Carmelite habit of the third order in a vault of the Discalced Carmelite Church, Clarendon St., where none but priests had hitherto been laid. July the 24th another postulant, Miss Anna Carroll, entered.

Early in the Summer means for supplying the wants of the sick poor falling short, Sister Anne O'Grady proposed that the Sisters should personally solicit subscriptions for the institution. The plan was adopted and for some months they were accustomed to go two together from door to door in the hopes of procuring a little relief for the suffering members of Christ Jesus; but this being found attended with inconveniences that were ill compensated by the success it obtained was after some months relinquished. Sister Anne who was alway[s] indefatigable in every good work exerted herself more than sufficiently in this, so that it was supposed to have occasioned her falling into an ill state of health which terminated in pulmonary consumption. In the autumn of this year a legacy of £31 having been bequeathed to the Very Revd. Dr. Blake he handed it over to the institution on which he had already bestowed sundry charitable donations.

The time of probation appointed for our three Sisters in the Convent at George's Hill was now drawing to a close but the Community there made great difficulty concerning the propriety of permitting them to make religious vows with liberty to visit the sick. At length however this objection having been overruled a chapter was held in which permission was granted for Sr. Mary Catherine McAuley, Sr. Mary Anne Doyle[24] and Sr. M. Elizabeth Harley to make their holy profession, which they did on the 12th of December, pronouncing their vows after the following form in presence of the Archbishop:

Act of Profession

In the name of our Lord and Saviour Jesus Christ and under the protection of His Immaculate Mother, Mary ever Virgin, I Sister Catherine McAuley, called in religion Mary Catherine, do vow and promise to God perpetual poverty, chastity and obedience, and to persevere until the end of my life in the Congregation called of the Sisters of Mercy established for the visitation of the sick poor and instruction of poor females, according to the Rule and Constitutions of the Presentation Order, subject to such alterations as shall be approved by the Archbishop; under the authority and in presence of you, my Lord and Most Revd. Father in God, Daniel Murray, Archbishop of this diocese, and Revd. Mother Elizabeth Knowd, called in religion Mary Francis of Sales, Superioress of this Convent of the Presentation, Dublin, this twelfth day of December in the year of our Lord one thousand eight hundred and thirty one.

Signed Sister Mary Catherine McAuley
in religion Mary Catherine
Sister M. C[lare] Doyle Assistant
Sister M. de Sales Knowd Superioress

D. Murray Abp. [Archbishop], etc.

They were professed in the habit of the Presentation Nuns, which much resembles ours in all but the coif and the smallness of the guimp which is round and made of linen double; the habit also is of serge with broader plaits round the figure. After the ceremony however they assumed the coif which it had been agreed should be worn by the Sisters of Mercy in future, the idea of which was borrowed from the Carmelites coif; they put on our usual black bonnets and cloaks and returned to our convent. The religious of the Presentation whom they left were not a little offended at their precipitate departure but Sister Mary Catherine was impatient of a longer absence from the Institution which had been the object of so much solicitude to her and for sake of which alone, hoping thereby to promote the greater glory of God, she had submitted to the trials and repugnances of her novitiate.

The next day, the feast of Saint Lucy V[irgin] M[artyr], the little Office of our Blessed Lady was recited by all the Sisters together, and in English, according to the Approbation of the Archbishop previously received. Henceforward the spiritual exercises were distributed as follows. After the Morning Office of Prime, Tierce, Sext and None, which began to be recited at the conclusion of the Angelus at six o'clock, there was a meditation 'till seven, when a Pater and Ave was said for the conversion of sinners, another for the perseverance of the just, and a third with the Collect "O God, the Creator" etc. for the faithful departed. At nine, unless there was a second Mass, a spiritual lecture was read to all the Sisters assembled according to their standing in Religion in the noviceship and community room. At three quarters past eleven particular examen was made; at twelve the Angelus etc., Acts of faith, hope and charity with the Litany of the holy name Jesus, were recited. Vespers and Compline with five Paters and Aves for the intentions of our holy Father in granting indulgences and the Litany of Loretto were said. Then came a lecture from the *Lives of the Saints,* and at six the Angelus, Matins and Lauds, De Profundis and Litany for a happy death, with the Litany for the dead on Monday. At nine was the general examen, Litany of the Saints and the subject of the next morning's meditation was read. On that day the Archbishop came to our convent and having appointed Sr. Mary Catherine McAuley Superior, gave permission for such of the Sisters as she thought sufficiently prepared to receive the holy habit on the 23rd of January next ensuing. These were to the number of seven and were severally presented to His Grace who discoursed with each in private concerning her vocation etc. The rest of this month was much occupied with preparations for this ceremony. The usual dinner was given to the children of the school at Christmas and was numerously attended by strangers of the first distinction.

1832

The first event worth noting which occurred this year was the reception of the seven Sisters nominated by Mother M. Catherine in the preceding month, which took place on the day appointed, the Feast of the Desponsation of our Blessed Lady [January 23]. The Sisters received were Sr. Catherine Byrne, in religion Mary Josephine, Sister Frances Warde, in religion Mary Francis Teresa,[25] Sister Margaret Dunne, in religion Mary Angela Teresa, Sister Mary Macauley, in religion Mary Joseph Teresa, Sr. Georgiana Moore, in religion Mary Clare, Sr. Mary Anne Delaney, in religion Mary Magdalen de Pazzi, Sister Anna Carroll, in religion Mary Agnes. The ceremony which was performed by the Archbishop was strictly private, none being admitted except clergymen, of whom however the attendance was numerous; and the postulants were presented to His Grace not in secular costume but in the black dresses they ordinarily wore, the habit received being in all respects the same as that now worn by us only that the sleeves were narrower and confined at the wrist. On account of their number and the difficulty of carrying on the business of the establishment without their cooperation, these Sisters had not entered into strict retreat as is usually prescribed before reception; they had indeed had the advantages of the spiritual exercises but by His Grace's direction they taught in the school and went on the visitation.

The resolution to have the ceremony private was adopted chiefly on account of the hopeless state of Sister Anne O'Grady's health as well as on the principle of religious poverty which Mother M. Catherine considered to be incompatible with the lavish expenditure of her own reception. Besides she had been favored with a visit from one of those very good friends with whom the world abounds, who are always ready to advise and inform in accordance with the preconceived opinions of their friends; and this person thought it was very prudent always to keep things quiet, but really the approaching ceremony was so spoken of, such crowds of people intended to come that it would be difficult to keep them out though there was nothing the Archbishop so much disliked as crowds and publicity. Now our dear foundress disliked crowds and publicity herself, so she gave orders that all seculars without exception should be excluded, and though carriage after carriage drew up and waited, though the space in front of the convent was crowded with friends of the Sisters, and benefactors of the Institution all were refused admittance. This naturally gave offence to a great many. Mrs. Carroll, mother to the Junior Novice that day received, who was standing on the steps before the door loudly expressed her indignation and determination to remove her daughter from a Convent where she was treated so unceremoniously. This threat she executed the very next week notwithstanding the entreaties of our good Sister who was very dear to all our community and who though she possessed no very remarkable talents and had received but a limited [education],[26] yet being active, docile and pious with a cheerful disposition and robust constitution might have proved a useful as well as an edifying member of our Order.

On the eighth of February Sister Anne O'Grady died in the [blank space in the text] year of her age having passed rather more than three in this Institution. She was greatly beloved by the Sisters for no one could be more meek, humble and charitable. She was indefatigable in every work of mercy and very pious though unhappily scrupulous and having an especial and exceeding dread of making the vows, a privilege which it pleased God should never be vouchsafed to her. Before the foundation of this Institute, when she was but sixteen she entered the Presentation Convent in Wexford where she remained more than a year and received the holy habit; but having been attacked with fever her health was so weakened that she had to leave. She soon however grew better and entered here, where her ardent zeal led her to make exertions beyond her strength. She suffered a great deal during the whole course of her long illness, yet when she was laid in the chapel preparatory to her interment her features looked even more lovely than when she was in the prime of her health and loveliness. She was buried with Sister Caroline in Clarendon Street in the vault which for years continued to be the burial place of our community.

While on the visitation a strange instance of human perversity fell under the observation of the Sisters. They were directed to attend an old woman that was dying and in making the usual enquiries discovered that for the last nineteen years she had not held the slightest intercourse with her husband though they inhabited the same house. They were natives of some part of Ulster where they were married and lived in rather comfortable circumstances. One of their sons, who was a great favorite with his mother, was guilty of some fault for which the father chastised him very severely, whereby such bitter resentment was excited in her that leaving her home with this lad she came to reside in Dublin. Thither her husband followed her; but though he used every means in his power to effect a reconciliation with her the unhappy sinner persisted in her enmity during that long lapse of years. It cost the Sisters much trouble to bring her to a sense of her guilty state, but they succeeded at length, and during the few days she survived she appeared cordially grateful for the many marks of kindness and attention she received from her husband.

About this time the Vicar General[27] who for many years had held the parish of SS. Michael and John was removed to the parish of St. Andrew within which our Convent stands. Immediately on his appointment he caused the parish books to be deposited here and the money received in the poor boxes etc. which is usually distributed by the Clergyman on duty, was placed at the disposal of the Sisters. This was a troublesome as well as an invidious task which Mother Mary Catherine managed to give up after a few months.

Sister Mary Elizabeth Harley, when she embraced the institute, was very healthy and continued so during [a] great part of her noviciate. But the Mistress of Novices at the Presentation Convent who was a convert and very zealous for the perfection of her charge thought she never could do enough to try the vocation of our three Sisters; therefore she placed all of them in laborious offices and Sister M. Elizabeth in the discharge of hers had to remain for a long time each day in a very cold damp underground room, 'till Mother M. Catherine perceiving that our dear Sister's health was giving way thought it her duty to represent the matter to the Mother Superior. When Sister M. Elizabeth returned to Baggot St. though by no means sickly she was evidently not so strong as when she left it. She attended Sister Anne as her infirmarian for some days before her death, and shortly after it took place she remarked that most persons wished that their last illness might be a protracted one but seeing how much that dear Sister's sufferings had impaired her intellect she hoped her own death might come on less slowly. On Ash-Wednesday she served in the refectory, but immediately after declined so rapidly that the physicians at once declared her case hopeless. She was not indeed confined to her cell but sat in [the] community room every day during the Lent; on Easter Sunday went to holy Communion in the choir and even came down to the refectory to take her portion of a pudding that had been prepared for the Sisters. On Easter Tuesday however she was much worse, unable to leave her bed and on Wednesday evening[28] she died about an hour after she had received the rites of the Church.

In this our holy Sister two virtues were especially remarkable, humility and obedience, and these she had acquired in so high a degree that no trial of either could disturb her equanimity. Of her humility it may be sufficient to give one instance out of the very many which she give [*sic*: gave]. After her profession she was for some time ranked below those postulants who entered before her yet she never complained, in fact never seemed to perceive that she was not in her place. No reproof however unmerited ever tempted her to justify herself, no contradiction, no want of attention ever seemed to give her pain and never by act, word or look did she give pain to others. On the subject of obedience she was particularly edifying; she never seemed to feel the slightest repugnance to any sacrifice it required. An hour or two before she died, having expressed a desire to perform some devotion Mother Mary Catherine feared would fatigue her, that kind Mother would not consent, telling her to say nothing but "Jesus,

Mary and Joseph". When she returned to the cell some time after, she found the patient had ever since continued to repeat the prescribed ejaculation, and would not change her prayer without permission. The Sisters were at Mattins not in the least supposing her death was so near, when to the great surprise of the two Sisters left with her she began to repeat the prayers of the dying and she departed before they could assemble the community. It was at the time of the annual bazaar, and poor Mother M. Catherine was called from beside the bed of death to a lady who wanted her in the parlour. Now this was an old lady who was very rich, very charitable and rather odd, having moreover a great dislike to bazaars, and she came to lecture on the impropriety, the utter sinfulness of these ways of raising money for the poor. To all this our dear Mother Catherine listened with exemplary patience which she thought amply rewarded when at length her visitor rising to depart presented her with £15 for the poor.

A Legacy of £700 Grand Canal Debentures bequeathed to the Right Revd. Dr. Blake was by him transferred to this Institution.

In the Spring of this year spasmodic Cholera broke out in Dublin and the Board of Health having fitted up the Depot Townsend St. as an hospital wrote to obtain the cooperation of our Order. Mother M. Catherine immediately wrote to the Archbishop expressing her desire that she might be permitted to acquiesce in the requisition which she enclosed; and the same evening his Grace came to the convent where having spoken with Mother M. Catherine for some time he came into the community room and gave his sanction to the good work which he said could not fail to be meritorious and pleasing in the sight of God. At the same time he required that the Sisters should take all due precautions for the preservation of their own health, make use of the prescribed remedies against infection, take port wine, broiled meats etc. He then spoke of the visitation in general and laid great stress on the unobtrusive manner in which they should appear and act, appealing to Mother M. Catherine's experience of the unpleasant feelings always excited in Protestants when certain points of difference were drawn prominently forth, on which account he wished our outdoor costume might exhibit no remarkable difference from that of secular persons of respectability who did not enter into the vanities of the world, and above all things that the cross and beads might be carefully concealed. That we should not wear in the streets any dress that would make us remarkable was not the opinion of the Archbishop only; the Vicar General, who though sufficiently cautious was not too much disposed to make many concessions to Protestant prejudices, at first objected to our wearing the coif out of doors and recommended a little English cap, but with our close bonnets and thick veils Mother M. Catherine conceived that this only glimpse of the religious dress would pass without notice so it has been retained.[29]

Excerpts from
THE ANNALS OF . . . SISTERS OF MERCY, ST. JOSEPH'S, TULLAMORE

This Convent is the First Filiation from the Parent-House of the Congregation, Baggot St. Dublin, and was founded under the patronage of the glorious St. Joseph on the 21st of April AD 1836.[1]

It received this title because the Community came to Tullamore on the Thursday before the Feast of the Protection of S[t]. Joseph, the 3rd Sunday after Easter—on which day they commenced the Duties of the Congregation, during the Episcopate of His Lordship The Most Rev. Doctor Cantwell, Lord Bishop of Meath, Very Revd. James O'Rafferty, Vicar General of the Diocese, being Parish Priest of Tullamore.

Mother Mary Anne Doyle, who assisted our Venerated Foundress from the beginning of the Congregation and who was one of the three that served their Novitiate in George's Hill, was appointed Mother Superior. Sister M. Teresa Purcell, a novice, and a native of the Diocese, accompanied her to make the Foundation. These two were judged sufficient, as two young ladies were awaiting the arrival of the Sisters to join them, and others were expected. . . .

Very Rev. Dr. O'Rafferty, Vicar General of Meath and Parish Priest of Tullamore, in whose hands the Bequest [of Miss Pentony][2] was placed, first applied to the Sisters of Charity, Stanhope St. Dublin, for a few sisters to form a foundation. The Superioress, Mrs. Aikenhead, declined when she became aware of the small means in hands to commence the Foundation. He next applied to the Sisters of Mercy who were only a few years established, and who had not yet begun to extend themselves beyond the Archdiocese. He had an interview with the Foundress, which so charmed him that he could never forget it. He spoke of it and her wonderful grace of manner, together with the supernatural virtues she manifested, until the day of his death which occurred about 20 years afterwards.

She made no hesitation, and when the poverty of the new house was made known to her, it was an additional motive for her to embrace it the more willingly, suggesting the idea of the poverty of Bethlehem which she desired to honor in this her first Foundation. Indeed it is even said that she set aside for the present an application made by a Bishop for a wealthy locality in order to give the preference to the poor priest from Tullamore.

The Very Rev. Redmond O'Hanlon, Provincial of the Carmelites, the special Friend and Confessor of the rising Congregation, gave his warmest sanction to the Foundation and encouraged it. He had been an old and particular friend of Miss Pentony's, and to manifest that regard, he accompanied the Sisters to Tullamore, that he might see for himself the scene and fruits of his saintly friend's labors.

The necessary arrangements having been concluded, Very Rev. Dr. O'Rafferty arrived in Dublin to conduct the appointed sisters to their new home. The Superior chosen for the Foundation was M. Mary Anne Doyle who, as remarked before, was Assistant to the Foundress. Only one sister more could be spared from Baggot St., Sr. M. Teresa [Purcell], who was preparing for holy Profession, but Rev. Mother brought Sisters with her who remained until two postulantes [*sic*] entered. These were Sisters Mary Clare Moore, who afterwards founded the convents of Cork and Bermondsey, and Mary Agnes McAuley [*sic*], niece of Revd. Mother's, who died next year. All five, accompanied by Dr. O'Rafferty and Father O'Hanlon, left Dublin the morning of the 21st April 1836 in the Fly-boat which at that time used to ply on the Grand Canal between Dublin and the Shannon, and arrived in Tullamore at 3 o'clock.

They were received with the greatest delight by the people and conducted to the Church where all united in invoking God's blessing on this grain of mustard-seed and to pray that it might take root and fructify. Dr. O'Rafferty entertained the little group and introduced them to Miss [Elizabeth] Locke, the expected postulante [*sic*], who had the honor of dining and supping with them. In the evening they were conducted to the convent in Store St. by this young lady and the Rev. Walter Murtagh [curate] who shewed great zeal and energy in procuring the Sisters of Mercy. . . .

On Sunday, the Feast of the Patronage of St. Joseph, the duties of the Congregation were commenced, and the house dedicated to this glorious Saint.

Dr. O'Rafferty, at the desire of Rev. Mother McAuley, employed tradesmen to fit up the house in the most conventual manner it would admit of, and one room in particular—the best they could boast of—was given up to serve for a Chapel in which they might have Mass occasionally, together with all the other duties prescribed by Rule. In the first years it was arranged that the sisters should go out to daily Mass. This domestic chapel was finished against the Feast of Pentecost and blessed by good Father Murtagh. The convent was indeed a small and a poor one, and notwithstanding the care taken to render it commodious for the sisters, it was but a sorry attempt at a religious establishment. Mother M. Anne, whose ideas of spaciousness in convents nearly coincided with those of S[t]. Peter of Alcantara, was well pleased with the straitness of the cells and parlor. Our V[enerated] Foundress notices this in a pleasant letter she wrote at the time to Baggot St., thus—"Mother M. Anne has met with her 'beau ideal' of a conventual building at last, for our rooms are so small that two cats could scarcely dance in them. The rest of us however would have no objection to larger ones". . . .

As the Community was increasing, much inconvenience was felt for sleeping room. Rev. Mother gave up the few cells they had to the postulantes as she did not think them sufficiently strong to bear the inconvenience of sleeping in small rooms. Indeed she always shewed this extreme consideration for the young. For herself and companions, they contented themselves with taking their short rest on the floor in one room, rejoicing at the opportunity of practising holy poverty and of experiencing some of its effects.

Our Venerated Foundress made it a practice all through life, which she commenced in Tullamore, to remain a month on a new Foundation, during which time she always said the Thirty Days' Prayer to our Blessed Lady to implore grace for the Sisters and a blessing on their work, through the intercession of the Mother of Mercy. During her stay in Tullamore she prepared Sr. Mary Teresa for holy Profession. This was a duty for which she was specially qualified. She seemed to inherit the great gift bestowed by God on the Prophet Isaias, who said, "The Lord hath given me a learned tongue, whereby to support with a word him that is weary." The eloquence that flowed from her lips when instructing the sisters, especially for making their Vows, went straight to their hearts and irresistibly inclined them to practise the perfection of their holy State. Her language was simple and unstudied but sweet and forcible, it was the fruit of prayer, and the sisters seemed impressed with the idea that whatever she inculcated was the holy will of God for them to do. Some notes of these precious lectures, carefully penned by Mother M. Teresa [Purcell], have been preserved in this house amongst its greatest treasures[3]. . . .

Friday in Ember Week, the 27th May, was the day appointed for Sr. Mary Teresa's Profession, His Lordship, Most Rev. Dr. Cantwell, the Lord Bishop of the Diocese, being then in the neighborhood. On Thursday, the 26th, he visited the convent for the first time, and canonically appointed Mother Mary Anne, Mother Superior. The Ceremony took place next morning at 10 o'clock in the Parish Church before a vast concourse of people. Many priests were present and Rev. W. Murtagh preached on the occasion, detailing the duties of the Order of Mercy and the good it would doubtless do in the church. This was, in truth, a great day for Tullamore, the first time that the holy Vows of Religion were pronounced within its walls. . . . On Monday morning, 30th May, Rev. Mother McAuley returned to Baggot St. accompanied by Father Murtagh and her two companions, Srs. M. Clare [Moore] and M. Agnes [Macauley], having left the new Foundation in working order. It being a large town, they had great field for their zeal. The Visitation of the Sick occupied a good portion of their time, and the Instruction of Adults engaged the Sisters almost continually. But one drawback they certainly had—there was no school attached to the premises—the only one in the town was held in a wretched little garret in Thomas Street. The Sisters attended this every day but allowed the paid-teacher, Miss Allwell, to continue her employment until the new schools were built.

We cannot form any idea of the grief of this young Community on the departure of Rev. Mother McAuley; until now she had been its stay and its support. No wonder then that when she left, poor Mother Mary Anne felt that she was *alone,* and that she was destined to govern a Community henceforth—a task for which she felt herself utterly unworthy; however she entered on her office with meekness and confidence in God, and was zealously upheld and aided by her young and fervent Community. . . .

. . . . Many valuable presents were made to the Sisters; indeed Dr. O'Rafferty and his priests thought they never could do enough in this way. Father Murtagh made an offering of a cow! This created great amusement, and was regarded as a great favor, it being the first *live-stock* of the Order, but the Community not possessing even a blade of grass at the time, the poor animal had to be sent to the country to graze. In the early correspondence, our Ven. Foundress often mentions this famous cow, desiring her best wishes to "*Madame La Vache*".

On Friday, the 29th July [1836], Rev. Mother McAuley returned to Tullamore accompanied by Srs. M. Clare, M. Elizabeth Moore (the foundress of Limerick convent), and M. De Chantal McCann, who died soon after, also by the Rev. Daniel Burke, a Franciscan Friar who was chaplain at Baggot St. at the time. Rev. Mother omitted nothing to give éclat to these first Ceremonies[4] on her Foundations; she would come herself and bring the Choir from Baggot St. to preside at them in order to make an impression on the public mind regarding the new Congregation and to induce them to enquire into its spirit and duties. Oftentimes too, young ladies were thus attracted to the new convent to dedicate their youth, wealth and energies to God and his poor. We see this expressed in a letter she wrote, thus—"I always find my visits to Foundations exceedingly useful—not for anything I can say or do, for my experience is so short that a good faithful sister may be said to know as much of the spiritual life as I! Yet it is most useful to give assistance for some time; it animates beginners and gives confidence to others. I have been told that it made parents and guardians more trusting and sanguine of success, saying they could not fear failure where so much attention is shewn to infant establishments." The Lord Bishop of Galway, Most Rev. Dr. Browne said from the Altar, in speaking of the Order of Mercy, "It is impossible it should fail where so much unity and affectionate interest are maintained, that its members will go hundreds of miles to encourage and aid one another. It is their established practice to look after what has been recently commenced."

On Monday, the 1st August, the Ceremony took place—the first religious Clothing of Sisters of Mercy in Ireland outside the Archdiocese of Dublin. Everything was done to add to its solemnity and splendour and the priests joined with their people in testifying their appreciation of the rising Institute in Tullamore. The Ceremony was held in the Parish Church to which the Sisters and numerous clergy walked in procession from the Presbytery amidst the prayers and blessings of the delighted people. The Very Rev. Dean Gaffney of Maynooth preached on the occasion. It added greatly to the interest of this beautiful Ceremony in the eyes of the people that both the young ladies who were candidates for the honors of the day were townswomen of their own, belonging to respectable and influential families. Miss [Elizabeth] Locke received the name of Sr. Mary Catherine and Miss [Mary] Delamere that of Sr. Mary Clare in Religion.[5]

After the Ceremony many of the clergymen and seculars visited the convent, all expressing their admiration of the imposing Ceremony. On Tuesday morning Rev. Mother and her companions returned to Dublin, truly gratified to see the amount of good likely to be effected by the sisters, and the truly religious spirit of their first Foundation.

The Annual Retreat came on in due time this August [1836]. Mother Mary

Anne conducted her little Flock through the Exercises of S[t]. Ignatius, as at that time it was not customary to have the aid of a spiritual Father on new Foundations. The most that could be procured was generally an Extraordinary Confessor to hear the Sisters' Confessions. Doubtless M. M. Anne's extreme humility and diffidence in self did not fail to add a special grace to her instructions, and to call down additional aid from on high for herself and her Sisters.

The Jesuits of Tullabeg showed the most lively interest in this establishment from its very beginning and should be regarded as our first spiritual benefactors. They kindly sympathised in its early struggles, being doubtless urged on by a "fellow feeling", as they had not been many years in Tullabeg and consequently well understood the disadvantages and inconveniences to which infant communities are often exposed. The Fathers often came to instruct the sisters, both privately and publicly in the Retreats which they offered to give, sent them books of instructions which, at that time, were very rare, and even left written lectures, which were most useful to the Community, and served for its guidance for many a year. Indeed this Community was considered as the richest in spiritual lore of the entire Institute, having so many precious manuscripts in its possession . . . .

On the 24th of September [1836], the Feast of our Blessed Lady of Mercy, which was always regarded as the Patronal Feast of the Congregation, a number of children made their First Communion, having been carefully prepared by the Sisters. Dr. O'Rafferty sang High Mass and gave an Exhortation to the children. After Mass they came in procession to the convent where they breakfasted. This sight of so many little innocent souls receiving the Holy Sacrament of the Blessed Eucharist for the first time made a lively impression on the minds of the people, and excited many an aged person to approach the Holy Sacraments who had been hitherto careless and indifferent in their religious duties. It was the first time First Communion was made in public by the children in Tullamore and they were all dressed neatly in white. In memory of this first great event, we always manage to have children make their First Communion in public on this Feast, if possible arrayed in white, and to give them breakfast at the convent.

The great success of this little Establishment encouraged our Venerated Foundress to undertake the work of another Foundation for which she was solicited, in Charleville, Co. Cork. In October, she visited Tullamore on her way in order to comfort and console her children there, as well as to give the Charleville Missioners an opportunity of seeing their old companions once more. She was accompanied on this occasion by the Superioress of the new Foundation, Mother M. Angela Dunne and her Sisters, together with her own companion, Sr. M. Clare Moore, and her chaplain, Rev. Mr. Burke. This was merely a passing visit but it served to encourage and animate the Sisters, and to draw still closer and closer the ties that bound each separate establishment to its Head. Our dear Foundress always wished to strengthen this, and often expressed her ardent desire that the first houses formed under her should keep up a mutual correspondence by letter, not only with the Parent House, but with each other.

It was on one occasion of a visit to Tullamore that the custom of wearing a crucifix in the cincture was introduced by the Foundress. From the beginning she wished each sister to have one in her possession in order to be able to inspire the sick and dying with sentiments of love for Jesus crucified, as well as with contrition for their sins which caused his sufferings and death. This small crucifix was always carried by the Sisters inside the Habit. At Sr. M. Teresa Purcell's Profession, by some mischance or other, she put the crucifix in her cincture, without adverting to the fact, on which Rev. Mother McAuley perceiving, said "Oh, Sister, how nice it looks! We shall henceforth wear the cross outside, that all may see to whom we are consecrated!"

From that day the professed sisters of this Community always observed the custom and in time it became general in the Congregation. Novices on Remote Preparation for Profession are allowed the privilege, although they may wear the cross inside during their Novitiate. . . .

All things were just progressing favorably in the new Community and the sun of public opinion shining around them when it pleased God to send them a few trials to test their patience, as well as to be a forerunner of future blessings. The cross chosen for them was the cross of illness, which appears to have hung close to St. Joseph's, if we may judge from the frequent recurrence of sickness that each year records in its annals. The town was visited by a frightful epidemic of fever of the worst type. The first person stricken in connection with the Community was their kind Father and Director, the Rev. Walter Murtagh. The sisters visited him every day and tended him with anxious care. This was surely the least they could do for one who had done so much for them, and who had at heart their slightest interest and happiness. . . .

Our V. Foundress, who is usually sparing in expressing her affections, is loud in praise of this humble priest. She felt she owed him a debt of gratitude and in her letters at this time to S[t]. Joseph's and elsewhere, she does not fail to desire her affectionate and most respectful regards to "*dear kind Father Murtagh*". Nothing could equal her regret at hearing of his illness and she had public prayers offered by the Sisters in Baggot St. for his recovery. It pleased God that he should recover, but shortly after, he was withdrawn from Tullamore, having been promoted by Most Rev. Dr. Cantwell to be Parish Priest of Eglish about 14 miles from Tullamore. On his removal, he was appointed Extraordinary Confessor to the Community. . . .

This was a severe winter [1836] for the poor. They suffered intensely from cold, hunger and disease, and as there was no fever hospital in the town the epidemic raged uncontrolled. The Sisters did not spare themselves, visited the sick, and established a regular system of collection for the poor. Michael Molloy, Esq., Distiller, was the foremost of the townspeople in this work of charity, and in kind appreciation of the labors of the Community. He even wished to endow an hospital and consign it to the Sisters' care, which benevolent wish was never carried out, being overruled later on by the Poor Laws [1838] which required a Workhouse to be built in the town with its accompanying Infirmary and Hospitals. . . .

As the Bishop was expected to administer the Sacrament of Confirmation in

Autumn [1838], the sisters were constantly employed in preparing the children both during the day and evening in the Parish Church for the reception of this Holy Sacrament. By their exertions and minute enquiries on the Visitation of the Sick, a great number of adults were discovered who had never received the strengthening grace of this Sacrament, and who were encouraged by the Sisters to make the necessary preparation for it. Many converts too appeared at this time, on one day no less than fourteen were received into the Church—such prodigies would remind one of the wonders of the First Pentecost. One thing it seems to indicate clearly is that the Faith of the poor Irish seemed to catch fire anew, after their long years of adversity and oppression, from the zeal of the young Institute which was destined to deck the Church with a new Band of fervent and zealous missionaries.

On Saturday the 22nd September, more than 930 children and others received the Sacrament of Confirmation from the hands of the Lord Bishop Dr. Cantwell, who was delighted and gratified at the answers of the children, shewing how well they had been prepared by the Sisters. On the next day, Sunday, the Bishop preached the Visitation Sermon after last Mass, and congratulated the people on the happy fruits of the labors of the sisters, as manifested in the proceedings of the previous day, and encouraged the united efforts of the Pastor and people in erecting a dwelling worthy of them.

The next day being the Feast of our B[lessed] Lady of Mercy, the good Bishop spent the day with the Sisters, and made some valuable presents to them, amongst the rest, a set of Rodriguez' *Christian Perfection* which are still regarded as a treasure in the convent, being one of the first gifts of its venerated Bishop. . . .

In August [1839] Rev. Mother McAuley again visited Tullamore on her return from Cork. She was accompanied by M. M. Clare Moore, Superioress of Cork, and four English Sisters,[6] all converts to the true Faith who having served their Novitiate in the City of the Lee were on their way to found a House of the Order in Bermondsey. The celebrated authoress of *Geraldine*, Sr. M. Clare Agnew, was amongst the number. . . .

Fever still continued to rage in the town [in early 1840], and of course, the poor were the victims. As the sisters were unceasing in their visits to the poor sufferers, they naturally caught the infection—the lay-sister Martha was the first who fell ill and two days afterwards, Mother M. Teresa [Purcell] and Elizabeth, the lay-postulante. There was much anxiety caused in the town by the illness in the convent, it being so full at the time. In course of time all, thank God, recovered. Owing to the prevalence of fever in the locality, and the Community usually suffering from it, the Bishop formally forbade the sisters to attend infectious cases, and although often called upon to revoke the prohibition, he could not be prevailed on to do so, especially after the establishment of the Fever Hospital. He often and often repeated that the sisters attend the sick for a twofold spiritual object—for instruction and consolation. Now he looked on this as out of the question in fever cases—not much good can be done for the poor sufferer in this way, but much, very much harm to the Sister Visitor and her Community, every member of which is so closely bound together by sympathy of avocation, constitution and education. He thought if the sisters attend infectious cases, they must lay aside other sick patients with whom they could do good and especially would they be obliged often to relinquish care of schools and such other Duties to which they are bound, not to speak of these many social ties of Community life which are so often snapped asunder by illness.

Many notes of condolence came at this time, but none were more welcome than our dear and Venerated Foundress; she says—"God has sent you an affliction but rest assured he will send you some distinguished consolation. You remember what Fr. Gaffney said to us in our first Retreat—'If the entire cross upon which Jesus died were sent to this house, how eager would each sister be to carry it and she who would be permitted to keep it the longest would be esteemed the most favored. Far better and more profitable is it to receive the cross which God sends you in any shape or form he pleases.' I earnestly hope you may receive this trial so as to make it valuable to you and your Community."[7]. . . .

In April [May 1840] Rev. Mother McAuley again visited on her way to Galway to found a convent. She had with her Sr. M. Teresa Whyte [White], the Superioress of Galway, her Sisters, and good Fr. O'Hanlon. She cheered her children after their heavy cross of sickness and was well pleased at the progress of the new building [school rooms and convent].

In June the new Schools were opened with great éclat and were numerously attended. Many very respectable families sent their children who did not disdain to mix with the poor in order that they might avail themselves of the superior instruction, both secular and religious, of the Sisters. There was general admiration expressed by all ranks at the ability and skill of the teaching power of the Sisters, and of their thorough knowledge of the system of the National Board of Education lately introduced into Ireland, which seemed incomprehensible to so many teachers at the time, and scarcely capable of being reduced to practice in poor schools. But they were faithful children of Catherine McAuley who had devoted herself so fully to Education, not only during the stormy time of her youth, and in her maturer years in the little village of Coolock, but later on when not being satisfied with her own attainments, which were of a superior order, she did not disdain to attend the schools of the Kildare Street Society which was then, as now, a very hotbed of Protestantism and Proselytism. This must have been an heroic act for one whose strong faith and indomitable courage urged her on to the great work of defeating the machinations of a hostile Government in its wiles for poisoning youth, but her only reason for these visits was to learn the most perfect mode of training teachers and of conveying knowledge in this far-famed Establishment, so that she might be enabled to meet its emissaries on their own ground, and defeat them by their own instruments. Doubtless Miss Doyle accompanied her on these visits for was she not her faithful co-operatrix in every good work?

. . . Doubtless Rev. Mother M. Anne did not fail to transmit to her young

Community many a lesson she learned by observation in the Model Schools of Kildare and Marlborough Streets [Dublin], and doubtless too, it was owing to them that the convent Schools of Tullamore acquired for the Infant Community a name of which they might be proud, as it enabled them to take a stand against the ignorant prejudice of the day, and to proclaim to their bigotted Protestant neighbors that the time was come at last when Ireland was becoming to be again "*Insula Sanctorum et Doctorum*", and its children be taught again the Truths of our holy Religion no longer by stealth in the way-side hovel or sea-girt cavern as heretofore, but in the broad daylight in the crowded city and the frequented thoroughfare of regenerated Erin.

It would appear as if our Ven. Foundress wished to confine the labors of the Sisters of Mercy to the instruction of the poor, and therefore in the beginning she did not intend to open special schools for the education of the upper and middle classes, leaving such to the Loretto [Loreto] and Ursuline Nuns. This want was keenly felt by persons where the Sisters were located who could not enjoy the advantage of sending their children to such Boarding Schools, either on account of distance or deficiency of means. Rev. Mother McAuley could not feel the want of such schools in the city, yet when it was laid before her she at once acquiesced and sanctioned them. Very Rev. Dr. O'Rafferty was the first applicant for Pension Schools in his Parish. He was delighted with the progress of the poor children of his Flock and was desirous that the richer ones should also share in these advantages. A Pension School was opened immediately, and it gave general satisfaction to all parties. It became in time the nursery of many a Religious, who imbibed in it their first lessons which they, in turn, imparted to others both at home and in foreign lands. . . .

On the 26th of December in this year [1840], our V. Foundress again visited on her way to Birr where she founded her last convent.[8] She was accompanied by Sr. Aloysius Scott, Superior of the new Foundation, and Srs. M. Rose [Lynch] and Teresa [White] from Baggot St. to form it. It was said that she was anxious that Birr should be founded from Tullamore, as it was in the same county, but Rev. Mother Mary Anne did not think her young Community sufficiently matured to send them out to form new colonies. Mother McAuley was a little vexed at this. Bishops and priests were constantly importuning her for foundations and she thought the younger houses ought to aid her. Half serious, half jesting, she wrote about this time in one of her notes—"Birr convent ought to be founded from Tullamore. It is a shame to be such creep-mouses in so good a cause. When we pass through Tullamore on our way to Birr, I will give a bitter scolding and three cheers for Carlow."[9]

The allusion she makes to Carlow was caused by this convent sending out Sisters to Wexford a very short time after its own foundation, in which respect it presented a striking contrast to its elder sister, Tullamore. Mother M. Anne might have been too cautious; however she erred on the safe side. Her zeal led her rather to perfect the sisters entrusted to her, before she sent them out to spread the new Institute, and surely she judged rightly, for the perfection and reputation of our Order ought to be dearer to us than its extension, and when she could not spare her more experienced subjects, she knew it would not advance the glory of God to form foundations of half-trained inexperienced members. Before many years, however, she sent out a colony and even went with it herself, as we shall see in its proper place. Notwithstanding Mother McAuley's threat it is superfluous to say that the "*bitter scolding*" was never delivered and that her visit at this time was as pleasing as ever and added a new charm to the festal time. Writing from Birr at this time, she says—"We travelled as far as Tullamore on Saturday. The new convent is a beautiful edifice. I had no idea of its extent, the staircase fine, the Community Room larger than ours, the infirmary as large, thirty cells, and water brought through the whole house by conductors, so that a pipe can be put anywhere. The School rooms are very fine and connected with the convent."...

In May [1841] Rev. Mother McAuley visited Tullamore again, for the sixth and last time. She was on her way from Birr, where she had assisted at the first public Ceremony. Her health was evidently breaking down, and the sisters saw with grief that she could not long withstand the labors and fatigues of her numerous foundations. She was accompanied by Mother M. Cecilia Marmion, the Mistress of Novices in Baggot St., and two other Sisters. Birr was her last Foundation in Ireland. She founded Bermingham [*sic*] a few months before her death.

In a letter she wrote at this time, she says of the convent and schools in Tullamore, "They are a grand tribute to Religion, and a very handsome sight from the canal boat; indeed they are quite an ornament to the town. I am sure God is preparing a distinguished place in heaven for the generous, benevolent priest who has been so instrumental in erecting them. If I said more it would [not] be too much. They will last for centuries. Yet Sister Marianne [*sic*] says she is grey with care notwithstanding all their seeming prosperity. She is, what I call, *doing the humble*, and, as ever, greatly afraid of that cunning thief, *vain-glory*."[10]...

The Lord Bishop, Dr. Cantwell, came again to the town on the 28th August [1841] to administer the holy Sacrament of Confirmation. A great number of children were prepared by the Sisters and confirmed. As usual, the Bishop visited the convent, and congratulated the Community and Dr. O'Rafferty on the new and beautiful convent just taken possession of. He was welcomed with more enthusiasm than usual at this time, for he brought with him the first copy of the confirmed Rule which he received on that day (1st Sep.) from Most Rev. Dr. Murray, Archbishop of Dublin.[11] The Original was in Italian and for some years after all the copies of our Holy Rule were written ones having been translated from the Originals sent from Rome. This was the last gleam of comfort vouchsafed our Venerated Foundress on earth and of course all her children participated in her joy. The confirmation of the Rule and Constitutions so speedily obtained excited universal surprise, the Order not being yet ten years old. It was obtained at the united request of the Lord Primate of Ireland and other

Bishops, in whose Dioceses Communities of the new Institute had been located. . . .

In September Mother McAuley applied to Mother M. Anne for permission to send her a sister who was in a very delicate state of health, thinking the change might benefit her. M. M. Anne consented and the invalid in question, Sr. M. Justina Fleming, came to Tullamore accompanied by Very Rev. Dr. O'Hanlon. . . .

A circumstance occurred at this time[12] which caused M. M. Anne no slight mortification. She wished to have this Ceremony performed with great éclat and for this purpose invited the great Apostle of Temperance, Rev. Theobald Matthew [Mathew], to preach on the occasion. When the Bishop heard of it, he thought it most imprudent just then, and ordered M. M. Anne to write immediately and decline his proffered services. The principal Benefactor of the Convent was a Distiller [Michael Molloy, Esq.] and many influential persons in the King's Co. also.[13] Dr. Cantwell judged it injudicious to excite them, when they were doing so much in promoting the service of God. Poor Mother M. Anne was dreadfully humbled and found her *act of obedience* hard in the extreme. Fr. Matthew was not in the least degree offended, and sympathised cordially with her on the occasion.

She wrote to M. McAuley, and unbosomed herself in this trial. This prudent mother poured consolation into her heart, but at the same time shewed her that such a proceeding without the express consent of her Bishop was reprehensible and added, "It will be a lesson to all our convents to be extremely cautious in seeking extraordinary favors. It might have been a little too presuming, but a great penance has followed. The kind, complying answer from 'the Apostle' might have excited some secret motions of self-complacency, but God in his mercy has sent the remedy."[14] And in a letter to another house she says, "You may judge how poor Sr. M. Anne feels at being obliged to decline Fr. Matthew's offer to preach at the Ceremony. Her Bishop thinks it would be imprudent to excite the Distillers there just now. I suppose he hopes the good work of temperance may go on quietly"[15]. . . .

On the 12th November [1841], the melancholy intelligence of the death of our Venerated Foundress arrived. She died the previous evening. No tongue can describe the grief of the entire Community for what did they not lose in losing her? And the account came so unexpectedly. True, they heard she was ailing, breaking down fast, but it would appear as if they never contemplated death in reference to her at all. They almost thought she could not, would not die so soon and leave the Institute still in its infancy and, as it were, but rudely formed.

The death of any one to whom the survivor has been united is a bereavement—it is hard to look the thought full in the face that we shall never see such a one again. But when that one has been light to one's feet, the stay and encouragement of one's very soul in the everyday difficulties and perplexities of life—the removal of such a one is a foretaste of death to those who remain behind. No wonder then that the poor sisters felt the blow keenly and required all the grace they could get to reconcile them to the loss of their sainted mother.

4

Mary Clare (Georgiana) Moore, 1814–1874

Georgiana Moore[1] was born of Protestant parents in Dublin on March 20, 1814.[2] The Bermondsey Register says that she was the daughter of George and Catherine Moore, and that she was born in the Parish of Saint Anne's where she was baptized and confirmed. Mary Austin Carroll says that "Her father died in 1817, and the family continued Protestant until 1823, when Mrs. Moore and her children had the happiness of being received into the Catholic Church" (*Leaves* 2:37).[3] Georgiana was then about nine years old.

Years later she wrote that she "became acquainted with dear 'Revd. Mother' [Catherine McAuley] in September 1828" and that she "went to reside in Baggot St. on the 13th October" (Letter of August 23, 1844). Baggot Street had been opened on September 24 of the previous year. Evidently Georgiana came "in answer to a call for a governess for Catherine Macauley and Teresa Byrn"—Catherine McAuley's younger niece and her adopted cousin, ages nine and seven, respectively (Degnan 75).[4] Eight months later Georgiana left temporarily. As she wrote on August 28, 1844, "I was not in Baggot St. from June '29 to June '30, so that I only know the occurrences of that year from hearsay." However, she returned on June 10, 1830 and remained at Baggot Street until she departed, at the age of twenty-three, to become the first superior of the Mercy community in Cork. Her sister, Clare Augustine Moore, writing to Bermondsey in 1875, several months after Georgiana's death, says of her: "She entered St. Catherine's [i.e., the Baggot Street convent] when she was little more than sixteen, not without a severe mental struggle. How she lived so long is wonderful for her lungs were diseased when she was fourteen and continued so for many years after, I know, perhaps to the last."[5]

Having stayed behind at Baggot Street while Catherine McAuley, Mary Ann Doyle, and Elizabeth Harley went to George's Hill, Georgiana was thus among the first seven to receive the habit at Baggot Street on January 23, 1832, and one of the first four women who professed their vows there on January 24, 1833. She was then not quite nineteen years old. At her reception of the habit she had adopted the baptismal name of her older sister Clare (who would later also enter the Sisters of Mercy) and so became known in religion as Mary Clare Moore. She was, by all accounts, an intelligent, trusted companion to Catherine McAuley and is acknowledged to be the person who most closely assisted her to prepare the completed manuscript of the Rule and Constitutions of the Sisters of Mercy. On July 6, 1837, Catherine and she then founded the first community of Sisters of Mercy in Cork.

On November 21, 1839, having left Cork—as she thought, temporarily—and journeyed from Dublin with Catherine and the rest of the founding party, she became the first superior of the Bermondsey (London) foundation. This appointment was intended to last only a year, until one of the English sisters, who had made her novitiate in Cork and come to Bermondsey as part of the founding community, was prepared to assume leadership. A year and a half later, in June 1841, Clare returned to Dublin, and thence to Cork where she resumed the role of superior, leaving Mary Clare Agnew as superior in Bermondsey. However, in the following six months Clare Agnew's grave misunderstanding of the ministerial vocation of the Sisters of Mercy nearly destroyed the spirit of the Bermondsey community, and, wanting a life more fully focused on contemplative practices, she was removed from the office of superior and subsequently left the community, on October 5, 1842, for a Trappist convent in Dorsetshire. So on December 10, 1841, Clare returned to Bermondsey, at the request of Bishop Thomas Griffiths, and was re-appointed superior on December 13, 1841.[6] She held this office until her death in December 1874—except for fifteen months, from June 5, 1851 to September 23, 1852.[7]

On October 17, 1854, while remaining superior of the community, Clare with four other Bermondsey sisters went to the Crimea to nurse the sick and wounded British, Scottish, and Irish soldiers who were involved in the war with Russia. They went, on three days' notice, at the request of Bishop Thomas Grant of Southwark, in response to a plea for volunteer nurses issued by the Secretary at War, Sidney Herbert. Clare was assigned to a hospital in Scutari, Turkey, and remained there until peace was declared. But having become dangerously ill with dysentery and pleurisy, she left Scutari before all the wounded had returned home, arriving back in Bermondsey on May 16, 1856.

In the Crimea, the Bermondsey sisters served under the leadership of Florence Nightingale. On April 29, 1856, the day after Clare left Scutari to return to England, Miss Nightingale wrote to her from the general hospital in Balaklava, at the front:

> Your going home is the greatest blow I have had yet. But God's blessing and my love and gratitude go with you, as you well know. . . .
>
> I do not presume to express praise or gratitude to you, Revd. Mother, because it would look as if I thought you had done the work not unto God but unto me. You were far above me in fitness for the General Superintendency, both in worldly talent of administration, and far more in the spiritual qualifications which God values in a superior. My being placed over you in our unenviable reign of the East was my misfortune and not my fault.
>
> I will ask you to forgive me for everything or anything which I may unintentionally have done which can ever have given you pain, remembering only that I have always felt what I have just expressed—and that it has given me more pain to reign over you than to you to serve under me. . . .
>
> My love and gratitude will be yours, dearest Revd. Mother, wherever you go. I do not presume to give you any other tribute but my tears. . . .
>
> Ever my dearest Revd. Mother's (gratefully, lovingly, overflowingly)
>
> Florence Nightingale (*Letters* 16–17)

Florence Nightingale (1820–1910) and Clare Moore remained close friends and corresponded until Clare's death eighteen years later. Clare served in some sense as a spiritual counselor for Florence, who once wrote to her: "I take great comfort in the thought that you offer me to God" (56). Two days before Clare's death, Florence wrote to a sister in the Bermondsey community: "I know not what to write. Perhaps she is at this moment with God. . . . It is we who are left motherless when she goes. But she will not forget us: I cannot say more. I send 2 or 3 eggs for the chance. And I have a little game which I send, for I think you, and perhaps others, must be so worn out with watching and sorrow that perhaps you cannot eat" (*Letters* 69).

Over the years, Clare's remarkable skills—of nursing, consoling, teaching, administering, and writing—served hundreds of people in England, the neglected and the well known, including the bishops of London and Southwark. It was she, and other sisters from Bermondsey, who attended the severely ill, and now almost blind, Bishop Thomas Griffiths, Vicar Apostolic of the London District, "day and night" before his death on August 12, 1847. Clare herself evidently stayed with him almost every night for over two weeks. On August 16, a few days after he died, Clare wrote to the sisters in Chelsea, a convent she had founded in west London in 1845, to give them "some little account of our good Bishop's illness and death". In her six-page letter, one senses what her presence must have meant to the dying man. She writes: "he told me to suggest to him what aspirations he should make, and what he should be thinking of—but I had no need to do this for he was praying incessantly when he was awake"; "he did not refuse any thing however unpleasant, the vomiting was continual, every thing he took"; "he told me the first day that his sight was gone entirely from one eye and almost from the other"; on Wednesday night, August 10, "as soon as he perceived I had come, he said . . . if I would cause the Holy Name of Jesus to sound in his ears, when he was dying, he would make me hear it at my death"; "his mouth was so parched . . ., and he could only get a teaspoonful at a time"; "when the sinking of death was coming he asked very often to be raised, and when we could not raise him as much as he wanted, he would say so quietly, what can you do for a dying man"; "he died so tranquilly that the Priest who was kneeling beside him did not know it." Clare's long, detailed letter, now in the Bermondsey archives, is a moving illustration of what the chapter of the Rule on the Visitation of the Sick had come to mean in her own life.

Clare also worked with Cardinal Nicholas Wiseman, Bishop Griffiths' second successor and later Archbishop of Westminster (1850–1865), and with Archbishop Henry Manning who succeeded Wiseman, but the bishop with whom she collaborated most closely was Thomas Grant, Bishop of Southwark from 1851, just after the restoration of the English hierarchy in 1850, until his death in Rome, at the Vatican Council, on June 1, 1870. A wealth of material in the Bermondsey archives, including correspondence, documents their relationship. In the summer of 1856, when Clare returned sick from the Crimea, Bishop Grant was anxious that she and Mary Gonzaga Barrie get away for a rest; at his suggestion she went to a convent of Visitation Nuns in Boulogne, and he assured her: "The money will not be wanting. I will send as much as you think necessary." His letters to her were always solicitous, and respectful of her judgment. He once wrote: "Pray much for me between now and Friday as I am in great anxiety of mind about two matters in which I have to decide. They do not regard the Convents of course."

It is clear from both sides of their correspondence, as extant in the Bermondsey archives, that Clare Moore served as a secretary to Bishop Grant, and that others in the Bermondsey community occasionally did copying for him. He once wrote: "I hope they will forgive me for troubling them so often with my MSS." Clare herself frequently mentions work that she has received from him, including letters to be translated. Once she reminds him: "I have delayed this, to send, at the same time, the copy of the French letter, but we have not yet received the conclusion which you promised to send by post." Bishop Grant evidently also relied on her to respond, when possible, to other requests that came to him. Thus he writes from Berkshire: "Sir Robert Throckmorton wants a Sister who can speak French and can nurse their governess. Have you any Sisters who could be spared? I do not like one to go alone and I fear you could not spare two." Many passages in the Bermondsey Annals, as well as many letters in the archives, tell of Thomas Grant's helpfulness to Clare, and of hers to him. For almost twenty years, until his death in 1870, their working relationship and mutual respect contributed steadily to the accomplishments of both. It was therefore fitting, as the Annals records, that when Clare was dying in December 1874, Bishop James Danell, the new Bishop of Southwark, "visited her every day and left with her his pectoral cross, which contained a relic, and which formerly had belonged to the revered Bishop Grant" (2:[228]).

During her thirty-five years in London (1839–1874) Clare Moore and the Bermondsey community founded eight additional autonomous houses in England: Chelsea (1845), Bristol (1846), Brighton (1852), St. Elizabeth's Hospital for Incurables on Great Ormond Street, London (1856), Wigton (1857), Abingdon (1859), Gravesend (1860), and Clifford (1870, where they replaced the Dublin sisters), as well as a branch house in Eltham. Clare was a solicitous and generous correspondent, and many of her autograph letters are preserved in the archives of the Sisters of Mercy, Bermondsey. What strikes one immediately, in the letters to her sisters, is her playfulness, good sense, and affection. While still in Turkey in 1856, she writes from Scutari to Mary Stanislaus Jones in Balaklava, to ease the latter's worry over the little opportunity she had for Mass or confession while working near the front: "You are a good old lady . . . do not be the least discouraged about your not getting Confession or H[oly] Communion—remember, our B [lesse] d Lord can supply for all"; when she finishes the letter the next morning, she writes: "Good morning, Miss Heathen—I ought not to be writing to an excommunicated old woman, ought I?" Mary Stanislaus was then about thirty-four! In March 1861, to a young sister, Clare writes, with playful grammar: "Dearest old Grandchild, You is bad to take the trouble of getting my nice clean Surplice washed again! Many thanks . . .," and then, like Catherine McAuley, she signs the note, "Your ever affectionate old Grandmother." On December 11, 1870, she writes to Mary Teresa (Elizabeth) Boyce in Brighton—

who had entered the Bermondsey community in 1839—to congratulate her on the anniversary of her reception of the habit and the anniversary of the Institute the next day: "We have set many favourite verses of our dear Foundress to music and we shall have them sung after supper with great glee—I wish you could come up to spend the evening with your old-fashioned relatives in Bermondsey—should we not give you a hearty welcome!!" On October 21, 1871, a week after Teresa Boyce's feast day, and while Clare herself is ill in the infirmary, she writes, "to offer you, though late, the most cordial and affectionate good wishes of all at Bermondsey, including pussy and the noisy sparrows."

Mary Austin Carroll quotes from numerous other letters of Clare Moore to her sisters. To one, Clare writes: "Experience is the best teacher—we grow wise through our blunders"; to another: "Do all with an upright intention, and never look back"; to yet another: "We are not angels; faults will be committed, mistakes made. Well, they can be remedied by quiet patience, and cheerfulness above all. Always look on the bright side of everything, and don't let anything trouble you"; and to one who was ill: "Yes, indeed, we must have pity on ourselves, and not believe in half the ghosts we see at such times. Did you think you were to march off to heaven and leave poor old me behind? No, truly; I will pray that you may be a jubilarian!" (*Leaves* 2:251–2, 260).[8]

Clare Moore had a wise sense of administration, a compassionate attitude toward human nature, and a tender devotion to the poor. For example, on October 30, 1856, she wrote to Bishop Grant: "Some of our poor children made their first Communion today and breakfasted here—will you give them your blessing—one poor child must stay out tonight 'till 12, selling onions in the street." In her younger years in Ireland Clare may have been rather quiet and reticent in conversation (as Catherine McAuley, Clare's sister, and Clare herself have claimed), but the letters and work of her later years reveal her remarkably outgoing kindness. The Bermondsey Annals for 1874 reports her personal involvement in establishing the Eltham house, nine miles from Bermondsey; this was to be her last major endeavor on behalf of the poor:

> On Sept. 23rd . . . Canon Wenham came, on behalf of the Bishop, to ask Revd. Mother if she would take charge for him of a Girls' Industrial School at Eltham, which had fallen into a very deplorable state, through neglect and mismanagement . . . . They went thither accordingly . . . and found the place in even worse condition than they had anticipated . . . . On Sept. 30th Revd. Mother, accompanied by Mother M. Camillus Dempsey and Sister Francis, lay sister, went to Eltham to take possession and begin the new work. No words can describe the dirt and disorder that everywhere prevailed . . . . The place had been stripped of everything but 25 bed steads with their miserable straw mattresses and threadbare coverings. There were 25 neglected looking girls, who had hardly a change of clothing. The house with everything in it was thoroughly cleaned and all necessaries speedily procured. The poor children were provided with good clothing and good food, and their numbers increased so fast, that in a very few weeks there were over sixty.

Clare was to live only ten weeks longer. As the Annals indicates, "the labour and anxiety entailed upon her by this new work, together with the fatigue of the constant journeys between Bermondsey and Eltham in the unusually severe weather soon produced fatal effects." On December 2, 1874 she caught a cold, but claiming that "a cold doesn't last for ever", rallied after a couple of days (Carroll, *Leaves* 2:268). However, on December 6, a doctor diagnosed her condition as pleurisy, and on December 14, 1874 she died in Bermondsey, in her sixty-first year.[9]

About a month before her death, Clare had written about the Eltham situation. In this letter one sees both her generosity and her sense of humor:

> We have been obliged to take from our own barely sufficient quarter's income almost half. We had to buy necessary furniture, and you would be amused at the scanty supply; clothing for the poor children, whose garments are next to rags; bed-covering and food, besides begging three months' credit from butcher, baker, grocer, etc.; afraid to light fire enough to warm us or cook our provisions. . . . One [child] only eight years old had stolen a perambulator with a baby in it; another a waterproof,[10] which she sold at a rag shop. What a blessing for these to be with us, but what an anxious charge for us! . . . I have been there six or seven times—no little cross to me, who do not care for travelling. We must accept our cross whatever it is made of, even a railway carriage. (Carroll, *Leaves* 2:268)

Like Catherine McAuley thirty-three years earlier, Clare had had her "surfeit" of travelling, but one also notes in this letter the same enlivening zeal which had led Catherine herself to proclaim: "Hurra for foundations, makes the old young and the young merry" (289). On November 14, Clare wrote a letter to "My very dear Children" at Eltham, telling them she was thinking of "getting up a Library" for them: "I thought if we had a book for each of the children marked for the charges [assigned chores] they might be the first contributors and by degrees we might have a very large Library of nice books to read on Sundays. You could write me a few letters to tell me what you would like."

The same Clare Moore, who in her last days writes to poor children, promising "nice books to read on Sundays", has also contributed to our knowledge of the early history of the Sisters of Mercy and of the life-story of Catherine McAuley three very important documents: the set of five letters about Catherine written to Clare's sister, Mary Clare Augustine Moore, from August 23, 1844 through August 26, 1845;[11] the long biography of Catherine McAuley entered into the Bermondsey Annals for the year 1841;[12] and the first compilation and publication of *A Little Book of Practical Sayings, Advices and Prayers of Our Revered Foundress, Mother Mary Catharine* [*sic*] *McAuley* (London: Burns, Oates & Co., 1868).[13] The complete texts of the first two of these manuscripts are presented below: "The Letters of Mary Clare Moore to Mary Clare Augustine Moore, 1844–1845" (no other title has ever been given to this set of autograph letters); and the Bermondsey Annals' entry for 1841: "A Life of Catherine McAuley" (often called the "London Manuscript" or the "Bermondsey Manuscript", though the latter title is also, unfortunately, sometimes used to refer to another manuscript, written by Catherine McAuley).[14]

Certainly Clare Moore is an extraordinary eyewitness source of firsthand knowledge about Catherine McAuley, principally for the years 1828 to 1837, but also, through correspondence and visits, for the years 1837 to 1841. A question that may be asked, however, is whether the Life of Catherine McAuley in the Bermondsey Annals is an original composition by Clare Moore, or a transcription of a manuscript life composed by someone other than Clare, and composed elsewhere—for example, in Limerick or Derry or Dublin. I do not think either Limerick or Derry is a likely candidate. Clare Moore would have had greater firsthand knowledge of Catherine McAuley than Mary Vincent Harnett, who entered Baggot Street in February 1837, and, in some respects, greater than Mary Elizabeth Moore, who entered in June 1832—the first, the author, and the second, a principal source, of the Limerick Manuscript. Moreover, the Limerick Manuscript contains numerous long passages from the Bermondsey Life, as well as from the Derry Large Manuscript, while the Bermondsey Life does not appear to contain passages *copied* from either, and has numerous internal clues which point to Clare Moore's authorship. Although Mary Ann Doyle, who lived in Derry, could conceivably have been the original author of the Life copied into the Bermondsey Annals, her evident association with the incomplete Derry Large Manuscript makes it seem unlikely that she would have *also* authored another life of Catherine McAuley, namely, the Derry Small Manuscript, a manuscript which is nearly identical to the Bermondsey Life, but which is not in Mary Ann Doyle's handwriting. The only other possible author might be someone in Dublin whom I cannot identify: although Mary Vincent Whitty copied this same Life from some source in 1860 (Cork MS. 3), she clearly says that Clare Moore composed it; Mary Cecilia Marmion, who died in 1849, might have composed such a Life, but there is no tradition which says she did; the same is true for Mary de Pazzi Delany, a possible but, in my view, not likely candidate; and Clare Augustine Moore was working on her own Life of Catherine McAuley as late as 1864.

The actual text as it appears in the Bermondsey Annals is probably a *transcription* of an *earlier* original manuscript written, as I assume, by Clare Moore. The location of the original manuscript, if it is still extant, remains to be determined. It may well be Cork MS. 2, which is in Clare Moore's handwriting, as noted by Mary Angela Bolster (*Documentary Study* 1:lxxxvii). Its presence in Cork, if this presence dates from the 1840s, could somewhat explain the inclusion of long passages of it in the Limerick Manuscript.[15] There remains of course the possibility that the Life in Cork MS. 2 was composed—*before* Clare Moore copied it into Cork MS. 2—by someone else whom no one has yet identified. Since the Derry Small Manuscript is almost identical to the Life in the Bermondsey Annals, and to Cork MS. 2, and, moreover, since transcriptions of various manuscript lives of Catherine McAuley were frequently made and shared with various houses, and since the present location of a manuscript is probably not sure evidence of its place of original composition, further research, especially to identify various handwritings, may still be needed to resolve the questions of *authorship* and *transcription* associated with several of these early manuscripts.[16]

If Clare Moore did indeed compose the Life which is copied into the Bermondsey Annals (the Annals' Life is not in her handwriting), she would have done so only *after* she had written her letters about Catherine McAuley in 1844–1845, for otherwise she would have sent her sister the Life itself, not her laborious and somewhat disjointed letters. Since she says in the Annals, in her own handwriting, that the Life "was written about eight or nine years after her [i.e., Catherine McAuley's] happy and holy death, 1849–1850" (by which she may mean, either *written into* the Annals, or *composed*), the period in which she may have composed the Life is either the four years from 1845 to 1849, or the year 1849–1850. Since she was in Bermondsey all this time, the presence of the manuscript in Cork is interesting. Mary Angela Bolster says that Clare compiled Cork MS. 2—"as mentioned on the brown-paper cover—for the Novices in Carlow" (*Documentary Study* 1:lxxxvii). Did Clare send the community in Carlow a copy of the Life after she composed it, before or after it was entered into the Bermondsey Annals; or did she have someone else's Life inserted into the Bermondsey Annals and copied for Carlow, the Carlow copy eventually making its way to Cork?

Clare Moore herself, whether or not she is the actual author, as such, of the Life in the Bermondsey Annals, would have been a principal source of its content. It can, therefore, be said to be, in some genuine sense, a record of her memories and perceptions of Catherine McAuley, as her five letters written to her sister in 1844–1845 most assuredly are. In the letters one gains a more personal insight into the mind and circumstances of the author-narrator. She wishes to be accurate and systematic in her presentations, but claims that she "was ignorant of what was passing around me except when told of something or when matters were so apparent that I should be not only nearsighted but blind all out not to see them." She feels that she "ought to apologize a thousand times for the confused medley I send"; and she takes care to "repeat some of the principal dates, as I could not feel positive whether I gave them correct after I had posted my last letter." Where she doesn't "know much about it", she says so. She experiences "various interruptions" as she writes, and moments when she has no time and feels "entirely stupid", or when she predicts that her sister "will be shocked at this scribbling but my hand is tired". If Clare is also the author of the Life in the Bermondsey Annals, as I believe, she is in that document much more at leisure to be her well-organized self.

In June 1841 Catherine McAuley welcomed Clare Moore back to Dublin. In writing about Clare at that time, she calls her "our old beloved companion" (345) and "our beloved old companion" (346). Clare was that indeed, not only in the quality of her life and work, but in the remarkable narratives she took the time to record, even when her hand was tired and poor girls in rags needed to be clothed. She was, throughout her life, one of the outstanding co-founders of the Sisters of Mercy and a remarkable contributor to the mission of the Catholic Church in England in the nineteenth century.

THE LETTERS OF MARY CLARE MOORE, BERMONDSEY, LONDON, TO MARY CLARE AUGUSTINE MOORE, BAGGOT STREET, DUBLIN AUGUST 23, 1844 - AUGUST 26, 1845

Convent of our Lady of Mercy,
Bermondsey August 23rd 1844

My dear Sister M. Clare,[1]

You could scarcely have applied to a worse person for information than to me—not that my memory fails me—but I never asked questions nor concerned myself about what did not concern me; consequently I was ignorant of what was passing around me except when told of something—or when matters were so apparent that I should be not only nearsighted but blind all out not to see them.[2]

This premised, I shall now endeavor to say what I did know, and first, I became acquainted with dear "Revd. Mother" in September 1828. I went to reside in Baggot St. on the 13th October. Baggot St. was opened Sept. 24th 1827. Mother M. A. Doyle and Sr. Josephine Byrn (now in St. Catherine's Convent) were there at first for some months and the House of Mercy was then opened—"Catherine Fay and Sister" first admitted, but there is a book of names of the young women—but not as now. It was only at night young women were there; they were obliged to provide their own support during the day. It was not until the Lent of 1829 that dinner was provided and then continued. It was at that time also the collection for the House of Mercy was commenced by means of notes, and the collection for the poor in 1830 or 1831, which at first was made by two of the Sisters who went from door to door begging subscriptions—*that* did not last long.

Are you aware that an account which appeared in the Newspaper soon after Revd. Mother's death was not quite true? *She never was a Protestant,* her father was an *excellent* Catholic, her mother nothing much—a *very good* woman but rather of a philosopher *above forms.* Dear Revd. Mother[3] was certainly much with Protestants and imbibed their sentiments, but I suppose you already know all about this so I will resume about Baggot St.

Revd. Mr. Armstrong died in May 1828,[4] after which dear Revd. Mother was enabled to come to Baggot St. with her two Nieces and Godchild; her eldest Niece was received into the Church and re-baptized by Archbishop Murray on St. Cecilia's Day 1828—unknown to her Father who was a Protestant. He died of fever the following January or February and Revd. Mother became guardian to his children, who all, after a while, became Catholics.

They commenced the Visitation of the Sick December 7th 1828, and at that time adopted the Postulants costume—the going out dress was a grey cloak with hood and Black silk bonnet and muslin veil, in summer a Black shawl. As to the form of life it was primitive Christianity. All rose at 6, but Revd. Mother and myself and sometimes Mother Frances used to rise at 4 and say the whole Psalter "by moonlight" often, read some of *The Sinner's Guide,* and transcribe I forget what, for after long labor it came to an untimely end. One winter morning poor dear Revd. Mother was looking for some letters in her desk and she held all those sheets of manuscript so close to the candle that they took fire and before she perceived it were consumed so far, that they could not be saved.

We all slept in one Dormitory, except Mother M. Ann and Sr. Josephine Byrn (Revd. Mother, her two Nieces, godchild, Mother Francis, Ellen Corrigan—Sr. Veronica, dead—*Ann Rice* and myself). Our sitting room and oratory was what is now, I don't know what. The last time I stopped in Baggot St. it seemed to be a waiting room for the poor; it was then the prayer room and work room. It had one chair, six *high* priezdieux, cut low after at Dr. Blake's request, some forms and tables; we said every morning the prayers in Gahan's *Catholic Piety,* made meditation; at night, prayers out of the same, and a lecture from the *Elevation of the Soul,* by Revd. Mother who always said the prayers and read. The young women joined us and at the night prayers the young girls from the neighbourhood used to come in also, for we kept open house with perfect safety until one day dear Revd. Mother began to boast of it, and before night the chair on which she was sitting disappeared.

The Sisters said the Rosary all together, walking up and down, and on Monday the Rosary for the dead, Wednesday that of St. Joseph, Friday that of the Sacred Heart. They had also a private oratory neatly fitted up in one of the cells. In Winter a fire was lighted on the corridor where they had Recreation. We had Mass only once in the chapel before it was dedicated; we used to go to Clarendon St. every Sunday morning, frequently in Revd. Mother's Swiss carriage, but that was sold in a few months after I went; they went on Saturdays to confession to Clarendon St. I think the Chapel was dedicated on the Octave of the Ascension 1829 or thereabouts. The House was thrown open to all visitors that day and a splendid déjeune laid out and Dr. Blake preached. On the following Saturday the Revd. Mr. L'Estrange said Mass and *O'Connell* served his Mass and went to Holy Communion; he then took collation with his daughter Kate and Mr. L'Estrange in the Community Room that was. The Confraternity of the Sacred Heart was established on the Feast of the Sacred Heart same year, and the Sisters then went into separate cells and the 2nd Dormitory was furnished for young women.

During this time I remember no one who proposed to join except a Miss Knaresborough from Kilkenny (I think). She was expected day after day, a fire lighted in her cell to air it for she was rather delicate. She did come to Dublin at length, but before she would enter Baggot St., went to consult Surgeon Colles of Stephen's Green as to the propriety of her doing so; he of course condemned the step, and she married a very old rich man.

Do you know that when Baggot St. was first opened it was much opposed by the Priests, especially Revd. Matthias Kelly. He went there one day, led Revd. Mother through the house telling her to select a room or two for herself, as it was the Archbishop's wish to give the house to the Sisters of Charity, but she could have a private entrance, etc. It was no such thing—he wished it. Dear Revd. Mother believed him at the time, and meekly said Dr. Murray could do as he pleased with the house, for it was his.

[Note][5] There was also another who left, Miss Ellen C. from Kilkenny, just before her Reception, but, after going to 2 or 3 Presentation Convents, she again entered in Carlow. Miss Jane Green (Sr. M. Josephine) got the Habit but was sent away, her health being bad. She went to Tullamore after. I told you that the Foundation to Tullamore went in April 1836. Mother M. Ann and Sr. Teresa Purcell (Novice) to remain. Revd. Mother, her youngest niece (who had got the habit the January before) and myself accompanied, Fr. O'Hanlon, our guardian. We went in canal packet boat, left Baggot St. before 7 o'clock, arrived in Tullamore 4 o'clock in evening—met by Dr. O'Rafferty, who took Revd. Mother and Mr. O'Hanlon in his own car while we 4 were put on an outside car and gazed at and followed in astonishment by *crowds*. We dined at Mr. O'Rafferty's and in the evening were sent to the future Convent. Other details of that Foundation you have no doubt heard from better authority but I thought well to give a hint of the journey. We returned to Baggot St. in about a month or six weeks (that is, Revd. Mother, Sr. M. Ann Agnes and myself). We went there again in August to assist at a ceremony. Mr. [Daniel] Burke was then our protector. He was such a good man. Did you know him? When we got to Tullamore it was desired that two more of the Sisters should come, and he went back for them. Before this Foundation Sister M. Agnes Marmion died of erysepilas [*sic*] on the brain—the particulars of her death you can easily obtain. In Autumn of this year, it was decided to send a Foundation to Charleville. We set out on the 27th of October, or 26th. Mother Angela and 2 (Sr. J. Delany and Sr. M. Agnes Hynes) Novices, to remain—Revd. Mother and myself companions. This journey was amusing.

I find I shall not have time to give particulars of this journey today and indeed I ought to apologize a thousand times for the confused medley I send. I can only say that I have a *good will* to render you any assistance, but *no ability*. I find I have forgotten much—and knew very little worth communicating. You can easily get the dates of receptions, Professions, deaths. I forgot to say that for Sr. M. T. Macauley we had a Dirge sung in our Chapel by Priests, the Vicar General Mr. Coleman, President. Mr. O'Hanlon sang the High Mass afterwards. This was the first and only time while I was there that the Solemn Office etc. was performed. Many things come into my mind but having often related them at Recreation I get puzzled and think, Oh I wrote that to her long ago,[6] and sometimes also I make foolish repetitions, but you would excuse if you knew how little time I have. I am glad to hear of Kate and children. I did not forget you in Retreat. I hope you are next door to a Saint if not one all out.

Remember me most affectionately to Mother de Pazzi, to Revd. Mother,[7] Mother Vincent, Sr. M. Magdalen, Sr. M. Camillus, and all our dear Sisters, not forgetting dear old Sr. Genevieve—and now I think I may for your "Sincerely and respectfully" much more truly subscribe myself—

Yours most obediently etc., etc., in J.C.

August 16th [26th?] Sr. M. C. Moore

Convent of our Lady of Mercy
Bermondsey August 28th 1844

My dear Sister Mary Clare,

Your note of the 25th I received this morning, the feast of your holy Father,[8] and in the first place allow me to wish you a happy feast—next you must excuse me if I repeat some of the principal dates as I could not feel positive whether I gave them correct after I had posted my last letter. Baggot St. was first opened 24th Sept. 1827. Revd. Mother went there herself in May or June 1828. The Chapel was dedicated the week before Whitsunday (I think the octave of Ascension) 1829.

I shall also go back to say that dear Revd. Mother's original intention was not to found a Convent. So little did she think of establishing a religious Institute, that when she went to see the building, she laughed at their putting a choir with a grated window in it. All she designed was that there might be an Establishment where pious ladies might retire for a while to exercise works of charity etc. and return again when they wished to their homes, in fact a Protestant convent plan, but Almighty God had greater designs. I believe Right Revd. Dr. Blake's advice was chiefly instrumental in inducing her to undertake what she so well accomplished. He returned from Rome about the year 1828–1829, bringing with him some Altar pieces, of which he gave dear Revd. Mother her choice. She selected that of our Lady, which now hangs over the Altar.

At this time she with his advice and the permission of Most Revd. Dr. Murray sent to the different Convents to request the loan of their Rules which she carefully reviewed and read aloud to those who were to form the Institute. They all chose the Presentation Rule and this was also most approved by Dr. Blake and Dr. Murray, altho' the Carmelite nuns were anxious to affiliate them to their order, and the Carmelite Friars, Clarendon St., who had been most kind from the beginning and rendered many services, wished it too.

The Poor Clares of Harold's Cross made the same proposal, but the Rule of the Presentation had the preference; however, matters did not at this time proceed further.

After the Chapel was dedicated, more regularity was observed. The Revd. Mr. Burke was appointed Chaplain, and Revd. Mr. O'Hanlon now came to the Convent to hear the Confessions, so that the Sisters went out no more to Clarendon St. or any place except to visit the sick. They were joined that year 1829 by Sr. Ann O'Grady, or as we called her, Sr. Aloysius O'Grady. She was niece to Father John McCormack of the Rock, a most pious young person. At 16 she entered a Presentation Convent in Wexford and got the Habit, but in a year or so she took fever and after recovery was obliged to leave. She remained a short time with her friends, and then obtained admission into Baggot St., where she was indefatigable in visiting the sick, etc. She was the beginner of the collection for the poor, and in the hot summer used to walk all day without being weary or annoyed, soliciting subscriptions. Whether that was too much for her, or the natural delicacy of her constitution was unable for the fatigues, she fell into decline in 1831. She was a long time ill, and died a few weeks after dear Revd. Mother's profession—in 1832. She was of a very scrupulous disposition, and above all had a great dread of making the Vows. She did not live to make them, poor thing. The same year November 1829 Sr. Elizabeth Harley entered, Sr. Magdalen had joined in the Summer, I don't know the date; and Sr. Angela Dunne also, and dearest Sr. M. Teresa McAuley [*sic*].

I think on the Feast of our Lady of Mercy 1828 Revd. Mr. Woods came to Baggot St. with Dr. Murray's permission for the house to be styled—"House of Mercy"— then *Convent* was not thought of. When the Chapel was dedicated Dr. Murray recommended Revd. Mother to get the gallery erected and permitted the Chapel to be public, saying the collection would support the poor young women in the House of Mercy. There used to be two Masses on Sundays and holydays—and 1 Mass every day—and the Sisters used to sing at last Mass.

For the support of the House of Mercy there had been a Bazaar in "Morrison's" in 1828, I think, and there was another in 1829—both went off well. I was not in Baggot St. from June '29 to June '30 so that I only know the occurences [*sic*] of that year from hearsay.

In 1830 Revd. Mother again turned her attention to the regular establishment of the Institute. She found that she must with two others serve a Noviciate and be professed in some Convent, and the selection of those two companions as well as the Convent to whose mercy she would commit herself engaged her thoughts. George's Hill was chosen, Dr. Murray permitted, Dr. Blake approved, and the Nuns consented, which was considered a very great act of condescension and kindness for them to profess persons for another Institute. Mother M. Ann and Sr. Elizabeth Harley were selected to accompany dear Revd. Mother and they entered George's Hill on the 8th Sept. 1830. Before she left us she did all she could for the preservation of order among us in Baggot St. No one was superior, it is true, but Mother de Pazzi, who had entered Baggot Street a little before and whose prudent manners seemed to fit her for having charge of others, was given the charge of the house—superior in effect tho' not in name. Mother Frances Warde was House keeper, and Revd. Mother made some other regulations, as—no more secular ladies to teach in the School, for formerly the Costigans, O'Connells, Miss O'B Butler and several others used to come and instruct in the School; at first it was all well, but afterward it degenerated into idle talk with the Sisters. The house was no more to be shewn to strangers except particular persons and for fear we should look out of the windows that white muffing was put on all that looked towards the street.

I forgot to mention about Miss Redmond, but I dare say you know it; well, as you may not, I shall inform you that in July before Revd. Mother went to George's Hill she was sent by Dr. Blake to attend a young lady with white swelling in her knee. Her Father and Mother were dead and she had no one with her but a young inexperienced cousin and an old country nurse. Her name was Mary Ann Redmond, she was from Waterford or Cork. The first Physicians were attending her and they judged it necessary to amputate the limb. Dr. Blake requested Revd. Mother to allow her to be in Baggot St. for the operation as she was so friendless and alone in her lodgings. Revd. Mother's charity readily consented. She was accommodated with the large room which is now divided into Noviceship and Infirmary. Mother Mary Ann and Mother Angela were present while the operation went on tho' her screams were frightful. We attended her night and day for more than a month, at the end of which time she was removed a little way into the country where she suffered for two or three months and died in great agony. Tho' she was rich, by some unaccountable chance, nothing was left by her to Baggot St., so we had no temporal reward for that work of mercy which included a *great many others,* I assure you.

You ask about a woman who did not speak to her husband for so many years. I know few of the particulars, only these: she had a favorite son who behaved ill and was chastised by his father, which she resented so bitterly that taking this son with her she left her home in the country and came to live in Dublin where her husband followed her and altho' he made every effort to obtain a reconciliation it was all in vain, until at last the unhappy woman falling sick the Sisters were sent to her. They prayed, etc., and at last on her death bed succeeded in making her forgive her husband, but I don't know much about it. We used to visit Sir P. Dunn's Hospital daily or any time we liked, besides the poor in *their* own houses.

I shall send you another sheet in a day or two, but perhaps I would not have time soon.

Sr. M. C. M.

*

Convent of our Lady of Mercy
Bermondsey Sept. 1st 1844

My dear Sister M. Clare,

Besides what I mentioned of the affairs of Baggot St. previous to dearest Revd. Mother's going to George's Hill, there are still some other little matters which I will write down at once and then you can if you like set about compiling your grand work up to that period, without fear of being interrupted by any fresh "reminiscences" of mine.

One thing was that from the Dedication of the Chapel [June 4, 1829] the spiritual exercises were changed. They were now separate from those of the young women. At six we assembled in choir and said morning prayer which was only the Act of Oblation from the big *Sacred Heart* book, then Meditation in the *Journal* 'till 7 I think, Mass 7 1/2, Breakfast 8 or 8 1/4, and immediately after in the Refectory, Revd. Mother read the Saint for the day. I do not think we had any more prayers then 'till near 4 when we assembled for examen, and after dinner we had a Visit to the B.S. [Blessed Sacrament] read out of Liguori, in the evening the Rosary, private reading and prayer.

Another thing I forgot was that during that time also they had Lay Sisters, who used to be, as in some convents, very much with the Choir Sisters and took their meals at the same table. This was found to be a bad practise and was discontinued. I think there were three Lay Sisters—two I am certain—one was a tall woman, Catherine. She was dismissed before dear Revd. Mother went to George's Hill. The other, Hannah Fulham, was retained for some time after. There was a grand tale about her—it may go in with the *Visions.* She was an [''*artful*'' is crossed out in ink] little person, a *very great* favorite with Mother Francis, but her conduct was not approved of, and Revd. Mother said she was to go (for all matters of importance were referred to her in George's Hill). Hannah did not like this, so one fine morning she got up with her head *quite shorn,* by supernatural agency, to be sure, as a sign that she was to remain and be a Nun. No trace of a single lock of hair could be found, nor where nor how it was done, but done it was, as we found out, *by herself.* One of the Sisters from whom she had borrowed a scissors perceived on the inside a little hair, and searching farther we discovered some more in the *Music Choir,* where, after much to do, she confessed she had cut it off; you may guess she was soon sent off.

Before Revd. Mother went to George's Hill, Sr. Caroline Murphy entered Baggot St. She was a very nice looking young person from Killarney. Most pious from her childhood, when very young she made a private vow of chastity, and I believe she never for a moment thought of any thing but of devoting herself entirely to the service of God. She came to us June 18th 1830, and died of consumption June 28th 1831. During the short time she spent with us, she edified all by her virtues. She used to obey all with cheerfulness, always laboring and humbling herself, and it gave her pleasure when any one saw her employed in the meanest offices. This is not a mere term of custom, for I know she used to clean out the floor of the school w.c.v. [w.c.u.?], and used to let herself be seen with her hands all black as if she was a mere servant, etc. I need not tell you she was patient and resigned in her tedious illness for she died like a Saint. Revd. Mr. O'Hanlon heard her general confession and assisted at her death. He read the last prayers for her. As we had then no Habit she was buried in the brown Carmelite Habit of the 3rd Order.

I said before that the Carmelite Priests of Clarendon St. were very kind to us—among other things, Revd. Mr. O'Hanlon and (when he was at Rome for some months) Revd. Mr. Whelan (now Bishop of Bombay) came regularly every week to hear the Sisters' confessions. They supplied us with Vestments and every thing almost for the Altar, and continued for nearly 3 years to *give* altar breads, Incense, charcoal and other things. When Mr. Whelan [actually, Mr. L'Estrange] was in Rome he obtained a special Rescript of Indulgences "for Sr. Catherine McAuley and the other pious women in Baggot St." which I daresay you have seen. It was that granting two days every month *plenary*, and *partial* for the Litanies. The good Priests of Clarendon St. also allowed us a place in their principal Vault where only Priests were allowed to be interred before, under the Altar. This you know but I put down what comes into my mind for if I stopped to select and place things in order you might wait long enough for any information. I send this in scraps also, lest if I kept it back to write it out fair—to revise and correct—you might never see it at all. I do not now remember any more previous to Revd. Mother's going to George's Hill.

[Note][9] Your enquiries about the good offices of Revd. Messrs. Nugent and Armstrong I cannot well answer, as I never made enquiries. Dear Revd. Mother often spoke (in general terms) of Mr. Nugent's great friendship and readiness to serve in any way, but this was said more to shew how much Almighty God intended the work should be entirely His own, as He was pleased to call away such good and efficient friends at the moment they were most wanted. Revd. Mr. Armstrong it was who undertook the charge of getting the Convent built. It was completed when he took his last illness. He had been the greatest friend of Archbishop Murray, and might reasonably have expected his Grace's friendship for an undertaking in which he was so much concerned, yet his last advice to dear Revd. Mother was not that she should confide in Dr. Murray, but most emphatically again and again he repeated, "Do not put your trust in any human being, but place all your confidence in God alone"—prophesying almost that all human aid would fail, but God's help would never be wanting. She often told me this when oppressed with care.

You ask about dear Revd. Mother's spiritual exercises. She was too humble to talk much about self—indeed, she disliked the words *my* or *myself* so much that I often felt ashamed when inadvertantly [*sic*] I had pronounced them. But I know that she was most pious from her childhood. Her first attempt at writing was to try and print the "Psalter of Jesus", her favorite prayer. This she had divided for every hour of the day when a little girl, and in whatever place she was she always was exact to this practise. I heard her say she once said part of it on the steps of a hall door. She was confirmed and made her first Communion in Arran Quay Chapel, and altho' her eldest sister and brother yielded to Protestant friends' solicitations and gave up the faith, she alone stood firm.

When living with Protestants she never neglected Religious duties. On Fridays she used to have nothing but two or three potatoes, as meat was always on table in those days. She used to pray before the cross moulding on the door, as she dared not have any emblem of catholicity. For many years she never tasted *any thing* on Good Friday. Obedience, when she was a Novice, made her conform to the Community, but after her return to Baggot St. she resumed her old custom for some years, but then she told me it was best to do as all did, and therefore she gave up this favorite practise. During the entire Lent in the world, besides strict fasting she made a law never to touch wine. Her charity and zeal, I need not say, were most remarkable, and when she resided at Coolock House, the residence of old Mr. and Mrs. Callaghan, her benefactors, she had much to exercise these virtues on account of the interference of a Protestant minister's wife with the poor, and there she formed her first idea of a community or some society devoted to the instruction and protection of the poor. But I do wrong to say any thing at all about her virtues and good works for I know so little of them; these circumstances I now mention came to my knowledge accidentally. Her successful efforts for the conversion of Mr. and Mrs. Callaghan you all know, but do you know that she brought her own Sister back to the Church during her last illness. She had married a person of the same name—Macauley—a Presbyterian who would not have suffered a Priest under his roof, but she was brought out to Dundrum for her health and there dear Revd. Mother contrived with much risk to bring Father McCormick to her, and she died a Catholic. Her children it was—and not those of a brother as stated in that Newspaper affair—that she adopted.

Whenever she was in doubt or difficulty she had recourse to prayer and the Thirty Days' Prayer as long as I knew her was the means by which she obtained all she wanted. She used always say it with *entire confidence* of obtaining what she asked. But you know her virtues and can describe them. But I must just say that her humility was truly profound and sincere—no affectation of it, but real self-contempt. If ever any affliction came to us she attributed the cause to herself. I used to grieve to hear her condemning and blaming herself so much. Tho' you know much about her, you did not know her as I knew her.

You will be shocked at this scribbling but my hand is tired.—

May God bless you. Sr. M. C. Moore.

*

Convent of our Lady of Mercy
Bermondsey Sept. 13th 1844

My dear Sr. Mary Clare,

I have had so many hindrances and interruptions to my promised account of old times that I almost fear you will deem me ungrateful, but I really could not help it and now I do not expect, tho' I have commenced this sheet of paper, to be able to write more than two or three lines today.

I told you that dearest Revd. Mother went to George's Hill on the 8th Sept. She often said it was so hard a struggle for her to remain on account of meeting there many things repugnant to her feelings that had she not had the establishment of the Institute most deeply at heart she would (that very evening) have sent for a coach to take her back to Baggot St. The Suprss. [Superioress] at George's Hill when she entered was Mrs. Doyle who treated her with great mildness, and for the first five months of her Noviceship as well as 3 months she was [a] Post[ulant] she was exempted from the jurisdiction of Mother Teresa Higgins, the Mistress of Novices, and only subject to Mrs. Doyle. She had also other privileges, but in May following there was an Election. Mother Francis Knowd was made Suprss. and she immediately placed Revd. Mother on the same footing as the other Novices, and Mother Teresa being very strict, poor dear Revd. Mother felt the change much. But perhaps I had better not waste time on this topic for I think it likely you have heard all the little stories of her Noviceship, or they might not be what you want to know—if you do, say so and I will try and remember them.

I shall then return to Baggot St. where as you may guess we were left very disconsolate. We had certainly enough of work to keep us from fretting, for besides the school which was more laborious under the old system, we had very many poor sick—Sir P[atrick] Dunn's Hospital, the Incurable Hospital at Donnybrook, and the Lying-In Hospital at the Coombe to attend, and indeed we labored hard.

The first effects of Revd. Mother's being at George's Hill which we experienced was [*sic*] an order to change our beds, for I forgot to tell you we used to sleep on the straw palliasses; those who desired to be comfortable used to cut the stiches, but most of us were quite happy on the hard stiched ones. The Presentation Nuns, however, thought that impossible. So they desired Revd. Mother to have hair mattresses got, and this was I assure you a penance, for to get so many at once was expensive, and some one offering to do it cheap, instead of horse hair, put in cow's or dog's or something so dreadful that the smell for several months was most sickening. Another change ordered by the good Nuns was that we should drink beer, as before we only had water at dinner.

I do not think there is much to relate about those 15 months of Revd. Mother's absence. Sr. Caroline Murphy took ill and died. Sr. A. O'Grady also got into consumption. But I only wonder more of the Sisters did not get ill for they were so zealous and fervent without any guide that one used to fast, another wear hair cloth, take disciplines, etc., stay up late praying, and many other pious indiscretions—but at the same time we kept on all the duties and customs. We had the usual High Mass on the Feast of the Sacred Heart. We had also the Christmas dinner, which even before Baggot St. Revd. Mother was accustomed to give to the poor children, and for some years in Baggot St. many respectable persons used not only send large presents of beef, etc., as I suppose they still do, but they use[d] to be present and serve the poor women and children. [Daniel] *O'Connell* used to carve for them—I think I said all this before.

Right Revd. Dr. Murphy visited us often during Revd. Mother's absence, said Mass and gave us the Mass book. He has been a *constant friend* to us from the *beginning.*

We had Sr. Josephine Byrn's illness during that time. The Physicians pronounced her recovery almost hopeless, tho' she might go on a long time. The Presentation Nuns wished Revd. Mother to have the relic of Fr. Tharesborough tried with her. Revd. Mr. de Luynes, a pious French Priest, said Mass that day (St. Joseph's), the relic was applied to her back, for it was a spinal disease, and altho' she had not been able to come down, or out of her cell for a long time previously, she came to benediction and continued quite well afterward. The Doctors said the nerves were in question, and there was nothing surprising in the suddenness of her recovery. I only know what I tell you, for I was not present when the relic was applied, and being then young I asked few questions and meddled in nothing. But the said relic got us into a scrape, for the Presentation Nuns said we stole a piece of it and were much annoyed.

As I have mentioned Revd. Mr. de Luynes, I had better inform you that he was a holy young Priest who being introduced to Revd. Mother at George's Hill she, ever mindful of her poor children, begged he would come and hold conferences with us, public and private—writing to us at the same time to speak to him of all our anxieties, doubts, etc., etc. We had but few public instructions from him. The private ones were numerous—but I can tell you nothing of them, for altho' I tried and thought to get some difficulty to propound with him, I was unfortunately too stupid. He afterwards went to America as Missioner.

Revd. Mother was much disappointed at being obliged to wait 3 months before she got the Habit. She complained of it to Dr. Blake who was not pleased at her seeking any exemption. She used to relate the conversation. When she represented to him the right she thought she had to get it at once, his answer was "The Devil is there." So you see he treated her as one far advanced in humility. Towards the end of her Noviceship she experienced great trouble and anxiety, as the Presentation Nuns made great difficulty about professing them with the liberty of going out to the Sick, and she often described the anguish she endured about the period of passing the Votes for her and the other two. She also had great uneasiness at her long absence from us, and so impatient was she to return that she offended the Nuns by leaving on the very day of her Profession.

Previous to that our costume had been a subject of much deliberation. At length the coif was chosen, the plan being taken from the Carmelite headdress. Black guimpes were for a long time decided on, but the Revd. Mother of George's Hill, representing to our dear Revd. Mother that Religious had in all ages been distinguished by the white guimpe, that too was settled. At first the Habit was to have sleeves tightened in, but (I need not tell you) by degrees we grew into what we are.

The expenses incurred during the 15 months of her Noviceship made Revd. Mother resolve on a plan of very strict economy when she came home to Baggot St. We were even spoken to at table to remember we were not come to a full and plentiful house, that we should be more sparing, etc., and we had been *most* sparing during her absence. Our Postulants dresses were altered and patched up into habits for us to be received in. We had only common brass crosses to our beads. We got their old white veils, only one new one, old guimpes, etc.

I think it was on the 13 of December 1831 Dr. Murray came to Baggot St. and after appointing Revd. Mother to her Office, gave permission for such of the Sisters as were ready to receive the habit on the 23 January. His Grace saw us all privately and spoke to us about our vocation, etc. There were 7 to be received, but as dear Sr. A. O'Grady was on her death bed and besides to save expense it was a very private ceremony, and we were not dressed in Secular clothes but as Postulants. Many Priests were present, and crowds outside the door, carriages, etc., but no admittance, which gave such offence to Sr. Anna Carroll's Mother who was there also that on the spot she declared she would remove her daughter which she did the week following. The 7 were Sr. M. J. Byrne, Sr. M. F. Warde, Sr. M. A. Dunne, Sr. M. T. McAuley [*sic*], myself, Mother de Pazzi, and Sr. Anna Carroll who took in Religion Mary Agnes.

On the 7th February Sr. A. O'Grady expired. She was, *I think,* interred in the brown Carmelite Habit,[10] and in Clarendon St. of course. During her last days Sr. E. Harley was attending her and after her death speaking of her sufferings, she observed that persons often wished for a long illness, but seeing her extreme sufferings had weakened her mind she, Sr. E., hoped she might not have a long illness. She [Elizabeth Harley] was well enough to serve in the Refectory on Ashwednesday immediately following, but soon became so ill that her recovery was despaired of. Still she was able to come down to the community room where she sat every day; on Easter Sunday she went to Holy Communion with us in the Choir and came down to the Refectory at the end of dinner to have a little pudding or something, but on Easter Tuesday she was much worse and on Wednesday evening about an hour after receiving the last Sacraments she died. This was a most severe trial, being one of the Professed and a very nice Sister, apparently blessed with good health. She was remarkably pious and exact to the least duty. She was very humble. I will mention one instance. Tho' professed she was for some time ranked below several of the Postulants, and even put in the most inconvenient place in Choir, Refectory, etc. Yet she never complained but was as happy and cheerful as if in the first place, not seeming to think of it. She was very obedient. An hour or two before she died Revd. Mother was in her cell and said "Now say nothing but 'Jesus, Mary and Joseph,' " meaning not to be anxious about any thing; some time after, when she went again, she was still repeating it and would not change her prayer without permission. Her death came the night before the Bazaar was to be held and you may guess how much we felt at being obliged to attend to the different arrangements for it. While she was dying,[11] poor Revd. Mother was called to the Parlor to old Miss Farrell[12] of Merrion Square who set about lecturing and scolding her for having such a means of procuring assistance for the poor as a Bazaar, which in her opinion was dangerous, sinful, etc. Dear Revd. Mother with her heart full of sorrow listened on patiently. When after a long tirade the old lady pulled out her purse and gave her £15 for the poor, which Revd. Mother quite regarded as a reward for enduring at such a time the lecture she gave.

I know I cannot write more today and all this has been done with various interruptions. I would scarcely send it only I fear you will think me negligent, and so I am but not wilfully.

Affte [Affectionate] love to your Revd. Mother and Mother de Pazzi—ask her to write. May God ever bless you.

Sr. M. C. Moore.

*

Convent of our Lady of Mercy
Bermondsey August 26th 1845

My dearest Sister,

Much as I desired to comply promptly with your wishes I was unable to find time, and now that I have succeeded in getting a few spare moments I want head, for I assure you I am entirely stupid.

I thought I told you that when dear Revd. Mother first came home she would have *no server*—it was to be a *carver*, for a week each, the reader too for a week. The table was not divided but like an ordinary Dinner table, and the carver occupied her own place as it came to her turn. I was appointed to carve the first week, Mother Angela of Charleville reader. I never shall forget it: a leg of mutton, and how I labored to cut it up, for I scarcely knew how to cut bread and butter. The next week I was reader and Mother Angela carver, which finished that plan. Revd. Mother took the carving entirely, and one was to serve, another read, one day at a time. Then Supper was at 8, no silence; that only lasted a few weeks. Supper went to 7 and silence.

When Sr. E. Harley died [April 25, 1832] or soon after I think we had no server at all, but the little girls waited at table; 5 or 6 used to stand against the wall and hand the plates, etc. Little Mary Quinn used to sit between Revd. Mother and Mother F. Warde, but no absolute want of silence. We went on this way until Sr. M. Teresa's death [November 12, 1833], when Revd. Mother reproached herself for not attending to these matters. She thought (she said to me) that perhaps the Sisters' health might be injured by the constraint of convent discipline, but Al[mighty] God had made her see that without it their health was lost —or something that way. For every affliction she used to imagine was a punishment for something she neglected or did wrong.

After that the Refectory took the form it now has pretty much, with a few minor changes, such as helping the juniors first, then the seniors were helped before them, then it went back to the juniors. I suppose they were considered to be the most hungry. Also Mother M. Ann got her to try dinner at 3 or thereabouts and no lunch, which lasted only a few days or weeks.

I cannot remember any thing about the sick poor, only the Cholera, and I think I told you that Revd. Mother wrote to Dr. Murray to get leave for us to attend the Depot Hospital. He came himself to bring the permission, it was evening, we were at Recreation. His Grace was brought in by Revd. Mother. He did not sit down, but standing at the end of the table spoke a few words about the work we were going to undertake, adding we should take great nourishment, *port wine* and *mutton* chops. This was litterally [*sic*] obeyed for a week or two when it was found to be too troublesome. We used also *at first* change our habits and use vinegar, we then got accustomed. We went early in the morning, 4 Sisters who were relieved in 2 or 3 hours by 4 others and so on till 8 in evening. Revd. Mother was there very much. She used to go in Kirwan's car, and once a poor woman being either lately or at the time confined, and died just after of Cholera, dear

Revd. Mother had such compassion on the infant that she brought it home under her shawl and put it to sleep in a little bed in her own cell, but as you may guess the little thing cried all night, Revd. Mother could get no rest, so the next day it was given to some one to take care of. I never knew what became of it, for I never asked questions; consequently I am but imperfectly acquainted with what occurred.

I went with Revd. Mother to Mrs. Lover, wife of Lover the portrait painter—who was a little crazy, thinking people intended to poison her—several times. I do not remember any thing about the sick. I suppose it is because I have been so much more out in Cork and here [Bermondsey] that the remembrance of the poor in Dublin has been effaced from my mind. I can just recollect the poor places, but no more.

As to benefactions I never knew of any. Oh no, if you want to know that, Mother F. Warde is the one. She knew every thing on that subject, or Sr. Teresa, the Lay Sister, since she was professed. Just after the Cholera Revd. Mother got printed tickets sent to each house begging old clothing, carpeting, bed covering, etc., and the result was that for a long time carriages used to stop and hand in great bundles so that the store room was filled, and the supply lasted a long time.

I mention Mother F. Warde, because she was always with Revd. Mother, even when a Novice, so that some little feeling was excited as she never took her turn in the duties which the other Novices had of sweeping, etc. At first we had charge of [the] Noviceship a week each in turn which she never took and I remember some complained to Revd. Mother, but I believe it was necessary she should attend to other business, for Mother M. Ann was of such a retiring disposition that she could not bear to see strangers.

Our cells for a long time had white curtains, quilts, etc. It was towards the end of my Noviceship—no, after I was professed [January 24, 1833]—we got that check.

In looking at the page I have written I see "shawl". We did at first wear shawls in Summer for our trains were *very short* before we got the religious habit. We always wore them in Summer, and in Winter grey cloaks bound with black—then the olive cloth. Our sleeves to[o] were *very narrow.* But just before the Cholera we had begun to wear black stuff cloaks with little hoods. I was much more than a year professed when we got merino cloaks lined, without hoods and fastened up the front, for Summer, and then the cloth cloaks were made in the same way. A fresh alteration, trifling, was made when we were going to Cork. I remember Dr. Blake objected to our wearing the Coif in the streets and thought a little *English* cap would look very neat, but this Revd. Mother did not yield to.

I have been interrupted and can write no more. May God bless you.

Sr. M. C. Moore

Don't forget to give my love to Mother de Pazzi, etc.
The wafers are a present. You need not be scandalized.

Excerpts from
THE ANNALS OF THE CONVENT OF OUR LADY OF MERCY,
BERMONDSEY ANNO MDCCCXLI [1841]

A Life of Catherine McAuley
[The Bermondsey Manuscript]

Towards the close of this year the whole Institute experienced a very serious loss and deep affliction caused by the death of our holy Foundress, The Reverend Mother Mary Catherine McAuley.[1] This admirable woman was born near Dublin about the year 1786, on the Feast of Saint Michael, of a respectable Catholic family. She was the second of three children,[2] and received the name of Catharine at her baptism.[3] She imbibed early impressions of piety from her Father, who was very exact in all religious duties, and was in the habit of assembling little children in his house to teach them the Catechism; but he died while she was yet very young, and her Mother, having met with pecuniary losses, was obliged to give up her establishment and take part of a house in Queen St. Dublin, the rest of the house being occupied by Mrs. George, the widow of an officer, a Protestant, and her intimate friend. Mrs. McAuley was a very amiable and accomplished person; her mind was highly cultivated, but her religious principles were defective; hence she considered liberty of conscience so essential that she thought constraint, or the obligation of performing any duties of religion foreign to its spirit—yet she educated her children as Catholics, and they were confirmed and made their First Communion in Arran Quay Chapel, and the little Catharine faithfully adhered to the pious practices she became acquainted with. When so young as to be unable to write, she copied in a kind of large print, passages from the Psalter of Jesus, a prayer for which she always retained great affection; she used to recite parts of it at different hours of the day, even when going through the streets. Her sister, who was older, was fond of dress and amusements, but Catharine felt only weariness and disgust for them. She was of a most affectionate and obliging disposition. When her brother in his fondness for play would lay aside his school exercises, she would try to write them for him, but he was often punished for her mistakes, which was a great trouble to her, for she would not willingly have caused pain to anyone, especially those she so dearly loved; and she always remembered with bitter regret having once told their Mother of some fault of pride committed by her sister, who was punished for it by being shut up in a dark room, where flames were represented, in order to give her an idea of the horror of eternal torments, for Mrs. McAuley had very strict and peculiar ideas on the education of her children.

Mrs. McAuley allowed her children to be very much with Mrs. George, whose conversation was not calculated to increase the spirit of Catholicity in their minds, but rather weakened it so much in the elder sister and brother, that on their Mother's death, when they were about twelve or thirteen years of age, being taken charge of by some Protestant friends, they unhappily yielded to false reasoning and relinquished their faith. The young Catharine alone remained firm and unshaken amidst the greatest temptations, for which she was much indebted to the instruction and kindness of the Revd. Dean [Andrew] Lubé, who was her steady friend for eighteen years. Her early life was one of much trial and sorrow. She lived some time with an Uncle [Owen Conway], her Mother's brother, and his daughter [Anne Conway, later married to James Byrn], to whom she was devotedly attached.

While she was with this Uncle, who was a Surgeon in the army, she had opportunities of settling in life which she declined. Surgeon Conway's affairs became embarrassed, and at last he was reduced to ruin, so that she suffered great poverty. Often after an entire day spent without food, they had nothing but a little bread at night, with many similar privations; but her cheerfulness never failed, and she has often said that she took her rest more contentedly on the boards than when surrounded by luxuries, and from these circumstances she used to conclude that we are much better able to endure hardships in God's service than we usually imagine, and that happiness does not depend on the enjoyment of temporal comforts, since many in great poverty are still most joyful, and Christ our Blessed Lord and His holy Mother had no temporal comforts, and yet were always full of peace and joy. She had a remarkable talent for thus drawing instruction from every occurrence, and made useful reflections on all passing events, teaching us to be careful in like manner to derive spiritual profit from all things.

After she was grown up, she was adopted by two wealthy Protestants, Mr. and Mrs. Callaghan, who had no children of their own. Being thrown so much among Protestants she read assiduously the best controversial works, and went often for instruction to the Very Revd. Father [Thomas] Betagh, whose learning and piety made every one revere his words, and who was also an able controversialist—hence her visits to him caused some to think that she had been a Protestant. She prayed unceasingly for the conversion of her friends, and succeeded so far that Mrs. Callaghan, shortly before her death, consented to see the Revd. Mr. [Michael Bernard] Keogh, but died before she could receive Baptism. Mr. Callaghan, who survived her three years, was received into the Church. Miss McAuley devoted herself to them with all the affection of a child, and gained their entire confidence, so that they left all the management of their household affairs to her discretion. All this time she was most fervent and exemplary in the performance of religious duties. She observed rigourously the days of fasting and abstinence, though in the midst of Protestants. She used to say that on Fridays her dinner generally consisted of two potatoes, for, when she had taken them, she would feel ashamed to stretch out her hand for more, lest it should be observed that she had taken nothing else. She never touched wine during Lent, and practised many other austerities. Prayer was her delight and her refuge—in all trials. She addressed herself to her good God with the utmost simplicity and confidence, even in the smallest difficulties. It was her chief recreation to copy prayers and pious books—and to unite with one of the

Catholic domestics in pious exercises.[4] Being unable to have any holy pictures or other objects of devotion, they used often to kneel before a Cross formed in the branches of the trees, or even the cross-shaped panels of the doors.

She was most careful to correct her faults, and to practise a genuine humility and patient forbearance; but charity was her characteristic virtue. She loved all, and sought to do good to all, but the poor and little children were her especial favourites; these she laboured to instruct, relieve and console in every possible way, so that she began even then to practise those works of Mercy to which she afterwards so fully devoted herself. One or two examples of her heroic charity will suffice to shew the spirit by which she was animated. It was her custom to visit the sick poor assiduously, as well in the wretched streets and lanes of St. Mary's Parish, Dublin, as in the village near her own residence; and having discovered in one of those abodes of misery in Liffey Street a poor old woman, a maniac,[5] who had formerly been in better circumstances, but was now deserted by every one (this poor creature was of good family, and a Protestant if she could be said to be of any religion), instead of getting her into an Asylum, Miss McAuley brought her to her own house, and took care of her till her death, which happened about five years afterwards, without her recovering even a gleam of reason so as to be able to receive any impression of a religious nature. During these years her Benefactress had much to endure from her, as, with the perversity of madness, she from the first conceived an absolute hatred for her, and her language in speaking of her was generally virulent and contemptuous; besides this, her habits were most filthy, and she had an inveterate custom of stealing every thing she could lay her hands on, hiding those things she could not use, so that the inconvenience was equally great. Miss McAuley's patience never seemed disturbed by these continual annoyances, nor would she permit the servants to teaze the poor creature on the subject. She also gave much attention to the poor school in St. Mary's Parish, spending several hours there daily; in the lower part of the school house she established a kind of shop or repository for the sale of articles of female clothing, the proceeds of which were applied to the poor.

Mr. Callaghan made his will some time before his death, and left all his property to her, saying he was convinced she would turn it to good account.

As soon as she had performed the duties of a Daughter of Mercy to her two beloved and wealthy benefactors, by attending them day and night during their last illnesses, until she closed their eyes in death, she was inspired by Almighty God to become a Sister of Mercy to the poor and afflicted members of Jesus Christ. Nor did she, among the great thoughts that occupied her mind relative to the Order she was about to establish for the relief of the poor, forget her own relations. She had long prayed most earnestly for the return of her beloved sister to the true faith, and at length had the consolation of seeing her reconciled to the Church on her deathbed through her own unwearied exertions. She then devoted her attention to the children; but their Father being a Protestant, she could only instruct the eldest, a most amiable young girl, in the principles of Catholicity.

She adopted the youngest daughter of her favourite cousin, before mentioned, whom she called Teresa, and carefully instilled into her sentiments of true piety, so that, when grown up, this young person had the happiness of devoting herself to religion, in the Institute founded by her beloved Godmother, as she always styled Miss McAuley.[6]

She was convinced Almighty God required her to make some lasting efforts for the relief of the suffering and instruction of the ignorant, and she thought of establishing a society of pious secular ladies, who would devote themselves to their service, with liberty to return to their worldly life when they no longer felt inclined to discharge such duties—for although our dear Revd. Mother was gifted with much piety, and was always a most zealous Catholic, she had imbibed certain Protestant prejudices, which she retained for a very long period. She did not like the idea of Religious vows, and disapproved of Conventual observances, etc., having constantly heard them ridiculed and misrepresented by Protestants. Her own house not being well situated for the purpose, she resolved to employ part of the large fortune she enjoyed in building one suitable to the designs she had in view. The site and the architect were chosen by the Revd. Dr. Blake, in Upper Baggot Street, before he went to Rome in July 1824.[7]

There was much difficulty in obtaining the ground, for the Protestants in the neighbourhood were opposed to it, supposing that an Establishment for the relief of the poor would injure the locality; however, she succeeded, and the house was completed in the beginning of the year 1827. It was built in Conventual style, which surprised and even amused her, for she has told us since that she never intended to establish a Religious Order, but Almighty God, Who disposes all things sweetly, brought her by degrees to see the necessity of regular discipline, and the advantages of the Religious state.

The Very Revd. Dr. Armstrong was the great friend and advisor of our dear Foundress, and had rendered her many services with the Archbishop, who loved him as a most holy and zealous Priest, and esteemed him in a particular manner. He had helped and encouraged her amidst many difficulties and contradictions, and she relied on him for future assistance in the great work she contemplated; but he had often said to her, "Place no trust or confidence in any man living, place all your trust and confidence in God alone", and God Who wished to do all things in her and by her, was pleased to call this good Priest to Himself, just after the house in Baggot Street was completed. Our Revd. Mother remained with him till his death, which happened on the Feast of the Ascension of our Lord 1828, and soon after she went to reside in Baggot Street, where there were already two young persons, waiting to unite with her in her holy undertaking, Miss Catharine Byrne, the eldest daughter of her beloved cousin, and Miss Anna Maria Doyle, sister to one of the Priests of St. Michael's and St. John's Chapel.[8] She brought with her her two nieces, Mary and Catharine Macauley, and her little God-child Teresa Byrn, and was joined by a young person desirous to labour for the poor, Miss Frances Ward.

The poor schools had been opened on the 24th of September 1827, under the care of Miss Byrn and Miss Doyle; and many young women had been received into the House of Mercy—they were not supported there, but only allowed to sleep in the dormitories, for at first it was intended merely to afford protection to those young women, who, being able to obtain a scanty subsistence, were forced to lodge in places where they were exposed to dangerous temptations; therefore after morning prayer and instruction they went out to their employments, and returned in the evening in time for similar devout exercises. Our dear Reverend Mother found that there was much to be regulated, and that constant watchfulness was required to maintain order and cleanliness. She also observed that these poor young women were still exposed to danger, by being out so late in the streets; her ingenious charity therefore made her adopt the plan of sending two of the poor school children, with an appeal in behalf of these destitute persons, to the principal Catholics in the neighbourhood. A very trifling subscription or donation was requested, and readily granted, so that abundant means of supplying all that was necessary for them were soon procured, and they were thus comfortably provided for within the Convent; and very many poor servants also, for whom there were no vacancies, had their meals daily, and were thus rescued from impending misery.

On the 24th of September 1828 she applied to Archbishop Murray for permission to have the Institute styled of our "Blessed Lady of Mercy", which he kindly granted, and he also gave leave for the visitation of the sick, on the 7th December the same year. About this time she had the happiness of seeing her two nieces received into the Church, tho' they were obliged to act without the knowledge or consent of their Father, who would by no means have allowed them to become Catholics. He died in the beginning of the following year, and she then took charge of his three boys, who, after being fully instructed, embraced the Catholic faith. She was a true Mother to these children—the boys she placed at College,[9] but her two nieces remained in Baggot St. with her. The eldest was about eighteen or nineteen years old; previous to her open profession of Catholicity she had long believed and practised all its duties, and, on the death of her Father, begged to become a member of the little Congregation, which began to increase and assume a Religious form. A plain black dress had been adopted, with a net cap and black muslin veil, resembling what is now worn by the Postulants. The manner of life was of the poorest kind, and they had only palliasses, with very scanty furniture in their cells, and other parts of the house.

Each hour of the day had its allotted duties. They rose early, and regular devout exercises of prayer and spiritual reading were practised. Although these were of some continuance, they did not satisfy the devotion of our pious Foundress, who besides private meditations used to rise at an earlier hour than the rest, with one or two of the juniors, to say the whole of her favourite Psalter, and read some spiritual book. One of these young persons had volunteered to call her, and it happened very frequently that, mistaking the time in the winter mornings, they used to get up at three o'clock instead of four, or half-past four as they had purposed. She would, on these occasions, fill up the remaining time by selecting, and transcribing from pious books, certain passages which might be useful for the instruction or consolation of the sick poor. She had made a good collection of them, when one day, searching for some important document in her desk, near which was a lighted candle, she held her manuscript too near the flame, and did not perceive that it had caught fire until it was nearly consumed; yet she never expressed the least annoyance at losing what had cost her so much labour.

They visited and relieved many poor sick persons in the neighbouring courts and lanes, and went daily to Sir Patrick Dunne's Hospital at a short distance from the Convent, where the effects of Miss McAuley's zeal and tender charity were soon very apparent. She spent much of her time in the poor schools, having an admirable method of conveying religious instruction, and considering the early culture of those poor children's minds as a work of paramount importance, and out of her affection for them and her devotion to the Divine Infancy of our Lord, she used to prepare a Christmas dinner for them every year, and wait upon them herself. In this act of humility she was for many years assisted by that great and good man Daniel O'Connell, who used to go to the Convent school on Christmas Day to carve for the little children.

Her compassion led her to make the greatest sacrifices in favour of the suffering and afflicted. The Revd. Dr. Blake having requested her to visit a young lady who had lost her parents, and was come to Dublin, to have medical advice about a white swelling on her knee, and amputation having been decided on, Miss McAuley offered her a home in Baggot St., that she might be able to assist and comfort her under this terrible operation, which was performed there, tho' without any beneficial result. During the month that this young person was in the Convent, she watched over her night and day with the solicitude of a parent, and neither sought nor received any remuneration for the expense and inconvenience such a serious illness must have caused.

On the Octave of the Ascension of our Lord, June the fourth 1829, the Chapel of the Convent was solemnly blessed by Archbishop Murray, and the Revd. Dr. Blake preached on the occasion. He had then just returned from Rome, and his kind feelings towards our Foundress had in no way diminished. He offered himself to assist her as far as lay in his power, and generously presented her with a beautiful Altarpiece of the Blessed Virgin and the Divine Infant, which is so justly admired by all who visit the Convent Chapel. He never failed to shew himself her friend, even after his removal from Dublin to a higher position in the Church, the Bishopric of Dromore.

A Chaplain being appointed, the Revd. Daniel Burke of the Order of St. Francis, the Sisters (as they were called) no longer went out to Mass or other religious duties, which they had formerly attended to in the Carmelite Church of St. Teresa, Clarendon St., their ordinary Confessor being the Very Revd. Father O'Hanlon, Provincial of the Carmelites, and our Institute is greatly indebted to this Order, as from it we have ever experienced kindness, support and encouragement.

The singularity of their customs having attracted notice, Miss McAuley was severely censured and condemned, especially by some among the Clergy, and a Priest, holding a post of authority, came one day to Baggot St. and told her that the Archbishop thought of giving the house to the Sisters of Charity, though she might have apartments and a private entrance. This intelligence was a great trial, yet she prepared her mind to submit with peaceful resignation. Having transferred all right over the house to Most Revd. Dr. Murray, she felt she ought not to dispute his wishes.[10] On enquiry, however, she ascertained that the Archbishop had not expressed such intentions, but he shewed much coldness, and when he visited her he said, alluding to the title of Sisters of Mercy being adopted, "the idea of a Convent starting up of itself, in this manner, never entered my mind." Our good Foundress in her affliction sought advice from the Revd. Dr. Blake, who went on her behalf to Dr. Murray without delay, and the result was, that the House would not be suffered to continue in the state it then was; that its inmates should either appear as secular ladies, or become Religious. The Archbishop gave her permission to examine the Rules of the different Religious Orders then established in Dublin, promising that he would obtain that she might serve a Noviceship in that which she thought best suited to her designs, so as to be prepared for establishing the Institute she proposed. [Footnote on the manuscript in Clare Moore's handwriting: "The permission for the establishment of the Congregation was granted by His Holiness Pius VIII."]

The Rule of the Order of the Presentation of our Blessed Lady, being the Rule of the great Saint Austin, with approved Constitutions, seemed to her the most fitting and after due deliberation, the Revd. Dr. Blake recommended that three of the Sisters (there were now twelve) should serve their Noviceship at George's Hill. She accordingly entered that Convent on the 8th of September 1830 as a Postulant, with two companions—Miss Anna Maria Doyle, who had been in Baggot Street from its first opening, and Miss Elizabeth Harley, a young person who had not been long associated with her, but whose fervent piety and amiable dispositions induced our holy Foundress to think she would be a great assistance in beginning the arduous work she had in view.

It was a severe trial to our Foundress to leave the house in Baggot Street, although she made every arrangement likely to promote and maintain order and stability; and frequently during her absence she procured that the Sisters might be assisted by the advice and instruction of pious Priests. She also felt difficulty in submitting to the usual restraints and trials of Conventual life, on account of the prejudices she had imbibed against them, but she offered herself cheerfully to God, to do and suffer all He should appoint in order to accomplish the great work which she felt He had marked out for her. She received the religious Habit with her companions on the 9th of December 1830, and the names given them were Teresa, Clare, and Angela—but our humble Mother reflecting that these Saints, after whom they were called, were all Foundresses of Religious Orders, was uneasy lest it might be thought she ranked herself with them, and therefore begged earnestly that they might retain their own names with the addition of Mary, which was granted at their Profession.

During her Noviceship, she evinced the cheerfulness of her natural disposition, even in conforming herself to trials which she felt very sensibly, especially as her Mistress thought fit to reprimand her publicly and often severely, for the most trifling omission, or inadvertent fault. She had also much care and anxiety about those Sisters who remained in Baggot Street—as it usually happens where regular discipline is not established (however good and pious persons may be) there will be some slight disagreements and irregularity; some amongst them, for want of prudent care, and being unrestrained in their austerities, lost their health and became seriously ill. Sister Caroline Murphy died on the 28th of June 1831. She was born in the South of Ireland, and from her childhood manifested dispositions of extraordinary piety. At the age of twelve or thirteen she made a private vow of perpetual Chastity, and her other devout and penitential exercises proved how sincerely she desired to give herself to God without any reserve. She joined the rising Institute in Baggot St. on the 18th June 1830, and although she lived there but a short time, she gave examples of virtue rarely to be met with. She practised an entire obedience to all, and on all occasions, though there was then no religious obligation to it. With profound humility she employed herself in the most abject offices, in such manner that it was not till after her death that many of her humiliations were discovered. As her appearance was highly calculated to attract admiration, she used, when she knew that strangers were to pass through the Convent, to blacken or otherwise disfigure her face, as it were accidentally, that she might be despised. She had very delicate health, but concealed her illness until it was too manifest, and too late for remedies, and when forced to yield to the violence of the malady (which was rapid consumption), she continued to evince her joyful resignation to the Divine will with sincere humility. She prepared for her last hour by a general confession of her whole life, and having received the last Sacraments on the Feast of St. John Baptist, she expired on the Eve of S.S. Peter and Paul, in sentiments of piety which edified and surprised, not only her companions, but the Confessor and Chaplain of the Convent, who knelt beside her in her dying moments recommending her soul to God.

This trial was followed by the illness of Sister Anne O'Grady, who had been then in the Convent for about eighteen months. She had received the Religious Habit in a Convent of the Presentation Order, when she was about sixteen years old, but was obliged to leave it on account of fever during the Noviceship. In two or three years afterwards she entered Baggot St. where her conduct was most exemplary. Her zeal and charity for the poor was such, that she begged permission to make a collection for their relief, and having by importunity obtained her request, she went from door to door, with one of her companions in turn, humbly soliciting the smallest alms for those destitute and suffering beings. This exertion made in the heat of the summer months was too great. She sank under it, and in August her case was pronounced hopeless. However, she lingered on for six months in great sufferings which she was anxious might be prolonged, and before she died was consoled by seeing once again, and experiencing the tender and unceasing care of our holy Foundress, who, while at a distance, was overwhelmed with grief and anxiety about her dying child.

And in addition to her many afflictions, her own favourite niece burst a blood vessel, and was dangerously ill; but her health improved again, though only for a time.[11] She suffered also herself from ill health, on account of the dampness of the Convent of George's Hill; but Almighty God supported her through all her trials, and she often said, that during no time of her life was she so happy as when a Novice, living under obedience, and were she to have a choice, it would be to continue always in that state. She had, however, one anxiety which sometimes occasioned moments of painful suspense. It was her fear that the Nuns would not unanimously give their votes for her and her two companions to be professed, as (perhaps to keep her in humility) some doubts on the subject had been mentioned, and she suffered intensely in mind when the time for the last Chapter, wherein the Profession or dismissal was to be decided on, drew near, and great was her joy to find that the decision was favourable. They made their vows according to the Rule of the Presentation Nuns, with the clause that they were subject to such alterations as might be approved of by Archbishop Murray, who had received full power from the Holy See for the establishment of the new Institute. The Habit chosen differed very little from that of the Presentation Order, though some change was deemed necessary; the coif with plaited frontal was substituted for the plain bandeau, and the silver ring with a pious motto engraved on it was added. The out-door dress was such as we now wear.

The Profession of our Foundress took place on the 12th of December 1831, and on the same day she returned to Baggot Street, from which time we date the foundation of our Institute.

The following day the Archbishop came to the Convent, and appointed Sister Mary Catharine McAuley Superioress and Mother of the Community. Such was her humility that she desired to be called only Sister Superior, and not to have the title of Mother amongst us, but Dr. Murray said that there must be at least one Mother. On the occasion of her being appointed Superior, she asked the Archbishop, as the Rule of the Presentation Order was not yet altered for our use, what Rule we were to go by. He opened the book of the Presentation Rule at the "Chapter of Union and Charity", saying: "If they observe that, it will suffice"; and for the space of six or seven years, during which the necessary alterations were being considered and decided on, the observance of this one Rule caused the greatest regularity and fervour to be invariably maintained. The Spiritual Exercises and the distribution of the hours of the day were similar to those they had followed during their Noviceship at George's Hill, with few exceptions. Only one half hour's Meditation daily was rendered obligatory, but the Spiritual Lectures were prolonged half an hour in the morning, and half an hour in the evening. She chose for Night Prayers the Litany of the Saints, having been much impressed with the beauty and efficacy of that devotion during the latter months of their Noviceship, when their Mistress had prescribed its recital as a means of their obtaining, through the intercession of those glorious citizens of Heaven, the more especial graces they required for their Holy Profession. The Litany of our Lady was added in the month of May following, at the solicitation of Sr. Mary Anne Doyle [Footnote on the manuscript in Clare Moore's handwriting: "His Holiness Pope Pius VIII having been pleased [in 1830] to grant a Plenary Indulgence on two days in each month for the daily recital of Our Lady's Litany. This Indulgence was granted to our Sisters in Baggot Street at the instance of Revd. Fr. L'Estrange OCD of Clarendon Street Dublin."], and then our Reverend Mother said, she thought the Litany of the holy Name of Jesus ought to be recited as well, in the course of the day, so she placed it after the Acts of Faith, Hope, and Charity. She also thought well of having the Litany for a Happy Death every evening after Matins, and that for the Souls in Purgatory on Mondays after Vespers. Archbishop Murray approved of her arrangements, only, with regard to the community observances, he desired that there should be recreation after dinner, which our Reverend Mother had omitted, intending, as she said, that we should labour all day like the poor, and have our rest and recreation after our work was finished.

Our Reverend Mother, having now to discharge the arduous functions of a Superior, applied herself with extraordinary zeal to correct the smallest faults, and establish the perfect practise of religious virtues. She yielded neither to human respect nor to human feelings—her exactitude with regard to poverty was extreme. Dr. Murray having given permission that those among the Postulants who had been in Baggot St. during her absence, and were considered fit, might receive the Holy Habit before the usual time, she caused their old black dresses to be made up into Habits, and would only allow of cheap brass Crucifixes to their Beads, thinking the ebony crosses in use among the Presentation Nuns, and which she afterwards adopted, too expensive. It was not only in dress she would have Poverty evinced, she was extremely watchful to retrench every other superfluity; and on one occasion, seeing a Sister take a little more milk in her tea than ordinary, she said aloud in the Refectory that the Sisters should remember they had not come to a house of plenty, but to a state of strict poverty.

The first public lecture she read after being appointed Mother Superior was the tenth Chapter of Rodriguez on Obedience—being an explanation of St. Paul's words, "Obey your Prelates and be subject to them, for they watch continually being to give an account for your souls"—and this duty she enforced very strictly, and desired to see it practised with child-like simplicity. She was also very particular that silence should be exactly observed, and would reprove for even one unnecessary word, being convinced that future regularity depended in great measure on beginning well and fervently; but, while she thus shewed her zeal for the perfection of those committed to her charge, she was equally careful that her own life should be a model of regular observance, and, in order that she might have the advantage of practising submission, she enjoined one of the junior Sisters to tell her of any fault or omission of duty she might perceive;

and when reminded that she had not performed some exercise, etc., though hindered by urgent business, she would humbly acknowledge it, and supply for it without delay.

It was on the 23rd of January 1832 that Archbishop Murray gave the Religious Habit of the new Institute to seven of the Sisters, in presence of a very large assembly of Priests, as on account of the approaching death of Sister Anne O'Grady, no secular persons were admitted, though many of the highest classes applied. This circumstance caused such great displeasure to the Mother of one of the Sisters who had on that day been clothed, Miss Anna Carroll, that she insisted on her immediately leaving Baggot St. and entering the Presentation Convent, which our good Foundress readily permitted. This was one of the first trials our Reverend Mother had; it was succeeded by the death of Sister Anne O'Grady on the 7th of February. And then Sister Mary Elizabeth Harley, one of those professed with her, whom she had hoped would be so useful in assisting to establish the rising Institute, fell into a rapid consumption. She had been assisting the last Sister who died, and observed to one of the Novices that she had often thought it would be a blessing to have so much time as lingering consumption affords for preparing to appear before God, "but," she added, "now that I see how much the mind is weakened, I hope Almighty God will permit that my last illness may be short"—and it would seem that He was pleased to hear her prayer, for she was only a few weeks suffering, and was able to come to Mass and Holy Communion on Easter Sunday, though she died on the following Wednesday, and enjoyed the perfect use of her faculties to the last moment of her life. She received the last Sacraments about three hours before her death. Such was the simplicity of her obedience, that our Reverend Mother having said to her, when called away about an hour before her death to attend to some business, "Now my dearest child, say nothing but 'Jesus, Mary, and Joseph, assist me in my last agony'," on her return found her still repeating the same words, and she would not, without asking leave, make any other prayer. She expired very soon after; and the bitterness of this sad scene was increased to our holy Foundress by being obliged to dissemble her grief, and attend to secular business, which she had undertaken for the relief of the poor, and which obliged her to have much communication with secular ladies who interested themselves in the Charity; and with others too, who disapproved of her plans:—and it happened that one of these latter had called for her, to condemn her conduct in severe terms, at the very time when the dear invalid above mentioned was in her agony. Our Reverend Mother listened humbly to the reproaches of this lady, without offering to justify herself; she did not even try to put a stop to such unpleasant conversation by telling her that a cherished Sister was at that moment dying in the House; and Almighty God, as it were to reward her patience and humility, so touched the person who had been reproving her, that, when she rose to go away, she handed her fifteen pounds for the poor. Our dear Reverend Mother, though grieved to the heart at the loss she sustained, gave example of willing submission to the Divine decree, and seeing the other Sisters in deep affliction, she repeated aloud the verse of the Benedicite said in the Refectory at Easter: "This is the day the Lord hath made; let us rejoice and be glad therein," reminding them that the trial came from Him Whose will we ought not only to obey, but love with our whole hearts. Sister Mary Elizabeth Harley died on the 25th April 1832.

Our Foundress's time being constantly occupied with necessary business, she could not devote herself so fully as she wished to the instruction of the Novices; nevertheless she provided excellently for the preservation of due order and regularity, by establishing the strict observance of silence. Her exhortations were most animated and impressive, especially on the duties of charity and humility. These were her cherished virtues, which she inculcated more by her example than by words. She taught the Sisters to avoid all that might be in the least contrary to charity, even the slightest remark on manner, natural defects, etc., so that they should make it a rule never to say anything unfavourable of each other. She was not content with their avoiding the smallest faults against this favourite virtue of our Blessed Lord; they were to evince it in their whole conduct. She instructed them to observe in speaking, mildness and great sweetness, to be always ready to yield and condescend to others, and careful to edify by word and example. On this subject her maxim was, that a Religious should never allege as excuse for saying what might give pain, even unintentionally, "I did not recollect"; she should be always recollected. Every word she says ought to edify, at least no one word should escape her which could disedify.

Her lessons on humility, being supported by her own unvarying example, necessarily made a deep impression on the minds of her spiritual children; the least shadow of pride was odious to her. She told them that their very tone of voice, and manner of walking should be humble and subdued; that they should carefully shun speaking of themselves, or of their works, and try as far as possible to banish even the words "me", or "myself", from their conversation; that they should never attribute to themselves anything but faults and imperfections, sincerely acknowledging that they were not merely incapable of promoting the good in which the Almighty deigned to employ them, but that their unworthiness would very likely obstruct its accomplishment. She taught them to love the hidden life, labouring on silently for God alone, for she had a great dislike to noise and shew in the performance of duties. "See how quietly," she would say, "the great God does all His mighty works; darkness is spread over us, and light breaks in again, and there is no noise of drawing curtains or closing shutters." She used often to tell them of the edification she had received in the Convent of George's Hill, from one of the Nuns who never spoke of herself or her employments, so that it was not until a change of offices, that our Reverend Mother discovered she had previously exercised an important and busy charge in the Community. But it was not only this Nun whose piety was remembered by her; the Superioress, Mother Mary Frances Knowd,[12] had been a subject of her admiration for her humble patience and extraordinary regularity. Though suffering greatly from rheumatism, this holy Religious never failed to rise at five, and was one of the first in Choir; with regard to humility she had so entirely overcome a naturally violent temper that she did not seem to know that anything unkind or disrespectful could be said to her, and as it happened one day that our Reverend Mother had, in ignorance of facts, said something which might seem a censure on her arrangements, and went as soon as possible to beg pardon, the good Superioress told her it did not signify, and added impressively the following maxim which our Reverend Mother used to repeat: "Never let anything cause you trouble or anxiety which is not an offence against God." Another of her sayings was, "If every one would mind their own business, the Convent would be a Heaven upon earth." She would readily obey the little school children, and disliked praise so much that, if any one commended her, even for knitting her stocking well, she would undo it all that very evening.

Our Reverend Mother, when instructing the Sisters, loved to dwell on those words of our Divine Lord: "Learn of me because I am meek and humble of heart," saying, "If His blessed words ought to be reverenced by all, with what loving devotion ought the Religious impress them on her memory, and try to reduce them to practise." Her own feelings of self-abasement she carried, it might be said, too far.[13] She could not be prevailed on to hold the prescribed Chapter of Faults for a very long time after being made Superior, and was pained when the Sisters manifested their faults to her in private. She allowed any of them to guide and direct her (being occasionally abstracted or forgetful of the ceremonies) and would good-humouredly call those, who perhaps had been rather importunate, "her Mistresses". She loved simplicity singularly in others, and practised it herself; telling the Sisters to adopt a simple style of speaking and writing, and if they were translating any work, she would tell them always to use simple, easy words; and never to affect worldly expressions, or manners, nor even those which are too decided. Her own beloved Niece,[14] saying once in an anxious tone, she hoped something would occur, our dear Reverend Mother checked her, saying, "The hopes and fears of a Religious ought to be centered in God." If a Sister said casually, "I hate such or such a thing," she would remark, "We ought to hate nothing but sin." Even in piety she disliked highflown aspirations or sentences, and to a Novice, who was writing something very exalted in that way, she observed, how much more suitable those simple phrases found in ordinary prayers would be; and then suggested as a favourite of her own, "Mortify in me, dear Jesus, all that displeases Thee, and make me according to Thine own heart's desire."

Fidelity to the inspirations of grace was a lesson she frequently and earnestly inculcated, shewing how important and necessary it was that they should listen attentively to that Divine voice, which silently and constantly whispers to the heart of the Religious, telling her how she may please the Heavenly Spouse of her soul; now, by avoiding some slight fault that self love or self indulgence urges her to commit; again, by practising those apparently little acts of humility, charity, patience etc. which are great in the sight of God. She was particularly desirous that they should adopt the practise of small acts of mortification, for example, in the Refectory, saying that they ought never let any meal pass without denying themselves something (being careful not to injure their health) and that these mortifications were often of far greater value before God, and caused Him to bestow more abundant graces, than rigid austerities which might spring from, or occasion vanity.

Not content with her own instructions, our Reverend Mother procured for her Novices the advantage of making their first Annual Retreat under the direction of a most pious and enlightened Priest, the Revd. Mr. [Myles] Gaffney, since made Dean of Maynooth College.[15] His simple but inflamed discourses were well calculated to excite in their hearts ardent desires of perfection, which were prudently regulated by his private instructions in the Confessional. His views accorded entirely with those of our holy Foundress. Humility was the virtue he recommended to all, desiring them to make that the subject of their particular Examens, and to let the first practise of it be never to speak of themselves either in praise or dispraise. It was to this Priest Dr. Murray confided the charge of assisting our Reverend Mother to adapt the Presentation Rule to our Institute.

About this time, the unsteadiness of purpose manifested by some of the first Novices caused her much anxiety, as several of them believed they were called to other Orders: her niece Sister Mary Teresa Macauley thought she had a vocation for the Carmelites, and requested that the second year might be added to her Noviceship; Sister Catharine Byrn resolved to join the Dominican Order, and effected her purpose under circumstances that were very painful to the feelings of our Reverend Mother.

Of the first seven who received the Habit, only four made their vows: Sister Mary Francis Warde, Sister Mary Angela Dunne, Sister Mary Clare Moore, and Sister Mary Magdalen de Pazzi Delany. The Most Reverend Dr. Murray received their Holy Profession, on the 24th of January 1833.

In the year 1832, when the cholera was raging in Dublin, the Sisters attended the cholera hospital in Townsend St. daily. There were always four there from nine in the morning till eight at night, relieving one another every four hours; and although our Reverend Mother had a natural dread of contagion, she overcame that feeling, and scarcely left the Hospital. There she might be seen among the dead and dying, praying by the bedside of the agonised Christian, inspiring him with sentiments of contrition for his sins, suggesting acts of resignation, hope, and confidence, and elevating his heart to God by charity. Almighty God preserved them all from the disease, and they continued to attend the Hospital, encouraging and consoling the poor patients, after that epidemic had ceased to prevail.[16]

The spirit of mercy and compassion for the poor, which animated and as it were consumed her, made her sometimes adopt plans for their relief which to some appeared beyond the limits of prudence, but the success with which her undertakings were usually attended shewed that she was guided by a heavenly wisdom. She wrote herself and sent the letter by post to Her Royal Highness the Duchess of Kent, entreating that she and the Princess Victoria would give some of their work for a Bazaar about to be held for the relief of the poor. A gracious answer was returned, and the Duchess of Kent sent her some of her own beautiful work, with drawings and transferred boxes done by her Royal Daughter. This extraordinary contribution was of considerable benefit to the Institute and realized as may well be supposed a very large sum of money.

During this and the succeeding year 1833 several Postulants were admitted, and the House was firmly established; but our dear Foundress was to have many crosses in order that her works might be blessed by God. In the autumn her niece, who was so deservedly beloved by her and all who knew her, again burst a blood vessel and only survived that fatal accident three months. From childhood her amiable disposition had endeared her to all, and as she advanced in years she gave proofs of great virtue and piety; having attained the happiness of becoming a Member of the true Church she from that moment devoted herself ardently to every religious duty, and listening only to her fervour, while her Aunt was at George's Hill Convent, practised austerities which seriously injured her health. From the time she put on the Religious Habit she applied herself to acquire the virtues of that holy state with so much ardour, that she was in some measure carried too far by her zeal, and anxious for greater perfection sought to join an Order too rigourous for her delicate frame, but on her deathbed she begged to be admitted to the holy Profession, and most fervently made her vows a week before her death, which took place on 12th of November 1833.[17] This was a grievous affliction to our dear Reverend Mother, but she submitted humbly, and always ascribed these trials which she felt so sensibly, and which were of frequent recurrence (for almost every succeeding year she lost one or two of the Community by death), to her own want of fidelity to God's holy inspirations; she would afterwards apply herself to correct or regulate whatever seemed to be amiss, and allowed those customs of Conventual life which, through prejudice, she had not hitherto permitted, to be introduced and practised.

In 1833 the Reverend J. Rice,[18] a venerable Augustinian Friar, brother to the holy man who founded the Christian Brothers in Ireland, on his way to Rome visited the Convent in Baggot St., and being much pleased with all he saw, asked if he could render any service to the Institute. Our Reverend Mother told him how anxious she was to receive the formal approbation of the Holy See, and he promised to remember her wishes. Some months after, she received directions to forward to Rome those additions to the Presentation Rule which were deemed necessary in order to adapt it to our duties, the Rule itself having been confirmed.[19]

On the Feast of our Lady's Immaculate Conception she sent the Chapters on the Visitation of the Sick and the Protection of Distressed Women, which she had previously submitted to Archbishop Murray, who then desired her to include them with the Rule altered as she considered necessary, and to send him a copy of it, that he might at leisure deliberate on it. Our dear Reverend Mother transcribed it herself with the greatest care, but it was not until the year 1835 that the Archbishop brought her the joyful intelligence that his Holiness Pope

Gregory 16th had given his approbation with his Apostolical Benediction to the Institute. His Grace then informed her that he had carefully collated the copy of the Holy Rule she had sent him, with that of the Presentation Order, that he had changed some points, and that as soon as it was again copied, such as he now gave it to her, he would affix his sanction to it, which was done accordingly, and Dr. Murray wrote the form of approbation with his signature, dating it from the time that the Institute received the approbation of the Holy See, the third of May 1835.[20]

In the year 1834, as the Community was much increased, our Reverend Mother sought to extend the good effected by it to the adjacent parts of Dublin. Kingstown[21] was then almost destitute of religious helps and there was no school for the poor children; she therefore purchased a suitable dwelling, which with Archbishop Murray's permission she made a branch house, and procured schools to be built where the Sisters assembled those hitherto neglected children, and instructed them assiduously in Christian duties, etc.; they also visited the sick, going often to a very great distance, and our good Foundress, notwithstanding the difficulty she experienced in walking, never spared herself in those labours of charity and mercy.

Although her zeal was great for the salvation of those poor little ones of Christ, it was far more ardent for the perfection of the Religious under her care. She felt all the value of a vocation to this holy and happy state, and sought to extend the blessing to very many. Like the glorious Saint Teresa, she never refused any Postulant for want of temporal means when it was at all possible to provide what was essential, and in order to facilitate this, as well as from her great love of holy poverty, she entirely retrenched those expenses which are usual in other Religious Establishments at the entrance of Postulants and at their Clothing. Every thing purchased for the use of the Sisters was of the poorest and plainest kind, and she would never allow a large provision of anything to be laid in, saying it was not according to poverty to have those kinds of stores. Although very careful to have her own exterior appearance and that of her Religious suitable to the holy dignity of their calling, her under clothing was always of the meanest description, and when it became necessary to repair it she would now and then go away from Recreation and employ herself at that work in the cell. With regard to other accommodation the worst and most inconvenient was her choice. Her meals were very scanty: as she thought best to carve the dinner for the Community in the Refectory, it generally happened that all had nearly dined before she could sit down, so that her repast was merely nominal, by which means she eventually destroyed her naturally good constitution. She rarely had a cell to her own use, being always ready to yield it up for the accommodation of others, and on one occasion when some Sisters arrived late in the evening from another Convent, and there were not cells for all, she quietly brought one of them to her's [*sic*], and next morning it was discovered that she had had neither cell nor bed that night. When she went to found Convents she invariably chose the poorest and cheapest mode of travelling, often to her own great inconvenience, and her bed was usually on the floor, as she never waited for a new Convent to be comfortably arranged, being satisfied to have any kind of opening to extend the good effected by the Institute. She relied on the loving Providence of her Heavenly Father that all necessaries would be supplied, and she was never disappointed; this her confidence in God's goodness was so well known that the late revered Bishop of Cork, the Right Reverend Dr. Murphy used to style her "Sister of Divine Providence".[22] If she were thus rigourous towards herself and solicitous that her spiritual children should disregard and be disengaged from temporal conveniences, she was nevertheless most tender and careful for the sick and infirm among them; no expense seemed to her too great when there was question of procuring them any comfort. She sought to alleviate their pains by every affectionate contrivance which the heart of a fond Mother could dictate, and spared no labour and fatigue in their service, but even in her extraordinary care of the sick she evinced her love for Religious Poverty. The Physician having advised that her beloved niece Sister Mary Teresa Macauley when in her last illness should be removed to some country place for change of air (there being then no other Convent of the Order), she told him not to recommend such things as were unsuited to poor people, who might indeed procure some little nourishment or delicacy for their invalids, but they could not have the means of removing them to a country place.

She applied herself with still greater earnestness to promote the spiritual welfare of her children, listening to them with patient kindness, and seeking to comfort and assist them whenever they applied to her in their difficulties; she would inspire the fearful and scrupulous with confidence, and rouse those who were slothful or negligent. She was very careful not to give many positive directions about any duty, or, as she used to call it, to make too many laws, giving her reason for it to a Sister who over-zealously requested her to desire the Community not to do some little thing rather out of order but not against [the] Rule. "It is better not," she answered mildly; "be careful never to make too many laws, for if you draw the string too tight it will break."

While she passed over without seeming to notice them many inadvertant [*sic*] offences, she was most watchful to correct in their conversation or manners the least failure against politeness, and anything which could discover the want of a good education, being convinced by experience that the inattention of some Religious persons to these minor points often lessens charity in a Community, as it tends also to diminish the respect which Seculars should have for the Religious State, and consequently our influence over them. "Even our nearest and dearest friends," she used to say, "expect to find us changed after we embrace this life; they look for something different from themselves, and I remember being very much struck with this truth on one occasion when I went with a person to visit a good Nun. On leaving the Convent her friend said to me with disappointed surprise, 'Well, her manners are not in the least changed, she is just the same she was in the world!' " She was full of concern when a Sister persevered in a fault, especially if it were against charity, though such rarely occurred, so unceasingly did she recommend this virtue to them. Once it did happen that some disagreement took place, and although fatigued by the exertions of the day, she requested a Sister[23] in whom she confided to remain with her in the Choir after night prayers that they might say the Thirty Days' Prayer to obtain the restoration of peace and union, a circumstance which shewed in what a serious light she viewed the least breach of charity, since she never performed that devotion except in some important case; for she had a particular reliance on its efficacy, saying she was careful what she petitioned for by means of it, as the request was sure to be granted. That devout prayer was always commenced by her on the first day of her arrival at a new foundation, and she endeavoured to remain at the place until it was completed.

Being of a remarkably cheerful disposition, she loved to see all under her charge happy and joyful. She tried to make them so, not only by removing whatever could disturb their peace, but also by contributing to the general cheerfulness of the Community especially at Recreation. Although burthened with many cares, she was at that duty as lively and merry as the youngest Sisters, who used to delight in being near her, listening to her amusing remarks and anecdotes. She had a natural talent for composing verses in a playful style, and would often sing them to some cheerful tune with admirable simplicity. She was a great enemy to that spirit of sadness and discontent which destroys true devotion, nor could she suffer them to take a gloomy view of passing events; her own recollections of former friends and occurrences were all of a benevolent nature, and only brought forward for the purpose of edifying and instructing the Sisters, and from her extensive knowledge of the human heart she could readily adapt her conversation to their wants. She did not possess worldly accomplishments, but she had read much and well, and her manners were most pleasing and agreeable; thus all in her was rendered subservient to the Divine honour and her neighbour's good for she never seemed to think or care for herself.

Her method of reading was so delightful that all used to acknowledge it rendered the subject quite new to them though they had perhaps heard it frequently, for she considered it most useful to adhere to a few solid spiritual works rather than to run over many without reflection. *The Following of Christ* was one of her favourite books, also Blythe's *Paraphrase on the Seven Penitential Psalms*;[24] her Prayer book was that entitled *Devotions to the Sacred Heart of Jesus.* Besides the spiritual exercises of the Community, at which she assisted with very great fervour, she had much devotion to the two Thirty Days' Prayers, the Psalter of Jesus, and the Universal Prayer. Some passages of the last she used to repeat often, especially this: "Discover to me, O my God, the nothingness of this world, the greatness of heaven, the shortness of time, and the length of eternity"; and she used to say no maxim could be more usefully impressed on the minds of children than the shortness of time—how quickly it passes—and the long durance of eternity. It was an ordinary topic with her, and she constantly expressed her regret at having to take so much pains for such a fleeting life. "We have scarcely put on our clothes in the morning, when night comes, and we have to take them off again, and then so soon to resume the same task. Oh! how nice it would be if we could make some contrivance only to dress and undress once a month!" She loved to expatiate on certain words: "Our mutual respect and charity is to be 'cordial'—now 'cordial' signifies something that revives, invigorates, and warms; such should be the effects of our love for each other." "Mercy" was a word of predilection with her. She would point out the advantages of Mercy above Charity. "The Charity of God would not avail us, if His Mercy did not come to our assistance. Mercy is more than Charity—for it not only bestows benefits, but it receives and pardons again and again—even the ungrateful." The very letters of that word were noted. "It has five, corresponding with the five Wounds of our Lord—with the letters of His holy Name Jesus—it begins with M like that of our Blessed Lady." These little dissertations formed part of her Recreation and then she would laughingly give the preference to those Sisters whose name consisted of five letters. She devised innumerable other little ways of making her spiritual children happy and united, and when duty permitted complied with all their wishes, especially when relating to their soul's good. A Sister asking her once what form of prayer would be best before leaving her cell in the morning, she immediately wrote for her the following: "O my most compassionate Lord and Saviour Jesus Christ, I humbly beseech Thee to look on me this day with pity and grant me the grace to be pleasing and acceptable to Thee even for one moment." This sweet compliance was not so much the effect of innate benevolence as of her desire to resemble our Blessed Lord, which was her daily resolution, and the lesson she constantly repeated. "Be always striving to make yourselves like Him—you should try to resemble Him in some one thing at least, so that any person who sees you, or speaks with you, may be reminded of His Blessed life on earth."

She meditated with heartfelt attention the great mysteries of Faith—and feeling as she did so sensibly for the sufferings of her fellow creatures, her compassion for those endured by our Blessed Lord was extreme, so much so that it was a real pain to her, as she once told a Sister in confidence, to meditate on that subject. She had for many years of her life fasted on Good Friday without taking any refreshment whatever, until she became a Religious, and then she conformed to the custom which she established for the Community, of taking a little bread and gruel standing. She had an extraordinary reverence for and confidence in the Holy Sacraments; her instructions on this subject, whether to seculars or her Religious, were calculated to awaken sentiments of lively faith and most confiding love. It was a cause of much sorrow to her when any Sister through scrupulosity or other motive absented herself from the Holy Communion, "for," she said, "it is by means of the grace therein bestowed on us, that we are enabled to persevere in our holy state, and the want of this grace is the reason why no Religious Communities can be formed among Protestants, however well disposed or anxious for such establishments." She directed the Sisters to make this a frequent subject of their instructions to the poor, whose happiness and eternal welfare depend entirely on their approaching the Sacraments with due dispositions, and she had always observed that Converts until they receive the Sacraments do not seem to understand fully the instructions given them, but afterwards they find many difficulties cleared up and their doubts removed. However, she did not at all like that the Sisters should spend a long time in preparing for or making the Confessions; they having so many other sources of religious instruction should be careful not to occupy the Priest's time unnecessarily, lest some poor person might be thereby disappointed and hindered from going to the Sacraments.

It would be needless to speak of her devotion to the ever Blessed Virgin, since she looked on the privilege of having our Institute so immediately under her powerful protection as one of the highest we could enjoy. She recommended this devotion with the greatest earnestness, and though she did not undertake many external practices in honour of the Most Holy Virgin, she required all to attend exactly and reverently to such as were prescribed. She would have them say the Rosary kneeling or walking, without any unnecessary interruptions, and was exact in performing the Novenas prior to our Lady's feasts, that of our Lady of Mercy especially, when she would have all in the house, even the poor little children, unite with the Sisters in calling on their Advocate and Mother to intercede with God for them, and during the month of September she always said the Thirty Days Prayer in her honour for the welfare of the Institute.

Our dear Reverend Mother entertained a profound respect for the sacred Ministers of Religion, and taught the Sisters to observe the same in word and manner. The Chaplain of the Convent, the Reverend D[aniel] Burke, had been there for eight years, and was consequently a very intimate friend, yet she always used the word "Sir" in addressing him, and told the Sisters they ought to say it also to all Priests; with other persons she did not like it, as she thought it quaint or old-fashioned, but she said they ought to venerate Priests, and not allow themselves the least familiarity of manner or expression in conversing with them; herein, she said, they could not be too guarded. She was particularly careful and vigilant to prevent unnecessary noise or other negligent conduct in the Choir, etc.; her veneration extended to all connected with our holy Religion. She would not allow any passage of our Rule to be repeated lightly or in jest, she loved to look on the Religious Habit, and a Ceremony day was one of the happiest to her. As for the sacred Vows, she cherished them with her whole heart; it was her greatest pleasure to make the Renewal of them, and she used to express this sentiment in her previous instructions to the Sisters. "When we first make our Vows" (she would say), "it is not surprising if we feel anxious, and pronounce them in a timid faltering voice, being as yet unacquainted with the full extent of His infinite goodness, to Whom we engage ourselves for ever—but when we renew them, it ought to be with that tone of joy and confidence which the experience of His unceasing mercies must inspire." This feeling was easily discerned in her manner of reading the Act of Renewal, and also in the joyful way she announced the usual Te Deum afterwards. The obedience and respect of our venerated Foundress towards her Ecclesiastical Superiors was that of a humble child; indeed, she often caused herself needless anxiety, through her fear of giving them the least displeasure.

When she went to found a Convent she would not take precedence of the Sister appointed Superior, though as Foundress she might reasonably have done so—and she would have been very glad to lay down her authority altogether, and place herself under entire obedience. [Footnote on the manuscript: "When the six years of her government had expired, she applied to Archbishop Murray, requesting that an Election might take place, according to our Holy Rule; but he would not permit her to resign her Office, saying that being the Foundress of the Order, she should continue 'Superior for life.' "] Very much more might be said of her humble submission and her other virtues, but one act of self abasement which occurred within the last four years of her life ought not to be passed over in silence; it was related with tears by the Sister who was the subject of it to a friend.[25] She had spoken, as she thought, rather sharply to her, and a few hours after she went to the Sister and asked her did she remember who had been present at the time. As several had been there, the Sister answered she could hardly say, for she had not noticed which they were, but as our Reverend Mother requested her to try and call them to mind and bring them to her, they were summoned, and when all assembled our dear Reverend Mother humbly knelt down, and begged her forgiveness for the manner in which she had spoken to her that morning.

According as the good resulting from the new Institute became known, application was made from different places for some of its members, that they might diffuse the blessings of religious instruction and consolation among the poor. A pious lady, who resided in Tullamore,[26] had bequeathed her house with a small annuity for the purpose of establishing a Community of Sisters of Mercy in that town; she had been a particular friend of the Revd. Mr. O'Hanlon and he employed his influence in engaging our Reverend Mother to undertake the foundation. She went there about the end of April 1836 accompanied by four of the Sisters; they were received most cordially by the townspeople, assembled in crowds to await their arrival, who joyfully conducted them to the Church and Presbytery, from which they proceeded to the new Convent. She remained about a month, and as they were joined by two young persons from the neighbourhood, she left only two of the Sisters from Baggot Street, her first companion Sister Mary Anne Doyle being appointed Mother Superior.[27] A beautiful Convent with extensive poor schools have [*sic*] been since erected in that place.

This foundation was followed by that of Charleville in the County Cork, where some efforts had been already unsuccessfully made to establish a Community of French Sisters of Charity. The lady[28] who desired to found the Convent offered five hundred pounds with a commodious house, and although this was a small beginning, our Reverend Mother would not refuse the opportunity of performing a work agreeable to God. She accordingly set out on this journey on the 29th of October the same year, taking with her three Sisters to remain at the new foundation, and a fourth for her companion. As she was very anxious to visit her dear children in Tullamore, she went there first, intending to go across the country afterwards by the Canal packet boat. When they reached Tullamore they found that the boat would not arrive until the middle of the night, and that it was a very slow and inconvenient mode of travelling; however she was not discouraged, and although she suffered very much from cold and fatigue all that night and the following day (for they did not get to Limerick until nine o'clock in the evening), her patience and cheerfulness never failed. The next morning they went on to Charleville and arrived there about five o'clock on the Eve of All Saints. She found the house very far from being as convenient as it had been represented to her, and, on account of a little stream running close by, extremely damp, so that their clothes were quite wet each morning when they got up. They had also to go some short distance to the Chapel and schools. Being a poor small town, there was very little chance of Postulants joining them, and our Foundress becoming uneasy, thought of withdrawing the Sisters; but she yielded to the solicitations of the good Parish Priest, Mr. Croke, as well as to her own compassion for the suffering members of Christ (being greatly touched by hearing a poor woman exclaim, "Ah! it was the Lord drove you in amongst us!"), and she exerted herself to the utmost of her power in promoting the interests of the Convent, which afterwards succeeded so well that a spacious Convent has been built in the best part of the town. The Superioress appointed there was Sister Mary Angela Dunne.

Our Reverend Mother left it on the 29th of November,[29] and on her way home gave a remarkable instance of her love for regularity, and her tender devotion towards the Adorable Sacrament, for it happened to be a day of Holy Communion, and although she had to rise at two o'clock in the morning to be ready for the stage coach which left Charleville at three, she said to her companion that they might be in time for Holy Communion when they reached Limerick at ten o'clock and therefore declined breakfasting; but as they did not arrive there till later (it was almost twelve when they heard Mass, and in order to find the Chapel they had to walk some distance without knowing the way, while it snowed very fast), it was one o'clock before she got back to the Inn for breakfast.[30] She arrived in Baggot St. next morning in time to assist at the Mass celebrated by the Right Revd. Dr. Murphy, Bishop of Cork, who was come to make arrangements for founding a Convent in that City, of which he had several times treated with her; but nothing definite was settled, and before it took place application was made from Carlow by the Bishop who had been entrusted with a large sum of money, the savings of a poor man who had a little shop in the town, and who at his death left it for the poor and destitute.[31] The Trustees feeling assured that it could not be better disposed of in their regard than by procuring a Community of pious Sisters, requested our Reverend Mother to give them a little colony of her children, and on the 10th of April 1837, she went to Carlow, and established there a small Community with every prospect of success; but she was not permitted to enjoy uninterruptedly these happy fruits of her labours, being summoned back to Baggot Street in a few days, on account of two of the Novices having been attacked with the worst description of typhus fever. They recovered, and she was enabled to return to the new Foundation, taking with her however the youngest of her nieces, now a Professed Nun, in an advanced stage of consumption.[32] Having completed the arrangements at Carlow, and placed the Community under the government of Sister Mary Frances Warde she began to prepare for the foundation at Cork.

The Foundress of this Convent, Miss Barbara Gould, sister to a wealthy merchant of that city, having placed a large sum of money in Bishop Murphy's hands, and provided a very suitable house, well furnished and disposed in Conventual order, his Lordship requested our Reverend Mother to make as little delay as possible in taking possession of it; but Almighty God required that she should first assist at the death bed of a Novice who was suddenly carried off by malignant typhus fever, and her own dear niece was evidently hastening to her last hour; nevertheless she conquered her grief and anxious affection, and before a week had elapsed from the death of Sister Mary Aloysia Thorpe she was on her way to commence the new establishment in Cork, where she arrived on the 6th of July 1837.[33]

She was welcomed with sincere goodwill by the Clergy and laity. The principal persons came to visit and offer kind services to her, and the poor blessed God for having sent her to them. Yet crosses were not wanting, and perhaps the greatest was the prudence of the good Bishop who would now allow her to admit any Postulants not possessed of ample funds, as he considered that precaution necessary in the beginning, lest debts might unwarily be incurred. This prohibition not being at first clearly understood by her, she ventured during the Bishop's absence on his Visitation, presuming on his permission, to admit a young person whose fortune was rather less than the required dowry, or not so well secured as the Bishop wished, which displeased him and was therefore a source of much grief to her. From this Foundation too she was called away on the 24th of July to her dying niece, who expired in the beginning of August,[34] and then business prevented her return to Cork until the middle of September. She continued there for about six weeks, during which she fully regained the favour of the kind hearted Bishop who had always entertained great affection and esteem for her and our whole Institute, often saying he carried all the Sisters of Mercy daily to the Altar in his Memento. Our holy Foundress revered and loved him as a Father, submitting her judgment to his wise and learned counsels, which she never had reason to regret. Here it may be observed in passing that her own great prudence and discernment were very evident in the choice she made of the most effectual means of promoting the interests of the different Foundations. Among others it was her custom to bring with the Nuns, a Novice near the time of her Profession, or a Postulant who had been sufficiently long in the Parent House to admit of her receiving the Habit soon after their arrival at the new Convent; so that it almost always happened a ceremony took place before she left, and thus many were attracted to enquire into the nature of the Institute and made desirous to embrace it.

On the 25th of October the Right Reverend Dr. Murphy gave the Habit to a

Postulant who had entered when the Sisters first arrived in Cork, and on the same day a Novice made her holy Profession. It was on this occasion that Bishop Murphy wished an alteration to be made in the formula of the Act of Profession; before that, only the three Vows of Poverty, Chastity, and Obedience, common to every Religious society, were expressed in it; but he proved to our Foundress the necessity of declaring the special object of the Institute distinct from others, and therefore the following words were introduced, "and the service of the poor, sick, and ignorant." But this was not generally adopted until after the Confirmation of our Holy Rule in 1841.[35]

In the year 1838 the Foundation in Limerick was proposed, and our Reverend Mother having selected the Sisters for it, and made all other suitable preparations, went there in September, but took Cork in her way, being anxious as well to revisit that House as to communicate with those Sisters who had been sent there from England, to serve their Noviceship, with a view to founding a Convent of the Order in Bermondsey. After some days spent in Cork to the great joy and comfort of her spiritual children, she proceeded to Limerick where she settled the Sisters whom she brought with her in the old Monastery of St. Clare. Our Sisters found here[36] large poor-schools, which had been for many years maintained under the care and guidance of two Lay Sisters, the only remaining members of that once flourishing Community.[37] The house though very old was commodious, with large well cultivated gardens. This foundation has been one of the most prosperous, and the liberal support granted to our Sisters afforded them the means of rendering their establishment most advantageous to the poor, especially by the opening of a large House of Mercy. The Mother Superior placed here by our Foundress was Sister Mary Elizabeth Moore. A new Convent was afterwards built.

The following year she accompanied the Religious from the Cork Convent to found the first House of the Order in England, having previously assisted at their Profession on the 19th of August, and then visited with them the Convents in Charleville, Limerick, Tullamore, and Carlow. They remained in Dublin more than two months, and during that time, in compliance with the Right Reverend Dr. Blake's wishes, she took them to the Convent of the Poor Clares in Newry,[38] who were most anxious to see them. On the 18th of November 1839 she sailed from Dublin, having with her, besides the three destined for Bermondsey, two Sisters from Baggot St. who were to return with her, and they reached London very late on the 19th.[39] With her usual love of Poverty, and disregard for all temporal comforts, she had written to inform Reverend Father [Peter] Butler, that if two rooms in the new Convent were finished, it would suffice for their accommodation. He had prepared six rooms, but the unfinished state of the other parts of the building, together with the severity of the season and her own increasing infirmities occasioned her serious indisposition. There were besides other causes of suffering, among the rest the death of one of her nephews. Her hopes in these three youths had been greatly disappointed; their amiable dispositions and fine talents had led her to expect that their career would have been prosperous, but deprived of the restraint and guidance of a Father's hand, they neglected the opportunities for their advancement. Scarcely had they passed their boyhood when consumption seized the eldest and carried him off.[40] Then the second was attacked, and our Reverend Mother not only left him in a very precarious state, but had quitted Ireland in displeasure with him on account of some foolish conduct; and the poor youth died during her absence, with expressions of deep regret for not having obtained forgiveness, which was a sore trial to her affectionate heart.[41] The youngest survived, but gave her continual uneasiness and trouble.[42]

Before she left Baggot St. for England the Reverend Mr. Colgan OCC, a faithful and long-tried friend to the Institute, offered to present the Holy Rule for confirmation at Rome where he was going, promising to translate it into Italian in order that it might be examined by the Sacred Congregation of the Propaganda Fide, and to further the business as much as he could; but his kindness stopped not here, he also instructed her in the means necessary to be adopted for its success. With the copy of our Holy Rule, she was to send a petition praying for its confirmation, signed by the Superioresses of the different Houses, and letters of recommendation from the Bishops in whose Dioceses they were located; all these our holy Foundress procured with much labour and anxiety, and despatched them from London by an opportunity kindly afforded her by the Right Reverend Dr. Griffiths.

She returned to Baggot St. on the 14th of January 1840, and during that year founded the Convents in Galway and in Birr; to this last she went in the end of December when the weather was particularly inclement, and while she remained there often went out to visit the sick when the snow was very deep on the ground. In August 1841 she again made a journey to England to found the Convent in Birmingham. This was her last foundation.

She had been very ill for some time previously, the great fatigues she had endured in the different Foundations joined to her other laborious exertions having quite exhausted her strength. She had also suffered much mental anguish in the painful separation from so many of her beloved spiritual children, some of whom had been sent to those Convents, and others had been called by God out of this world; in one year (1837) three died of typhus fever and two of consumption. Indeed the last years of her life had been strongly marked with crosses and afflictions, and trials seemed to flow in upon her from various sources. She was obliged to sacrifice the Branch-house in Kingstown on account of the debt incurred in building the schools, for which she had unwarily rendered herself liable by confiding in the promise given her, that the money should be obtained from the National School fund, and she was for some time in danger of being arrested for it. This loss was, however, replaced by the liberality of Mrs. [Barbara] Verschoyle who built a small but well adapted Convent with a garden for the Sisters at Booterstown. The house at Kingstown remaining undisposed of was a heavy expense, and influential persons prevailed on her to send Sisters there again, but they again met with difficulties which were opposed to the well being of the Establishment, and so it was at last finally relinquished. Just then, by the misconduct of a person to whom she had entrusted a considerable sum of money, she experienced heavy losses which she felt the more keenly as she had always shewn him especial kindness, and even after this ingratitude she did not diminish the exertions of her friendship for his unhappy family.[43]

Our dear Reverend Mother was also grieved to be obliged to shut up the little Convent Chapel in Baggot St., for the contributions offered there by those persons who availed themselves of the advantage of its being in their neighbourhood had been a great means of supporting the House of Mercy, and had been allowed by Archbishop Murray as such. In 1836 the Chaplain was prohibited to celebrate more than one Mass on Sundays; in 1837 it was ordered to be closed, and there was difficulty made respecting the Chaplaincy, which occasioned her so much trouble that it seemed to be one of the greatest trials she had experienced since the commencement of her arduous task,[44] and no doubt was ordained by Almighty God to purify the soul of His servant, and keep her humble amidst such great successes; but His tender mercies were not forgotten, and with these crosses He was pleased to mingle consolation and joy.

She lived to see her Institute confirmed by the Holy See on the 20th of June 1841, and although ten years had not elapsed since her Religious Profession, she saw fourteen Houses of the Order established in Ireland and England.[45] She might say with holy Simeon: "Now Thou dost dismiss Thy servant, O Lord, according to Thy word in peace. Because mine eyes have seen Thy salvation"; and such were her dispositions. Her immense exertions for God's glory would have been capable of destroying the most robust constitution, and although she bore up under these fatigues, her health was for many years far from good. She endured constant and violent pain in the stomach, perhaps the beginning of that disease which terminated her existence; she was also subject to inflammatory attacks in the head, with extreme soreness in her mouth, yet she would go on reading the public Lectures, and reciting the Office until absolutely incapable of uttering a word; in truth she never spared herself, and sought alleviation from her pains only when forced to do so. During the last year of her life her sufferings were great, and foreseeing that they must shortly end in death, she prepared herself calmly for that last hour:—in life she dreaded it, but now her fears were dispersed by the bright beams of God's infinite Mercy—"Blessed are the merciful, for they shall obtain mercy." The day of her happy departure out of this world was the eleventh of November 1841.

The following short account of her death was written by the Mother Superior of the Limerick Convent [Mary Elizabeth Moore], who went to Baggot St. to assist her in her last moments:

> Of our dear Reverend Mother what shall I say but that she died the death of the just. Cautious as she was from bringing herself into notice unnecessarily in health, she was still more so in sickness, waiting on herself even in her last agony, preserving to the last moment the same peace and serenity of mind which so

eminently distinguished her through life; omitting not an iota of what was essential, and totally disregarding all but what was of moment.

I was not at all aware that her death was so near. I was full of hope till Wednesday morning about eleven o'clock: that is, the day before her death; had I then known what I since heard I should not have been so unprepared for the shock. She was herself well aware that she was dying for the last six months, and since her return from Birmingham cautiously avoided anything like business: it is only by her acts we can judge of her mind. She was perfectly silent as to what she thought; arranged all her papers etc. about a month or six weeks since, and said to Sister Teresa[46] on leaving the parlour that now they were ready . . . .[47] About four (on Thursday morning) she desired the bed to be moved to the centre of the room saying that she would soon want air; about seven she desired the Sisters to be brought to her, said to each one individually what was most suited; but her first and last injunction to all was to preserve union and peace amongst each other, that if they did they would enjoy great happiness, such as they would wonder where it came from—told Sister Genevieve [Footnote on the manuscript: "A venerable Sister who entered Baggot St. in 1833 at the advanced age of 63"] particularly, that she felt exceedingly happy, as if to encourage her to die—recognised all; told little Sister Mary Camillus Byrn [Footnote on the manuscript: "Her God-child Teresa"] to kiss her and go away, that she would see her again, as if to prevent her from weeping. The Holy Sacrifice was offered in the room at about half past eight. She said it would be a comfort to her to see the White Cloaks on the Sisters, for she had been anointed without the usual ceremony on Monday, more to hasten her recovery than that she was thought in immediate danger.

I think her agony commenced about eleven o'clock, she spoke very little, but was visited that day by the Dean Gaffney, her brother etc., Dean Meyler, Reverend Mr. Walsh of Kingstown, Reverend Mr. O'Hanlon, Reverend Mr. O'Carroll . . . to the Doctor she said, "Well, Doctor, the scene is drawing to a close." About five in the evening she asked for the candle to be placed in her hand; we commenced the last prayers, then I repeated one or two she herself had taught me; she said with energy, "God may bless you!" When we thought the senses must be going, and that it might be well to rouse attention by praying a little louder, she said, "No occasion, my darling, to speak so loud. I hear distinctly"—in this way she continued till ten minutes before eight when she calmly breathed her last sigh. I did not think it possible for human nature to have such self possession at the awful moment of death, but she had an extraordinary mind in life and death. . . . She left for you, and all the Reverend Mothers a special blessing for themselves and Communities.

We will here subjoin the beautiful letter of the venerable Bishop of Dromore, the Right Reverend Dr. Blake, on this sad occasion, to one of the Sisters:

We have all reason to weep for the loss which Ireland, and England too, must sustain in consequence of the death of the ever-memorable foundress of your holy Order. A more zealous, a more prudent, a more useful, a more disinterested, a more successful benefactress of human nature, I believe never existed in Ireland since the days of St. Bridget. She has been taken from us after bestowing incalculable services and benefits upon her fellow creatures here below. What she accomplished would have been sufficient to attach celebrity to many individuals.

Her course was long enough to render her name immortal in the remembrance of the virtuous and truly religious. But, judging of what she would do, had she been left longer amongst us, from what she executed, amidst difficulties and trials of no ordinary magnitude, we cannot but lament her departure, and we are tempted to cry out—"Oh! it was too soon!" But God's holy will be adored at all times: to Him we are indebted for all that she did; from Him she received the spirit which animated her pure soul—His providence guided her steps, removed her difficulties, strengthened her heart, and ensured her success. By His ever watchful care and ever assisting grace, every opportunity of doing good was turned to advantage—every undertaking was well pre-considered—every work was made solid and permanent; and, though her sojourn here was, alas! too short for our wishes, it was, nevertheless, so far prolonged as to have enabled her to finish the great machine which, for His glory, and the sanctification of souls, as well as for the corporeal relief of the destitute she planned and constructed. Let the holy will of God then be ever adored: let us bless His Name at all times, and in this moment of bereavement, while we lament the loss which such a removal has caused, let us be grateful for the benefits He has conferred, and profit by the great example which is still fresh before our minds.

I most sincerely and deeply sympathise with you, and with all the members of the holy Order of Mercy. Most earnestly do I beseech the God of all consolation to pour his healing comforts into your and their wounded feelings, and in this trying conjuncture, while your hearts are mellowed with love, grief, and gratitude, to fill you with the spirit of prayer.

Although your Foundress was holy, and eminently holy, she was still a human being, liable to human temptations and infirmity, and obliged every day to express sincerely that hallowed petition, "Forgive us our trespasses." Let us now be mindful of her, and by our fervent supplications obtain for her, if she need it, that entire remission of every, even the smallest debt, which could retard her admission to the realms of bliss.

Your letter reached me this morning just when I was going to the Altar. On seeing the black seal, I hastily opened it; my heart was instantly filled with grief, but I used it, I hope, in making me offer with more fervour the divine sacrifice of propitiation for the happy repose of the dear departed friend whom I ever esteemed and reverenced, and whose memory I shall ever esteem and reverence.

The Very Reverend Dean Gaffney writes of her as follows:[48]

It is not necessary in speaking of the revered Foundress of the Sisters of Mercy, to draw much upon the fancy, or to conjure up, as is sometimes done, by ingenious invention, an imaginary picture of perfection and benevolence, and then apply it to the character we wish to praise. No, her eulogy would be written by the mere mention of the one-hundredth part of what she has done for suffering and destitute humanity. . . .

In the year 1830 Mrs. McAuley entered the Convent of the Presentation Nuns of George's Hill, to prepare herself for the great work she was about to undertake for the glory of God, and the salvation of souls. In the year 1831 she began the foundation of the Order of the Sisters of Mercy, in Baggot Street, in this city, and she died in the year 1841. How short the time, but how numerous and how wonderful the works of that mighty mind, of that expansive heart! They would hardly appear credible if they had not happened in our own time, and passed before our own eyes.

This great and good woman had three objects in view in founding the Order of the Sisters of Mercy: the first—the visiting and relief of the sick poor. The second—the instruction of poor female children. The third[49]—the spiritual and temporal care of poor destitute female servants of good character, whilst out of place. And did she succeed in realising her wishes? She did succeed, and succeed even beyond her own most sanguine expectations. . . .

Whoever visits the schools of the female children in Baggot Street will be consoled and delighted by the scene that will present itself to his view. But what shall I say of Mrs. McAuley's charity towards poor female servants of good character, whilst out of place, who had no resource, no friends, no home? She built a house for them, adjoining the Convent, she supported them—she clothed them—she instructed them—she provided situations for them. The ordinary number in the house, during her life, was sixty at a time, and in the course of ten years of her religious career she procured comfortable situations for more than a thousand female servants, whom she had rescued from all the appalling dangers, to which needy and unprotected females are exposed. If all this good has been effected by one Convent of the Order of the Sisters of Mercy, how much good may be expected from the fifteen[50] Convents which Mrs. McAuley has been instrumental in establishing?

Few left the world in 1841, that can, with more confidence than the revered Foundress of the Order of Mercy, expect to hear on the last accounting day the following words from the lips of our Divine Redeemer: "Come, you blessed of my Father; I was hungry and you gave me to eat, I was thirsty and you gave me to drink, I was a stranger and you took me in, naked and you covered me, sick and you visited me. As much as[51] you did it to one of these my least brethren, you did it to me."

Mrs. McAuley's death was such as might be expected, after a life replete with good works. It was the death of the just, which is precious in the sight of the Lord. Her soul was calm and peaceable, and perfectly resigned to the Divine will. The Sisters of Mercy have one more advocate, one more protectress before the throne of God. . . .

May the Order of Mercy prosper! May Mrs. McAuley's spiritual children always have before their eyes the example left them by their revered Foundress! May they imitate her virtues, and they will have glory in the sight of God and man.

[Footnote on the manuscript: "The foregoing Memoir of our revered Foundress was written about eight or nine years after her happy and holy death, 1849–1850. What follows was added in the year 1868."][52]

A new source of grief to the Sisters on the death of their revered Foundress was that they had no cemetery of their own. Hitherto the Sisters had been buried in the Vaults of the Carmelite Church, Clarendon Street; and although our Foundress had often expressed her desire to have a portion of the Convent Garden consecrated for that purpose, something always happened to cause delay. She had often said also that she should like to be buried in the same way as poor people, in the earth, without the expense attending interment in Vaults, and

Divine Providence ordained that she should be the first laid in that chosen spot which Mother Mary M. de Pazzi, her faithful Assistant and successor in the Office of Superior, obtained leave to have consecrated. The Archbishop, Most Revd. Dr. Murray, was too ill at the time to officiate himself, but he deputed Right Revd. Dr. Kinsella, Bishop of Ossory, who, assisted by V. Rev. Fr. O'Hanlon, performed the Ceremony of consecrating the little Cemetery, and on Saturday November 13th [*sic*] the Solemn Office and Mass were celebrated.[53] Bishop Kinsella officiated, being assisted by the aged Bishop Murphy of Cork, Right Revd. Dr. Blake of Dromore, Right Revd. Dr. Browne of Galway and about sixty of the Clergy; her mortal remains were then carried to the grave, where only the small cross erected for the consecration marks the resting place of her whose name is in benediction in every part of the world.[54]

In a letter written many years later (October 13, 1864) by this same Sister M.M. de Pazzi Delaney, she expresses her grief that no monument had been raised: "I feel daily increased reproach that in this Parent House of the Institute, we have nothing to represent her, that the place of her interment is justly said to be the least ornamented spot within the precincts, nothing to distinguish her grave. When we succeeded in getting the ground consecrated and permission to keep her holy remains, I was determined on having the best monument to be had placed over her, but doubts arose and rumours were afloat that we would not be allowed to have a burial ground where buildings were so much increasing in the neighbourhood. So according to the best advice I was obliged to let the place remain, as I thought only for some years, without anything but one Cross (to mark consecration) hoping after some years no objections would be made and a monument could be erected to her memory at least—for years I have in vain attempted to get even a simple stone— . . . I sincerely deplore not doing so at first, not foreseeing the difficulty. Our good God will accept my desire". . . . "would that I may see some little decoration even of ironwork round the grave of our dear venerated Foundress."

This, her ardent desire, was at length accomplished. In the year 1868, twenty seven years after the death of our Foundress, she renewed her petition and in a letter of October 21st wrote joyously: "I told you my request to our Revd. Mother on my last Feast was for some simple shrine to distinguish the place of our revered Foundress' interment. I am happy to hear it is in hands and I hope will soon be erected. It is to represent our Blessed Lady as Mother of Mercy, praying for and blessing Her children". . . .

Our Reverend Mother and Foundress, Mary Catharine McAuley, was born on the 29th September 1786–7.[55] She received the Religious Habit in the Presentation Convent, George's Hill, on the 9th December 1830, made her holy Profession on the 12th December 1831, and died on the 11th November 1841. She was in stature rather above the middle height, well proportioned and erect, with a fair complexion and high colour; her eyes were large and penetrating, of a very bright blue, with a most kind expression; her manner dignified and reserved, while tender and compassionate to the poor, and maternally affectionate to the Sisters; her movements quiet, and her words few; her whole demeanour shewing constant recollection of the presence of God[56]. . . .

The last Sister who received the holy Habit from the hands of our venerated Foundress was Sr. M. Juliana Delaney, a younger sister of Mother Mary de Pazzi Delaney, and the Silver Ring of Profession worn by our Foundress was bestowed on this Novice[57]. . . .

Twenty five years had not elapsed from the death of the Foundress when her Institute numbered one hundred and fifty Houses spread throughout the world.

It is observed by a pious writer that the history of Religious Orders tells to us that the Institutes which have lasted longest are those which from their commencement spread rapidly; the same Divine Providence which watched over their foundation, watched also over their extension.

Mary Vincent (Anna Maria) Harnett
1811–1865

In 1868 Richard Baptist O'Brien, dean of the Limerick diocese, published the second edition of his *An Eight-Day Retreat, Intended Principally for The Sisters of Mercy and The Active Orders*. Publication of this volume fulfilled a longstanding promise he had made to Elizabeth Moore and Mary Vincent Harnett, the founding members of the Limerick community, who were now both dead.[1] In his Preface to the work, O'Brien—former president of St. Mary's College, Halifax, and former professor of moral theology and sacred scripture at All Hallows College, Dublin—speaks of his esteem for these "two great women". Of Mary Vincent Harnett he says:

> It would be quite impossible to imagine any thing more perfect than Mother Mary Vincent's possession of Mother Mary Catherine M'Auley's spirit. She had an unbounded reliance on Providence, such as is inspired for grand achievements; . . . her gentle, loving nature, that knew how to minister to every want but her own, and the large span of allowance she made for peculiarities of character and circumstances in every case that made a difficulty, rendered Mother Mary Vincent almost an object of reverential affection to every one. (ix–x)

O'Brien's view coincides with the perceptions of Sisters of Mercy who knew Mary Vincent. Mary Austin Carroll would later write that she was "one of the most saintly women the foundress ever admitted" (*Leaves* 1:310); she quotes a friend of Mary Vincent who said: "She had a heart of gold and a great head; she was large in person and rather plain, but her eyes were very lovely" (*Leaves* 2:39).

The widely beneficial effects of Anna Maria Harnett's gentle temperament and of her many educational and literary talents all lay ahead on February 5, 1837—the day she entered the Sisters of Mercy on Baggot Street, Dublin. Anna Maria was then twenty-six, the daughter of Maurice and the late Anne Harnett of Milltown, Co. Dublin. Her mother had died when she was eight or nine years old. On July 1, 1837, she was received into the community, taking the name, Mary Vincent. In the course of that year she saw that the Institute was indeed "founded on Calvary", as she and the rest of the Baggot Street community grieved the deaths of five sisters from typhoid fever or consumption: Veronica (Ellen) Corrigan, whom Catherine had cared for since she was a child, died on February 9, four days after Anna Maria entered; Mary Rose Lubé—the sister of Andrew Lubé, Catherine's long-time but now deceased friend, the former parish priest of Saint James—on March 11; Mary Aloysius Thorpe, on June 30; Mary Anne Agnes (Catherine) Macauley, Catherine McAuley's young niece, on

August 7; and Mary de Chantal McCann, who with her inheritance as a widow had made the purchase of the Kingstown house possible, on October 27. Mary Vincent, who had known young Catherine Macauley for six months at Baggot Street, must have understood well what her aunt meant when she wrote to Andrew Fitzgerald in Carlow on August 8: "We feel just now as if all the House was dead. All are sorry to part our animated, sweet little companion" (94).

In late 1838, when Catherine was finally able to act on Bishop John Ryan's and Miss Helena Heffernan's request that she found a community in Limerick, Mary Vincent, then a novice, was chosen as a member of the founding party, to assist Mary Elizabeth Moore, the new superior. She professed her vows in Limerick, on October 24, 1838, a month after they founded St. Mary's Convent. It was Catherine's general practice, whenever possible, to schedule a profession or reception ceremony soon after their arrival at each new foundation so that the people of the town might see what religious life was all about, and hear a sermon descriptive of the work of the Sisters of Mercy. In this way their purpose was made known, laity and clergy had the opportunity to contribute to their efforts if they wished, and young women were encouraged to see membership in the community as a possibility for their own lives.

On the occasion of Mary Vincent's profession, Helena Heffernan, the principal financial benefactor of the Limerick community and an extraordinarily self-effacing woman, did not attend; evidently she wished to remove from the public eye her own particular role in the founding. The next day Catherine wrote of her with admiration: "We have never seen the foundress, this is gospel perfection. She did not even ask for a ticket to the Ceremony" (141). Miss Heffernan's generosity to the community continued—with one unusual consequence. In 1858 she settled her large estate in Ardagh on the Limerick community. Ten years later, on this property, which the sisters had leased through an agent to various tenants, a farmer by the name of Quinn unearthed, while digging potatoes in an old fort, a splendid hoard of late eighth- or early ninth-century silver treasures. Today these celebrated objects, including the magnificent Ardagh Chalice and Brooches, are housed in the National Museum of Ireland.[2]

Among Mary Vincent's many accomplishments, two are outstanding: her public work as an educator, and her all but anonymous work—at least in her own lifetime—as a published writer. The scores of poor schools and pension schools set up in Ireland and England by the first Sisters of Mercy were remarkably successful in responding to the religious, educational, and employment needs of thousands of young Irish and English girls—to such a degree that this topic deserves extended historical research beyond the scope of this study, and any analysis of the development of the Irish and English churches in the nineteenth century is incomplete without reference to this contribution. The first Mercy schools in Limerick were, thanks to the talents of Mary Vincent, a particularly successful example of this work of mercy.

When the sisters came to Limerick they found in operation on the premises of their new convent a poor school begun over two decades before by the Poor

Clares, and affiliated since 1833 with the National Board of Education, the system established in 1831 by the British parliament to provide government-sponsored primary education to the children of the Irish poor, including Catholics. While some bishops feared these schools, as one more means of subtle Protestant proselytizing of Catholic children, Daniel Murray of Dublin and John Ryan of Limerick did not—nor did Catherine McAuley, who in 1834 applied to have the poor school at Baggot Street connected with the National Board.[3]

In Limerick, therefore, Mary Vincent Harnett joined the two surviving members of the Poor Clares—Mary Shanahan and Anne Hewitt—in the school which they had kept running, as best they could, after the departure of the rest, but one, of the Poor Clare community in early 1831, and the death of their colleague, Catherine Shanahan, in 1834 (Courtney, "The careful instruction" 16). To this school, to which she was appointed by the board of commissioners in 1838, Mary Vincent brought her considerable genius for education. Her earliest biographer, Mary de Chantal Meagher, says that Mary Vincent urged the teachers "always [to] bring out the good traits of the children, never the bad ones; these will wear off gradually as both cannot subsist together—for when the good are strengthened the bad must necessarily die away of themselves."

As Marie Therese Courtney points out, the children "were taught partly on the Lancastrian plan", a modified system wherein senior girls served, under the direction of the sister-teachers, as monitresses who heard the recitations in secular subjects and corrected the written assignments of small groups of younger children. This was the method generally followed in many of the early Mercy schools, there being too few sisters to handle the complete instruction of the hundreds of children who attended each school. The competence achieved under this system was evidently very high. Courtney quotes a Visitor's report on the Limerick curriculum in 1849:

> The morning classes were taught consecutively for an hour and a half. They formed the classes which supplied monitresses to the juniors during the greater part of the day after. . . . Besides their correctness in parsing, derivation, mathematics, physical and practical geography, etc., they could also examine their classes with much tact and success for seculars. . . . Their style of reading too was both expressive and natural. This can also be said of the whole body of the school. Pronunciation was excellent. The penmanship of the senior classes met admiration from every visitor, while their acquaintance with Scripture History crowned the entire. ("The careful instruction" 18)

According to Courtney, the monitresses "from the beginning were paid by the community even during the hard years of the Famine", and Saturday classes in singing, drawing, and piano were provided to them. They, in turn, if they "aspired to be governesses", gave piano lessons in the school where "there was a piano for lessons and also one for practice" (19).

Under the national system of education, Catholic (and Protestant) religious instruction, as such, was not permitted during regular school hours, but only before or after the school day. The sisters in Limerick and elsewhere accommodated to this regulation. Catherine McAuley found it workable and welcomed the financial support which the system provided. On November 15, 1838, she wrote from Limerick to Mary de Pazzi Delany:

> They [the board of commissioners] give forty pounds per year to this school which is as much under the direction of the superintending priest and the Sisters as could be desired. I think the inspector would not make a remark which could be objected to. Religious instructions are given every day from three till half past three, and any hour in the day we may say what we please to them. Hence, I could have no objection to be subject to the regulations anywhere. In Charleville and Tullamore the inspectors are equally unobtrusive. The priests and our Sisters are in full authority, sometimes three priests teaching in the school at once. (144)

Mary Vincent served as assistant to Mary Elizabeth Moore, the superior in Limerick, for twelve years, until 1853 when she was named the superior of the new foundation in Roscommon. In addition to her teaching in the school and her other duties in the convent—and her service in severe crises such as the Great Famine (1845–1849) and the cholera epidemic of 1849—she began sometime in the 1840s to write two important works: her *Catechism of Scripture History* which was used in manuscript form in the Limerick schools until it was published in London in 1852; and her handwritten biography of Catherine McAuley which became known as the Limerick Manuscript, and which served as the basis for her *Life of Rev. Mother Catherine McAuley*, edited by Richard Baptist O'Brien and published in Dublin in 1864. Evidently she did not anticipate publication when she began these manuscripts. Moreover, neither of these published works bears her name as the author: the title page of the *Catechism* says only that it was "compiled by The Sisters of Mercy, for the use of the Children Attending Their Schools"; and that of the *Life* says simply, "By a Sister of Mercy".

The *Catechism*, which according to its title page was "revised by Rev. Dr. [Edmund] O'Reilly", then professor of theology at Maynooth, is a 300-page summary of "the principal events" in the Old and New Testaments, arranged in question and answer form: that is, "the historical narrative [has] been copied from the sacred text" in selected responses to interspersed questions ([iii]). As its Preface states, the manuscript

> was commenced in rather a limited form, and was gradually added to as the children advanced. It is now deemed advisable to print it, both to prevent the inaccuracies likely to arise from frequent transcripts, and to meet the wishes of those who desired to procure copies. ([iii])

Knowing the early Mercy penchant for transcribing and sharing manuscripts, with the inherent possibilities of miscopying—to say nothing of the considerable amount of time required in handcopying—one can appreciate the decision to publish. But as one reads the *Catechism* one is even more impressed by the thoroughness of the instruction in scripture and by the sensitivity to the students' learning capacities which the *Catechism* exhibits. As the Preface acknowledges, the catechism form was "adopted to render it less difficult to commit the facts to memory" (iv). While scripture scholars today would question the precision with which the book dates events and sets down the ages, birth years, and death years of Old Testament figures—for example, "from the Creation to the Deluge includes a space of 1656 years" (v), and Adam died at the age of 930 years (5)—the chronological tables, which Edmund O'Reilly may have had a hand in developing, are a very small part of an otherwise thoughtfully constructed book. In response to the question, "What parable did our Lord relate on the lawyer's asking, Who is my neighbour?" the complete text of the parable of the Good Samaritan (Luke 10.30–37) is given (244–5); and to the question, "In what manner did our Lord foretel [*sic*] He would address the just on His second coming?" the entire text of Matthew 25.34–40 is printed (265). If Mary Vincent's pupils acquired command of even a fraction of this *Catechism,* they would probably have to search a long time today to find their equals among their age group.

Her work as a biographer of Catherine McAuley is a more complicated story to unravel. Her collection of data on Catherine, and the preparation of her two major and related writings about her—the Limerick Manuscript, and its eventual expansion into the printed *Life of Rev. Mother Catherine McAuley*—spanned at least twenty years, from sometime after Catherine's death in 1841 to 1864 when the *Life* was published in Dublin. Copies of the *Life* are now rare, and a number of intriguing questions about it await further investigation. For example, the exact editorial role of Richard Baptist O'Brien, who wrote the "Introduction" to the *Life* and is prominently featured on the title page as its editor, cannot be fully ascertained without considerably more research, beyond the intended scope of this volume. In addition, since the *Life,* as published, is a greatly enlarged version of the Limerick Manuscript, a page-by-page comparison of these two works would reveal the added materials in exact detail and would raise important questions about their source and authorship. Finally, work remains to be done on any correspondence or other archival documents, if such are extant—perhaps in Roscommon, Athlone, Limerick, or Dublin—related to the final preparation and publication of the *Life,* about one year before Mary Vincent's death.

In the *Life* Mary Vincent's Limerick Manuscript is altered in the following ways, among others: although the *Life* is clearly dependent on the content and order of the original manuscript, it rewords the manuscript throughout, only occasionally picking up exact phrases and sentences; sections of the original manuscript are expanded by general explanations and theological reflections; numerous long quotations from Catherine's letters are interpolated; sentences about Catherine's young adulthood which might have been seen—I think, incorrectly—to prejudice her eventual canonization are omitted or reworded; more information is provided on the subsequent histories of the first foundations and their founders; activities at Baggot Street in the years following Catherine's death are added; material which Richard Baptist O'Brien knew firsthand is inserted, such as his conversation with Catherine in 1838 about a possible foundation in Nova Scotia, and her expressed willingness to go there herself;

and, at the beginning of the book, the Limerick Manuscript's extensive account of Catherine's early religious isolation and difficulties, and yet her increasingly Catholic practice, is expanded, to correct once and for all what was apparently O'Brien's own earlier claim—in his obituary on her in the Halifax *Register*—that she was a convert to Catholicism. (In the intervening years both Mary Ann Doyle's and Clare Moore's protests against this interpretation had, it seems, settled the matter, by providing a more subtle account of Catherine's religious development.)

That Mary Vincent Harnett's published *Life* enjoyed good circulation in Ireland and England and commanded respect as an authoritative account, even though her primary authorship was not specifically acknowledged, is evidenced in the use made of it immediately after publication by at least one writer on Catherine McAuley. In England in February 1866, Henry James Coleridge SJ published in *The Month* (4:111–27) an article entitled "The First Sister of Mercy" which, while not a review of Harnett's book, condenses and summarizes its content. Coleridge notes that Catherine McAuley's life "has been written by one of her own religious" and that the book is "sufficiently rich in detail" (111). He acknowledges his dependence on "the artless and humble biography on which we have been drawing" (125), but nowhere in his article does he mention Mary Vincent Harnett or Richard Baptist O'Brien, or give the title of the book. Coleridge understandably may not have known who "a Sister of Mercy" was, but the editor's name is on the title page, with the title of the work. Coleridge's article appeared too early in 1866 to have been a summary of Carroll's biography published for the first time later that year in New York (Muldrey 351).

Since Harnett's published *Life* is an expansion and alteration of her Limerick Manuscript—in the ways indicated above, and by means which are presently not altogether clear—it seems desirable that the Limerick Manuscript itself, representing as it does her own unaltered account, should be made more easily available to scholars and students of Catherine McAuley's life. It is the longest of the early biographical accounts. While it incorporates numerous passages from the Derry Large Manuscript and the Life in the Bermondsey Annals (or a copy of it, such as Cork MS. 2, or the Derry Small Manuscript)—and therefore was finally completed after them, probably in the early or mid 1850s[4]—it also presents Mary Vincent's own eyewitness knowledge of Catherine, from early 1837 onwards, as well as the recollections of others from whom she sought information. As she notes in her introduction to the manuscript, she wishes to capture these memories in a more enduring record "while the events are still fresh in the recollection of those who have witnessed them, and while many are still living who took an active and prominent part" in the establishment of the Institute.

What distinguishes the Limerick Manuscript from the other early biographical accounts about Catherine McAuley is, particularly, the recollections of Mary Elizabeth Moore, the superior of Limerick and Catherine's close friend. Although Elizabeth is not identified in the narrative as a contributor, she would have been Mary Vincent's principal, and most easily accessible, personal source of information, one who had been privy to Catherine's own memories and confidences and to her frank assessments of situations. However, in addition, according to the Limerick Annals, both Frances Warde and Mary Ann Doyle visited Limerick in the 1840s: Frances, for "one night" in 1843, "on her way from Westport to Carlow"; and Mary Ann, for "a couple of months at the close of the year", in 1846.[5] Of Mary Ann's visit, the Annals says: "Having been professed with Mother McAuley and known all of the early days of the Order, Mother M. Vincent Harnett committed her details to writing for her after Memoir of our Foundress.[6] The 12th Dec[ember] was kept with unusual rejoicings on her account. Appropriate verses were read before Mother McAuley's wreathed portrait." Thus, despite its dependence throughout on the Derry Large and the Bermondsey accounts, and hence on Mary Ann Doyle's and Clare Moore's recollections and interpretations therein, the Limerick Manuscript also has many sections of original material—obtained from conversations with Elizabeth Moore, Frances Warde, and Mary Ann Doyle—all of which provide new angles of vision on Catherine's life and character.[7]

For example, by comparison with the other early biographical manuscripts, the Limerick Manuscript contains more detailed treatment of Catherine's childhood, her years of residence with the Callaghans, Mrs. Callaghan's illness and conversion, the role of Edward Armstrong in the building of the Baggot Street house, the clerical opposition Catherine experienced in 1829 and 1830, her niece Mary Teresa's desire to be a Carmelite and her deathbed profession of vows as a Sister of Mercy, her niece Catherine's virtues and final illness, the activities of her three nephews, and Catherine's own final illness. However, here one needs to recall that though the opening pages (how many?) of the Derry Large Manuscript are now missing, the manuscript was undoubtedly complete when Mary Vincent used it, and material in the now missing pages—on Catherine's years prior to 1823—may have dealt with some of these aspects of Catherine's early life.[8] Nonetheless, the Limerick Manuscript now provides important first-hand information and insights, not available in other documents, and, unlike the published *Life,* the compilation is clearly Mary Vincent Harnett's own.

At least three manuscript copies of the Limerick Manuscript are now extant: two in the archives of the Sisters of Mercy in Limerick, and an incomplete one in Ennis, founded from Limerick in 1854, the year after Mary Vincent went to Roscommon.[9] I am not able to say definitively which one of the Limerick copies is in Mary Vincent's own handwriting. The Ennis copy clearly is not. While it would be highly desirable to locate or identify one of her own handwritten manuscripts—there were evidently two, written at different times, one of which may have been the text given to Richard Baptist O'Brien—the almost verbatim correspondence between the three available manuscripts suggests that Mary Vincent's own autograph of the Limerick Manuscript (if we do not already have it in hand) would not, in any significant way, be different from these copies of it. The manuscript presented in this volume is one of the two now preserved in the Limerick archives.[10]

But Mary Vincent Harnett did not spend all her time writing manuscripts. In fact, as one reads Mary de Chantal Meagher's Memoir of her life, one is struck by all she struggled to accomplish in Roscommon, after the community was founded there on September 24, 1853. "Pending the erection of their own school", she had the sisters "attend the National one in their street dress for some hours daily." Yet she felt that "the labours of the Community still would be limited unless permission were procured to have them visit the Work House, the Jail, and the Co[unty] Infirmary." The priests of Roscommon thought getting such permissions from the Protestant trustees of the institutions would be impossible, but their "strongest representations on the matter made no change whatsoever in Mother M. Vincent's design". The Board of Guardians, by a "mere majority", soon gave permission for them to visit the workhouse and its adjoining hospitals, though "for a length of time the Sisters were always accompanied by an official." Mary Vincent then worked on getting into the jail, aided by a longstanding motion on the books to the effect that "Ladies likely to have influence in reforming female prisoners in the Jail . . . had access thereto for the purpose of doing so." The governor of the jail was "deeply tried by the concession, but the coolness of two nuns having entered within his jurisdiction 'without even the complimentary form of bringing the Prison Chaplain to introduce them' quite uncontrolled his warm temper." However, he soon got used to their visits; and they eventually got leave to "introduce cut muslin work for those [prisoners] competent to do it . . . and thus they earned something to bring them home after liberation; besides that, it also took up their thoughts in weary hours."

The County Infirmary was next on Mary Vincent's list. Happily for her, the vice-president of the Infirmary board, finding himself alone at a meeting of the board which no other member attended, "without dissent . . . wrote an order in their book 'to have the Sisters of Mercy allowed henceforth to visit the Co. Infirmary.' " (Even Mary de Chantal Meagher admits that the way access to the jail and the infirmary was gained "will perhaps read to some 'more like pious fables, to inspire confidence in prayer, than real facts!' ") Though their visits to the infirmary were restricted to a specified weekday at first, the community eventually gained greater freedom to visit the patients whenever they wished. Thus Mary Vincent's twelve years in Roscommon were, like her years in Limerick, passionately committed to the spiritual and bodily needs of the poor and afflicted. About a month before she died, she signed a contract for building an orphanage next to the convent.[11] When she died, the women of Roscommon openly wept.

Catherine McAuley was fond of Mary Vincent Harnett. She relied on her educational skills, and referred others, such as Mary Ann Doyle, to her expertise in these matters (Neumann, ed. 232–3). Catherine also looked forward to letters from her, and once wrote to Elizabeth Moore, half in jest: "tell my Dear Sister

M. Vincent she must write to me or I will be out with her'' (195). For her part, Mary Vincent saw—to the extent that one humanly could—the deep sanctity of Catherine McAuley. Yet years later, as Carroll notes, she wrote her own assessment of the prospect of Catherine's canonization, if, as was then apparently the case, Rome were to require the evidence of confirmed miraculous cures:

> ''We often smile at what we believe to be Reverend Mother McAuley's plan. She cannot find it in her heart to leave the sufferer in pain, while she seems equally determined to lead the hidden life, and, therefore, she obtains the cure, but in such a manner that we cannot *prove* it to be done by her; she obtains it *certainly,* but not *instantaneously*.'' (Carroll, *Life* 271)

The Limerick Annals records that Mary Vincent Harnett ''died of Anthrax in the neck at the Convent of the Immaculate Conception, Roscommon'' on July 9, 1865.[12] She was then fifty-four. The annalist says of her:

> Her own mind was very cultivated and refined; her manner of explaining any subject she ever studied was clear and satisfactory. Her goodness of heart and straightforwardness of purpose were admirable.

One can see these qualities of mind and heart in the Limerick Manuscript.

THE LIMERICK MANUSCRIPT[1]

Introduction

The Institute of the Sisters of Mercy is well known to the Irish Catholic public. Of late years its services have been extended to many cities and towns, not only in Ireland, but also in England, America, Australia, New Zealand, etc.[2] Yet of those who have been benefited and edified by the exalted virtues for which it is conspicuous, how few are acquainted with even the name of the great and holy woman to whom that Institute is indebted for its existence; much less with the circumstances from which it originated, and the means by which in the designs of God it was brought to its present condition.[3]

While the events are still fresh in the recollection of those who have witnessed them, and while many are still living who took an active and prominent part in its establishment, it has been deemed desirable to commit to a more enduring record than that of mere traditional record a narrative in which the working of the Divine Spirit has been signally manifested, and which is replete with incidents of no ordinary interest.

MEMOIRS OF THE LIFE OF REVD. MOTHER MARY CATHERINE McAULEY FOUNDRESS OF THE ORDER OF OUR LADY OF MERCY[4]

Miss Catherine McAuley was born on the 29th September 1778 at Stormanstown House, in the county of Dublin, the residence of her parents, James and Eleanor McAuley. She was the eldest of a family of three children.[5] At a very early age she had the misfortune of losing her father who was a truly religious and edifying Catholic tho' he lived at a time when the practical exercise of religion was far from general or fashionable, but even then she was old enough to remember how on Sundays and Festivals he was wont to collect about him the poor boys and girls of his neighbourhood for the purpose of instructing them in his own homely and impressive manner in the great truths and duties of religion. His wife was a very amiable and accomplished person, but her religious principles were defective. She was completely a woman of the world, had no great liking for this sort of business, and often remonstrated on what she considered the unsuitableness of such an occupation for a man of his age and condition.[6] But no opposition or entreaty of hers could induce him to abandon the good work, or neglect a duty which he felt was attended with such advantages.

If the religious instruction of the poor be, even in our days, a work of such decided utility and merit, with all the means that the charity of individuals and institutions have [*sic*] established for the purpose, how much more necessary and meritorious must it have been when the religious institutions of the country were then only in their infancy, or just beginning to emerge from the pressure of those restrictions to which they had been so long subjected.[7]

The poor children in the vicinity of Stormanstown House must have suffered a great and irreparable loss, and have been overwhelmed with a proportionate affliction when it pleased God in the mysterious dispensations of His Providence to deprive them of their good friend and benefactor. Yet greater must have been the affliction of his own poor family when at an early age the death of their good father made them orphans. Their extreme youth while it perhaps diminished the sense of the affliction, but made that affliction more calamitous. Catherine was the only one of the three children who was at an age to appreciate her loss, and in after life she always cherished the most grateful recollection of his Christian worth, and the most hallowed veneration for his memory. After his death Mrs. McAuley having met with pecuniary losses was obliged to give up her establishment. She removed to Dublin with her children, Catherine, Mary, and James then almost an infant. Altho' Mrs. McAuley considered that being under obligation to perform any duties of religion was foreign to its spirit, and an infringement on liberty of conscience, yet she educated her children as Catholics, and Catherine was Confirmed in Arran Quay Chapel.

The little Catherine faithfully adhered to the pious practices she then became acquainted with, and to the fervent preparation she made for receiving this Sacrament, and her faithful co-operation with grace, may be attributed the special grace she received of preserving her faith amidst the temptations to which she was afterwards exposed. Ever after, even to the end of her life, she was most solicitous to have children well prepared and instructed for Confirmation.[8]

When she was still very young, before she knew how to write, she copied in a kind of large print passages from the Psalter of Jesus, a prayer for which she always retained great affection and used to repeat parts of it at different hours of the day, even when going thro' the streets.

As she grew up she evinced an utter distaste for dress, and the ordinary amusements of young persons, and became much attached to reading, to which she often devoted part of the night. She sometimes hid a lighted candle in a box on going to her bedroom, and when the family had retired to rest, would take it out to resume her favorite occupation. She was of a most affectionate, obliging disposition and this she manifested not only in the communications with the members of her family, but towards all with whom she had intercourse. Nothing but a sense of duty could induce her to give a reprehension or make a complaint of anyone. She often called to mind with regret having told her mother of some fault of pride committed by her sister who was punished for it by being shut up in a dark room where flames were represented in order to give her an idea of the horror of eternal torments, for her mother had very strict and peculiar ideas on the education of her children.

Mrs. McAuley did not survive her husband many years, and Catherine's early life was one of much trial and sorrow. In all her difficulties she was consoled by Very Revd. Dean Lubé,[9] who till his death was her steady friend. She lived for some time with her mother's brother who had been a surgeon in the army; to this uncle and his daughter she was devotedly attached, and she had the grief to witness their affairs become embarrassed to an extreme degree. She shared their privations, and by her cheerfulness endeavored to lighten them.

A Protestant gentleman,[10] who was probably some connection, or at least friend of the family, took compassion on the children and assumed the care and responsibility of their education. Whatever pecuniary means remained to them was vested in his medical establishment, and the revenue that accrued therefrom was applied as a provision for their instruction and subsistence. In their new position they seem to have been amply supplied with every thing that their worldly wants required; but their guardian, whether from any indifference of his own on such an important subject, or not wishing to interfere with the children of Catholic parents, took no interest in their religious instruction. Thus brought up in the midst of a Protestant family, completely separated from all intercourse with the members of the persuasion to which they belonged, hearing day after day the usual misrepresentations of its rites and practices, and having no opportunity of having these misrepresentations removed, the result may be easily conjectured. The brother James adopted the creed of those with whom he lived. His sister Mary lost by degrees the few Catholic impressions that were made upon her mind in childhood, and having married a Protestant gentleman of the name of Macauley, a surgeon in the army, she finally surrendered her few remaining sentiments of religion at the shrine of her conjugal affection. Catherine, the eldest, having been more perfectly impressed with Catholic principles, was more proof against the influence to which she was subjected. A Protestant she was not, but yet she could scarcely be called a Catholic.[11]

The memory of her beloved father and her veneration for his virtues would now and then come strongly before her mind to sustain her in her trials, and endear to her the faith of which he was a member; but such a sentiment however it may have encouraged her to persevere could not have produced conviction, and she grew up without any settled religious opinions. If a remark was made injurious to the Catholic religion it always gave her pain, tho' she knew not in what manner to refute it, and the misrepresentations to which she was often forced to listen were always to her the source of inward and scarcely suppressed indignation. In this state of doubt and anxiety she spent several years of her life, feeling however daily more and more the want of some spiritual assistance, and the necessity of some external guide to conduct her in the way of salvation. She resolved to try whether by her own study and examination she could determine which of the two religious communions had the most cogent arguments in its favor, and to which she could with most safety and confidence commit the guidance and guardianship of her spiritual interests. Having a sincere regard and affection for the persons with whom she lived and who had always treated her with uniform kindness and attention, she wished to try whether it was possible for her with a safe conscience to adopt their sentiments, and join them in religion, as she was already united with them in a friendly communion. She read their books, heard their explanation, discussed with them the several points on which they differed, and sought anxiously by long and deliberate reflection to persuade herself that the Protestant religion was that she was bound in conscience to embrace. But the more she read, and studied, and thought upon the subject the stronger did her doubts become.

Baffled and disappointed in her efforts in this direction, her mind turned to the consideration of the Catholic doctrines. She procured some books and read them with the most serious and profound attention. She had always cherished a secret partiality for the religion of her parents, and therefore was rejoiced to find that the objections she had so frequently heard urged against it had their source in ignorance and misrepresentation of its dogmas; and having naturally a strong and instinctive yearning after piety and perfection she found to her great delight that her most sanguine desires in this respect admitted of being realized. The antiquity of its institution, which she could so easily trace back to the Apostles themselves; the universality of its diffusion, which marked it as the Church that was to fulfil the Divine injunction of "teaching and baptizing all nations"; and the holiness of its institutions and observances which were calculated to realize the highest expectation of her devotional fervor, made the most prompt and favorable impression and dispelled any shade of doubt and uncertainty that may have hitherto obscured her religious convictions. During this time she occasionally sought for instruction from the late Dr. Betagh SJ, whose learning and piety made everyone revere his words, and who was also an able controversialist. In mind and heart she was a confirmed Catholic and she only waited for a favorable opportunity to make known her sentiments and give practical effect to her resolve. This did not present itself as soon as she wished for or expected.

About this period Mr. Callaghan became connected with the establishment over which her guardian presided;[12] he was but a short time returned from India, where he had realized a considerable fortune, and was a gentleman of great scientific attainments. Mr. and Mrs. Callaghan became constant visiters of the family, and Miss McAuley's agreeable manners and amiable disposition soon made her a great favorite with them. They had no children, and were therefore the more ready to appreciate and esteem the good qualities both of mind and heart which they discovered in her. From their habit of familiar intercourse they became more and more attached to her, and instead of meeting her only occasionally they desired at length to have her entirely with them, and to make her their daughter by adoption.

The advantages of this proposal were too many and decided to be rejected, and at their repeated solicitations she removed to their beautiful country residence at Coolock near Dublin; neither of the parties had any reason to regret the consequences of this arrangement; they were to her all that the fondest parents could be, and her grateful and devoted attachment led them to forget that she was only their adopted child. But neither the advantages of her new position, nor the comforts she enjoyed, nor the attention of her sincere and anxious friends could relieve the anxiety, or quiet the troubles of her mind on the great subject of religion. She still continued determined in her intention of professing herself a Catholic, and longed anxiously to communicate her sentiments to her friends, and to have an interview with some Catholic clergyman, for notwithstanding all her study and examination there were a few points on which she still required some explanation, and this she felt could not be satisfactorily obtained by a written communication. Her agony of mind was very great when she found herself about to take a step on which she felt her eternal interests depended, for this inward trial was aggravated by difficulties of a worldly and scarcely less painful nature; such as, the giving offence to valued friends; the separation from long cherished connections; the probability of being exposed to obloquy, and censure, and ridicule from those whose good opinion it had ever been an object to secure. Her friends were unaware of her secret partiality for the Catholic religion, and she, from a feeling that will be easily understood, had a difficulty in making her intention known. Yet without making it known it was morally impossible to effect the object she had at heart; for her residence was some miles from the city, and so strong was the attachment of her adopted parents that they would scarcely permit her to be absent from them. But everything is preferable to the agony of suspense. One day she alleged some excuse for going into Dublin alone; she went to a Milliner's shop, and having purchased some trifling articles of dress, desired the servants to wait with the carriage until she should return. It was not far from the Roman Catholic church then in Liffey Street, and almost breathless with haste, and trembling from the excitement of her feelings, she applied at the residence of the clergymen, and inquired whether any of them were at home. The answer was in the affirmative, and she was introduced to the presence of the Revd. Dr. Murray then a curate attached to that parish, and afterwards Archbishop of Dublin. No one could be better suited to the occasion, or make a more favorable impression. When the agitation of her excited feelings permitted her to make known the object of her visit, and the peculiar circumstances in which she was placed, he gave her whatever instruction and advice she needed, removed any remaining difficulties she may have had, and appointed a day on which she was, if possible, to return to him again, and commence her preparation for the Sacraments.

Many were the difficulties she had to encounter in accomplishing her purpose, difficulties which, as the issue proved, might have been avoided by promptly and openly avowing her resolution. But she wished to put off as long as possible a disclosure which she apprehended would prove so painful to those she sincerely loved, and it was only after she had been admitted to Sacraments that she made them acquainted with the step she had taken.[13] It was but natural to suppose that they would have wished her to be of the same religious persuasion as themselves, but as her conscience and conviction led her otherwise they were unwilling to exert even the smallest influence, and allowed her the same freedom of choice in the matter of religion, which in similar circumstances they would have desired for themselves. She continued to go to Mass and they to Church without any diminution of their mutual esteem and affection. Thus at liberty she soon proved by her regularity and piety the strength of her religious conviction.

To Mr. and Mrs. Callaghan she devoted herself with all the affection of a child;

while they placed entire confidence in her, and left her the management of their affairs, allowing her also, to a certain extent, to practise those works of charity to which she had so much devotion; but their objection to Catholic practices made her restrict herself in devotional exercises and deny herself the use of the crucifix, and holy pictures. In the absence of these she and a Catholic domestic used sometimes kneel before a cross formed by the branches of the trees, and at other times before the cross-shaped panels of the doors; and with Heavenly prudence managed to observe the fasts and abstinences of the Church without offending the prejudices of those by whom she was surrounded. By constant humble prayer she fortified herself against the temptations incident to her position; it was her delight and her refuge, and with childlike confidence and simplicity she had recourse to her Heavenly Father even in her least wants. Her chief recreation was to copy prayers and pious books, which together with reading occupied her leisure moments, for, as has been already remarked, she took no pleasure in the ordinary amusements of young persons, but she conformed her taste for dress to that of her good friends.

She was most diligent in the observance of all the duties which religion requires, and indefatigable in her exertions to relieve the wants and sufferings of the poor. She had, indeed, little of her own to give beyond a kind word of advice, or an affectionate expression of sympathy, but her adopted parents were good charitable people, and she was, on almost every occasion, the organ of their benevolence.

Her charity did not confine itself to the relief of their temporal wants only; she took pity on their spiritual ignorance and destitution, and remembering the example of her father's usefulness, she wished in all things to prove herself the faithful imitator of his virtues. She collected the poor children of the neighbourhood in the lodge, which was placed at her disposal, and devoted a great portion of her time to their instruction. Her solicitude for the interests of the poor soon drew around her many who hoped to derive from her advice, relief, and consolation. Everyone who had distress to be relieved, or affliction to be mitigated, or troubles to be encountered came to seek consolation at her hands, and she gave it to the utmost of her ability; her zeal made her a kind of missionary in the small district around her.

Her generous solicitude was on one occasion exerted for a poor girl whose virtue was in danger, but unfortunately she could not obtain timely protection for her in consequence of the delays attendant on secular committees, which were attached to the then existing houses of refuge.

It will be seen hereafter that the lesson however melancholy which it afforded was not lost upon Miss McAuley, and that in the Institute which Providence made her the instrument of establishing she took the most effectual precautions against the possibility of such a calamity. God may, in His foreseeing wisdom, have permitted an individual to fall that thousands may in after times be saved and rescued from impending destruction.

From this time she took great delight in projecting means of affording shelter to unprotected young women.[14] She had then no expectation of the large fortune which afterwards was hers, but she fancied that if she had a few hundreds at her disposal, she would hire a couple of rooms and work for and with her protégées; the idea haunted her very dreams.

To these works of charity, limited and unobtrusive as they were, she continued to devote much of her time, but after a few years her kind friend Mrs. Callaghan was taken ill, and from this illness she never recovered. It was a lingering and tedious one, and though not attended with any violent pain, was sufficient for the most part to confine her to her bed. This was a new source of affliction to Miss McAuley, and a new occasion of merit also. For many a long month did she watch by that bed, and prove the sincerity of her attachment by unremitting assiduity and care. Everything that the most filial love could suggest to alleviate the pains of the poor sufferer was done by her dear adopted child, who was ever near to smoothe the pillow on which her wasted and restless head reclined, or to soothe her in the fitful moments of infirmity. She often read for her some book of moral and religious instruction, though this was a matter of no slight inconvenience, for the tender eyes of the invalid could bear no light but that of a shaded lamp placed on the floor. For many weeks the only sleep Miss McAuley had was on a couch in the sick room, during the patient's intervals of repose; yet even then was her mind engaged in visions of charity and mercy to the poor; at one moment it was a group of orphan children to whom she was administering the kind offices of humanity; at another it was a crowd of young women engaged in the various occupations of household industry. Then the scene would suddenly change and picture to her a number of destitute females, deprived of their natural protectors and deserted by their friends, some flying with horror from the suggestions of the tempter. Alarmed and amazed at the wild revelling of her imagination she often started from her slumbers and burst into tears. "Catherine," the sick lady would sometimes say to her, "I almost wish you never went to sleep, you frighten me so much, and seem to suffer such agony."

Was it that her charity overflowing the ordinary stream of usefulness to which it was confined, loved to unbody[15] itself in visions of benevolence to her kind; or could it be that God was thus to manifest to her, as to many of His sainted children of old, the extended sphere of usefulness, and mercy, and generous benevolence to which a few years later she was to be called.

But her solicitude was not confined to the bodily infirmities and pains of her dear and valued friend; she wished to make her a partaker of the religious advantages which she herself enjoyed; and the great object for which she prayed with many sighs and tears was that the sick patient should die in the true Faith, and receive all the spiritual helps which the holy Sacraments afford. For this important step she had endeavored in some measure to prepare her, by speaking from time to time on religious subjects, and explaining the nature of Catholic truths and practices; and availing herself of a favorable opportunity most earnestly recommended its adoption. But there were many difficulties in the way; Mrs. Callaghan said she had herself no objection to die a member of the

Catholic Communion, but she was sure it would afflict her husband beyond measure; he had always been attentive to her, and proved himself on every occasion most affectionate and devoted, how could she thus requite him for all his kindness? They had lived in peace and harmony together, how could she by embracing another creed sever, as it were, the bonds that united them together, and embitter his declining years? There was, she said, another reason that influenced her and rendered it impossible to think of such a change; this reason she was unwilling to disclose, her kind attendant was pressing in her entreaties, and at length Mrs. C. said, "I think my husband would be so dissatisfied and displeased with your interference that he would be very likely to deprive you for ever of any portion of his property, and I cannot consent to any measure that would prove so disastrous to you."[16]

Surprised at such a proof of generous affection and determined that in an affair of such vital consequence this consideration should have no influence, Miss McAuley continued to urge her proposal, entreated her friend to lay aside such apprehensions, and assured her that the poorest habitation, and the humblest position in life, would be a thousand times more acceptable than the wealth of the universe, if it were to be purchased at such a price, and secured by the loss of one so valued and esteemed; she was content to live in the meanest cottage for the remainder of her life if she could only see her benefactress a Catholic before she died. Such disinterested and self-sacrificing love was irresistible, and Mrs. Callaghan at length consented, provided arrangements could be made to effect the object in view without the knowledge of her husband, and added, "Surely the Faith that leads you to work by charity, must be holy and sent by God; you have with saintly sweetness borne with all my peevishness and impatience, and I rejoice to embrace the religion which has sanctified you." Delighted at her success Miss McAuley lost no time in availing herself of the permission thus given, and Mr. Callaghan's absence on business having afforded a convenient opportunity, she applied to a Clergyman who was then residing in the vicinity;[17] he received Mrs. Callaghan into the Church, heard her confession, but being much engaged in other duties he postponed the administration of the other Sacraments for a few days. But the hours of the good lady were already numbered and before he could repeat his visit she had expired in the arms of her devoted child.

The goodness and generosity of the deceased lady may be inferred from what has been stated in the preceeding [*sic*] pages; the following incident may serve to show it in a still stronger light. Mr. Callaghan having amassed all his wealth by his own exertions had a number of relations not as well off in the world as he was, and who therefore hoped to come in for a share of his riches as he had no family. It was a source of great annoyance and jealousy to them that Miss McAuley held the place which they thought they should have occupied themselves; they envied her the happiness and good fortune she possessed, and attributed it all to Mrs. Callaghan's partiality, and resolved to wreak their vengeance on her. In furtherance of their intentions they tried to sow dissension between her and her husband. They sent anonymous letters full of the most insulting language, and outrageous to her feelings. She knew the handwriting, and was able to trace them to a young man, a connexion of the family. Sometime after, the mother of this young man waited on her to solicit her interference with Mr. Callaghan in his behalf. She went down stairs to see her, and having heard the nature of the application returned to Miss McAuley with whom she had been previously conversing. "Mrs. N . . . ," said she, "has been talking to me about her son; he has been offered, it seems, a commission in the army provided he can pay down immediately £300. Such an opportunity may never present itself again, and she wishes me to induce my husband to give the money." "Well," replied Miss McAuley, "and will you not do so." "Can I," exclaimed she, "exert myself in favor of one who has in so malicious a manner endeavored to destroy my domestic happiness, who has tried without any provocation to wound my feelings and insult me." Then taking from a drawer the letters she had received said, "Were I now to read these I could not be prevailed on by any solicitations; but I will act nobly and generously towards him." Saying this she cast them into the fire, went to Mr. C., stated the object of the request and got the money.

After her death matters went on in the family as usual, Mr. Callaghan attending to his professional engagements, and Miss McAuley to the works of charity she had again resumed. But after some time advancing years brought with them to him increasing infirmities, aggrevated [*sic*] perhaps by his late domestic affliction. He only survived his wife three years, but if the most untiring solicitude could arrest the progress of age and illness, he would have long continued a healthy man; for his adopted daughter did all that a child could to comfort his declining years. Yet though she may delay or lighten the progress of infirmity no care however devoted could avert it altogether; and her kind friend's health began rapidly to decline. A little while and he was confined entirely to his house. One evening as they were conversing together he abruptly said to her, "Catherine, what shall I leave to you at my death, will you be satisfied with £1,000?" Annoyed and disturbed at the question she expressed her grief at being thus addressed on the subject, and assured him that such a thought had never occupied her mind; she did not want money, she said, and would not know what to do with £1,000. "You would not know what to do with £1,000," observed he, falling back in his chair laughing, "well, I know what you would do; you would do a great deal of good with it at all events."

Each day he became weaker and more infirm, and soon began to exhibit symptoms of approaching dissolution. Miss McAuley who had his spiritual, much more than his temporal interests at heart, became filled with the most serious apprehensions, and prayed earnestly that before his death he might be reconciled to the Church by a sincere conversion. He was a good, kind-hearted man, blameless in all the relations of life, and generous in his charities to the poor; but she desired he should add the treasure of the true Faith to the number of his other virtues, and secure for himself the possession of the one thing that of all others was the most necessary. He had devoted somewhat of his attention to the subject of religious controversy, read many religious works, and was most liberal and unprejudiced in his opinions. Although Miss McAuley enjoyed his confidence and regard to a greater extent than any other person, yet she felt the utmost difficulty in addressing him on such a topic, however great its importance, and could only pray fervently and earnestly that God, in His great mercy, would confer this favor upon him. At length he began to sink rapidly, and she determined to leave nothing undone on her part to secure his conversion. She begged the attending physician to let her know what length of time his life was likely to be prolonged. "That is quite uncertain," said he, "the nature of his illness is such that he may live for a month, and he may die tomorrow." Alarmed at the urgency of the occasion she knew not what to do. The Revd. E. Armstrong was her friend and spiritual adviser, since the elevation of Dr. Murray to the Episcopacy.[18] She had recourse to him for counsel, and told him what she had just heard from the doctor; he advised her to lose not a day in speaking to her benefactor on the subject, and promised to pray for a blessing upon her efforts in his customary ministration at the Altar.[19]

The very next morning she resolved to introduce the topic of religion, but when the moment came for doing so, she had not strength, she made several attempts but could not give utterance to a word; at length she made up her mind to do it, no matter what the consequence might be, and went to his bed-side, but there unable to give expression to her feelings, sank down upon her knees, clasped his hands in hers, and overpowered by her emotions burst into an agony of tears. The sick man was frightened, and thought that some dreadful calamity had happened; he asked her again and again what was the matter, and did all in his power to calm her agitation. When he had in some degree succeeded she told him that her excitement was caused by a matter concerning which she was most desirous, yet afraid to speak to him. Not being able to conceive what this matter might be, and feeling hurt at the idea of there being any subject on which she could be afraid to speak to him, he enquired whether he had ever refused her anything she had asked of him; or had he ever given her reason to doubt the sincerity of his affection. "No, no," said she, "it is not for myself, it is on your account I am uneasy." A thought flashed[20] across his mind. "It is," he said, "that you think I am in imminent danger." "I do indeed think you are in danger," replied she, "and know that you are very bad, but it is not the state of your health which troubles me so much, it is the peril of your immortal soul, which I believe to be endangered by your dying in any other than the Roman Catholic Church; and without the aid of those spiritual advantages which Christ has appointed for persons in your condition; the very thought of such a calamity is to me most painful." "Dear Catherine," said her friend, "be tranquil, you have excited yourself most unnecessarily on my account; I have a firm confidence in God, and reliance on His mercy; I have read a great deal on religious matters, and have, I trust, acted uprightly in following, according to my conscience, the religion I profess." Seeing that she was far, very far, from being satisfied with this answer, he told her to be calm for the present, and promised to speak to her some other time on the subject. She requested him not to postpone the consideration longer than the following day; and on the ensuing morning he was himself the first to resume the conversation. "Well," said he, "am I to introduce this exciting subject again. I suppose I must do so to gratify you; I dare say you wish me to be a Roman Catholic whether I am convinced or not." After a few more remarks, she asked him if he would read some good and approved works on the differences between their respective Churches, and on his observing that the state of his health did not then permit him to do so, she requested that he would at least allow her to introduce her friend the Revd. E. Armstrong to discuss with him the subject that was at issue between them. "As you desire it," said he, "I have no objection; and if he can succeed in proving the faith of Roman Catholics to be better and holier than that of which I am a member, I promise to embrace it on the instant."

She lost no time in availing herself of the permission thus given, but sent for her reverend friend and introduced him without delay. The sick man received him with politeness, and listened to his explanation of doctrinal subjects with marked and anxious attention. At his rising to depart Mr. Callaghan begged of his own accord that he would be good enough to repeat his visit at his earliest convenience. What was at first mere courtesy soon ripened into the deepest interest, and his mind began to open by degrees for the reception of the Truth. Difficulties that he thought insuperable ceased to be such when presented to him in a different light from that in which he had been accustomed to consider them. And the conviction was at last brought home to his mind, that the true Church of Christ was that, which owing to his mistaken opinions, and the involuntary prejudices of his early education, he had always looked on as apostate. He had no motive to do violence to his convictions; no views of self-interest to dispute the supremacy of his conscience; no link to bind him to error, other than the persuasion that error was truth; and when that link was broken, its hold upon his mind was lost for ever.

He avowed his intention of becoming a Catholic, and sought immediate admission into the pale of that Church from which the circumstances of his birth, together with his position in society, and not any insensibility or obduracy of his own, had hitherto excluded him. Who can tell the feelings of Miss McAuley when her prayers, her solicitude, her untiring exertions in his behalf were at length crowned with success, and she saw him admitted into the Church, and to the participation of the Sacraments; which he received with sentiments of the most sincere and heartfelt piety.

He survived his conversion but a short time, during which his piety was truly exemplary. It may be supposed that the assiduity of his adopted daughter was not diminished by a circumstance which endeared him to her yet more. He died the 11th [*sic*] of November 1822,[21] leaving her sole heiress of his property, which amounted to £20,000 in ready money, and £400 a year, being convinced she would make good use of it. In this he was not mistaken.

As soon as her last duties were performed to him who had been a parent to her, she devoted herself unreservedly to the performance of those works of mercy which afterwards formed the characteristics of the holy Institute Almighty God made her the instrument of founding; and looking on herself only as executrix of the large fortune placed at her disposal, she resolved to devote it to the greater glory of God, and the benefit of the poor.

A short time after the death of Mr. Callaghan, Miss McAuley was honored with the attentions of many distinguished individuals, who would scarcely have condescended to notice the poor orphan girl dependent on the bounty of her friends; but money is able to make great changes. However she at once made known her determination of leading a single life. This avowal was not at all displeasing to her more immediate friends, in as much as it seemed to secure to them the reversion of her fortune and property after her death, and the partial enjoyment of it during her life. What her intentions were she made known to the Revd. E. Armstrong, who was aware of every circumstance of her life since she had become a practical Catholic; he knew also the events of the last few years, by which Providence seemed to be preparing her for some exalted destiny, and the achievement of some great destiny[22] which It had in view.

To him and to Very Revd. Michael Blake, V. G. of the Diocess [sic], and afterwards Bishop of Dromore,[23] she alone communicated the design she had formed of devoting her means to the relief of the needy and the destitute; and of establishing some permanent Institution for the mitigation of their many sufferings. It was a project she had been long contemplating, it was ever present to her mind, even when dependent on the bounty of [o]thers, and there seemed no human probability of her ever being able to carry it into effect. Now that God gave her the means of doing so she resolved on commencing the good work without delay.

Her two friends and advisers, after deliberating on her pious and charitable designs, decided on selecting a suitable site in some public and respectable quarter of the city. "For," said Revd. E. Armstrong, "if you would have a public Institution be of service to the poor, place it in the neighbourhood of the rich." It was his opinion that it had been too much the custom for Catholics to have their charitable Institutions in the bye places of the Capital, in some obscure street or lane that was almost inaccessible. He considered it was desirable to make a change in this respect and bring the Institutions of Catholics more prominently before the world; thus their light would not be hid under a bushel, but so placed that all may see, and admire, and be edified at the good works they witnessed. Nor did he think it right that in this respect they should be placed at a disadvantage when compared with their Protestant fellow citizens.

It was also considered more likely to bring the blessing of God on the proposed good work, to take—not a house already built and occupied for other purposes, and which probably they should have some difficulty in adapting to their own—but a plot of ground that had not been built upon, and erect for the honor and glory of God an edifice that never had been profaned by the vices or follies of fashionable life, nor sullied by any insult to their religion; which would be holy in its erection as in its use, and dedicated to Him from its very foundation. Accordingly a piece of ground in Upper Baggot St., a healthy and respectable part of the city, was purchased for £4000, subject to the yearly rent of £60. The first stone of the new building was laid by Very Revd. Dr. Blake, previous to his going to Rome to found the Irish College there, in July 1824. The contractors received £4,000 for the mere shell, which they took three years to raise.

As Miss McAuley knew little of building and besides, had no object in view but to accommodate the poor, she merely told the architect that she wanted a commodious house with very large rooms, one of which she wished to be loftier than the rest to serve as a chapel. These rooms she intended to appropriate as poor schools; dormitories for young women who for want of proper protection might be exposed to danger; and apartments for ladies who should choose for any definite or indefinite period to devote themselves to the service of the poor, remaining at liberty to visit their relations, or return to their worldly occupations when they no longer felt inclined to continue their pious labors.

To meet her views and make the building suit the ground, the architect erected it in conventual style, and even placed a conventual grate between the chapel and the room adjoining, at which she was much surprised and amused; for though she felt convinced from the first that God required from her some exertion to secure the lasting relief of the suffering, and the instruction of the ignorant, yet the idea of founding a religious Institute never entered her mind. But Almighty God whose will alone she sought to know and do, designed her as His instrument, and led her step by step to the accomplishment of His work.

While the building was carried on Miss McAuley resided chiefly at Coolock House, keeping her intention a secret, as she had reason to know that her family would resent it extremely. She lived in what is usually called good style, that is, she kept a carriage, dressed well, went into society, gave parties at her own house. But the greater part of her time she employed in works of piety and charity, especially in the instruction of poor children in the female schools of St. Mary's parish, Abbey St.; in the lower room of which she established a repository or shop, for disposing of the various kinds of needle-work done by the girls attending it. This she considered a better way to assist them than to give them money or clothes by way of alms, as they were thus trained to industrious habits.

In her visits to the poor in their own habitations she evinced great compassion for such as had been formerly in better circumstances, and aided them as far as was in her power.

On one occasion she discovered a poor maniac who had once enjoyed the comforts of life, being of a good family, but was then deserted by all and suffering from extreme poverty. She immediately took charge of this poor creature, and instead of getting her into an asylum, brought her to her own house where she kept her till her death. Miss McAuley had much to suffer from this woman, as she, with the perversity sometimes attending madness, conceived an absolute hatred of her benefactress, and ordinarily used most virulent and contemptuous language towards her. Besides she was of very dirty habits, and had an inveterate custom of stealing everything she could lay hands on, hiding such things as she could not use, which caused great inconvenience in the family. Yet the patience of her protectress never seemed disturbed by these continual annoyances, nor would she permit the servants to teaze [*sic*] the poor creature on the subject. She had not the consolation of being ever able to impart to her any religious instruction, for she had been a Protestant (if she could be said to be of any religion), and she died without recovering even a glimpse of reason.[24]

Miss McAuley was most regular in the performance of every duty of religion, fasted rigorously, and during Lent made it a law never to taste wine, nor to break her fast from dinner on Holy Thursday till collation on the morning of Easter Eve. She rose very early, prayed much, and was most assiduous in her attendance at sermons, and at the public Offices of the Church.

The new building had already made considerable progress, and the people in the neighbourhood, and also those passing by, often asked each other what the large house was intended for. But not one could tell; neither the laborers who were employed at it, nor the tradesmen; not even the contractor or the architect: they only knew that it was being erected at the expense of a Miss McAuley; and some said that having lately come into the possession of a great deal of money she did not know what to do with it. Her brother too would come frequently to see what his sister was doing in Baggot St., look about attentively, and make enquiries like any of the others; for as little as they did he know what she meant to do. There could be no doubt, he would say, that it was a useless and wasteful expenditure of money. But not one ventured to ask a word of explanation of herself. It was her own money she was expending, and none felt warranted in calling her to an account for the use she wished to make of it.

In the meantime the work of God met with many difficulties, and the faith and confidence of Miss McAuley were often rigorously tested. The relatives of the late Mr. Callaghan contested his will, trying to prove him insane when he made it. In this emergency she was much indebted to the Revd. Joseph Nugent of Sts. Michael and John's parish, who deserves to be considered a special benefactor by the whole Institute. He was a very holy and highly gifted man, and during Very Revd. Dr. Blake's absence in Rome, continued to render her most efficient service. But it pleased Almighty God soon to deprive her of his counsel and assistance. On the 30th of May 1825 she had the affliction to lose her good friend, after fifteen days of severe suffering, during which she attended him assiduously day and night.[25]

Still there remained her excellent and faithful friend, Very Revd. Dr. Armstrong, who had undertaken to inspect the building. This was a very great service as she was quite unacquainted with business; and besides as she saw the building rise, and reflected on the magnitude of the work (in which she had almost imperceptibly engaged), with the expense it would necessarily entail, she began to be much troubled with apprehensions that her charitable projects could never be realized. Dr. Armstrong supported and encouraged her in all difficulties; he comforted her with the assurance of using all the influence he possessed to promote the good work, and suggested that if necessary, a subscription could be raised. He was above all things solicitous that she should purify her intention, and place all her confidence in God alone. To this he repeatedly and emphatically exhorted her, saying over and over again, "Do not put your trust in any human creature, place all your confidence in God alone." Those who knew her afterwards, when she was a religious, thought she possessed holy confidence to an eminent degree of perfection; but it was a virtue she did not suddenly acquire, her friend had often to repeat the lesson to her.

About this period she took charge of a little orphan that she saw cast into the street from a cellar which her parents had occupied; as there were doubts as to the fact of her being baptized, Miss McAuley procured conditional baptism to be administered. Thenceforward the protection of orphans became to her an object of special interest.

At this time also a severe family affliction befel her. Her sister had long been laboring under a serious indisposition which had gradually undermined her constitution. This lady, though she had early forsaken the Catholic Faith, married a rigid Protestant, and reared her children, three sons and two daughters, in the same persuasion; yet she was far from participating in the disapprobation with which her husband and brother regarded the use her sister was making of her money; she had indeed no precise idea of the nature of the benevolent object for which it was intended, but she would frequently speak of the delight she hoped to experience in seeing the poor enjoying the comforts of that great house. She did not live to witness it; for the disease from which she had been so long suffering having at length developed itself in an unequivocal manner was pronounced by the physicians to be an internal cancer. The invalid claimed and obtained from her sister the most unwearied attention.

Finding it impossible to attend the poor patient as she wished, and at the same time look after the building in Baggot St., and keep up her establishment in the country, Miss McAuley resolved on giving up the last. Accordingly she sold the house and demesne at Coolock, dismissed her servants, and took up her abode with her brother-in-law at his residence on the Military Road.[26] Here she was able to act the part of a parent to his children, and without much difficulty pay a visit every day to the new building.

All possible diligence being used to prevent any Catholic friend from endeavoring to recall Mrs. Macauley to her first faith, she prepared herself to die, by receiving the Communion according to the Anglican Rite. But the state in which she now was, and the danger to which she was exposed, induced her sister to make a last effort to bring her back to the knowledge and profession of the Truth. She spoke to her of their father's zeal and piety, of the example which he had bequeathed to them; said that her abandonment of the Church was rather owing to want of instruction in early life, and the accidental circumstance of being united to a prejudiced Protestant, than to any real conviction of the truth of that form of worship to which she had given her adhesion. And in frequent conversations explained to her the leading doctrines of Catholicity. Her labors, and still more perhaps her prayers, were crowned with complete success, and the sick lady expressed herself desirous of being reconciled and restored to the communion of that Church which she had so long and so ignorantly forsaken.

But an obstacle seeming insurmountable presented itself from the bigotry and opposition of Dr. Macauley. No one could be kinder or more indulgent on every point except religion; on that alone he was inflexible. He had been reared in the rankest prejudices, and brought up with a perfect horror, nay an abomination, of what he was pleased to designate popish practices; and his wife knew he never could consent to have her return to a Faith which he so hated.[27] She dreaded arousing his naturally impetuous temper, and therefore considered the most prudent and peaceable thing she could do, was to request change of air, and this Dr. Macauley most willingly granted. Dundrum was the place selected, and thither she went accompanied by her sister, and her eldest child. In the quiet seclusion of the country she was enabled to receive the visits of Revd. Mr. McCormack, a Roman Catholic Clergyman, without the knowledge, and therefore without the opposition of her husband. There she was reconciled to the Church, admitted to the participation of the Sacraments, and in about three weeks after departed this life in the most edifying sentiments of compunction and piety, August 1827. She had previously informed her daughter concerning her faith, exhorting her likewise to embrace it; yet at the same time recommending that the most profound secrecy should be observed in everything relative to the matter, for she dreaded the consequence of acting otherwise.

After her sister's death Miss McAuley returned to the house of her brother-in-law and continued to devote herself to the care and superintendence of his children. She had promised their dying parent that she would be a mother to them, and such she proved herself to be, providing for their wants, and anxious for their improvement with a solicitude as devoted as any mother.

Her eldest niece was now in her sixteenth year;[28] nature had bestowed on her more than an ordinary share of personal attractions, and a mind of much power and capacity; while her angelic sweetness gained her the love and admiration of all who had the happiness of knowing her. She was a great favorite with her father, and he heard with much regret that she usually accompanied his sister-in-law to her customary places of devotion, though her only motive at the time was not to be separated from her aunt to whom she was much attached. But in her father's eyes such a temporary compliance was a violation of duty that merited his severest displeasure, and he resolved by his remonstrance to prevent a recurrence of it for the future. One night after supper when they were seated round the fire in the drawing room, he suddenly introduced the topic which was occupying his mind; and having expressed his perfect confidence in Miss McAuley's prudence and good sense in most matters, said that on the subject of religion alone did he disagree with her, and on that point he would permit no interference with his children. She replied that she had used no influence beyond that of her example, and that if her niece thought fit to accompany her of her own accord to her place of worship, it was not her duty to prevent it; on the contrary she had prayed incessantly that the grace of conversion might be vouchsafed to her.

The conversation became warm by degrees, and at length he said, "You know how her mother thought on the subject, how she lived, and you may thence conclude how she would be grieved if she could foresee that her treasured child would become a papist."

Miss McAuley had long wished for an opportunity of telling him of the change that had taken place in his wife's sentiments on the subject of religion before her death, but she always trembled at the shock it was likely to give. The occasion that now presented itself was too favorable to be neglected, and such a one may never occur again; so summoning up all her resolution and firmness she replied, "William, you are mistaken; my sister always loved the Faith in which she was born; as your wife she did not, and could not follow it, but she died a Catholic." With much emotion he exclaimed, "Did you make Mary die a papist."[29] Uttering a frightful oath he rushed up stairs perfectly beside himself with the fearful paroxysm of his fury, and utterly reckless as to what his anger might prompt him to do. Perhaps in the rage of the moment some calamity may have been the result, if Miss McAuley, terrified at the storm which she had excited, had not resolved to escape the danger by flight. To this she was still more urged by the fright of the domestics who told her they heard their master muttering dark threats of vengeance. It was an unseasonable hour, but even unprepared as she was, it was better to encounter the darkness of the night than the violence of a frenzied man. The servants secured the hall door so that she could not be suddenly pursued; and when Dr. Macauley returned to the drawing room, it is said with a dagger in his hand, she was gone. He sought her everywhere through the house; his servants could only say they heard the street door shut violently. Startled at the excess of his passion, and what its consequences may be, he sent messengers in all directions to bring her back, and when they returned unsuccessful his mind was agitated beyond description; he found his children weeping, and anxiously enquiring what he had done to their dear Aunt, who had always been so affectionate and good to them.

When Miss McAuley became conscious that she was alone on the road, she commenced running until she thought, as she was afterwards wont to say, she would have died of terror and fatigue; fortunately she met no one until she reached the house of a friend. She mentioned her name and solicited admission, which was immediately granted. It was only then she recollected the extraordinary appearance she presented, and the singular circumstances under which she sought protection; how to account for it she knew not, her kind heart would not permit her to state a matter that may prove so injurious to the character of her brother-in-law, so she apologized for her untimely intrusion, saying it was caused by a passing domestic disturbance.

Morning came, and with it more calm reflection to Dr. Macauley; he soon discovered where his sister had taken refuge; some friends undertook the work of reconciliation, and he, ashamed of his violence and wishing as far as he was able to repair the injurious treatment of which he had been guilty, made an apology for his conduct, and solemnly engaged that the topic which had been the occasion of his anger should never again be alluded to. The apology was accepted, and to the great happiness and joy of the children their beloved Aunt returned to them.

Throughout all her anxieties she had not lost sight of the great work before her. As the instruction of poor children was one of the principal objects she had in view, she resolved to prepare herself for the more efficient accomplishment thereof, by becoming acquainted with the method of instruction adopted in the most approved, and best regulated schools.

The Kildare Street Society was then in active operation, and though its faults were many and considerable there can be no doubt but that the plan of education pursued by it was the very best of its time, and a great improvement on any that had gone before. To acquire a practical knowledge of its details, which she could afterwards render available for her own purpose, Miss McAuley visited the schools, and while she admired the utility and great efficiency of its educational system, she was sorry to find that many Catholic children, attracted by the worldly advantages it held out, were brought within the sphere of its peculiar influence, and while receiving earthly knowledge, were forced to imbibe the poison of error, which was insidiously infused into the draught. Although Miss McAuley as a Catholic was looked on with no very favorable eye by the managers, yet being connected with a respectable Protestant family, and occupying an independent position in society, she was entitled to some degree of attention. Her visits were frequent and protracted, and while she inspected the progress of the pupils, and saw how knowledge was communicated, her zealous and attentive eye noted the Catholic children who were present; she learned from them the names, residence, and occupations of their parents, in order that at a subsequent period she could have them withdrawn to attend the schools in Baggot Street.

Whilst residing with her brother-in-law early in the year 1827,[30] she was visited by Miss Anna Maria Doyle. This young lady whilst out walking had remarked the building in Baggot St. with a feeling of indescribable attraction; she eagerly watched its progress, and at length asked the person in charge of the premises to allow her to enter and view the work. She was delighted with the place, and after hearing from Miss McAuley its destination, she resolved to become a member of the projected society. Her intention had been to enter a convent; but as she was the only daughter then left to her aged parents the hope of being permitted to visit them, united to a strong interior impulse made her prefer joining the new association. Her family were of course desirous to confirm her in this decision, so she offered to share in the good work. Early in Autumn the building was in some degree habitable and it was determined that she should remove to it at once, tho' she was to have but one companion, Miss Catherine Byrne, still very young. Miss McAuley could not then possibly make it her place of residence, on account of the recent death of her sister, her niece not being old enough to undertake the management of her father's household. Yet she occasionally took up her abode there[31] according as the nature of her duties required.

The 24th of September was finally fixed on for commencing the work; Miss Doyle suggesting that "House of Mercy" would be a good name for the Establishment. Nor can we think it was without a singular providence of God that a day was chosen which in a special manner placed the house under the protection of His Immaculate Mother, and caused it to be named from the most amiable of her attributes, by which she chiefly resembles Him, whose mercies are above all His works. Therefore on the appointed Feast some young women were admitted to the dormitories, and the schools opened, to which the poor children came in great numbers. A few kind and charitable ladies volunteered their services, and the good work began its career of usefulness. The pious foundress visited almost daily, and took an active part in the schools; she was always accompanied by her eldest niece, who, though not yet a Catholic, took a deep interest in the various works of charity, and worked as zealously and devotedly as any of the others.

The dress adopted by Miss Doyle and her associate[32] was a wide dress of black valentia made in one from the throat to the ground, with full sleeves confined at the wrist, plain lace cap with black linen, having a very high caul, and full quilling round the face. This costume excited the disapprobation of some who considered it an assimilation to a religious dress, to which they had no claim; but Miss McAuley would not find fault with the taste of her young friends, perhaps on the whole she was rather pleased as it seemed to promise stability, and showed they had an intention to persevere. Through love of holy poverty they excluded all superfluities, and retrenched even necessaries to a greater degree than they would be allowed in a religious community, their zeal and desire of perfection being the only bounds to their pious practices. But it was to themselves alone they were austere, to the children and others connected with the Institution they were all kindness, and with pleasure entertained their little pupils with roast beef and plumb [*sic*] pudding the first Christmas Day they were in their new abode; Miss McAuley having a particular devotion to making as many poor people as she could happy and joyful on that holy Feast. On that day also the holy Sacrifice of the Mass was celebrated for the first time in the house.

A short time after the opening of the schools Miss Frances Warde was introduced to the Foundress; she was a lively, animated, fashionable young lady; her parents being dead, she had lately gone to reside with some friends in Dublin, where she spent her time in a round of visits and amusements, but yet never gave up the pious habit in which she had been reared of approaching regularly the holy Sacraments. On one occasion her confessor enquired how she spent her time, and finding she was quite her own mistress, he represented to her the necessity of doing some good, and recommended her to teach, for a few hours daily, in the poor school lately opened in Baggot St. She acquiesced, and from that time attended very regularly at the school, and often visited Miss McAuley, with whom and her elder niece she contracted a solid and lasting friendship. A young friend of Miss Warde's, Miss Elizabeth Harley, daughter of Captain Harl[e]y, offered herself at the same time—under similar circumstances—to aid in the good work. There were now several efficient assistants who attended more or less regularly according to circumstances, and the poor school was soon filled with about three hundred children, whose teaching, as yet, formed the business of the day. The inmates of the House of Mercy consisted chiefly of workwomen who went to their employments every morning after prayers and instruction, and returned in the evening, when their work was done, to lodge for the night; this they continued to do for nearly the first year, one or two orphan children alone being entirely provided for.

In this manner the good work went on to May 1828, when it pleased God to send Miss McAuley a severe trial in the death of her sincere and long tried friend Very Revd. Dr. Armstrong, then parish priest of St. Michan's North Ann Street. He had been her helper in many difficulties and contradictions, and on him she relied for assistance in carrying on the good works she had undertaken, and in which he had encouraged her from the commencement. Just at that time too she thought his advice indispensable as many were beginning to murmur at the new Institute. He had already rendered her many services with the Archbishop—whose confessor he was, and who loved and esteemed him in a particular manner as a most holy and zealous priest. And now when he was on his death-bed he requested an interview with his Grace; when Dr. Murray entered the apartment he told him that the motive which urged him to seek the favor then conferred, was his solicitude for Miss McAuley and her infant establishment in Baggot St. He said he knew her worth and had watched over the progress of her undertaking, seeing it was one that promised to be of great and signal utility to the Church and to the poor; and added that he was convinced its Foundress was raised up by Providence as a special instrument of mercy to His suffering and afflicted children. He then most earnestly besought his Grace to watch over and protect the Institution, and to extend to it and its members the benefit of his patronage. It is scarcely necessary to add the appeal was most favorably received, and that the holy prelate realized the confidence thus reposed in him.

Miss McAuley attended her reverend friend with unremitting care till his death, which happened on the Feast of the Ascension of our Lord. He did all in his power to encourage and fortify her, telling her he had spoken to his Grace and urged every motive likely to secure his protection for the rising Institute, and that he had also applied to others whom [*sic*] he knew were able to serve her. Yet after having mentioned all this, and the favorable assurances he had received, he repeated to her emphatically for the last time his favorite lesson, "Do not place your confidence in any human being, but place your confidence in God alone." He had furnished the first dormitory in the House of Mercy on its opening, and at his death gave fifty pounds more to the charity.

In the month of June [1828] Miss McAuley began to make Baggot St. her occasional residence, dividing her time between it and the house of her brother-in-law; her two nieces did the same, for they were greatly attached to her, and would not be separated from her. Towards the end of the same month Miss Warde also began to reside occasionally, though the house was still in quite an unfinished state, and in the October following she assumed the black dress and cap, and became a resident member.

When the Foundress took up her abode in Baggot St., she perceived that the poor young women protected in the House of Mercy were still exposed to many dangers by being out so late after laboring all day for their scanty subsistence, and felt that her mission would not be fulfilled until she should have completely secured them. Her ingenious charity then suggested to her to adopt the plan of sending two of the school children in whom she could confide to the principal inhabitants in the neighbourhood with an appeal in behalf of those industriously inclined, but destitute persons. A very trifling donation was requested, and in so many cases granted, that sufficient means were had to support as many as the House could accommodate at that time (about 30). There were, as might be expected, a good many refusals, and some of them given in rather unmeasured terms; on such occasions she would animate her associates, telling them not to be troubled or disheartened; and would playfully say that when they personated the poor, whose claims they advocated, they should expect sometimes to receive the treatment of beggars.

On the 24th of September this year [1828], Archbishop Murray most kindly granted permission to have the new Institute styled "of our Blessed Lady of Mercy"; and on the 22nd of November following, to the inexpressible happiness of her Aunt, he received her beloved niece Mary Macauley into the Holy Catholic Church; the ceremony was private, and performed in the Sacristy adjoining the new unfinished chapel. On the same day his Grace gave leave for the visitation of the sick,[33] which was commenced on the 30th of November, the Feast of St. Andrew, he being the Patron Saint of the Parish. The outdoor costume adopted for winter was a coarse grey cloak with a hood, a black silk bonnet, and black muslin veil; in summer the cloak was replaced by a black rock-spun shawl.

It was not permitted at this time for the members of any religious body in Dublin to visit the public hospitals. Miss McAuley wished to remedy this evil, and knowing that the greater number of the patients received into these hospitals were Roman Catholics, she resolved to make an effort to gain access to them for the purpose of communicating instruction and consolation. As she knew that persons would more willingly accede to the request of those who occupied a good position in society, rather than to that made by individuals of humble rank, she resolved for the furtherance of the object she had in view to make her first visits in her own carriage. This she did, not from any motive of ostentation or display, but from a wish to remove the obstacles the world might raise to the fulfilment of her charitable designs; she wished to vanquish the world's prejudices with its own weapons, and having happily succeeded, she disposed of her carriage in the course of a few months and never resumed it again. Her first visit in this way was to Sir Patrick Dunne's [*sic*] hospital where one of her Protestant friends was head physician. She was accompanied by three of her associates, and while one or two of the governors brought her through the establishment, and showed her several objects of curiosity as the means[34] which modern science has employed for the mitigation of human pain, her young friends were dispersed through the wards ministering comfort to the patients. In the course of conversation she took an opportunity of asking whether there would be any objection on the part of the managers to her visiting from time to time, for the purpose of imparting religious consolation to the poor suffering inmates; the reply was that not the smallest objection should be thrown in her way, and that she was perfectly welcome to visit the patients as often as she wished to do so. She paid a similar visit to Mercer's Hospital and met with the same success.

In December another associate was added to their numbers: Miss Anne O'Grady, niece to the Revd. M[r]. McCormack, who, ever since he had prepared Mrs. Macauley for death, took a deep interest in her sister's undertaking, and now brought his niece, a most zealous, pious young lady to assist in the good work.

The Christmas dinner this year attracted much attention; it was liberally contributed to by many charitable persons in the neighbourhood. Some sent beef, others fruit, etc. Several of the highest Protestants as well as Catholics attended, and kindly assisted in carving for the poor children. The next day a Lottery of fancy work was held, the proceeds of which were so considerable that great hopes were entertained of being able to continue the support of the young women in the House of Mercy.

In the beginning of the year 1829 a circumstance occurred which brought forcibly to Miss McAuley's mind the sad fate of the poor girl alluded to earlier in her life, and which confirmed her in the resolution she had formed in consequence, of never allowing the House of Mercy to be subject to the interference of a non-resident committee; at the same time she determined not to refuse re-admission to any who were deserving and who had previously received protection in it. Late one evening in answer to a violent ring, the door, secured by a chain, was cautiously opened and admitted the flushed face of a very young girl who implored shelter for the night, saying she had travelled a very long distance on foot, and knew no one in Dublin. The wild glare of her large dark eyes, and the disorder of her hair and dress naturally excited unfavorable suspicions, but as she was evidently in great distress, Miss McAuley would not refuse her relief. So she was brought into the hall and had some bread and milk given her. She then, though very incoherently for she was stupefied with fatigue, hunger and terror, told her name, and how on account of a quarrel with a severe stepmother she had run out of her father's house; when not knowing in what manner to retrieve this imprudence she had walked all the way to Dublin in the hope of getting into some house of refuge in the city. On her arrival she made application to one, but the good woman who answered her knock at the door told her that unfortunately there existed not the slightest chance of her obtaining admission, so strict were the regulations. In vain did she declare that she knew no one in Dublin, that she had no home to go to, and no one to give her even a morsel of bread. In the anguish of her mind, and the utter hopelessness of her position, she asked whether if she remained at the street door till morning there would be any chance of her being then admitted, but there was still no hope held out as it was not the day on which the committee assembled to attend to such applications. She continued importuning so piteously that at last she was recommended to make application to the house in Baggot St. Miss McAuley heard her account, and though she did not give implicit credence to it all, she yet thought it would be prudent to give her shelter for the night. In the morning one of the associates happened accidentally to see the poor girl, and recognized her immediately as one with whom she had been previously acquainted. The father of the young person, she said, was an attorney who had married a second time; the introduction of a stepmother was not very agreeable to his family, particularly to the grown up daughters, and in all probability it was the dissension arising from this circumstance that had led this young girl to the rash step she had taken. On enquiry, her story was found to be true, she was allowed to remain in Baggot St. for some months, and was then provided with a situation as governess in a respectable family; in which, however, she did not long remain, as her father forgave her and took her home.

In February this year Dr. Macauley died of ulcerated sore throat attended with fever, having been not quite three days ill.[35] His pious sister-in-law made every effort to induce him to embrace the true Faith, but could not prevail; though to the surprise of all by an express clause in his will he left his children at perfect liberty to choose for themselves on the important subject of religion, and also to select as guardian either their Aunt or her brother Dr. James McAuley who continued a Protestant. They unhesitatingly chose their Aunt, who then removed permanently to Baggot St., taking with her [her] two nieces; her nephews she placed in Carlow College, for they like their sisters were determined to be Catholics.

When she became a permanent resident she found the necessity of establishing a certain degree of uniformity in the daily exercises. She appointed fixed duties for the different hours of the day. The Sisters, as they now called themselves (each of whom had assumed the black dress etc. selected at the commencement), rose early and had regular devout exercises of prayer and spiritual reading. Although these were of considerable length they did not suffice for Miss McAuley's devotion, who besides private meditations used to rise earlier than the rest with one or two of the Sisters to say the whole of her favorite Psalter,[36] and read some spiritual book. One of these Sisters had volunteered to be caller, and it frequently happened that mistaking the hour in the Winter mornings, she used to call at three o'clock instead of half past four, the hour they had proposed to rise at. On these occasions Miss McAuley would fill up the intervening time by selecting and transcribing from pious books certain passages that might be useful for the instruction and consolation of the sick poor. She had made a good collection of them when one day while searching for some document in her desk, near which was a lighted candle, her manuscript happened to catch fire which she did not perceive until it was too late to save it. Yet she never expressed the least annoyance at losing what had cost her so much labor.

Besides regulating the Sisters' time, she introduced a regular system for the inmates of the House of Mercy. On account of some acts of petty pilfering and other little irregularities, it was now found necessary to put an end to the indiscriminate admission of strangers to prayer in the work room. The first article missed was the chair on which Miss McAuley usually sat, and it was taken one day on which she had been congratulating with her companions on the honesty of their poor visiters, and that though they had so long kept open house nothing had been stolen. Therefore while she still continued to allow numbers to come and join in prayer, and receive partial subsistence, she resolved to have a room apart for themselves in order to guard against the danger of persons of exceptionable character mixing with the inmates of the House of Mercy—which exclusively protected persons of irreproachable lives.

In Easter week this year a Bazaar was held for the Institution in Morrison's Hotel, the proprietor most charitably gave the use of his rooms gratis, and the ladies who presided at tables exerted themselves so zealously that they realized nearly three hundred pounds.

The works that God has specially favored, and which He has destined to be the means of great and enduring good, have, almost always, been humble and unpretending in the beginning; they have also been exposed to trial and opposition. It was thus with His Church, it was thus with the Religious Institutions of many an age, and thus also it was to be with the House of our Lady of Mercy. Miss McAuley had to endure much unkindness and opposition from many. Our Saviour says that a man's enemies are those of his own household, and her trial arose chiefly from the misconceptions of Catholics, whose piety and benevolence engaged them in similar pursuits, and who dreaded lest this new Establishment should divert the public attention from those objects in which they took an interest. Several Clergymen made no secret of their dissatisfaction, though obliged to confess that it was not grounded on any mismanagement that had come to their knowledge, but on an opinion that hereafter evil consequences might ensue from some arrangements which were not such as they thought advisable. It may be, and in charity we are bound to think, that those who thus expressed themselves thought they were doing well in censuring and condemning an undertaking which they deemed dangerous or unsafe; nevertheless it was very painful to one who had made such disinterested sacrifices, to hear disapproval from any, particularly from those whose zeal for the Divine glory, and charity for the suffering poor, she considered to be greater than her own. This contradiction continued for a long time to thwart and impede as far as it could the object and progress of the Establishment, but God watched over it and brought it to a prosperous issue.

Depressed very much by the opposition she encountered, and fearing in her humility lest it may be an intimation from above, that her designs however well meant were not approved by God, she sought advice from her ecclesiastical superior to guide and comfort her in the difficulty. His Grace the Most Revd. Dr. Murray had been from the beginning her sincere friend; he was also the person to whom Religion bade her have recourse, and whose authority was to be in her regard even as the authority of God. She felt that if he sanctioned her undertaking, it mattered little what others said or did; if he objected to the Establishment it was to be a sign that her views and undertakings had not been dictated by the Spirit of God; accordingly she sought an interview with him and laid before him the nature of her benevolent foundation, the objects she sought to accomplish, and the methods by which those objects were to be attained. She said that fame, or distinction, or notoriety she sought not; she wished not to interfere with any others that may be laboring in the same field, and offered to resign into his hands the house she had nearly completed, for any purposes of Religion he wished, asking for herself some apartment in the house, and the merit of laboring in any capacity, however humble, to carry out his charitable intentions. No one could have better appreciated the generosity of such an offer than the prelate to whom it was made. He knew her worth, and had no difficulty in perceiving that her conduct throughout had been entirely influenced by the purest and most devoted charity. To her proposal of committing the Establishment to the care of some one of the religious Institutions in Dublin,[37] he answered in the most decided negative; he felt that the same benevolent spirit to which it was indebted for its existence would best preside over its subsequent workings, and conduct it to eventual success. Every good work, he said, was destined to be opposed and contradicted, and for trials she should be prepared.

Meanwhile the interior of the building was progressing, one part after another being finished as it was required. At length the wing which contained the Chapel was begun to be set in order, as great inconvenience arose from so large a number as were now in the house going out to a public Church. Very Revd. Dr. Blake who had but lately returned from Rome kindly presented a painting of the Blessed Virgin and Divine Infant as an Altar piece. His long absence had in no way abated his friendship for Miss McAuley; he still took the same interest in her works and offered himself to assist as far as was in his power.

On the Octave day of the Ascension of our Lord the Chapel was dedicated by the Archbishop under the invocation of "Our Lady of Mercy". There was Pontifical High Mass on the occasion, and Very Revd. Dr. Blake preached a brilliant sermon in which he highly eulogized the Foundress (who was not present, having remained in prayer within the house) and prognosticated much lasting good from the infant Establishment. In alluding to the opposition she had to contend with, he said, "I look on Miss McAuley as one selected by Heaven to be specially endowed with benediction; her heart is overflowing with the charity of the Redeemer, whose all consuming fire burns within her. No female has ever done more for sorrowing, suffering humanity than she has done. She may well rejoice over those whom she has been instrumental in snatching from the enemy's grasp; and confidently claim a blessing from Heaven on her future exertions. I would venture to say her name is written in the Book of Life, and I feel convinced that any individual in society presuming by word or deed to injure her Establishment will draw down on himself the lash, the scourge of the Almighty even in this world." This prediction was unhappily realized in one instance soon after.

At the déjeuner[38] prepared for the strangers present some unpleasant feelings were manifested. Many enquiries were made as to who was this very extraordinary person Dr. Blake mentioned; amongst others to whom this question was addressed was a Clergyman, whose answer indicated anything but a concurrence with the sentiments of the preacher; in fact he said a great deal that showed he neither liked the Foundress nor the Establishment. As soon as he ceased speaking another Clergyman who stood listening turned to one of the Sisters who was near—and who appeared in the greatest surprise and confusion at this angry oration—and asked her if she were not one of the members; on her replying in the affirmative, "Then my dear," said he, "have the goodness to assure Miss McAuley of my respect for her, and my good wishes for the prosperity [of the] Institution; I am but a poor Priest, yet I will contribute my mite, I wish I could do more"; he gave her a sovereign. There was no more said on the subject just then, but a day or two after, Miss McAuley received an anonymous note containing the most mortifying and insulting strictures on her proceedings; she knew the hand writing, and so did Dr. Blake to whom she showed it.

Another evidence of displeasure excited on the morning of the dedication was very convenient to the Establishment, and rather amusing. The trustees of the Protestant house of refuge which was next door, had previously refused to permit that the par[t]y wall which divided their premises should be raised tho' it had been proposed to do it without any expense to them. The wall was extremely low, and the ceremonial of the dedication having required that his Grace should pass down the walk beside that wall, the inmates protected in the Asylum could not be prevented from looking on, which circumstance, joined to the horror excited by a large quantity of holy water having passed over their low boundary, forced the unaccommodating neighbours to set about raising the wall themselves the very next morning.

Before the Archbishop left the house on the day of the dedication, he gave permission to have the Chapel opened to the public, and recommended that a gallery should be erected, saying that the collection would pay the expense, and help to support the inmates of the House of Mercy. He also appointed a Chaplain, the Revd. D. Burke of the Order of St. Francis, who entered on his duties, and said Mass in the new Chapel of our Lady of Mercy, on the following Sunday, June 7th, it being the Feast of Pentecost. From this time forward the Sisters no longer went out to Mass or other religious duties, which they had hitherto attended in the Carmelite Church of St. Teresa, Clarendon Street; and their ordinary Confessor, Very Revd. R. O'Hanlon, then provincial of the Carmelites, went on the appointed days to Baggot St.

The Institute has ever been much indebted to the Order of Carmelites who from the commencement never failed to give every possible assistance, and for a long time supplied vestments and other requisites for the Chapel.

There was now Mass on every week day, and two on Sundays and Holidays; this was considered a great convenience by the inhabitants of the neighbourhood who showed their appreciation of the benefit by their contributions, which enabled an increased number to be supported in the House of Mercy. On the Feast of the Sacred Heart of Jesus, the Sodality of the Sacred Heart was erected in the Chapel.

The following month, July, Miss Marcella Flyn[n] was introduced by Very Revd. Dr. Blake and numbered among the Sisters. On the eighth of the ensuing September, the Feast of the Nativity of the Blessed Virgin, Miss Margaret Dunne entered. This lady admired the rising Institute and liked all its duties, but wishing to dedicate herself to God for life, she was at first deterred from entering a house which she feared would have no stability until encouraged to do so by two or three Clergymen who assured her it would ultimately settle into a Religious Institute. Her feelings were in many respects similar to the two first associates, each of whom had an earnest desire to become a Religious; Miss Byrne was only withheld by circumstances from entering the Order of St. Dom[i]nick, which she eventually did, when these obstacles were removed.

On the twenty second of November Miss McAuley was rejoiced by the request of her beloved niece, Mary Macauley, to be admitted a member of the little community. She had adhered to her Aunt in her various struggles, taken a part in her works of charity, embraced the Catholic Faith, and finally on this the anniversary of her reception into the Church, resolved to devote herself and talents to the glory of God and the interests of Religion. Her example was followed on the ninth of December by Miss Elizabeth Harley who, it will be remembered, began to attend the schools at the same time as her friend Miss Warde. Miss Harley made the ninth member, and with her closed the admissions of the year 1829.

With the year 1830 began a new era. Everything was going on prosperously; the annual Bazaar, which was held in Easter week in the round room of the Rotunda, was very productive; the schools were crowded; the House of Mercy had proved an asylum for many young persons, and created universal interest; the benefits arising to society from the protection and recommendation of servants was [*sic*] duly appreciated; still the Catholic visiter, however much he may value its services, and be edified by the piety of its members, must have missed the religious character which should ever pervade similar establishments, and the religious organization which alone can give stability and efficiency to its operations. It was at best but the work of private charity, presided over by individual zeal, and dependent for its continuance on the good will of her to whom it was indebted for its existence. It must necessarily be insecure if those whose labors should uphold it were to continue merely an association of seculars, bound together by no bond, save their mutual regard, and an abstract love of doing good; whose fervor or caprice might find sanctuary in a convent, or solace in the enjoyments of the world. No one was more sensible of these defects than Miss McAuley herself, and no one more ardently desired to have them remedied.

Many well disposed Catholics had taken offence at the strange and unusual appearance which the Establishment presented; it was observed that it had assumed a religious character without having any claim to it; it was neither a convent, nor a private house; neither a religious community, nor yet a public Establishment. Remonstrances were made to the Foundress by friends, as well as by those who were by no means friendly, sometimes in the language of kind and well meant expostulation, and not unfrequently in terms of unqualified disapproval. She often received by post letters written and addressed in the most insulting manner. For her own part she could have borne it all in patience, and found strength and consolation in prayer to Him who was Himself insulted and reviled, and who has said to His followers, "Blessed are ye when they shall revile you, and persecute you, and speak all that is evil against you untruly for my sake; be glad and rejoice for your reward is very great in Heaven." Matt. v. 11. But she would not that those who were united with her in the sacred work of charity should suffer also, nor that the Institution at which she had labored so long and anxiously, and at such expense, should be injured in the public estimation, and be thereby obstructed in its career of usefulness. She therefore applied to his Grace to take the house and its associates under his immediate protection, and give them whatever religious form he might deem advisable; and though at the time he seemed not to heed her application, he afterwards showed that he had by no means lost sight of it altogether.

In the midst of these contradictions she received a pledge of the Divine protection by a grant of Indulgences for herself and associates from our Lord's Vicar on earth, his Holiness Pius 8th. It was granted on the twenty third of May, on the application of Very Revd. Dr. Whelan, a father of the Discalced Carmelites, afterwards raised to the Episcopal dignity. The arrival of the Rescript was hailed with joy by the Sisters, who were thereby animated to renewed exertions in their pious labors. They were joined on the tenth of June following by Miss Georgiana Moore, and on the eighteenth of the same month by Miss Caroline Murphy; these were followed by Miss Mary Anne Delany, who entered on the twelfth of July. In this same month Very Revd. Dr. Blake requested Miss McAuley to visit Miss Marianne Redmond, who was suffering from white swelling in the knee. Though wealthy, this young lady was peculiarly unprotected, for she had no friends in Dublin whither she had come accompanied only by an inexperienced young girl, her cousin, and an old country nurse; her parents being both dead. The most eminent physicians and surgeons attended her with so little success that amputation was soon judged necessary. Dr. Blake pitying her lonely situation entreated that she would be permitted to remove to Baggot St. in order that the operation might be performed there. This being acceded to, she was accommodated with a large room in the centre of the house; two of the Sisters[39] remained with her during the amputation. For the month this young person stayed in the house Miss McAuley watched over her day and night with the solicitude of a mother, and neither sought nor received any remuneration for the expense and inconvenience attendant on such a serious illness. The poor patient removed a little way into the country, where she lingered for some time in great agony and died; and strange to say, though she bequeathed some legacies for charitable purposes she forgot to mention the Establishment to which she owed so much.

About this time Almighty God permitted the former complaints and murmurs to be renewed with increased vigor, and laid before the Archbishop, and though that wise and enlightened prelate saw the inconvenience of adopting singularity of costume, with many of the observances of religious life, yet he would by no means stop the progress of the good work. While disapprobation was at the highest on the part of those who were anxious for religious discipline and fearful of innovations, one more zealous than the rest called on the Foundress to tell her that Dr. Murray thought of giving up the Establishment entirely to the Sisters of Charity; but that she might retain apartments and a private entrance. This intelligence pained her, but she prepared to submit with peaceful resignation considering that as she had transferred her right over the house to his Grace, she ought to acquiesce in his disposal of it; yet she could not conceal from herself that it would be a sensible affliction to her to separate from the pious associates of her charitable labors. However, rising superior to mere human feeling, she meekly replied, that the Archbishop could dispose of the house as he considered best. On the departure of the visiter she wrote to his Grace relating what had happened, and saying that if such were his determination she would acquiesce. He called on her next day and informed her that he had not commissioned any person to make such a communication, that he had no idea of putting any obstacle to her benevolent intentions, but he added in allusion to the title "Sisters of Mercy" being adopted, "The notion of a Convent starting up of itself in this manner never entered my mind." The coldness of his manner troubled her, and in her affliction she sought advice from her old and tried friend Very Revd. Dr. Blake; he went on her behalf to the Archbishop, and the result of the conference was that the house would not be suffered to continue as it then was; that its inmates should either appear as secular ladies, or become religious; they unanimously chose the latter, and in a few days his Grace announced his determination to meet their wishes, and at once invest the Establishment with a solemn religious character. With a view to this he gave Miss McAuley permission to examine the Rules of the different Religious Orders then established in Dublin, that she might select that most suited to her designs. She sent to the Mother Superior of each, to beg she would lend a copy. The greater number most kindly complied with her request; the Carmelites and Poor Clares even offered to affiliate the house to their Order. She laid all before her companions, and read for them the several Rules. After mature deliberation she and they decided that among those submitted to them that of the Presentation Order was most in accordance with their vocation, and that they were willing to adopt it with modifications suited to the performance of the duties they had undertaken, and which were to form the characteristics of the new Institute. Dr. Murray had promised that they could go through a novitiate in a Convent of whatever Order should be decided on, and application was accordingly made at the Presentation Convent, George's Hill, for the Foundress and two other Sisters to serve it there. The request was most willingly acceded to, and immediate preparations were made.[40]

Before leaving Baggot St. she made every arrangement likely to promote order and stability, appointing to the Sisters their respective charges. The assistance of secular ladies was henceforth to be declined; and, except in particular cases, strangers were not to be shown through the house; the windows were entirely muffed. It was arranged that she should be informed of all that passed in the Establishment and that business of importance should be referred to her decision. Then after many exhortations to act always with charity, humility, fervor and prudence, and having procured for them the advice and instruction of holy and enlightened Clergymen during her absence, she took leave of her little Community, and on the eighth of September, the Feast of our Blessed Lady's Nativity, entered the Presentation Convent, George's Hill, taking with her Miss Doyle and Miss Harley as her companions in the Novitiate. They were clothed with the Holy Habit on the ninth of December following, the usual time of probation being shortened in their regard to the term prescribed by the Canons of the Church. The names given them at their Reception were Teresa, Clare, and Angela, which gave the humble Foundress some uneasiness, lest it might seem that they ranked themselves with any of the Saints after whom they were called. She therefore earnestly begged that they might be permitted to retain their own names, with the addition of "Mary"; which was granted at Profession.

Owing to her advanced age, she found great difficulty in conforming to the usual restraints of conventual life, but she offered herself unreservedly to God to do and suffer all He should appoint in order to accomplish the work which she felt He had marked out for her. During her novitiate she evinced the naturally happy disposition of her mind in cheerfully submitting to trials which she felt very sensibly. She made the virtues of humility and poverty her special study; in this she was aided by her wise and zealous Mistress, who, reflecting that the time was short and the proposed work arduous, spared no pains to lay a deep and solid foundation of humility. To exercise her in this virtue she often reprimanded her publicly and severely for the most trifling omission or inadvertent fault. These reproofs and trials were far from disturbing the serenity of her mind; she knew the motive whence they originated, and earnestly devoted herself to acquire the virtues peculiar to the religious state. She afterwards often said that during no time of her life was she so happy as when a novice, and were she permitted to have a choice it would be to continue always living under obedience, rather than to have the government of others.

She suffered much solicitude for her dear spiritual children in Baggot St. who undertook more labors for the poor than their strength was able for, and mistaking the real nature of religious mortification some addicted themselves to fasts of supererogation, others wore hair-cloth, used the discipline, and remained in prayer during hours of the time appointed for rest, not considering that the fatigue attending the duties of the Institute was in itself a most salutary mortification, and that by their want of spiritual discretion in thus undertaking supererogatory works more than was recommended, they effectually incapacitated themselves for the performance of those that were obligatory. Three of them became dangerously ill; one of these, Sister Caroline Murphy, had concealed her illness until it was too late to remedy it, and even then rather admitted than made it known. She was very beautiful and engaging in the eyes of the world, but still more lovely and precious in the sight of Him whom by a private vow she, even in her childhood, had chosen for her spouse. For the short time she resided in the house her piety and uniform practice of performing each duty in the most perfect manner, edified and endeared her to every member of the community; she practised an entire obedience to all, and on all occasions with cheerful alacrity, though as yet there was no obligation to it. She rejoiced in humiliations, nor is it a mere form of words to say that she loved the meanest offices, for she selected them in preference to all others; many of her humiliations were not known till after her death. When she was no longer able to go through her accustomed duties and perceived her mortal labors were nearly at a close (having got rapid consumption), she prepared for death with the same joyful conformity as had distinguished her during life. She made a general confession and received the last Sacraments on the twenty fourth of June, Feast of St. John the Baptist, and expired on the twenty eighth in sentiments of piety which edified and surprised not only her companions, but also the Confessor and Chaplain who knelt beside her in her dying moments. She was buried in the habit of the third order of Carmelites and laid in the vault of the Church of St. Teresa, Clarendon St.

The death of this dear Sister was followed by the serious illness of Sister Anne O'Grady, who also sank under excessive exertion made in the heat of Summer. She was indefatigable in every work of mercy, her ardent zeal led her to labor beyond her strength, and in August her case was pronounced hopeless, yet she lingered on six months in great suffering. Before her death she had the consolation of again seeing and experiencing the tender care of her beloved mother in Christ, who when at a distance was overwhelmed with grief and anxiety for her dying child. While thus a prey to anxious suspense Miss McAuley had to endure the additional pang of hearing that her much cherished niece had burst a blood vessel and was dangerously ill; but it pleased God she should rally though only for a time.

Along with these exterior trials she suffered intense anxiety respecting her own and companions' admission to holy Profession, as some of the Religious at George's Hill entertained doubts that they would be justified in permitting those to make Profession who were not to live exactly according to their Institute. These doubts transpired and she feared they would influence in the final Chapter to be held for their Profession. In this trouble the Archbishop comforted her, telling her to keep her mind in peace for even if what she feared should come to pass, he would himself admit her to holy Profession, if her religious Superiors could assure him that she had been humble and obedient during her novitiate. He also took on himself the responsibility of seeing that she had so disposed of her property as to be truly poor at the time of Profession; for which considerate kindness she ever felt most grateful, as it prevented the necessity of making known to others, not concerned, the amount and appropriation of the funds of her Establishment.

In the mean time the number of the Sisters in Baggot St. was increased by the entrance of two: Miss Mary Jones and Miss Anne Carroll; the former entered in May; the latter, who was niece to one of the Community in George's Hill, in June. Miss Jones had become a Catholic only a short time previously; she was a native of Bridgenorth in North Wales, and had not even a Catholic acquaintance, but a circumstance which happened in her childhood recurred so often to her mind as she grew up that she could enjoy no peace till she got an explanation. When a very small child she got hooping [*sic*] cough and her mother sent her in care of a domestic to a priest who lived several miles off to beg he would give her a drink out of a chalice, as she considered it would cure her. Her request was complied with, and Miss Jones never forgot the chalice, but she could get no information concerning it nor the priest (there being no Catholics in her part of the country), except that it was used in Catholic worship, and that he was a Catholic. After many years she was taken on a visit to some friends in London, who in showing her all the objects of interest among other places took her to a Catholic Church. There she recognised a chalice similar to that seen in her childhood, and having now an opportunity of satisfying herself on the subject of her long and anxious enquiry she applied for instruction and became convinced of the truth of the Catholic doctrine. On her return to Bridgenorth she mentioned what had occurred and the change that had taken place in her religious opinions, at which her family were much surprised and troubled, but seeing her happiness depended on it, they gave her permission to return to London to be received into the Church, and soon after consented to her entering the new Establishment in Baggot St. to which her attention was drawn by some newspaper publication.

As the time drew near for the final Chapter that was to decide the Profession or dismissal of Miss McA. and her companions, she could not divest herself of anxiety, notwithstanding the Archbishop's kind assurance, and great was her joy when after an unusually long deliberation she learned the decision was favorable. On the twelfth of December 1831 they made their Religious Profession according to the Rule of the Presentation Order, with a clause that it was subject to whatever alterations should be deemed necessary by Archbishop Murray, who had received full power from the Holy See for the establishment of the new Institute; and from this day its foundation is dated.

Soon after the ceremony the newly professed Sisters were conducted home by Very Revd. Dr. Blake to the heartfelt joy of the little community in Baggot St.

On the following day they were visited by his Grace, who appointed Mrs. McAuley (as we shall now call her) Mother Superior.[41] On that occasion she asked him what Rule they should observe pending the proposed alterations. Opening the book of the Presentation Rule and pointing to the chapter "On Union and Charity", he said, "If they observe *that,* it will suffice." She immediately applied herself to draw up a regular distribution of time and of spiritual exercises. The Archbishop approved of these arrangements, except that he desired there should be a short recreation after dinner, which she had omitted, intending that the Sisters should labor all day like the poor, and have their rest and recreation after their work was finished.

The first public lecture she read after being appointed Mother Superior was the tenth chapter of Rodriguez "On Obedience", which is an explanation of St. Paul's words, "Obey your prelates and be subject to them, for they watch as being to render an account of your souls . . . that they may do this with joy and not with grief." Heb. xiii. 17.[42] She used often expatiate on this latter part, earnestly exhorting and entreating all to acquit themselves of the duty of obedience, not only perfectly, as regarded the performance of the precept and because it was the will of God, but likewise with such alacrity and cheerfulness as would be calculated to lighten rather than increase the weight that devolves on Superiors.

She was also most solicitous that silence should be observed with the utmost exactness, and that the Sisters should be most punctual in attending all the community exercises, as she felt convinced that future regularity depended in a great measure on a good and fervent beginning. But while she thus showed her zeal for the perfection of those confided to her charge, she was equally careful to be herself a model of regular observance, and in order that she might have the advantage of practising submission she enjoined one of the Sisters to tell her of any fault or omission of duty she might perceive.

The Archbishop having given permission that those who were considered fit among the postulants that had been in Baggot St. during her absence might receive the holy Habit of Religion, she made choice of seven, and his Grace performed the ceremony of their Reception on the twenty third of January 1832. This being the first ceremony excited considerable interest, and great numbers applied for permission to witness it; but on account of the approaching death of Sister Anne O'Grady, no seculars were admitted. This caused much dissatisfaction, so much that one of the Sisters received was removed by her mother to another Convent in a few days. This trial was followed by the death of Sister Anne O'Grady which took place on the seventh of February.[43] She was interred in the same vault with Sister Caroline Murphy, which was then set apart as a burial place for the Sisters by the ever kind and charitable Fathers.

Very soon the young Community had the additional pang of losing one of its most valued and useful members, Sister Mary Elizabeth Harley, one of the three professed in George's Hill. During her novitiate she had suffered much from delicacy but her fervent spirit concealed or disregarded the sufferings under which she labored; she neither omitted any of her duties, nor sought any relaxation from her severe and trying occupations. Shortly after her Profession the disease that had been working its way in secrecy and silence developed itself in a manner that admitted of no concealment, and that bid defiance to any remedy. Confirmed and rapid consumption marked her as its victim, and neither the skill of the physician nor the tears and prayers of an afflicted and affectionate sisterhood could check the rapid progress of the disease. Revd. Mother had hoped that this Sister would have proved most valuable in assisting to establish the rising Institute, but God ordained otherwise. During the illness of Sister Anne O'Grady she said to one of the other Sisters, that she formerly thought it would be a blessing to have so much time as lingering consumption affords for preparing to appear before God, but she added, "Now that I see how much the mind is weakened, I hope Almighty God will permit that my last illness may be short." And it would seem that He was pleased to hear her prayer, for she was only a few weeks suffering, and was able to be at Mass and Holy Communion on Easter Sunday, though she died on the following Wednesday, April 25th 1832. She enjoyed the perfect use of her faculties to the last moment of her life, and received the last Sacraments about three hours before her death. Such was the simplicity of her obedience that Revd. Mother having said on being called away from her about an hour before her death, "Now my dearest child, say nothing but 'Jesus, Mary, and Joseph, assist me in my last agony'," she found her on her return still repeating the same words, nor would she, without asking permission, make any other prayer.

Mrs. McAuley's religious feelings were severely tested that day. She was obliged to dissemble her grief and attend to secular business, in consequence of a Bazaar which she had undertaken for the relief of the poor. This caused her to have much communication with those who interested themselves in the charity, and with others too who disapproved of her plans. It happened that a lady[44] called for her to condemn her conduct in severe terms, at the very time Sister Mary Elizabeth was in her agony. Revd. Mother listened humbly and silently without offering to justify herself, she did not even try to put a stop to so unpleasant a scene by saying that a cherished Sister was then dying in the house; and Almighty God, as if to reward her patience and humility, so touched the person who had been reproving her that on rising to go away she handed her fifteen pounds for the poor. Sister M. Elizabeth's death was a great affliction to the whole Community, but Revd. Mother, who was always averse to any great manifestation of feeling, encouraged them to bear up cheerfully under it; for this purpose she repeated aloud, "This is the day which the Lord hath made, let us be glad and rejoice therein," reminding them that the trial came from God, whose will we ought not only to obey, but love with our whole hearts.

After the Community received a Religious form it began to increase rapidly; Revd. Mother, who spared herself in nothing, retained the charge of the Novices, and continued it for three or four years; the only office she got filled being that of Mother Assistant, for which she proposed Sister Mary Anne Doyle, who was confirmed in the office by his Grace.

Her exhortations were most animating and impressive, especially on the virtues of humility and charity. These were her characteristic virtues, and on St. Paul's description of charity she loved to expatiate, most earnestly striving to reduce it to practise herself, and induce all under her charge to do the same. She loved all, and sought to do good to all, but the poor and little children were her special favorites; these she labored to instruct, relieve, and console in every possible way. She taught the Sisters to avoid all that might be in the least contrary to charity, even the slightest remark on manner, natural defects, etc., so that they should make it a rule never to say anything unfavorable of each other. She was not content with their avoiding the smallest faults against this favorite virtue of our Blessed Lord; she wished their whole conduct should evince that this virtue reigned in their hearts. She instructed them to be always ready to yield and condescend to others, and to observe in speaking mildness and great sweetness. On this subject her maxim was, that a religious should never allege as excuse for saying what might give pain, even unintentionally, "I did not recollect"; she should be always recollected, every word uttered by her ought to edify, at least no word should escape her which could disedify. Her lessons on charity and humility being supported by her own unvarying example necessarily made a deep impression on the minds of her spiritual children. The least shadow of pride was odious to her; she told them that their very tone of voice and manner of walking should be humble and subdued; that they should carefully shun speaking of themselves or of their works, and to try as far as possible to banish the words "me" or "myself" from their conversation; that they should never attribute anything to themselves but faults and imperfections, sincerely acknowledging that they were not merely incapable of promoting the good in which the Almighty deigned to employ them, but that by their unworthiness they were calculated to obstruct its accomplishment. She loved to dwell on those words of our Divine Lord: "Learn of me, because I am meek and humble of heart," saying if His blessed words ought to be reverenced by all, with what loving devotion should the Religious lay them up in her heart, and try to reduce them to practise. Her own feelings of self-abasement she carried, it might be said, too far; in trifling matters she allowed any of the Sisters to guide and direct her, and would good humouredly call those who perhaps had been rather importunate "her mistresses". When founding convents she would not take precedence of the Sister appointed Mother Superior, tho' as Foundress she might reasonably have done so.[45] She singularly loved simplicity in all and practised it herself, telling the Sisters to adopt a simple style of speaking and writing, and when translating any work she would tell them always to use simple, easy words, and never to affect worldly manners or expressions, nor those which are too decided. Her niece saying once in an anxious tone, she hoped something would occur, she checked her saying, "The hopes and fears of a religious ought to be centred in God." If a Sister said casually, "I hate such or such a thing", she would remark,

"We ought to hate nothing but sin." Even in piety she disapproved of high flown aspirations or sentences; to a novice who was writing something very exalted in that way, she observed how much more suitable those simple phrases found in ordinary prayers would be, and then suggested a favorite of her own, "Mortify in me, dear Jesus, all that displeases Thee, and make me according to Thine own heart's desire."

Fidelity to the inspirations of grace was a lesson she frequently and earnestly inculcated, showing how important and necessary it was that they should listen attentively to that Divine voice which silently and constantly whispers to the heart of the religious, telling her how she may please the Heavenly Spouse of her soul, now by avoiding some slight fault, that self-love or self-indulgence prompts her to commit; again by practising those apparently trifling acts of humility, charity, patience, etc., of which the daily occurrences of life present occasions, and which from their very nature and unobtrusive character are unlikely to attract human applause, while they are of special value in the sight of God. She was particularly desirous that they should adopt the practice of small acts of mortification, for example, in the refectory, saying they ought never let any meal pass without denying themselves in something (being careful not to injure their health or strength), and that these mortifications were often of far greater value before God, and caused Him to bestow more abundant graces than rigid austerities which might spring from or occasion vanity.

She taught them to love the hidden life, laboring on silently for God alone; she had a great dislike to noise and display in the performance of duties. Often she was heard to say, "How quietly the great God does all His mighty works; darkness is spread over us, and light breaks in again, and there is no noise of drawing curtains or closing shutters." Again she would say, "How silently and brilliantly the lamp in the Sanctuary burns, before the Most Holy Sacrament, when the oil is pure and good; it is only when it is otherwise that it twinkles and makes noise." She had a remarkable talent for thus drawing instruction from every occurrence, and made useful reflections on all passing events which she taught all subject to her likewise to do, and to derive spiritual profit from all.

When the cholera was raging in Dublin [in] 1832 Mrs. McAuley was solicited by the board of health to attend the great cholera hospital fitted up in Townsend Street. Having obtained the Archbishop's permission and approval she joyfully entered on her labors there, and scarcely left the hospital the entire day, though she had the remainder of the community to relieve each other every four hours. The distress of the poor this year being necessarily augmented, she redoubled her exertions to relieve them. The spirit of mercy and compassion for them which animated her made her sometimes adopt plans which to some would appear to exceed the limits of prudence; but the success with which her undertakings were usually attended evinced that she was guided by a Heavenly wisdom. When preparing for the Bazaar she wrote a letter which she sent by post to her Royal Highness the Duchess of Kent entreating that she and the Princess Victoria would give some of their work to be disposed of at it for the relief of the poor. A most gracious answer was returned, and her Royal Highness sent some of her own beautiful work, with drawings and transferred boxes executed by her Royal daughter. This extraordinary contribution was of considerable benefit, and realized a very large sum of money.

Revd. Mother had obtained permission for an annual charity sermon, and in the summer of 1831 the first appeal was made by the late Right Revd. Dr. Kinsella, Bishop of Kilkenny,[46] in the convent chapel, Baggot St., but as the smallness of the chapel admitted only of a limited congregation she had it now arranged with[47] the consent of the Parish Priest that in future the sermon should be preached in the Parish Church on Sexagesima Sunday.

By this time the charitable objects of the Institute began to be rather generally known, and many besides contributing money sent plain-work to be done by the young women of the House of Mercy, the payment for which helped to defray some of the expense of their maintenance. When the number of inmates amounted to between fifty and sixty, Revd. Mother perceived the necessity of adopting some further means of contributing to their support, for the average time of residence being only about four months, and the greater number requiring instruction in almost everything necessary for them to know, they could not consequently earn much; she likewise saw the great good likely to arise from giving constant occupation to such a large number of persons residing together, and therefore set herself to devise some suitable, and at the same time remunerative work. After some deliberation she decided on erecting a building for a public Laundry; but as this was an arduous undertaking and the many calls for immediate support and protection keeping a constant drain on the funds, she had to defer the execution of her project for some years.

The annual retreat this year was conducted by the Revd. M. Gaffney afterwards appointed Dean of Maynooth College.[48] His views entirely according with those of the Foundress, to him the Archbishop confided the charge of assisting her in making the necessary alterations and additions in drawing up the Holy Rule. In the month of October this year the second ceremony of Reception took place, on which occasion four were clothed with the Holy Habit; the Archbishop acted as Celebrant, and the Chapel being opened to seculars on this occasion a large concourse attended.

The first Ceremony of Profession took place the 24th of January 1833, at which the Archbishop also presided. Of the first seven received only four made their vows, namely, Sr. Mary Francis Warde, Sr. Mary Angela Dunne, Sr. Mary Clare Moore and Sr. Mary De Pazzi Delany. Two had gone away to other religious Orders, as before mentioned;[49] and the third, the niece of the Foundress, now called Sr. Mary Teresa, hesitated about making her Profession. For some time past her health had been very precarious, yet her piety often led her to pay but little attention to the suggestions of prudence, and to make exertions which a due regard to the natural delicacy of her constitution should have deterred her from making; her Aunt was often obliged to use her influence, and to make her moderate her austerities and labors. To her timid conscience this exercise of authority looked like an indication from God that she was not called to the state of life in which she was then engaged; because she was not able to do all that her charity and devotion would prompt her to do, or all that she saw the members of the community doing, she persuaded herself that Providence did not wish that she should constitute one of their number. Her Aunt who had ever watched over her with the tenderest solicitude, who knew how zealously and sincerely she was devoted to the service of the poor, and with what single-mindedness she had ever cooperated in all the plans for their welfare, endeavored from time to time to remove this erroneous impression but in vain. Doubts were ever and anon presenting themselves to her mind; she imagined that her incapacity for the active duties of the Institute of Mercy was, as it were, a warning from Heaven to devote herself exclusively to the spirit of pious contemplation, and for the better attainment of that object to become a member of the Order of Carmelites. While in this state of uncertainty, praying for grace to know the Divine Will, and like Saul, exclaiming in the sincerity of her heart, "Lord, what wilt Thou have me to do," the Archbishop came on important business to the convent; her Aunt, having much confidence in his wisdom, requested an interview for her niece. Sister Mary Teresa made known to him her desires, what she wished to do, and what she believed herself capable of doing; his Grace heard her with attention, pointed out to her the advantages and merits to herself and others of the state of life in which she was already engaged, that the Almighty required of her only what her strength and constitution enabled her to do, and said he considered that, without some stronger indication of the Divine Will than what she had already received, it would be rash and insecure for her to turn aside when once she had put her hand to the plough.

After this interview her doubts and fears were altogether removed; her health, indeed, became each day more and more feeble, but each day also her life became more saintly and edifying to the community. Of herself she scarcely seemed to take any heed, but all her solicitude was directed to the wants of others. If she ever thought or spoke of herself it was but to say how unworthy she was of the happiness she enjoyed. One evening walking in the garden of the convent, she happened to see one of the children of the Establishment on the top of a shed, to which she had climbed with childish carelessness, and from which she was every moment in the most imminent danger of falling. In the excess of her anxiety for the poor child's safety, she screamed out to her to take care, and in the effort a second time burst a blood vessel in the lungs. This accident brought with it serious and alarming consequences, consumption set in and made rapid strides. When her recovery became hopeless she was permitted, as is customary in similar instances, to make her Profession upon her dying-bed. After receiving the last Sacraments she requested to have the Sisters summoned to her bed side that in person she might ask pardon of them individually for any disedification which she said she may have ever given them, and at her earnest entreaty each member of the community was compelled to give forgiveness of offences that never existed. Her uncle[50] came to see her and as he embraced her in an agony of grief she said to him, "Dear Uncle, you never refused me anything; now as my dying request I ask you to become a member of that Church in which I rejoice to expire."

On the morning of the day before she died, a physician who had known her from her infancy was sitting beside her; she asked him how many hours he thought she should live. He was moved to tears and gave an evasive answer to the question; perceiving the objection he had to tell her, she said, "You need not fear to tell me; people in the world are terrified at the approach of death, but a religious rejoices and see[s] in it an end of banishment, and a beginning of happiness: is not this the chill of death which is on me, and which you are trying to keep off?" This was said in reference to some hot flannels in which the doctor ordered her to be wrapped, and of which she conjectured the cause. He was at length compelled to declare that he thought she would not survive the night that was approaching. He was right, for she calmly expired on the morning of the 12th of November 1833.

Some short time after the death of this dear Sister, Revd. Mother's second niece expressed her intention of becoming a member of the community. She had been educated in the convent from her youth, and when she arrived at an age to warrant her in deciding on the choice of a state in life, she proved herself animated with the same heroic and generous spirit of charity of which her Aunt had given her so noble an example. She wished to devote herself entirely and for ever to those works of mercy to the poor and suffering which from her earliest years she had seen performed by the edifying community in which she lived. But some obstacles were thrown in her way. Her Uncle, not appreciating the spirit of religious sacrifice that prompted the choice she made, or perhaps wishing to try still further the sincerity of her resolution, insisted on her spending some time in his own house. He hoped that estrangement from the scenes and companions to which she had been until then accustomed, and the attractions of the gay world with which she would be made acquainted, would produce a change in her opinions, and induce her to abandon the determination which, in his opinion, was adopted in a moment of unreflecting enthusiasm. But neither the persuasions of her uncle, nor the fa[s]cinations of the society to which he took care to introduce her, could prevail with her to change her original intention; God had called her, and she proved herself faithful to His inspiration, and though her vocation was tried, its sincerity remained unshaken in the ordeal to which it was exposed. At length her uncle seeing that her resolution remained unchanged left her at liberty to follow her wishes, and she immediately returned to her former abode in Baggot St. and received the Habit of the Sisters of Mercy.

When Revd. Mother had carefully transcribed the Rule of the Presentation Order with such additions as she found by experience suited for the Visitation of the Sick, and Protection of distressed Women of good character, and having also made such alterations as were necessary for religious who should appear abroad, she sent it to Archbishop Murray at his desire, as he wished to deliberate on it at leisure. His Grace most carefully revised it, and at the end of about two years (which existing circumstances made appear very long), returned it with those alterations he thought advisable, saying that as soon as it was copied such as he now gave it, he would affix his sanction to it. This was done accordingly and he wrote the form of approbation and signed it the 3rd of May 1835, the very day on which his Holiness Pope Gregory 16th gave his approbation and apostolical benediction to the Institute. This approbation was notified in a letter to Dr. Murray of which he without delay informed her, knowing how anxious she was to have the approbation and benediction of the Holy See. And most joyful intelligence it was, for by this time the number of the community had become considerable, so much so that early in the previous year 1834,[51] they were able to spare a sufficient number to extend the good work to Kingstown. This rising town was then almost destitute of religious helps, and there was no school for the poor children. Revd. Mother, therefore, purchased a long fronted house in Sussex Place at the rere of the parish Chapel, which, with the Archbishop's permission she made a branch house, and had commodious schools built on part of the ground attached to it. Here she labored from time to time, dividing her cares between this and the Convent in Baggot St. and devoting herself to the instruction of the poor children and the visitation of the sick.

She was no less assiduous in training to the perfection of their holy state the Religious under her care; she felt all the value of a vocation to religious life and sought to extend the blessing to many, like St. Teresa never refusing admission to any postulant for want of temporal means, when it was at all possible to provide what was essential. In order to facilitate this, as well as from her great love of holy poverty, she retrenched those expenses which are usual in other Religious Establishments at the entrance of postulants and at their Clothing. Everything purchased for the use of the Sisters was of the plainest kind, and she never would allow a large provision of anything to be laid in, saying it was not according to poverty to have those kinds of stores. Although very careful to have her own exterior appearance and that of her Religious suitable to the holy dignity of their calling, her under clothing was always of the meanest description; and with regard to other accommodations the worst and most inconvenient was her choice. She rarely had a cell to her own use, being always ready to yield it up for the convenience of others; and on one occasion when some Sisters arrived late in the evening, and there were not cells prepared for all, she quietly brought one of them to hers, and next morning it was discovered that she had neither cell nor bed that night. When she went to found Convents her bed was usually on the floor, as she never waited to have the house comfortably arranged, being satisfied to have any kind of opening to extend the good effected by the Institute. She relied on the loving Providence of her Heavenly Father that all necessaries would be supplied, and she never was disappointed.[52]

Rigorous as she was towards herself, and solicitous that her spiritual children should disregard, and be disengaged from temporal conveniencies, she was, nevertheless, most tender and careful of the sick and infirm among them; she sought to alleviate their pains by every affectionate contrivance which the heart of a fond mother could dictate, and spared neither labor nor fatigue; yet even in her extraordinary care of the sick, she evinced her love for religious poverty. The physician having advised that her beloved niece, Sr. M. Teresa, when in her last illness should be removed to some country place (there being at the time no other Convent of the Order), she told him not to recommend such things as were unsuited to poor people, who might indeed be able to procure some little nourishment or delicacy for their invalids, but would not have the means of removing them to a country place.

She applied herself with great earnestness to promote the spiritual welfare of the Sisters, listening to them with patient kindness, and seeking to comfort and assist them whenever they applied to her in their difficulties; she used to inspire the fearful and scrupulous with confidence, and rouse those who were slothful and negligent. She was very careful not to give many positive directions about any duty, or as she used to term it, to make too many laws. A Sister having once over zealously requested her to desire the Community not to do some little matter which was rather out of order but not against [the] Rule, she mildly replied, "Be careful not to make too many laws, for if you draw the string too tight it will break."

Whilst she passed over many inadvertant [*sic*] offences without seeming to notice them, she was most watchful to correct in conversation and manners the least failure in politeness, or anything which could discover the want of a good education, being convinced by experience that the inattention of some Religious to these minor points often lessens charity in a community, and tends also to diminish the respect which seculars should have for the Religious State, and consequently the influence that Religious ought to possess over them. She often said, when giving instruction on the regulation of manners, that the most spiritual and enlightened persons could not form a more correct judgment on what the manner of a Religious ought to be than seculars do.

Being of a remarkably cheerful disposition she loved to see all under her charge cheerful and happy. She tried to make them so not only by removing whatever could disturb their peace, but also by contributing to the general cheerfulness of the community especially at recreation. Although burthened with many cares she was at that duty as lively and merry as the youngest Sisters, who used to delight in being near her, listening to her amusing remarks and anecdotes; she had a natural talent for composing verses in a playful style, and would often sing them to some cheerful tune with admirable simplicity. What solid instruction these verses generally contained the following will show. The first was in reply to some lines sent her by one of the Sisters;[53] the second was her parting advice to a newly appointed Revd. Mother.[54]

Dear Sister . . . .
I hope you don't think I've been very
remiss
In not answering all your nice rhyme
I should have done so indeed long ere[55]
this
Could I snatch but one hour from Time
That monarch who bears us away
In his chariot of measureless flight
To whom we can never oh never say nay
But go with him from morning till night
Stern foe to our beauty and youth
Which he steals as he passes along
While he makes us acknowledge as truth
That life is no more than a song
Oh what shall we do to defeat him
While he is smiting us so
Let us try by what art we can cheat him
And make him a deep fallen foe
Let us now with the new year begin
To wrest from this tyrant his power
Not only avoiding all sin
But piously passing each hour
Our humours and pride we'll subdue
And be mild and be meek as we can
We will try to become quite a new
And entirely cast off the old man[56]
The thirty eighth year is now passed
Its cares and its pleasures are gone
The thirty ninth may be our last
Since the last is so surely to come
Let us beg for renewed animation
In discharge of our duties each day
Let us smile under every privation
That Religion has strewed in our way
All coldness and choler we'll smother
And watchfully shun all dejection
We will cordially love one another
Since that is the mark of election.

My Dearest Sister N.N.[57]
Don't let crosses vex or teaze
Try to meet all[58] with peace & ease
Notice the faults of every day
But *often* in a playful way
And when you seriously complain
Let it be known to give you pain
Attend to one thing at a time
You've fifteen hours from six to nine
Be mild & sweet in all your ways
Now & again bestow some praise
Avoid all solemn declaration
All serious close investigation
Turn what you can into a jest
And with few words dismiss the rest
Keep patience ever at your side
You'll want it for a constant guide
Show fond affection every day
And above all devoutly pray
That God may bless the charge He's
given.
And make of you their guide to
Heaven.[59]

Revd. Mother was a great enemy to that spirit of sadness which destroys true devotion, and to inculcate the contrary used often to quote the Scripture which describes our Divine Lord as being neither "sad nor troublesome". She could not suffer the Sisters to take a gloomy view of passing events; her own recollections of former friends and occurrences were all of a benevolent nature, but she very rarely spoke of them, and then only for the purpose of edifying. She did not possess worldly accomplishments, but she had read much and well, and her manners were most pleasing and agreeable. She had an extensive knowledge of the human heart, and could readily adapt her conversation to the wants of those by whom she was surrounded. Everything in her she rendered subservient to the Divine honor and her neighbour's good, for she never seemed to think or care for herself. Her method of reading was so delightful that all used to acknowledge it rendered quite new to them a subject which perhaps they had frequently heard before, for she considered it most useful to adhere to a few solid spiritual works, rather than to run over many. The "Imitation of Christ" was one of her favorite books, also "Rodriguez on Christian Perfection"; her prayer book was that entitled, "Devotion[s] to the Sacred Heart of Jesus". Besides the spiritual exercises of the Community, at which she assisted with very great fervor, she had much devotion to the two "Thirty Days Prayer", the "Psalter of Jesus", and the "Universal Prayer"; some passages of the last she used to repeat often, especially the following: "Discover to me, O my God, the nothingness of this world, the greatness of Heaven, the shortness of time, and the length of eternity." This was an ordinary topic with her, and she constantly expressed her regret at having to take so much pains for the passing events of such a fleeting life.[60]

"Mercy" being the title which it pleased Almighty God should be given to the Institute He made her the instrument in founding, she used sometimes at recreation turn the conversation on the merits of that virtue, comparing it with Charity, and showing how peculiarly appropriate it was for the Sisters and how often they were called on to exercise it. The mercy of God, she would say, comes to our assistance and renders practical His charity in our regard; Mercy not only bestows benefits, but receives and pardons again and again, even the ungrateful; how kind and charitable and merciful, then, ought not "Sisters of Mercy" to be. She devised innumerable little ways of making her spiritual children happy, and when duty permitted complied with all their wishes. A Sister asked her once what form of prayer would be best before leaving her cell in the morning; she immediately wrote for her the following: "O my most compassionate Lord and Saviour Jesus Christ, I humbly beseech Thee to look on me this day with pity, and grant me the grace to be pleasing and acceptable to Thee even for one moment." This sweet compliance for the wishes of others was not so much the effect of innate benevolence, as of her desire to resemble our Blessed Lord which was her daily resolution, and the lesson she constantly repeated. "Be always striving," she would say, "to make yourselves like your Heavenly Spouse; you should try to resemble Him in some one thing at least, so that any person who sees you may be reminded of His holy life on earth." She meditated with heartfelt attention on the great mysteries of religion and feeling as she did so sensibly for the sufferings of her fellow creatures, her compassion for those endured by our Blessed Saviour was extreme, so much so that it was real pain to her (as she once told a Sister in confidence) to meditate on the Passion.

She had an extraordinary reverence for and confidence in the holy Sacraments; her instructions on this subject, whether to seculars or her Religious, were calculated to awaken sentiments of lively faith and confiding love. It was a cause of much sorrow to her when any Sister through scrupulosity or other motive absented herself from holy Communion; for, said she, it is by means of the grace therein bestowed on us that we are enabled to persevere in our holy state; and to the want of this strengthening grace may be attributed the instability of all religious communities formed outside the pale of the true Church. She did not wish the Sisters to spend much time preparing for, or in making their Confessions; having so many other sources of religious instruction she considered they should be careful not to occupy the priest's time unnecessarily. She was solicitous to have the Sisters avail themselves of every opportunity of instructing the poor in the nature of the Sacraments, and the benefits to be derived from them, exhorting them to approach frequently those of Penance and the Blessed Eucharist, convincing them that their temporal and eternal happiness depends on their doing so. She observed that with regard to converts she had always noticed they did not seem fully to understand the instructions given them until they had received Sacraments, but that afterwards they used to find many difficulties cleared[61] away and doubts removed.

Her devotion to the ever Blessed Mother of God was most tender and filial, and she looked on the privilege of having the Institute under her special protection as one of the highest it could enjoy. She was most exact in having the community perform the Novenas prior to her Feasts; that of our Lady of Mercy she always desired to be accompanied with as much solemnity as possible, and at an hour that would enable all the inmates of the House of Mercy to attend. During the entire month in which that Feast occurs she said in choir the Thirty Days Prayer in honor of the Blessed Virgin for the spiritual and temporal welfare of the Institute. To all whom she could influence she recommended with the greatest earnestness to invoke with confidence her intercession in all their doubts and difficulties.

She entertained profound respect for the sacred Ministers of Religion, and taught the Sisters to observe the same; she said they should so venerate their sacerdotal character as not to allow themselves the least familiarity of manner or expression in conversing with them, and that herein they could not be too guarded. She wished them when writing or speaking to priests, even though they might be near relatives, to address them as "Revd. Father" or "Revd. Sir", and this she invariably practised herself. Her veneration extended to everything connected with our holy Religion, and she would not allow any part of the holy Rule to be repeated lightly or in jest; she was particularly careful and vigilant to prevent unnecessary noise or other negligent conduct in the choir, etc. She loved to look on the religious Habit, and a ceremony day was one of the happiest to her. As to the sacred vows, she cherished them with her whole heart, it was her greatest pleasure to make the renewal of them, and she used to express the following sentiments in her instructions to the Sisters during the retreat previous to it. "When we first make our vows it is not surprising if we feel anxious, and pronounce them in a timid faltering voice, being as yet unacquainted with the full extent of His infinite goodness to whom we engage ourselves for ever; but when we renew them it ought to be with that tone of joy and confidence which the experience of His unceasing mercies must inspire." This feeling was easily discerned in her manner of reading the Act of Renewal, and also in the joyful way in which she repeated the usual Te Deum afterwards.

According as the good resulting from the new Institute became known, application was made from different places for some of its members, that they might diffuse the blessings of religious instruction and consolation among the poor. A pious lady[62] who resided in Tullamore had bequeathed her house with a small annuity for the purpose of establishing a Convent of Sisters of Mercy in that town. This lady had been a particular friend of Very Revd. R. O'Hanlon and he employed his influence in engaging Mrs. McAuley to undertake the foundation. She went there about the end of April 1836 taking with her Mother Mary Anne Doyle as the Mother Superior, and three other Sisters. They were received most cordially by the good parish priest and by the town's people, who assembled in crowds to await their arrival, and joyfully conducted them to the Church from which they proceeded to the house prepared for them. The community was immediately joined by two young ladies from the neighbourhood whom Revd. Mother had the consolation to see clothed with the holy Habit of religion before she returned to Baggot St. A beautiful Convent and extensive poor schools have since been erected in that locality, through the zealous exertions of the parish priest aided by the contributions of the kind and charitable people of the neighbourhood.

The Tullamore foundation was followed by that of Charleville in the county Cork. The lady[63] who desired to found the Convent offered five hundred pounds, with a house; and although this was a small beginning Revd. Mother would not refuse the opportunity of performing a work agreeable to God. Accordingly on the 29th of October the same year she set out on this journey accompanied by Mother Mary Angela Dunne, as Mother Superior, and three Sisters, two to remain at the new foundation, the other as her travelling companion. Being very anxious to see her dear children in Tullamore she went there first, intending to go across the country afterwards in the canal boat. On reaching Tullamore she discovered that the boat was a very slow and inconvenient mode of travelling; however she was not discouraged and although she suffered extremely from cold and fatigue, her patience and cheerfulness never failed. She arrived in Limerick at nine o'clock on the evening of the 30th and set off next morning for Charleville, where she found the house very far from being as convenient as it had been represented; it was not only damp, but some distance from the schools of which the Sisters were to take charge. These circumstances, together with the fact of Charleville being a small poor town and consequently little chance of postulants joining, made her feel uneasy, and she thought that perhaps it would be prudent to withdraw the Sisters; but her feelings of compassion for the suffering members of Christ, joined to the pressing solicitations of the parish priest soon determined her to place the little community courageously in the arms of Divine Providence. She was greatly touched by hearing a poor woman exclaim, "Ah! 'twas the Lord drove you amongst us," and exerted herself to the utmost of her power in promoting the interests of the house; in less than two years she had the consolation of assisting at the ceremony of laying the first stone of the new Convent. On her return from this foundation she gave a remarkable instance of her love for regularity, and tender devotion towards the most holy Sacrament. The day fixed for travelling was a Communion day and although she had to rise at two o'clock in the morning to be ready for the stage coach, she declined taking any refreshment, saying to her companion that they might reach Limerick in time for Holy Communion. They did not arrive till after ten o'clock, and then as neither of them knew the way to a Chapel, they walked some distance in a heavy fall of snow, but at length succeeded in hearing Mass and satisfying her ardent piety; it was after twelve when they got back to the hotel to breakfast. The next morning they arrived in Baggot St. in time to assist at the Mass celebrated by the Right Revd. Dr. Murphy, Bishop of Cork, who had come to make arrangements for founding a Convent in that city. Nothing definite was settled on that occasion so that she was free to meet an application made from Carlow by the Right Revd. Dr. Nolan. He had been entrusted with a large sum of money, the savings of a shop-keeper in the town who at his death left it to the poor and destitute, and the trustees feeling assured that it could not be better disposed of in their regard than by procuring a community of Sisters of Mercy, his Lordship requested she would give him a little colony. On the tenth of April 1837 she, and the newly appointed Mother Superior, Mother Mary Francis Warde, left for Carlow. This Convent was established with every prospect of success; however, she was not permitted to enjoy uninterruptedly the happy fruits of her exertions, being summoned in a few days back to Baggot St. on account of the illness of two of the novices who were attacked with the worst description of typhus fever; they, however, recovered, and she at once returned to Carlow to complete all necessary arrangements, taking with her as companion her surviving niece (now a professed Sister) in an advanced stage of consumption.

As soon as the foundation was settled in Carlow, that for Cork was again revived. The Foundress Miss Barbara Goold having placed a large sum of money in Right Revd. Dr. Murphy's hands, and promised a very suitable house well furnished, his Lordship requested that as little delay as possible would be made in taking possession of it. She began to make preparations, but Almighty God required that she should first assist at the death-bed of a novice who was suddenly carried off by typhus fever; her own dear niece was evidently hastening to her last hour; nevertheless she conquered her grief and anxious affection, and before a week had elapsed from the death of the novice, she was on her way to commence the new Establishment in Cork where she arrived on the 6th of July 1837. She took with her Mother Mary Clare Moore as Mother Superior, and three others; they were welcomed with sincere good will by the Clergy and laity; many of the most influential persons came to visit and offer their kind services; and the poor blessed God for having sent them to them. Yet many difficulties accompanied the establishment of this foundation, from which she was recalled on the 24th of July to her dying niece who expired in the beginning of August. The career of Sister Mary Ann Agnes[64]—for so she was called in Religion—promised to be one of great virtue and great usefulness; she was to her attached sisterhood a model of the most devoted charity and the most fervent and exact religious observance. Her great delight was to teach and provide for the poor children in the schools, and to perform for the orphans that were inmates of the house, acts of charity and kindness, such as, dressing their hair, attending to the cleanliness of their person, etc., which acts though trifling in themselves, and perhaps little deserving of being thus mentioned, were yet proof of a generous and affectionate heart, and a soul overflowing with charity. Those who had the happiness of being associated with her long preserved the recollection of her worth, and still speak of her with the most affectionate remembrance.

Whether it was that God designed to try the young community in the hard ordeal of tribulation—or that He wished to reward a devotedness so perfect, and a charity so ardent as theirs, by a speedy admission to the promised crown, it would be hard to say—but it is a singular circumstance attending the commencement of the Institute, that for the first few years no less than fifteen members were struck down by death, and passed in the very freshness and vigour of youth, and the prime of their usefulness to the possession of that crown which has been promised to those who leave father and mother, brothers and sisters, and lands, and take their Divine Master as the portion of their inheritance.

Revd. Mother felt most deeply the separation from those she so fondly loved. But she was still more to be tried in the crucible of affliction; for God, who is jealous of His creatures' love, knowing with what deep affection she cherished those children, whom from childhood she had watched over with a mother's tenderness, permitted that those very children should be the channel through which a portion of her cross was to reach her. Her eldest nephew died young of consumption, just as he had finished his education. The second, a young lad of great promise, after a course of study of no ordinary distinction was preparing for the bar; but owing to the indiscretion of youth he had the misfortune of incurring the displeasure of his Aunt, and for some time mutual estrangement was the consequence. During her absence to found a house of the Order in England, he was seized with an alarming illness, the most fatal consequences threatened to be the result, he became a penitent and sought a reconciliation with her whom he had so deeply grieved. It is needless to add that pardon of the past was at once and fully given, but before it reached the poor sufferer for whom it was intended death had put an end to his existence. He had received the last Sacraments, been attended by the Sisters of her community in Baggot St., and expired in great sentiments of sorrow and repentance; but the fact of his departing this life without having received her letter or having known her altered sentiments, was beyond measure afflicting to her who had loved him even in his errors with all the fond affection of a mother.[65]

Her youngest nephew manifesting a strong predilection for a seafaring life was bound on board a vessel engaged in foreign trade; he went to sea, but what became of him his Aunt was never able to discover.

Revd. Mother's prudence and discernment were very evident in the choice she made of the most effectual means of promoting the interests of the different foundations. Among others it was her custom to bring a novice near the time of her Profession, or a Postulant who had been sufficiently long in the parent house to permit of her receiving the Holy Habit soon after their arrival at the new Convent, so that it almost always happened that a ceremony took place immediately, and thus many were attracted to enquire into the nature of the Institute, and become desirous to embrace it.

About the middle of September she returned to Cork to complete the arrangements for that foundation, and on the 25th of October Right Revd. Dr. Murphy gave the Habit to a postulant, and on the same day a novice made her holy Profession. It was on this occasion that his Lordship wished an alteration to be made in the formula of the Act of Profession, in which only the three vows of Poverty, Chastity, and Obedience common to every Religious Institute were expressed; he proved to the Foundress the necessity of declaring the special object of her Congregation, distinct from others, and therefore the following words were introduced: "And the service of the Poor, Sick, and Ignorant"; which were not, however, generally adopted until after the confirmation of the Holy Rule in 1841. This foundation became in a short time most flourishing; it was not quite a year established when two Postulants from England entered it for the purpose of serving a novitiate and returning to found a Convent in Bermondsey near London. This being the first step towards introducing the new Institute in England, it necessarily excited great interest, and ultimately, when the Sisters had served their novitiate and were Professed the Foundress accompanied them to Bermondsey in November 1839. Mother Mary Clare Moore was appointed Superior, and was succeeded in Cork by Mother Mary Joseph Warde.

The Right Revd. Dr. Ryan, Bishop of Limerick, applied to have a foundation established in that city, funds for the purpose having been assigned to him and other trustees by a benevolent lady.[66] After making all necessary arrangements Revd. Mother set out for Limerick early in September 1838, taking with her Mother Mary Elizabeth Moore as Mother Superior, and three others. She travelled by the steamer to Cork being anxious to revisit the convent there, and also to have an interview with the English Sisters who were serving their novitiate there; she remained some days to the great joy and comfort of her spiritual children, after which she proceeded on her journey by Charleville, where she also spent some days, and had the gratification of witnessing the ceremony of laying the first stone of the new convent; which was performed on the 24th of September. Immediately after she left with a clergyman who had been sent from Limerick to conduct her, and arrived there with the Sisters on the evening of the same day—the Feast of our Lady of Mercy. The place prepared for them was the old Convent of St. Clare, of which two lay Sisters, who still remained of that once flourishing community, were the sole occupants. The Convent itself was an old building, but commodious, and had a large well cultivated garden, and extensive poor schools attached. This foundation has been one of the most prosperous; and the liberal support given from the commencement enabled Revd. Mother to have the gratification of opening a House of Mercy before she left, which was not till the 9th of December.

Previous to her leaving Baggot St. for England in the close of the year 1839 the Revd. R. Colgan OCC, a faithful and long tried friend to the Institute, offered to present the Holy Rule for confirmation at Rome, whither he was going, promising to translate it into Italian in order that it might be examined by the Sacred Congregation of thc Propeganda [*sic*] Fide, and to further the business as much as he could. But his kindness stopped not here; he instructed her in the means necessary to be adopted for its success. With a copy of the Holy Rule, she was to send a petition praying for its confirmation signed by the Mother Superiors of the different convents, and letters of recommendation from the Bishops in whose Diocesses [*sic*] they were located. All those she procured with much labor and anxiety and despatched from London, an opportunity of doing so being kindly afforded her by the Right Revd. Dr. Griffith[s].

She returned to Baggot St. on the 14th of January 1840, and during that year founded the Convents in Galway[67] and Birr.[68] She went to the latter towards the close of December, when the weather was particularly inclement, and while she remained there often went out to visit the sick when the snow was very deep on the ground. Her exertions were most unsparing to withdraw the people from the Schism which had unhappily disturbed the peace of that town. Almighty God blessed her efforts most wonderfully, and she had the consolation to see numbers restored to their lawful pastors, who had obstinately held out for so long a time against all the efforts made for their conversion.

In August 1841 she again made a journey to England to open the Convent in Birmingham, which was the last founded by her. For some time previously she had been very ill; she had also suffered much mental anguish; indeed, the last years of her life were strongly marked by crosses and afflictions, and trials seemed to flow in upon her from various sources. She was obliged to sacrifice the branch house in Kingstown on account of a debt incurred in erecting poor schools; for which she had unwarily made herself liable. This loss was however replaced by the liberality of Mrs. [Barbara] Verschoyle who built a Convent for the Sisters at Booterstown, in a field adjoining the parish Church. The house in Kingstown remaining undisposed of, influential persons prevailed on her to send Sisters there again; they remained during her lifetime, and for one or two years after, when it was thought well to relinquish it entirely, and in consequence the house was sold.

Among other things she was grieved to be obliged to shut up the little Convent Chapel in Baggot St. for the contributions offered there had been a great means of supporting the House of Mercy. Indeed this seemed to be one of the greatest trials she had experienced since the commencement of her arduous task, and no doubt was ordained by Almighty God to purify the soul of his servant and to keep her humble amidst such great success; still His tender mercies were not forgotten and with these crosses He was pleased to mingle consolation and joy.

She lived to see the Institute confirmed by the Holy See on the 6th of June, 1841;[69] and although ten years had not elapsed since her Religious Profession, she saw fourteen houses of the Order established. She might say with holy Simeon, "Now Thou dost dismiss Thy servant, O Lord, according to Thy word in peace"; and such were her dispositions.

The pressure of the many works of charity in which she had been hitherto incessantly engaged had left traces upon a constitution which never was very strong. The numberless cares and troubles attending the foundation of so many houses; the fatiguing journeys to which she was necessarily subjected; and the obligation of providing all things necessary for the efficient working of the several communities, were enought [*sic*] to break down a constitution much stronger than hers. She endured very frequent and violent pain in the stomach, perhaps the beginning of that disease which terminated her existence. She was also subject to inflammatory attacks, accompanied by extreme soarness [*sic*: soreness] in her mouth, yet she would go on reading the public lectures, and reciting the Office until absolutely incapable of uttering a word; in truth she never spared herself and sought alleviation from her pains only when forced to do so; during the last year of her life her sufferings were great.

On her return from Birmingham it was perceived by the debility and exhaustion under which she was laboring, that the term of her usefulness was drawing to a close. After struggling with her increasing infirmity some time, she was at length obliged to confine herself to her room. It was her desire to continue still to encourage her spiritual daughters by her example to the punctual fulfilment of their meritorious duties; but her Divine Master had proved that such was not His will by depriving her of the power to perform them. Her good works were full, she had labored long and faithfully in the vineyard, and now the Master of the vineyard was about to confer upon her the rich and abundant reward of her devotion and fidelity. About the beginning of November a sudden attack of inflammation seriously alarmed her anxious children. She received the last Sacraments on the 8th with sentiments of great peace and holy resignation and appeared fully aware of her approaching dissolution though no one else thought it so near. On the morning of the 11th—in order to satisfy her ardent devotion to the Blessed Eucharist—Mass was offered in her room, and her soul was strengthened by union with our Lord in the most holy Sacrament. Her patience and submission under suffering, and her conformity to the holy Will of God, were most edifying and instructive. The following little prayer composed by herself expresses most truly her sentiments.

> My God, I am Thine for all eternity; teach me to cast my whole self into the arms of Thy Providence with the most lively unlimited confidence in Thy compassionate,

> tender pity. "Grant, O most Merciful Redeemer, that whatever Thou dost ordain or permit may always be acceptable to me; take from my heart all painful anxiety, suffer nothing to afflict me, but sin; nothing to delight me, but the hope of coming to the possession of Thee, my God, in Thy own everlasting Kingdom. Amen."[70]

She preserved the perfect use of her faculties till the last moment, and though hitherto she had dreaded death, yet as it drew near even her spiritual trials seemed to have an end, and her soul was replenished with unbounded confidence in the mercy of her heavenly Father, who thus most graciously gave her a foretaste of the fulfilment of His own Divine promise, "Blessed are the merciful, for they shall obtain mercy." Her agony lasted for about nine hours;[71] and in the evening her holy soul passed calmly to the enjoyment of its eternal rest, Nov[embe]r 11th 1841. Her death was truly characteristic, nothing very unusual or extraordinary in word or action, but full of that quiet self control for which she was remarkable; and which in such an awful extremity can be experienced only by those spiritual souls whose heart, soul, and whole being has been unreservedly laid at the feet of their Saviour and Judge.

The Community were so anxious to keep her remains that instead of burying her in the vault of the Carmelite Church—where all the deceased Sisters had hitherto been interred—they applied for permission to have a cemetery[72] consecrated within the walls, and His Grace having given his sanction, Right Revd. Dr. Kinsel[l]a consecrated part of the garden for that purpose. On the 13th [*sic*] Inst.[73] after a Solemn Office and High Mass, her remains were laid in the little cemetery; and a small wooden cross was placed at the head of the grave to mark the spot, with an inscription inviting all to pray for the repose of her soul.

"May she rest in peace"

The following short account of her death was written by one of the Mother Superiors who went to Baggot St. to assist her in her last moments:[74]

> Of our dear Revd. Mother what shall I say but that she died the death of the just. Cautious as she was in health of bringing herself into notice unnecessarily, she was still more so in sickness, waiting on herself, even in her last agony; preserving to the last moment the same peace and serenity of mind which so eminently distinguished her through life; omitting not an iota of what was essential, and totally disregarding all but what was of moment. I was not at all aware that her death was so near. I was full of hope till Wednesday morning about eleven o'clock, that is, the day before her death. Had I then known what I since heard, I would not have been so unprepared for the shock. She was herself well aware that she was dying for the last six months, and since her return from Birmingham cautiously avoided anything like business. It is only by her acts that we can judge of her mind. She was perfectly silent as to what she thought, arranged all her papers etc. about a month or six weeks since, and said to Sister N. on leaving the parlour, that now they were ready. . . . About four o'clock on Thursday morning she desired the bed to be moved to the centre of the room, saying, that she would soon want air; about seven she desired the Sisters to be brought to her, said to each one individually what was most suited, but her first and last injunction to

all was to preserve union and peace amongst each other, saying that if they did they would enjoy great happiness such as that they would wonder where it came from. Told Sister N. that she felt exceedingly happy, as if to encourage her to die; recognized all, told little Sister N. to embrace her and go away, that she would see her again, as if to prevent her from weeping. The Holy Sacrifice was offered in the room about half past eight; she said it would be a comfort to her to see the white cloaks on the Sisters, for she had been anointed on Monday without the usual ceremony, more with a view to hasten recovery, than that she was thought in immediate danger.

I think her agony commenced about eleven o'clock. She spoke very little, but was visited that day by Dean Gaffney, Dean Meyler, two or three other clergymen, her brother, etc. To the doctor she said, "Well, doctor, the scene is drawing to a close." About five in the evening she asked for the candle to be placed in her hand, we commenced the last prayers, then I repeated one or two she herself had taught me, she said with energy, "God may bless you."[75] When we thought the senses were going and that it might be well to rouse attention by praying a little louder, she said, "No occasion, my darling, to speak so loud, I hear distinctly." In this way she continued till ten minutes before eight when she calmly breathed her last sigh. I did not think it possible for human nature to have such self-possession at the awful moment of death, but she had an extraordinary mind in life and death. . . . She left for you and all the Revd. Mothers a special blessing for themselves and communities.

We will here subjoin the beautiful letter of the Venerable Bishop of Dromore, Right Revd. Dr. Blake, on this sad occasion:[76]

My dear Revd. Mother,

We have all reason to weep for the loss which Ireland and England too must sustain in consequence of the death of the ever memorable Foundress of your holy Order. A more zealous, a more prudent, a more useful, a more disinterested, or a more successful benefactress of human nature, I believe, never existed in Ireland since the days of St. Bridget. She has been taken from us after bestowing incalculable services and benefits upon her fellow creatures here below. What she accomplished would have been sufficient to attach celebrity to many individuals. Her course was long enough to render her name immortal in the remembrance of the virtuous and truly religious. But judging of what she would do had she been left longer amongst us, from what she executed amidst difficulties and trials of no ordinary magnitude, we cannot but lament her departure and we are tempted to cry out, "Oh! it was too soon," but God's holy will be adored at all times. To Him we are indebted for all that she did, from Him she received the spirit which animated her pure soul; His Providence guided her steps, removed her difficulties, strengthened her heart, and ensured her success. By His ever watchful care, and ever assisting grace, every opportunity of doing good was turned to advantage, every undertaking was well preconsidered, every work was made solid and permanent; and though her sojourn here was, alas! too short for our wishes, it was nevertheless so far prolonged as to have enabled her to finish the great machine which, for His glory and the sanctification of souls, as well as for the corporal relief of the destitute, she planned and constructed. Let the holy will of God then be ever adored, let us bless His name at all times, and in this moment of bereavement, while we lament the loss which such a removal has caused, let us be grateful for the benefits He has conferred and profit by the great example which is still fresh before our minds. I most sincerely and deeply sympathize with you, and with all the members of the holy Order of Mercy; most earnestly do I beseech the God of all consolation to pour His healing comforts into your and their wounded feelings, and in this trying conjuncture, while your hearts are mellowed with love, grief, and gratitude, to fill you with the spirit of prayer.

Although your Foundress was holy, and eminently holy, she was still human, liable to human temptation and infirmity, and obliged every day to express sincerely that hallowed petition, Forgive us our trespasses. Let us now be mindful of her, and by our fervent supplications obtain for her, if she need it, that entire remission of every, even the smallest debt, which could retard her admission into the realms of bliss.

Your letter reached me this morning just as I was going to the Altar, on seeing the black seal I hastily opened it. My heart was instantly filled with grief, but I hope it only served to make me offer with more fervor, the Divine Sacrifice of propitiation, for the happy repose of the dear departed friend whom I ever esteemed and revered, and whose memory I shall ever esteem and revere.

Very Revd. Dean Gaffney writes of her as follows:[77]

It is not necessary in speaking of the revered Foundress of the Sisters of Mercy, to draw much upon the fancy, or to conjure up, as is sometimes done by ingenious invention, an imaginary picture of perfection and benevolence, and then apply it to the character we wish to praise; no, her eulogy would be written by the mere mention of the one hundredth part of what she has done for suffering and destitute humanity.

In the year 1830 Mrs. McAuley entered the Convent of the Presentation Nuns at George's Hill, to prepare herself for the good work she was about to undertake for the glory of God, and the salvation of souls. In the year 1831 she began the foundation of the Order of Sisters of Mercy in Baggot St. in this city; and she died in 1841. How short the time, but how immense and how wonderful the works of that mighty mind, of that expansive heart! They would hardly appear credible if they had not happened in our own time, and passed before our own eyes.

This great and good woman had three objects in view in founding the Order of the Sisters of Mercy, *viz.*, the Visitation and relief of the sick poor, the Instruction of poor female children, and the spiritual and temporal care of poor destitute female servants of good character, whilst out of place. And did she succeed in realizing her wishes? She did succeed, and succeed beyond her own most sanguine expectations.

Whoever visits the schools of the female children in Baggot St. will be consoled and delighted by the scene that will present itself to view. But what shall I say of Mrs. McAuley's charity towards poor female servants of good character whilst out of place, who had no resource, no friends, no home! She built a house for them adjoining the Convent, she supported them, she clothed them, she instructed them, she provided situations for them. The ordinary number in the house during her life time was about sixty, and in the course of ten years of her religious career she procured comfortable situations for more than a thousand female servants, whom she had rescued from all the appalling dangers to which needy and unprotected females are exposed. If all this good has been effected by one Convent of the Sisters of Mercy, how much good may be expected from the fourteen Convents which Mrs. McAuley has been instrumental in establishing? Few left the world in 1841 that can with more confidence than the revered Foundress of the Order of Mercy expect to hear on the last accounting day the following words from the lips of our Divine Redeemer: "Come, ye blessed of my Father" etc., etc. Matt. xxv. 34.35.36.[78]

Mrs. McAuley's death was such as might have been expected after a life replete with good works. It was the death of the just which is precious in the sight of the Lord. Her soul was calm and peaceable and perfectly resigned to the Divine Will. The Sisters of Mercy have one more advocate, one more protectress before the throne of God. . . .[79]

May the Order of Mercy prosper, may Mrs. McAuley's spiritual children have always before their eyes the example left them by their revered Foundress, may they imitate her virtues, and they will have glory in the sight of God and of man.

Mary Clare Augustine (Mary Clare) Moore 1808–1880

Among the early biographers of Catherine McAuley, Mary Clare Augustine Moore is remarkable in several ways: apparently she was among the first (in 1844 or before) to solicit from those who had known Catherine written and oral contributions for a projected memoir about her; of the manuscripts presented in this volume, hers was completed last (in 1864 or later), yet it appears to be an entirely fresh and original composition; and Catherine's relationship to her was, from Catherine's perspective though perhaps not from Clare Augustine's, the least naturally harmonious. Clare Augustine was a painter, an artist who took her time to complete projects to her own satisfaction, and Catherine sometimes did not have sufficient patience with the pace of her careful brush-work.

Mary Clare Moore—Mary Clare was her baptismal name—was born in Dublin on August 1, 1808, and was an older sister of Georgiana Moore. She entered the Sisters of Mercy on Baggot Street five years after her sister Georgiana had taken the name Mary Clare as her name in religion. Thus when Mary Clare herself received the habit on February 21, 1838, she was given the name, Mary Clare Augustine. However, Catherine McAuley and Mary Clare (Georgiana) Moore tended to address her simply as "Sister Mary Clare". This exchange of name—and the frequent shortening of Clare Augustine's—can be very confusing to readers. Happily, the personalities and careers of the two sisters were quite distinct.

In her Memoir, Clare Augustine says that she first met Catherine McAuley in early 1829, just after the death of Catherine's brother-in-law, Dr. William Macauley. With the trained eye of a fine artist she describes Catherine's appearance on that occasion—her face, lips, eyes, nose, hair, hands, and figure—and thus provides a precise verbal portrait of the woman for whom there is no painted portrait from life. Although Clare Augustine underestimates Catherine's actual age by several years, she still claims that she "looked at least 10 years younger". However, she also notes that Catherine "broke down very soon after, for when I saw her again in about 6 months I scarcely knew her."

Clare Augustine entered the Baggot Street community on August 8, 1837, a month after her sister had gone to Cork as the first superior of that new foundation. She professed her vows on February 27, 1840. Although in her early years at Baggot Street she undoubtedly had other daily responsibilities related to the various works of mercy undertaken by the community, her artistic talents were employed in preparing an illuminated Register (a volume recording the entrance, reception, and profession dates, the major assignments, and, eventually, the date of death of each member of the Dublin community), and, later, an illuminated copy of the Rule. It was in reference to her progress in this artistic work that the temperaments of Clare Augustine and Catherine McAuley occasionally collided.

One of the touching ironies of Clare Augustine's Memoir about Catherine is the absence in it of any hint of Catherine's impatience toward her, as indicated, for example, in three of Catherine's letters to Frances Warde. In January 1839, commenting on some calligraphy done in Carlow, Catherine refers to Clare Augustine's opinion:

> The Invitation is very nicely done. I think the printing remarkably good. *The Judge* thinks the etching would be exceedingly good if not so heavy, which she says gives it the appearance of a print, but I do not mind half what she says on these scientific points, which she delights in unfolding to the fools that will hearken to her. She will do anything in the Register you wish, but what is mentioned. She calls three weeks work, and she could not give that time until the Bazaar is over. She is very slow. (158)

In early March 1841, Catherine wrote, in even greater exasperation:

> Sister Mary Clare [Augustine] Moore is a character not suited to my taste or my ability to govern, though possessing many very estimable points. She teased and perplexed me so much about the difficulty of copying the two pages, that I was really obliged to give up, unwilling to command lest it should produce disedifying consequences. She said it would take the entire Lent. Indeed, you can have no idea how little she does in a week. As to a day's work, it is laughable to look at it. She will show me 3 leaves, saying, "I finished these today." 3 rose or lilly [*sic*] leaves. (311–12)

Obviously the amiable Catherine McAuley could become angry on occasion. Her speed of action and Clare Augustine's apparent meticulousness evidently did not mix well in matters such as the production of illuminated pages. Writing from Birr earlier in the same year to Cecilia Marmion at Baggot Street, Catherine sent a terse message to her Assistant, Mary de Pazzi Delany: "Tell her to keep Sr. M. Clare close to the Register" (289)! Clare Augustine had of course other daytime duties which adequately accounted for the pace of her art work in her own eyes, but apparently not in Catherine's. Having promised to show the illuminated Dublin Register to the Carlow community, so they could model their own Register on it, Catherine wrote at the end of March 1841:

> Sr. M. Clare is working indeed at the Register. She is quite ashamed to leave it unfinished. I hope to find a safe way of sending it to you, for Sr. M. Cecilia [Maher] to copy what she likes. (Bolster, ed. 214)

On the cover to this letter, in a postscript evidently referring to Clare Augustine, Catherine wrote:

> *That one* has more of her own ways yet than ours, and it is not easy to fix her to a point. She finds the duties sufficient to fill up her time, and as her constitution is strong, she is much employed in outdoor work. (Bolster, ed. 214)

Clare Augustine Moore's constitution was indeed strong. She outlived Catherine McAuley and her own younger sister, dying at Baggot Street on October 7, 1880. Except for a brief period of time in Cork, she generally lived and worked in Dublin. She was back at Baggot Street in the late summer of 1844 when she began to receive the letters of reminiscences about Catherine which she had solicited from Mary Ann Doyle and Clare Moore.[1] By 1854, her artistic talent was so well known that, according to Mary Nathy O'Hara, "when the Irish bishops wished to send a memorial of congratulation" to Pius IX, celebrating his declaration of the dogma of the Immaculate Conception, Clare Augustine was "deputed to illuminate the address in Gaelic" (26).[2] In 1856 she began teaching in the school associated with the Goldenbridge Refuge, an institution operated by the Dublin Sisters of Mercy for women prisoners about to be discharged from prison. The Refuge provided supportive housing during the final stage of their sentences and, more importantly, instruction and guidance which enabled them to secure work upon their release or to return to their families. In 1870 she became the supervisor of the Refuge (Carroll, *Leaves,* 1:54–5 and Neumann 316).

Clare Augustine was in Cork when Catherine McAuley died. She says she saw Catherine for the last time on the morning of June 29, 1841, the day before she went to Cork "to open a day school for the wealthier class". She recalls that Catherine was then "greatly broken in health, but she concealed half her illness, in fact never complained of any." The Limerick Annals claims that when Catherine died, a cast of her face was taken, and that Clare Augustine later attempted to paint her likeness:

> Not long after Mother McAuley's death, an attempt was made in Baggot Street to draw her portrait from memory and her cast taken after death. One of the Sisters skilled in painting executed it, but the disadvantages were so great under the circumstances that we cannot wonder why it does not bear more likeness to the Revered Departed. We soon procured a copy, from which others were taken by a good artist—O'Halloran of Limerick—who however never *saw* her. Yet tho' those familiar with her features and expression clearly described both here anew, still it was not possible to throw their ideas into the brush of the painter, and consequently little if any improvement was made in the new ones, save a more intelligent expression! The photograph in the frontespiece of this book [i.e., volume 1 of the Limerick Annals] was got up by one of the English Houses in years and years after—it was partly from the original which may be seen in the Infirmary at our Parent House, Dublin.

Clare Augustine was in Cork for some time after Catherine's death—at least until after her sister Clare left Cork again for Bermondsey in mid December 1841—but probably longer.[3] Consequently her portrait of Catherine, if she used the death mask, which was presumably kept in Dublin, would have been executed some considerable time after Catherine's death.[4]

Whatever may have been Catherine McAuley's occasional "frets" with Clare Augustine, it is to the latter's credit that within three years of Catherine's death she began to encourage her sister Mary Clare, Mary Ann Doyle, and perhaps others, to put their memories of Catherine in written form, and she began herself to collect other data, with a view to writing "A Memoir of the Foundress of the Sisters of Mercy in Ireland", the long narrative now known as the Dublin Manuscript. As she notes in the opening paragraph, her Memoir was

> compiled from circumstances related to me by the Foundress herself, by Miss Byrne, whose brother married the cousin and most intimate friend of our dear foundress; by Mary Murphy, for many years servant to Mr. and Mrs. Callaghan; by M. M. Clare Moore . . . and communications from the Right Revd. Dr. Blake, late Bishop of Dromore; M. M. A. Doyle who was her first companion; [and] Mr. Daly, a very eminent apothecary who was constantly thrown in her way.

The reference to Michael Blake indicates that at least this portion of the manuscript was written or revised after March 7, 1860, the day of his death (Mac Suibhne 2:353). References midway in the document to the "Surgeon General, the late Sir P[hilip] Crampton", who died in June 1858, and to Catherine McAuley's own original manuscript of the Rule "in a blue cloth cover [which] is (1864) still among the papers of the Convent" signify that although the initial impulse to write the Memoir occurred about 1844, the manuscript was probably not begun and certainly not completed until much later, in 1864 or thereafter.

Of all the autographs of the early biographical narratives about Catherine McAuley, Clare Augustine Moore's manuscript is in the most delicate state. It consists of two parts: the first part (slightly over half) is written in black ink on small sheets of white paper; the second part is written in pencil on slightly larger, thin gray paper, some sheets of which are very faded and can be read only with a magnifying glass and good lighting. The handwriting appears to be the same in both parts, although the hand in the second part is that of an older person. Alterations of the first part have been made in pencil, and there are three lacunae, all fairly long, where some pages of the manuscript are missing.

Yet, with all its physical fragility, Clare Augustine's "Memoir of the Foundress" is a marvelously lively narrative, filled with stories, observations, and insights that appear in no other early document. In certain respects it is the most independent and the least mannered of the early biographical accounts, using direct and sometimes even colloquial language, and informed throughout by Clare Augustine's obvious effort to be objective about Catherine, despite her evident admiration and affection for "Foundress", as she so often names her.

Clare Augustine finds fault with the "unfit" diet at Baggot Street; with the disruption caused by the poor of Saint Andrew's parish who for a year or more came daily for soup—"through the office down to the dining hall in squadrons"; with the priests who let Catherine down; with the "freaks" of austerity practiced by some of the early community during Catherine's absence at George's Hill; and with the extent of Catherine's own practice of poverty: "at first [she] thought there never could be enough of it." She notices Catherine's "weakness for pretty faces", her "frets", and the "uncatholic nature" of her original plan, and she claims that Catherine "doated [*sic*] on children and invariably spoiled them".

But she is also indignant at the "atrocious calumnies" hinted about Catherine by those who opposed her early initiatives, and sarcastic about the "kind friends [who came] to enlighten her on the Archbishop's views as well as on her own." She is explicit and detailed in her treatment of Dean Walter Meyler, parish priest of St. Andrew's and a highly respected Dublin priest, who was for several years, as she says, "not friendly". After his death on January 5, 1864, she may have felt some greater freedom to write about his strictures. But, most strikingly, one finds throughout Clare Augustine's Memoir the strong, clear statements of a devoted friend of Catherine McAuley: "every talent and every penny that our dear foundress possessed had been devoted to the poor"; "Poor Revd. Mother's patience and humility seemed to increase with her trials"; "How much she grieved" for her nephews "few knew so well as I"; and, "She had a really tender affection for us."

The extent of Clare Augustine's research, her narrative ability, and her sharp eye for detail, as well as her fresh vocabulary, give her manuscript a special strength and appeal. If she was aware of any tension in her relationship with Catherine McAuley, or of the latter's impatience with the pace of her artistic work, she shows no sign of it in her Memoir. She seeks only to do justice to the woman who "endured ingratitude and even insolence so sweetly that those who behaved ill towards her never felt they were doing wrong."

Seven months after her sister Mary Clare's death in London on December 14, 1874, Clare Augustine wrote from Dublin to the superior in Bermondsey, in response to a request for reminiscences about her sister. Although Clare Augustine had seen very little of her sister in the community—having entered in 1837 after Mary Clare went to Cork—she writes a wonderfully informative eight-page letter.[5] She discusses Georgiana's "very violent temper" when she was three years old; her childhood beauty, courage, and truthfulness; her firmness, at age eleven, in facing down a potential robber of the family's "outdoor wraps, shawls, furs and mantles"; and her entrance into the Baggot Street community "when little more than sixteen, not without a severe mental struggle". But then she concludes her letter about her sister: "The writing of this has been painful, for I am an old woman and her memory is linked with many others." Indeed. And in her Memoir, Clare Augustine has served those memories well.

On October 7, 1880, Mary Clare Augustine Moore died in Dublin. She is buried in the cemetery in the garden of the Baggot Street convent, where Catherine McAuley is buried.

A MEMOIR OF THE FOUNDRESS OF THE SISTERS OF MERCY IN IRELAND [THE DUBLIN MANUSCRIPT][1]

These memoirs are compiled from circumstances related to me by the Foundress herself; by Miss Byrne, whose brother married the cousin and most intimate friend of our dear foundress; by Mary Murphy, for many years servant to Mr. and Mrs. Callaghan; by M. M. Clare Moore, Mother Superior of our Convent in Cork and afterwards at Bermondsey; and communications from the Right Revd. Dr. Blake, late Bishop of Dromore; M. M. A. Doyle, who was her first companion; Mr. Daly, a very eminent apothecary who was constantly thrown in her way. I shall note my authority.[2]

M. M. Catherine was born at Stormanstown House, County Dublin on Michaelmas day 1787.[3] Her father was an architect in very good business, a very devout Catholic, who married when rather advanced in years a young, very beautiful, very vain, but not very devout Catholic. She had a great deal of natural talent but in those times, and for some years after, Catholic education was a thing of impossible attainment, so Mrs. McAuley was a liberal Catholic. Her husband, whose business occupied him incessantly during the week, offended her greatly by devoting . . . [lacuna].[4]

. . . very much and took little trouble to conceal his [Mr. Powell's] sentiments when Mr. C. [Callaghan] was not present, his reasons being that he could not conceal from himself her old friend's affection for her and that she was a Catholic, while he if not a pious, was undeniably a determined Protestant. One warm summer's day when the old gentleman was to[o] ill to come down, but had got out of bed to sit at the open window, Mr. Powel[l] began to discuss the subject of his wife's expectations at the open window just beneath. According to him the idea of Miss McAuley's ever being mistress of Coolock House was too absurd to be entertained for a moment. No, she should never make it a resort for her priests. As soon as the invalid should depart this life she should quit the place. Unfortunately for him not one word of this was lost on the invalid in the room above, and the consequence was that a will which had made Mrs. Powell and Miss McAuley residuary legatees to share equally in his property, was revoked by a codicil which placed £1,000 in the hands of trustees quite out of her husband's power, for the benefit of the former, and left the latter sole residuary legatee.[5] I asked Miss Byrne the amount of the property bequeathed; she said it was £25,000, but between Mr. Powel[l], who either borrowed £4,000 or got it to invest and did not, and two [or] three other worthies, she did not get more than £20,000, [and][6] first heard about the conversation at the window from . . . [lacuna].[7]

. . . was his. He reserved the Most Holy in the lower part. Father Nugent succeeded him in Liffey St. but in little more than a year he too was dead. He was always delicate but he took ill suddenly and for a few days Miss McAuley heard nothing of it. When she did she went to him immediately and found him in a sad state of dirt and neglect. She hardly left him till his death. I was told he left something to the Institution, but it could not be much for he was a true disciple of Dr. Blake's, always giving. There were a few books of his in the Library.

Her sister [Mary] soon after Mr. C's death fell into ill health. Her brother-in-law, whose name was the same as hers only he spelled it differently (Macauley), was so frightfully bigotted [*sic*] that he quite discouraged a prolonged visit from her. Of several children Mrs. Macauley had, 5 were surviving. The eldest was a lovely and highly gifted child, Mary, her aunt's favorite of all her family, of whose Protestantism the parents were particularly jealous. When she was about 12 years old the mother went on the car with the children to the Protestant service at St. Catherine's Church. On their return Mary turning round called to her mother who sat at the other side of the car. "Mamma, why do we say at our prayers, 'I believe in the holy Catholic Church'? I don't believe in the Catholic Church; I believe in the holy Protestant Church." Mrs. Macauley like any other Protestant in the same predicament tried to persuade . . . [lacuna].[8]

. . . but even if he were he could not be exactly very angry as he never partook in that rite: for though he went to the Anglican church sometimes, he was really a dissenter. The poor mother was greatly agitated and no longer felt that security in Protestantism to which till this incident she had clung most firmly.

Our dear foundress was at this time in rather a puzzle about her great house.[9] Its destination was no longer a secret and her plan met with general approbation, but no one offered to cooperate with her. One evening, however, a Mr. and Mrs. Doyle with their daughter, who had just obtained their consent to enter a Presentation Convent, were walking down Baggot St. wondering at the big house and asked the caretaker to let them see the inside. While shewing it the man spoke of the foundress and her purposes, Miss Doyle expressed her admiration, and her parents told her how glad they would be if she were to join this institution. They were too pious to oppose God's holy will in her regard, but they thought if she would be allowed to console them in the infirmities of age and stand beside the death bed, it would be far less painful to part with her for the present. So an introduction to Miss McAuley was obtained and Anna Maria Doyle, in religion Mary Anne, was her first associate. Soon after a very young lady, Miss Frances Warde, in Religion Sr. Mary Frances Xavier, offered herself. She has founded more houses of our order than almost any other Superior.

But now poor Mrs. [Mary] Macauley was so ill that she required all her sister's care and attention, so that half of the year 1827 had already passed and there was no appearance of the new Institution being opened. Miss Doyle began to grow uneasy at the delay and wrote to the foundress that if this were much longer to be delayed she should feel it her duty to enter a Presentation Convent at once.

Thus urged, Miss McAuley wrote to the contractors to know how soon they could finish off a portion of the building sufficient to begin the good work. Their answer, which was at once forwarded to Miss Doyle, named the 24th of September. Miss Doyle was delighted at the thoughts of beginning her work on such a feast as that of Our Lady of Mercy, and suggested that the name of the Institution should refer to it, and so the House and Order got their name.

On the Feast of Our Lady of Mercy 1827 the work of the Institute commenced, that is, a school was opened, if I remember rightly, in the central part of the first floor, where the infirmaries are now, and two sisters were lodged in the dormitory which was where St. Anne's Corridor is.[10] St. Mary's Corridor[11] was for the accommodation of the Sisters, who were Anna Maria Doyle, Frances Warde, Mary Byrne, the eldest daughter of Foundress's deceased cousin. The foundress was at the house that day but could not remain on account of her sister. In the Spring of the next year that sister died a Catholic.[12] It was with great difficulty that she was able to procure her the Sacraments, so fierce was her husband's bigotry, and he watched her so closely. At the Military Road[13] it would have been impossible, but under pretence of satisfying an invalid's longing for change of air, our foundress hired a house near Dundrum, where his professional duties would not allow him always to remain, and the children being sent out for some amusement Fr. McCormac [McCormick] from Booterstown was able to be with her three or four times.

After her death Foundress lived at Baggot Street, though occasionally she staid [*sic*] for a day or two at her brother-in-law's. Her nieces were with her, as the eldest could not stay at a house so necessarily frequented by military men as her father's was without some female protection. She had also adopted her goddaughter, Teresa Byrne, the youngest of her cousin's numerous family. She was then 7 years old, 2 years younger than little Kitty [Catherine] Macauley. I cannot say that our dear foundress had a talent for education; she doated [*sic*] on children and invariably spoiled them.

Coolock House was sold soon after her sister's death and most of the furniture removed to Baggot Street. Mary Macauley [Catherine's niece] became a Catholic and indeed so did little Kitty.[14] For a time it was managed to conceal this from their father, but when he discovered Mary's conversion he was actually insane in his fury. After he had loaded her with reproaches he rushed into the next room and returned holding a carving knife which he thrust at her, but his sister-in-law caught his arm and before he could disengage himself his daughter had escaped from the room.[15] The servant locked her into the coal vault and threw the key among her pots and pans. He attempted to force the door of the vault but in vain. His fury then turned against his sister-in-law, but she too had hid herself. He spent the night raging through the house like a baffled beast of prey. Next morning his violence had quite exhausted him. She ventured to meet him and alternately soothing and expostulating got him to promise not to behave violently and see his daughter, but the interview was a most painful one. She had been his favorite child, but he told her that her conversion made a marked difference in his affection between her and his other children; it certainly did in his manner.

He took fever in the January of the following year [1829] and died, notwithstanding all the efforts of his sister-in-law, a Protestant. He repeatedly said all her arguments were good but he could not believe. Before he made his will he had his sons called into the room—the eldest was about 15—and asked them whether they would wish for their guardian their uncle James who would have them educated Protestants, or their aunt who if she undertook the charge would require them to become Catholics. They unanimously choose [*sic*] their aunt. When their father died they were brought to Baggot Street for a few days and then sent to Carlow College.

When after her sister's death the foundress came to live in Baggot St., the Institution which had hitherto been confined to the instruction of the children in the school and of the young women who occupied the dormitory took a farther [*sic*] development. As the young women who were received into the dormitory had not constant employment and as it was not proposed to maintain them, a great [deal][16] of misery was endured by the greater number. To relieve them she took in needlework, the present office, office parlor and that portion of the hall which now divides them from the hall being then the workroom; "the Sisters'", or as they were then called, "the Ladies'" sitting room being entered from it. Some externs now came for instructions and she also tried to find situations for servants.

Every evening at 8 or 8½ o'clock, I forget which, she said night prayers, in which the sisters, the young women and many people of the neighbourhood joined, the door towards Herbert St. being left open to admit any who choose [*sic*] to come in. For a long time this led to no inconvenience, but one day the foundress, who was always inclined to look at the sunny side of things and shew it to others, extolled the honestty [*sic*] of her little congregation. "We have never lost a pin's worth by them," said she. Unfortunately there were no street police then and that very evening the only portable piece of furniture in the room, her own chair, was gone. The ice of honestty [*sic*] broken, other matters were soon after missing; so the side door was shut early and the devotions confined to the inmates. The prayers she used then were those in the *Catholic Piety* with an additional Litany or the Psalter. She then read a chapter from a devout book: *The Sinner's Complaint, The Elevation of the Soul*, and *The Sufferings of Christ.*

From the very beginning the Discalced Carmelites Fathers from Clarendon St. were active and efficient friends. Through their Provincial, Fr. L'Estrange, our foundress became acquainted with the family of the great O'Connell and the Misses Costello of Merrion Square, sisters to the much regretted Eastern traveller. Both these families distinguished for their talents and accomplishments assisted her in every way, taught in the school and sometimes in the work room. On the 22nd of November 1828 Mary Macauley received conditional Baptism from the late Archbishop Dr. Murray. The chapel had been floored and ceiled and a temporary altar set up. He gave permission for the visitation of the sick and told her to build a gallery in the chapel which he permitted to be opened to the public in order to furnish funds. Accordingly this good work began the next day, by a visit to Sir P. Dunne's [Dun's] Hospital. I think too that it was on the next day that the first Mass was said in [the chapel].[17] The celebrating priest was the Very Revd. Fr. L'Estrange OCD; his acolyte was O'Connell.

Every Xmas day she gave a dinner of roast beef and plum pudding to the children of the school and all friends of the Institution were invited to be present. That given at Xmas 1828 (I am not sure if it were [*sic*] the 1st or 2nd) excited great interest. The Liberator carved, the other ladies and gentlemen served. O'Connell was excessively fond of children. Now among these children was the orphan of one of the nurses at Sir P. Dunne's Hospital who died about a week before—the ugliest, most il[l]formed, uncouth being you could fancy. She was almost an idiot with a most startling voice. Beside her sat 3 or 4 pretty little girls, orphans which were some time longer in the house and had learned to behave prettily before company. These were the pets with the ladies and many remarks were made on the contrast between them and their il[l]favoured companion. Not so with the illustrious orator. He helped her to dainty pieces, said droll things to make her merry, and when she had done eating took her in his arms, kissed her (she was about 4 years) and told her she was his favorite of all the little girls there. He was then "the Member for Clare" and Catholic Emancipation was obtained a few months later.

On the 21st January '29 an associate joined our foundress, Miss Anne O'Grady, a very pious and very lovely girl. A few days after it was that Surgeon Macauley died.[18]

And a very few[19] days after his death I saw our foundress for the 1st time. My brother took me to introduce me. She was sitting in the little parlor on the right side of the hall as you enter. She was then upwards of 40 but looked at least 10 years younger.[20] She was very fair with a brilliant color on her cheeks, still not too red. Her face was a short oval but the contour was perfect. Her lips were thin and her mouth rather wide, yet there was so much play and expression about it that I remarked it as the next agreeable feature in her[21] face. Her eyes were light blue and remarkably round with the brows and lashes colorless but they spoke. In repose they had a melancholy beseeching look; then it would light up expressive of really hearty fun, or if she disapproved of anything they could tell that too. Sometimes they had that strange expression of reading your thought[s],[22] which made you feel that even your mind was in her power, and that you could not hide anything from her. Her nose was straight but thick. She wore bands made from her own back hair which were so well managed as to be quite free from the disagreeable look bands of the kind usually give. The color was pale golden not in the least sandy, very fine and silky. She was dressed in black British merino which according to the fashion of the time fitted tight to her shape. She was remarkably well made, round but not in the least heavy. She had a good carriage, her hands were remarkably white but very clumsy, very large with broad square tips to the fingers and short square nails. She broke down very soon after for when I saw her again in about 6 months I scarcely knew her.

She was not as yet undeceived as to the uncatholic nature of her project. True, she had got but one associate since the house opened, but as she got one she supposed she should get more. Therefore when she returned to Baggot Street after her brother-in-law's death it was with great surprize and no pleasure that she saw a grating in front of that part of the chapel which she had reserved for herself and companions. "What," she said, "could be the use of a grating where there never would be nuns?" Her companions prevailed on her to let it remain.

I believe the 1st time she tolerated the idea of having the House of Mary of Mercy, as it was then called, turned into a Convent was when Sr. M. Magdalen Flinn [Flynn] was about to enter, but her old dislike to it returned and held on for more than half a year after. It was Dr. Blake who introduced Sr. M. Magdalen, and his heart was set on having it a religious house. She entered in July. In September another joined them, Margaret Dunne, in Religion Sister M. Angela, the 1st Revd. Mother of Charleville.[23] Mary Macauley on the anniversary of her baptism also associated herself; next month Miss Harley, Sr. M. Elizabeth, entered.

But before this the Institution excited attention and a most unpleasant feeling among the higher rank of Catholics. The most atrocious calumnies were hinted at. She was sneered at as an upstart, as uneducated. To give some relief to the poor creatures sheltered in the Dormitory she began to solicit subscriptions by notes in her own name. They began, "C. McAuley takes the liberty of soliciting etc.," and from Catholics, good Catholics and rich Catholics, she got the most insulting answers. In one it ran thus: "N— knows nothing of such a person as C. McAuley and considers that C. McAuley has taken a very great liberty in addressing her. She requests that C. McAuley will not trouble her with any more of C. McAuley's etc., etc." We never could find out from her who wrote that note. She said that if we knew we should be surprised, that lady was so true a friend and so large a benefactress to the Institute. However, we had some real friends, among the earliest I may mention James and John O'Ferrall. With Mr. Cavanagh our foundress became acquainted through Fr. [Daniel] Burke OSF, our first chaplain.

It became a subject of debate among the pious ladies whether the Archbishop would sanction the Institute, though it had had his sanction from the very beginning. However, they settled quite independent of his Grace that he would allow the work to go on but that he would put it under the control of the Sisters of Charity; indeed the report was prevalent that Miss McAuley meant to join that order herself. Nor were there wanting kind friends to enlighten her on the Archbishop's views as well as on her own. At last a priest asked to be shown through the house and as she accompanied him he informed her that the Archbishop had come to a resolution concerning her affairs. The Sisters of Charity were to take charge of the house. The foundress and her friends were to have certain apartments which he pointed out, with leave to help in the school, visit some of the sick, work for the poor, etc., under their direction. Believing him to be authorized by his Grace, she said she was quite willing to place herself and house at the Archbishop's disposal and as soon as he left wrote to Dr. Murray to that effect and to request his orders if any previous arrangements were to be made. He was quite puzzled and drove over to know what she meant. He then assured her that far from deputing that clergyman he had never entertained such an idea. The house was her own and she should dispose of it as she pleased for he was sure she never would do anything that he could not sanction.

Now, however, she was convinced that to carry on the Institute she must be a religious. This point had often been discussed with her associates who were all in favor of it, but still she shrank from deciding on it. She was no longer young, her habits were formed among Protestants, she did not like ceremony, and some of the ceremonies used in Convents, as kneeling to the Superiors, were particularly distasteful. But Dr. Blake was urging her and dear Fr. O'Hanlon managing it, and in fact I may say he did manage to bring her to the point. All along he had it in view, and by drawing her attention to particular bits of propriety now and then, prepared her mind to appreciate the advantages of uniform observances. Now he procured her the Theresian[24] Rule and Observances, offering her if she would take the Rule of the Tertian and so much of the Observances as would bring the Community into form, that the Discalced Carmelites would adopt them as a Third Order. But some of the observances appeared ridiculous and then came [the] weighty consideration of subjecting her community to the Fathers who must change their superiors so often, in which she foresaw great inconvenience. Still, the having been given that Rule shewed her how to proceed, and Dr. Blake procured for her the Rules of all Religious Houses near Dublin except that of the Sisters of Charity who refused to allow its inspection, though, by way of parenthesis, I got and made a week's study of it. The only one which at all suited her views was that of the Presentation Order, so negotiations were entered into with the Superiors of the convent on George's Hill to allow her with two companions to serve a novitiate there. She had to wait, however, for some young persons who promised to join her, in order to leave enough to carry on the business of the Institute. She had also a good many arrangements to make.

In the first place, the ladies who came in to teach in the school were with many thanks excluded, The Costelloes and the O'Connells had been very useful, those who came after not quite so much so and a deal more fond of gossipping [*sic*]. Then there were the lay sisters in the management of whom she utterly and always failed. She had a weakness for pretty faces and had taken, I think, 5 pretty young girls; of these two had evidently no vocation,[25] but she left 2 after her who had both to be dismissed before her return. In June Georgiana[26] Moore and Caroline Murphy entered, in July Marianne Delany (Sr. De Pazzi), and at length, having made the best arrangements in her power for the well being of the Institute during her absence, she with Miss Doyle and Miss Harley entered the Convent at George's Hill early in September 1830.

The Superior when she entered was M[other] M. Clare Doyle (or Sr. Angela Taylor)—I am not sure which[27]—who was very kind to her and for whom she felt great affection. This religious considering her age, her position past and future, and the many other circumstances which made hers an exceptional case, treated her with a certain degree of deference and in accordance to her wishes the Mistress of Novices did the same. But the close of her 2nd triennial drew nigh and at the next election M[other] M. de Sales Knowd was chosen Revd.

Mother, who had opposed the admission of subjects not to be professed for their own order, and openly declared herself against differences and privileges. Of course she named a Mistress of Novices who held the same opinions and so the subjects from Baggot St., especially Sr. M. Catherine, which was the name our foundress had in religion, were pretty severely tried. Sr. M. A. Doyle was the favourite. Sr. M. Elizabeth Harley they pronounced a living saint, but by keeping her employed cleaning shoes and cooking utensils in a damp underground kitchen without fire fostered her constitutional tendency to consumption. Foundress ventured to remonstrate but it was then too late, she was incurable before her Profession.

As for the foundress herself, a few of the nuns understood her and valued her highly, but the Revd. Mother and Mistress of Novices kept her in perpetual agitation by giving her to understand that they would receive her companions to Profession at the end of the year and postpone hers, or even reject her altogether. This had it been done would have ruined the Institute altogether, for much less than the charge of the Mother House proved too much for Sr. Mary Anne and, as I have said, Sr. M. Elizabeth was dying. She was also anxious about the sisters who were left in Baggot St. Sister Marianne Delany had been left in charge of the household affairs and of the duties of the Institute, but as to spirituals,[28] the others were not much inclined to be guided by the junior of all, so every one mismanaged her own spiritualities in her own way. One took to fasting, another took the discipline, another slept in haircloth, while a fourth and fifth thought proper to remain up half the night at their prayers. To this last piece of perfection, however, Fr. O'Hanlon put a stop. I am not sure whether it was he or Fr. Burke who having to go late at night to Upper Baggot Street saw lights in the cells, but it was he who came the next day to forbid it and went to George's Hill to tell the foundress, who also forbid it. Moreover, he and Fr. Burke made it a point to walk round the house of odd nights just after 10 to see that all the lights were out. However, these freaks told on their health; all grew more or less sickly and Sr. Caroline died of disease of the heart. She was a most pure and holy creature, very young and exceedingly beautiful. She was especially humble, and her great delight was to be taken for a lay sister or told she was very silly. Then the lay sisters had to be dismissed after giving a deal of trouble.

The soliciting of subscriptions which had at first been carried on by notes had for some time before her departure been carried on by the orphans in the house, but after she left they quite fell off, and poor Sr. Anne, or as she would be called, Aloysius O'Grady, in her zeal for the service of the poor proposed that the sisters themselves should collect and wrung a reluctant consent from the foundress. But the sisters soon found this quite an unsuitable thing and at length it was with great difficulty she could get a sister to accompany her; as for anyone going *en chef*, she could not hope it. Soon the fatigue and anxiety preyed on her constitution. She was dying when the foundress returned from George's Hill.

On the 12th of December 1831 the foundress and her companions were professed and immediately after the ceremony returned to Baggot Street. On the following day Dr. Murray came and appointed her Superior. For a long time she would not be called Revd. Mother but only Mother Catherine. Even to the last she would not allow the least ceremony to be used towards her. If a sister spoke to her on affairs of conscience, she drew a chair beside her Revd. Mother and talked on. At Recreation she moved about the room but the sisters were not to stand up or she went off. I had a trick for keeping her. She liked to look at me drawing or working and I always contrived an empty chair I could reach without standing up and by drawing it to her I have often got her to sit half an hour at the end of the table. At the first Recreation the business of the convent was talked of as freely as if it were a Chapter of Discreets. She was with us precisely as my own mother was with her family, or rather we used less ceremony than was used at home.

The Archbishop ordered that the Office should be said in English, and as long as he lived we were not permitted to say it in Latin (Dr. Cullen gave the permission). She was a great lover of poverty and at first thought there never could be enough of it. In consequence she resolved that all ceremonies should be strictly private, but the first attempt shewed her that the plan would not answer. Six sisters[29]—one of whom she had received while at George's Hill, with very little means, at the request of [an] aunt, one of the Presentation Nuns whom she liked most—were to be received in the sacristy and orders were given that no visitors should be admitted. But there was such ringing of bells. Friends of the sisters, friends of the Institute, everyone sure that some one else had been admitted, everyone indignant, then the mob that collected round them increased the confusion. But loud above all rose the voice of the junior Postulant's mother who declared she would not allow her daughter to remain in the convent where she herself was so affronted, and the aunt's death, which occurred about a week after, having a vacancy at George's Hill, she actually forced her daughter to remove thither. So many indeed were offended by their exclusion that the ceremonies were ever after more public. Still, she insisted on the postulants being dressed very simply, and white muslin was the only costume allowed in her time.

Another department in which her poverty shewed itself injuriously was the refectory. She had a fine constitution, and a superior could not be like the others always employed in the active duties such as the school or the visitation, and therefore she did not feel so soon, though she did as effectually, the consequences of their wretched dietary; but the sisters overworked in these departments soon sank. Three were attacked with virulent scurvy, all the others ill. This took place soon after Sr. M. Elizabeth's death on Easter Monday.[30] Revd. Mother who notwithstanding her love of austerities was always and most kind to the sick did her best to restore them. The Surgeon General, the late Sir P[hilip] Crampton,[31] was called in, I forget to which of them; as [and?] he, having always less faith in medicine than management, inquired into their food and occupations, and at once declared that an amellioration [*sic*] of the diet would be the best cure, and especially he ordered beer. He tried to convince her of the real unwholesomeness of the visitation, but she never could understand, and always maintained that fresh air must be good, forgetting that it must be taken by us mostly in Townsend St. and Bull Alley. Even when I entered the diet was most unfit for persons doing our duties. Leg of Beef with onion sauce, beef stakes [*sic*] that seemed as if they had lain in a tanpit, hash of coarse beef, salt beef, and for a dainty, fried liver and bacon, though boiled and roast mutton came in sometimes.

The breakfast table was a trial to one's nerves: sugar of the very blackest and coarsest kind with no sugar spoon, and for that matter the juniors seldom had a little lead spoon apiece, weak tea, very little milk, plates of very stale thick bread with a very thin scraping of butter. But Crampton also said that the silence Religious observed at meals was unwholesome and so more recreation days were appointed than she afterwards found convenient.

The Institute had now got a firm footing, subjects and work came in. A Bazaar this year held at Morrisson's [*sic*] was most successful. The next year it was held in the Rotunda, and the Queen, then Princess Victoria, as well as her excellent mother, then patronized and contributed work which the Duchess of Leinster sold. All the nobility in Ireland were at that Bazaar. It was like a drawing room; but they fell off greatly after that.

The first cholera broke out in Ireland in 1832, and the people were most injuriously prepared for it by the terrible accounts of its virulence in other countries. It certainly was an awful visitation. The deaths were so many, so sudden, and so mysterious that the ignorant poor fancied the doctors poisoned the patients, and as immediate burial was necessary it was reported that many were buried alive. Some no doubt were, but there is reason to believe very few indeed. It was under these circumstances that Revd. Mother offered her services to the cholera hospital, Townsend Street, which were thankfully accepted. The Archbishop having approved of this step the sisters entered on their duties to the great comfort of the patients and doctors; but the fatigue they underwent was terrible. Revd. Mother described to some of us the sisters returning at past 9, loosening their cinctures on the stairs and stopping, overcome with sleep. All the sisters were not allowed to the cholera hospital but those who had to stay from it had to do double work in the school and visitation, so they lost no merit. Numberless conversions both of Protestants and old sinners were the consequence of their attendance.

I ought to have mentioned before that Fr. L'Estrange, when at Rome in 1830, desirous to do us all the good in his power, spoke of us to the Holy Father and procured as a mark of his approbation the first rescript of indulgences granted. In 1832 Dr. Whelan was in the Holy City and called the attention of the Pope to all the good the order was doing and in consequence the Archbishop received the most flattering congratulations from his Holiness on the foundation taking place in his time, and sending us through him the Papal Benediction.[32] But poor Revd. Mother was not without her troubles. Sr. M. Catherine Byrne, one of her first associates, besides a strong preference to the Order of St. Dominic, had a most decided love and talent for manoeuvering, with a most fertile imagination. She had during Revd. Mother's noviciate made acquaintance with a rather wealthy Dominican priest to whom, after her own reception, she gave such a distorted picture of her benefactress and her position that he thought it the most meritorious action in the world to remove her to Cabra. In the mean time she carefully concealed her project which she effected by means of her office of sacristan, which enabled her to keep one of the orphans sent to assist her in cleaning the chapel watching at the visitation entrance then opening on Baggot Street, till the answers to her notes were brought her by one of the school children. Revd. Mother had not the least idea of what was going on till the Revd.[33] friend came to remove her cousin. She never uttered a single word of remonstrance nor made any effort to shake her purpose though she felt it painfully, a circumstance which puzzled the good friar and perhaps disappointed his protégée. It was himself who told me [a] great deal of this; the rest I learned from Revd. Mother herself and the child employed to watch who was, when I came in, a lay sister.

If it were only the loss of an intriguing subject, however gifted as Miss Byrne undeniably was, it might have been accounted a gain, but it made others of the Sisters uneasy concerning their vocations, so that when the year of novitiate, which was all that at [that] time was required, had elapsed, 2 who were most unfitted for Carmelites found out that they had a Carmelite vocation. One, however, thought better of the matter and was professed with 3 others, but the other, Sr. M. Teresa Macauley, though then manifestly consumptive, could not bear the thoughts of any Profession except in the Carmelite Order. She was professed, however, on her death bed in the year 1833.[34]

As well as I can recollect, it was early in 1833 that the rule was drawn up. The Archbishop sent a priest, I think his name was Kelly,[35] to confer with the foundress on the subject. The Presentation rule, amplyfying [*sic*] that of St. Augustine, is the foundation of ours.[36] Some clauses were omitted; others relative to the objects of the Institute were added, which were drawn up by the foundress and Mother M. Clare. When they were satisfied with their labors, the manuscript was sent to his Grace. He kept it for several months, added a little and struck out a great deal. This copy in a blue cloth cover is (1864) still among the papers of the convent. Mother M. Clare wrote out a fair copy to which the Archbishop's approval was given, signed and sealed. This copy was taken to Cork.

When the house was first opened the parish belonged to the archbishop who appointed as Administrator the Revd. Mr. [Matthias] Kelly. This gentleman had no great idea that the unlearned sex could do any thing but mischief by trying to assist the clergy, while he was prejudiced against the foundress whom he considered a parvenue. His opinions perhaps influenced the curates by whom he was greatly beloved, for certainly they did not affect to be glad of the establishment, either as a secular or religious Institute. Fr. McDermott, a Trinitarian, [was] for very many years our only friend among St. Andrew's parochial clergy.[37] Fr. Kelly was a great favorite with them, but having got the parish some thousands of pounds into debt by altering the dirty, ugly, inconvenient chapel into something uglier and far more inconvenient, quarrels with the parishioners had ensued, so that the archbishop, to put an end to them, had promoted Fr. Kelly to the parish of Clondalkin which happened to be vacant, and unwilling to entangle himself assigned the parish of St. Andrew to his Vicar General, Dr. Blake.

Even very good people consider great Saints great torments. Dr. Blake was not coveted by his new curates. He was a great friend of our dear foundress and held her in absolute veneration, and soon after his appointment he identified her with his views by sending to her all the contents of the poor boxes, that food might be provided for the poor whom he should send to us. This I think was in 1830, but I am not sure.[38] It was a measure most distasteful to the clergy who before distributed it, and to a set of old but not very worthy pensioners who used to receive the greater part and whom we could not consciencioul[s]ly [*sic*] continue to keep up, to the prejudice of those who wanted and deserved it more. It was a most troublesome duty. There was the labor of accounts, which was no trifle. I saw the account books. There was soup to be made for a hundred, sometimes more, and they had to pass through the office down to the dining hall in squadrons, and this by a wooden staircase now replaced by stone, so there was work and dirt and discontent, as well as derangement of the office business and inconvenience in the management of the House of Mercy. Mother M. Clare, M. Anne and, more graphically than all, Sr. M. Magdalen Flynn have described it to me. In 1832 Dr. Blake was made Bishop of Dromore,[39] and Revd. Mother requested his successor, Dean [Walter] Meyler, to relieve her from this onerous and invidious duty, and he was very glad to do so.

A circumstance which had occurred years before had left an unpleasant feeling in Dean Meyler with regard to our foundress.[40] One of the first things he did was to forbid the 2nd Mass on Sundays, which cut off a great resource for the charity, and he tried not to have the Charity Sermon preached in the Parish Church, but the Archbishop decided it was to be so. Many other trials sprang from the same source.[41]

But I believe the greatest trial of all to her were the frequent deaths of the Sisters. While she preserved her health she had a great awe or even fear of death, and she never saw the approach of a Sister's death or spoke of one who had died without great emotion. She had a really tender affection for us. A great many of the Sisters died in the early years of the foundation. The first Professed who died was Sr. M. Elizabeth Harley, who was her companion in her own noviceship, on Easter Monday 1832 and before the close of the year 1836 [six][42] had died.

In 1834 the first branch house was established at Kingstown.[43] There had been a great deal of sickness. Sr. M. Elizabeth [Moore], afterwards the first Superior at Limerick, had a dreadful fever and hardly escaped death. The doctors said the house was overcrowded; besides, that for persons engaged in our laborious duties a change of air was often indispensable. Fr. O'Hanlon and the chaplain, Fr. Burke, seconded their representations, and the latter having heard of a suitable house to be sold in Kingstown, one of the novices, the widow of a Dr. McCann who had a good property,[44] offered to buy and fit it up, which decided the business. It was in Sussex Place, now Clock Lane, and is the monastery and school of the Christian Brothers. The whole history of this place may as well be told here.

It was intended merely as a place where a sickly or overworked sister might recover, and the only work of the Institute contemplated was the Visitation. But the proselytizers there were very active; there were no National schools and the parish school was worthless, so, as of course some healthy sisters should be there, it was proposed to fit up the stables and coach house of our new acquisition as a school room. Foundress was willing enough to undertake the teaching if the parish would be answerable for the expense of alterations, furniture, etc. Nobody expected the parish priest would. All the richest parishioners said they would be delighted to contribute, and the most influential of the curates considered that a subscription for the purpose could not possibly fail, though it would not do to open it just then, at least not publicly. The proprietor of a timber yard offered long credit. Poor Foundress[45] fell into the snare. The work was executed, if not in the best at least in the most expensive manner. That which might have been well done by a Dublin builder for £200, was clumsily got up and charged £400. The P. P. [Parish Priest] would not countenance a subscription, none of our good friends came forward to assist, so that in November 1837 [actually, 1838] the Sisters had to come into Baggot St. with all haste to avoid being in the house when an execution should be laid upon it. In the beginning of 1840, at the close of some troublesome litigation, the debt was paid by the Institute and Foundress was persuaded to open the House again. Other inconveniences occurred, however, and within a few months after her death it was sold.

One evening soon[46] after I was received I happened to sit next her at first recreation and said something about the general[47] appreciation of the Institute. She turned round to me and said very emphatically, "Do not be too sure of that. It is not every one, even of those who are benefitted, that feels thankful. If you work with that expectation, you will often be disappointed." Then, as usual, she illustrated her opinion with an anecdote. When Sr. M. Elizabeth was in fever the least noise caused her intense agony and the doctors had so impressed Revd. Mother with the danger of the least disturbance that even the wire of the hall doorbell was cut, and a girl set to watch all comers from the side window, that the door might be opened and shut without noise. Nevertheless the women in the House of Mercy would put no restraint on themselves and took their recreation in the yard, schouting [sic][48] at the top of their voices. Revd. Mother went down to remonstrate. As she turned to go away she heard one of them say, "Humph, indeed, what a fuss she makes! I thought the House was built for us and not for them." Now this anecdote occurred forcibly to me when in 1840 I had the charge of the House at Kingstown for a couple of months. A truly pious, charitable lady called to make arrangement which regarded the charity, but in the course of our conversation she said, "You see after all, your clever Mrs. McAuley had to pay that £400." She never reflected that every talent and every penny that our dear foundress possessed had been devoted to the poor. But she endured ingratitude and even insolence so sweetly that those who behaved ill towards her never felt they were doing wrong.

One instance of her sweetness I may mention. Judge Fitzgerald's mother had a servant, a widow who was anxious to get her only child into some Catholic establishment where she would be taken more care of than in a lodging and be educated. She was willing, she said, to pay, and Mrs. F. with some difficulty prevailed on Revd. Mother to take her. As soon as this matter was arranged to her satisfaction, the mother got married privately and had sailed for America before her mistress had the slightest idea she was leaving her service. The lady felt naturally indignant, especially at having been the means of burdening the Institution with the maintenance of a child who for years could not contribute to her own support. But when in the midst of her excitement she came to tell Revd. Mother she was heard with so much kindness and calmness and found that excuses were offered for the fugitive, while the child was promised care and protection more cheerfully than when payment was expected, she was more than surprized. Speaking to her sister, then a postulant among us, she admired the ascendancy of the meekness which calmed her own anger. "She has made me feel," said Mrs. Fitzgerald, "what real charity and real religion is."

In 1836 she led out her first foundation. Tullamore was the first place after Dublin which had a Convent of Mercy. In the same year there was another foundation at Charleville. In 1837 there were founded Houses in Carlow and Cork; in 1838 one in Limerick, and a branch house was established at Booterstown, which was built for us by Mrs. [Barbara] Verschoyle. In 1839 she went down to Cork for the Profession of the Sisters who had entered there for our first Convent in England, that at Bermondsey, and in November she went with them to form the foundation; in 1840 she founded Convents in Galway and Birr, and in 1841 she went with her last foundation to Birmingham and came home to die.

Her method was to give two Sisters—a Professed for Superior, and a Novice near profession. Immediately on her arrival she began the Thirty Days Prayer to the B[lessed] Virgin, and at the close of it the novice was professed. Generally she returned home at the end of that time, but not always. She was 3 months in Cork. She would lend another Sister or two till subjects came in, but unless Sisters entered specially for the foundation she would give but two. The only instance where she departed from this rule was in Cork, where she gave three besides a Sister who entered specially for that house.

During these years a great number of postulants entered in Baggot St., and we were accounted a very prosperous Convent, but the foundress had plenty of sorrows. Death had taken so many fine subjects, and in 1837 five departed, among them the younger of her nieces. The conduct of her nephews was most unsatisfactory. The youngest went to Australia without asking her advice or bidding her farewell and died there very soon; the two elder died of consumption brought on by reckless dissipation. She had by every means in her power striven to keep them in the right path and afterwards to reclaim them; how much she grieved for their errors few knew so well as I.[49] They both died penitent.

Then Dean Meyler was not friendly. In 1837 our chaplain, Fr. Burke OSF, went to the Cape Colony with Bishop Griffiths,[50] and the Dean closed the chapel to the public. He then refused to let the Institution have a chaplain of its own, proposing to have the duty performed by one of the clergymen attached to St. Andrew's. Poor Foundress, who foresaw the inconveniences of such an arrangement, refused to acquiesce, and he at once put an interdict on the chapel so that for some months we daily, and the young women on days of obligation, went out to Mass. After almost two months, he with much difficulty permitted Fr. [Richard] Colgan OCC, who was most uneasy concerning the length of time the Blessed Sacrament was reserved, to say Mass and give Holy Communion on Christmas Day; but as he declared he would not renew the permission she had to yield, and plenty of inconveniences, especially as regarded confessions of the school children, we had to endure.

In 1838 a legacy of £1,000 was bequeathed to the Institute, and Foundress resolved to build the laundry, hoping that the labour of the inmates might be able to render the House of Mercy self-supporting, as the closing of the chapel had so greatly curtailed our resources. But the expense of the building greatly exceeded her calculations, and the building itself was a continual worry. Neither were the returns when it was built at all equal to her expectations; in fact, for long enough after her death they were miserably insignificant.

Until the year 1839 Revd. Mother had enjoyed good health. She always suffered from rheumatism in her head, and now and then, but certainly not often, had sick days when she caught cold by being out in rain, but when she left us in order to begin the Foundation at Bermondsey she seemed likely to live many healthy years. But this the first of Pugin's convents was built most inconveniently, and she got cold immediately on her arrival. The air of London was uncongenial to her, but more so still the spirit of one of the Sisters. This lady, who all through life, when she was a Protestant, when a convert in secular life, when a Sister of Mercy, and when no longer so, was always consistently actuated by the desire of concentrating everyone's admiration and, if possible, affection on herself, could not live without manoeuvering.[51] She contrived to create a misunderstanding [between] our foundress and Mother M. Clare which though of short duration was very painful to the former, who loved her younger Sister very fondly. She also contrived to make M. Cecilia Marmion discontented with our customs and bent on making changes, which was also a fret to our dear Superior.

In May she went to Galway and left there for the foundation Mother M. Teresa White and Sister M. Catherine Leahy. The former was, I think, her favorite of all the Sisters. She said to me once: "Of all the sisters Sr. M. Teresa has most of my spirit and I trust more to her guiding the Institute as I wish than to any other Sister." She disliked the spirit of change which possessed some of the Sisters under pretence of seeking greater perfection, saying that if they adopted the practices of other orders it was making out that ours was not requisite in the Church.

Though above all objects of devotion she most loved a crucifix, she insisted that Mother M. Clare should not wear one in her cincture and forced from her a promise that she would always keep hers concealed under her habit.[52] She was an ardent lover of poverty, yet it was with great difficulty she was induced to change the expensive gossamer veils the Professed wore for woollen ones, saying that if once changes began no one knew where they would stop. She loved to pray before the Most Holy Sacrament and finding that in Carlow they used after the mid-day prayers one of the beautiful Effusions of Love at the end of *The Soul United to Jesus,* she liked them so well that she began to use them herself. After a month, however, she ceased this devotion and when I asked her why said that if she added prayers herself some very devout successor would add more and another more till, especially in poor convents, the sisters would be incapable of the duties of the Institute and we should end like the Presentation Nuns after Miss Nagle's death in being enclosed. Still she told me she would always use these prayers herself and advised me to do the same.

When she returned from Bermondsey she filled up all the Offices of the Discreets, which had not been done before. I fancy she thought Sr. M. de Pazzi too austere a Mistress of Novices and named her Mother Assistant.[53] The Sister who replaced her soon shewed, however, how little she had of her spirit and how much of the spirit of change. The practice of silence during the five minutes preceding our common duties was not observed then on recreation days. I was directed to observe it. A senior Professed spoke to me, I made a sign of silence, she drew Revd. Mother's attention to the circumstance. Now Revd. Mother when displeased with any of us usually called us by our sirnames [*sic*]. She called me over and said, "Pray, little girl, why did you not answer Sr. M. Teresa?" I told her. She replied, "You are not to attend to such commands in future. Mrs.—[54] shall make none of her improvements here while I live," and she laughed and chatted with me till the next duty. Soon after, she went into the Noviceship and saw a very pretty green card on which were written extracts from the 5th Chapter of our Constitutions with some other directions, concluding with this notice: "If any of the Senior Professed should require the services of a Novice she shall apply to her Mistress." She took down the card and wetting her handkerchief effaced the paragraph. About half an hour after, the Mistress of Novices was observed with tearful eyes and there were no more improvements while she lived.

For several years there had been a fearful schism on Birr which was the source of innumerable sins. It had originated on the appointment of Dr. Vaughan as P.P. in preference to a popular curate. The Bishops of the province had hoped that by elevating Dr. V. to the Bishoprick and replacing him in the Parish by Fr. [John] Spain, a man of great talent and popularity who had fought the battle of the tythes [*sic*], to the admiration of all Munster, would put an end to the scandal, but it [did] not.[55] True, Dr. Spain's life was not threatened, but his excommunicated rival lost no partizans, and only a few well-instructed families [went to] his Mass. Father Matthew[56] went there to administer the pledge (the temperance movement was then at the height of its success) but appearing as the partizan of the P.P. could do no good. But he gave an advice; which was to found there a Convent of Mercy, and though there were no funds, he undertook to negotiate the matter with the Archbishop and Revd. Mother. In spite of the express prohibition of the Rule he succeeded. On the feast of St. John the Evangelist 1841 [actually, 1840] Revd. Mother with Mother M. Aloysius Scott, Sr. M. Rose and another Sister left Dublin for Birr, and the Convent was founded without any ascertained revenue. Their appearance produced an almost miraculous effect. Within a year there was scarcely a vestige of the schism, and the unfortunate author of it, forsaken by his faction, went to Manchester where he met with little favor even from Protestants. He afterwards repented and made his submission to the Bishop.

But our dear foundress had a deal to fret her just then. The school at Kingstown opened directly on the street, so that seculars could enter it without any Sister being aware of it, except her who taught there, nor even had she been willing could she at all times communicate the entrance of a visitor to the local Superior. Unfortunately the school Sister was by her vanity and selfishness most liable to err in such a position, and err she did, most injuriously for the Institute. The Superior with a multitude of virtues had no talents, and her mistakes proved almost as troublesome as the other's sins.[57]

Poor Revd. Mother's patience and humility seemed to increase with her trials. One instance I will give. A Sister[58] whom I know she loved and trusted more than others was afflicted with severe disease which injured her mental much more than her bodily powers, so that she became inconceivably melancholy and captious. Revd. Mother, too large-minded herself to understand a groundless jealousy, indeed any jealousy at all, tried in vain to find out what was the trouble. At last one morning I was drawing at Lecture, which was then given in the Bishop's Parlor, and not finding it convenient to rise the moment it was concluded, was left the last. Revd. Mother, who knew this Sister often spoke to me, said: "Sister M. Clare, what ails Sr. N—?" Now it would not have answered at all to tell her Sr. N—'s grievances, so I only said, "Revd. Mother, I wish you could sit in the Community room as you used to do when it was down stairs." She answered that she could not, on account of her failing strength, but she wished we would sit with her, and there was room enough for there were but four of us [professed] in Community, including the Mistress of Novices. And she told me to bring down the paint box. In the Community room I found the Sister who asked me with some warmth what had detained me. I told her Revd. Mother wished us to sit with her and that she ought to bring down her desk, but she refused, saying she could not speak to Revd. Mother if Sisters her juniors were to be constantly present, etc. I went back and said, "Revd. Mother, it will not do for us all to sit here so, if you please, I shall take away my things, but you could ask Sr. N— only." About an hour after, I met Sr. N—, quite radiant, her desk in her hand. Revd. Mother had complained of loneliness and asked her to sit with her. I escaped the visitors and poor Sr. N— gave less annoyance for a while.[59]

On the morning of SS. Peter and Paul that year (1841) I saw our foundress for the last time, being sent to Cork to open a day school for the wealthier class. I had no idea her death was so near. True, she was greatly broken in health, but she concealed half her illness, in fact never complained of any. She almost always rose with the rest of us and still insisted on using the ordinary fare of the refectory. She was then preparing for the foundation at Birmingham, which was established in the third week of August, but a Sister whom I parted in her ordinary health had before that time fallen into hopeless consumption. Sr. M. Justina's virtues and talents were of no common order, and Revd. Mother had formed great hopes of her, and her approaching death was a serious affliction, but her own death preceded it. When she returned from Birmingham the Sisters could no longer deceive themselves: she was evidently dying. An abscess had formed internally; her debility was most painful so that to walk from room to room fatigued her, she coughed incessantly, her appetite was gone, she could not sleep. The highest medical advice was procured but it was useless, and she knew it, but she took all that was ordered and submitted to all the little alleviations in the way of diet which the Sisters presented to her, though a foul taste with which she was now constantly afflicted prevented any comfort from them. This was perhaps the reason she accepted them, for when she was ill after her return from Bermondsey she lectured the infirmarian for buying her a chicken, and absolutely refused to touch it. The infirmarian was Mother M. Catherine Leahy.

She immediately began to set the affairs of the house in order, looked over her papers and destroyed a few. She was greatly harassed by pecuniary difficulties, in fact so much so that she feared the Community might be obliged to disperse. Next to Mr. Cavanagh the most useful friend she had was Sister M. De Pazzi's brother, Mr. Bernard Delany. She always liked him very much and had great confidence in his business talents and discretion, and he fully justified it. He spared no pains to serve us, and if things are all right with us now, as I believe they are, much of it is due to his activity and liberality also.

As far as I can make out she was not more than a week or 10 days confined to bed. Besides the internal abscess she had a hideous ulcer on her back,[60] brought on by the use of haircloth and a large chain. This she had concealed. Her brother,[61] how I know not, became aware of it and wanted to see it, which she refused to allow, but consented to let the Sister (M.T[eresa] Carton) who slept with her in the infirmary dress it. She told me it was almost as large as the palm of her own hand, with green matter in the middle. On the 9th of November when Dr. Stokes[62] had seen her he told this Sister to watch her closely as he expected the abscess would burst and that would be the immediate forerunner of death. At this time the only Sisters she would have much with her were Sr. M. Vincent Whitty, Mother M. Elizabeth Moore who came up from Limerick to be with her, a step she did not approve of, and this lay sister (M. T. Carton) for whom she entertained a great affection, and whom she preferred should remain with her at night. All through this evening of the 9th she suffered intensely and I believe it was after 10 that the pain increased so much that she got out of bed and the dreaded lesion took place. It left her so weak that she had to call her companion to help her back to bed. After a few minutes she asked if she was asleep. The sister who had remained sitting up in bed quite frightened replied in the negative, and was then asked if she could get brown paper and cord, and to bring plenty.[63] She rose, procured four or five large pieces, some very coarse indeed, and a good bundle of strong twine. She was then told to draw the curtains of both beds and lie down, the first part of which injunction she obeyed, but though she returned to her bed she could not lie down for terror. After a short interval of silence she heard a great rustling which seemed to come from under the bedclothes and continued for a good space. Revd. Mother then called her to her bedside and shewing her a packet she had wrapped in the brown paper and tied up most curiously told her she was to go to the kitchen, stir up the fire, and when it blazed strong to put the parcel in it and turning her back to it remain till it was quite consumed, "but", she continued, "I forbid you under obedience to attempt to open this parcel or look at it while it is burning." The Sister did not stir. The idea of standing in the kitchen where the cockroaches would be crawling about her was not a pleasant one, but the prohibition under obedience made the matter worse. Revd. Mother then said, "Would you be afraid, dear?" "Oh, Revd. Mother, I would be afraid I might look." "Well, call Sister M. Vincent." Sr. M. Vincent [Whitty] was awakened, came down and received the same injunction and solemn prohibition, with the further direction that when she put the parcel in the fire she was to draw red coals over it. She burned the parcel but disobeyed that prohibition. She hinted to me of a haircloth, but as I could not approve of a breach of trust under any circumstance, I asked her no questions. She told Fr. Vincent, the Passionist,[64] she saw a discipline. However that be, she returned to the infirmary, was asked if she had done as she was required, answered in the affirmative, and received the thanks of her dying Superior.

The next morning Revd. Mother executed some business with Mr. Cavanagh, saw her brother for the last time, and also Dr. Murphy, B[ishop] of Cork, and Fr. O'Hanlon, her confessor. Later in the day she sent for each of the Sisters, exhorted them, each according to her need, to advance in the way of perfection, and bade her a loving farewell. Early on the 11th she fell into her agony. Mass was said in the infirmary and the Sisters went to the chapel for Holy Communion while she still struggled between life and death, nor was it till that she breathed her last. The Right Revd. Dr. Kinsella, B[ishop] of Ossory, consecrated the burial ground in which her body was the first laid.[65]

Mary Frances Xavier (Frances) Warde 1810–1884

Less than three years before her death at the age of seventy-four, Frances Warde wrote from Manchester, New Hampshire, to Mary Austin Carroll in New Orleans:

> How full of joys and deep sorrows my life has been none can tell. It is a long time in which much good could have been accomplished, and I fear much *neglected.* . . . The memory of the past is filled with humbling reflections for me.[1]

It was a letter Catherine McAuley might have written: passionate, humble, grateful. It was written by the woman whom Catherine—in more than her usual affection and tenderness—had called "my ever dearest Child" (Neumann 142).

Frances Warde was born about 1810, the daughter of Mary Maher and John Warde of Belbrook House, Abbeyleix, County Laois.[2] She was the youngest of six children: Daniel, William, John, Helen, Sarah, and Frances (Healy 5–6). Shortly after her birth her mother died, and the younger children were then cared for at Belbrook House by their father and a maternal aunt. In 1819 Belbrook House and the accompanying lands were lost to the Warde family through certain residual practices of the penal code which permitted the transfer of the lease to Sir Robert Staples who opened the Abbeyleix Institution for the Education of the Upper Classes of Society on the property (Healy 10–13). Consequently, the Warde family was dispersed. The girls went to live with their uncle, William Maher, at Killeany in the parish of Mountrath (Healy 13–14, 488). When Frances was about fourteen, one of her brothers and her sister Helen died within a year, and not long after this her father also died.[3] Surely these deaths, and the early loss of her mother, were among the "deep sorrows" to which Frances referred in 1882.

Frances was thus an orphaned young woman in her late teens when she first met Catherine McAuley, through her friendship with Catherine's niece, Mary Macauley. Frances, who apparently resided with friends in Dublin at this time, often visited the Macauley residence on Military Road where Catherine was living before and after the death of her sister Mary in August 1827. In June 1828, after Catherine began to reside more regularly at Baggot Street, Frances began to help out in the poor schools there. The Derry Large Manuscript describes her activities in this period:

> On the 22nd of June [1828] Miss Frances Warde was associated to the pious labors of the institute, though rather as an amateur in good words than as one meant to give up the world for the service of God's poor; for though she resided pretty

> constantly at Baggot St., yet she did not assume the black dress and plain cap of the resident members, but went out to drive and visit her friends 'till the following November.

The same manuscript says that the visitation of the sick "began on the 30th of November" in 1828, and that "Our dear foundress, Miss Doyle, Miss Byrne and Miss Warde who had become a member in the preceding month, went in the carriage to Sir Patrick Dunne's Hospital where the Physicians knowing Miss McAuley's family and friends to be all Protestants and probably supposing she and her companions were of that persuasion not only allowed them to speak to the patients, but also gave a general order for their admission in future." Thus Frances began to live permanently at Baggot Street in early November 1828, as one of Catherine's earliest associates. She was, therefore, present for the dedication of the chapel at Baggot Street on June 4, 1829, and heard firsthand the clerical criticism directed against Catherine at the breakfast which followed the ceremony.[4]

When Catherine went to George's Hill in September 1830, Mary Anne (later, Mary Magdalen de Pazzi) Delany—a somewhat older woman who had joined the Baggot Street community on July 12, 1830—was left in charge of household affairs related to the works of mercy, and Frances Warde was put in charge of finances. In her letter of August 28, 1844, Clare Moore explains these arrangements: "no one was superior, it is true, but Mother de Pazzi, . . . whose prudent manners seemed to fit her for having charge of others, was given the charge of the House—superior in effect, tho' not in name. Mother Frances Warde was House keeper." It was probably in this period that the seeds of tension between the vivacious, decisive Frances and other members of the community, including Mary Anne Delany, began to develop—not over finances, but over the closeness of Frances's relationship to Catherine. Clare Moore was a life-long friend of Mary de Pazzi Delany, yet she is nonetheless objective in her assessment of the situation, as it took shape in 1832, when Frances served as Catherine's secretary, even though Mary Ann Doyle was Catherine's Assistant:

> I mention Mother F. Warde, because she was always with Revd. Mother, even when a Novice, so that some little feeling was excited as she never took her turn in the duties which the other Novices had, of sweeping, etc. At first we had charge of [the] Noviceship a week each in turn which she never took, and I remember some complained to Revd. Mother, but I believe it was necessary she should attend to other business, for Mother M. Ann was of such a retiring disposition that she could not bear to see strangers.[5]

Frances Warde received the habit on January 23, 1832, in the first reception ceremony held at Baggot Street. A year later she professed her vows with three others—Mary Clare Moore, Mary Angela Dunne, and Mary de Pazzi Delany—at the first profession ceremony of the new Institute, on January 24, 1833. Her name in religion was Mary Frances Teresa, and her chosen patron was Saint Francis Xavier. Catherine McAuley always refers to her as "Sister Mary Frances" or "Sister M. Frances", and the Dublin and Carlow Registers spell her name "Mary Frances Teresa". However, the Carlow community Annals sometimes calls her "Mother M. Francis" or "Mother M. F. Xavier" or "Mother M. Francis X. Warde". Moreover, in the United States where Frances founded the first Mercy community in 1843—and numerous other communities thereafter—she often used the name "Xavier" as part of her name, and she was in later life generally known as "Mother Xavier Warde".[6] In this study, "Frances Warde"—the simplest form of her name in religion—is used for the sake of consistency, even though it does not correspond to her own use of "Xavier" in the United States, nor explicitly reflect her life-long devotion to Francis Xavier's missionary spirit.[7]

Frances became the first superior of the Mercy foundation in Carlow in 1837, and from there she founded three more communities in Ireland: Naas (1839), Wexford (1840), and Westport (1842). Then, on November 4, 1843, she and six other sisters departed from Carlow, going by way of Naas and Dublin to Liverpool, whence they sailed to North America where on December 21, 1843 they founded the first convent of Sisters of Mercy in the United States—in Pittsburgh, Pennsylvania. A year and a half before, in June 1842, the first Mercy convent in North America had been founded in St. John's, Newfoundland.

In the almost forty-one years of her life which remained after the founding in Pittsburgh, Frances traveled the length and breadth of northeastern United States. She personally founded, or was instrumental in founding, autonomous convents of Sisters of Mercy in Chicago, Loretto (Pennsylvania), Providence (Rhode Island), Hartford (Connecticut), Rochester (New York), Manchester (New Hampshire), Philadelphia, Portland (Maine), Burlington (Vermont), and Bordentown (New Jersey).[8] She also sent founding communities of sisters to Omaha and to Yreka, California. She had a hand—whether directly, or by virtue of her earlier activity—in founding numerous schools, academies, night schools, orphan homes, hospitals, and other service institutions in these and various other cities in the United States where convents were affiliated with the above foundations.[9] From 1851 to 1858 Frances was superior of the new foundation in Providence, Rhode Island, and from 1858 until her death on September 17, 1884, she was the superior, except for three years (1880–1883), of Mount St. Mary Convent, Manchester, New Hampshire.[10]

On January 24, 1883, Frances celebrated her fiftieth anniversary as a professed Sister of Mercy. She was the last living member of the "first seven" who had received the habit at Baggot Street in January 1832, and one of the last of the "first-born", as Catherine had called her earliest companions. Years before, when Catherine wrote to Frances in the summer of 1841, she had contrasted their approach to things to that of Mary Clare Agnew, then superior in Bermondsey: "She wrote to me in the greatest alarm about a most trifling matter. If you and I were to write on such subjects we would never be done" (354). This observation is an important clue to the large-mindedness of both Catherine and Frances. Their capacity to focus on the truly important, outward-directed tasks of the Sisters of Mercy was at the heart of their greatness and explains the natural basis of their affection for one another. Even though separated by over thirty years' difference in their ages, they were from the beginning kindred spirits. They had the same zest and human sensitivity, and enjoyed one another's complete confidence.

The death of Catherine McAuley on November 11, 1841 was, therefore, a grave loss for Frances. Her apparent absence from Catherine's bedside as she lay dying probably cannot be explained by anything overt on Catherine's or Frances's part—except perhaps Catherine's own uncertainty about the terminal nature of her illness and her reluctance to alarm any of her earliest associates, or to request their presence too explicitly. The sisters present at Baggot Street early in the week of November 7 did not anticipate that Catherine would die later that week. They knew that her debility was severe, but not until November 10 did Mary Ursula Frayne write, on their behalf, to the superiors of the other foundations to tell them that "our very dear and much beloved Reverend Mother is considered to be past hope of recovery."[11] Years later, Frances Warde said to Mary Austin Carroll: "I don't know how I survived the parting from Reverend Mother . . . I often think of the heaven to which [death] will give entrance, but to me it would be heaven in itself to see dearest Reverend Mother once more" (*Leaves* 1: 175).

Perhaps Frances did not fully interpret the few indirect clues in some of Catherine's last letters to her. On June 3, 1841, Catherine wrote: "I do not despair of visiting Saint Leo's [Carlow] again, please God" (343–4); on October 4, she concluded her letter: "God bless you and all your charge. *You will not forget* your ever affectionate M. C. McAuley" (Bolster ed., 264); on October 12 she apparently wrote: "I have just received your welcome letter. How grateful I ought to be for all your anxiety. We shall meet again, please God, *but not at present*"(Carroll, *Life* 427); and to this letter she evidently added: "I wish Rev. Mr. Maher would bring you to see me" (Burke Savage 370–1).[12] Such a meeting may not have occurred. As Mary Vincent Whitty notes, in her letter of November 13, Catherine's illness took a sudden turn for the worse, and her strength declined rapidly. Toward the end she "did not seem to take an interest in any thing. Some of Mother Francis' notes remain unopened."

The obvious question must be asked: if Frances wrote notes, why did she not just *come* to Baggot Street, with or without James Maher? In responding to this question considerable weight must be given to the general incomprehension of the finality of Catherine's illness, and to the fact that during Catherine's lifetime no superior of the foundations outside of Dublin ever simply visited Baggot Street on her own—except Clare Moore on her return from Bermondsey via Kingstown in June 1841. Elizabeth Moore, the superior of Limerick, came when Catherine was dying because she was, as she says, "sent for", and had a chance to come to Dublin with her bishop. According to Mary Vincent Whitty's letter of November 16, at some point during her last illness Catherine apparently "told Sister de Sales not to allow Sr. M. Teresa from Galway [to] come for some time at least." But Teresa—of whom Catherine once reportedly said, "Of all the sisters, Sr. M. Teresa has most of my spirit, and I trust more to her guiding the Institute as I wish than to any other Sister"[13]—came as soon as she got word of the gravity of Catherine's condition, perhaps from her sister, Mary de Sales White, who was attending Catherine, or through Ursula Frayne's letter of November 10. She arrived four hours after Catherine died (*Leaves* 1:49–50). Frances Warde, Mary Aloysius Scott (Birr), and Mary Ann Doyle (Tullamore), who were relatively nearby (though it was a six-hour coach ride from Carlow), apparently held back, as did those much farther away: Clare Moore in Cork, and Mary Angela Dunne in Charleville. Mary Vincent Whitty mentions none of these superiors—except Elizabeth Moore and Teresa White—as having attended Catherine's funeral on November 15, though their presence may be unrecorded. Some tacit understanding, or accepted practice, or inability, or shock almost to the point of disbelief, may have kept them from coming.

One cannot, however, ignore the *possibility* that Frances Warde did, in fact, visit Catherine earlier, during the month before her death, perhaps after receiving her letter of October 12, and that this visit is simply unrecorded. There are apparently only three extant letters of Catherine McAuley written after October 12, none of them to Sisters of Mercy, and these are the only eyewitness written records up to November 7. If such a visit occurred, it is conceivable that Catherine, Frances, and Mary de Pazzi Delany might have remained silent about it, then and later, so as not to alarm or disappoint others, and that in such a meeting Catherine and Frances might have agreed that this would be their last visit. The "parting from Reverend Mother", to which Frances later referred (Carroll, *Leaves* 1: 175), may have been, literally, just such a face-to-face leave-taking.[14]

Frances Warde's fidelity to Catherine McAuley was primarily manifested, not in her presence at Catherine's bedside during her final days, if this occurred, but in her lifelong commitment to the works of mercy to which Catherine's own life had been dedicated. To the end of her life, even when her eyesight was almost totally gone, Frances continued to instruct adults in the consolations of the Christian faith—an educational work in which she was particularly skilled. As she once said: "I did not dream of the good to be done in educating the grand, sturdy New England character" (Healy 456).

On Easter Sunday in April 1851, Catherine McAuley's godchild, Mary Camillus (Teresa) Byrn, who was then serving in New York City, wrote to Mary Ann Doyle in Derry. In the letter she comments on the recent visit of Frances Warde, who was on her way to Providence, Rhode Island:

> Mother Francis Warde, a true Apostle of the Order of Mercy, has just begun, for the fourth time, all the toil and labor attending the establishment of a Convent of Mercy. You are aware I suppose that she was not in Office in Pittsburg [*sic*] for better than a year.[15] Right Revd. Dr. [Bernard] O'Rielly [*sic*], Bishop of Providence [actually, of Hartford], having succeeded in obtaining a Community of Sisters for his Diocess, she was appointed Mother Superior. They all stayed in our Convent for a few days; it gave us all great pleasure to see them, but will you

> believe it? I did not know Mother Francis when I first saw her; she is greatly changed in appearance, quiet and subdued, indeed almost as quiet as yourself. Upon my remarking it to her, she said "that it was time for her now to look old and careworn, her charge in Pittsburg had been so heavy and accompanied by many trials".... She was accompanied by Mother M. Joseph[ine] Cullen (Sister to the Primate of Ireland)[16] who came from Carlow with her and who succeeded her in the Superiorship of Pittsburg .... When I told Mother Francis that I sometimes heard from and wrote to you, she desired me give you her fondest love .... They left us early in March to begin their career in Providence ....[17]

Frances was only forty-one in 1851. She may have been half joking about her right "to look old and careworn", but her years as superior in Pittsburgh (1843–1850) had not been easy. While the Pittsburgh sisters had opened three convents in the diocese, two academies, five poor schools, an orphanage, and Mercy Hospital; had served the poor, the sick, and the imprisoned in countless other ways; and had founded a convent in Chicago (1846) and a house in Loretto, Pennsylvania (1848), they and Frances had also suffered. Two of the sisters who came from Carlow had died: Mary Philomena Reid, on October 2, 1845; and Mary Aloysia Strange, on July 6, 1847. Four other sisters had died of ship-fever (typhus) early in the following year. In late 1845, Frances and Mary Xavier Tiernan (one of those who died in 1848) had also made a long journey back to Ireland with Michael O'Connor, Bishop of Pittsburgh, to invite other Irish Sisters of Mercy and lay women to join them in ministering to the needs of people in the United States.[18] Although Frances's health was evidently sound, it is small wonder she was "greatly changed in appearance" from the woman Mary Camillus remembered. Yet her Xavier-like zeal carried her forward for another three decades. In 1878–1879, when she was nearly seventy and living in Manchester, she sent out sisters for three missions among the Penobscot and Passamaquoddy Indians in Maine. When she visited Indian Island herself, in late 1879, they welcomed her as the "Great Mother", gave her baskets they had woven, and presented each of their children for her blessing (Healy 419–20).

So far as we know Frances Warde did not write her own personal memoir or narrative about Catherine McAuley. However, she was one of the principal sources of the knowledge about Catherine which Mary Austin Carroll amassed in her biography, the *Life of Catherine McAuley,* first published in 1866.[19] In fact, in 1859 when Mary Austin began this work, she understood herself to be commissioned to do so by Frances herself, and she sought data from other sources under Frances's sponsorship (Muldrey 54). Moreover, in the course of the next twenty-five years, during which Austin Carroll completed her *Life* and then extended the narrative history of the Institute through four volumes of *Leaves from the Annals of the Sisters of Mercy,* Frances sent her numerous letters, transcriptions, and accounts, often using the help of other sisters in Providence or Manchester in order to get what Austin needed down on paper. Unfortunately, some years after Mary Austin Carroll's death on November 29, 1909, her trunk "stuffed full of the notes and letters of a lifetime, was sacrificed," as Mary

Hermenia Muldrey puts it, "upon the altar of a typical convent *faire le ménage,* clearing an attic because cleanliness is next to Godliness" (331–2). Whatever Frances Warde had committed to writing and sent to Austin Carroll was, with few exceptions, in this trunk.[20] Moreover, Frances's letters to other correspondents, many of which may have contained some commentary on Catherine McAuley's life, have not for the most part been preserved, and those that have been preserved have not yet been published in a single collection. Kathleen Healy has identified only twenty-two letters of Frances Warde in diocesan and Mercy archives, and notes the irony of this, given Frances's great care in preserving the many letters written to her by Catherine, and by others (428–30, 504).

Seventy-two of Catherine's letters to Frances Warde are published: all but three are in Mary Ignatia Neumann's *Letters of Catherine McAuley;* all seventy-two are in Mary Angela Bolster's *The Correspondence of Catherine McAuley.* The preservation of these letters is Frances's second major contribution to our present knowledge about Catherine. To the extent that, as John Henry Newman claimed, "a man's life lies in his letters" (*Letters and Diaries* 20:443), and the same is true of a woman's, these letters constitute documentation about Catherine which is more precious than any memoir Frances might have written.

In addition, verbal portraits of Catherine and accounts of her involvement in the early history of the Sisters of Mercy in Carlow are preserved in the Carlow Annals, especially for the years 1837 through 1843. While Frances Warde did not write these Annals herself—they are clearly the reflections of novices—they represent the perceptions of the community of whom she was the first superior. As such, excerpts from these Annals may in some way stand as the indirect testimony of the woman to whom Catherine felt free to confide such plain, human statements as the following: "Pray fervently to God to take all bitterness from me" (129); "This is a shameful letter. I am nervous" (201); "I think the name of another foundation would make me sick. . . . Indeed the thought of it at present would greatly distress me" (237–8); "The ceremony just over and I as usual tired doing nothing" (269); and "I look forward with fear and trembling to my Birmingham journey. I have really got a surfeit" (343).

To Frances Warde, therefore, historians are singularly indebted: for her extensive contributions to Mary Austin Carroll's *Life of Catherine McAuley* and her *Leaves from the Annals;* for nearly half of Catherine's published letters addressed to Sisters of Mercy; and, indirectly, for the refreshing observations about Catherine which appear in the early years of the Carlow Annals. Frances thus takes her place among those who serve as primary sources of historical knowledge about Catherine McAuley.

Jürgen Moltmann has written that "Friendship is an unpretentious relationship, for 'friend' is not an official term, nor a title of honour, nor a function. It is a personal designation" (115). One ought not to underestimate the enabling power of friendship in Catherine McAuley's life, nor fail to consider how limited her endeavors might have been had she not been endowed with co-workers and supporters who were, like Frances Warde, also her good friends. Catherine's relationship with Frances was not unlike that of Teresa of Avila to Maria de San José Salazar, the prioress of the Carmelite monastery Teresa had founded in Seville: an affectionate mutual love between two collaborators dedicated to demanding Christian work which they both regarded as more urgent and important than themselves or the solace of their friendship. A year before her death in 1581, Teresa wrote from Avila to Maria de San José:

> It was a great comfort to me to get your letter, not that that is anything new, for your letters rest me as much as other people's letters weary me. I assure you that, if you love me dearly, I for my part return your love and like you to tell me of yours. How unmistakable a trait of our nature is this wish for our love to be returned! . . . Our Lord wishes it too . . . . let us be like Him, even in a thing like this. (878)

Catherine McAuley has often been likened to Teresa of Avila: in her constant reliance on the mercy of God, in her humility and self-deprecating humor, in her passionate spirit of social reform, and in her fatiguing but nonetheless persistent traveling, by whatever means and in all weathers, to establish new foundations of the work she had initiated. She is like Teresa also in her human dependence upon, and gratitude for, good friends. Frances Warde was such a friend, in a special sense: she had a mind and sensitivities comparable to Catherine's. While Catherine often wrote to her in a motherly way, urging, for example, that she take care of herself in the cold winter air—"Have your shawl crossed on your chest and your feet very warm" (151)—what most moved Catherine was Frances's vigorous, intelligent commitment to their common goals. Moreover, Frances's confidential understanding permitted Catherine to be entirely open with her, not only about administrative problems facing the Institute, but also about the little daily "frets" that Catherine shared with no one else. Only to Frances could she write, when notice of the confirmation of the Rule was delayed and arrangements for the Liverpool foundation were still up in the air: "These good Bishops take their own full time to consider any little affair and those that are, like myself, rather impatient for an answer may just as well make up the mind to wait for one" (363).

Catherine McAuley loved all her early associates; that is abundantly clear from her letters. But in Frances Warde, perhaps more than in anyone else, she found the sort of organizational assistance which made much that was accomplished in the initial founding of the Sisters of Mercy in Ireland and England, if not possible, certainly much easier. There was in the affectionate closings of Catherine's letters to Frances—though the wording of each was slightly different—a deeper vision for the Institute and a deeper need for personal support than the words of any one of them alone might seem to convey. Thus, in August 1841, three months before her death, Catherine concluded a letter to her:

> God Almighty bless you and all with you.
> Pray much for your ever affectionate — M. C. M. (363)

Frances was then thirty-one. Speaking of Catherine's death, the Carlow annalist says of Frances:

> The whole Community were in deep affliction, those Sisters especially who had the happiness of seeing and conversing with her when she visited St. Leo's, but to dear Rev. Mother who shared her joys and sorrows in the early days of the Institute, and who was now deprived of her holy guidance in her own responsible office, the trial was a very bitter one indeed.

Excerpts from
THE ANNALS OF SAINT LEO'S CONVENT OF MERCY, CARLOW[1]

The holy Foundress of our Congregation, Mother Mary Catherine McAuley, at the earnest request of Right Rev. E. Nolan D.D., Bishop of this diocese, came to found a House of her newly formed Institute in this town, on the 10th of April 1837; accompanied by Sisters Mary Francis[2] Warde; M. Josephine Trennor (Novice); M. Teresa Whyte; M. Xavier O'Connor [actually, M. Ursula Frayne], and M. Cecilia Marmion. The three last named were to remain for a limited time, until postulants would enter, and be trained to take part in the visitation of the sick, and the instruction of the poor.[3]

It so happened, that a Mr. Michael Nolan,[4] shopkeeper in this town, had a short time previously, bequeathed the sum of seven thousand pounds sterling (funded property), for the relief of the sick and poor roomkeepers of the parish. The interest amounted to a large sum, which the Bishop proposed to have disbursed by the Sisters, under the supervision of the trustees of said bequest.

The mail coach from Dublin drew up at the gate of the old "College Academy", which was kindly given by the Very Rev. President, Andrew Fitzgerald D.D., for the temporary residence of the young Community. There, they received a most friendly welcome from the Bishop and several of the clergy who awaited their coming. They were then conducted by their Rev. friends to see the College (Saint Patrick's), thence to the Presentation Convent, from whose kind Superioress, Mother Mary Joseph Costlett, they had a very cordial invitation "to dine and spend the afternoon", which invitation they most thankfully accepted. Having spent a few hours most agreeably with the kind Presentation Community, the travellers returned to the old College Academy.

Strange to say, our foundress became suddenly dejected; she had not asked the Bishop, if there was any endowment for the support of the Community, and the residence chosen for the Sisters was a dingy, dilapidated concern. The furniture was scanty, so that when the Sisters went from one room to another, they were obliged to carry their chairs with them; six being the total number provided. The zeal and spirit of sacrifice of our dear Rev. Mother was such, that personally she would encounter very considerable inconvenience, but she shrank from putting her children in a position of an embarassing [*sic*] nature. She therefore told them of her trouble and anxiety regarding them, adding, that she could only give from the parent house, the dower of the novice, £100; and offering to bring them back to their first convent home, if they wished. However, Sisters Mary F. Xavier Warde and Mary Josephine Trennor preferred casting their solicitude upon Divine Providence, and commencing the works of the Institute, at once.

After some days, our venerated Foundress having learned that fever had visited the community in Baggot St., returned there, bringing for companion Sister M. Cecilia, and leaving the little band in charge of Sister M. F. Xavier Warde, whom the Right Rev. Dr. Nolan had appointed Mother Superior, and (for the time being) also Bursar and Novice Mistress. His Lordship named the Adm[inistrator] Rev. James Maher, for Ordinary confessor; and Rev. Daniel Nolan C.C. Graigue,[5] Extraordinary confessor to the young Community . . . .

The Sisters had not long to wait, ere they experienced that their trust in Divine Providence was not confounded. Early in the month of May, Mr. John Nolan (brother to Mr. Michael) signified his intention of bestowing two thousand pounds sterling in order to the erection of a Convent. . . . And for this special favour, vouchsafed us by a Fatherly Providence, we were solely indebted to the generosity of this one, truly charitable and worthy man; who, in a very humble position had worked on with persevering industry, for years, and who found, when the autumn of life approached, that God had given the "increase". . . .

The first stone of the new Convent, was laid on the 20th May [1837], by His Lordship Right Rev. Dr. Nolan, who, attended by all the clergy of the town and College, placed it under the protection of Saint Leo. Our Mother Foundress, accompanied by her niece, Sr. Mary Catherine McAuley,[6] came down from Baggot Street, in order to be present at the little ceremony; and was greatly gratified by the brightening prospects of the young colony. . . .

In the month of October, a heavy cross fell on the Community. The amiable Bishop and father of the flock caught fever, while holding his visitation in Maryboro', and had much difficulty in returning to Braganza. The physician who first attended him, unfortunately prescribed the now obsolete remedy of bleeding, so that the more experienced of the medical faculty on seeing him, pronounced his case—hopeless.

Mother M. F. Xavier Warde and Sr. M. Teresa Whyte were permitted to assist in nursing his Lordship, during the last few days of his life. A short time before he expired, being still perfectly conscious, he looked in the direction in which Fathers Maher and Rafter were kneeling, and pointing to the Sisters at the same moment, said "Take care of them." Father Rafter leaned over his Lordship, and asked, "Is it I?," to which the dying Prelate answered, "No," and again looked towards Father Maher. How faithful the latter was, to the trust confided to him at so solemn an hour, will be seen further on. In the evening of the 14th instant, the holy Bishop was summoned to his reward at the early age of forty-four, having borne the episcopal dignity scarcely three years . . . .

After the death of the holy Bishop, the College Clergy increased (if it were possible) their kind attentions to the orphaned Community. The generous

President, Dr. Fitzgerald, familiarly styled "Father Andrew", consoled the Sisters both by word and deed. Being aware of their limited finances, he replenished the bursar's purse with £34; and promised that the rent would not be called for until the Community would be in a position to meet the demand. A piano, a sofa and chairs for the community room were likewise his gifts; the musical instrument was indeed a great boon to the Community, although it was something the worse, from having made the acquaintance of the lay boys in St. Patrick's [College]. . . .

The spring of this year [1838] was ushered in with a cross. On the 12th of February, Sr. Kate [Coffey] being on the Visitation of the Sick, slipped in the snow, and fell; she only seemed a little stunned for the moment, but after retiring to bed that night, she got a severe attack of hemorrhage of the lungs, which put an end to her earthly career on the 14th inst. . . .

On the 23rd February Miss Maria Kelly, Castletown, Queen's Co., entered the Novitiate. She had presented herself for admission in Baggot St. but our Foundress, mindful of the wants of St. Leo's advised her to choose it for her Convent home. . . .

The community had now grown so large [by November 1838], that the sleeping apartments including the two garrets were insufficient for their accommodation. Indeed Rev. Mother often likened her position to that of "the little woman who lived in the shoe, and who had so many children, that she knew not what to do." However a means of surmounting this difficulty, as well as all others which came in her way, was afforded her by that Fatherly Providence, that was never trusted in vain. Mrs. Nolan (widow), sister to Messrs. Michael and John Nolan, and like them a warm admirer of the Sisters of Mercy, came to reside in a small house adjoining our temporary Convent.[7] She, poor woman, was so completely paralysed, that the rooms on the first story were the only ones she required for her use; she was even quite unable to move from her bed to the easy chair without assistance. Rev. Mother, therefore, asked her to allow the Sisters the use of her two bedrooms upstairs, which request was most willingly granted: also permission to make an entrance thereto through her back yard. It was rather a source of amusement than an inconvenience to the five Sisters who were directed to "take furnished lodgings next door".

Father Maher becoming aware that a postulant had presented herself for admission, who was possessed of many most desirable qualities, but on whom her friends were unable to bestow a dower, very generously undertook to supply the deficiency. Having £400 in the funds, he handed the interest thereof to Rev. Mother, every year as it became due; and later on, signed the "Power of Attorney" which authorized the Superioress to receive it directly from the Stock-brokers, Messrs. Woodlock and O'Donnell. The same Rev. friend, soon afterwards presented a very fine Piano to the Community on whom he bestowed many other valuable gifts, but seemed to forget he had done so, the next moment.

On the 10th December [1838], three of our postulants were clothed in the Holy Habit. The ceremony took place in the Cathedral; the new Bishop [Francis

Haly] officiated, and Rev. B. Fitzpatrick, Dean of the College, preached. It was no small gratification to the congregation to be present at a nun's reception, which being the first and last function of the kind that took place in the Cathedral, it may interest young Sisters to hear of it more in detail. The professed Sisters, Novices and postulants walked in processional order through the College grounds to the back door of the Sacristy; there they put on their Church cloaks and preceded by Cross bearer entered the Sanctuary. The Bishop very kindly lent his carriage for the Novices elect; they being lightly dressed, could not, without danger to their health, accompany the other Sisters on foot. At that period the dress of the candidates for the Holy Habit was of the humblest style, and most inexpensive texture: a thick white muslin dress, a homemade lace veil and a wreath of flowers, was the simple attire worn for years, on such occasions. The expense of supplying a luncheon used not exceed £5. Our Holy Foundress came down from Baggot Street with two of her children, to assist at the Ceremony; and also to assure herself that all at St. Leo's were endeavouring to imbibe the spirit of the Rule which she had compiled with so much care, anxiety, and trust in God's helping grace. The postulants, *viz.*, Charlotte [Johnson], Ellen [Maher], and Eliza [Maher] henceforward were known as Srs. Mary Angela, Cecilia and Clare. . . . [8]

On the 2nd of April [1839] we took a loan of our new chapel which having received a blessing (pro tem.) from His Lordship, he offered there the Holy Sacrifice and presided at the ceremonies of Profession and Reception. Sr. M. de Sales [Mary Maher] made her Vows; and Srs. Rosina [Strange] and Margaret [Kenny] were clothed in the Holy Habit, receiving for patron Saints, Rose of Lima and Vincent of Paul. Our Foundress always seeking to gratify her children came down for the ceremony—it was the last in St. Leo's which she favoured with her presence.

Although properly speaking the education of the middle class is not a feature of our Institute, yet our venerated Foundress gave her fullest sanction to its being undertaken by this Community. The Presentation Nuns having been established in Carlow for some years prior to our coming, and having devoted themselves most zealously to the instruction of poor girls, the Bishop directed that we should leave that portion of the vineyard entirely to them, as their exclusive work. Right Rev. Dr. Haly, considering of almost equal importance the religious education of children of the better class, requested Rev. Mother to undertake it, and accordingly, on the 1st of May [1839], our pension day school for girls was opened. . . .

On the 6th June, Miss Kate Maher, Kilrush, Co. Kildare, entered the Noviciate. . . .

The dress which the postulants wore during their probation, was of coarse black stuff plaited from the throat with a cape of same material. The skirt was cut with a train a finger long, so that after reception, by putting a large plain piece at the shoulders, it served as a second habit. The cap was rather grotesque, having a large caul lined with black calico: this style of head-dress was quite unfashionable at the time, but as a mark of special attention to a young sister of small dimensions, was[9] supplied with a high horn comb and a large paper sugar-bag to keep her cap set to full height the round of the week: this addition to the head-dress, already burdensome enough, made it doubly penitential. The veil was of black lace, very heavily worked. . . .[10]

Everything in and about the new Convent was now beginning to assume a neat and finished appearance. The garden was laid out, and a few bright flowers in the newly-formed beds shed a sweet perfume; while evergreens and poplar trees planted by Rev. D[aniel] Nolan's own hand adorned the front entrance.

The 2nd July, the Feast of the Visitation [1839], was the day chosen for our removal to our new home; and on that morning, Right Rev. Dr. Haly attended by Father Maher and followed by the Community, proceeded through its various apartments and blessed them as he passed. His Lordship then celebrated the Holy Sacrifice of the Mass, as did also Father Maher and Dr. Fitzgerald.

We were very grateful indeed for the many comforts afforded by the spacious choir, cool refectory and cells, in our new Convent; yet we had ample opportunity for the practice of religious poverty. Like most new foundations, ours possessed no funded property, and the pensions[11] of the Sisters were insufficient for their support unless rigid economy was observed in every detail. Our food was plain, simply served, and sparing in quantity; more meat would have been quite acceptable at dinner, and more butter at breakfast and supper. Plates of very thick slices of bread thinly buttered placed between every three or four sisters, and three or four knives for the use of all was the arrangement for morning and evening meals. Mattrasses [*sic*] were no longer placed on the floor, as three bedsteads had been purchased, but only three cells were furnished with cabinets and chairs. Our supply of candlesticks, sweeping brushes, and dust pans was very scanty; however we had the Convent well swept every morning before ten O'clock, and the four brushes in their appointed places. As there was no matting on the corridors the sweeping of them was easy and rapid. . . .

Towards the close of the month of August [1839], our venerated Foundress paid us a visit, on her way from Cork, where she had been to assist at the profession of Miss Agnew and Miss Taylor, both destined for a foundation to Bermondsey, England. The first named was the authoress of *Geraldine*—a controversial novel, very popular at the time. She received for her patron in religion St. Clare, and her companion, St. Ignatius. The newly professed left for their mission the day after the ceremony, accompanied by Mother M. Clare Moore Superioress of the Convent at Cork. Our amiable Foundress, being desirous that they should see the houses of our Institute in Limerick, Charleville, and Tullamore brought them thither for a short visit, before leaving the Emerald Isle for ever. Father O'Rafferty P.P. of Tullamore kindly drove them thence to St. Leo's, where with our Foundress and her travelling companion, Sr. M. de Sales White, they remained for four or five days. Previous to their visit, the young sisters got a very vigorous lecture to act religiously, affectionately and politely, whence they concluded that a great restraint would be imposed on them during their stay, but this grave apprehension was removed after a few hours acquaintance with their amiable guests. Rev. Mother McAuley was liked by all, except one Novice on whose stocking she had unluckily espied a hole, at a previous visit. Our revered Foundress seemed greatly pleased with the accession to our numbers in the Noviciate, while the young people there were flattered by the notice taken of them, and kept faithful watch on her every movement. She rose at first call every morning, and joined in all the common exercises, taking the place assigned to the Mother Assistant. She looked very devout at prayer and was very cheerful and maternal in her intercourse with every member of the Community. The most amiable trait in her character which we believed we discerned was a total absence of everything in her manner telling, I am the Foundress. She spent much of her time conferring with the professed Sisters; a foundation to Naas being in contemplation we supposed that she had many matters to discuss relative to it. During her stay in St. Leo's, she visited Mr. Gerald Cullen,[12] Crawn, who was then seriously ill; and whose two daughters were in the Noviciate—on which happy circumstance she congratulated him, observing, "that if an earthly Prince had called them to his service, he would consider himself greatly honour[ed] thereby, how much more glorious when the call came from the King of Kings."

A word or two about our other visiters. Mother M. Clare Moore's whole demeanour was that of one who had been well schooled in religious discipline; Sr. M. de Sales [White] was very lively and a very agreeable companion at recreation. The English Sisters not young but most ladylike; we thought them a little eccentric, especially in their attitude at prayer, but excused ourselves for so thinking by saying that "they were English converts." The sequel proved however that our opinion, if premature, was not wholly incorrect. . . . On the morning our visiters left, our holy Foundress being in the refectory, asked Rev. Mother M. F. Warde if she might take three twists of bread from table, for the use of the travellers who would be six hours on the road. The request was made in a most unostentatious manner, with an air of natural simplicity that seemed to say—"It is refreshment quite good enough for poor religious." Rev. Mother M. Francis begged to be allowed to add some meat and wine to the scanty store, but both were declined—humbly but decidedly. The stage coaches were then the quickest mode of conveyance, and by one of them did the little band of missioners leave St. Leo's. . . .

On the morning of the 23rd [September 1839] the first detachment of sisters destined for the Naas foundation left St. Leo's by car accompanied by Father Maher, and in the afternoon were followed by Father A. Fitzgerald bringing Rev. Mother and M. Josephine Trennor in the Bishop's carriage. M. Josephine the Superioress, and Srs. M. Catherine Meagher and M. Agnes Greene were to form the new filiation. . . . Rev. Gerald Doyle, P.P. Naas, gave the nuns a most hospitable reception; they dined at his house, and slept at the National School which had been just converted into a Convent. . . .

. . . We entered our annual retreat [August 1840] on the day named in our

Holy Rule, and were favoured with the guidance of the same zealous Priest who directed us last year.[13] The lectures were for the most part a repetition of those which he then gave, and altho' they were very good and very practical, we should have been better pleased had he unfolded to us the truths of Eternity under a new form of words.[14] We were a little surprised on seeing a strange Sister join in the Spiritual Exercises, and on the morning of the Assumption, we had the pleasure of making her acquaintance. Our visiter, Sr. M. Aloysius Scott, a native of Kilkenny, and now a professed member of the Baggot Street Community, had just recovered from a severe attack of hemorrhage of the lungs, and our holy Foundress gladly accepted Rev. M. M. Francis's invitation for her to spend some time in St. Leo's. Father Maher who was then in Dublin took charge of the invalid on her way from Baggot Street, and during her stay allowed her the use of [a] horse and car of which he then could boast the possession. . . .

In the first days of our Congregation, it was usual in each newly-founded Convent, to give the Holy Habit after three months' probation to the first seven who entered the Novitiate; and to permit the said number to make their Profession when their first year in the white veil would have expired. Waiting the will of the Holy Father for the confirmation of our Rule, our venerated Foundress had obtained this permission, in order that a Chapter might be formed in each House at an early date[15]. . . .

On the above named feast [Our Lady of Mercy: September 24, 1840], we undertook another branch of our Institute, *viz.*, the protection of poor distressed women of good character, and on that day three were admitted, and the old domicile known as "Mrs. Nolan's" was their House of Mercy for the time being. . . .

Rev. J. [Myles] Gaffney, Dean of Maynooth College, whose cordial interest in the welfare of our Institute dated from its birth, paid a visit to St. Leo's about this time, and at Rev. Mother's request, gave us a very practical instruction on our Holy Rule, praising its beautiful simplicity, urging us to its observance, and promising us Heaven without Purgatory if we were faithful to it. He assured us of a remembrance in his daily Mass, and in return Rev. Mother appointed a general Communion for his intentions every month. . . .

During her three months' residence at St. Leo's, Sr. M. Aloysius Scott had much improved in health and had edified all by her amiability, and her industrious employment of every moment of time. She assisted in forming the Choir, for which she copied music; she taught the Sisters painting, printing and fancy-work; indeed she seemed quite a book of references on such matters, and sought to oblige those around her by every means which her weak health would allow.

Towards the end of November [1840], Rev. Mother McAuley came to take home her amiable child, having for travelling companion Sr. M. Juliana Hardiman [Hardman], then wearing the white veil, and destined for the Birmingham foundation. We observed with deep regret that the health of our venerated Foundress was declining, and that she did not take the necessary care of herself.

She rose at first call and attended punctually all the common exercises, read lecture for us one morning, and gave religious instruction in the school, where she seemed pleased with the demeanour of the pupils. To Rev. Mother M. Francis Warde she remarked, that the education of the children of the middle rank was of the utmost importance, forming as they did, the connecting link between the high and the low classes. Before leaving, she presented the four professed Sisters with black veils of the same material as that now generally worn; the gossamer she considered, was "too like a bit of millinery". . . .[16]

On the 7th December [1840], the Sisters named for the Wexford foundation left St. Leo's by covered cars, purposing to remain that night in Enniscorthy at the residence of the good Bishop, Right Rev. Dr. Keating, and proceed to Wexford next morning, the feast of the Immaculate Conception. Our kind friend Father Maher took charge of the little band, including Sr. M. Teresa Kelly (Superioress), Sr. Mary Gertrude Kinsella, Sr. Mary Aloysius Redmond, and Bridget Hackett, lay Sister, who were to make the foundation, and Rev. Mother F. Warde with Sr. M. Cecilia [Maher] for travelling companion. The weather was most unpropitious; a violent storm arose, and the rain fell in torrents, so that when the party just reached Enniscorthy, one of the horses backed into the ditch, and kept the Sisters prisoners there for nearly two hours. They could not seek for shelter in cottage or cabin, owing to the deluged state of the roads, so the driver consigned them to the care of a poor man who chanced to be passing by, whilst he went to the Bishop's residence in order to provide a fresh horse. . . .

On the eighth of December [1840] the little Community took possession of their temporary Convent [in Wexford], and a few days after had the honour of a visit from Right Rev. Dr. Keating, who appointed Sr. Mary Teresa Kelly to the offices of Mother Superior, Assistant, Bursar, and Novice Mistress. . . . Miss Susan Wall of Wexford had entered the Novitiate in Baggot Street some months previously, but our Foundress thinking that it would be an advantage to the new Branch to get a postulant, transferred her thither at the earliest opportunity. . . .

A county election caused great excitement in the town just at this time [Summer 1841], the great "Liberator" Dan O'Connell having come to solicit the votes of the freeholders for his younger son John. He remained a month in town, and every evening from a raised platform in front of his hotel, he addressed his crowded audience, and having done speaking he would retire as if to take a short rest, but really to beg God's blessing on his labours; Father Maher told us that these moments were always employed by the grand old patriot, in saying his beads. On Sundays he went to Confession in our Sacristy or rather in the screened off portion of our chapel, whence his fervent act of Contrition could be distinctly heard by all outside, then heard Mass and received Communion most devoutly. He also breakfasted here on these occasions together with His Lordship and some of the priests.

The 20th July will be ever memorable throughout the whole Order, as on this day our Holy Rule received its approval from the lips of the saintly Pontiff Gregory 16th. . . .[17]

About this time [after the August retreat in 1841], Right Rev. Dr. Haly held a Visitation of the Convent, and appointed Rev. James Walshe ordinary Confessor. Up to this period the Novices were not allowed the use of the Holy Rule, but once a week at morning lecture a Chapter was read and explained to them by their Mistress, and the Constitutions in like manner during the retreat before Profession. This, however, His Lordship did not deem sufficient, so directed that each Novice should be supplied with a copy of the Rules and Constitutions, exhorting to a careful study of the obligations she intended to contract. There being no English translation of the Rule in print the Sisters were obliged to set to work to provide themselves with manuscript copies. . . .

The 12th November [1841] brought us a very heavy cross in the death of our revered Foundress. The whole Community were in deep affliction, those Sisters especially who had the happiness of seeing and conversing with her when she visited St. Leo's, but to dear Rev. Mother who shared her joys and sorrows in the early days of the Institute, and who was now deprived of her holy guidance in her own responsible office, the trial was a very bitter one indeed. . . .

As there were ten professed Sisters in the Community [after June 16, 1842], Rev. Mother considered it full time to appoint a Novice Mistress and chose for this important Office Sr. Mary Cecilia Maher.[18] She made the appointment herself and in doing so outstepped the limits of her authority, as Rt. Rev. Dr. Haly informed her when, having said Mass here a few days afterwards, he heard the little piece of news at breakfast, and gave his blessing to the new Novice Mistress as requested. The selection met his warmest approval, but he reminded Rev. Mother that she should have conferred with him on the matter, as he only could make the appointment. She should also have taken the votes of the Sisters, for altho' all had not been two years professed, yet there was the required number for a Chapter. But the Congregation was in its infancy, and matters of religious discipline were but very imperfectly defined. Rev. Mother's fault was one of ignorance, not committed in a spirit of independance [*sic*], therefore she very easily obtained his forgiveness. Mother M. Cecilia was in many respects highly qualified for the Office of Mistress of Novices; she was very holy, gentle in disposition, and polished in manners, rather disposed to be austere, but regulating this tendency by piety and unqualified obedience to Superiors. . . .

The foundation for Westport left us on the 6th September [1842], the Srs. chosen for it being Sr. M. Paul Cullen (Superioress), Sr. M. Gertrude and M. Magdalene O'Brien; a young person named Mary Walshe, anxious to be a lay Sister joined the little band of missioners. Rev. Mother took as travelling companion Sr. M. Xavier Peppard, who was not very strong just then, to whom it was hoped the change of air would prove beneficial. . . .[19]

Our evening recreations [in 1843] were most cheerfully sustained, they were such as our venerated Foundress would quite approve of.[20] On Sundays it was left to our choice, either to do some trifling work at our desks or gather round Rev. Mother [Frances Warde] on the sofa, and listen to the oft told early history of the Order. The subject was ever most pleasing to dear Rev. Mother, awakening as it did so many bright happy holy recollections of her first days in Baggot Street; and twenty years afterwards, when the *Life* of Mother M. Catherine McAuley was presented to the public by another of her devoted children, Mother Mary Vincent Harnett (Roscommon), we renewed acquaintance with very many interesting incidents.[21] The story of the infant days of our own house possessed of course still greater charms for us, while Rev. Mother's vivid description always lent a novelty to it. Of a very cheerful disposition herself, Rev. Mother encouraged the Sisters to be so too; she would laugh heartily at little innocent witticisms, and invariably gave recreation at its proper time, a most gracious approval. Like our holy Foundress she was particularly fond of music, and often called on the Sisters to contribute to the general amusement by their vocal and instrumental attainments.

Mary Vincent (Ellen) Whitty, 1819–1892

Among Catherine McAuley's associates the youngest, and first, to commit her observations of Catherine to writing was, so far as we know, Mary Vincent Whitty, who entered the Baggot Street community on January 15, 1839. She was only twenty-two when she wrote her series of five letters about Catherine's final illness and death. Of her Catherine had written to Frances Warde on January 6, 1839: "a new sister was concluded this day, from Co. Wexford. She comes in a week . . . . She will not be 20 till next month. Very pleasing and musical" (150).

Ellen Whitty, the daughter of William and Johanna Whitty, was born near Oylegate in Co. Wexford on March 1, 1819, and was baptized in Oylegate church, near Enniscorthy, on the same day.[1] She had two sisters and three brothers: Mary, who married Edward Lucas of London, the brother of Frederick Lucas, founder of the English Catholic newspaper, *The Tablet* (O'Donoghue 6); Anne, who became a Sister of Mercy in the Dublin community (Mary Agnes Whitty), worked as a nurse in the Crimea, and served for a time with the Mercy community in Buenos Aires (Carroll, *Leaves* 4:123); Robert—a friend of John Henry Newman—who after ordination in Ireland became a priest of the diocese of Westminster (London), was vicar general and provost of the cathedral under Cardinal Nicholas Wiseman, and later, having joined the Society of Jesus in 1857, served as provincial of the English province from 1870 to 1873 and as assistant to the father general of the Society from 1886 to 1892 (Mac Suibhne 2:179–80); William, who died while studying for the priesthood at the English College, Rome; and Peter, who became a successful civil servant in Dublin and was secretary of the General Post Office at the time of his death (O'Donoghue 6).

On July 23, 1839 Ellen Whitty received the habit of the Sisters of Mercy, taking the name, Mary Vincent. Two years later, on August 19, 1841—less than three months before Catherine's death—she professed her vows, with Mary Justina Fleming, then seriously ill, and four English women destined for the Birmingham foundation. She was thus one of the last young women to profess her vows in Catherine McAuley's presence. Moreover, since the mistress of novices, Mary Cecilia Marmion, had been ill and recuperating in Birr for most of Spring 1841, Mary Vincent received much of her novitiate training and preparation for profession directly from Catherine. With the rest of the Baggot Street community she also made her August retreat prior to profession under Catherine's guidance; as Catherine wrote: "'Father' McAuley conducts the retreat in poor Baggot St." (360).

The day after Mary Vincent's profession Catherine left for Birmingham with the foundation party: four professed sisters and two novices who were to establish the new community; Mary Cecilia Marmion who was to remain in

Birmingham for some months to assist the young superior, Mary Juliana Hardman; and Myles Gaffney and Redmond O'Hanlon who accompanied them. While Mary Cecilia was gone, Mary Vincent served as assistant in the novitiate. When Catherine returned to Baggot Street on September 21, exhausted and suffering from a constant cough, Mary Vincent assumed the further role of "head cook" in the infirmary. She made such "nice rennet whey, light puddings, etc.," that Catherine—who was never one to be waited on—says of herself in a letter to Mary Aloysius Scott:

> I am very sure her Majesty is not attended with half so much care, often most ungraciously received by a poor, unfortunate, peevish old sinner, who never required any particular care or attention before, and who is more weary of it than of the delicacy that occasions it.
>
> To the affectionate, often repeated question: "Revd. Mother, what could you take?" the best answer is: "My heart, you tease me very much." (375)[2]

In the last week of September Mary Vincent also had the sad task—with Redmond O'Hanlon, the confessor at Baggot Street—of accompanying Mary Justina Fleming to Tullamore. Catherine had asked for Mary Ann Doyle's help in providing a "change of air" for this young sister, who was now dying.[3]

After Catherine McAuley's death on November 11, Mary Vincent Whitty served as acting mistress of novices until Mary Cecilia Marmion returned to Baggot Street some time after the December 6, 1841 profession ceremony in Birmingham. On May 23, 1844, when Mary Cecilia was elected superior of Baggot Street, succeeding Mary de Pazzi Delany, who in December 1841 had been elected to succeed Catherine, Mary Vincent was chosen mistress of novices. She retained this post for five years until a new election was suddenly called. Mary Cecilia Marmion whose health had often been fragile contracted typhus and died in office on September 15, 1849 (Carroll, *Leaves* 2:529).[4]

The Chapter held at Baggot Street on September 26, 1849 elected Mary Vincent Whitty as the new superior. She was re-elected in 1852, and thus served the maximum number of consecutive years in this office permitted by the Constitutions: two three-year terms. At the elections held on May 24, 1855, she was named assistant to the new superior, Mary Xavier Maguire. Later that year, Mary Vincent also assumed the role of mistress of novices once again, holding both positions until elections were held in 1858. Then on December 8, 1860, as the leader of five other women, she sailed from Liverpool to found the first community of Sisters of Mercy in Brisbane, Queensland, Australia.

The record of Mary Vincent's life prior to December 1860 demonstrates several important facts about her: her sustained influence—as mistress of novices or as superior—over the novitiate training offered at Baggot Street, unequaled in length of time by any of the early sisters except Catherine McAuley herself; her missionary spirit—as superior, or as a member of the council—in agreeing to send Sisters of Mercy to Perth, Australia (1845), New York (1846), and Buenos Aires (1856), as well as encouraging the Naas community to send sisters to Little Rock, Arkansas (1850) and referring to the Kinsale community the request for a foundation in San Francisco (1854); her generosity toward new foundations in Dundalk (1847), Loughrea (1850), Athy (1852), Belfast (1854), and Clifford, England (1855); her daring in purchasing land on Eccles Street in 1851 and beginning the development of Mater Misericordiae Hospital which opened in 1861; her wisdom in sending sisters to France to study the structure and operation of large-scale hospitals for the poor; her acceptance in 1854, on behalf of the community, of the responsibility of managing the old Jervis Street Hospital; and during the Crimean War, her energy and skill, in late 1854, in quickly assembling fifteen Irish and English Sisters of Mercy, under the leadership of Mary Francis Bridgeman, the superior of Kinsale, to nurse with Miss Mary Stanley in the British military hospitals in Koulali and Balaklava.[5] She was, as Mary Austin Carroll claims, "the all-accomplished Mother M. Vincent Whitty" (*Leaves* 4:132).

In late 1860, James Quinn—the newly consecrated bishop for Queensland, Australia, who had for several years served as chaplain at Baggot Street—asked Mary Vincent to accompany him to Queensland, to found a Mercy community in Brisbane. She formally asked the Baggot Street community for permission to go, writing to them on November 15: "I have placed before my mind all the possible difficulties . . . and still they do not discourage me" (quoted in O'Donoghue 28). On November 20 the community responded, refusing permission on the understandable grounds that they could not spare her from Dublin. However, Dr. Quinn then asked the Archbishop of Dublin, his long-time friend and former mentor in Rome, to intervene. On November 27 Paul Cullen, as ecclesiastical superior of the Baggot Street community, wrote to Mother Mary of Mercy Norris, the superior, saying in part:

> Dr. Quinn is anxious to secure Mrs. Whitty's assistance in establishing a house of Sisters in Brisbane. If Mrs. Whitty be willing to go, I am perfectly satisfied that she should go, and as she has so much experience, I think she would secure the success of the mission.[6]

Archbishop Cullen's letter settled the matter, to the sorrow of Baggot Street community. He also asked that two novices volunteer to accompany her. So on December 3, 1860, Mary Vincent Whitty, Mary Benedict McDermot and Mary Cecilia McAuliffe left Dublin, after less than a week's preparation; they were joined by two Irish women whom Dr. Quinn had secured as prospective postulants—Jane Townsend and Emily Conlan—and, in Liverpool, by another Sister of Mercy who volunteered, Mary Catherine Morgan (O'Donoghue 29). They set sail on December 8, 1860 with Dr. Quinn and the five priests he had assembled, and reached Brisbane in May 1861. The human and religious needs they faced there were overwhelming. Over the years Mary Vincent wrote numerous appeals for more sisters to come to Brisbane, and in 1871–1872 visited Ireland and England to secure yet more Sisters of Mercy to work in Queensland. The communities in Athy and Tralee were particularly helpful.

In her full-length biography devoted primarily to Mary Vincent Whitty's thirty years in Brisbane, until her death there in 1892, Frances (formerly, Mary

Xaverius) O'Donoghue RSM presents not only Mary Vincent's wide-ranging accomplishments in Queensland, but also the tensions she experienced, arising from both church and state. With all her educational talents and administrative expertise, she still had to deal with state-entrenched bigotry as well as with Bishop James Quinn's inability to delegate initiative or permit appropriate control, all of which made for a difficult life (2–4).[7]

When Mary Austin Carroll completed the fourth volume of her *Leaves from the Annals of the Sisters of Mercy* in 1895, she was not able to present the same kind of summary portrait of Mary Vincent Whitty, who had so recently died (1892), as she had written for other deceased early Mercy founders. In her second volume published in 1883, and devoted to England, the Crimea, Scotland, Australia, and New Zealand, Carroll, in speaking of Queensland, tends to focus more specifically though not exclusively on the good works and holiness of Bishop Quinn, noting, with an interesting shift of attribution, that "He opened forty schools under the Sisters of Mercy alone, and founded seventeen Convents of Mercy" (2:565). However, Carroll also recognizes the immense zeal of Mary Vincent Whitty. Speaking of her earlier life in Dublin, Carroll quotes a description of "this eminent religious" written by a Sister of Mercy "*en route* for the East in 1854". Carroll's unnamed source says of Mary Vincent: "She had a very earnest look when listening to one speaking, set her eyes quietly on the speaker, listening with all possible sweetness. Indeed, she seemed more disposed to listen than to converse. I look on her as one of the gems of the Institute" (*Leaves* 2:541).[8]

Of Mary Vincent Whitty's ministry in Queensland, Carroll remarks, "This holy and accomplished woman devoted herself heart and soul to the . . . country which for the love of God she chose for her future home" (2:541). She does not hesitate to speak of Mary Vincent as Bishop Quinn's "venerable coadjutrix" (2:565) and his "zealous coadjutrix" (2:566)—a title which was undoubtedly accurate, even though not ecclesiastically recognized. Mary Vincent's passion to accomplish with the people of Queensland what their needs required is evident in one of her letters of appeal for more sisters, which Carroll quotes:

> "You could not be here . . . and see the necessity for religious education, without making every sacrifice to secure it for the numbers settling down with their families in this vast colony. I have sent a paper on education to Cardinal Cullen, hoping it will excite his zeal, for he could not bear to have St. Patrick's children lose the faith even in Queensland. Do . . . send me some good, sensible nuns whose happiness will be found in the faithful discharge of appointed duties and implicit obedience, and not in anything external—places, companions, etc. Such only are the right ones, especially for a mission." (*Leaves* 2:563)

When Mary Vincent Whitty died in All Hallows Convent, Brisbane, on March 9, 1892, a sister there prepared a long obituary on "The Late Mother Vincent" which appeared in the *Brisbane Australian* on March 19, 1892.[9] Speaking of Mary Vincent's work in Queensland, the author notes that within a month of their arrival in Brisbane in 1861, "the Sisters of Mercy opened their first school at St. Stephen's, without desks or appliances"; she describes Mary Vincent's struggle until 1872 to liquidate the heavy financial debt (£6,000 plus ten percent compound interest) incurred in building All Hallows, their first convent; and she comments on Mary Vincent's "two strongly marked traits—of gentleness and perseverance", noting that she "always distinguished between a matter being 'troublesome' and being 'impossible'; no amount of 'trouble' intimidated her from pressing on to the accomplishment of a project once she had undertaken it."

But the Mary Vincent Whitty who is of special significance in the present study is not so much the superior of Baggot Street or the foundress of Queensland, but the young professed sister who attended Catherine McAuley during the last ten days of her life, after she became bed-ridden about November 1, 1841. Mary Vincent was then twenty-two. Her detailed firsthand accounts of Catherine's last days, her death on November 11, and her funeral Mass and burial on November 15 are preserved in the five letters she wrote to Mary Cecilia Marmion in Birmingham over the course of nine days, from November 7 through November 16, 1841. One of these letters was written on two days: Saturday, November 13 and Sunday, November 14. The other four letters were written on November 7, 11, 12 and 16. While the letter of November 7 is hopeful, and confident of Catherine's recovery, the remaining four letters are hastily written, under the overwhelming stress and grief Mary Vincent felt at Catherine's imminent, and then actual, death. They are the ardent letters of a young woman who admired and trusted Catherine deeply, and whom Catherine once called "a great favorite, most deservedly" (334).

Katherine O'Brien RSM, former congregational archivist at All Hallows Convent, Brisbane, where the autograph letters are preserved, has described these documents well:

> there is a recognised literary style, the term for which is highly apt in its application to the style of the letters. It is that of the stream of consciousness. Any page of the letters is strongly reminiscent of a page from James Joyce: no paragraphs, little indication of lengths of sentences, apart from some dashes. Indeed, S. M. Vincent was reporting the details of the Foundress's condition as they streamed from her consciousness. As a result we have these personal, vivid, loving descriptions of Catherine's last days and hours.[10]

The letters are remarkable for other reasons as well. First, Mary Vincent is silent, as one would expect, about what she saw—what Catherine had not wanted anyone to see—during the task she performed for Catherine on the night of November 10: the burning of the parcel Catherine had prepared, containing her shoes and instrument(s) of penance.[11] Moreover, as a young sister who did not imagine that she was in any way writing for posterity, Mary Vincent is straightforward and uninhibited in her comments on the people and events surrounding Catherine. She thus provides a fresh narrative perspective on Catherine and the community. Finally, and in much greater detail than Mary Elizabeth Moore—who provides the only other known eyewitness account of Catherine's last days—Mary Vincent records numerous instances of Catherine's own words as she lay dying, including her request that the sisters should "get a good cup of tea . . . when I am gone."[12] She thus extends our knowledge of Catherine's final thoughts and dispositions well beyond October 26, 1841, the date of Catherine's last known letter.

In 1860, before she left for Brisbane, Mary Vincent Whitty transcribed, as a feast day gift for Mary of Mercy Norris, then superior of the Baggot Street community, a copy of a Life of Catherine McAuley composed by Clare Moore. At the beginning of her transcription she inserted a short prefatory statement about her own perceptions of Catherine.[13] In this preface, written almost twenty years after Catherine's death, Mary Vincent speaks with the same attachment and admiration as in her November 1841 letters. She says, in part:

> If you had known her, dearest Revd. Mother, how you would have loved and venerated her, and still, be as familiar with her as with an intimate friend. I have often wished her lovely character could be *Photographed* for the admiration and instruction of posterity; it seems to me that words are slow and imperfect, in conveying all the lineaments of that gifted soul—she was so humble yet dignified, so playful and witty, yet reserved and charitable, so pious and strict, yet amiable and kind, but to me at least the climax of her attractions was that she *was always the same,* always ready to listen, to consider and to direct whenever applied to.

Other than Catherine's own writings—and, in a certain sense, the present-day actions of Sisters of Mercy around the world—the biographical documents presented in this volume, including Mary Vincent Whitty's five letters, are the only available "photographs", however flawed, which history possesses of Catherine McAuley. While these verbal portraits are, as Mary Vincent admits, "slow and imperfect in conveying all the lineaments", they do at least sketch some of the features of her personality and character which impressed her associates. But the present-day act of coming to "know" Catherine McAuley, to the extent that any such knowledge can be real and is attainable, involves two movements: interpreting, in the context of her own time, the data of her character and actions—which these biographical documents, themselves also interpretive, provide—and then interrogating these data from the perspective of present-day realities. The early biographical accounts offer rich occasions for such fusions of horizons, and without them present-day commentary on Catherine's life, values, actions, and spirituality can run the risk of being unmoored speculation or wishful thinking. For instance, if one seeks to comment precisely on Catherine McAuley's final dispositions in the experience of human dying, one needs to engage, as best one can, with the dying Catherine, as represented, even though fragmentarily, in the almost hour-by-hour "careless" notes of Mary Vincent Whitty. In these pages a trustworthy "voice" of Catherine McAuley in her last hours can be discerned.

THE LETTERS OF MARY VINCENT WHITTY
CONVENT OF MERCY, BAGGOT STREET, DUBLIN, TO
MARY CECILIA MARMION, CONVENT OF MERCY, BIRMINGHAM, ENGLAND
NOVEMBER 7, 11, 12, 13 AND 14, AND 16, 1841

Sunday
Nov[embe]r 7, [18]41

My dear Mother Cecilia[1]

Revd. Mother is more restless and feverish last night & to-day than she was yesterday or the day before. The attack in her stomach Sr. de Sales[2] mentioned has returned to-day but not so frequent as on Thursday—her mouth is very sore. Altogether the Doctor[3] is not so much pleased with her—yesterday he thought her very much improved—indeed it is difficult to say any thing of her, she gets so many changes—yet we have great hopes in the prayers that are offering for her. Mother Elizabeth [Moore] from Limerick is here since Thursday. She brought a relic that has wrought I believe many cures. She says she is determined to cure Revd. Mother. Srs. Ursula, de Sales, Xavier, M. Catharine & I are the principal sitters up.[4] Sr. de Sales & Sr. Teresa[5] are almost always with her—indeed you would be astonished to see how Sr. Teresa keeps up. She still sleeps in the Infirmary & hears every stir of Revd. Mother's—yet never was better—although she is up very frequently during the night. She says she is head nurse. Indeed you would pity Mother de Pazzi—in the beginning of the sickness she told Revd. Mother the Doctor must be sent for; since then Revd. Mother does not ask her for any thing. Mother de P went to remain up one night & Revd. Mother would not allow her, which of course Mother de Pazzi feels much more than a week's staying up. This is indeed a cross for Mother de Pazzi—although I do not think Revd. Mother intends to hurt her feelings for she told me she was afraid to let Mother de P remain up. No one goes to see her excepting Mother de Pazzi but those that are employed about her. Although so far from her I believe you have less to suffer than poor Mother de Pazzi. Sr. Camillus[6] is in Booterstown since Wednesday. She had no inflammation on her chest this time—but the hiccup still returns at intervals. Doctor Carroll has given her a bottle which stops it almost immediately. She is better since she went to Booterstown. Sr. Xavier sends you her affectionate love—as she found me writing to you when she returned from the Assylum [*sic*]. She defers hers until Tuesday when she hopes to have better news—indeed I at least have great hopes—God is too good to take Revd. Mother from us yet. I have just had an order to make beef tea for her—give my affectionate love to each Sister. Will you sometimes pray for your truly attached in Jesus Christ

Sister Mary Vincent

6 weeks will not be long passing & you will be here once more to assist in nursing Revd. Mother.[7]

Thursday 4 O'clock, Morning
[November 11, 1841]

Dearest Mother Cecilia

You can not have much hopes from our last accounts. Dear Revd. Mother is sinking fast. Mother de Pazzi is beside her—it is indeed edifying to be with her—we had some hopes until last night about 12 O'Clock.

9 O'Clock—We have had Mass in the Infirmary. Revd. Mother received Holy Communion & all were present with white cloaks & lighted tapers—she wished for this. Each Sister in the house has got her blessing and a parting advice.

May God assist & strengthen us & make us truly resigned to His holy will—we can not be sufficiently grateful for being with her—I'm sure God in His mercy must reward you for this privation. She is so calm & recollected.

10 O'Clock—The Sisters from Booterstown & Kingstown[8] are here—each get their blessing, after which I asked her to bless the Mothers with their foundations. She went over every name—saying, oh, I remember them all—May God bless them—May the Holy Ghost pour down His choicest blessings—Make them truly good Religious—May they live in Union & Charity & May we all meet in a happy Eternity. You would be astonished—she is so calm & each of us crying about her. She looked up to Sr. Genevieve[9] & said— I'm *very* happy. Her stomach gives her great pain. She says, 'tis a hard struggle.

11—read prayers for the dying

12 O'Clock—Mr. & Mrs. McAuley[10] come—she says to her brother, 'tis come to a close. We've all left the room but Sr. Teresa—he[11] wished it—we were not long from it—she is in great pain. Mr. Gaffney, Dr. Meyler, M[ess]rs.[12] Quin & O'Grady has [*sic*] been here to see her.

I think I may as well close this now—3 O'Clock—for she is very cold yet may linger until tomorrow. May God be our help and comfort.

I will go on writing & send it tomorrow. She appointed me to remain up all last night[13]—this I believe is too great a comfort for your truly attached in J.C.

Sister M. Vincent

September [*sic*][14] 11th 1841

*

Friday [November 12, 1841]

My dear Mother Cecilia[15]

I believe I left off yesterday at 3 O'Clock—our dear Revd. Mother continued very quiet but suffering intense inward pain until 6 O'Clock when we lighted her candle. She continued breathing & so sensible until 7½ when she expired. The Sisters were all with her from 6 until 7 when we went to supper after which we said Matins & some one sent for me & I had the consolation, for it is a pleasing though melancholy consolation, to read the last prayers for her, close her eyes & that mouth, from which I have received such instruction. May God grant us all grace to remember & practice it. Mother de Pazzi, Mother Elizabeth, Srs. Magdalen, de Sales, Lucy, Martha[16] & I were in the room—you can not think how calmly & quietly she drew her last breath—I am sure she is now an advocate for us all in heaven.

She is not to be interred until Monday on account of an Office that is to be in Westland Row tomorrow. I believe I told you of Mr. O'Hanlon's having a Cemetry [*sic*] formed in the garden immediately after his return from Birmingham. It is to be consecrated & we will have her laid here near us.

She begged Dr. Meyler's pardon yesterday—if she ever did or said any thing to displease him—he said she ought not to think of [''any thing'' is crossed out] that now & promised, I will take care & do all I can for your spiritual children—she looked at him so pleased & said, will you—then May God help & reward you for it. She told Sr. Teresa, now fearing I might forget it again—will you tell the Srs. to get a good cup of tea—I think the community room would be a good place—when I am gone & to comfort one another—but God will comfort them.[17] She said to me, if you give yourself entirely to God—all you have to serve Him—every power of your mind & heart—you will have a consolation you will not know where it comes from.

Speaking of the Birmingham foundation to me one day, she said we are to have the Birmingham cross here—for had none there. Sr. Julianna[18] should be happy when she hears all our dear Revd. Mother said (before her illness) of the consolation Sr. Julianna gave her, she was so true a Religious. The second last lecture she gave us she spoke of all the English Sisters—how edifying they were—& that they indeed made 2 months of one—that no instruction not even the least was lost on them. She told me—one day she asked how we were going on in the Noviceship—that you would soon be back to take care of us. I do not think she made any arrangements, wished for any thing to be done or given to any one—indeed she looked the picture of entire abandonment of herself and all that belonged to her into the hands of God.

We had three Masses here this morning—Mr. O'Carroll, Mr. Gaffney & Dr. Brown[e] of Galway.[19] Mr. Smyth[20] of St. Michael's & John's called last night & took notes begging prayers for the repose of her soul to each of the Chapel Houses.

Poor Mother de P is completely knocked up—Revd. Mother called to her for many little things yesterday. Sr. Teresa is surprising—she says she feels so strong & so comforted. Revd. Mother promised her this—if she would be entirely resigned to the Will of God. I forgot to tell you—Mother de Pazzi had a most kind note from Dr. Meyler this morning—wishing the Office might be deferred until Monday—that he was coming to say Mass for us this morning when he was prevented by some necessary duty. Dr. Murray saw Revd. Mother on Saturday[21]—the Priests I think look upon her death as an universal loss.

I can not believe she is really gone from us—but God will assist us & He Himself will supply her place over her cherished Order. I would like to hear from you soon. I'm sure God will comfort you for being deprived the consolation of being with her—I hope I am not doing wrong in letting such a careless note as this is leave me, for I know you will excuse it. I must now try to be very exact in every thing.

Mother Elizabeth here—her Bishop[22] allowed her to remain a little time longer when he heard Revd. Mother was so bad—how good God is—I do not know what Mother de P would do but for her. I wish you would soon write to Mother de P, it would console her.

We will now really be longing for your return. Give my affectionate love to each of the Sisters & believe me, my dear Mother Cecilia, your truly attached in J.C.

Sister Mary Vincent

*

Saturday [November 13, 1841]

Dearest Mother Cecilia

Although my letter of yesterday gave you the last account of our dear dear Parent, yet I imagine it will be a comfort to you to hear all that passes with us. Sister Mary Teresa from Galway arrived here this morning hoping to see our dear Revd. Mother[23]—she was I believe uneasy as Revd. Mother made no final settlement concerning her remaining in Galway—but Revd. Mother did not speak of any one's return but yours. She told me you were soon to be back, the only day she asked during her illness, how we were going on in the Noviceship—for she did not seem to take an interest in any thing. Some of Mother Francis'[24] notes remain unopened.

She is to be put in the coffin to-night and brought to the choir where she will remain until Monday—preparations are making for the consecration[25]—is it not a great comfort that she is to be left with us. She spoke to me 2 or 3 times of your "tender affectionate care" of her in Birmingham. I suppose you will this day receive my letter of Thursday—indeed I pity you—but God will assist you to bear up against it. I do not know what poor Mother de P would do but for Mother Elizabeth. I often think of what Revd. Mother said to me on Monday last—When we give ourselves entirely into the hands of God he will so sweetly ordain all things for our greater comfort, even in this life.

Sunday [November 14,1841]

I have just received your letter, my dear Mother Cecilia. I suppose now there remains nothing to be done but that you execute faithfully her last wish in your regard & hasten the ceremony as much as possible. Will you pardon me, dear Mother Cecilia, for saying this, but I fear you might now think it unnecessary to do so, knowing all poor Sister Julianna will feel—but you are now really wanting here. I say this as I know Revd. Mother wished for your return to the Noviceship so much—at least I think I do.[26]

Doctor Kinsella has consecrated the ground & gave us a nice little exhortation after it[27]—1 cannot tell you what he said for indeed I can only thing [think] of our dear dear Parent for she was truly such to each of us. I believe you are to see all you love go before you—but God has His own wise ends in view & He Himself will be all to you.

When I think she is so happy it is almost selfish to grieve for her—we must endeavor all we can, as you say, to be united to her. I do pray for Sr. Julianna every Friday. I give her a very particular remembrance, as she told me to remember, at the foot of the Cross—will you ask her for one for me in return. We will not forget you on Saint Cecilia's day.[28]

You can not think the want in every place—the Choir, Refectory, Community Room—but God's holy will be done. I will write to you on Tuesday or Wednesday again—which I suppose will be the last for some time. May God comfort you & may He teach us all entire unreserved submission to His ever adorable & holy will. Give my love to each Sister & will you pray for your sincerely attached in J.C.

Sister Mary Vincent

*

[Tuesday][November 16, 1841]

My dear Mother Cecilia

I received your letter yesterday morning & would have immediately answered it, but I recollected some of your inquiries had been answered in my last letter. Revd. Mother did mention your name three or four times during her illness & wished, as she said, from her heart, you were come back—& when I asked her to bless the Sisters that were absent your name was said—the only one she did not name was Mother Angela[29] altho' I'm sure she blessed her with the rest. I would have asked a particular blessing for you, but the third night before she had given me a nice lecture on universal charity & told me above all things to avoid all appearance at least of preference for one more than another for it is the [bane?][30] of religion. I do not believe she thought she was near death at this time—but this it was that prevented me from asking for you in particular altho' I would have done so had I received your note in time. And does it not prove, my dear Mother Cecilia, she thought of you when she got Mother Elizabeth to write to you to hurry home—when she even told Sister de Sales not to allow Sr. M. Teresa from Galway come for some time at least.[31] I do indeed pity you but I'm sure God will comfort you & strengthen you to bear this trial—the time we are to remain after her too will be so short—we have only to endeavor to imitate her that we may die like her—& she was such a picture of total abandonment of herself & all that belonged to her into the hands of God.

I send you the coppy [*sic*] of a letter Mother Elizabeth received from Doctor Blake[32]—I think it is so consoling. I've heard there were 62 priests at the Office—Doctor Brown[e] & Doctor Healy [*sic*][33]—there were two rows of seats at each side the choir & all were full. We were on the gallery & followed the coffin with our white cloaks on[34] & lighted tapers to the garden or cemetry [*sic*] now. The singing was delightful. Mr. O'Hanlon[35] sang High Mass—it all appears like some scenery for I can not think we are never to hear her in[36] the choir or see her go through the different parts of the house again—but God's holy will be done, it is indeed difficult to say this sincerely now. Mother M. Teresa returns to Galway this evening—Mother Elizabeth goes on Thursday. Doctor Rien [*sic*][37] is to have High Mass & Office for Revd. Mother some day next month in Limerick. I would wish to hear from you soon—in the mean time we will pray that God may assist & strengthen you to bear up against this trial—for it is indeed one to those particularly that were from her [*sic*].[38] I had great comfort—she spoke so beautifully to me several times—but I'm sure she did not think she was in immediate danger until the night before her death.

She once said to me—pray with confidence & you will surely be heard, that is, if the request be for your sanctification. She spoke to me twice on charity & most of all to be unwearied in my little exertions to promote the glory of God—to let nothing stop me. But what she said to Sr. Teresa was beautiful—she told her to prove to the world that her exertions for the poor was [*sic*] not for Revd. Mother's sake but only for love of God & that her sweet Jesus would assist her—she said this when she knew she was dying.[39] I fancy you will like to hear some of what she said—I wish I could tell it in her own words. Will I soon hear from you? Believe me, my dear Mother Cecilia, your sincerely attached in Jesus Christ

Sister Mary Vincent

Tuesday

I can not finish without telling you—this day month[40] our dear Revd. Mother was down to office at 6 [o'c, or ½].[41] Thursday 3 weeks was her first day in bed.[42]

Mary Elizabeth (Anne) Moore, 1806–1868

In planning the first ceremony for the reception of novices at Baggot Street, held on January 23, 1832, Catherine McAuley made what she soon regarded as a big mistake. Remembering the expense, as she saw it, of her own novitiate and reception and profession ceremonies at George's Hill, she had decided, as Clare Augustine Moore explains, that "all ceremonies should be strictly private." Moreover, one of the prospective novices, Anne O'Grady, who died two weeks later, was severely ill. So Catherine planned that the seven other sisters were to be received in a ceremony open only to clergy, and "orders were given that no [other] visitors should be admitted." On that day Clare Augustine herself had evidently come to the convent to see her sister Georgiana receive the habit. And she was not alone. Such a great "ringing of bells" ensued that, as she records:

> Friends of the sisters, friends of the Institute, everyone sure that some one else had been admitted, everyone indignant, then the mob that collected round them increased the confusion. . . . So many indeed were offended by their exclusion that the ceremonies were ever after more public.

In fact, as Catherine's letters show, the ceremonies held later in each new foundation were almost always held in the nearby parish church.

Standing outside the front door of the Baggot Street convent on that January day—and, as she later acknowledged, joining "cordially . . . in the murmuring" (Harnett 75–6)—was Anne Moore.[1] She was a twenty-five year old Dublin woman who had earlier entered the Sisters of Charity on Stanhope Street, but had since left that congregation (Carroll, *Leaves* 1:323–24). Her friend and confessor was Michael Blake, then parish priest of Saint Andrew's, Townsend Street. Despite the lack of a warm welcome on this visit to Baggot Street, Anne soon entered the community—on June 10, 1832, which was Pentecost Sunday and her twenty-sixth birthday. In the years that followed she became one of Catherine McAuley's closest friends, and, as the superior of the Limerick community from 1838 to 1862, one of the impressive early founders of the Sisters of Mercy. Whether she ever teased Catherine about the closed-door policy is not known, but is likely, given the ease of their relationship.

Since Anne had entered during the peak of the 1832 cholera epidemic in Dublin she was immediately pressed into service, to nurse for the remainder of the year with Catherine and the others at the cholera hospital on Townsend Street. She became a novice on October 8, 1832, taking the name, Mary Elizabeth, and choosing Elizabeth of Hungary as her patron saint. On October 8, 1834, she professed her vows—after a two-year novitiate, rather than one-year, because she was not one of the first seven professed sisters in the community. From October 1836 through most of 1837 she was in charge of the branch house in Kingstown (now Dún Laoghaire). Though this house had been purchased initially as a place of convalescence for sick sisters, the condition of the poor girls in Kingstown had moved Catherine early on to open a poor school in a renovated coach house on the grounds. Elizabeth was thus in Kingstown at the beginning of the controversy over payment for this renovation.[2]

In 1838, Catherine fulfilled her promise to Dr. John Ryan, Bishop of Limerick, and, indirectly, to Miss Helena Heffernan, to found a community of the Sisters of Mercy to serve the destitute poor in that city. Elizabeth Moore, then thirty-two, was chosen to be the superior. On September 8, 1838, the founding party, including Mary Vincent Harnett, a novice who was to remain in Limerick, set out by steamer to Cork. They visited the Cork community for a few days, and then proceeded to Charleville, where they witnessed the laying of the cornerstone for the new Mercy convent. They finally reached Limerick in the evening on September 24, took possession of a convent building formerly belonging to the Poor Clares, and welcomed into the Sisters of Mercy the two remaining members of that order, Mary Shanahan and Anne Hewitt.

Catherine's correspondence from Limerick, where she remained until December 9, provides valuable commentary on Elizabeth Moore. In these letters one can see evidence of the human process that was at work in the development of all the early Mercy founders: the nurturing presence and guidance of Catherine McAuley, gradually assisting somewhat timid and inexperienced young women to become competent, courageous, and decisive leaders in their respective communities. Writing on October 25 to Frances Warde, Catherine—who had an uncanny sense of how long to help another person and when to leave her on her own—describes the beginning stages of this growth in Elizabeth Moore:

> I cannot go for a full month. No person of less experience could manage at present, and I am very insufficient for the task. As to Sister Elizabeth, with all her readiness to undertake it, we never sent forward such a faint-hearted soldier, now that she is in the field. She will do all interior and exterior work, but to meet on business, confer with the Bishop, conclude with a Sister, you might as well send the child that opens the door. I am sure this will surprise you. She gets white as death, and her eyes like fever. She is greatly liked, and when the alarms are a little over and a few in the House, I expect all will go on well. (140)

In time, according to the Limerick Annals, the poor school on the property—which had been opened in 1812, connected with the National Board of Education in 1833, and kept in operation by the two remaining Poor Clares—was expanded; the visitation of the numerous sick poor commenced; a House of Mercy for the Protection and Training of Women was opened in the lower part of the school on November 19; a Sunday School for poor girls was started, and "hundreds of the lace workers then so numerous in Limerick thronged to it"; Mary Vincent Harnett professed her vows on October 24; and three young women entered the community. Thus the Limerick foundation took hold, and with it, Elizabeth Moore. One of the most useful things Catherine taught Elizabeth was respect for local needs and preferences; for, as Catherine wrote from Limerick on November 17: "Every place has its own particular ideas and feelings which must be yielded to when possible" (147). Because the Limerick poor would deal only with "real nuns", not with the "caps" (postulants), Catherine dispensed with part of the required probationary period before reception into the community so that the first two Limerick postulants could receive the habit on December 4, 1838.

When Catherine departed for Carlow and Dublin on December 9, she left behind, for Elizabeth Moore's encouragement, a kindly poem-letter about how to be a good superior. In Catherine's best doggerel verse, it reads:

> *My dearest Sister M. E.*
> Don't let crosses vex or teaze
> Try to meet *all* with peace & ease
> notice the faults of every Day
> but *often* in a playful way
> And when you seriously complain
> Let it be known to give you pain
> Attend to one thing at a time
> you've 15 hours from 6 to 9
> be mild and sweet in all your ways
> Now & again bestow some praise
> avoid all solemn declaration
> all serious, close investigation
> Turn what you can into a jest
> and with few words dismiss the rest
> keep patience ever at your side
> you'll want it for a constant guide
> Shew fond affection every Day
> and above all—Devoutly Pray
> That God may bless the charge He's given
> And make of you—their guide to Heaven
> *The parting advice of your ever affectionate* M. C. M.[3]

For the next thirty years, until her death on January 19, 1868, Elizabeth tried to take these large-minded words to heart. Although she had a conscientious regard for good order, even to the point of strictness, she was ever for the Limerick sisters "our loved Mother Elizabeth"—who wept when they told her of the sufferings of the sick poor they visited, and "whose kindness and friendship were sincere", and, as one of them wrote to Mary Austin Carroll, "greatest where most needed" (*Leaves* 1:339, 331).

After Catherine McAuley left Limerick in December 1838, her letters over the next two years express her pride in the progress made in Limerick, her desire to return, her continuing joy in exchanging poems with Mary Teresa Vincent (Ellen) Potter who had entered while she was there, and her profound anguish when this "sweet little poet" suddenly died of typhus in March 1840. But these letters written in 1839 and 1840—comprising fourteen of the eighteen published letters to Elizabeth—also manifest Catherine's deepening personal affection for Elizabeth herself, and her increasing gratefulness for her support and comfort. Although Elizabeth's letters to Catherine are apparently not extant—perhaps Catherine herself destroyed them just before her death—there are in Catherine's letters to her numerous indirect indications of Elizabeth's solicitude.

Apparently Elizabeth saw and responded to certain needs of Catherine's heart in a way that Catherine's other close friends in the community, for example, Clare Moore and Frances Warde, did not. While Catherine certainly turned to Clare and Frances for intellectual and administrative help, even after they moved from Baggot Street, and loved and trusted them deeply, Elizabeth evidently offered, and Catherine accepted, a kind of emotional support that was unique in her relationships. This bond may have had something to do with Elizabeth's being slightly older than the others and with her initiative and thoughtfulness. For example, she knew that Catherine liked flowers, so she sent them to her. As Catherine wrote on July 24, 1839:

> We have this moment received your sweet fruits and flowers. I seldom see any so fragrant to me. The offering of genuine affection, has everything to enhance its value. I am looking at them now and think the roses have some unusual shade—and such bright purple and rich yellow flowers. The gooseberrys—liqueur —jams and jellys—all safe—apples, etc. . . .
>
> Every one who came in since I began [this letter] said, "oh, the sweet smell, where did you get all the lovely flowers," and when answered, "from Limerick," I think they fancied them somewhat out of the common way. (165–7)

Perhaps. And so were Catherine's responsibilities and cares.

Catherine visited Limerick in August 1839 on her way from Cork to Dublin with the sisters destined for the Bermondsey foundation. As her letters indicate, she then tried from mid March 1840, immediately before Mary Teresa Potter's death, until early October that year to get to Limerick again, as she had promised and as she herself wished. Something always intervened to change her plans. She finally made it, for a very brief visit on her way home from Galway, between October 9 when she was still in Galway and October 12 when she was back in Dublin (Neumann 235–36).[4] Throughout this seven-month period Catherine's letters to Elizabeth speak, often only in single sentences here and there, of her gratitude for their friendship. She writes: "Your letters are always most acceptable to me. I rejoice to see one" (202); "I owe you all in my power and I take pleasure in giving you my poor tribute of affection and esteem" (203); "The prospect of my visit to Limerick will animate me. I need scarcely tell you that it will be a source of great happiness, for which I thank God, a pure, heartfelt friendship which renews the powers of mind and body" (206); "If you have time, write me a few words of comfort, and say you are well and happy" (218); "Absence has much increased my affection for you. Even the new Sisters here [in Galway, in July 1840] are sorry for our mutual disappointment this time, I have talked so much of it" (222); "I could not recollect any circumstance that inflicted such painful disappointment on me as not going to Limerick before my return, and I suppose it is for this very reason I was not permitted to go, because I desired it too ardently" (225–6);[5] and finally on September 9, "It is decreed that I am to be in Galway on the first of October for what Mr. Daly terms the grand reception. . . . I will not venture even to hope that I shall return by Limerick" (233). As it turned out, Catherine's eventual visit to Limerick in October 1840 was her last personal visit with Elizabeth Moore before they met at Baggot Street a year later, in the final week of Catherine's life. Although Catherine must have written other letters to Elizabeth in 1841, apparently only one letter to her in that year is extant (and published). Perhaps Elizabeth, who carefully preserved so many of Catherine's letters, destroyed some of the 1841 letters, or they were especially treasured and then lost.

A significant clue to the ease of their relationship is the fact that Elizabeth was, according to the available evidence, the only person outside of Catherine's own family who ever called her "Kitty", as her brother James often did (Carroll, *Life* 269). Catherine seems to have enjoyed this, and used the name herself on at least one occasion. When she writes to Elizabeth from Bermondsey on December 17, 1839, describing arrangements there and the recent reception ceremony, she refers to herself as "Kitty" six times in the course of the letter, and claims, no doubt with tongue-in-cheek, that "Every application [for admission] is referred by the Bishop to Kitty, who is major domo" (187). Catherine is partly playing up to English expectations about the "wild Irish", as she notes (188); partly speaking from the great exuberance she felt in being able to establish the first new convent of Catholic sisters in London since the English Reformation; and partly writing in intimate affection to her good friend. She concludes this letter to Elizabeth: "Pray for your fondly attached—Kitty—M. C. McAuley" (189).

Like the rest of the superiors of the first foundations outside of Dublin, Elizabeth Moore did her share of founding new communities where they were needed, thereby contributing to the extension of the Institute of the Sisters of Mercy throughout the world in the two decades following Catherine's death. In the eighteen years from 1844 to 1862, when she left the office of superior, Elizabeth and the community founded twelve houses from St. Mary's, Limerick: branch houses at Mount St. Vincent's (1850), Newcastle West (1850), Rathkeale (1850), Adare (1854), and St. Camillus City Home and Hospital (1861); and new foundations in Kinsale (1844), Killarney (1844), Mallow (1845), Glasgow (1849), Roscommon (1853), Ennis (1854), and Edinburgh (1858). These foundations, in turn, eventually founded other communities in Ireland, England, Scotland, Australia, New Zealand, and the United States.

As Catherine McAuley had rightly predicted, Elizabeth Moore did not remain "faint-hearted" in Limerick.[6] In time her creativity in responding to human needs instituted new aspects of the works of mercy. She opened poor schools in outlying parishes, and in late 1839 started a Christian Doctrine Society for the women of Limerick, mindful, as the Rule says, that "no work of charity can be more productive of good to society, or more conducive to the happiness of the

Poor than the careful instruction of women" (2.5). This group also served as a temperance sodality and library club, the members taking the pledge as testimony to the sufferings consequent on the abuse of alcohol, and enjoying the use of books presented to them each week (Courtney, "Elizabeth Moore" 33). When, after the ravages of the Famine, a prolonged cholera epidemic struck Limerick in the spring of 1849 (and, less severely, again in 1854), Elizabeth sought volunteers from among the community to nurse with her in two cholera hospitals in the city: St. John's Fever Hospital and Barrington's Hospital. The sisters had charge of these hospitals and remained there day and night in shifts (Courtney, "Cholera" 38). After the sisters gained access to the city and county jails in 1843, prison ministry was an important aspect of Elizabeth's work as well, and she and other sisters often spent long hours with prisoners, including those condemned to be hanged. Courtney tells of a rare occurrence, the execution of a woman for alleged complicity in the murder of her husband, and notes that prior to her being hanged, Elizabeth visited her every day, "even during the August retreat, a time of seclusion and silence" ("Mission" 10–11). As one reads such stories of Elizabeth's life in Limerick—whether in Carroll's volumes, Courtney's articles, or the Limerick Annals themselves—one remembers Catherine's words in her essay now called "The Mercy Ideal" or "The Spirit of the Institute": "the spirit of prayer and retreat should be most dear to us, yet such a spirit as would never withdraw us from these works of mercy; otherwise it should be regarded as a temptation rather than the effect of sincere piety" (Neumann 389).

Early in 1839, Elizabeth Moore was instrumental in getting Catherine to write a statement on the "history" of the Sisters of Mercy, an account which she was very reluctant to attempt but which she nonetheless provided, in obviously abbreviated form, in her letter to Elizabeth of January 13, 1839 (153–6). Although Catherine, regretting her random style, charged Elizabeth in a postscript "not to let this out of your hand", the documentary sources of the Sisters of Mercy are immensely enriched by Elizabeth's request (made on behalf of a curate, John Clarke, who was to preach a charity sermon for the Limerick poor school) and by Catherine's subsequent response: her brief sketch of how the Institute "commenced" and how "it evidently was to go on" (154–5). In the letter Catherine acknowledges both the gift of charity which the community savored, as from God's Spirit, and their own human deficiency and resolve:

> One thing only is remarkable, that no breach of charity ever occurred amongst us. The sun never, I believe, went down on our anger. This is our only boast—otherwise we have been deficient enough—and far, very far, from cooperating generously with God in our regard, but we will try to do better—all of us—*the black heads* [professed sisters] will try to repair the past. (155)

The death of Catherine McAuley—"our darling foundress", as Elizabeth called her (Carroll, *Leaves* 1:299)—must have been a severe loss to her good friend. Yet Elizabeth had the privilege, singular among the superiors of the nine independent houses Catherine had founded outside of Dublin, of being with her for a week before she died and of being at her bedside that night. Consequently, she was able to add to historical knowledge of Catherine's life not only the text of Catherine's prayer of resignation—commonly called her "Suscipe"—but also a detailed account of Catherine's last days and death, as recorded in the letters she wrote afterwards to various superiors of houses Catherine had founded.

The Limerick Manuscript which incorporates Elizabeth Moore's recollections contains an extended account of Catherine's final illness and death. Much of this account is fresh, not identical to the wording in the Bermondsey Life. In this section the author describes Catherine's "patience and submission under suffering". She then says of the dying Catherine:

> The following little prayer composed by herself expresses most truly her sentiments.
>
> "My God, I am Thine for all eternity; teach me to cast my whole self into the arms of Thy Providence with the most lively unlimited confidence in Thy compassionate, tender pity. Grant, O most Merciful Redeemer, that whatever Thou dost ordain or permit may always be acceptable to me; take from my heart all painful anxiety; suffer nothing to afflict me, but sin; nothing to delight me, but the hope of coming to the possession of Thee, my God, in Thy own everlasting Kingdom. Amen."

In the earliest eyewitness accounts this is probably the first recording of the words of Catherine's "Suscipe."[7] Undoubtedly Catherine had composed this prayer, or transcribed it from some source, much earlier in her life, and Elizabeth Moore either had a copy or had memorized it. Given the openness of their relationship, it is more than conceivable that Catherine would have shared this prayer with her. Its placement in the Limerick Manuscript at this point in the narrative implies that Elizabeth—who alone of the Limerick community was present at Catherine's death—was probably the person who supplied the text to Mary Vincent Harnett. A fairly thorough search through prayer books available in Catherine's day, including her own *Devotions to the Sacred Heart of Jesus,* has not so far turned up any printed source from which Catherine might have transcribed the prayer. On the contrary, the available evidence suggests rather strongly that this prayer, so typical of Catherine's lifelong attitudes, is, as the Limerick Manuscript and Mary Austin Carroll say, her own composition. Carroll says she wrote it "in compliance with the request of a Sister" (*Life* 237).

After Catherine died, Elizabeth wrote letters about her death to Michael Blake, then Bishop of Dromore, and to several if not all of the superiors of foundations outside of Dublin. I have not so far been able to locate either the autograph or a copy of the letter to Dr. Blake written on November 12. But evidently his response to her, written from Newry on November 13, was widely shared, since it is transcribed with a few slight variations in both the Limerick Manuscript and the Bermondsey Annals' Life, and a handwritten copy of it, which Mary Ann Doyle may have taken with her from Tullamore, is in the Derry archives.[8] Transcriptions of it also appeared in at least two published obituaries.[9]

Perhaps Elizabeth's letter to Michael Blake was similar in content and wording to the letters which she wrote to various superiors of the foundations. These letters to superiors were apparently somewhat alike, since several versions of this communication to early associates of Catherine McAuley are now extant or recorded. The Bermondsey Annals incorporates the text of a letter which Clare Moore may have received—while in Cork, or later in Bermondsey—or a transcription of a letter received by someone else. Mary Ignatia Neumann quotes the entire text of a copy which is now in the Cork archives (45–6).[10] The Limerick Manuscript incorporates a text of this letter, noting that "The following short account of [Catherine's] death was written by one of the Mother Superiors who went to Baggot Street to assist her in her last moments," and this text is included in Mary Vincent Harnett's published biography. In her *Life,* Mary Austin Carroll also gives a version of this letter; she dates it "November 12, 1841" and notes that it was written from Baggot Street (461–63). She is quoting a letter similar to the one sent to Mary Ann Doyle, but does not indicate to whom it was sent. Frances Warde may have brought the letter she received in Carlow to the United States, and Carroll may be quoting that letter. Elizabeth Moore would have known of Catherine's and Frances's very close friendship and would surely have written to Frances immediately after Catherine's death. Finally, two autograph letters are extant: one in Derry, written to Mary Ann Doyle in Tullamore; and one in Rath Luirc (Charleville), written to Mary Angela Dunne. The latter autograph is incomplete.[11]

The differences between these versions are generally, though not always, minor. Some versions of the letter evidently had a sentence or two about the burning of Catherine's shoes, and some did not, or else these sentences were simply not copied in the later transcriptions. The Limerick Manuscript uses the marks for an ellipsis at this point, as does the Bermondsey Annals. However, the autograph letters to Mary Ann Doyle and Mary Angela Dunne do contain the reference to the burning of the "boots" (45), as does the Cork copy.[12] Some versions use names of individuals, and some do not. All have differences in wording and details. Of the available versions I have seen, only in the Rath Luirc (Charleville) autograph and in the Cork transcription does Elizabeth acknowledge that "I was sent for", though perhaps she said this in other letters as well.[13]

The letters of Elizabeth Moore which are presented below are those written from Limerick to Mary Ann Doyle in Tullamore on November 21, 1841, and from Limerick to Mary Angela Dunne in Charleville on December 10, 1841. They are the letters of a long-time friend of Catherine McAuley, and, unlike the letters of Mary Vincent Whitty written in the same period, they contain the mature reflections of a somewhat older woman (Elizabeth was then thirty-five, whereas Mary Vincent was twenty-two), and of one who knew Catherine well. In these letters Elizabeth records the calm and gracious dying of a beloved woman, and gives a clear and concise account of the major events in Catherine's last days, from November 8 to the night of November 11. Although Elizabeth could have spoken, with some credibility, about the loss felt by all Catherine's earliest companions, her writing is restrained and factual, recounting Catherine's last words and actions undramatically, but with dignity.

When she returned to Limerick shortly after Catherine's burial on Monday, November 15, Elizabeth brought with her, as keepsakes, Catherine's cloak, one of her coifs, and one of her prayer books (*Devotions to the Sacred Heart of Jesus,* edited by Joseph Joy Dean). These tokens of Catherine's human life are still treasured in the Limerick archives. But nothing which Elizabeth Moore carefully saved is so irreplaceably important to a knowledge of Catherine's life as are the clear images of her hours of dying which Elizabeth preserved in the letters she wrote to Catherine's grieving companions.

THE LETTER OF MARY ELIZABETH MOORE, LIMERICK TO MARY ANN DOYLE, TULLAMORE

Convent of S.S. [Sisters] of Mercy
Limerick 21st Nov[embe]r '41

My own dear Mother Mary Anne[1]

It was my intention to write to you immediately on my return from Baggot St. I know you have received an account of the Consecration of the Cemetery, the Office, etc., in a letter directed to your poor patient; of our beloved Revd. Mother what shall I or what can I say but that she died the Death of the Just. Cautious as she was from bringing herself into notice unnecessarily in Health she was still more so in sickness: waiting on herself even in her last agony, preserving to the last moment the same peace and serenity of mind which so eminently distinguished [her][2] through Life, omitting not an iota of what was essential, and totally disregarding all but what was of moment.

I was not at all aware that her Death was so near. I was full of hope till Wednesday morning about 11 o'clock; that is, the day before her death; had I then known what I since heard, I would not have been so unprepared for the shock. She was herself well aware she was dying for the last six months and since her return from Birmingham cautiously avoided anything like business; it is only by her acts we can judge of her mind. She was perfectly silent as to what she thought, arranged all her papers etc. about a month or six weeks since and said to Sr. Teresa on leaving the parlor that now they were ready.

On Wednesday night or rather Thursday morning about two o'clock she called for a piece of paper and twine, tied up her boots and desired them to be put in the fire. The Sister to whom she gave them did not know what they were, but had directions to remain at the fire till all was consumed. Before she gave them to her she inquired was I out of the way, as the only one she supposed would venture to open the Parcel.

About four she desired the Bed to be moved to the centre of the room, that she would soon want air; about seven she desired the Sisters to be brought to her, said to each one individually what was most suited, but her first and last injunction to all was to preserve union and peace amongst each other—that if they did they would enjoy great happiness such as that they would wonder where it came from; told Sr. Genevieve particularly that she felt exceedingly happy, as if to encourage her to die; recognized all, told little Sr. Camillus Byrne to kiss her and go away, that she would see her again, as if to prevent her from weeping.

The Holy Sacrifice was offered in the room about ½ past 8; she said it would be a comfort to her to see the white Cloaks on the Sisters for she had been anointed without the usual Ceremony on Monday, more to hasten her recovery than that she was thought in immediate danger.

I think her agony commenced about 11 O'Clock. She spoke very little but was visited that day by Dean Gaffney, her Brother, Sister-in-Law, and nieces[3]—Dean Meyler—Mr. Walsh [of] Kingstown—Mr. O'Hanlon—Mr. O'Carroll, and the Doctor. To the last she said: Well, Doctor, the scene is drawing to a close. About five in the evening she asked for the candle to be placed in her hand. We commenced the last prayers; when I repeated one or two she herself had taught me, she said with energy: God may bless you.[4] When we thought the senses must be going and that it might be well to rouse attention by praying a little louder, she said: No occasion, my darling, to speak so loud, I hear distinctly. In this way she continued till 10 minutes before 8 when she calmly breathed her last sigh.

I did not think it possible for Human Nature to have such self-possession at the awful moment of Death but she had an extraordinary mind in Life and Death. Her Sister-in-Law remained with her the entire day till she expired, and attended the Office. I think we ought all pray for her conversion and her family, as the thing of all others our dear dear Revd. Mother had most at heart.

I know you got an acc[ount] of the Office and Burial. She left for you and all the Revd. Mothers a special blessing for themselves and Community.

Now my own dear Mother M. Anne, can I in any way lighten your affliction—if so command me now and at all times.

A letter from Baggot Street: His Grace desires them prepare for an Election. Say what are your feelings about the dear Sister that is dying with you.[5] I mean, say would you like any suggestion from me to Baggot St. How it happens I don't know, but all there appear to like me to say any thing I wish.

I am afraid I will be late for the Post; I will send you a lock of our beloved Revd. Mother's hair next letter; I now enclose copy of a letter sent to me from Dr. Blake.[6] I wrote to him the day after she died.

Get no translation of our Holy Rule till I have time to explain further; our dear Revd. Mother did not sanction the alterations with the exception of one or two—not certain how they crept in, but I have my suspicions. I will write again when I hear from you. Ask me any thing I have not told and that you are anxious to know. Your fondly attached

Mary Elizabeth

*

THE LETTER OF MARY ELIZABETH MOORE, LIMERICK
TO MARY ANGELA DUNNE, CHARLEVILLE

I commenced Friday—
could not finish till this day, Sunday—
on the 10th the sister departed[1]

Convent of S.S. of Mercy—
Limerick 10 Dec[embe]r '41

My dearest Sister[2]

What shall I say of the death of our dear Revd. Mother, but that she died the Death of the Just. She was preparing for it some months before, without saying any thing on the subject. Since her return from Birmingham she avoided in every possible way any thing like business or giving an opinion on any subject—arranged all her papers—made her will—and all this without its being known except to the persons absolutely necessary. At four O'Clock of the morning of the day she died, she tied up her boots, and you know they were generally of her own making, gave them to one of the young Sisters with directions not to open the parcel but wait at the fire till all was consumed—then ordered her bed to be moved into the middle of the room, that she would soon want air. At nine Mass was celebrated in the room. All the Sisters assisted with Cloaks and candles at her own request; she gave each her blessing separately and said a few suitable words to each. Poor Sr. Genevieve, she told her she was very happy.

Her agony commenced about 11 O'Clock and continued till 10 minutes before eight. During the day she saw the Doctor, told him with her usual calmness, the scene was drawing to a close. She also saw Dean Gaffney, Dean Meyler, Mr. O'Hanlon, Mr. O'Carroll, her Brother, Nieces, and Sister-in-Law who remained with her all day till she expired.

About ½ after six, when we supposed the senses must be going, we prayed in a louder tone; she sweetly smiled and said: No occasion, my darling, I hear distinctly, and desired the candle be placed in her hand. I did not think it possible for human nature to have such self-possession to the last breath of life. She left a special blessing for the Revd. Mothers who were absent.

None of the old Sisters were with her but Mother Di Pazzi, Sr. M. Magdalen, and your humble servant. I was sent for. Sr. M. Teresa, Galway, arrived the morning after she expired. She returned to Galway the day after the Burial. 60 priests at the Office. Their own Cemetery consecrated the day before interment and they have the consolation of having her remains. Sr. Agatha[3] is also dying, and another sweet Sister[4] in deep decline went to Tullamore a few months since to see would there. . . .

An Introduction to Catherine McAuley's Manuscript of the Rule and Constitutions of the Sisters of Mercy

The most important of Catherine McAuley's writings is the original Rule and Constitutions of the Sisters of Mercy. The manuscript, handwritten in black ink in a copybook, is preserved in the Archives of the Sisters of Mercy, Dublin. It is the most comprehensive written expression of Catherine's thought now available, and when it is compared with the Rules and Constitutions of the Presentation Sisters, which was its basis, the qualities of Catherine's composition emerge in striking ways. Respect for her thought and values and for her linguistic sensitivity only increases as one follows her, word by word and sentence by sentence, and sees the sometimes bold and sometimes subtle, but always deliberate, choices she made as she modified the Presentation Rule to suit the purposes of the Sisters of Mercy.

Simplicity was a hallmark of Catherine McAuley's style. In early 1840, when she made arrangements for a foundation of Sisters of Mercy in Birmingham, England, she wished to avoid some features of Augustus Welby Pugin's architectural design of the Bermondsey Convent which she had found impracticable. She therefore wrote to Bishop Thomas Walsh, Vicar Apostolic of the Midland District, outlining for him and Pugin the number of rooms needed in the proposed building and the desired dimensions:

> . . . all executed in the plainest style without any cornice. Cheap grates and stone chimney pieces.
>
> This could be completed in ten months and would not cost more than a small building where ornamental work would be introduced. . . .
>
> The Convent in Bermondsey is not well-suited to the purpose. The sleeping rooms are too large, the other rooms too small, the corridors confined and not well lighted, all the Gothic work outside has made it expensive. A plain, simple, durable building is much more desirable. (198)

Catherine's preference for what was "plain, simple, durable"—as well as for what was unconfined and well lighted—also characterized her composition of the first Rule and Constitutions of the Sisters of Mercy. Insofar as she was free to do so, and in some matters she was not, she avoided what was merely ornamental or so precise as to be time-bound. She had an instinct about the danger of prescribing in too great detail, and did not share the hidden lack of trust in others' judgments that minute prescriptions can imply. As the Bermondsey annalist notes:

> She was very careful not to give many positive directions about any duty, or, as she used to call it, to make too many laws, giving her reason for it to a Sister who

> overzealously requested her to desire the Community not to do some little thing rather out of order but not against [the] Rule. "It is better not," she answered mildly; "be careful never to make too many laws, for if you draw the string too tight it will break."

Even after the Rule was composed Catherine guarded against so-called "improvements" which would have added to the specificity of its interpretation or to Rule-like customs. Though she once discovered new prayers which she herself liked, and for a while prayed them with the community, Clare Augustine Moore notes that

> After a month . . . she ceased this devotion and, when I asked her why, said that if she added prayers herself some very devout successor would add more and another more 'till, especially in poor convents, the sisters would be incapable of the duties of the Institute. . . .

This same spirit of restraint and of respect for the future guided her as she composed the Rule.

I. HISTORY OF THE COMPOSITION

Five stages in the history of the original Rule and Constitutions of the Sisters of Mercy can be identified and will be discussed: Catherine McAuley's own manuscript, which is a detailed revision of the Rules and Constitutions of the Presentation Sisters; Archbishop Daniel Murray's penciled revisions of Catherine's manuscript; Mary Clare Moore's fair copy, which incorporates Daniel Murray's revisions, adds one chapter, and revises the chapter sequence; the Italian translation which was returned from Rome in 1841 as the official form of the Rule approved by the Congregation for the Propagation of the Faith and confirmed by Pope Gregory XVI; and the earliest published English translations of the Italian text—those published in Birmingham in 1844, in London in 1856, and in Dublin in 1863.

At the beginning of the process of composition, Archbishop Murray appointed Myles Gaffney (1798–1861)—a curate at Saint Andrew's Church, Dublin, and, after September 1834, senior dean at Maynooth College—to assist Catherine. Although several early biographical accounts of her life mention this assistance, none of them describes the exact nature of it, or ascribes any particular portion of the document to his guidance. That Myles Gaffney became a close friend of Catherine and the community is, however, evident: he frequently gave them spiritual instructions, directed their first eight-day retreat in August 1832, and was present at Catherine's bedside on the day she died. Burke Savage claims that he was asked to "help her draft additional chapters for the revised Rule" (134), and that "in January 1832 . . . at the Archbishop's request, [he] came to Baggot Street to assist Catherine in drafting the proposed Rule" (263). Myles Gaffney was undoubtedly extremely helpful to Catherine as she drafted the two chapters on the distinctive works of the Sisters of Mercy—"Of the Visitation of the Sick" and "Of the Admission of Distressed Women"—but after his departure for Maynooth in 1834, he may have been less able to give her close assistance as she completed her rather extensive revision of the Presentation Rules and Constitutions.[1]

The source from which Catherine wrote was the approved Rules and Constitutions of the Presentation Sisters, founded by Honora (Nano) Nagle in 1775. Catherine's choice of this text as her model had been made, a few years earlier, when she and her associates in the Baggot Street community first decided to found a new congregation of women religious devoted to the service of the poor. Sometime in 1830, during intense clerical and lay criticism of their unusual way of life—as a community of lay women, living together, who professed no religious vows and yet *appeared* to be a religious community—the decision was made that Catherine McAuley, then about fifty-two years old, and two of her companions in the House of Mercy on Baggot Street, Anna Maria Doyle and Elizabeth Harley, would enter the Presentation Convent on George's Hill, Dublin, for the purpose of serving an approved novitiate prior to their profession of religious vows as the first Sisters of Mercy. They entered the Presentation Convent on September 8, 1830, and professed their vows there on December 12, 1831. Having previously studied the Rules of several other religious congregations, they had chosen in 1830 to make their novitiate with the Presentation Sisters and eventually to use their already approved Rules and Constitutions (hereafter: Presentation Rule) as a guide for their own, because they admired the spirit and purposes of the Presentation Sisters and of Nano Nagle herself (she had died in 1784), and felt that the Presentation document—despite its chapter on enclosure which they intended to modify—came closest to describing their own intentions as the future Sisters of Mercy.

The particular edition Catherine used was undoubtedly the English translation published in 1809, entitled, *Rules and Constitutions of the Institute of the Religious Sisterhood of the Presentation of the Ever Blessed Virgin Mary . . . for the Charitable Instruction of Poor Girls* (Cork: James Haly, 1809).[2] This Rule was clearly at Catherine's side as she wrote her own Rule, and it was also obviously at Daniel Murray's side as he reviewed her manuscript. Therefore, one can best follow Catherine's mind at work as she composed her Rule if one thinks about three elements of her method: her *additions* to the Presentation Rule of chapters, paragraphs, and words; her *deletions* of chapters, paragraphs, sentences, and words; and her *changes* of sentences, words, and the chapter sequence itself. Similarly, Daniel Murray penciled in additions, deletions, and changes, and altered the chapter numbering.

The two full chapters Catherine added—"Of the Visitation of the Sick" and "Of the Admission of Distressed Women"—were composed first, that is, before she revised the rest of the Presentation Rule for her purposes. They were probably written in 1832 or early 1833. The Bermondsey annalist reports that:

> In 1833 the Reverend J. Rice, a venerable Augustinian Friar, brother to the holy man who founded the Christian Brothers in Ireland, on his way to Rome visited the Convent in Baggot St., and being much pleased with all he saw, asked if he

could render any service to the Institute. Our Reverend Mother told him how anxious she was to receive the formal approbation of the Holy See, and he promised to remember her wishes. Some months after, she received directions to forward to Rome those additions to the Presentation Rule which were deemed necessary in order to adapt it to our duties, the [Presentation] Rule itself having been confirmed.

On the Feast of our Lady's Immaculate Conception [December 8, 1833] she sent the Chapters on the Visitation of the Sick and the Protection of Distressed Women, which she had previously submitted to Archbishop Murray, who then desired her to include them with the Rule altered as she considered necessary, and to send him a copy of it, that he might at leisure deliberate on it. Our dear Reverend Mother transcribed it herself with the greatest care, but it was not until the year 1835 that the Archbishop brought her the joyful intelligence that his Holiness Pope Gregory 16th had given his approbation with his apostolical Benediction to the Institute. His Grace then informed her that he had carefully collated the copy of the Holy Rule she had sent him, with that of the Presentation Order, that he had changed some points, and that as soon as it was again copied, such as he now gave it to her, he would affix his sanction to it, which was done accordingly and Dr. Murray wrote the form of approbation with his signature, dating it from the time that the Institute received the approbation of the Holy See, the third of May 1835.

Although the early manuscript sources are somewhat unclear in their dating of these events, the chronology with respect to the Rule seems to have been as follows: in 1832, or very early 1833, Catherine composed, with Myles Gaffney's help, the two chapters noted above, and only these two chapters were sent to Rome in December 1833, the rest of the Rule being temporarily presumed to be identical to the Presentation Rule which had already been confirmed by Pius VII on April 9, 1805; on March 24, 1835, the Holy See gave formal approval for the establishment of the new Institute, as defined by these two chapters and by the Presentation Rule, and sent notice of this to Archbishop Murray; on May 3, 1835, when he received this news he communicated it to the community on Baggot Street (hence the importance of this date in their eyes); meanwhile Catherine had begun to revise the Presentation Rule, perhaps as early as 1832 or 1833; she submitted her manuscript of a complete Rule and Constitutions to Daniel Murray sometime in the mid 1830s, and he then made penciled revisions on it (there is no date on her manuscript or on his revisions—Clare Augustine Moore says that Dr. Murray kept the document "several months", while the Limerick Manuscript says he kept it "about two years");[3] at some point after this, Archbishop Murray received a fair copy of the Rule (prepared by Mary Clare Moore), incorporating all his revisions, which he approved, sealed in red wax, and dated retroactively "3d May 1835"; he received at least one other fair copy for his approval, signature, and seal which he also dated "3d May 1835", again to correspond with the date when the Holy See's approval for the establishment of the Institute was received at Baggot Street; and by January 23, 1837, he received another fair copy of the completed Rule, on which he also wrote, "We approve of these Rules and Constitutions compiled for the Religious Congregation of the Sisters of Mercy. . . . + D. Murray, Abp., Etc., Dublin." He dated this copy "23d January 1837", and again affixed his archepiscopal seal.

The fair copy dated "3d May 1835" which is now preserved in the Bermondsey archives and the "23d January 1837" fair copy, which is now called the Dundee Manuscript and is preserved in the Dublin archives, are the ones used in this study.[4] These two fair copies are nearly identical except for copying errors, a few variations in spelling and capitalization, a handful of minor differences in wording, and three more significant differences which will be discussed later in this chapter. Undoubtedly Archbishop Murray received other fair copies for his signature and seal, perhaps before but certainly after the one he signed on January 23, 1837.[5]

II. CATHERINE McAULEY'S MANUSCRIPT AND DANIEL MURRAY'S REVISIONS

The complete text of Catherine McAuley's manuscript (incorporating Daniel Murray's revisions) is presented in the next chapter. All of her revisions of the Presentation Rule, as well as all of Dr. Murray's revisions of her text, are documented in the notes which accompany the text.[6] I here list only some of the more important additions, deletions, and changes Catherine made as she transformed the Presentation Rule. (In this summary I also note the changes in chapter sequence which appear in Clare Moore's fair copy, to be discussed later in this chapter.) Catherine's entire manuscript, reflecting as it does her deliberate choice of concepts and wording, invites in-depth analyses of various kinds—which lie beyond the scope of this study, but which, I trust, the detailed presentation of her Rule will support and encourage.

Catherine makes the following important revisions of the Presentation Rule as she composes the First Part of her Rule:[7]

- She begins the first article of the first chapter, on the purposes of the Institute, with the wording of article 1, chapter 1 (untitled) of the Presentation Rule (hereafter: PR), but she composes a completely new conclusion to the article, naming as "peculiarly characteristic" of the Sisters of Mercy: "the Instruction of poor Girls, Visitation of the Sick, and protection of distressed women of good character."
- In article 2, chapter 1, Catherine changes the PR reference to Jesus' "tender love for little children" to his "tender love for the poor" and changes the scriptural quotation from "whosoever receiveth these little ones in his name, receiveth himself" (Matt. 18.5), to "He would consider as done to Himself whatever should be done unto them" (Matt. 25.40).
- Catherine's chapter 1 is entitled "Of the Schools", but Daniel Murray separates the first two articles of this chapter from the rest of the chapter and forms a new chapter 1 to which he gives the title, "Of the Object of the Institute." He leaves the remaining articles of her original chapter 1 as a

new chapter 2, "Of the Schools". The numbering of Catherine's subsequent chapters in the First Part is thus altered. Therefore, in the following commentary and throughout this study the new chapter numbers are used.

- In the chapter, "Of the Schools", Catherine makes countless small but significant changes which are best understood by examining her manuscript against the PR, as I have done in my notes on the text. Basically, she uses in this chapter parts of only four articles in chapters 1 and 2 of the PR. In other words, of the *seventeen* articles in the first two chapters of the PR she uses parts of *six* of them, in what are now, after Daniel Murray's division, her first two chapters: "Of the Object of the Institute" and "Of the Schools".

- The fifth and last article in "Of the Schools" is, apparently, entirely Catherine's own composition. With Daniel Murray's slight revisions (Catherine's original wording is given in brackets), it reads as follows: "The Sisters shall feel convinced that no work of charity can be [so] more productive of good to society, or [so] more conducive to the happiness of the poor [as] than the careful instruction of women, since [however] whatever be the station they are destined to fill, their example and advice will always possess influence, and where ever a religious woman presides, peace and good order are generally to be found" (2.5). Here "religious woman" does not refer to a "sister", but to any woman informed and motivated by her religious faith.

- Catherine composes a completely new chapter 3 (originally, her chapter 2): "Of the Visitation of the Sick", consisting of eleven articles and having a remarkably Christological emphasis. It begins with the words: "Mercy, the principal path pointed out by Jesus Christ to those who are desirous of following Him. . . ."

- She also composes a completely new chapter 4: "Of the Admission of Distressed Women", an astute, business-like chapter consisting of five articles about the care, instruction, and employment of women and girls sheltered in the House of Mercy.

- In chapter 5, "Of the Perfection of Ordinary Actions" (which is chapter 17 in the PR), Catherine makes dozens of small changes in wording, some of them very subtle and significant. Daniel Murray also makes a few minor revisions in three of Catherine's five articles. Clare Moore places this chapter later in the First Part, as chapter 14.

- Catherine's chapter 6, "Of the Employment of Time", corresponds to chapter 12 in the PR which consists of one long article. Catherine revises and considerably shortens this article for her article 1; she omits two statements, one of which says that the sisters "shall never be found running giddily thro' the convent" (!). She then composes a second article which Daniel Murray completely deletes by crossing it out with a large X. This second article has to do with "religious modesty . . . dignified deportment" and a "countenance . . . ever serene and cheerful". It is actually a sensible, thoughtful paragraph that probably says a good deal about Catherine's own manner and facial expression.

- Catherine's chapter 8 is the very important chapter, "Of Union and Charity", which is chapter 15 in the PR. Catherine uses the first five articles of this long chapter almost verbatim, although she makes well over a dozen small changes in wording, some of which are significant. The most emphatic alteration Catherine makes in her use of this chapter is her complete omission of article 6, which Daniel Murray does not restore. That article in the PR reads:

  > In speaking to the Superioress all the Sisters shall call her *Mother,* not only while she is in office, but ever after. The Assistant, Burser [*sic*], and Mistress of Novices shall also be called *Mother,* by all the other Sisters, except by the Mother Superior. The other Religious shall call each other *Sister.* (PR 15.6)

  In Clare Moore's fair copy, "Of Union and Charity" is chapter 17.

- In chapter 9, "Of Humility" (which is chapter 14 in the PR and chapter 19 in Clare Moore's fair copy), Catherine uses both articles almost as they are in the PR. However, in article 2 she inserts "and affection" after "respect" and she changes "mutual honor and respect" to "tender concern and regard". Daniel Murray crosses out both of these revisions and composes the concluding phrase: " 'in honor,' as St. Paul expresses it, 'preventing one another'."

- Catherine's chapter 14 (originally her chapter 13) is titled only "Of Spiritual Retreat". She uses almost verbatim only the first article in the PR, omitting in her title reference to the "Renewal of Vows" which she places later as chapter 9 in the Second Part. Archbishop Murray, following the order and content of the PR, restores the full chapter title and writes "Renewal of Vows" after article 1. Here Clare Moore, in what is her chapter 10, inserts the text of the PR "Form of the Act of the Renewal of Vows", but she alters it to match the formula used in the profession of vows of the Sisters of Mercy.

- Catherine moves the chapters, "On Devotion to the Passion of Jesus Christ, to the Blessed Sacrament, and to the Sacred Heart of Jesus" and "On Devotion to Our Blessed Lady", forward to the First Part of her manuscript, as chapters 15 and 16 respectively. They are chapters 9 and 10 in the Second Part of the PR. She uses these chapters almost verbatim, although she makes a number of significant word changes, some of which Daniel Murray alters. In Clare Moore's fair copy these are moved forward as chapters 12 and 13.

- In her chapter 16 Catherine makes four significant changes in the list of "Saints to whom the sisters of this religious Institute are recommended to have particular devotion": she adds "Saint John of God" and "Saints Catherine of Sienna and Genoa" and deletes "St. Francis Regis" (16.4).

- The three chapters "Of the Vows" are chapters 3, 4, and 5 in the First Part of the PR. Catherine moves these chapters to the end of her First Part, as chapters 17, 18, and 19. However, in Clare Moore's fair copy, these three chapters are moved forward again as chapters 5, 6, and 7, right after the four chapters on the works of the Sisters of Mercy. It is not clear from Daniel Murray's notations on Catherine's manuscript that he intended this placement.

- Catherine makes a number of small but noteworthy changes to chapter 17, "Of the Vow of Poverty", though the memorable first article of this chapter is almost verbatim from the PR: ". . . they should frequently revolve in mind how tenderly He cherished Holy Poverty. Born in a stable, laid in a manger, suffering hunger, cold, and thirst in the course of His mortal life . . . He consecrated this virtue in His sacred Person and bequeathed it as a most valuable patrimony to His followers" (17. 1).

- In chapter 18, "Of the Vow of Chastity", Catherine omits one clause in the first article ("they carry this most valuable treasure in brittle vessels") and, far more significantly, she omits the entire second article of the chapter in the PR, which Daniel Murray does not restore. It reads:

> They shall most cautiously avoid every occasion that may be a stumbling block in their way: profane books of any kind, which are apt to beget worldly affections, they never shall read. When spoken to by men of any state or profession they shall observe and maintain the most guarded reserve, never fix their eyes on them, nor shew themselves, in conversation or otherwise, in the least degree familiar with them, how devout or religious soever they may appear to be. They shall turn with abhorrence from every object that may in any shape tend to excite unclean ideas, in order to keep their minds and hearts always spotless and pure, and preserve with the most scrupulous integrity the faith which they have so solemnly plighted to their heavenly Spouse. (PR 4.2)

- Catherine makes a number of thoughtful changes in chapter 19, "Of the Vow of Obedience", some of them involving greater modesty about the role of the mother superior and greater deference toward the good judgment of the sisters. In addition to other smaller changes, she entirely omits the two concluding sentences of article 2 of the PR, which Daniel Murray does not restore. They read:

> They are not only to fulfil the commands of their Superior, but should also endeavour to anticipate her wishes, if they can discover them. They shall undergo with humility the penance enjoined by her, and, should she happen to reprimand them undeservedly, they are not to murmur, nor complain, but with a submissive mind and pious affection receive her rebukes, striving to

justify them in their own minds, in order the more perfectly to obey with all the powers and strength of their souls. (PR 5.2)

- The last chapter in the First Part of Catherine's manuscript is her original chapter 19, on "Enclosure", which Catherine copies directly from the PR (where it is chapter 6). She follows the PR exactly except that she changes the name of the Institute involved and inserts as a "first" reason for legitimately passing beyond "the limits of the enclosure" the need "to comply with the duties of their Institute". Daniel Murray excises the entire chapter from Catherine's manuscript, without comment, simply by drawing a large X through it.

The Second Part of Catherine McAuley's Rule and Constitutions is about half the length of the First Part. I here note, as briefly as possible, only the major changes she makes in this section of the Presentation Rule, even though the smaller changes, involving a single word or phrase, are often more telling. Catherine's entire text deserves very close examination against the Presentation text, as my detailed notes on her text illustrate.

The following are the major revisions in the Second Part, again presented here without extensive comment:

- Catherine places the chapter on the "Reception of Postulants, their Admission to the Habit, and Religious Profession" as the first chapter in the Second Part of the Rule. Archbishop Murray moves it to be the last chapter (that is, chapter 20, after his deletion of the chapter on Enclosure) of the First Part, whereas Clare Moore places it in the First Part as chapter 8. Catherine makes a number of changes in the first four articles, places article 4 *after* the Form of the Act of Profession, and omits entirely the fifth article in the PR. Daniel Murray re-positions article 4, and restores article 5 of the PR, which refers to the guidance of the young professed, and their lack of active and passive voting privileges during the first two years of profession unless they are among the first seven professed sisters in a new foundation.
- With the foregoing revision, the entire first chapter of the Second Part is now "Of the Superior and the Visitation of the Convent", consisting of six articles. It is taken verbatim from the PR by Clare Moore, interpreting Daniel Murray's notation. The Superior referred to is the ecclesiastical superior—i.e., "the Diocesan Bishop" or "a Priest . . . appointed by him". Catherine herself uses *only* article 1 of this chapter and the last clause of article 2 which she combines into a single unnumbered paragraph and places as the penultimate paragraph of her manuscript. However, Daniel Murray circled Catherine's paragraph and wrote above it: "N.B. This belongs to the 1st Chap. Part 2nd", and at the beginning of Catherine's Second Part he wrote: "2nd Part. Chapter 1st Superior, Visitation, etc." Thus, in making the fair copy Clare Moore did not use Catherine's single paragraph for article 1, but rather the exact text of all the articles of the PR. Catherine had

provided the substance of this chapter in her single paragraph, but perhaps would not have wished to incorporate some aspects of the internal role given to the Priest-Superior appointed by the Bishop, e.g., that "He shall sign . . . the annual accounts of the receipts and expenditure of the Convent" (II.1.3), "give such orders and directions, as in his prudence and discretion he shall judge most likely to reform every abuse" (II.1.5), and "for the purpose of clearing the debts suppress all unnecessary expenses", except those related to "such food and raiment as had been promised" to the sisters (II.1.6).

- Chapter 2, "Of the Election of the Mother Superior", is a revision of the chapter in the PR. Catherine fuses parts of some articles and omits others. Significantly, she completely omits article 1, which Daniel Murray restores. In Clare Moore's fair copy ("3d May 1835") it reads:[8]

  > A Superioress shall be elected from amongst the Vocals, distinguished for her virtue, prudence and discretion. She shall be at least thirty years old and of five years profession, except in new establishments, and must have the majority of votes for the validity of her election. (II.2.1)

  Undoubtedly the reference to the "virtue, prudence and discretion" of the superior was something Catherine would not write of herself, nor, initially, of the young women who would have to lead the new foundations and develop these qualities through experience. She also knew that some of the superiors she would be designating for these foundations would be in their twenties.

  Article 2 of the "23d January 1837" fair copy contains a clause which has been erased in the "3d May 1835" fair copy. Both copies note that the mother superior can be re-elected to serve a second three-year term, but the 1837 copy then says, "after which another Superioress shall be elected," as in Catherine's original manuscript (although she uses the word, "Superior"). Throughout this chapter, and the subsequent chapter Catherine usually changes "Superioress" to "Superior".

- Catherine's chapter 3, "Of the Office of Mother Superior", is a slight but sensitive revision of the corresponding chapter in the PR. In each of the eight articles she uses, Catherine makes some changes. She omits article 9, having to do with the Bishop's (or his delegate's) examination of novices before profession, and with his signing the Acts, accounts, and other written documents of the community. Daniel Murray restores this article as in the PR.

- In chapter 4, "Of the Office of the Assistant", which consists of two articles, Catherine makes, among other changes, one particularly thoughtful revision: she changes "She shall make it her particular study to assist and comfort the Mother Superior in all doubtful and difficult matters" to simply, "She shall assist the Mother Superior in all doubtful and difficult matters."

- In chapter 5, "Of the Office of the Depositary or Burser [*sic*]", which consists of one article, Catherine makes several significant changes, notably in the direction of removing the bursar's responsibility to "receive and keep the money of the convent, and pay all the disbursements." She also inserts "patience" as a quality of the bursar, and deletes the last clause requiring the weekly auditing of the accounts and the signature of the mother superior. Daniel Murray deletes her "patience" and restores the last clause.

- Catherine's chapter 6, "Of the Mistress of Novices", consisting of eight articles, is a thoughtful revision of the corresponding chapter in the PR. Each article reveals important aspects of Catherine's theological sense. Her revisions of article 1 express the role of the mistress of novices more humbly and modestly than does the wording of the PR, though Daniel Murray does not accept these revisions and restores the PR wording. However, he generally accepts her revisions in the subsequent articles. For example, in article 3 Catherine omits "especially in the female sex" in the sentence: "She shall instruct them in modesty, meekness and humility, encouraging them to conquer those pettish and childish humours which, especially in the female sex, weaken the spirit, and render it vapid and languid . . ." (PR II.6.3). Daniel Murray does not restore the omitted words.

- In chapter 8, "Of Capitular Assemblies", Catherine makes one significant change in the PR wording. In article 1, having to do with the admission of candidates to reception of the habit, and to profession of vows, she omits the last sentence: "But should it be notorious before these meetings that the Candidate has not the requisite qualities and dispositions for the Institute, she shall be immediately dismissed." Daniel Murray restores this sentence.

  The PR, Catherine's manuscript, and the "3d May 1835" fair copy all contain article 3, which requires that "All transactions in chapter shall be kept inviolably secret", and prescribes the prayers to be used in these meetings. However, the article is missing in the "23d January 1837" fair copy, undoubtedly due to a copyist's error.

- The chapter, "Of Correction", is chapter 16 in the First Part of the PR; Catherine places it in the Second Part, as chapter 10 (but with the new placement of her chapter 9, "Of the Renewal of Vows", as noted earlier, it becomes chapter 9), and she modifies it considerably. Clare Moore, for some reason which is not evident, places it as chapter 18 of the First Part, right after "Of Union and Charity" and before "Of Humility", not exactly in conformity with its placement in the PR. Given Catherine's persistent reluctance to hold the Chapter of Faults (specified in the chapter on the office of mother superior)—as the Bermondsey annalist notes: "She could not be prevailed on to hold the prescribed Chapter of Faults for a very long time after being made Superior, and was pained when the Sisters manifested their faults to her in private"—it is possible that the advancement of this chapter, was one of the "mistakes" in the Rule which Catherine noted, especially since this chapter was altered in Rome to contain a second reference to the Chapter of Faults.

- Finally, the last two chapters of Catherine's manuscript, "Of the Care of the Sick Sisters and Suffrages of the Dead" and "On Establishments", contain a number of significant revisions: for example, Catherine does not call death a "danger", and she speaks of the support of the establishment (foundation) itself, rather than of "the support of the Sisters who undertake it". Catherine places "Of the Care of the Sick Sisters . . ." as chapter 11, in the Second Part; in Daniel Murray's sequence it would become chapter 10 in the Second Part. However, Clare Moore makes it chapter 22 of the First Part. Beyond this change in chapter sequence, and the one noted above, she follows Catherine's chapter order in the Second Part, as this Part is revised by Daniel Murray.

- However, Clare Moore inserts into the fair copy a new "Chapter 9th", entitled "Of Lay Sisters", which is not found in Catherine's manuscript or in the PR, nor indicated in Daniel Murray's revisions. The chapter contains four articles—on the requisites, religious habit, meals, spiritual exercises, and important role of lay sisters, whose state "is very similar to that which our humble Redeemer made choice of in this world; for He was constantly engaged serving others, but never requiring any care or attendance for Himself" (article 4). The "23d January 1837" fair copy contains article 3: "In speaking to or of the Choir Sisters they [the Lay Sisters] shall call them by their Sirname: Mrs. N—if Professed; Miss N—if Novice or Postulant." However, in the "3d May 1835" fair copy in Bermondsey this article has been erased, or in some way deleted; the text moves from the second article to the fourth, so numbered, with an intervening blank space. In the comparable fair copy in Birmingham, the article is also missing, with no space for it, and the fourth article is numbered "3d." Evidently, whatever the origin of this chapter on Lay Sisters, and of article 3, there was a movement early on to avoid unnecessary distinctions in the speech and relationships between lay and choir sisters. (It may be noted here that article 3 is not contained in the 1841 Italian text of the confirmed Rule nor in the published English translations of it.)

- Catherine concludes her manuscript with an unnumbered statement about the nature of the binding force of the Rule: "We declare it is not our intention that these rules and constitutions compiled for the Religious Sisters of Mercy shall oblige under pain of mortal or venial sin, only in as much as the transgression of any article may be a violation of the vows and in itself a sin independantly [*sic*] of the rule." This paragraph is not altered by Daniel Murray as he reviews her manuscript, but neither is it included in the text of the fair copies examined in this study. Rather, Daniel Murray uses the wording of this paragraph, with one revision (changing the last "and" to "or"), as part of his own formal statement of approval, written on the last page of each fair copy.

III. CLARE MOORE'S FAIR COPY

It may be helpful here to focus briefly on the important role Clare Moore played in the preparation of the Rule—at least in transcribing the first fair copy, but perhaps also in the initial composition. Since she was the primary source for the information on Catherine McAuley in the Bermondsey Annals, these Annals do not allude to Clare's own role in compiling the first fair copy. The Limerick Manuscript, which, at this point, uses the same wording as the Bermondsey Annals, also does not mention her role. Only Clare Augustine Moore, Clare Moore's own sister, presents this detail:

> As well as I can recollect, it was early in 1833 that the Rule was drawn up. The Archbishop sent a priest, I think his name was Kelly [actually, Myles Gaffney], to confer with the foundress on the subject. The Presentation Rule, amplyfying [*sic*] that of St. Augustine, is the foundation of ours. Some clauses were omitted; others relative to the objects of the Institute were added, which were drawn up by the foundress and Mother M. Clare. When they were satisfied with their labors, the manuscript was sent to his Grace. He kept it for several months, added a little and struck out a great deal. This copy in a blue cloth cover is (1864) still among the papers of the Convent. Mother M. Clare wrote out a fair copy to which the Archbishop's approval was given, signed and sealed. This copy was taken to Cork.

Probably the fair copy Clare Moore took to Cork (where she became the founding superior in July 1837) was one which Daniel Murray had dated "3d May 1835". She may have subsequently taken this copy to London when she and Catherine founded the Bermondsey convent in November 1839, or when she returned to Bermondsey permanently in December 1841. The "3d May 1835" fair copy now in the Bermondsey archives is hand-printed, so it is difficult to be sure that it is in Clare Moore's hand. Were it in cursive handwriting the task of verifying this would be relatively easy since numerous specimens of Clare Moore's cursive handwriting are preserved. But if it could be established with confidence that the Bermondsey fair copy is in Clare Moore's printing, then it is probably the first fair copy referred to in the early biographical manuscripts. The Dundee Manuscript is not, I believe, in Clare Moore's handwriting, and I have not so far been able to locate a fair copy that I am confident *is* in her handwriting.[9] It is also probable that Clare handwrote the copy which was sent to Rome in late 1839, but I have not been able to verify this.[10]

Nonetheless, in this study, I refer to both the Dundee Manuscript (dated January 23, 1837) and the Bermondsey fair copy (dated May 3, 1835) as "Clare Moore's fair copy". I do so for two reasons: all fair copies of Catherine's manuscript (with Daniel Murray's revisions incorporated) were intended to be identical copies of the first fair copy; and it was Clare Moore who performed the meticulous task of writing out the first fair copy of the corrected manuscript. Moreover, Clare certainly handwrote or hand-printed more than one fair copy, as is evident in Catherine's October 3, 1837 letter to Mary de Pazzi Delany: "There will be great *woe* if the Rule gone to Carlow has *half* as many mistakes as the one for Charleville—poor Sister Mary Clare was worn out at the work when she wrote it" (Bolster, ed. 34).

In Clare Moore's fair copy, as thus understood, Catherine McAuley's manuscript with Archbishop Murray's revisions, deletions, and additions is copied exactly except for two notable changes: the placement of some of the chapters and the addition of one chapter. Archbishop Murray had divided Catherine's first chapter into two chapters, deleted one entire chapter ("On Enclosure"), moved a chapter forward ("Of the Reception of Postulants"), and included a chapter of the Presentation Rule from which Catherine had used only one paragraph ("Of the Superior and the Visitation of the Convent"). However, it is not clear from his penciled notations on Catherine's manuscript that he advised any other changes in the sequence of the chapters.

Whatever the impetus for the changes in placement, Clare's fair copy of the Rule differs from Catherine's manuscript in the sequence of several of its chapters (see the charts at the end of this chapter). In the First Part, Clare follows the order of the manuscript through the first four chapters, then moves the three chapters on the vows forward, then inserts the chapter on the reception of postulants, and then places the three chapters on prayer, spiritual retreat, and confession and communion as chapters 9, 10, and 11—following, in all this, the sequence in the Presentation Rule. She then skips around, following exactly neither Catherine's sequence nor the Presentation sequence. She places some of Catherine's earlier chapters at the end of the First Part (for example, "On Humility"), places some of Catherine's later chapters earlier (for example, "On Devotion to the Passion . . ."), and inserts in the First Part a chapter from the Second Part of Catherine's manuscript ("Of Correction"). In the Second Part, Clare generally follows Catherine's chapter order as revised by Daniel Murray, but she inserts a "Chapter 9th, Of Lay Sisters," not found in Catherine's manuscript or in the Presentation Rule, nor indicated for inclusion by Daniel Murray. Perhaps this chapter was inserted at Catherine's request, and perhaps Mary Austin Carroll is correct in believing that it was "entirely composed by the Foundress" (240). Although no such chapter appears in Catherine's original manuscript, she may have composed it later, for inclusion in the fair copy.

With respect to the changes in chapter sequence that appear in Clare Moore's fair copy, there are a number of plausible but not verifiable explanations: that Clare received oral (or written) instructions to make these changes from Daniel Murray, or from Myles Gaffney, or from Catherine herself; that she misunderstood someone's instructions; or that, on her own, which seems unlikely in view of her character, she thought the new sequence more appropriate. It must be said that Clare Moore was a meticulous scribe and that she copied exactly both

Catherine's wording and the wording of the Presentation Rule, wherever Daniel Murray indicated the latter.

On the other hand, we know that Catherine discovered "mistakes" in the Rule in 1841 when she received one of the approved Italian copies sent to Daniel Murray. On October 12 she wrote to Frances Warde: "The Very Rev. Dr. Kirby, Vice-President of the Irish College, Rome, called here the day before he sailed. I mentioned to him some evident mistakes in the copy of our Rule. He told me to select them and forward the document to him, with Dr. Murray's signature, and said we would, without any more trouble, obtain permission to rectify the evident mistakes" (381–82).[11] Moreover, on November 21, 1841, ten days after Catherine's death, Elizabeth Moore wrote to Mary Ann Doyle: "Get no translation of our Holy Rule till I have time to explain further. Our dear Revd. Mother did not sanction the alterations with the exception of one or two. Not certain how they crept in, but I have my suspicions."

Unlike Elizabeth Moore, we do not presently have sufficient evidence for accurate "suspicions" about the identity or origin of the "evident mistakes" which troubled Catherine. The alterations to which Elizabeth referred may have been among those already noted (Daniel Murray's revisions, or the changes in chapter sequence in Clare Moore's fair copy), some or all of which Catherine, in the press of other concerns, may have innocently missed in the fair copy which she sent to Rome in late 1839. Or, more likely, they may have been the alterations which occurred in Rome, to be discussed below.

IV. THE 1841 ITALIAN TEXT OF THE RULE

On January 30, 1840, two weeks after her return from Bermondsey, London, Catherine wrote to Frances Warde about the packet, containing the Rule, which she had sent to Rome from London:

> I received your letter in London. As to what you said of the application to Rome I did exactly what was marked out for me. A Petition from the "Mother House"—a Memorial from the A[rch]bishop of Dublin praying a confirmation of the Rule, to which his approbation is attached—and letters of recommendation from the Bishops in whose Dioces [*sic*] Branches of the order were established. This has been most fully executed, the letters were as favorable as they could be. (195–6)

The final complete text of the Rule was sent to Rome for the first time with this packet, conveyed under the auspices of Bishop Thomas Griffiths, Vicar Apostolic of the London District. Prior to leaving for London with the Bermondsey founding community on November 18, 1839, Catherine had written to Bishop John Murphy of Cork:

> His Grace called here yesterday to affix his approbation and seal to the copy of our Rule going to Rome and left with me his memorial to the Holy Father. Your own Mary Clare [Moore], the best Latin reader amongst us, finds that your name is not introduced. . . . I am sure that you who have so long honored us with your

> patronage and valued friendship will not withhold what would certainly give great weight to our application.
>
> My Lord, in the year 1830 His Holiness gave permission for our noviciate to be served in a Presentation Convent. In 1835 our venerated Archbishop represented the successful progress, when the Holy See imparted to us full approbation. Doctor Murray then prepared our Rule, and finding it after due trial well suited to our different duties, we now seek for its final confirmation. We take all our documents with us to London on Monday next. (Bolster, ed. 103–4)

While the correspondence accompanying the Rule was evidently in Latin, the Rule itself was apparently sent to Rome in English. However, in Rome it was translated into Italian.

Paraphrasing "the substance" of a letter which James Maher, parish priest of Carlow, had received from his nephew, Paul Cullen, then Rector of the Irish College in Rome, the Carlow Annals for 1843 says that "Right Rev. Michael O'Connor, lately consecrated for the diocese of Pittsburgh, America had been called on when a student at the Irish College, Rome to translate our Rule into Italian before presenting it to the Sacred Congregation." After Bishop O'Connor assumed the episcopacy—so, the Annals continues—"remembering the Institute of our Lady of Mercy the rules of which he had furthered the confirmation, he requested Dr. Cullen to write to Carlow and engage a foundation for his distant mission. . . ."

Michael O'Connor was ordained a priest in Rome on June 1, 1833, and in the following year served as Vice Rector of the Irish College, and as a member of the faculty of the Urban College of the Congregation for the Propagation of the Faith. He returned to Ireland, as parish priest of Fermoy in the Diocese of Cloyne, from about 1834 to 1839, and then went to Philadelphia. In Rome on August 15, 1843, he was consecrated Bishop of Pittsburgh. It does not appear, therefore, that Michael O'Connor could have translated the final text of the Rule into Italian, since he was not resident in Rome after 1834. However, he may have been the translator of the two chapters which Catherine had sent to Rome in late 1833—those entitled, "Of the Visitation of the Sick" and "Of the Admission of Distressed Women"—although these two chapters were probably again translated into Italian after the entire text of the Rule arrived in Rome in late 1839 or early 1840. The translator on this occasion may have been Richard Colgan, OCC. The Bermondsey Annals, whose main source of information about the 1830s was Clare Moore, explains that

> Before [Catherine] left Baggot St. for England the Reverend Mr. [Richard] Colgan OCC, a faithful and long tried friend to the Institute, offered to present the Holy Rule for confirmation at Rome where he was going, promising to translate it into Italian, in order that it might be examined by the Sacred Congregation of the Propaganda Fide, and to further the business as much as he could. . . .

Documentation in the archives of the Sisters of Mercy, Dublin—which includes copies of documentation in the archives of the Congregation for the Propagation of the Faith in Rome and in the Dublin Diocesan Archives—

indicates that on June 6, 1841, Pope Gregory XVI granted papal approval and confirmation to the Rule and Constitutions of the Sisters of Mercy. He acted in response to the positive recommendation of a General Meeting of the Congregation for the Propagation of the Faith held almost a year before, on July 20, 1840.

The year-long delay in papal confirmation may be explained in part by the recommendations of Paul Gavino Secchi-Murro, who, as a Consultor to the Congregation for the Propagation of the Faith, had been asked to review the text of the Rule and Constitutions prior to the July 1840 meeting of the Congregation. Secchi-Murro issued his report to the Congregation on March 3, 1840. In it he recommended a number of ways in which the specificity of the document should be increased. He noted, in particular, that greater detail should be provided to the members of the Institute about their "conduct" and "the means of perfecting themselves in the service of God". He supported this view by reference to St. Francis de Sales' belief that "The Rule teaches what is to be done, the Constitutions teach how it is to be done." Among Secchi-Murro's recommendations for improving the document were the following: clearer expression of the "literary teaching . . . to be given to the children" in the schools; removal of the provision—unwise, in his view—that a bishop might, in extraordinary circumstances, reduce the time of the novitiate from two years to one year; insertion of a horarium: "an orderly distribution of time for attending at prayer and at the various works"; insertion of "some regulation" about whether, how, and when externs might be admitted into the convent; and provision for a system of penances and for "the expulsion of those who are incorrigible . . . . [and] the reasons for expulsion." Secchi-Murro also commented on "inexactitudes even of expression" which appeared in the Italian translation of the document and which he felt "should be corrected". But his overall assessment was that, "on account of the truly evangelical doctrine taught in them, . . .the maxims of solid piety inculcated in them, and . . . the spirit of most perfect charity which is manifested in them," the Rules and Constitutions of the Sisters of Mercy deserved the "highest approbation" of the Congregation. However, he also noted that "by means of a few additions that could be made to them, these Constitutions would be satisfactory, just as the Rules are most perfect."

Evidently Secchi-Murro's recommendations were to have been sent to Archbishop Murray. The members of the Congregation for the Propagation of the Faith were told prior to their meeting in July 1840 that "the distinguished Consultor agrees fully that the required approval should be given, except for some slight alterations which are to be sent, together with instructions, to His Grace the Archbishop of Dublin." The question put to the vote on July 20, 1840, was therefore: "Should His Holiness the Pope be petitioned for the Approbation which is asked for, with only those modifications recommended by the Rev. Consultor?" The members of the Congregation "replied Affirmative and left it to the Cardinal Prefect and the Cardinal Petitioner [who had presented the question] to have some things in the Constitutions, to which attention had been drawn, suitably improved or more accurately expressed."[12]

I have not so far been able to discover whether these recommended modifications were, in fact, ever sent to Archbishop Murray, or, if they were, how he chose to respond to them. In any event, three of the five recommendations noted above were eventually somewhat accommodated by alterations made in the Rule and Constitutions sometime before the final Italian text was published in 1841: the two-year novitiate was prescribed, without exception; reference to a "fixed horarium, approved by the Ordinary" was inserted in chapter 15, "Of the Employment of Time"; and a second reference to the Chapter of Faults was inserted, in chapter 18, perhaps as a general response to Secchi-Murro's comment about penances. (Many other alterations of Catherine's text also appear in the Italian text, but these will be discussed later in this chapter.)

Catherine McAuley's correspondence during 1840–1841 does not indicate that she was aware of any need for modification of the text she had submitted to Rome. She was, however, well aware of the long delay between approval of the Rule and Constitutions by the Congregation for the Propagation of the Faith on July 20, 1840, and her receiving word of its confirmation by Gregory XVI. On August 5, 1840, after a visit of Richard Colgan to Baggot Street on July 29, she wrote to Frances Warde, referring, probably not to the meeting of the Congregation for the Propagation of the Faith on July 20, but to the positive preparations for that meeting:

> . . . You say Doctor Cullen might call during the retreat. I would, of course, see him. . . .
>
> I am not surprised at what you say as to the confirmation of our Rule, though we have been led to expect it all the past month; but these matters seldom go on so rapidly at the Holy See. It is however certain that the process of examination has been gone through, and most strong promises made for the conclusion, so much that a Priest coming to Ireland [Richard Colgan (296)] was asked could he wait a few weeks to carry it with him. Yet I suppose all possible interest and attention may be necessary to prevent its being delayed. (230)

Frances Warde had probably heard something of this in conversation with James Maher, who would have received information from his nephew Paul Cullen, then Rector of the Irish College in Rome. Perhaps Rev. Maher had offered to urge his nephew to assist in hastening matters in Rome. On October 14, 1840, Catherine herself wrote to Cardinal Giacomo (James Philip) Fransoni, Prefect of the Congregation for the Propagation of the Faith. While the language of her letter appealing for confirmation of the Rule was restrained and indirect, she represented to him the hope of "Ecclesiastical authorities who are anxious to establish more Houses in England and Ireland, which they think would be greatly facilitated by the full approbation of the Holy See, as all orders of the clergy would then cooperate in promoting an order which they deem very conducive to the Interests of Religion." She noted further that "when the petition was presented in December [1839] there were twelve Houses in operation. Two have since been added. One hundred forty-two Sisters are now devoted to God and His poor in this order" (Bolster, ed. 153). Three months later, on January 20, 1841, Catherine wrote in response to Mary Angela Dunne's "enquiry about the Rule": "I spoke with Dr. Cullen, President of the Irish College at Rome, when in Dublin last summer. He said it was certainly granted, but that they were slow in issuing final documents" (296).

Finally, on June 6, 1841, Gregory XVI confirmed the Rule and Constitutions of the Sisters of Mercy. This confirmation was published in a decree issued by the Congregation for the Propagation of the Faith on July 5, 1841. On July 31, 1841, in a letter written in Latin to Archbishop Murray, Cardinal Fransoni said: "Along with this letter Your Grace will receive ten copies of the Rule and Constitutions of the Congregation of the Sisters of Mercy," and he requested that Dr. Murray "take care that the Superior of the House of the above-mentioned Congregation which has been erected in your diocese gets one copy of the Rule and Constitutions" (Burke Savage 417).[13]

The printed and bound document thus forwarded was *La Regola e Le Costituzioni delle Religiose nominate Sorelle della Misericordia.* This Italian text is the first ecclesiastically approved and confirmed Rule and Constitutions of the Sisters of Mercy, founded in Dublin, Ireland in 1831. It was printed and bound in Rome sometime after Gregory XVI's approval on June 6, 1841, and the promulgation of the decree of confirmation on July 5, 1841. The decree itself is printed on the last page (p. 26) of the bound text.[14]

When, exactly, Catherine McAuley received a copy of the confirmed Rule and Constitutions, and how soon she obtained a translation of it are questions which do not admit of clear answers. In an undated letter, written shortly before August 19, 1841, the day on which four of the English novices destined for the Birmingham foundation professed their religious vows, Catherine told Frances Warde: "I was aware the confirmation of the Rule was granted but I have not received it yet. Probably His Grace may bring it on Thursday to the Ceremony" (362). However, on Thursday, August 19, she again wrote to Frances: "Dr. Murphy of Cork received an account of the confirmation of our Rule. Dr. Murray has not yet, and is much surprised" (363). Mary Ignatia Neumann claims that, "Since the Rule went to Rome through Dr. Thos. Griffiths, Vicar Apostolic of London, it may have returned the same way. The Bishop of London and the Bishop of Cork were in frequent communication, especially over the superior of their respective convents, i.e., Mother M. Clare Moore" (363).[15] However, Cardinal Fransoni's letter of July 31, 1841, addressed to Daniel Murray in Dublin, indicates that with Fransoni's letter ten copies of the Rule and Constitutions were on their way to him. Perhaps these came to Dublin through London, but this seems unlikely. Whatever the case, they had not arrived by August 19, and it is not clear when in fact they did arrive.

Catherine and the sisters chosen for the Birmingham foundation sailed for Liverpool on August 20, 1841, and from there traveled to Birmingham. She was back at Baggot Street by September 21, and probably studied her copy of the confirmed Rule at this time. No further mention of the Rule appears in her extant letters until October 12, when she wrote to Frances Warde—who had by then undoubtedly received a copy from Francis Haly, Bishop of Kildare and Leighlin. This is Catherine's last extant written reference to the Rule, penned a month before her death; in it she discusses, as we have seen earlier, Tobias Kirby's offer to arrange "permission to rectify the evident mistakes" in the Rule, but adds that she was "cautioned not to speak of any mistake in the R[ule]" (381–2).

It is not clear from available documentation whether Catherine examined the Italian text of the Rule with the help of a translator (there is no evidence that she could read Italian); whether the "mistakes" to which she referred were obvious changes that even a person not fluent in Italian could pick out; or whether she had been quickly provided with an English translation of the Italian text. An entry in the Carlow Annals, referring to the period in Carlow just after their August 1841 retreat, is somewhat unclear as to timing, but it nonetheless reveals that at least in Carlow in late 1841, and presumably elsewhere, there were handwritten copies of a translation of the Rule, or at least translated corrections inserted in the earlier version of the Rule:

> About this time Right Rev. Dr. Haly held a Visitation of the Convent. . . . Up to this period the Novices were not allowed the use of the Holy Rule, but once a week at morning lecture a chapter was read and explained to them by their Mistress, and the Constitutions in like manner during the retreat before Profession. This however His Lordship did not deem sufficient, so directed that each Novice should be supplied with a copy of the Rules and Constitutions, exhorting to a careful study of the obligations she intended to contract. There being no English translation of the Rule in print the Sisters were obliged to set to work to provide themselves with manuscript copies.

The Tullamore Annals for 1841, noting that John Cantwell, Bishop of Meath, received his copy of the Italian text of the Rule on September 1, presents a similar comment about handwritten translations:

> The Lord Bishop, Dr. Cantwell, came again to the town on the 28th August to administer the holy Sacrament of Confirmation. . . . As usual, the Bishop visited the convent, and congratulated the Community and Dr. O'Rafferty on the new and beautiful convent just taken possession of. He was welcomed with more enthusiasm than usual at this time, for he brought with him the first copy of the confirmed Rule which he received on that day (1st Sep.) from Most Rev. Dr. Murray, Archbishop of Dublin. The Original was in Italian and for some years after all the copies of our Holy Rule were written ones, having been translated from the Originals sent from Rome.

Considerably more archival research must be done to clarify the processes whereby, in various places, handwritten English translations of the confirmed Rule and Constitutions were obtained, prior to the publication—in Birmingham in 1844, in London in 1856, and in Dublin in 1863—of approved English translations. One suspects that, for a while at least, some communities were using fair copies of the Rule in English as it had been sent to Rome in late 1839, not

English translations of the Rule as it returned from Rome. Perhaps only Catherine McAuley and a few other superiors were aware of the differences between the English original and the confirmed Italian text. One recalls the caution in Elizabeth Moore's letter from Limerick to Mary Ann Doyle in Tullamore on November 21, 1841: "Get no translation of our Holy Rule till I have time to explain further; our dear Revd. Mother did not sanction the alterations with the exception of one or two." But five months later, on April 20, 1842, Elizabeth wrote to Mary Angela Dunne in Charleville: "If you send me the copy of our Holy Rule after the next Wednesday I will have the necessary alterations made in it, but when I have a copy that I am sure will be correct I will get a nice one written for you. Until then you can manage with the one you have by sending it to me."[16] Presumably Elizabeth means that she will have the alterations which appear in the Italian text inserted into Charleville's pre-1841 copy of the Rule, and not that she will have corrections made to a translation of the Italian text.

In the apparent absence of documentary evidence to the contrary (at least I have found none), it is possible that Richard Colgan, a member of the Calced Carmelite Friars on Whitefriar Street, Dublin, was, as noted above, the person who, while in Rome in early 1840, translated into Italian the final text of the Rule and Constitutions which Catherine had sent to Rome, although it is also possible that others affiliated with the Congregation for the Propagation of the Faith may have had a hand in the translation.[17] Whoever the translator or translators were, it is clear that many alterations were made to Catherine's text at this time, if not in the course of translating it into Italian then by some other intervention prior to the 1841 printing of the confirmed Rule and Constitutions in Italian.

V. THE ALTERATIONS OF CATHERINE'S TEXT IN THE ITALIAN TEXT

The English translation published in Dublin in 1863 was certified by Canon Laurence Forde,[18] who declared on the final page of the text:

> I have examined carefully this translation of the Rule and Constitutions of the Sisters of Mercy, and having compared it with the original, certify that it is substantially accurate. I would recommend, however, that the better to decide any doubts or questions that may arise, the Italian original should be printed along with it. (58)

The "original" to which Forde here refers is not Catherine's text as sent to Rome, but the approved Italian text. The imprimatur for this 1863 publication was given by Paul Cullen, then Archbishop of Dublin, and successor to Archbishop Murray who had died in 1852.

In the Italian text which was returned from Rome in 1841, and therefore also in the approved English translations of it,[19] there are numerous alterations of Catherine's original intentions, provisions, and wording, as these can be presumed to be presented, for example, in the extant fair copies which Daniel Murray approved, signed, and sealed on May 3, 1835 and January 23, 1837. (In view of Elizabeth Moore's reference to "one or two", one of the alterations—that affecting the wording of the vow formula—and possibly another which cannot now be positively identified were evidently sanctioned by Catherine herself, either before the document was sent to Rome in late 1839, or, by some means, later.) Some of the changes appearing in the Italian text may have been judged necessary by officials at the Congregation for the Propagation of the Faith; others seem to reflect personal preferences on the part of unidentified persons, presumably in Rome; and, finally, some may have resulted simply from inaccuracies in the translation into Italian or from misinterpretations of Catherine's text. While it must be recalled that after papal confirmation in June 1841 the only ecclesiatically approved version of the original Rule and Constitutions of the Sisters of Mercy was this Italian text, or approved translations of it, nevertheless it remains true that in the process of official confirmation much that Catherine had deliberately and sensitively formulated was almost irretrievably lost or muted—hence the present necessity and value of studying the text of her original manuscript as corrected by Daniel Murray, and of comparing it with the subsequently approved versions.

Among the major alterations of Catherine's original intentions which appear in the Italian text are the following, here presented in the wording of the 1863 English translation, unless otherwise noted:[20]

- In article 10 of chapter 3, "Of the Visitation of the Sick", an entire sentence and a half are omitted and two long sentences are substituted, to the effect that when the sisters visit the dying they are no longer free, in Catherine's simple language, to "promise attention to whatever object engages [the patient's] painful anxious solicitude, that the mind may be kept composed to think of God alone," but rather, now, even in dire circumstances:

  > Should the conversation turn on disposal of property by will, let the Sisters dexterously avoid taking part in it, and confining themselves to general matters, let them suggest to the patient to make known his intentions to a suitable person, and deserving his confidence. When again the subject turns on procuring relief for the indigence of the sick person's family, let them promise, as far as depends on them, to attend to it, in the manner their state permits; so that, removing all anxiety from the mind of the sick, they may be able with tranquillity to give every thought to God alone. (10)

- In chapter 4, "Of the Admission of Distressed Women" into the House of Mercy, "distressed" is changed to "poor" (*povere*), with a consequent loss of wider meaning. More importantly, the very limitation which Catherine had strenuously sought to avoid—namely, the referral of admissions decisions about strangers to non-resident personnel, with the consequent delay in providing shelter—is here included. Into Catherine's sensible and qualified general provision that "Although it shall be considered as a general rule to require suitable testimonials as to character and distress, yet. . . . The daughters of reduced tradesmen . . . should be admitted on the recommendation of a pious, orderly woman," the following wording is inserted after "testimonials":

> and particularly that of the Parish Priest, concerning their character and poverty, nevertheless there are some deserving of assistance, though they cannot procure them. Still, about even these, the Parish Priest shall always be consulted, in order the better to know their dispositions, for the guidance of Superiors. But with this precaution, the daughters of reduced tradesmen . . . may be admitted. . . . (12)

Whoever made this alteration may not have remembered that the text is talking about the admission of needy women and girls into the House of Mercy, not about the admission of candidates into the religious community.

- In article 5 of the same chapter, Catherine's realistic provision that the young servant girls and women sheltered in the House of Mercy "shall be required to go regularly to confession to the Chaplain, and all who are prepared shall approach the Holy Communion on the first Friday of every month" is made a far more stringent requirement, with several impracticable ramifications. The altered article reads:

  > They shall be required to go regularly to Confession, to the Confessor appointed by the Ordinary; and the days for Communion shall be the Feasts of Obligation (including also those now retrenched), all the Solemnities of the Blessed Virgin, although falling on ferial days; and the first Friday of every month. (13)

  Often there were fifty or sixty residents in the Baggot Street House of Mercy, and during the chaplaincy controversy (1837–1839) there was no regular chaplain at Baggot Street. Moreover, Redmond O'Hanlon, the confessor for the religious community, who happened to be also a superior of the Discalced Carmelites, had not been expected to hear the confessions of the women and girls in the House of Mercy. This is presumably why Catherine had designated "the Chaplain". Again, whoever made this alteration may have been thinking the article applied to the sisters in the community, not to the residents of the House of Mercy.

- In the formula for the profession (or renewal) of religious vows, which appears in chapter 8 (and chapter 10) of the Rule, after the words, "Poverty, Chastity, and Obedience", the words, "and the service of the Poor, Sick, and Ignorant" are added. These words are not in the earlier fair copies, but they were probably added, with Catherine McAuley's consent, in the copy that was sent to Rome.[21]

- In article 4 of chapter 13, where Catherine lists the saints to whom the sisters of the Institute are to have particular devotion, St. Francis de Sales is omitted, and St. Peter Nolasco, St. Ignatius, St. Camillus of Lellis, and St. Aloysius Gonzaga are added (27–28). All but St. Peter Nolasco are in

Catherine's earlier list of saints who were devoted to the sick (3.2), but none of these is listed in her original chapter 13.

- In chapter 15, "Of the Employment of Time", the following sentence, in quotation marks in the Italian, is added to the end of the article: "In every House there shall be a fixed Horarium, approved by the Ordinary, suited to the circumstances of the place, and the duties of the Congregation" (31). This addition in the Italian text was undoubtedly made in response to one of Paul Gavino Secchi-Murro's recommendations noted above. In her own composition Catherine had chosen not to include a revision of chapter 20 of the Presentation Rule, entitled "The Order of the Exercises of the Day", wisely believing that an appropriate horarium should be developed, as this insertion suggests, to suit the circumstances and duties of each convent. Catherine herself may have sanctioned this addition.

- In chapter 18, "Of Correction", two sentences are added to the end of the paragraph. These sentences, in quotation marks in the Italian, refer specifically to the Chapter of Faults, a practice which Catherine includes later in the Constitutions under the office of the Mother Superior (II.2.11), and which she herself, as was well known, was reluctant to inaugurate. The sentences added here in chapter 18 are:

  > Once every month each Sister, kneeling in public chapter, shall, for the exercise of humility, accuse herself of her public faults and transgressions. The Superioress shall lovingly correct and sweetly admonish the Sisters on these occasions, without lessening the gravity of their faults. (35–36)

  Again, this insertion in the Italian text may be a mild response to Secchi-Murro's recommendation that a system of penances be introduced into the text.

- In chapter 21, "Of the Refectory", where Catherine had provided that silence be observed at all meals and a spiritual lecture be read only at dinner, the words, "and at supper, except when there shall be recreation", are added.

- Throughout the Second Part of the Italian document, and occasionally in the First Part, the word "Monastery" is substituted for "Convent", and "Congregation" for Catherine's term, "Institute"; and in the Second Part of the text the title "Assistant" is changed to "Mother Assistant", a maternal designation Catherine had initially wished to avoid even for the Mother Superior.

- Finally, in chapter 17 of the First Part, "Of Union and Charity"—the chapter which in its Presentation form served for several years as the only "Rule" of the first Sisters of Mercy and which so deeply expresses Catherine's characteristic emphasis on mutual love, and communal union in the love of God—an entire sentence in article 3 of her text is eliminated in the Italian text. Catherine's sentence reads as follows:

> They shall as true followers of God walk in love, as Christ loved us, preserving above all things charity, which is the bond of perfection, gaining over souls in the obedience of charity, and in sincerity of heart fervently loving each other.

For this positive invitation to companionship in love, the following prescriptive clause is substituted: "and they shall be solicitous to repair the smallest offence, by promptly asking pardon, which should be immediately granted, without contention, and without reserve" (32).

Among the changes in the Italian text which seem merely to reflect the personal preferences of some person or persons handling the document in the process of its translation into Italian, or its confirmation, are the following, as presented in the 1863 English translation:

- In the First Part, chapter 10, Catherine's chapter title, "Of Spiritual Retreat and Renewal of Vows" is changed to "Of the Spiritual Exercises [*Degli Esercizj Spirituali*] and Renewal of Vows", and Catherine's opening sentence, "Spiritual exercises being justly considered . . . "is changed to "The Spiritual Exercises [*Gli Esercizj spirituali*] . . . ", thus narrowing Catherine's provision to a particular Ignatian form of spiritual retreat. In the same article, Catherine's provision that "the Sisters . . . shall make every year a spiritual retreat of eight days immediately before the Feast of the Assumption . . . and another retreat of three days the last of the year", is changed to read: "the Sisters . . . shall every year devote to them [the Spiritual Exercises] the ten days immediately before the Feast . . . and in addition, the last three days of the year" (20). The spirituality of the community, at least in retreat, is thus given a specifically, and required, Ignatian orientation, and the length of the annual retreat is extended by two days.
- In article 3 of chapter 12, which deals with "Devotion to . . . the Sacred Heart of Jesus", two additions are made to Catherine's text. These two additions are as follows: the phrase, "Fount of all grace, and sweetest (*tenerissimo*) object of our love", is inserted; and later, after Catherine's reference to the Passion and Death which Jesus suffered for our redemption, the words, "and which he daily evinces to us by the treasures of grace, and the immense benefits which flow from His loving and amiable Heart", are added (24).

VI. THE ENGLISH TRANSLATIONS

As the Tullamore and Carlow Annals indicate, English translations of the Italian text of the Rule and Constitutions of the Sisters of Mercy were begun in the fall of 1841. To make or verify these translations, the sisters in Dublin and elsewhere were presumably dependent on persons outside these communities who were proficient in Italian, many of whom were undoubtedly priest friends who had studied abroad and knew Italian well. The names of these translators can perhaps be guessed in some instances, but not known for certain.

But understanding the process by which these translations were produced is also complicated by the question which Catherine McAuley herself had raised about "some evident mistakes in the copy of our Rule", and by the fact of Tobias Kirby's assurance—which Catherine reported to Frances Warde, and evidently also to Elizabeth Moore—that, with Archbishop Murray's approval, "we would without any more trouble obtain permission [in Rome] to rectify the evident mistakes" (381–2).[22] I have not so far been able to ascertain whether, in fact, any such attempt at rectification ever occurred, and if so, exactly which corrections, if any, were ever proposed or approved.[23] This investigation, which would require additional collaborative research, is, however, rendered moot by the fact that the first published translations—in Birmingham in 1844, in London in 1856, and in Dublin in 1863—appear to me to contain no alterations of the provisions of the original Italian text. Although Elizabeth Moore's letter to Mary Angela Dunne in Charleville, on April 20, 1842, promises that she will "make the alterations" in Angela's copy of the Rule for her, Elizabeth is probably here referring to the alterations already contained in the Italian text as originally received from Rome, which must now be incorporated into Charleville's earlier handwritten copy of the Rule, and not to subsequent alterations of the Italian text following correspondence with Rome.

In some ways the most perplexing piece of this puzzle is the fact that Mary Austin Carroll, who is in many respects a very careful researcher—and who, following correspondence with him in 1883, became a fairly close friend of Bishop Tobias Kirby in Rome—says in her *Life of Catherine McAuley,* first published in 1866, and in subsequent editions of this book, that:

> The Rules and Constitutions were originally written in English. They were translated into Italian for the greater convenience of the Sacred Congregation by whom they were examined. Very Rev. Mr. Colgan, of the Carmelite Order, certified the translation to be "substantially accurate". After their confirmation they were translated back into English, and this new translation Mother McAuley found did not agree exactly with the original; the errors she pointed out were, however, immediately rectified. The first printed copies of the Rule were those sent from the Propaganda to the Bishops in whose dioceses convents of the Order were located in 1841.
>
> The examination of the Rule, and the effort to have its inaccuracies rectified, occupied the time of the Foundress, and the rectifying of these was almost the last act of her life. (427–8)[24]

Whatever may yet be discovered about attempts to correct "mistakes" in the Italian text, no alterations of it appear in the first three published translations examined in this study. I believe Carroll's account of this matter is simply inaccurate.

The English translations published in Birmingham in 1844 and in London in 1856 are excellent translations, for one very important reason: apparently unlike the 1863 Dublin translation, they avoid the damaging alterations of Catherine McAuley's original manuscript that would have been inherent in double translation, by using Catherine's original wording wherever the Italian text permits. Consequently, these translations are not really "translations", but rather—as ideally they should be—simply corrected copies, by reference to the confirmed Italian text, of the original fair copy as it was sent to Rome. As such, they preserve whatever Rome did not explicitly alter, including Catherine's own language and concepts in the sections of the Rule and Constitutions which Rome left untouched.

One can easily imagine the reverence for Catherine's language with which Mary Juliana Hardman and Mary Clare Moore, the superiors of the Birmingham and Bermondsey communities, prepared these documents for publication. Although the actual dissemination of the Birmingham and London publications needs further study, surely the foundations which emanated from these two communities, and from their affiliates, used these translations for many decades, perhaps well into the twentieth century. They were thus fortunate, since their approved *Rule and Constitutions* in English, although it carefully incorporated all the revisions in the confirmed Italian text, was nonetheless as faithful a rendering as possible of Catherine McAuley's own original language.

Such was not the case with the Dublin translation published in 1863. When this approved English translation was published, in an edition giving the parallel Italian and English texts, the English translation was apparently made directly from the Italian text, without preference for the English wording in the text which Catherine had submitted to Rome. The most damaging of the unnecessary changes appearing in this translation are therefore those which involve the almost irremediable loss of Catherine's own carefully chosen vocabulary, and with this, the early and official loss, in this most important document, of her characteristic conceptions, expressive of her own particularly thoughtful and sensitive cast of mind and heart. I say that these transformations of Catherine's text are unnecessary because they are the result of double translation, without any apparent reference to the English wording in Catherine's own original manuscript or in the fair copies of it. In some sections of the Rule this loss may be borne more easily, but in the more distinctive or theological sections of the Rule, the loss, if it is, as I believe, unnecessary, is grievous.

For example, in the distinctive chapter 3, "Of the Visitation of the Sick", an original chapter which Catherine herself composed (presumably with Myles Gaffney's help), there are well over two dozen changes of wording in the 1863 English text, only a few of which are required by the explicit language in the Italian text. These alterations unnecessarily deprive the text of much of the simplicity, practicality, and tenderness of Catherine's wording. The same is true of the distinctive chapter 4, "Of the Admission of Distressed Women", which becomes "Of the Admission of Poor [*Povere*] Women"; here again, some of Catherine's own diction—her "great care", and "protection", and her language expressive of a humble attitude towards the women in the House of Mercy—

has been lost by needless variations in diction, as a consequence of double translation. In the "Act of Oblation and Consecration to the Blessed Mother of God" (chapter 13)—to be prayed by the whole community on the Feast of Our Lady of Mercy, and by each newly professed sister on the day of her profession—countless wording changes also occur which in effect nullify the care with which Catherine had only slightly revised this prayer as she found it in the Presentation Rule, though the changes in the 1863 English translation do not in fact restore the prayer to the previously approved Presentation wording.

In the chapter, "Of Union and Charity", the superbly Augustinian chapter in the Presentation Rule which served so irreplaceable a role during the first years of the Sisters of Mercy, Catherine had made only a few changes in language; basically she had used the first five articles of the chapter almost verbatim. However, in the course of double translation the language of the original text is unnecessarily altered and its human tone diminished. For example, Catherine's "our Blessed Saviour desires" becomes "our Saviour wishes (vuole)"; "His last dying injunction" becomes "His last precept"; "the last conference of His mortal life with His beloved disciples" becomes "His last conference with His disciples"; the "Institute, founded and grounded on charity" becomes the "Congregation, founded and established (*stabilita*) on charity"; Catherine's provision that the sisters study to maintain and cherish this virtue "so perfectly amongst themselves as to live together as if they had but one heart and one soul in God" becomes "so perfectly among themselves, that it may be truly said, there is in them only one heart and one soul in God"; and the complete quotation of 1 Corinthians 13.4–7, with which Catherine had concluded article 4, is abbreviated in both the Italian and English texts to "Charity is patient, etc., etc., etc."

Some may argue that these changes are minor, and not to be regarded as damaging to Catherine's text. On the contrary, I would argue that to the extent that these and countless other alterations of the original vocabulary were unnecessary and not explicitly required by Roman regulations, they tampered with Catherine's original inspiration, reduced the original ardor and femininity of her Rule, and led, though presumably unwittingly, to the almost complete historical effacement of Catherine McAuley's own choice of wording.

VII. COMMENTARY ON CATHERINE'S TEXT

Editing can be a highly creative and revealing mode of expression. The more extensive and thoughtful the editing, the more original the whole composition can be said to be, because the mind of the person who is doing the editing shows itself as decisively active. Here it is useful to reflect on the process of composition of the Rule of Saint Benedict. As R.W. Southern notes in his *Western Society and the Church in the Middle Ages:* "It now appears almost certain that St. Benedict took a very large part of his Rule, including some of the most famous passages of spiritual teaching, almost verbatim from the Rule of a slightly earlier writer known as 'the Master' "(221). But, nevertheless, as Southern points out, "we can read the mind of Benedict in his silent omissions, alterations, and additions, as well as in the material he was content to take without alteration from the Master. The difference between the two documents is immense . . . it is in his short additions that he shows his personality most vividly. All the examples of the mild wisdom of the Rule . . . are Benedict's additions to his source" (222). The similarity between Benedict's method and Catherine's, particularly in terms of their outcomes, is striking. For with respect to the Rule of the Master and Benedict's Rule, Southern claims that:

> A comparison of the two documents leaves an unexpected impression on the reader's mind. Benedict, the most influential guide to the spiritual life in western history, appears as an uncomplicated and self-effacing man who was content to take nearly all his doctrine from the Rule of his predecessor. Yet with a few changes, omissions, and additions he changed the whole character of his source. (223)

Similarly, Catherine produced a Rule and Constitutions for the Sisters of Mercy which, while it is dependent in no small measure on the structure, concepts, and wording of the Presentation Rule and Constitutions, has nonetheless a noticeably different character from its source. It is, I believe, more tender in its expression, more humbly stated, and more confident in the good judgment of those who will observe the Rule. In this Catherine no doubt benefited from the forty years which intervened between the writing of the two Rules, from her own considerable experience and maturity at the time of composition, and from her already well-founded respect and affection for her co-workers. But also significant is the fact that Catherine was a woman, whereas the author of the Presentation Rule and Constitutions was a man, Rev. Laurence Callanan. He produced, apparently without the help of the kind of model Catherine followed, a document which is rich in its Augustinian structure, emphases, and language, and in the teachings of St. Francis de Sales, but he evidently also felt some constraint, from within the community and perhaps from within himself, to incorporate traditional perspectives about and prescriptions for women religious. Honora (Nano) Nagle, the founder of the Presentation Sisters, died in Cork, at the age of sixty-five, on April 26, 1784—seven years before Callanan began his task, at the request of Francis Moylan, Bishop of Cork; nine years before he completed it; and eighteen years before the Presentation Rule and Constitutions was sent to Rome in 1802. Had she lived longer Nano Nagle might have written her own Rule and Constitutions in a different way, but still with Laurence Callanan's help. He was her friend and guide, and T. J. Walsh claims that "No priest was more fitted to interpret her religious ideals in a religious rule and constitutions" (139).[25]

While Catherine's method of composition may have resembled Saint Benedict's, the content and emphases of her Rule, and of the Presentation Rule which was her immediate source, were influenced by another early monastic document: the Rule of Saint Augustine. The lineage of the Presentation Rule, in terms of its spirit and content, evidently goes back through the Rule of the Visitation Nuns—founded in Annecy, France, in 1610 by St. Francis de Sales and St. Jane Frances de Chantal; to the Rule of the Order of St. Ursula (Ursulines)—founded in Brescia, Italy, in 1535 by St. Angela Merici; and thence to the Augustinian prototype. Throughout Christian history the appeal of the Rule of Saint Augustine has been so great, especially to religious communities committed to apostolic works, that more than 150 contemporary religious orders and congregations have regarded their original Rules as modeled on that of Saint Augustine.[26]

The outstanding feature of Augustine's Rule is the primacy he gives to union of mind and heart in a religious community, that is, to the oneness which the love of God and the love of one's neighbor inspire and effect. For Augustine, mutual charity is both the source and the outcome of a profound interior union of spirit—between God and the human person, and between human persons and one another. In George Lawless's scholarly edition of Augustine's Rule, the opening chapter of the feminine version of the Rule announces this fundamental ecclesiology:

> The chief motivation for your sharing life together is to live harmoniously in the house, and to have one heart and one soul seeking God. . . .
>
> Live then, all of you, in harmony and concord; honour God mutually in each other; you have become his temples. (110–111)

Augustine identifies three essential outcomes of this union and charity: the common surrender and common possession of all the goods of the house; genuine humility of mind and heart, such that one recognizes and honors the dignity and unity of the members of the community in God; and obedience, respect, and compassion towards "your superior as a mother . . . who serves you in love, not as one who exercises authority over you" (117). In Augustine's view, a further consequence of such attitudes is that the community will seek to "Be assiduous in prayer": there will be both personal and communal unity of lips and heart, for "when you pray to God in psalms and hymns, the words you speak should be alive in your hearts" (111). Tarsicius Van Bavel has pointed out that the principle upon which Augustine builds his Rule is the God-desired wholeness of the human person and of the human community, such that interior dispositions animate exterior behavior. Consequently, as Van Bavel claims:

> It is immediately obvious how few concrete regulations and detailed laws are given in the Rule. Nowhere is it a question of details, but of the core of things and the human heart. Thus, the way of interiorization is repeatedly applied in the Rule: the external alone is not sufficient, for it must be the symbol of what happens inwardly. The external ought not to remain empty, but should be animated from within. (7)

Thus the entire Rule of Augustine has but one theme which it variously paraphrases: fidelity to the continuing gift of the Spirit of God, as manifested in the union and charity of the first community of Jesus' followers and portrayed in the Acts of the Apostles:

> Now the whole group of those who believed were of one heart and soul, and no one claimed private ownership of any possessions, but everything they owned was held in common. With great power the apostles gave their testimony to the resurrection of the Lord Jesus, and great grace was upon them all. There was not a needy person among them, for as many as owned lands or houses sold them and brought the proceeds of what was sold. They laid it at the apostles' feet, and it was distributed to each as any had need. (Acts 4.32–35)

Both the Presentation Rule and Catherine's Rule exhibit these Augustinian priorities and emphases, not only in their descriptions of voluntary poverty and humility, their specific concern for the care of sick sisters, and their definitions of the offices of mother superior and mistress of novices, but especially in the emphasis they give to the example of Jesus Christ. In both texts this emphasis culminates in the chapter, "Of Union and Charity". For many years this one chapter of the Presentation Rule served as the only designated "Rule" of the Sisters of Mercy. The Bermondsey annalist reports that on December 13, 1831, the day following the founding of the Institute, Daniel Murray visited Baggot Street. On that occasion Catherine "asked the Archbishop, as the Rule of the Presentation Order was not yet altered for our use, what Rule we were to go by." His response was to have a profound effect on the character of the young Institute:

> He opened the book of the Presentation Rule at the "Chapter of Union and Charity," saying: "If they observe that, it will suffice"; and for the space of six or seven years, during which the necessary alterations were being considered and decided on, the observance of this one Rule caused the greatest regularity and fervour to be invariably maintained.

Thus, when Catherine undertook the task of altering the Presentation Rule she retained the wording of this chapter almost verbatim, omitting only the final section on the titles of "Mother" and "Sister". The memorable opening paragraphs of her version of this chapter are as follows:

> "Love one another as I have loved you." This was the special command of Jesus Christ to His Apostles, and in the accomplishment of this Divine Precept, inseparably united as it is with the grand precept of the Love of God, consists, according to the Apostle, the plenitude of the Law. This mutual love, our Blessed Saviour desires, may be so perfect as to resemble in some manner the Love and Union which subsists between Himself and His Heavenly Father. This He inculcated in the strongest terms at the last Conference of His Mortal Life, with His Beloved Disciples. This was His last Dying Injunction, which as a most valuable legacy, He bequeathed to all His followers, and by this they were to prove themselves to be really His Disciples. (8.1)
>
> This mutual union and love should therefore eminently characterise religious souls. This should distinguish them above all others as faithful spouses, and servants of Jesus Christ. The Sisters of this pious Institute, founded and grounded

> on charity, should therefore make that favorite virtue of their Divine Master, their own most favorite virtue. This they should study to maintain and cherish so perfectly amongst themselves as to live together as if they had but one heart and one soul in God. This love for one another should be such as to emulate the love and union of the Blessed in Heaven. (8.2)

Catherine seems to have had an instinctively Augustinian sense of the centrality of mutual love and humility in religious life. In the final paragraph of this chapter, in words similar to those in Augustine's Rule, Catherine urges the community to remember that "the love and union of religious persons should be founded not on flesh and blood or any human motive, but on God alone, as their hearts should be united together in Jesus Christ, their Spouse and Redeemer, in whom and for whom they should live and love one another" (8.5). Thus the same spirit of tenderness, freedom, and spiritual modesty which characterizes Augustine's Rule informs the language and emphases of her Rule. The "spiritual beauty" which she, like Augustine, sought was resemblance to Jesus Christ who, in responding humbly to human need, "had no form or majesty that we should look at him, nothing in his appearance that we should desire him" (Isaiah 53.2).

While Catherine's Rule certainly depends initially on the text of the Presentation Rule, and benefits enormously from its language and content, it is in the end a fresh and original composition, a masterwork of sagacious editing. The Augustinian elements are subtly strengthened, and, in sentence after sentence, Catherine's own wisdom, humility, trust in her companions, and compassion toward human need reshape the tone and character of much of the earlier text. The two chapters and one paragraph which she added are excellent statements of her theological understanding and pastoral practice, but equally revealing is her editorial treatment of the wording in the Presentation Rule. Here one can see the hundreds of theological *choices* she made, in diction and emphasis: choices which manifest, almost more than do the passages composed from scratch, the perspicacious character of her thinking and the gracious dispositions of her mind and heart.

The over-arching attitudes disclosed in her choices, as she accepts or transforms the wording of the Presentation Rule, are more numerous than can be mentioned here. But among them are the following:

- her modesty of language and idea, and her preference for "a simple style of speaking and writing" (Bermondsey Annals);
- her reserve and self-effacement in the treatment of the role and functions of the superior;
- her maturity with respect to gender and sexuality;
- her expectation of and trust in the dependability of her sisters, and her affection for them;
- her restraint in terms of prescriptions;
- her respect for those served, as seen in countless indications of deference

toward them, especially in her language about the poor, the sick, children, and distressed women;

- her care to avoid unnecessary clerical or ecclesiastical supervision that could intrude upon the direct responsibility of the members of the Institute;
- her placement of the vows and of intra-institutional matters in a supportive rather than in a primary position;
- her consciousness throughout of the primacy of the external ministry ("duties") of the sisters;
- and her characteristic emphasis on the example of Jesus Christ and of the saints.

VIII. THE PRIVILEGED STATUS OF CATHERINE'S TEXT

One crucial question remains: Which text should one regard as *the* text of the original or first Rule and Constitutions of the Sisters of Mercy? The 1841 Italian text as confirmed in Rome? One or other of the early approved English translations of it? Clare Moore's fair copy, on the last page of which Daniel Murray wrote his declaration of approval, signed his name, and affixed his episcopal seal? Or Catherine McAuley's own manuscript with Archbishop Murray's penciled revisions?

In view of the two layers of alteration of Catherine's original manuscript, in addition to Daniel Murray's revisions—namely, Clare Moore's chapter sequence and the changes made in Rome—it seems proper to regard Catherine's own original manuscript as revised by Daniel Murray with her concurrence as the primary expression of her thought and intentions, and, in this respect, as *the* text of the original Rule. It would not be in accord with Catherine's wishes if one were to regard just her own original manuscript, *without* Daniel Murray's revisions, in this privileged way. Catherine wrote the document as a woman of the Church, and she wrote it for the Church. She submitted it to Archbishop Murray for his critique and approval, and his revisions written in pencil directly on her manuscript are, in general, helpful and restrained. They were inserted, one presumes, only with a view to the document's eventual approval in Rome. Therefore, Catherine's own ecclesial attitude is best served by treating Daniel Murray's revisions as she presumably did: as welcomed refinements of her original manuscript. In presenting her text in the following pages I have been at great pains, wherever his revisions occur, to preserve Catherine's own original wording and format, in square brackets and in the notes on the text. But I believe that with Daniel Murray's revisions and his accompanying approval, Catherine's manuscript can indeed be regarded as *the* text of the original Rule.

It is true that only the Italian text of the Rule as it was returned from Rome in 1841, or an approved English translation of it (such as that in 1844, 1856, or 1863), is, strictly speaking, the first official, because the first ecclesiastically confirmed, Rule and Constitutions of the Sisters of Mercy. Nevertheless, Catherine's manuscript with Daniel Murray's revisions serves not only as the privileged original statement of her intentions and conceptions, but also as a primary guide for translating and interpreting the 1841 Italian text, and as a necessary corrective for reading the 1863 English translation of it published in Dublin, from which so many nineteenth- and twentieth-century printings derived.[27]

Catherine McAuley's own manuscript, with Daniel Murray's revisions, remains, therefore, the primary foundational document of the Sisters of Mercy, and the most comprehensive and deliberate articulation of Catherine's original inspiration as their founder. As such this important manuscript is presented in its entirety in the next chapter.

CATHERINE McAULEY'S ORIGINAL TABLE OF CONTENTS* FOR THE FIRST PART OF THE RULE OF THE SISTERS OF MERCY

Chapter Sequence in the Presentation Rule	*in Catherine McAuley's Manuscript*	*Chapter titles in Catherine McAuley's Manuscript (or the Presentation Rule)*	*Chapter Sequence in Daniel Murray's Revision*	*in Clare Moore's Fair Copy*
1 [no title]		[Of the Object of the Institute]	1	1
2	1	Of the Schools	2	2
-	2	Of the Visitation of the Sick	3	3
-	3	Of the Admission of Distressed Women	4	4
17	4	Of the Perfection of Ordinary Actions	5	14
12	5	Of the Employment of Time	6	15
11	6	On Silence	7	16
15	7	On Union and Charity	8	17
14	8	On Humility	9	19
10	9	Of Confession and Communion	10	11
8	10	Of the Office and Mental Prayer	11	9
13	11	On Fast and Abstinence	12	20
19	12	Of the Refectory	13	21
9	13	Of Spiritual Retreat [D.M. inserts here "Of the Renewal of Vows" from C.McA.'s Second Part, ch. 9]	14	10
Second, 9	14	On Devotion to the Passion of Jesus Christ, Etc., Etc., Etc.	15	12
Second, 10	15	On Devotion to Our Blessed Lady, Etc.,	16	13
3	16	Of the Vow of Poverty	17	5
4	17	Of the Vow of Chastity	18	6
5	18	Of the Vow of Obedience	19	7
6	19	Of Enclosure	-	-
7	Second, 1	Of the Reception of Postulants, Their Admission to the Habit, and Religious Profession	20	8
16	Second, 10	Of Correction	Second, 9	18
18	Second, 11	Of the Care of the Sick Sisters, and Suffrages of the Dead	Second, 10	22
20	-	The Order of Exercises of the Day	-	-

* Catherine made this table of contents and numbered her chapters before Archbishop Murray divided her chapter 1 into two chapters; hence, in the First Part, her chapter numbers and his are subsequently off by one. She put some of the Presentation chapters in the Second Part of her Rule, and vice versa.

CATHERINE McAULEY'S ORIGINAL TABLE OF CONTENTS FOR THE SECOND PART OF THE RULE OF THE SISTERS OF MERCY

Chapter Sequence			*Chapter Sequence*	
in the Presentation Rule	*in Catherine McAuley's Manuscript*	*Chapter titles in Catherine McAuley's Manuscript (or the Presentation Rule)*	*in Daniel Murray's Revision*	*in Clare Moore's Fair Copy*
1		Of the Superior and the Visitation of the Convent*	1	1
First, 7	1	Of the Reception of Postulants	First, 20	First, 8
2	2	Of the Election of the Mother Superior	2	2
3	3	Of the Office of Mother Superior	3	3
4	4	Of the Office of the Assistant	4	4
5	5	Of the Office of the Depositary or Burser	5	5
6	6	Of the Mistress of Novices	6	6
7	7	Of the Discreets and Their Office	7	7
8	8	Of Capitular Assemblies	8	8
First, 9	9	Of the Renewal of Vows	First, 14	First, 10
First, 16	10	Of Correction	9	First, 18
First, 18	11	Of the Care of the Sick Sisters, etc., etc.	10	First, 22
12	12	On Establishments	11	10
1		*Of the Ecclesiastical Superior, etc. (Catherine McAuley uses only one paragraph of this chapter, which she places, unnumbered, at the end of her manuscript.)	1	1
11	-	Of Registers	-	-
9	First, 14	On Devotion to the Passion of Jesus Christ, to the Blessed Sacrament, and to the Sacred Heart of Jesus	First, 15	First, 12
10	First, 15	On Devotion to Our Blessed Lady and Other Saints	First, 16	First, 13
-	-	[Of Lay Sisters]	-	9

11

Rule and Constitutions of the Religious Sisters of Mercy

The following text is Catherine McAuley's complete manuscript for the Rule and Constitutions of the Sisters of Mercy, as revised by Daniel Murray, Archbishop of Dublin. The text is presented exactly as it appears in the manuscript in the archives of the Sisters of Mercy, Dublin, except for the deletion of some commas and the insertion of a few commas, semicolons, and periods. In the printed text the use of capital "C", "R", and "H" is inconsistent, especially for such words as "congregation", "community", "chapter", "confession" and "communion"; "religion" and "religious"; and "holy". In each case I have tried to follow Catherine's handwriting exactly, and to capitalize, or not, accordingly. The spelling is also Catherine's own, even where it may seem unusual. I have chosen not to use "[*sic*]" in these instances, lest such insertions disrupt the reading of the text. Where Catherine occasionally departs from her usual spelling of a word (e.g., "endevour" for "endeavour") I have given her usual spelling, assuming that she intended it.

Since Catherine McAuley submitted her manuscript to Archbishop Murray for his review, and revision where necessary, his penciled additions and deletions are here incorporated into the text. However, since it is also necessary to preserve in this published form Catherine's own original wording, the material which Daniel Murray crossed out is always provided in square brackets. Where Dr. Murray wrote in his own wording in place of Catherine's wording, the wording he crossed out is usually inserted *before* his wording.

The text is accompanied by over one hundred notes which record nearly every change Catherine McAuley made as she transformed the Presentation Rule and nearly every change Daniel Murray made in her manuscript. Only very minor changes are unrecorded. The notes are provided primarily for those who wish to do research on Catherine's thought, or simply to explore these insights into her thinking. For these readers the notes will repay patient attention and study, because the numerous changes Catherine made in the Presentation wording are wonderful, though sometimes subtle, revelations of her own thought, feelings, and values. The revisions Daniel Murray made, or chose *not* to make, are also revealing.

The idea of publishing the Presentation text side by side with Catherine's text, in parallel columns, was considered but abandoned. Aside from not wanting to presume to present, in such an edition, the first Rule of another, and existing, religious congregation, I did not, in the first instance, wish so much to draw attention to the differences between the two texts, as to present Catherine McAuley's text clearly and completely, and, for the first time, in printed form. I hope I have done this with something of the "greatest care" with which she "transcribed it herself".

Rule and Constitutions of the Religious Sisters of Mercy*

AD MAJOREM DEI GLORIAM

CHAPTER 1
[OF THE SCHOOLS]
OF THE OBJECT OF THE INSTITUTE[1]

1st The Sisters admitted into this religious congregation besides the principal and general end of all religious orders, such as attending particularly to their own perfection, must also have in view what is peculiarly characteristic of this Institute of the Sisters of Mercy, that is, a most serious application to the Instruction of poor Girls, Visitation of the Sick, and protection of distressed women of good character.[2]

2nd In undertaking the arduous, but very meritorious duty of instructing the poor, the Sisters whom God has graciously pleased to call to this state of perfection, shall animate their zeal and fervor by the example of their Divine Master Jesus Christ, who testified on all occasions a tender love for the poor and declared that He would consider as done to Himself whatever should be done unto them.[3]

* Catherine McAuley's own manuscript does not contain a title. This title appears on the fair copies prepared by Mary Clare Moore.

1 In Catherine's manuscript, chapters 1 and 2 are a single first chapter entitled "Of the Schools". Archbishop Murray separated the first two articles into a new chapter 1 to which he gave the title, "Of the Object of the Institute"; he left the remaining articles of the original chapter 1 as a new chapter 2, "Of the Schools". The numbering of Catherine's subsequent chapters is thus affected.

2 In the first article of the Rule Catherine outlines the purposes of the Sisters of Mercy; she uses the wording of the first article of the Presentation Rule (hereafter: PR) up to "attending particularly to"; she then substitutes "their own perfection" for "the perfecting of themselves in the way of the Lord". She keeps the Presentation wording, "must also . . . Institute", adding "of the Sisters of Mercy", and substitutes "that is, a most serious application . . . good character" for the Presentation wording: "that is, a most serious application to the Instruction of poor female children in the principles of Religion, and Christian Piety."

3 Catherine uses as her article 2 the sentence that immediately follows in the PR, omitting "very" before "arduous", changing "meritorious task" to "very meritorious duty of instructing the poor", changing "is graciously" to "has graciously", omitting "encourage themselves, and" before "animate", reversing the order of "fervor and zeal", adding "Jesus Christ" after "Divine Master", changing "little children" to "the poor", omitting "expressed the greatest pleasure on their approaching him", and substituting the scriptural reference, "He would consider . . . unto them" (Matt. 25.40) for the Presentation reference: "whosoever receiveth these little ones in his name, receiveth himself" (Matt. 18.5).

CHAPTER 2 : OF THE SCHOOLS

1st The Sisters appointed by the Mother Superior to attend the Schools shall with all zeal, charity and humility, purity of intention and confidence in God undertake the charge and cheerfully submit to every labor and fatigue, annexed thereto, mindful of their vocation, and of the glorious recompense attached to the faithful discharge of this duty.[4]

2nd Before the Sisters enter School they shall raise their hearts to God and to the Queen of Heaven, recommending themselves and the Children to their care and protection. They shall endeavour to inspire them with a sincere Devotion to the Passion of Jesus Christ, to His real presence in the Most Holy Sacrament, to the Immaculate Mother of God, and their Guardian Angels.[5]

3rd The Sisters shall teach the Children to offer their hearts to God when they awake in the morning, adore His Sovereign Majesty, return thanks for all His favors, and arm themselves with the Sign of the Cross. They shall instruct them how to direct all their thoughts, words, and actions to God's glory, implore His grace to know and love Him, and to fulfil His Commandments, how to examine their conscience, and to honor and respect Parents and Superiors.[6]

4th They shall teach them the method of assisting devoutly at the Holy Sacrifice of the Mass, how to prepare for confession, and be ever attentive to dispose them for the Sacrament of Confirmation, and for Holy Communion. At a quarter before twelve, silence shall be observed, and the Children taught how to examine the fault which they most frequently commit and to make resolutions of amendment. The Angelus and Acts of Faith, Hope and Charity being said, general instructions shall be given by an appointed Sister for about half an hour, adapted to their state and capacity and rendered practically useful by explanation.[7]

4 In the first article of this chapter (the third article of chapter 1 as she originally composed it) Catherine copies almost verbatim the first sentence of chapter 2, article 2 of the PR; she omits "their" before "duty" but Daniel Murray inserts "this". (The chapters in the PR are numbered with roman numerals; in these notes I have changed them to arabic numerals. Where it seems necessary to provide the page reference to the PR, I do so in parentheses.)

5 Article 2 is an almost verbatim transcription of article 3, chapter 2 of the PR except that Catherine changes "When the Mistresses" to "Before the sisters", makes "Schools" singular, omits "and then salute with all reverence interiorly the Guardian Angels of the children" after "Queen of Heaven", and changes "the dear little ones" to "the Children".

6 Article 3 is a re-working of article 3, chapter 1 of the PR. Catherine omits "from the first use of Reason, and" before "when they awake", omits "to raise up their hearts to him" before "adore", omits "to him" after "thanks", changes "offer" to "direct", omits "they are" before "to examine", omits "every night" after "conscience", and changes "their Parents" to "Parents and Superiors".

7 The first clause of article 4 ("They . . . mass") is Catherine's own composition; the remainder of the first sentence comes from article 4, chapter 1 of the PR. The second and third sentences are modifications of article 7 and part of article 8, chapter 2 of the PR: she omits "to accustom the children to recollect themselves in the presence of God" after

5th The Sisters shall feel convinced that no work of charity can be [so] more productive of good to society, or [so] more conducive to the happiness of the poor [as] than the careful instruction of women, since [however] whatever be the station they are destined to fill, their example and advice will always possess influence, and where ever a religious woman presides, peace and good order are generally to be found.[8]

CHAPTER 3 : OF THE VISITATION OF THE SICK[9]

1st Mercy, the principal path pointed out by Jesus Christ to those who are desirous of following Him, has in all ages of the Church excited the faithful in a particular manner to instruct and comfort the sick and dying poor, as in them they regarded the person of our Divine Master, who has said, "Amen, I say to you, as long as you did it to one of these my least brethren, you did it to Me."

2nd The many miraculous cures performed by our Saviour, and the power of healing given to the Apostles, evince His great tenderness for the Sick. The most eminent Saints have devoted their lives to this work of Mercy—amongst whom Saint Vincent of Paul, Saint John of God, Saint Camillus of Lellis, Saint Ignatius, Saint Francis Xavier, Saint Aloysius, Saint Angela De Merici, Saints Catherine of Sienna and Genoa were particularly distinguished. Such bright examples and the great recompense promised must be strong motives for the Sisters of this Holy Institute, to fulfil with fervor and delight every part of this meritorious duty.

3rd Let those whom Jesus Christ has graciously permitted to assist Him in [His labors] the Persons of his suffering Poor, have their hearts animated with gratitude and love and placing all their confidence in Him, ever keep His unwearied patience and humility present to their minds, endeavouring to imitate Him more perfectly every day in self-denial, [composure] patience and entire resignation. Thus shall they gain a crown of glory and the great title of Children of the Most High which is assuredly promised to the merciful.[10]

"observed", substitutes "and the children . . . amendment" for "and to afford the sisters the opportunity of making their particular Examen", drops "Domini" after "Angelus", omits the Act of Contrition, and transforms the PR reference to a half-hour "spiritual lecture" in the evening by substituting "general instructions . . . explanation." Archbishop Murray placed an asterisk before the second sentence and noted in the margin, "In Schools connected with the National Board this practice could not be attended to." Consequently, in Clare Moore's fair copy of the Rule, which Archbishop Murray approved, the last two sentences of this article do not appear.

8 Article 5 is, apparently, entirely Catherine's own composition. Her original wording is in brackets, followed by Dr. Murray's substitutions: "more", "more", "than" and "whatever be".

9 Chapter 3 is, apparently, entirely Catherine's own composition.

10 Archbishop Murray substituted "the Persons of his suffering Poor" for Catherine's "His labors", and substituted "patience" for her "composure".

4th The Sisters appointed by the Mother Superior to visit the Sick shall prepare quickly and when ready shall visit the Blessed Sacrament to offer to their Divine Master the action they are about to perform, to ask from Him the graces necessary to procure His glory and the salvation of souls.

5th Before the Sisters leave the Convent they shall endeavour to understand perfectly the way they are to go, and if some places cannot be found without making enquiry it will be most prudent to go into a Dairy, Huxter or Baker's shop where the poor are generally known, always speaking with such reserve as ensures respect but not to continue looking about since charity is not only kind and patient, but doth not behave unseemly.

6th Two Sisters shall always go out together. The greatest caution and gravity must be observed passing through the streets, walking neither in slow or hurried pace, not stopping to converse, nor saluting those whom they meet, keeping close, without leaning, preserving recollection of mind and going forward as if they expected to meet their Divine Redeemer in each poor habitation, since He has said, "Where two etc. etc. are in my name I will be."[11]

7th One of the Sisters should be capable of reading very distinctly and have sufficient judgment to select what is most suitable to each case. She should speak in an easy, soothing, impressive manner so as not to embarrass or fatigue the poor patient. The other Sister can be very conducive to the good which is accomplished, by uniting in fervent prayer.

8th Great tenderness must be employed and when death is not immediately expected it will be well to relieve the distress first and to endeavour by every practicable means to promote the cleanliness, ease and comfort of the Patient, since we are ever most disposed to receive advice and instruction, from those who evince compassion for us.[12]

9th The Sisters shall always have spiritual good most in view; hence when they find habits have been careless, religious duties long neglected, and coldness and indifference seem to prevail, it is most necessary they should endeavour to create alarm—by speaking of the dreadful judgments of God towards impenitent sinners, and admonishing the Patient that if we do not seek His pardon and mercy in the way He has appointed, we must be miserable for all Eternity. They should add the strongest entreaties with evident deep concern, for if our hearts are not affected in vain should we hope to affect theirs; above all, [to] they should pray in an audible voice and most earnest emphatic manner, that God may look with pity on His poor creatures and bring them to repentance. This will be most likely to dispose them for a good confession upon which all depends and for the

11 Archbishop Murray inserted "not stopping to converse, nor saluting those whom they meet."

12 Archbishop Murray inserted "and to endeavour by every practicable means to promote the cleanliness, ease and comfort of the Patient."

accomplishment of which every prayer and instruction shall be offered. The Sisters shall question them on the principal mysteries of our Holy Faith, and if necessary instruct them.[13]

10th When recovery is hopeless it must be made known with great caution and if time permit done by degrees, assuring them of the peace and joy they will feel when entirely resigned to the will of God, inducing them to pray, that He may take all that concerns them into His Divine care and dispose of them as He pleases. Let the Sisters if possible promise attention to whatever object engages their painful, anxious solicitude that the mind may be kept composed to think of God alone.

11th When the Sisters return to the Convent they shall again visit the Blessed Sacrament, thank Jesus Christ for His protection, humble themselves before Him for any imperfections they have fallen into and most earnestly pray that whatever assistance has been afforded through His grace and mercy, may conduce to His own glory, the salvation of their souls and of those whom they have instructed.

CHAPTER 4 : OF THE ADMISSION OF DISTRESSED WOMEN[14]

1st Distressed women of good character, admitted to the House of Mercy, shall if necessary be instructed in the principal mysteries of Religion, and required to comply with their religious obligations. They shall be induced to repair as much as possible their past neglect by piously preparing to approach the Holy Sacraments, and conforming their minds to the regular discharge of the duties of the state in which God has placed them.

2nd Suitable employment shall be sought for and great care taken to place them in situations for which they are adapted, in order that they may continue such length of time in their service, as shall establish a character, on which they can depend for future support. Many leave their situations not so much for want of merit as incapacity to fulfil the duties they unwisely engaged in. They shall not be encouraged to remain long in the House, as it will generally be found more conducive to their good, to get them soon into the state and employment by which they are to live.[15]

3rd Although it must ever be considered a general rule to require suitable testimonials as to character and distress [from a Priest or respectable Lady], yet there are some who have a strong claim for protection, who could not obtain them. The Daughters of reduced tradesmen, who were not practically instructed in religion or known [to any Lady] beyond the humble circle of their Parents'

13 Archbishop Murray inserted "admonishing the Patient" in the first sentence, the second "they should" in the following sentence, and "a good" before "confession" in the next sentence.

14 Chapter 4 is, apparently, entirely Catherine's own composition.

15 Archbishop Murray inserted "for future support" at the end of the first sentence.

home, [these] should be admitted on the recommendation of a pious orderly woman, who had lived some years in the same neighbourhood; and they should be allowed to remain in the House untill practised in servitude, and entitled to character from the Institution.[16]

4th The Sisters shall most carefully avoid all familiarity with these persons, never allowing them to speak of the families with whom they lived or asking the reason of their leaving their respective situations. The Mother Superior or the Sister she appoints shall make every necessary enquiry.

5th They shall be required to go regularly to confession to the Chaplain and all who are prepared shall approach the Holy Communion on the first Friday of every month.

CHAPTER 5 : OF THE PERFECTION OF ORDINARY ACTIONS

1st The perfection of the religious soul depends, not so much on doing extraordinary actions, as on doing [extraordinary] extraordinarily well the ordinary actions and exercises of every day. In this particularly consists the difference between the perfect and imperfect in a religious community. The daily duties are the same for all, the manner of performing them distinguishes the one from the other.[17]

2nd The Sisters of this religious [Institute] Congregation shall therefore endeavour to acquit themselves of the ordinary duties of their Institute with all possible care and attention, according to the advice of the Holy Ghost, "The good you ought to do—do it well," *viz.*, Prayer, Examen of conscience, assisting at Mass, Office, spiritual lecture, meals, recreations, and their respective employments. By performing each and every one of those duties well, they shall perfect themselves and their day shall be full of merit and good works.[18]

3rd But in order to perform these ordinary exercises well, with a view to their own perfection, they must have the purest intention of pleasing God. God and God alone must be the principal motive of all their actions—it is this pure intention of pleasing God that renders the good work valuable and meritorious. Without this the most laborious [application] duties of the Institute, the greatest

16 Archbishop Murray inserted "suitable" and deleted "from a Priest or respectable Lady" in the first sentence. In the next sentence he deleted "to any Lady, these" and added "beyond the humble circle of their Parents' home" and "they should be" in the last clause.

17 Catherine changes "in every Religious Community" to "in a religious community" and omits "common, and" before "the same for all". Dr. Murray changed her "extraordinary well" to "extraordinarily well".

18 Catherine deletes "and functions of their Institute" after "ordinary duties", changes "Their daily prayers" to "Prayer", drops "their" before "Examen", "assisting" and "office", omits "meals" and "school duties", and changes "all" to "each". Archbishop Murray substituted "Congregation" for "Institute", inserted "of their Institute", added "meals" to the list of ordinary duties, and inserted "their" before "respective employments".

austerities, the most heroic actions and sacrifices are of [no] little value, being divested of that merit which flows from a pure and upright intention, while on the contrary, actions the most trivial when accompanied by it become valuable and meritorious of Everlasting Life, nothing is lost, every word and action fructifies, the religious soul enriches herself every moment and lays up treasures of glory for an endless eternity.[19]

4th The Sisters should consider purity of intention in all their works, not merely as a simple practice of piety, but as an essential duty of Religion. They shall therefore most studiously watch over themselves and guard against the insinuations of self love, lest they lose the merit of their labors and good works by self complacency, vain glory, or by having in their actions any other motive or end in view, than to please Almighty God. They are never to act from mere inclination, whim or caprice, but all should be performed with regularity and exactness, and be referred with the utmost fervor [be referred] to the Divine Honor and Glory, in union with the most holy actions and Infinite Merits of Jesus Christ. They shall therefore not only make a general offering in the morning to God of the works and actions of [each] the day, but also renew that offering frequently in the day, having always in mind and engraved in their hearts, this important advice of the Apostle, "Whether you eat or whether you drink, or whatever else you do, do all for the Glory of God and in the name of our Lord and Saviour Jesus Christ."[20]

19 In Article 3 Catherine omits "in doing them" after "must" in the first sentence; she omits "principal" and "of pleasing God" in the second sentence and changes "that characterizes the good work, and renders it valuable" to "that renders the good work valuable"; and in the third sentence she shortens "the most laborious functions of the Institute" to "the most laborious application", changes "little value" to "no value" and "and are divested" to "being divested", leaves out "and indifferent in themselves" after "trivial", deletes "virtuous" before "valuable", changes "eternal" to "Everlasting", and changes "work" to "word". Archbishop Murray re-inserted "principal" and "of pleasing God" in the second sentence; in the third sentence he substituted "duties of the Institute" for Catherine's "application", changed her "no value" to "little value", inserted "and" in "pure and upright", and added "when accompanied by it". He also provided the end punctuation of the first two sentences.

20 In article 4, Catherine omits "this" before "purity" and omits "in all their works" after "intention" in the first sentence; in the second sentence she omits "subtle" before "self love", "or" before "vain glory", and "in their actions" after "view"; in the third sentence she omits "much less from passion" after "caprice", changes "their every action" to "all", moves "be referred", deletes "by them solely" after "referred", and deletes "most holy" before "actions"; in the fourth sentence she deletes "not only", "in the morning" and "but also at the commencement of every action in particular purify their motive." Archbishop Murray added "in all their works" in the first sentence, and "in their actions" in the second sentence. In the third sentence he moved Catherine's "be referred", and added "most holy" before "actions". In the fourth sentence, he added "not only" and "in the morning", changed "each day" to "the day", and inserted "but also renew that offering frequently in the day."

5th The means by which the Sisters may preserve this purity of intention and perform well all their actions, are first to keep themselves always in the Presence of God, remembering that He sees them and that on the manner in which they perform these works depends the judgment He will pronounce on them. Secondly, to do each work in particular as if it were the only one they had to do. By this they will avoid all hurry and precipitation in their actions. Thirdly, to do the duty of every day, as if that day were to be the last of their mortal life, ever mindful of this advice of their Heavenly Spouse, "Watch, be always prepared, you know not the day nor the hour in which you may be called upon."[21]

CHAPTER 6 : OF THE EMPLOYMENT OF TIME

1st As Idleness according to the Holy Ghost teacheth much evil and as we must render an account in Judgment of every moment of our precious time, the Sisters shall be careful never to indulge Idleness but to be always engaged in some useful employment.[22]

[*2nd* They shall at all times appear with those cheerful yet reserved manners which characterise religious modesty and form the dignified deportment that becomes persons consecrated to God. This deportment will be the index of a mind equally free from restraint and levity, it will give to the eyes that humble expression which bespeaks a feeling recollection of mind almost natural because wholly unaffected. The countenance should be ever serene and cheerful and exhibit that sweet religious gravity which is never lost by loud laughter, hasty or noisy words; every action and gesture, even the walk of a religious, should shew a recollected mind, free from all that agitates and disturbs; haste may be necessary, but hurried steps or precipitation shall be carefully avoided.][23]

21 In the first sentence of article 5, Catherine omits "both ordinary and extraordinary" after "actions", changes "to perform all their actions in the presence of God" to "to keep themselves always in the Presence of God", changes "considering that God sees them" to "remembering that He sees them", and changes "he will pronounce sentence on them" to "depends . . . pronounce on them". In the second sentence, she changes "every work" to "each work" and "only work" to "only one". In the fourth sentence, she changes "duties and works of every day" to "duty of every day".

22 In article 1, Catherine adds "but to be always engaged . . . employment" after "Idleness" at the end of the first sentence. She then omits the second and third sentences that complete article 1 in the PR: They read: "Wherefore whatsoever time they may have to spare from the functions of the Institute, they shall diligently employ in manual works, or such other corporal or spiritual occupations as the Mother Superior shall appoint. They shall never be found running giddily thro' the Convent, but shall always, and in all places preserve in their deportment a gravity becoming Religious persons" (p. 29). Archbishop Murray started to add to this article the rest of the article as it appears in the PR ("Wherefore . . . persons."), but then crossed out his own addition.

23 Article 2 appears to be entirely Catherine's own composition. She modifies the concept of "gravity" by the adjectives "serene", "cheerful" and "sweet". Archbishop Murray deleted this entire article, crossing it out with a large X.

CHAPTER 7 : ON SILENCE

1st Silence being the ornament of Religious souls, and the faithful guardian of interior recollection, the Sisters shall observe it as much as circumstances admit except at the time appointed for recreation. They shall keep silence in the Dormitory, in the Chapel, and during meals in the Refectory. When ever it may be necessary to speak in time of silence, they shall do so in a very low voice and as briefly as possible. In observing silence exteriorly, they shall endeavour to keep their minds recollected and fixed on what may tend to their greater perfection.[24]

CHAPTER 8 : OF UNION AND CHARITY[25]

1st "Love one another as I have loved you." This was the special command of Jesus Christ to His Apostles, and in the accomplishment of this Divine Precept, inseparably united as it is with the grand precept of the Love of God, consists, according to the Apostle, the plenitude of the Law. This mutual love, our Blessed Saviour desires, may be so perfect as to resemble in some manner the Love and Union which subsists between Himself and His Heavenly Father. This He inculcated in the strongest terms at the last Conference of His Mortal Life, with His Beloved Disciples. This was His last Dying Injunction, which as a most valuable legacy, He bequeathed to all His followers, and by this they were to prove themselves to be really His Disciples.

24 Catherine broadens the intended meaning of the first sentence on "Silence" in the PR by substituting "shall observe . . . recreation" for "shall strictly observe it from the end of the evening recreation untill after they have recited the small Hours together in the Chapel next morning." She omits the next sentence: "They shall keep silence in the Chapel, in the Dormitory, and in Refectory during meals." In the sentence beginning "When ever . . ." she changes "at the hours and places of silence" to "in time of silence", and changes "in a low tone of voice" to "in a very low voice". In the last sentence she changes "keep themselves recollected in the Lord, their minds fixed" to "keep their minds recollected and fixed . . ." Archbishop Murray inserted the entire second sentence of this article, copying it almost exactly as it appears in the PR.

25 Catherine uses the first five articles of this chapter in the PR almost verbatim. She makes only the following changes. She omits "together" in "so perfectly . . . as to live together as if . . ." in article 2, fourth sentence. In article 4, she changes "ready" to "willing" in the first sentence; omits "or altercations" after "disputes" in the second sentence; changes "their" to "the" and "the" to "a" in the third sentence; and omits the adjective "low" before "jealousy" in the fourth sentence. In article 5, Catherine makes the following changes: she omits the preposition "on" before "any human motive"; omits "common" before "Spouse"; omits "from themselves" after "banish"; adds "from amongst them" after "affections"; and omits "amongst themselves" after "connections". In article 2, Archbishop Murray changed "them" to "themselves" and re-inserted "together" in the fourth sentence; changed "each other" to "one another" and added "love and" before "union" in the fifth sentence. In article 4, he changed "weakness" to "weaknesses" in the first sentence, and inserted "of charity" after "noble description" in the fourth sentence.

2nd This mutual union and love should therefore eminently characterise religious souls. This should distinguish them above all others as faithful spouses, and servants of Jesus Christ. The Sisters of this pious Institute, founded and grounded on charity, should therefore make that favorite virtue of their Divine Master, their own most favorite virtue. This they should study to maintain and cherish so perfectly amongst [them] themselves as to live together as if they had but one heart and one soul in God. This love for [each other] one another should be such as to emulate the love and union of the Blessed in Heaven.

3rd They shall, therefore, in conversation, manners and conduct most cautiously avoid whatever may in the least disturb their union, or lessen in the smallest degree, their mutual love and charity. They shall as true followers of God, walk in love as Christ loved us, preserving above all things charity, which is the bond of perfection, gaining over souls in the obedience of charity, and in sincerity of heart fervently loving each other.

4th They shall be willing on all occasions to help and assist one another, bearing with patience and charity each other's defects, [weakness] weaknesses and imperfections. They shall never enter into disputes, but should they happen to differ in opinion on any subject they shall propose their reasons with coolness, moderation and charity. They shall never speak of the faults of the Sisters, except to the Mother Superior, and then only with a charitable desire of their amendment and after consulting God in prayer, and their spiritual director. They shall avoid all rash suspicions and judgments, all jealousy and envy, and shall always bear in mind in order to regulate their sentiments and conduct on this head the noble description of charity given by the Apostle, "Charity is patient, is kind, envieth not, dealeth not perversely, is not puffed up, is not ambitious, seeketh not her own, is not provoked to anger, thinketh no evil, beareth all things, hopeth all things, endureth all things."

5th As the love and union of religious persons should be founded not on flesh and blood or any human motive, but on God alone; as their hearts should be united together in Jesus Christ, their Spouse and Redeemer, in whom and for whom they should live and love one another, the Sisters of this religious Institute shall banish all particular friendships, attachments and affections from amongst them, and shall scrupulously avoid all private parties and connections, as the source of discord and divisions, and as hostile to purity of heart, to charity, and to the spirit of religion.[26]

26 The most significant alteration Catherine makes in her use of this chapter of the PR is her omission of article 6, which reads as follows: "In speaking to the Superioress all the Sisters shall call her *Mother,* not only while she is in office, but ever after. The Assistant, Burser [*sic*], and Mistress of Novices shall also be called *Mother*, by all the other Sisters, except by the Mother Superior. The other Religious shall call each other *Sister*" (p. 33). Archbishop Murray did not insert article 6.

CHAPTER 9 : ON HUMILITY

1st Humility being the abridgment of all the discipline of a religious life, the ground work of the spiritual building, and the surest mark of true servants of Christ, the Sisters shall be particularly attentive to the practice of this virtue, studying the nature and extent of it, and performing all their actions in the spirit of the most profound, sincere and unaffected humility.[27]

2nd They shall bear to each other great and cordial respect [and affection], not in outward behaviour, looks, and words only, but also really indeed in heart and in mind. The young shall reverence the more advanced in years, and all shall with true humility, endeavour to vie with each other [in tender concern and regard.] in exhibiting towards their Sisters a respectful demeanor, "in honor" as St. Paul expresses it, "preventing one another".[28]

CHAPTER 10 : OF CONFESSION AND COMMUNION

1st The ordinary days of Confession for the Sisters shall be the Saturdays of every week and the Eves of great feasts.[29]

2nd The Bishop shall appoint a Confessor. He shall also provide extraordinary Confessors as recommended by the holy Council of Trent, to whom the Sisters shall present themselves at the appointed times.

3rd The Most Holy [Sacrament] Eucharist having been instituted by Jesus Christ for the nourishment of our souls, as well as for our Sacrifice, and as in it He imparts to us the Most Precious Pledge of His Love, the Sisters shall cherish in their hearts the [most tender affectionate] tenderest and most affectionate devotion towards this Adorable Sacrament. They shall assist daily at the Holy Sacrifice of the Mass, with the greatest possible devotion, and approach the Holy Communion, with lively faith, profound humility, and the utmost purity, as often

27 Catherine uses both articles almost as they are found in the PR. In article 1 she omits "a" before "religious life", "distinctive and" before "surest", and "the" before "true servants". Archbishop Murray restored the "a"!

28 In article 2 Catherine changes "one another" to "each other," inserts "and affection" after "respect," and omits "in" before "mind" in the first sentence. In the second sentence she omits "cordial" after "true", changes "in mutual honor and respect" to "in tender concern and regard", and concludes the article there. However, Archbishop Murray eliminated Catherine's "and affection" and "in tender concern and regard", re-inserted "in" before "mind", and composed the concluding phrase: "in exhibiting . . . 'preventing one another.' "

29 Catherine omits the second sentence of this article in the PR, which reads: "Should any one in particular desire to confess on other days, the Mother Superior shall grant her permission" (p. 27). She shortens the next article, retaining its substance.

as their spiritual director may permit. They shall not however go to Communion three days successively without permission from the Mother Superior.[30]

CHAPTER 11 : OF THE OFFICE AND MENTAL PRAYER

1st As the Sisters of this Institute must employ a great part of their time instructing the poor, they shall be obliged only to the short Office of our Blessed Lady, which they shall daily recite together. Before they begin, they shall consider the Infinite Majesty of that God whom they are about to praise, and they shall endeavour to perform that holy exercise with all attention and devotion.[31]

2nd Mental Prayer, or Meditation, has ever been considered most effectual, to imprint deeply on the mind the sublime truths of religion, to elevate the soul, and enflame the heart with the love of God and of Heavenly things. By it the Saints attained perfection in all states. It is the way which they marked out to all who aspire to any degree of sanctity. This practice the Founders and Institutors of all Religious orders have recommended and expressly established in their Constitutions. Though differently inspired to compose that admirable variety of rules and observances which decorate the Church of God, they all had and have but one and the same spirit with respect to the necessity and advantage of Mental Prayer.[32]

3rd The Sisters of this religious Institute shall therefore most sedulously attend to this salutary exercise; in this shall they take delight and seek their comfort and refreshment from the labors and fatigues of the Institute.[33]

30 Catherine changes "Eucharist" to "Sacrament"; Archbishop Murray changed it back to "Eucharist". In the first sentence she also changes "cherish in themselves" to "cherish in their hearts" and "the tenderest and most affectionate devotion" to "the most tender affectionate devotion"; Archbishop Murray restored the wording of the latter phrase. She changes the entire second sentence of this article in the PR, which reads: "They shall approach it on Sundays and Holidays with a lively faith, the most profound humility, and the utmost purity of heart; and as often as their spiritual Director may recommend" (p. 28).

31 Catherine shortens this article, changing "in instruction" to "instructing the poor", omitting "as at the end of the Roman breviary" after "Blessed Lady", omitting "in the chapel" after "together", changing "Before they begin the Office, they shall recollect themselves a while, to consider" to "Before they begin, they shall consider . . . ," and omitting "whom" after "God". Archbishop Murray re-inserted "whom".

32 Catherine omits "their disciples" after "marked out to all", changes "aspired" to "aspire", and makes two other minor changes in this article.

33 Catherine uses only the first two sentences (which she combines) of the article in the PR, omitting the remaining three sentences. Archbishop Murray started to add "They shall, etc." and then crossed out his own addition. The omitted sentences read as follows:

They shall employ, every morning, in the chapel three quarters of an hour, and in the evening, half an hour in meditation. They shall take for the ordinary subject of this Meditation the four last things, the life, passion, and death of our Redeemer, and other mysteries of our Faith and Redemption. They shall read the subject of the morning meditation the preceding night, before they retire to rest. (p. 25)

[*4th* The Sisters shall read a spiritual lecture every day. No books shall be used in the Convent without permission from the Mother Superior.][34]

CHAPTER 12 : ON FAST AND ABSTINENCE

1st The Sisters of this religious Institute, being constantly employed in spiritual and corporal works of mercy, shall be obliged to fast and abstain only on the days commanded by the Church, and on the Eves of the Conception, Nativity, Presentation, and Purification of the Blessed Virgin, also on the Eve of the Feast of Our Lady of Mercy.[35]

CHAPTER 13 : OF THE REFECTORY

1st The Sisters shall breakfast, dine and sup together in the Refectory, which shall be kept with perfect regularity and neatness. Silence shall be observed, and a spiritual lecture read at dinner from such pious and instructive books as the Mother Superior shall direct.[36]

34 This article, which Archbishop Murray deleted, is two fragments of the much longer article in the PR. The entire article in the PR reads:

> The Sisters shall assist devoutly every day at the holy Sacrifice of Mass, and make their particular examen of conscience at a quarter before twelve, and at their night prayers. They shall also daily make a spiritual lecture in private for a quarter of an hour in the book that shall be appointed by the mother superior, or mistress of Novices, and shall read no other without permission. They shall accustom themselves to read but little at a time, and to digest well by reflection whatever they read. No books shall be introduced into the Convent, for public or private reading, but such as shall be approved of by the Bishop or Confessor. (p. 25)

35 Catherine changes "congregation" to "Institute", and "being . . . almost constantly employed in the arduous and laborious functions of instructing poor children" to "being constantly employed in spiritual and corporal works of mercy"; she also adds the last phrase, "also . . . Mercy".

36 Catherine uses two parts of the two articles in the PR, but basically writes her own article, adding the references to the upkeep of the Refectory and to silence, and limiting the spiritual lecture to dinner. The two articles in the PR read as follows:

> 1. The sisters shall all breakfast, dine, and sup together in the Refectory, and on the same Viands, without any distinction or difference whatsoever, except when sick; and then such diet shall be provided for them in the Infirmary, with the permission of the Mother Superior, as may be deemed necessary.
>
> 2. During dinner and supper a lecture shall be made by one of the Sisters out of such pious and instructive books as the Mother Superior shall direct. It shall not be lawful for the sisters to eat, out of the Refectory, without the permission of the Mother Superior. (p. 38)

CHAPTER 14 : OF SPIRITUAL RETREAT AND RENEWAL OF VOWS[37]

1st Spiritual exercises being justly considered one of the most powerful means for the advancement of Religious Persons in the perfection of their state, the Sisters of this Institute shall make every year a spiritual retreat of eight days immediately before the feast of the Assumption of Our Blessed Lady, and another retreat of three days the last of the year. They shall also devote the first Sunday of every month to a preparation for a happy Death.

2nd The Sisters shall on the first day of every year make a renewal of their vows to excite in their hearts an encrease of fervour in the service of their Heavenly Spouse by so solemn a recollection of the obligations they have contracted.[38]

FORM OF THE ACT OF THE RENEWAL OF VOWS

Omnipotent and Eternal God, I, Sister N.N., do ratify this day in the presence of the Heavenly Court the vows which I made at my profession, and promise faithfully to observe Poverty, Chastity and Obedience according to the rules and constitutions of this Institute of our Blessed Lady of Mercy, and under her Protection. I most earnestly supplicate [the] thy Divine goodness through the merits of Jesus Christ to grant me grace to fulfill these obligations. Amen.[39]

CHAPTER 15 : ON DEVOTION TO THE PASSION OF JESUS CHRIST, TO THE BLESSED SACRAMENT, AND TO THE SACRED HEART OF JESUS[40]

1st The Sisters of this Congregation shall have the most affectionate devotion to the Passion of Our Lord and Saviour Jesus Christ. They shall often recall to mind and meditate on the different circumstances of it in order to excite in themselves an ardent desire of conforming [their hearts] themselves to their

37 Catherine titles this chapter "Of Spiritual Retreat" and uses, almost verbatim, only the first article in the PR, omitting reference to the renewal of vows and the Form for the renewal, which she places later as chapter 9 in the Second Part of her manuscript. Archbishop Murray, following the order of the PR, restored the full chapter title and wrote "Renewal of Vows" after article 1; hence, following his notation, Clare Moore's fair copy places Catherine's article and Form for Renewal, from the Second Part, chapter 9, in this chapter.

38 Catherine copies this article almost verbatim except that, again, she changes "in themselves" to "in their hearts."

39 Catherine alters the Presentation form as follows: she deletes "and to continue to the end of my life in this pious Institute for the instruction of poor female children" after "obedience", changes "Rules and Constitutions of the Presentation of our most Blessed Lady", and changes "I most humbly and earnestly beseech" to "I most earnestly supplicate". Archbishop Murray changed Catherine's "the Divine goodness" to "thy Divine goodness," as in the PR.

40 This chapter, which Catherine places in the First Part of her Rule, is chapter 9 of the Second Part of the PR, i.e., the fourth last chapter of that Rule.

suffering Redeemer, persuaded that to share hereafter in His glory, they must here participate in His [great humiliation] suffering and humiliation. They shall offer the fatigues and labors of their state, the mortifications they undergo, and all their pains of mind and body in union with the sufferings of their crucified Spouse. They shall make some part of the Passion the subject of their meditation on every Friday, and at three o'clock in the afternoon, they shall adore on their knees in Choir, Jesus Christ for us made obedient unto death, nay to the death of the Cross. They shall then say five Paters and five Aves, in honor of His sacred wounds and death, for those who are in their agony or in mortal sin, and for all the souls in Purgatory.[41]

2nd Jesus Christ really present in the most Holy Eucharist shall be the constant object of their affection and devotion. They shall often reflect on the infinite Charity He displays for them in that ever Adorable Sacrament and, by frequent visits every day, they shall pay most assiduous court to their Heavenly Spouse on the throne of His Love, uniting by acts of adoration, praise, and thanksgiving their homages to [the homage] those which the Angels who constantly attend Him in the Holy Tabernacle incessantly offer to Him. In all their sufferings and anxieties of mind, in all their fears, afflictions and temptations they shall seek at the foot of His Altar, their comfort and consolation as He lovingly invites them in these words, "Come to me all you who labor and are heavily laden and I will ease and refresh you."[42]

3rd They shall also profess the most tender devotion to the Sacred Heart of Jesus, concurring with the pious wishes and sentiments of the Holy Catholic Church, by raising their minds and affections to that boundless love which the Divine Redeemer has shewed for mankind in the Institution of the Eucharist, and in His Dolorous passion and death suffered for our Redemption. They shall on their part endeavour to atone for the outrages thus endured, and for which the malice and ingratitude of mankind make so base a return.[43]

41 Catherine uses the wording of the first article of the PR except for the following: in the first sentence she omits "of this Congregation" (but Dr. Murray restored the words), omits "in themselves" after "excite" (which he, again, restored), changes "conforming themselves" to "conforming their hearts" (which he restored), omits "hereafter" after "share" (which he restored), and changes "his humiliations and sufferings" to "His great humiliation" (which Dr. Murray changed to "His suffering and humiliation"). Evidently, Archbishop Murray wanted this article to be nearly identical to that in the PR, although in the remainder of the article Catherine makes several insignificant changes which he did not alter, and she changes "the agony" to "their agony" and "the state of mortal sin" to simply, "mortal sin"—which, again, Dr. Murray left as worded.

42 Catherine omits "also" after "shall," adds "constant" before "object" in the first sentence, and adds "most" before "assiduous" in the second. She changed "their homages to the homages" to "their homages to the homage," but Dr. Murray changed "the homage" to "those". Catherine makes both "Tabernacles" and "Altars" singular nouns. In the last sentence she spells "loveingly" thus, which I take to be a slip of the pen, and therefore correct.

43 Except for changing "likewise" to "also" in the first sentence, Catherine copies this article verbatim.

CHAPTER 16 : ON DEVOTION TO OUR BLESSED LADY, ETC.[44]

1st Devotion to Mary ever Virgin and Mother of God has always been the favorite of religious persons, and is particularly recommended in every regular Institute. But as this congregation is immediately under Her special protection and as she is under God its principal [Patron] Patroness and Protectress, the Sisters shall always have the warmest and most affectionate devotion to her, regarding Her in a special manner as their Mother, and the great Model they are obliged to imitate, that by Her intercession and Powerful protection, they may be enabled to fulfil the obligations of this Holy Institute, and implant Jesus Christ in the hearts of the poor, whom they are charged to instruct.[45]

2nd They shall have individually unlimited confidence in Her, have recourse to Her in all [spiritual] their difficulties and spiritual wants, and by the imitation of Her virtues, study to render themselves worthy of Her Maternal Protection. They shall solemnize Her festivals with spiritual joy and devotion and shall impress on the minds of all [those] whom they can influence, the greatest respect, veneration and love for Her. They shall recite every day five decades of the Rosary in Her Honor.[46]

3rd On the Feast of Our Lady of Mercy every year, the whole community with lighted tapers in their hands shall on their knees before the Altar make the following Act of Consecration, which the Mother Superior shall read in an audible voice in the name and on behalf of the Community, and every newly professed Sister shall read it on the day of her Profession.[47]

44 This chapter is chapter 10 of the Second Part of the PR, i.e., the third last chapter of that Rule; its title, which Catherine does not fully transcribe, is "On Devotion to Our Blessed Lady, and Other Saints." Clare Moore copies the title as Catherine has it. In the first two articles of this chapter, Catherine nearly always capitalizes "Her". I have left the capital letters where she uses them.

45 Catherine omits "all" before "religious persons", adds an "and", uses "Patron" for "Patroness" (which Archbishop Murray restored), adds "always" before "have the warmest," and changes "tender hearts of those poor dear little ones" to "hearts of the poor".

46 Catherine changes "all their difficulties and spiritual necessities" to "all spiritual difficulties and wants". Archbishop Murray changed this to "all their difficulties and spiritual wants". She omits a few words, the most significant of which are "to please her, and to" after "study" and "the poor children and of" after "the minds of". Archbishop Murray inserted "the" before "imitation" and changed her "those" to "whom".

47 Catherine substitutes the Feast of Our Lady of Mercy for the Feast of the Presentation, omits "the titular Feast of this Institute," omits "of the Blessed Virgin" after "the Altar", omits "of themselves, and of the Congregation" after "Act of Consecration" and changes, in the case of newly professed, "make it privately" to "read it".

ACT OF OBLATION AND CONSECRATION TO THE BLESSED MOTHER OF GOD

Most Holy and Glorious Virgin Mother of God, we thy humble Suppliants, convinced how much we stand in need of the Grace of God to fulfil the arduous duties and obligations of our Pious Institute and of the greatness of Thy power with Jesus Christ, Thy Beloved Son, and of Thy goodness towards [us,] poor Christians, [we] most [humbly] earnestly address ourselves to Thee this day as the Mother of Mercy, and in full confidence of obtaining, through thy Holy intercession, the divine assistance. We therefore, most clement Virgin, prostrate before Thee, with all humility earnestly beseech Thee to be most graciously pleased to accept the oblation which we all irrevocably make on this Holy day of ourselves to Thy love and service, proposing with the divine assistance to bear always towards Thee the most cordial respect and veneration, and to engage as far as in our power all others to love, honor and respect Thee. Deign, Most Pure and immaculate Virgin Mother of God, to receive us all and every one of us in particular under Thy Holy protection. We look up to Thee as our Mother, our Lady, and our Mistress, as our [Patron] Patroness and Protectress, advocate and directress, humbly entreating Thee to obtain, through the merits of thy adorable Son, the pardon of all our sins and transgressions against the Divine Majesty, and of all our negligence in Thy Holy Service. We beseech thee to obtain of [the] His Infinite goodness [of Thy Beloved Son] that we may always and on all occasions be favored with Thy singular assistance, especially in the arduous functions of our Institute, and in the practice of every religious virtue; in fine, we most earnestly request thou wilt be graciously pleased to obtain that perfect union of hearts and minds may always reign amongst us, that we may ever be faithful to the observance of our rules, and persevere to the end of our lives in the spirit and grace of our vocation, that having with fidelity, served Thy Beloved Son by imitating Thy virtues on earth, we may with Thee, and all the Elect praise and glorify Him in Heaven for all Eternity. Amen.[48]

The Saints to whom the Sisters of this religious Institute are recommended to have particular devotion are Saint Joseph, Saint Ann and Saint Joachim, the Holy Apostles, Peter and Paul, and Saint John the Evangelist, Saint Patrick, Saint Bridget, Saint Augustin, Saint Monica, Saint Francis of Sales, Saint Vincent of

48 Catherine copies almost verbatim the "Act of Oblation and Consecration" as it appears in the PR, making one paragraph out of what is there three paragraphs, eliminating the two references to the "Religious Congregation of Charitable Instruction", inserting "us" before "poor Christians", changing "the fullest confidence" to "full confidence", omitting an "up" and an "our", and changing "Patroness" to "Patron" and "the Institute" to "our Institute". Archbishop Murray made a number of changes: he added "we thy humble Suppliants", deleted Catherine's "us" and "we", changed "humbly" to "earnestly", restored "Patroness", inserted "through the merits of thy adorable Son", changed Catherine's "the infinite goodness" to "His infinite goodness", and deleted "of Thy Beloved Son".

Paul, Saint John of God, Saint Joseph Calasanctius, Saint Francis Xavier, Saint Angela of Merici, Saints Catherine of Sienna and Genoa.[49]

CHAPTER 17 : OF THE VOWS[50]

OF THE VOW OF POVERTY

1st As the Sisters in order to become more conformable to their Heavenly Spouse Christ Jesus, have in quitting the world renounced all property in earthly things, they should frequently revolve in mind how tenderly He cherished Holy Poverty. Born in a stable, laid in a manger, suffering hunger, cold and thirst in the course of His mortal life, not having a place to lay His head, naked on a cross, He consecrated this virtue in His sacred Person and bequeathed it as a most valuable patrimony to His followers.[51]

2nd The Sisters shall therefore keep their hearts perfectly disengaged from all affection to the things of this world, content with the food and raiment allowed them and willing at all times to give up whatever had been allotted to them. They shall not give or receive any present without permission from the Mother Superior, and if with her permission they receive any present from their relatives or others, it must be considered as for the use of the community, and not for the particular use of the receiver.[52]

49 Catherine does not number this article but Clare Moore makes it the "4th" in this chapter. Catherine changes "the Members of this Congregation" to "the Sisters of this religious Institute". To the list of recommended Saints in the PR, the order of which she slightly changes, Catherine adds: "Saint John of God" and "Saints Catherine of Sienna and Genoa". She deletes "St. Francis Regis" and after the name of Saint Joseph Calasanctius, she deletes "Institutor of the Pious Schools for children in Italy".

50 The three chapters "Of the Vows" are chapters 3, 4, and 5 in the First Part of the PR. Catherine moves these chapters to the end of her First Part, as chapters 16, 17, and 18. She follows the PR wording very closely though she makes some significant changes which are noted below. In Clare Moore's fair copy these three chapters are moved forward as chapters 5, 6, and 7, right after the four chapters on the purpose of the Institute and the works of the Sisters of Mercy. It is not clear from Archbishop Murray's notations on Catherine's manuscript that he intended this placement. He explicitly re-numbered her chapters 2 through 15, because all the chapter numbers were one off after he formed the new chapter 1. He also re-numbered these chapters, 17, 18, and 19, but in addition appears to have crossed out the numbers 18 and 19, perhaps intending that all three chapters would be moved forward. It is also possible that the re-numberings or the crossings out are not in his handwriting.

51 Catherine makes relatively minor changes in articles 1 and 3 of the chapter on the vow of poverty as it appears in the PR. In article 1 she omits "consider and" before "revolve", changes "their Divine Master" to "He" before "cherished," omits "where" before "to lay," and changes "most eligible patrimony" to "most valuable patrimony." Archbishop Murray made no changes here or in article 3.

52 Catherine simplifies article 2 by omitting a number of words and phrases and shortening others. The most significant changes are these: she omits "from the common stock of the Community" after "raiment allowed them", changes "ready" to "willing", omits "at the will of the Superior" after "allotted to them" at the end of her first sentence, and changes "applied to the use of the community" to "considered as for the use of the community". Archbishop Murray inserted "for" in the last phrase.

3rd Nothing shall appear in their dress, but what is modest and grave, nor can they keep in their cells any thing superfluous, costly or rich, in furniture or decorations. All must be suitable to religious simplicity and poverty.[53]

CHAPTER 18 : OF THE VOW OF CHASTITY

1st As Chastity is a most angelical virtue, consecrated in the Person of Jesus Christ and recommended in the Evangelical Law, with the most distinguished encomiums, the Sisters shall esteem nothing more precious than this Heavenly Gift, and [shall] they should always observe the strictest guard on their senses, lest the enemy who is constantly on the watch should penetrate through these avenues to their souls, and tarnish in the least the purity of their hearts.[54]

CHAPTER 19 : OF THE VOW OF OBEDIENCE

1st The Sisters are always to bear in mind that by the vow of obedience they have forever renounced their own will, and resigned it without reserve to the direction of their superiors. They are to obey the Mother Superior, as having authority from God, rather through love than servile fear. They shall love and respect her as their Mother, and in order that she may be enabled to direct them in the way of God's service it is recommended to them to make known to her their penitential works and mortifications, with the advantages derived from them.[55]

53 In article 3, Catherine simply deletes "of any kind" after "decorations".

54 In article 1 of the chapter on chastity Catherine makes only one change: she omits the clause, "But as they carry this most valuable treasure in brittle vessels, they are always to" before her "observe the strictest guard . . . ." More significantly, Catherine deletes the entire second article of the chapter in the PR, which reads as follows:

> They shall most cautiously avoid every occasion that may be a stumbling block in their way: profane books of any kind, which are apt to beget worldly affections, they never shall read. When spoken to by men of any state or profession they shall observe and maintain the most guarded reserve, never fix their eyes on them, nor shew themselves, in conversation or otherwise, in the least degree familiar with them, how devout or religious soever they may appear to be. They shall turn with abhorrence from every object that may in any shape tend to excite unclean ideas, in order to keep their minds and hearts always spotless and pure, and preserve with the most scrupulous integrity the faith which they have so solemnly plighted to their heavenly Spouse. (p. 18)

Archbishop Murray did not restore this paragraph. In article 1, he made one small change, substituting "they should" for her "shall" before "always observe".

55 Catherine considerably alters the chapter on obedience as it appears in the PR. In article 1, besides five minor word changes, she makes three significant alterations: she deletes the sentence, "Wherefore they are with a ready and chearful [*sic*] mind to undertake and exactly fulfil whatever is commanded, provided it be not manifestly sinful" after the first sentence; she deletes "They are to reverence her interiorly and exteriorly, and" before "love and respect her as their Mother"; and after her last phrase in this article, she deletes an entire long clause: "and likewise their practices of devotion and of virtue, sincerely desiring to be brought back to the strait road to perfection, should it have happened to them to stray from it, and never to presume to rely on their own judgment as their guide" (p. 19). Archbishop Murray made no changes in Catherine's article 1.

2nd They shall without hesitation comply with the directions of the Mother Superior, in all matters of great or little moment, agreeable or disagreeable. They shall never murmur, but with humility and spiritual joy carry the sweet yoke of obedience.[56]

3rd They shall not [be] absent themselves from the common exercises without her leave, except in a case of pressing urgency; [but if they cannot have previous access to her, they shall make known the reason afterwards.] and if they cannot then have previous access to her, they shall make known the reason of their absence as soon afterwards as an opportunity shall offer. They shall obey the call of the Bell as the voice of God.[57]

[CHAPTER 19: OF ENCLOSURE]

[*1st* The religious of this Institute of the Sisters of Mercy, always keeping in mind that in consecrating themselves in this holy state, they have totally renounced the world, shall hold themselves obliged to a strict, exact and faithful observance of enclosure, so that after having made their vows it shall be no longer in their power to pass the limits of the enclosure which shall be marked out,

56 Besides five minor word changes, Catherine makes three other, more significant changes in her use of the PR text of article 2: she substitutes "directions" for "orders" of the Mother Superior; she substitutes "never murmur" for "never give way to murmuring or discontent" and she deletes a clause and two additional sentences, after "the sweet yoke of obedience". The omitted passage reads as follows:

> . . . which they assumed when they devoted themselves to Christ. They are not only to fulfil the commands of their Superior, but should also endeavour to anticipate her wishes, if they can discover them. They shall undergo with humility the penance enjoined by her, and, should she happen to reprimand them undeservedly, they are not to murmur, nor complain, but with a submissive mind and pious affection receive her rebukes, striving to justify them in their own minds, in order the more perfectly to obey with all the powers and strength of their souls. (p. 20)

Dr. Murray did not restore the omitted passage.

57 Article 3 is much re-worked by Catherine and by Archbishop Murray. Catherine writes "They shall not be absent . . .," but Archbishop Murray restored the PR wording: "They shall not absent themselves . . . ." She deletes "express" before "leave", and then says simply, following the language of the PR: "but if they cannot have previous access to her, they shall make known the reason afterwards", omitting only the longer PR phrase, "as soon afterwards as an opportunity affords". Archbishop Murray, however, re-worked the whole clause, strengthening it to read: ". . . except in a case of pressing urgency; and if they cannot then have previous access to her, they shall make known the reason of their absence as soon afterwards as an opportunity shall offer." In the last sentence, Catherine omits "without delay" after "obey", and "to the different exercises of the Community" after "Bell".

except, first, to comply with the duties of their Institute, second, for the reasons assigned in the Sacred Canons and Apostolical Constitutions.][58]

CHAPTER 20 : OF THE RECEPTION OF POSTULANTS[59]

1st [No person will be admitted unless of unblemished character. Should any present themselves who are not known, care must be taken not to admit them untill it be fully ascertained if they are worthy.] Such as desire to embrace this Religious Institute shall be previously examined with respect to their vocation by the Bishop or Priest delegated by him and by the Mother Superior. When admitted they shall continue Postulants for six months and employ their time as shall be appointed.[60]

2nd If their conduct during this time be truly humble and conformable to the spirit of the Institute, they shall be allowed to solicit in Chapter the religious Habit, and if the majority of votes which must be secret be in their favor, they shall receive it and commence their noviciate.[61]

3rd The time of their noviciate shall continue two entire years. The Bishop can however in extraordinary cases reduce it to one year. Two months before the expiration of the period of their probation, they shall with the permission of the Mother Superior, present their request in Chapter to be admitted to Profession. If the Chapter accede thereto a scrutiny shall be made, with white and black

58 Archbishop Murray did not change Catherine's chapter number, as he had done throughout, because he here excised the entire chapter on enclosure from Catherine's manuscript by drawing a large X through it. In her text, Catherine follows the PR exactly except for the following changes: where the PR reads, "The Religious Sisters of this new Institute, so well calculated for the Christian education and improvement of poor girls in particular, to which they are bound by vow to attend, always remembering . . . ," Catherine simply writes, "The religious of this Institute of the Sisters of Mercy, always keeping in mind . . ."; she omits "to God" after "consecrating themselves"; she changes "their Religious Profession" to "their vows"; and after "except" in the final phrase, she inserts, "first, to comply with the duties of their Institute, second," and here changes "for such weighty reasons as are assigned in the Sacred Canons" to "for the reasons assigned in the Sacred Canons . . . ."

59 Catherine places this chapter as the first chapter of the Second Part of her manuscript. Archbishop Murray crossed out "Second Part", and inserted "2d Part" *after* this chapter, thus making "Of the Reception of Postulants" the last chapter—chapter 20—of the First Part of the Rule.

60 Catherine apparently composed her own article 1, not using the much longer, more detailed article in the PR. Archbishop Murray excised her first and second sentences, shown here in brackets, substituting for them, as the first sentence, nearly all of the first sentence in the PR, omitting only "the Assistant, and Mistress of Novices" as examiners. The last sentence is Catherine's composition.

61 Catherine's article is almost identical to the second article in the PR, except that she makes it one sentence, changes "be admitted to it, and begin their novitiate" to "receive it and commence their noviciate," and omits the requirement at the end of the PR article: "provided they be of sufficient age."

beans, and if the majority be in their favor, they shall spend the remainder of the time of their probation, as circumstances may allow, in prayer and other spiritual exercises.[62]

4th As many shall be received on the Establishment as the funds will admit of and no more, unless the subject bring with her a sufficient dower for her support in every necessary. Lodgers shall not be admitted, with an exception in favor of a foundress or very particular Benefactress.[63]

5th The young professed shall remain under the direction of the Mistress of Novices for two years, without either active or passive vote, except the first seven professed in each House who shall have both active and passive vote immediately on their profession.[64]

FORM OF THE ACT OF PROFESSION[65]

In the name of Our Lord and Saviour Jesus Christ and under the protection of His Immaculate Mother Mary ever Virgin, I, Sister N.N., called in religion N.N., do vow and promise to God perpetual poverty, chastity, and obedience, and to persevere untill the end of my life in this Institute, according to the rules and constitution of this congregation of Our Lady of Mercy, under the authority and in presence of you, my Lord and Most Reverend Father in God, N.N., Archbishop of this Diocese and of our Reverend Mother N.N., called in religion N.N., Superioress of this Convent of Our Lady of Mercy, on this — day of — in the year of our Lord —.

62 Article 3 follows exactly the text of article 3 in the PR, except that Catherine omits the second and third sentences: "The first six months shall be employed chiefly in spiritual exercises, and in the study of the duties and functions of the Institute. They shall afterwards attend more closely to the schools, and to the instruction of the poor children." She also changes "received to Profession" to "admitted to Profession" and omits "of the votes shall" after "majority".

63 Catherine places this paragraph below, unnumbered, *after* the Form of the Act of Profession. She copies almost verbatim the complete text of article 4 in the PR, and then adds the sentence, "Lodgers shall not . . . Benefactress." Archbishop Murray moved the paragraph, without change, to its present location by his notation inserted after article 3: "4th As many shall be, etc."

64 After the above notation, Archbishop Murray wrote, "5th The young professed, etc." In her fair copy, Clare Moore copied article 5 verbatim from the PR. It was not originally in Catherine's manuscript.

65 Catherine generally follows the Presentation "Form of the Act of Profession", but makes several changes: she adds "perpetual" before "poverty, chastity, and obedience"; she omits the Presentation purpose after "this Institute": i.e., "for the Charitable Instruction of poor girls in this Enclosure"; after "congregation" she substitutes only "of Our Lady of Mercy", for "of the Presentation of our Blessed Lady, approved of and confirmed by the Apostolical Authority of our holy Father Pope Pius VII"; she changes "Right Reverend" to "and Most Reverend" and uses "Archbishop of this Diocese" for the longer PR wording: "Bishop of N.N. (or in presence of the Priest who officiates by the appointment of the Bishop)"; and she adds "on this — day of —" to the date.

Should the Mother Superior through sickness not attend, they shall, instead of naming her, name the Assistant.[66]

SECOND PART

CHAPTER 1 : OF THE SUPERIOR AND THE VISITATION OF THE CONVENT[67]

1st This religious congregation of the Sisters of Mercy shall be always subject to the authority and jurisdiction of the Diocesan Bishop, and the Sisters shall respect and obey him as their first Superior after the Holy See. If on account of his many avocations he should not have leisure to attend immediately to the direction of the Community, a Priest shall be appointed by him on whose prudence, piety and experience he can depend to govern and direct under him and to whom he will give the necessary faculties. [Nothing of importance relating to the House or community shall be undertaken without the consent of the Bishop.][68]

2nd The Priest thus appointed shall duly attend to the government and good order of the Community in spirituals and temporals; he shall watch over the exact observance of the Constitutions for the purpose of maintaining good order, peace and charity, and shall also assist the Mother Superior with his advice in all weighty matters. Nothing of moment shall be attempted by her without consulting him nor any matter of importance relating to the House or Community be undertaken without the consent of the Bishop.

3rd When the Bishop is not at leisure to attend in person the Superior appointed by him shall officiate at the Reception of Sisters to the Habit and at their Profession. No person shall be admitted as Postulant or if admitted, be rejected without his advice and the consent of the Bishop. He shall sign the Acts of Profession, and the annual accounts of the receipts and expenditure of the Convent.

66 In this note, Catherine copies the wording in the PR, only omitting "instead of naming her", which Archbishop Murray re-inserted.

67 This entire chapter is taken verbatim from the PR by Clare Moore, at Archbishop Murray's request. In her manuscript, Catherine uses only article 1 and the last clause of article 2 of the PR, which she combines into a single unnumbered paragraph and places as the penultimate paragraph of her manuscript. However, Archbishop Murray circled Catherine's paragraph and wrote above it: "N.B. This belongs to the lst Chap. Part 2nd"; and at the beginning of Catherine's Second Part (the chapter "On the Reception of Postulants" having now been moved to the end of the First Part), he wrote: "2nd Part. Chapter 1st Superior, Visitation, etc." In making the fair copy, Clare Moore did not use Catherine's single paragraph for article 1, but rather the exact text of all the articles in the PR. However, article 1 as presented here is Catherine's paragraph; the rest of the articles of this chapter are taken from Clare Moore's fair copy.

68 See note 67. Catherine's last sentence (here in brackets) differs from the last sentence of article 2 in the PR.

4th This Superior shall visit the Convent every year, in the third week of January (should not the Bishop himself think fit to do it) to examine whether the rules and Constitutions be exactly observed, the obligations of the Institute duly fulfilled, and whether the Sisters live in perfect harmony, union and charity.

5th That the visitor may come to the knowledge of the real state of the Convent, all the Sisters shall individually appear before him, one after the other, beginning with the youngest, and shall answer such questions as he shall deem expedient to put concerning the said matters. Should he by this enquiry discover any irregularity or disorder to exist or any thing whatever contrary to the spirit of the Institute he shall give such orders and directions, as in his prudence and discretion he shall judge most likely to reform every abuse and to restore good order, regularity and union in the Community. He shall cautiously avoid mentioning the name of the person or persons from whom he may have his information, and shall make only such use of it, as may tend to promote the spiritual and temporal advantage of the Establishment.

6th Before he closes the Visitation, he shall examine the accounts of the annual receipts and disbursements, signed by the Mother Superior and the Burser. If he find that the expenses exceed the income, he shall for the purpose of clearing the debts suppress all unnecessary expenses (which however must not relate to such food and raiment as had been promised to the religious on their embracing the Institute). It were better for the Sisters to submit to a temporary inconvenience than suffer the Establishment to fall into ruin, which cannot be avoided where debts are inconsiderately allowed to accumulate. He shall render to the Bishop an account of the actual state of the Convent. The Bishop shall make a visitation every third year, or more frequently, if he deem it expedient.

CHAPTER 2 : OF THE ELECTION OF THE MOTHER SUPERIOR

1st A Superioress shall be elected from among the Vocals, distinguished for her virtue, prudence and discretion. She shall be at least thirty years old and of five years profession (except in new Establishments) and must have the majority of votes for the validity of her election.[69]

2nd The Superior when duly elected shall govern for three years. She can with the approbation of the Bishop be re-elected and govern three years more

69 The first article of this chapter is in the PR but not in Catherine's manuscript. Undoubtedly its reference to the "virtue, prudence and discretion" of the Superior was something she would not write of herself. She begins with article 2 of the PR. However, Archbishop Murray indicated that article 1 of the PR should be included by writing above Catherine's first article, "1. A Superioress, etc." In general, Catherine uses the rest of the PR chapter almost verbatim, making only a few significant changes which are noted below.

after which another Superior shall be elected. In new Establishments or foundations, the first Superior shall continue for six years unless there be canonical reasons for her being removed from office during that time.[70]

3rd On Saturday immediately after the feast of the Ascension of our Lord, the Chapter shall assemble in presence of the Bishop or his Delegate at an appointed hour. The Mother Superior shall then resign her office into his hands, who accepting her resignation, shall dismiss her from the exercise of it, saying: "We dismiss thee, Sister N.N., from the office of Superioress of this Community, in the name of the Father, and of the Son, and of the Holy Ghost. Amen." He will then transfer the authority to the Assistant by giving her the keys of the Convent, after which he will exhort [them seriously] the Sisters to think seriously on a new election against the following Thursday, that is, the Octave of the Feast of the Ascension, and to have no view in the choice they will make but the greater glory of God and the good order, peace and welfare of the Community. They shall then repeat the Hymn "Veni Creator Spiritus," the versicle "Emitte Spiritum" and the prayer "Deus qui corda" with the "Salve Regina," and then retire.[71]

4th On the Sunday within the octave, there shall be a general Communion for the approaching election, and every morning after Mass and at night after the Litany, the "Veni Creator" shall be said to direct the choice of the Community.[72]

5th On Thursday, the day of the Election, Mass shall be offered and a general Communion made for this Intention. [About ten o'clock] The election shall begin with the Hymn "Veni Creator."[73]

6th The Billets which should be all of the same form, and folded in the same manner shall be prepared and distributed the day before among the vocals, [of the same form and folded in the same manner,] each of whom shall write down on her respective billet the name and sirname of the Sister for whom she intends to vote. The Sisters shall never intimate in any manner for whom they vote, nor be curious to see the billets of others. They shall carefully avoid all conversation on the subject. If any of the vocals be sick and not able to attend the election, two Sisters shall receive her vote enclosed in a sealed cover which shall be thrown in with the rest.[74]

70 In this article and throughout this chapter and the next, Catherine generally changes "Superioress" to "Superior", unless she is quoting a ceremonial formula.

71 In the second last sentence of this article Catherine inserts "peace" after "good order".

72 Catherine deletes "of the Blessed Virgin" after "Litany".

73 Catherine omits reference to the exact time of Mass ("seven o'clock") and she changes, "At ten o'clock the Election shall begin" to "About ten o'clock . . . ," but Archbishop Murray crossed out the reference to time.

74 Catherine slightly alters articles 6 and 9 of the PR and combines them into this single article. Archbishop Murray further altered her wording, inserting some words in the first sentence ("which . . . manner"), and deleting others.

7th When all the billets are collected in a box prepared for the purpose, the President shall reckon them and if they do not correspond with the number of vocals, another scrutiny shall be made. [When the number is exact] If they do correspond, the President shall open each one and shew it to his Assistant. On inspecting each billet, the Assisting Priest shall write down the name mentioned on it. Should there be an equality of votes, for two or more, a new scrutiny shall be made and if neither in this nor in a third, there be found a majority of votes, the Election shall devolve to the Bishop.[75]

8th The billets having been duly examined, if there appear [a majority] the requisite majority in favor of one, the President shall call on her to come forward. Being on her knees, he shall declare her canonically elected without mentioning the number of votes which concurred to her election. He shall then confirm the election saying, "We confirm this election, and declare you, Sister N.N., Mother and Superioress of this Community, in the name of the Father, and of the Son, and of the Holy Ghost. Amen." The Billets shall then be burned.[76]

9th The Mother Superior being thus confirmed shall take her place as Superior. The Bell shall be rung to announce the election, and all the Sisters according to seniority in the Order shall on their knees kiss her hand. The "Ave Maris Stella" shall be sung, with the Psalm "Laudate Dominum omnes gentes." The Assistant shall write down the day of the election and the Act shall be signed by the President.[77]

10th The Mother Superior thus elected, shall make choice of such Sisters as she shall in conscience deem most fit to execute the offices of Assistant, Burser and Mistress of Novices, and propose them to the Chapter. The election shall be made according to the plurality of votes by white and red beans. Should they or any of them be negatived, the Mother Superior shall propose others. The election made, she shall with the advice of these three Sisters make choice of such other Sisters as she may judge qualified for the other different offices, and these shall remain in their several charges untill the Mother Superior shall think fit to remove them.[78]

75 Catherine completely omits articles 7 and 8 in the PR (the place of the election, the scrutineers, and the reading of the ballots). Her article 7 (formerly her article 6) is almost identical to article 10 in the PR though she omits some detail, including the phrase "expressing the name and surname in a low voice, but so as to be distinctly heard by them" after "shew it to his Assistant". Archbishop Murray altered her wording slightly.

76 This article is almost identical to article 11 in the PR. Catherine shortens the formula for the confirmation of the election. Archbishop Murray made three minor changes.

77 Catherine makes no significant change in article 12 in the PR. Archbishop Murray inserted "to" before "announce" and capitalized "Dominum".

78 Catherine inserts "most" before "fit", changes "black beans" to "red beans", and makes three other minor changes in article 13 of the PR. In her fair copy Clare Moore wrote "black beans".

11th When there are not seven professed to make the election, the Bishop shall appoint to the Office of Mother Superior and to the other principal charges, after having consulted the senior sister of the Community.[79]

CHAPTER 3 : OF THE OFFICE OF MOTHER SUPERIOR

1st The Mother Superior to govern with advantage to the Community and merit to herself, must shew herself a model of regular observance, that becoming a pattern to the Community, she may by example more powerfully engage them to the strict accomplishment of the duties of the Institute.[80]

2nd She shall take care that regular discipline be duly maintained, that the rules and constitutions be strictly observed, and that the Sisters diligently apply to their respective charges.[81]

3rd She shall tenderly comfort and support the dejected if there be any such, admonish with charity those who may transgress, and inflict such penances as may be judged expedient.[82]

4th She shall take due care that the Sisters be provided with all necessaries and that every thing superfluous be excluded.

5th Whatever the Sisters disclose of their interior, she shall keep an inviolable secret, nor shall it be lawful for her to speak thereof even to the Bishop except to ask advice and even then she cannot give the least hint who the sister in question is without her own express permission.

6th The Mother Superior shall preside at all the public exercises and meetings. The Sisters are obliged at all times and on all occasions to respect her as their Mother in God and to shew a ready obedience to her.[83]

79 Catherine makes two significant changes in article 14 of the PR: she changes "eldest sister" to "senior sister", and omits "and the Priest appointed to have the direction of it" after "Community".

80 Catherine changes "pattern to her little flock" to "pattern to the Community", omits "her" before "example" and "all" before "the duties," and makes two other minor changes.

81 After "respective charges" Catherine omits "and particularly that they most sedulously attend to the instruction of the poor children, of which she shall herself give the example." She also deletes two other words: "particular" before "care", and "themselves" after "apply".

82 Catherine simplifies and softens this article. The PR reads: "She shall tenderly comfort and inspirit the dejected, and troubled of mind, if there be any such; admonish with charity those, who may transgress; and inflict, if necessary, such punishments, and enjoin such penances, as she may judge suitable, and expedient for their amendment" (p. 50). In the next two articles she makes no changes in the PR wording. Archbishop Murray incorrectly changed her "who" to "whom" in article 5. Her "who" is retained here.

83 Catherine omits "always" before "preside", and changes "obedience to her commands" to "obedience to her". She also omits "But" at the beginning of the second sentence.

7th She shall assemble the Discreets, on the first Wednesday of every month, and oftener if circumstances require, to examine the accounts and to consult on the measures most expedient for promoting the spiritual and temporal welfare of the Community. She shall attend to their [councils] counsels, and not be the least displeased should any of them dissent from her, but shew herself disposed to coincide with their opinion when convinced by the force of their reasons.

8th She shall call a meeting of all the Sisters, on the last Wednesday of every month, to enquire into the observance of the constitutions, and if any be found remiss in strictly complying with them, the Mother Superior shall rebuke them with charity, exhort them to observe them with exactness in future, and if necessary impose such penance as she may deem expedient.[84]

9th The Mother Superior shall take care that every novice be examined by the Bishop or his Delegate one month before the time of her profession. She shall sign the Acts of her Profession and of the Chapter, the accounts and all the written documents relating to the spiritual and temporal concerns of the Community.[85]

CHAPTER 4 : OF THE OFFICE OF THE ASSISTANT

1st The Assistant being the first of the Discreets, shall in the absence of the Mother Superior preside at Choir and all other public meetings. She shall assist the Mother Superior in all doubtful and difficult matters. She shall undertake nothing against the will of the Superior, and shall give her an account of whatever she orders in her absence.[86]

2nd She shall carefully enquire into the wants of the Sisters and inform the Mother Superior thereof, that they may be provided with every necessary.[87]

CHAPTER 5 : OF THE OFFICE OF THE DEPOSITARY OR BURSER

1st The Burser, second in rank among the Discreets, should be acquainted with household business, a prudent and careful economist and qualified by her [patience and] affability to engage the good will and respect of all those with whom she may have business to transact. She shall keep an exact account in

84 Catherine makes two minor changes, omitting unnecessary words. She also changes "penances" to "penance" and omits "on them" after this word.

85 Catherine completely omits this article in the PR, but Archbishop Murray inserted it by writing after article 8, "9. The Mother Superior, etc."

86 In the second sentence Catherine changes "She shall make it her particular study to assist and comfort the mother Superior" to simply, "She shall assist the Mother Superior . . . ," and makes two other minor changes.

87 Catherine deletes "and necessities" after "wants," and "all" before "be provided".

writing of all the receipts and expenditures, which she shall lay every week before the Mother Superior in presence of the Discreets to be audited and signed by her.[88]

CHAPTER 6 : OF THE MISTRESS OF NOVICES[89]

1st As the order and preservation of a religious Institute [depends] depend much on the good direction and the pious [regular] and religious conduct of the Novices, the Sister appointed to this important office should be [humble and devout, of great prudence and very patient, in order to form those under her care in humility and solid virtue.] discreet, meek and devout, of great prudence and experienced in all the duties of the Institute, judicious in discerning the dispositions of such as are under her care, and endowed with talents to form their minds to the practice of every virtue.[90]

2nd She shall study to make them truly sensible of the end they should have in view in quitting the world which [is] should be to unite their hearts perfectly to God by dying to themselves and to the world so as to apply all the powers and faculties of their souls to the service of their Heavenly Spouse, by a spirit of evangelical poverty, divested of all inordinate attachments, by the purest chastity and by an unlimited obedience, grounded on self-denial and an entire surrender of their own will; [and as] in short, that this Institute is in a special manner founded on Calvery, there to serve a crucified Redeemer. By [His] whose example the Sisters ought to crucify their senses, imaginations, passions, inclinations and caprices for the Love of their Divine Master.[91]

88 Catherine simplifies and shortens the two articles in the PR, combining them into one article, and she makes several significant changes, notably in the direction of removing the Bursar's responsibility to "receive and keep the money of the Convent, and pay all the disbursements". She changes "courteousness and" to "patience and" before "affability", but Archbishop Murray deleted this. She deletes the last clause, "which she shall . . . signed by her", but Archbishop Murray re-inserted this clause from the PR.

89 Catherine makes many changes in this chapter, not all of which are noted here. In general, she shortens the articles and expresses the role of the Mistress of Novices more modestly.

90 Catherine inserts reference to virtues important to her, and ends the article at "solid virtue", but Archbishop Murray restored all the concluding wording of the PR, by crossing out "humble and devout . . . solid virtue" and writing in "discreet, etc."

91 Catherine omits "and entering into the Religious state" after "quitting the world," omits "no other than" before "to unite," changes "unite themselves" to "unite their hearts", changes "more perfectly with God" to "perfectly to God", changes "their soul and body" to "their souls", and, after "dying to themselves and to the world", deletes "mortifying their outward senses, and more particularly their interior passions". She also changes "earthly attachments" to "inordinate attachments"; omits "self-denial" after "grounded on", though Archbishop Murray restored this; changes "a total abnegation" to "an entire surrender"; omits "Mount" before "Calvery [*sic*]"; changes "crucified Jesus" to "crucified Redeemer"; and omits "aversions" after "inclinations" and "sake and" before "Love".

3rd She shall instruct them in modesty, meekness and humility, encouraging them to conquer those pettish and childish humours which weaken the spirit, and render it vapid and languid, to the end that they may bring forth fruits of solid and vigorous sanctity. And because this undertaking is arduous, she shall teach them to place all their trust and confidence in God and in the Protection of the Blessed Virgin. She shall teach them the method of prayer and meditation, how to confess their sins briefly, distinctly, and contritely, and how to profit by their Confessions and Communions.[92]

4th As religious obedience is the principal virtue of religious life, and as in it chiefly consists the perfect sacrifice of the soul to God, the Mistress of Novices shall give her greatest attention to instruct them in the nature, extent, motives and advantages of this sublime virtue, that knowing its excellence, they may apply themselves with earnestness to the practice of it, not only by complying without hesitation in their actions, but also by submitting their will and judgment to the will and judgment of their Superiors. For this end she shall teach them to consider God in their Superiors and in their direction His guidance, being as certainly convinced that God speaks to them by their Superiors as if an angel had spoken, according to those words of Jesus Christ, "Whoever heareth you heareth me."[93]

5th She shall impress on their minds, that by the virtue of obedience the religious soul becomes most intimately united to God; that His will so governs and directs her as to entitle her to say with the Apostle, "I live, not I, but Christ liveth in me"; that [God] it is God that then regulates all her thoughts, words, and every action of her life; and that, in consequence, actions in themselves the most trivial become in some manner divine, of great value and merit for Eternity. In fine, that in Holy Obedience, she has an infallible [rule] means of knowing and fulfilling the will of God in all perfection, an advantage of the greatest

92 In the first sentence Catherine changes "exercise them" to "instruct them", changes "root out, as much as possible" to "conquer", and omits "especially in the female sex" before "weaken the spirit". In the second sentence she omits "not to depend on themselves, but" before "to place all their trust . . . ," and in the last sentence, she changes "make good use of" to "profit by", and deletes the last clause: "how to read well, pronounce, and recite the Office in Choir".

93 In the first sentence, Catherine changes "the virtue which principally characterizes the true spirit of Religion" to "the principal virtue of religious life"; deletes "great" before "excellence" and "and to what it obliges" after it; and omits "instantly and" after "complying", "exterior" before "actions", and "in all things" after "submitting". In the second sentence she omits "always" before "to consider" and changes "in their orders" to "in their direction", and "the orders of God" to "His guidance". She omits "to them" after "as if an angel had spoken".

importance, which the Religious soul enjoys over even the most regular and devout who remain in the world.[94]

6th She shall endeavour to penetrate them with a sublime idea of and most cordial love and reverence for their Holy Institute, and fill their hearts with the tenderest pity and charity for the Poor. She shall inculcate the sincerest desire for the salvation of mankind [and to], that so they may pour forth fervent prayers for all, but in particular for the Most Holy Catholic Church, its Chief Pastor, Prelates, and Clergy, often applying their communions and prayers for the encrease of true religion, especially in these Kingdoms.[95]

7th She shall particularly impress on them, that the Sisters should have but one heart and soul in Christ their Heavenly Spouse, mindful that as our Divine Saviour has by the grace of their vocation united them together in one Body [by the grace of religious vocation], they should always remain united in the spirit of Charity which is the bond of perfection.[96]

8th The Novices shall in all their wants apply to their Mistress who shall inform the Mother Superior, or in ordinary matters redress them herself. The Mistress of Novices should be as far as circumstances admit disengaged from all other offices [when there shall be sufficient number of Novices to engage her undivided attention.] that she may be enabled to give her undivided attention to this very important charge.[97]

CHAPTER 7 : OF THE DISCREETS AND THEIR OFFICE

1st The Assistant, Depositary and Mistress of Novices shall be the Discreets or Council of the Mother Superior, who shall consult them in all weighty matters,

94 At the end of the first sentence, Catherine changes "all her steps" to "all her thoughts", omits "prayers, lectures, recreations" after "words", and changes "the meanest, the most trivial, and indifferent actions in themselves" to simply, "the most trivial"; Archbishop Murray changed her "God" to "it is God that" and inserted "actions in themselves". In the next sentence, she changes "a sure and an infallible rule and means" to simply, "an infallible rule"; Archbishop Murray inserted "that" after "In fine" and changed her "rule" to "means". She omits "and fulfilling" after "knowing," but he restored it. Finally, Catherine ends the article with "enjoys", but Archbishop Murray added the concluding phrase in the PR.

95 Catherine changes "charity and affection for the poor children" to "pity and charity for the Poor", omits "Roman" before "Catholic Church", omits "visible Head and" before "Chief Pastor," and changes "propagation" to "encrease".

96 Catherine changes "inculcate" to "impress on them" and omits "same" before "spirit of Charity". Archbishop Murray moved her reference to the grace of vocation to a position earlier in the sentence.

97 Catherine changes the PR wording, "as far as circumstances admit, disengaged from all other affairs and occupations of the Community that she may the more closely attend to this very important charge" to her own wording (in brackets), but Archbishop Murray re-inserted some of the PR wording and added his own conclusion: "that she may be enabled . . . ."

and determine with their advice what is best to be done. They are to propose whatever may appear most expedient for the advantage of the Community and Institute but cannot without the express leave of the Mother Superior mention out of the meeting what has been discussed thereat.[98]

2nd Each Discreet is to give her opinion candidly and assign with humility her reasons, without affectation, or strong attachment to her own judgment. One of the Discreets shall be appointed by the Mother Superior to write down whatever is agreed on, should it be deemed necessary to do so.[99]

CHAPTER 8 : OF CAPITULAR ASSEMBLIES

1st The Sisters who can vote shall assemble in Chapter as often as the Mother Superior may think it expedient to have their opinion on matters of importance to the Community. They shall assemble every six months to consult on the qualities and dispositions of the Postulants and Novices. They shall also assemble a month before the Postulant be received to the Habit and two months before the Novice is admitted to Profession, to determine by votes on their admission. But should it be notorious before these meetings that the candidate has not the requisite qualities and dispositions for the Institute, she shall be immediately dismissed.[100]

2nd In the Chapter, [they] all shall listen with attention to whatever may be proposed for consideration, weighing well before God every matter in their mind. They shall give their opinion with modesty, candour and humility. In the meetings relative to Postulants and Novices, the Mistress of Novices shall declare what she knows of the temper and disposition of each, their abilities and attachment to the Institute. In all their deliberations, especially respecting the admission or dismissal of Sisters, the vocals shall take great care to divest themselves of all human respect and to have nothing in view but the greater glory of God.[101]

98 Catherine omits "at their meetings" after "propose", and "spiritual and temporal" before "advantage." She also deletes "proposed and" before "discussed," as well as the entire last phrase in the PR: "nor the opinion given by any one, or the subject of their deliberation".

99 Catherine changes "an obstinate attachment" to "strong attachment". She omits "by the Mother Superior Secretary" after "appointed" but Archbishop Murray restored "by the Mother Superior". She substitutes "should it . . . to do so" for the PR wording: "and decided in Chapter, or in the Discretory".

100 Catherine omits "on matters of importance to the Community" (which Archbishop Murray restored), changes "ballot of white and black beans" to "votes" and omits "or dismissal" after "admission." Archbishop Murray added the entire last sentence from the PR, by his indicating "But should it be, etc."

101 Catherine omits "and in silence" after "attention," changes "deliberation" to "consideration," changes "dispositions of the subjects" to "disposition of each," changes "affection

3rd All transactions in chapter shall be kept [inviolable] inviolably secret. They shall begin always with the Hymn "Veni Creator Spiritus" and the prayer "Deus qui corda" with the "Sub tuum praesidium", and close the meeting with the "Salve Regina".[102]

CHAPTER 9 : OF CORRECTION[103]

1st When any of the Sisters shall commit a fault the others shall not reproach her for it. If it be grievous they shall mildly and lovingly give her sisterly reproof three different times as prescribed by the Gospel, after which, should she persist in her fault, the Mother Superior shall be informed of it, but should the fault on account of the scandal or bad consequences which might follow require to be immediately put a stop to, whoever first observes it shall take the advice of the Mother Superior and spiritual director without making known the guilty person until she is desired to do so.[104]

CHAPTER 10 :
OF THE CARE OF THE SICK SISTERS AND SUFFRAGES OF THE DEAD

1st Special care shall be taken of the Sick and proper remedies provided for them according to the prescription of the Physician. The Sisters, particularly the Mother Superior, shall frequently visit them, treat them with the tenderest charity and piously console them. If Death be apprehended, the Mother Superior shall be careful to have the Holy Sacraments administered in due time. The whole community shall attend with lights in their hands at the administration of the Viaticum and Extreme Unction.[105]

for" to "attachment to," and, before the last sentence, omits an entire sentence: "And in the Scrutiny the majority of white or black beans shall decide either their admission or dismissal." She also changes "subjects" to "Sisters", inserts "great" before "care", inserts "greater" before "glory of God", and omits after "God" the phrase, "and the good of the Institute".

102 Catherine omits "*fidelium*" after "*corda*". Archbishop Murray changed her "inviolable" to "inviolably".

103 The chapter, "Of Correction", is chapter 16 in the First Part of the PR; Catherine places it here, near the end of her Second Part, and modifies it considerably.

104 In the first sentence Catherine omits "small" before "fault" and "immediately" before "reproach". She omits the entire second sentence of the PR: "But in case she persist in it, the Mother Superior shall be apprized of it." In her next sentence she omits "and secret" after "grievous"; changes "this secret grievous fault" to simply, "the fault"; changes "attend it" to "follow"; omits "mentioning, or" before "making known"; and changes "be advised" to "is desired". She also omits the entire last sentence of the PR: "If the grievous fault be notorious, the Sister who knows it shall immediately give notice of it to the Mother Superior."

105 Catherine follows article 1 of the PR except that she deletes "in the Lord" after "console them", substitutes "If Death be apprehended" for "If danger be apprehended", and deletes the entire last clause of the article: "and from the time the sick person shall be declared to be in danger of death, the Sisters shall watch alternately two hours each, and assist her with their prayers, and pious exhortations."

2nd On the Death of a Sister, the Office for the Dead shall be said by the Sisters for the repose of her soul and three Masses, and three general Communions, shall be offered for her. Should the Mother Superior die in office six Masses shall be offered for her.[106]

CHAPTER 11 : ON ESTABLISHMENTS

1st As the Sisters of this holy Institute are devoted to the Poor from whom they cannot receive any temporal emolument and as they are strictly forbidden to take lodgers, no new Establishment shall be undertaken unless a certain revenue adequate to its support be duly ascertained and approved of by the Bishop and by the Discreets of the Convent.[107]

We declare it is not our intention that these rules and constitutions compiled for the Religious Sisters of Mercy shall oblige under pain of mortal or venial sin, only in as much as the transgression of any article may be a violation of the vows and in itself a sin independently of the rule.[108]

106 Catherine makes minor changes in the first sentence, including the deletion of "(as in the Lady's Primer)" after "Office for the Dead". She also deletes the entire third and fourth sentences of this article in the PR: "As soon as the account be received of the death of a Sister of this Religious Institute in any other House of the Order, one Mass with a general Communion shall be offered up for her soul. The Office of the Dead shall be said in common on every Sunday for the Souls in Purgatory, particularly for the friends and benefactors of this Religious Institute" (p. 38).

107 Catherine alters the initial wording of the PR which reads as follows: "As the Sisters of this holy Institute are entirely devoted to the instruction of the poor, for which they can receive no temporal emolument . . . ." She also deletes "or Boarders" after "lodgers," and changes "adequate to the support of the Sisters, who undertake it" to "adequate to its support".

108 This paragraph is exactly as it appears in the PR except that Catherine substitutes "Sisters of Mercy" for "Congregation of the Sisters of Charitable Instruction". Clare Moore did not conclude her fair copy with this paragraph, but Archbishop Murray used the wording in it for his declaration of approval, written at the end of each fair copy.

Epilogue

When one wishes to understand the basic orientation of an individual human life, one searches not just for traits of temperament but for indirect revelations of something deeper: the characteristic images, actions, and vocabulary which expose the inner shape and direction of the life in question. One seeks to discover the order of priority in that life: the arrangement of concerns and relationships which direct and energize it. One wishes to locate, if possible, the person's *character*: the perspective and intention underlying, and resulting from, her attachments and detachments, her activities and passivities. In this quasi-archeological search among the fragments of a particular human life, its riches and poverties, one is grateful for the concrete: those specific graspable realities that somehow represent the contours of that life and, in so doing, illuminate its intangible or less tangible aspects. One is glad for these tokens which seem to connect and gather to a concentration not all but much of the meaning and intention of that life. Of course such symbols do not summarize the life completely, but they do open up, to the understanding of those who wish to appreciate that life, key aspects of the inner journey of the person in question.

Such is the promise of the "affectionate" closings of Catherine McAuley's letters to her sisters, her nightly care of Mary Ann Redmond (after the amputation of her leg), the chapter of her Rule on the "Visitation of the Sick", the poverty of her community on Baggot Street, her persistent desire to build a commercial laundry to provide financial support for the poor women and girls in the House of Mercy, her repeated use of the words "comfort" and "console", her deliberate reference to Jesus' claim: "I have come to cast fire upon the earth" (Luke 12.49), her abiding memory of "dejected faces", and, at the very end, her disposal of her homemade boots, and her asking for the blessed candle to be placed in her hand. I would like to dwell briefly on the last four of these symbols of Catherine McAuley's life.

Of the English postulants preparing in Dublin, Catherine once wrote, evidently thinking of Luke 12.49: "They renew my poor spirit greatly—five creatures fit to adorn society coming forward joyfully to consecrate themselves to the service of the poor for Christ's sake. This is some of the fire He cast on the earth—kindling" (226). About two months before, she had used the same scriptural reference to describe them. As her letters, her Rule, and the biographical documents presented in this volume reveal, Catherine evidently felt moved by a deep personal vocation, however intuitive and unself-conscious, to be herself a maternal and sisterly "kindling" in her world of what she understood to be the tender fire of Jesus Christ's merciful purpose: "by bearing some resemblance to him"; by receiving and going out to meet him and love him in the poor and distressed; by suffering in solidarity with them; and by being for them, in God's name, the instruction, visitation, protection, and consolation which she believed God desired for them. All the stories of her life seem to embody this simple merciful fire: her ardent self-donation to those she loved and served, and her passionate commitment to the merciful, life-bestowing tasks she felt God asked of her.

For Catherine could not forget the faces of those in need. She seems always to have put herself in the position of those who suffer and to have felt their suffering as her own. In November 1840 she wrote in sorrow to Catherine Meagher in Naas about the widespread unemployment in Dublin and her inability to house a young woman whom Catherine Meagher wished to send to Baggot Street for shelter:

> I . . . regret exceedingly that it is impossible to admit the young person. We are always crowded to excess at this season [50–60 in the House of Mercy]—so many leaving Dublin, dismissing servants and few engaging any. We have every day most sorrowful applications from interesting young creatures, confectioners and dressmakers, who, at this season, cannot get employment, and are quite unprotected. I am sure I spoke with two yesterday who were hungry, tho' of nice appearance. Their dejected faces have been before me ever since. I was afraid of hurting their feelings by offering them food and had no money. (255–6)

Similarly, at the height of the Kingstown (Dún Laoghaire) crisis in late 1838, when the convent and poor school there had to close because of lack of funds—a £450 bill (later, a lawsuit) was wrongfully hanging over her head because in donating £50 (the entire proceeds from a bazaar) toward the renovation of two buildings for the school, she had allegedly incurred the entire cost—she wrote to Mary Teresa White in Kingstown:

> Do not be afflicted for your poor, their Heavenly Father will provide comfort for them. . . . He will not be displeased with me, because He knows I would rather be cold and hungry than the poor in Kingstown or elsewhere should be deprived of any consolation in our power to afford. (142–3)

Here Catherine was seeing again the "dejected faces" of those for whom she had desired to build a poor school in Kingstown in the first place: "the poor girls whom we every day saw loitering about the roads in a most neglected state" (86–7).

But the distinctive orientation of Catherine McAuley's life reveals itself not only in her characteristic mercifulness but also, and intimately related to this, in her persistent confidence in God's will, care, help, and protection—the mystery which she called the "Providence of God" or God's "Providential Guidance".

Catherine had made her own the strong Hebraic faith in divine providence which is presupposed in the New Testament. She was confident that in and through their personal histories God leads human beings toward the final reign of love, tenderly maintaining this movement by directing, caring for, and bestowing life upon God's beloved people. Moreover, she was convinced that the reality of God's constant care is definitively proclaimed in the mercifulness of Jesus, as manifested in his life, death, and resurrection. Thus God's providence was for her the hidden but sure presence of God's merciful care in all human moments, even the most painful, and the trustworthy mode of God's intimate, active engagement in the forward journeys of all human lives, including her own. She had this in mind when, in the "Universal Prayer", she prayed daily:

> I adore thee as my first beginning. I aspire after thee as my last end. I give thee thanks as my constant benefactor. I call upon thee as my sovereign protector. Vouchsafe, O my God, to conduct me by thy wisdom, to restrain me by thy justice, to comfort me by thy mercy, to defend me by thy power.[1]

In Catherine's thinking there was a direct correlation between her awareness of the continuing presence in the world of the "Cross of Christ" and her resolute confidence in the accompanying providence of God—a correlation which enabled her to be profoundly sensitive both to human suffering and to God's life-giving participation in that very suffering.

A year before she died, Catherine had rejoiced, in a letter to Catherine Leahy in Galway, that, at last, homemade boots were being made at Baggot Street:

> They have lately made some very nice cloth boots, and got them soled and capped with leather. When finished they do not cost quite 4 shillings. Dear Sister M. de Sales [White] commenced the work and it now goes on rapidly. They are exceedingly neat and warm—any kind of stocking will do. I have been long recommending these homemade boots, both for neatness and economy. (254)

Catherine's wanting inexpensive shoes was in keeping with her desire to live in solidarity with the circumstances of the poor, and to direct whatever financial resources the community had to the works of mercy. As the Bermondsey annalist notes, when she initially planned the daily schedule of the Baggot Street community, she deliberately omitted—contrary to the custom in other religious orders—a period of recreation after the noonday meal, "intending, as she said, that we should labour all day like the poor, and have our rest and recreation after our work was finished." She had the same attitude toward her homemade shoes.

The final collapse of Catherine's health is recorded in nearly all of the biographical documents written by her earliest associates, but the letters of Mary Vincent Whitty and Elizabeth Moore, who were present when Catherine died, and certain pages in the Limerick Manuscript which incorporate Elizabeth Moore's recollections, are apparently the only extant (or discovered) eyewitness accounts of her last days. The Limerick Manuscript describes Catherine's gradual surrender to death as she approached her final personal encounter with the mystery of God's providence:

> The pressure of the many works of charity in which she had been hitherto incessantly engaged had left traces upon a constitution which never was very strong. The numberless cares and troubles attending the foundation of so many houses; the fatiguing journeys to which she was necessarily subjected; and the obligation of providing all things necessary for the efficient working of the several communities, were enough to break down a constitution much stronger than hers.

She endured very frequent and violent pain in the stomach, perhaps the beginning of that disease which terminated her existence. She was also subject to inflammatory attacks, accompanied by extreme soreness in her mouth, yet she would go on reading the public lectures, and reciting the Office until absolutely incapable of uttering a word; in truth she never spared herself and sought alleviation from her pains only when forced to do so; during the last year of her life her sufferings were great.

On her return from Birmingham [September 21, 1841] it was perceived by the debility and exhaustion under which she was laboring, that the term of her usefulness was drawing to a close. After struggling with her increasing infirmity some time, she was at length obliged to confine herself to her room.

Throughout her life Catherine had prayed two different "Thirty Days Prayers"—one of them "To Our Blessed Redeemer, In Honour of His Bitter Passion"—when she established new foundations of the Sisters of Mercy, and when she felt in particular need of God's help. As Clare Moore says:

Whenever she was in doubt or difficulty she had recourse to prayer and the Thirty Days' Prayer as long as I knew her was the means by which she obtained all she wanted. She used always say it with *entire confidence of* obtaining what she asked. (September 1, 1844)

Now, when she was nearing death, the words of the prayer to the Redeemer must have been even more profoundly important to her, as she contemplated her own final act of confidence in God's providence:

. . . By the anguish thou enduredst when, the time of thy designed passion drawing nigh, thou prayedst to thy eternal Father, that if it were possible that bitter chalice might pass away from thee, yet concluding with a most perfect act of resignation, Not my will, but thine be done. . . .

By all those sorrows, joys, passions, compassions, and whatsoever else is dear to thee in heaven and on earth, take pity on me, O compassionate Redeemer! . . . Give me, O gracious Saviour, speedily to experience thy divine succour and comfort, who, according to the accustomed sweetness of thy tender heart, art wont to grant the requests of those who fear and love thee, even to their soul's desire and satisfaction; bestow on me also, O blessed Jesus, a constant faith, a firm hope, a perfect charity, a true contrition . . . a zealous imitation of thy exemplary life and conversation, an entire accomplishment of my vows . . . a willing readiness to die for thy love and honour, a final perseverance in grace and good works. . . .[2]

What occurred during Catherine's last days, as the eyewitness accounts indicate, was the gradual conversion of her active confidence in God's providence into deeper, more passive, surrender to that faithful presence. Her attachment to the merciful work she had felt called to do and to her co-workers was slowly transformed into detachment from her role and contribution, and from her very life. She made herself more and more unnecessary to the future of the community and service she had founded and inspired. Thus the final distinctive feature of her life was abandonment of herself and of all that was dear to her to the care and protection of God. As Mary Vincent Whitty wrote on Friday, November 12: "I do not think she made any arrangements, wished for any thing to be done or given to anyone. Indeed she looked the picture of entire abandonment of herself and all that belonged to her into the hands of God."

Catherine McAuley died about ten minutes to eight in the evening on Thursday, November 11, 1841. Early that morning she disposed of her home-made shoes in a quiet but definitive gesture which has rich symbolic import as a revelation of her character. She had established an unenclosed religious order of women—"walking nuns", as they were popularly called—one of whose chief purposes was to visit the poor, the sick, and the dying in their own homes and in hospitals. She had urged her associates, and herself, to go forward through the streets to those in need, "as if they expected to meet their Divine Redeemer in each poor habitation" (Rule 3.6). But now, as Elizabeth Moore records:

> On Wednesday night or rather Thursday morning about two o'clock she called for a piece of paper and twine, tied up her boots and desired them to be put in the fire. The Sister to whom she gave them did not know what they were but had directions to remain at the fire till all was consumed.

This simple gesture of quietly burning her boots in the middle of the night stands as a remarkable symbol of Catherine's final abandonment of herself to the providence of God. In this act of self-surrender she accepted the end of her walking, she relinquished her historical work as a Sister of Mercy, and she turned barefoot toward the God who stood before her in death. Like Moses who removed his sandals before the burning bush (Exod. 3.5), and Joshua who put off his sandals before the messenger of God (Josh. 5.15), Catherine McAuley deliberately and reverently entered the holy encounter of her death.

*

About five o'clock in the evening on November 11, 1841, Catherine "asked for the candle to be placed in her hand," and "we commenced the last prayers." This candle remains the final, fitting symbol of her attitude toward her own death, and life. She had once told her young community that their lives should be like the noiseless burning of a pure candle:

> How silently and brilliantly the lamp in the sanctuary burns . . . when the oil is pure and good; it is only when it is otherwise that it twinkles and makes noise. (Limerick Manuscript)

Now, in the last hours of her life, she reached for the blessed candle, the ancient symbol of the presence of the risen Christ. How long she was able to hold it is not known, but her positive gesture of reaching for it marks her final, decisive turning toward the merciful God in whose providence she had always confided.

In grasping this candle, she left behind, to the care of God and of her "darling" companions, all that she had created and animated. With the total self-abandonment that is the final act of true Christian self-possession she surrendered herself and her life's work to the mysterious Easter consummation who is Christ, without claim or ceremony.

Appendix 1

REDMOND O'HANLON, ODC

After the chapel of the house on Baggot Street was dedicated on June 4, 1829, Daniel Murray appointed Daniel Burke OSF as chaplain to the community, and Redmond J. O'Hanlon ODC (1789–1864) as confessor. Daniel Burke remained affiliated in this capacity until late 1837 when he was reassigned to accompany Bishop Patrick R. Griffith to Cape Colony, Africa. Redmond O'Hanlon remained confessor to the community until his death in February 1864.[1] However, his exact relationship with Catherine McAuley and the first Sisters of Mercy appears to have been much more than this, although it is not clear whether his additional service was formally assigned or informally assumed, or whether, strictly speaking, it pertained only to assisting Catherine in her responsibilities as founder, or to assisting the whole Institute.

The copy of the Rule and Constitutions of the Sisters of Mercy which was prepared in the mid to late 1830s—after Daniel Murray's revision of Catherine McAuley's manuscript—designates the diocesan bishop as the ecclesiastical superior of the congregation, but provides for the episcopal appointment of a priest to serve as his deputy if the bishop himself cannot give the requisite time to this role. The priest is to be one on whose "prudence, piety and experience" the bishop "can depend to govern and direct under him and to whom he will give the necessary faculties" (II.1.1). Catherine had not initially transcribed this chapter ("Of the Superior and the Visitation of the Convent") beyond its first paragraph, to which she had added a revised sentence from the second paragraph. The complete second paragraph in the text finally approved by Daniel Murray reads as follows:

> The Priest thus appointed shall duly attend to the government and good order of the Community in spirituals and temporals; he shall watch over the exact observance of the Constitutions for the purpose of maintaining good order, peace and charity, and shall also assist the Mother Superior with his advice in all weighty matters. Nothing of moment shall be attempted by her without consulting him, nor any matter of importance relating to the House or Community be undertaken without the consent of the Bishop. (II.1.2)

The priest so designated is also charged with visiting the convent "every year, in the third week of January"—unless the bishop does so himself—"to examine whether the Rules and Constitutions be exactly observed, the obligations of the Institute duly fulfilled, and whether the Sisters live in perfect harmony, union and charity" (II.1.4). Archbishop Murray required the inclusion of this entire chapter in the Rule and Constitutions, presumably to put the document in conformity with prescriptions preferred in Rome and with provisions of the already confirmed Presentation Rule.

However, after the founding of the Institute in December 1831, Archbishop Murray himself does not appear to have ever acted personally in so meticulous and formal a way as the six articles of this chapter seem to require. When Catherine and the community were asked in April 1832 to take charge of nursing in the cholera depot on Townsend Street she formally applied to Archbishop Murray for permission to do so. He came immediately to Baggot Street to meet with her and the community and give them his permission, at the same time suggesting that they "take great nourishment, port wine and mutton chops" (which, as Clare Moore observes, "was literally obeyed for a week or two, when it was found to be too troublesome"). But there is no clear indication that he ever personally examined "the accounts of the annual receipts and disbursements, signed by the Mother Superior and the Bursar" (II.1.6). He "visited" the convent every time he presided at a ceremony for reception of the habit or profession of vows, but the character of these visits probably did not amount to the formal Visitation envisioned by this chapter of the Rule and Constitutions.

The question which arises then is whether, in the first decade, Daniel Murray appointed a priest to act in these matters on his behalf. If he did, the probable candidate would seem to be Redmond O'Hanlon. No other priest was so consistently involved in the daily workings of the community. No other priest so regularly participated in Catherine's decisions, such as those about new foundations or the placement of sisters who were ill. He is, in fact, more frequently mentioned in Catherine's extant letters than any other priest.

While none of the documentation consulted for this study explicitly states that Redmond O'Hanlon was formally appointed to the supervisory role described in the Rule and Constitutions, this possibility is not automatically ruled out. Given the gentle style of both Daniel Murray and Redmond O'Hanlon, such an appointment may actually have been the technical arrangement, even though it does not adequately describe the manner of O'Hanlon's relation to Catherine or to the community. In view of the way his helpfulness is described in Catherine's correspondence and in the eyewitness accounts of her life, one may reasonably conclude that Redmond O'Hanlon's role was a far more informal one, though also a far larger and more important one, than that of episcopally-designated ecclesiastical superior, even if in some low-keyed sense he *was* so appointed as Archbishop Murray's deputy.[2]

The documentation in Mercy archives for the period, 1827–1841, suggests that in addition to his service to the Baggot Street community as confessor, Redmond O'Hanlon devoted himself, with her full gratitude and confidence, to the role of advisor to Catherine herself; that he did so unobtrusively, with evident respect for her personal authority and for her more formal relationships with Archbishop Murray and the other bishops in whose dioceses she arranged new foundations; and that his service in this capacity increased as the foundations beyond Dublin became more numerous and as Catherine's health simultaneously began to decline. In assuming this role he may have offered Catherine what no member of her own community initially could have offered, or offered so effectively: he confidentially counseled with her about leadership decisions; he helped her to say No, when she was pressed beyond her own or the community's resources by requests she could not meet; he advised her on ecclesiastical matters; he helped her anxious assistant, Mary de Pazzi Delany, when Catherine was away on foundations; and he defended her own physical well-being when she was inclined to neglect it. Mary Bertrand Degnan interprets his relation to Catherine and the community as that of "spiritual director of the Institute" (177, 307). This may well be the proper designation, although perhaps not in the full modern sense of the term. Catherine's correspondence does not speak of his helpfulness to her in precisely this way, but given her personal reserve, one would not expect her to have told others who it was from whom she was seeking and receiving spiritual direction in her own religious life. Roland Burke Savage calls him simply, "her ever faithful counsellor" (305).

Redmond O'Hanlon was seventeen when he was received into the Carmelites in 1806; he studied in Spain, and was ordained in Dublin in 1809. A member of the Discalced Carmelite priory at St. Teresa's Church on Clarendon Street, he was from 1826 to 1856 either provincial or prior of the community—except for three years (1829–1832) when Francis L'Estrange was provincial, for part of which time O'Hanlon was in Rome, and for one year (1838–1839) when he had just completed two terms as prior.[3]

All the early biographical accounts of Catherine's life speak of the generous association of the Dublin Carmelites, both Calced and Discalced, with the Baggot Street community.[4] Mary Ann Doyle writes: "We had much consolation in the support and kindness which the Revd. gentlemen of St. Teresa's Church always evinced for the establishment, particularly the Very Revd. R. O'Hanlon." Clare Moore, speaking of the death of Caroline Murphy (June 28, 1831), says:

> Revd. Mr. O'Hanlon heard her general confession and assisted at her death. He read the last prayers for her. As we had then no Habit she was buried in the brown Carmelite Habit of the 3rd Order. . . the Carmelite Priests of Clarendon St. were very kind to us—among other things, Revd. Mr. O'Hanlon and (when he was at Rome for some months) Revd. Mr. Whelan (now Bishop of Bombay) came regularly every week to hear the Sisters' confessions. They supplied us with Vestments and every thing almost for the Altar, and continued for nearly 3 years to *give* altar breads, Incense, charcoal and other things. . . . The good Priests of Clarendon St. also allowed us a place in their principal Vault where only Priests were allowed to be interred before, under the Altar.

But in the earliest days Redmond O'Hanlon did more for the women on Baggot Street than hear their confessions or assist them as they died. He was, apparently, especially vigilant about their health while Catherine was at George's Hill, and tried to direct them away from dangerous, self-chosen forms of mortification unsuited to their young age and their daily duties. Clare Augustine Moore, who also did not favor such practices, recounts Catherine's worry during her absence and O'Hanlon's watchfulness on her behalf:

> She was . . . anxious about the Sisters who were left at Baggot St. Sister Marianne Delany had been left in charge of the household affairs and of the duties of the Institute, but . . . everyone mismanaged her own spiritualities in her own way. One took to fasting, another took the discipline, another slept in haircloth, while a fourth and fifth thought proper to remain up half the night at their prayers. To this last piece of perfection, however, Fr. O'Hanlon put a stop. I am not sure whether it was he or Fr. Burke, who having to go late at night to Upper Baggot Street saw lights in the cells, but it was he who came the next day to forbid it, and went to George's Hill to tell the foundress, who also forbid it. Moreover, he and Fr. Burke made it a point to walk round the house of odd nights just after 10 to see that all the lights were out.

O'Hanlon had earlier exerted some influence in Catherine's decision to begin a religious congregation: as Clare Augustine Moore says, "Dr. Blake was urging her and dear Fr. O'Hanlon managing it, and in fact I may say he did manage to bring her to the point. All along he had it in view." Now, in 1830–1831, he did what he could to carry her messages from George's Hill to Baggot Street, though upon her return in December 1831, he withdrew to a much more subordinate role.

Catherine's letters and the early eyewitness accounts indicate that Redmond O'Hanlon accompanied the founding parties to Tullamore (1836), Galway (1840), and Birmingham (1841), and that over the years he visited the Carlow, Charleville, Limerick, Birr, Cork, and Tullamore communities. He was instrumental in urging Catherine to let Mary de Chantal McCann, then a novice, offer her inheritance as a widow to purchase a house in Kingstown (Dún Laoghaire) as a rest home for sick sisters, and he helped to procure a £1000 legacy with which Catherine built the public laundry on Baggot Street. By 1838 he had become so enthusiastic a proponent of new foundations that on August 23 Catherine wrote to Frances Warde:

> Mr. O'Hanlon is just returned from Cork, Charleville and Tullamore and is pleased beyond every expectation. When we said, oh not in Carlow! he said that that was his *first* visit last year. He never was such an advocate for founding as he is now, so that I do not mention to him where we are asked, for fear he would be pressing what cannot be done. We are very near a Stop—I should say a full Stop. Feet and hands are numerous enough, but the heads are nearly gone. (132)

But on the eve of the founding party's departure for Bermondsey in late 1839, he was sufficiently "alarmed at the angry things which are said in the English papers" that, as Catherine wrote, "He gave me 10,000 cautions yesterday" (Bolster, ed. 105).

Catherine regarded Redmond O'Hanlon as "our ever dear good Father" (376). When serious illness struck the Wexford community in February 1841, she wrote to Frances Warde:

> Please God it will not end in death. I feel very anxious to hear, and Mr. O'Hanlon will expect me to let him know. His care and anxiety for us all increases every day. He said yesterday: "This is my fourteenth year amongst you." (306–7)

And when the chaplaincy controversy was at its height in December 1837, Catherine wrote to John Hamilton, archdeacon of the Dublin diocese, about O'Hanlon's long years of unpaid service as confessor. To explain her perspective on the complaints brought against her by Walter Meyler, parish priest of St. Andrew's (who wished her to increase the chaplain's salary), she recounted exactly what O'Hanlon had given to and received from the Baggot Street community:

> It is said that we all dislike the Parish Clergy—God forbid—and that we give freely elsewhere. Indeed, Reverend Sir, I should fear that God would be displeased with my ingratitude, did I not declare that Mr. O'Hanlon has been the most generous friend, and that all he ever received for his nine years' constant attendance—often every day for two weeks preparing for Profession—was thirty-two pounds (£32) in different sums from the Sisters—to get Mass for them etc., etc. In all, the entire sum—£32—in nine years. (Bolster, ed. 44)

In addition to his other kindnesses, Redmond O'Hanlon was always solicitous that those who were sick had a change of air. He was especially so towards Catherine herself, though she could not always accede to his advice. In the last year of her life he clearly sensed the seriousness of her fatigue and increasing debility. His willingness to accompany the founding party to Birmingham in late August 1841, and to go in Catherine's stead to fetch the two sisters who had been temporarily loaned to the Bermondsey community is evidence that he interpreted her cough and weakness correctly. When they returned from Birmingham it was he who urged her to consult an eminent Dublin physician, and to curtail her normal community activities. In her most explicit account of her own last illness, written in late September 1841 to Mary Aloysius Scott in Birr (who also suffered from a disease of the chest), Catherine puts a realistic but humorously cheerful face on the situation, while noting O'Hanlon's interventions:

> My cough very variable, one night bad, another good. Five minutes in a room with a window ever so little open brings on an hour's coughing . . . yet I am not weak, tho' I cannot say I have any appetite. Mr. O'Hanlon particularly requested I would consult Dr. Stokes. I have seen him twice. On his first visit he looked like a person who had made a great discovery. On his second, Mother de Pazzi conducted him out and returned with such sorrow in her countenance that I entreated her to tell me his opinion. My right lung was "diseased". I have now less confidence than ever in the faculty [the medical profession] and you know my stock was small enough. I do not think my lung is affected. I am now dead to the poor children—not to read, speak, give out Office, etc. I tell you all these particulars to give you the benefit of experience. If my lung is actually engaged, the progress will not be checked, and the fact of no debility, not half so much as I have had when my gums were inflamed, shews that it cannot be. . . .
>
> As we should carefully examine the motive of our actions, I here humbly confess that my chief motive just now is to shew that one of the most distinguished amongst our medical professors may be mistaken and that we should not immediately take up their opinions. . . .
>
> I should add that it was not the Dr. desired me not read, etc. It was Fr. O'Hanlon. The Dr. in a melancholy tone left me to my own wishes. . . . (375–6)[5]

William Stokes (1804–1878) had earned an M.D. degree at Edinburgh in 1825. In 1837 he had published an acclaimed work, *A Treatise on the Diagnosis and Treatment of Diseases of the Chest.* In 1839, Trinity College, Dublin, had also conferred on him an M.D. degree, and the King and Queen's College of Physicians in Ireland had elected him a Fellow (Fitzgerald 1:268–70).[6] Hence, the possibility that Dr. Stokes might "be mistaken" was not high.

One further, and very private, aspect of Catherine McAuley's personal life is related to Redmond O'Hanlon: her apparent use of instruments of penance, as evidenced in her disposal of them during the night before she died. Catherine had always counseled her sisters that the duties, labors, and fatigues of their way of life were their chief physical mortifications, and that "the perfection of the religious soul depends, not so much on doing extraordinary actions, as on doing extraordinarily well the ordinary actions and exercises of every day" (Rule 5.1). While she had apparently suggested that they mortify their taste in some inconspicuous way at each meal, she had also insisted that they maintain their health and that the daily demands of true union and charity were the most effective austerities God asked of them. Why then did she herself, perhaps only in the last year or years of her life, use, if she did, the haircloth, the discipline, the shoes studded with nails, or the chain mentioned in various early documents? The reported "nails" in the shoes might be simply explained as the unintended effect of the cobbler's putting leather soles on her handmade stocking-boots and of her own extensive walking, but what of the other instruments?

It seems clear that Catherine would not have chosen to use such means of bodily penance without consulting her confessor, and in the last decade of her life Redmond O'Hanlon evidently fulfilled that role for her. One can not presume to formulate her reasons for making this request, or his reasons for granting it, but surely her use of such an instrument or instruments, if it was requested and granted, was intended to be forever unknown, and was in some way related to the personal responsibility she must have felt she bore as founder of the Sisters of Mercy. One might speak of possible motives: her deep-rooted humility, her sorrow for her faults, her grief before the passion of Jesus Christ, her thorough dependence on God's providence, and her belief that the weaknesses of the community were caused by her own failings, but to do so is to presume to enter the privacy of her conversations with Redmond O'Hanlon. From all we know of him and of her, these conversations and the decisions they reached would have been utterly simple and prayerful.

Catherine had always wished that when her own death came she might be "laid in the earth like the poor"—not for sentimental reasons, but to avoid, as the poor must, what seemed to her the unnecessary expense of the sturdier coffin which interment in church vaults required (Carroll, *Life* 438). She had often spoken of this when sisters died at Baggot Street and were interred in St. Teresa's Church. Seeing that her death was near, Redmond O'Hanlon evidently acted on her wish, as Mary Vincent Whitty reports on November 12, 1841: "I believe I told you of Mr. O'Hanlon's having a Cemetery formed in the garden immediately after his return from Birmingham. It is to be consecrated & we will have her laid here near us."

To the end Redmond O'Hanlon stood by Catherine McAuley. He anointed her, visited her on the day she died, and sang the Requiem Mass for her burial on Monday, November 15, 1841. In countless unobtrusive ways, over fourteen years, he had eased her burdens and done helpful things for her—like telling her on a lovely March day in 1841 to "take off the cloak and drive out to Booterstown" for some refreshing air (Neumann 313). Though he was, from 1832 on, prior of the Carmelite community at Saint Teresa's for all but one year, he still found time—and "prudence, piety and experience"—to assist her. The first decade of the Sisters of Mercy would have been considerably more difficult had it not been for his unassuming presence and help.

Appendix 2

CATHERINE McAULEY'S READING AND PRAYERS

Listed here are books on the spiritual life and prayer books which Catherine McAuley is known to have read. Each title is explicitly mentioned in the early biographical manuscripts written about her.[1] Since most of these books were reprinted numerous times, often over centuries, I do not give the dates of publication, but rather the dates of the authors or editors, where these names are known, and, in the case of works not originally published in English, the date of *an* English translation which I have been able to examine and which, in most cases, was published prior to Catherine's death:

Abbé Barthélemy Baudrand SJ (1701–1787). *Elevation of the Soul to God* (Dublin: Richard Grace, 1833), and *The Soul on Calvary, meditating on The Sufferings of Jesus Christ* (Dublin: Catholic Book Society, 1840). This edition of *Elevation of the Soul* is revised and corrected by Francis J. L'Estrange ODC (1788–1833), Prior (1826–29) and Provincial (1829–32) of the Discalced Carmelites, Clarendon Street, Dublin.

Francis Blyth ODC (1705?–1772). *A Devout Paraphrase on the Seven Penitential Psalms; or, A Practical Guide to Repentance* (Dublin: Catholic Book Society, 1835).

Louis Bourdaloue SJ (1632–1704). *Spiritual Retreat* (Dublin: Printed by E. M'Donnel, 1810).

Alban Butler (1710–1773). *The Lives of the Fathers, Martyrs, and Other Principal Saints* (Dublin: James Duffy, 1866). 12 vols.

Joseph Joy Dean (–   ), ed. *Devotions to the Sacred Heart of Jesus* (Dublin: Printed by Chambers and Hallagan, 1820). Catherine McAuley's own copy of this edition is in the archives of the Sisters of Mercy, Limerick.

William A. Gahan OSA (1730–1804). *The Christian's Guide to Heaven; or, A Complete Manual of Catholic Piety* (Dublin: Printed by T. M'Donnel, 1804).

John Gother (–1704). *The Sinner's Complaints to God* (Dublin: Hoey, 1792).

Louis of Granada OP (1505–1588). *The Sinner's Guide* (Dublin: Printed by Richard Coyne, 1820).

A Journal of Meditations for Every Day in the Year; Gathered out of Divers Authors (London, 1630, and Dublin: Reprinted by Richard Coyne, 1823). Catherine McAuley's own copy of this edition is in the archives of the Sisters of Mercy, Tullamore.

Thomas à Kempis (1380?–1471). *The Imitation of Christ* (Dublin: Catholic Book Society, 1834). The copy of this edition of the *Imitation,* translated from a French edition by Bishop Richard Challoner (1691–1781), which Catherine McAuley gave to Mary de Pazzi Delany is in the archives of the Sisters of Mercy, Bermondsey (London).

Alphonsus Mary Liguori (1696–1787). *Visits to the Most Holy Sacrament* (Dublin: James Duffy, n.d.).

Alonsus Rodriguez SJ (1526–1616). *The Practice of Christian and Religious Perfection* (Kilkenny: John Reynolds, 1806). 3 vols.

Ursula Young OSU (1783–1830). *The Soul United to Jesus in the Adorable Sacrament; or, Devout Methods of Hearing Mass Before and After Communion.* An edition of this book is contained in Volume I of *Duffy's Standard Library of Catholic Divinity* (1883).[2]

To this list may be added at least some of the transcribed books in the Dublin archives, some of which were presumably copied under Catherine's direction. A complete listing of all early Mercy transcriptions (1827–1841) will eventually also include some of the transcribed books in Mercy archives elsewhere in Ireland and in England, some of which were probably copied at Baggot Street during Catherine's lifetime and given to the respective communities at the time of their founding.

Among the transcriptions in the Dublin archives are the following. In all but one case (Augustine Baker), the authors of the works listed below are not given in the transcriptions, and most of these authors have not yet been positively identified. Except for the three books listed by author, I have not yet located published editions of these works. In some of the transcriptions it is evident, or one suspects, that the original books, or at least parts of them, have been abridged or only partially transcribed:

Augustine Baker OSB (1575–1641). *Sancta Sophia.* First Part and Second Part.

Jean Pierre Camus. *The Spirit of St. Francis de Sales.* First published in 1726.

Discourses on the Sacred and Immaculate Heart of Mary.

An Easy Method of Prayer Reduced to Practice.

Letter from a Carthusian Priest: On Zeal for Souls.

Life of Saint Catharine of Sienna.

Michel-Ange Marin. *The Perfect Religious.* Translated from the French, 1845.

On the Three Vows.

Spiritual Maxims, or An Abridgement of the Interior Life.[3]

Notes

NOTES TO INTRODUCTION

1 "Catherine McAuley's Theological and Literary Debt to Alonso Rodriguez," in *Recusant History* 20 (May 1990): 81–105, and "Catherine McAuley's Spiritual Reading and Prayers," in *Irish Theological Quarterly* 57 (1991): 124–46.

2 Congregatio de Causis Sanctorum. "*Decretum Dublinen. Canonizationis Servae Dei Catharinae McAuley, Fundatricis Congregationis Sororum a Misericordia (1778–1841).*" I am grateful to Mary Angela Bolster RSM, Vice-Postulator for the Cause of Canonization of Catherine McAuley, for a copy of this Decree.

NOTES TO CHAPTER 1

A Chronology of Catherine McAuley's Life

1 In preparing this chronology I have consulted the biographies of Catherine McAuley written by Mary Vincent Harnett, Mary Austin Carroll, Roland Burke Savage, Mary Bertrand Degnan, and Mary Angela Bolster; the chronology compiled by Mary Angela Bolster in the *Documentary Study* (1:xvi–xliv); and the published letters of Catherine McAuley, as edited by Mary Ignatia Neumann *(Letters)* and Mary Angela Bolster (*Correspondence*). I am particularly grateful for the research recorded in the notes accompanying Degnan's biography and Neumann's *Letters,* and for the detailed research presented in the text and notes of Bolster's *Documentary Study,* vols. 1 and 2. However, I have also consulted the handwritten and the illuminated Registers of various early communities of Sisters of Mercy, especially those at Baggot Street, Dublin; the early biographical manuscripts about Catherine McAuley which are presented below in the present volume; the Annals of various early Mercy communities; and numerous autographs of Catherine's letters, of many of which I have obtained photocopies.

Inevitably, given the multiplicity of handwritten sources, a few discrepancies have occurred over the years, between various unpublished and published works. While I have not been able to resolve these completely, I have tried to base my choice of dates on my best assessment of the evidence. Where I give a date or other information which differs from that previously published I have been guided by data in the earliest manuscript sources, Registers, and autograph letters. I have not, however, noted every instance where my date differs from that in a particular published work, nor have I always cited my reasons for giving the particular date I give. While these instances are relatively very few in number, readers familiar with the published works may note the discrepancies, and so I offer this explanation of my method in preparing this chronology.

To illustrate the problems, let me note two random examples. First, the important letter which Catherine wrote from Birmingham to Teresa Carton at Baggot Street was not written on September 8, 1841, as in Neumann (373), but on September 6, as in Bolster (256–7). The autograph letter, in the archives of the Sisters of Mercy, Dublin, is dated, and the earlier date makes possible Bolster's correct reading of a later part of this very fragile autograph. (Neither published text, however, corresponds exactly with the autograph.) Similarly, the obituary notice for William Callaghan, printed in the *Dublin Evening Post* on Thursday, November 14, 1822 (quoted in Burke Savage 40–1), indicates correctly that he died on November 10, as in Neumann (49), not on November 11, as in Carroll (109).

I have included in this chronology some dates associated with members of Catherine's family and some of her closest friends, as well as certain dates associated with the women who are the authors or principal sources of the biographical manuscripts published in this volume. These men and women played important roles in Catherine's life, and she cherished her relationships with them. The dates associated with Catherine's parents, siblings, and brother-in-law cannot always be verified directly because of the absence or destruction of some records; hence, they may be inaccurate as listed here.

2 There are two published editions of Catherine McAuley's letters: *The Letters of Catherine McAuley,* edited by Mary Ignatia Neumann (1969), and *The Correspondence of Catherine McAuley, 1827–1841,* edited by Mary Angela Bolster (1989). References in this volume to Catherine McAuley's letters are generally to the Neumann edition, since it is the first such edition. When the Neumann edition is cited, *only* the page reference is given in parentheses; when the Bolster edition is cited, the editor's name and the page reference are given. Occasionally, where I have a photocopy of the autograph of a particular letter and the autograph shows slightly different wording or punctuation, I have followed the autograph, but have usually also given the page reference for the published letter. The two published editions have over 175 letters in common; differences in some of the dates and wording of some of these letters in the two editions are no doubt due to the state of the autographs and the difficulty of reading Catherine's handwriting and punctuation. Bolster's edition contains about seventy additional letters: forty of these were written by Catherine McAuley; the rest, with one exception, by clergy and church officials. Neumann's edition contains one letter not in the Bolster edition, written by Myles Gaffney. Some work remains to be done on the extant letters of Catherine McAuley: verifying some of the texts and dates once again, providing additional notes, and creating an index. Neumann's and Bolster's editions also contain Catherine McAuley's "Spirit of the Institute" essay (also called "The Mercy Ideal") and her "Personal Act of Consecration."

3 The birth years for James McGauley and Elinor Conway, and the year of their marriage—as noted here—are those given by Mary Angela Bolster (*Documentary Study* 1:xvi). These dates roughly correspond to those estimated or implied by Roland Burke Savage (6, 418–19). James McGauley was evidently much older than Elinor Conway, perhaps as much as thirty years, although Mary Nathy O'Hara says Elinor was "twenty years younger" (1). On James McGauley's woodwork in Liffey Street Chapel, see Degnan (353).

4 There remains a presently irresolvable uncertainty about the date (September 29, or September 17) and the year (1778 or 1781) of Catherine's birth. Neither her nor her sister Mary's birth record or baptismal record is extant. The earliest biographical accounts written by Catherine's contemporaries give various years, some of which are clearly inaccurate (for example, 1786 and 1787). Mary Vincent Harnett RSM gives the year 1778; Roland Burke Savage SJ gives 1781. The will of Catherine's father, James McGauley, was probated on August 2, 1783. See Burke Savage, *Catherine McAuley,* 418–19, and Muldrey, *Abounding in Mercy*, 77–79. I have chosen to use the birth date and year now most frequently cited: September 29, 1778. It is plausible that Catherine was indeed the eldest of the McAuley children—as Mary Vincent Harnett's Limerick Manuscript claims—and that Catherine's sister Mary was born sometime between mid 1779 and mid 1782. Mary would then have been at least twenty-two when she married William Macauley, a Dublin physician, in 1804 (Degnan 29). However, Mary Ann Doyle (Derry Large Manuscript) and Mary Clare Moore (Letter of September 1, 1844)—both of whom were Catherine's early associates— refer to Mary as Catherine's elder sister. The author of the *Dublin Review* article in 1847, presumably Myles Gaffney, gives September 17, 1778 as Catherine's birthday, but no other early source does so. Mary Hermenia Muldrey tells me that the Archival Repository of the British Library houses a collection of early Irish newspapers which may contain announcements of significant events in the lives of Catherine's parents and siblings, as well as notice of her own birth.

5 Nearly all biographical accounts of Catherine McAuley's life give Catherine as Mrs. Callaghan's first name. However, Mary Nathy O'Hara RSM, *Catherine McAuley, Mercy Foundress,* notes that "There is a marriage licence in 1776 showing that William Callaghan

and Anna Ryan were married but whether or not the Mrs. Callaghan who became so attached to Catherine was formerly Anna Ryan is not known" (3). Catherine McAuley wrote the name, "Cath. Callaghan", on the mottled cover of a notebook where she wrote the names of other deceased friends and relatives for whom she prayed. This notebook is now in the archives of the Sisters of Mercy, Dublin. According to Mary Bertrand Degnan RSM, *Mercy Unto Thousands,* the Callaghans leased the house in Coolock on July 27, 1803; they purchased twenty-two acres of land in Coolock "with all the houses and buildings thereon" on April 26, 1809 (354).

6 Burke Savage (32), Degnan (29), and Neumann (15) all say that Mary McAuley and William Macauley were married in 1804. Bolster gives 1805 as the year of their marriage (*Documentary Study* xviii). However, Carroll says they were married in 1810 (*Life* 119). Their eldest child, Mary, was evidently born about 1811, according to Degnan (30) and Neumann (54), although there may have been earlier births of children who did not survive. In his letters written years later William—born in 1821, and the youngest of their five children—says he was "the third attempt" his mother "made in her great love for my fond father to call a child after him" and that the two earlier Williams "both died in infancy". Burke Savage says explicitly that they were married "in St. Mark's (Protestant) Church, Dublin, on 18th August 1804" (32).

7 In the early documents the surname of this family is spelled in two ways: "Byrn" and "Byrne". For example, Mary Ann Doyle, who worked with Catherine Byrn at Baggot Street, permits "Byrne" in the Derry Large Manuscript; Clare Moore uses "Byrn" in her 1844–1845 letters about Catherine McAuley; Clare Augustine Moore, who in preparing her Memoir interviewed a "Miss Byrne", the sister of Anne Conway's husband, uses "Byrne"; and in Catherine McAuley's last Will and Codicil—neither of which is in her own handwriting—Teresa Byrn's name is spelled both ways. Mary Austin Carroll, who knew Mary Camillus (Teresa) Byrn in the United States, uses "Byrne" throughout her writings. However, Mary Bertrand Degnan, who did extensive research into the Byrn family, uses "Byrn", as does Roland Burke Savage. Moreover, in autograph documents preserved in the Dublin and Bermondsey archives, the three Byrn sisters—Catherine, Teresa, and Anne—consistently spell their surname, "Byrn". Therefore, I follow this spelling.

Considerable work remains to be done to bring together in one study all the available information on this family, so dear to Catherine McAuley, two of whom were her adoptive children (Catherine and Teresa), and three of whom entered the Sisters of Mercy: Catherine (Sister Mary Josephine), who subsequently left to join the Dominican Sisters where she took the name, Sister Mary Raymond; Teresa (Sister Mary Camillus), who eventually served in New York and Baltimore; and Anne (Sister Mary Margaret), who entered the Bermondsey community. Such a study might usefully include the texts of the various extant letters of the Byrn sisters, as well as those of William (Willie) Armstrong Montgomery Macauley—their cousin and Catherine McAuley's nephew. William died in Australia in 1904. The Byrn and Macauley letters propose important supplements and possible corrections to some information in the early biographical accounts of Catherine's life.

8 Of the biographical manuscripts presented in this volume only the Limerick Manuscript names the priest who received William Callaghan into the Catholic Church; it says he was Edward Armstrong. However, in her letter of October 23, 1867, to Mary Clare Moore, in which she complains about errors and omissions in Mary Vincent Harnett's published *Life*, Mary Raymond (Catherine) Byrn OP says that it was Joseph Nugent, and that "Mr. Armstrong had never been in the house." Her letter is preserved in the archives of the Sisters of Mercy, Bermondsey (London). Burke Savage and Degnan also say that it was Joseph Nugent, but Carroll, apparently following at this point the wording of the Limerick Manuscript, says it was Edward Armstrong. I would like to accept Mary Raymond Byrn's recollection here, since Joseph Nugent was a curate in Coolock at the time. However, he was then only twenty-six, and perhaps less experienced in this sort of theological

conversation than Catherine's older friend, Edward Armstrong, then a curate at Liffey Street Chapel, which Catherine is known to have attended. For me, at least, the question is still open.

9 Mary Anne Delany's baptismal name is evidently not "Marianne", but her surname (Delany or Delaney?) has been a conundrum for me. There are early sources for each spelling. For example, the earliest Dublin Register has "Mary Anne Delaney", and Catherine McAuley addresses her October 3, 1837 letter to her as "Mrs. Delaney". Clare Augustine Moore, who lived with her for many years, spells the name, "Delany", although her sister, Clare Moore, spells it "Delaney" in the Bermondsey Annals. The Limerick Manuscript spells it "Delany", as do Degnan and Bolster. I am grateful to Mary Magdalena Frisby RSM and Mary Francis Lowe RSM for their researches into the ownership of lands in Durrow, County Laois, which confirm that Mary Anne's father's name is William Delany. I therefore use "Delany" in this volume, except when presenting a manuscript that uses "Delaney".

10 The remains of these thirteen sisters are still buried in the Carmelite vault. Carroll is incorrect in saying that they were later moved to the cemetery at Baggot Street (*Life* 172).

11 Although this was her full name in religion, as given at her reception, she was nearly always called "Mary Teresa" by her aunt and the rest of the community.

12 At her Uncle James's insistence, young Catherine Macauley left Baggot Street for a period of time and lived with his family. Degnan says (168–69) that her departure occurred in 1833; she implies that it was after the death of her sister, Mary Teresa (November 12, 1833), and before young Catherine's own entrance into the community at age fifteen (January 28, 1834). While Catherine would have been required to serve a two-year novitiate, the interval of twenty-seven months between her reception of the habit (July 3, 1834) and her profession of vows (October 22, 1836, as given in the Dublin Register) seems long; it may indicate that she was too young to be permitted to profess vows any earlier, or that the profession ceremony was delayed for other, external reasons (see note 14 below), or that she had left Baggot Street after her reception of the habit.

The Limerick Manuscript—a reliable early source on the life of Mary Anne Agnes (Catherine) Macauley, since Mary Vincent Harnett was her friend at Baggot Street—is not precisely clear on this topic. It says: "Some short time after the death of this dear Sister [Mary Teresa Macauley], Revd. Mother's second niece expressed her intention of becoming a member of the Community .... But some obstacles were thrown in her way. Her uncle . . . insisted on her spending some time in his own house .... But neither the persuasions of her uncle, nor the fascinations of the society to which he took care to introduce her could prevail with her to change her original intention .... At length her uncle seeing that her resolution remained unchanged left her at liberty to follow her wishes, and she immediately returned to her former abode, in Baggot St. and received the Habit of the Sisters of Mercy."

This manuscript seems to suggest that young Catherine was gone from Baggot Street only a few months: from the death of her sister (November 12, 1833) to her entrance, as recorded in the Dublin Register (January 28, 1834); or from the death of her sister to her reception of the habit as recorded in the same Register (July 3, 1834). While her name in religion is Mary Anne Agnes, she is nearly always called "Catherine" in her aunt's correspondence.

13 Teresa Carton will become a choir sister in 1844, and add the name Mary. Consequently many of the early manuscripts refer to her as "Sister Mary Teresa Carton", even when referring to the 1830s or early 1840s.

14 See note 12 above. See also Catherine McAuley's letter of October 14, 1836, to Archdeacon John Hamilton, requesting that Archbishop Murray set a date for a profession ceremony: "Two Sisters whose noviciate ended in June have been most anxiously waiting the return of His Grace" (Bolster, ed. 22).

15 Although the Dublin Register says that Mary Anne Agnes (Catherine) Macauley died on

August 8, 1837, in writing to Andrew Fitzgerald OP, Carlow College, on August 8, Catherine McAuley says, "Our innocent little Catherine . . . died a little before twelve o'clock last night" (Neumann 94 and Bolster, ed. 29).

16 A photocopy of William Armstrong Montgomery McAuley's long letter, written to "My very dear child Sr. M. Catherine, Revd. Mother and Sisters," is in the Archives of the Sisters of Mercy, Carlow. The "Sr. M. Catherine" addressed is presumably his tenth child, his daughter Fannie Theresa (1871–1952), who had become a Sister of Mercy in Kyneton, Victoria, Australia, with the name Mary Catherine. William signs his surname "McAuley". He is an important source of information about his aunt and other members of their family.

17 See Memoir of Mary Clare Augustine Moore.

18 The autograph of this letter is undated. The date given in Neumann (374) and Bolster (259)—that is, September 20, 1841—cannot be correct, in view of the content of the letter and Catherine's claim on Friday, September 17, that she would depart Birmingham "on Monday", that is, September 20 (Neumann 373–4 and Bolster 258). Since she writes ""Sunday morning—Baggot St." at the head of this autograph, it was probably written on September 26, the Sunday after her return from Birmingham.

19 Mary Ignatia Neumann and Mary Angela Bolster give as the addressee of this letter the "Board of Trustees—Booterstown" (Neumann 383) or "Board of Trustees, Booterstown Convent" (Bolster, ed. 266). The salutation of the letter is "Gentlemen". I have not been able to examine the autograph. The signature on the October 13, 1841 letter which prompts Catherine's letter is almost illegible: it may be "Dowling". It is written from "Poolbeg St., Dublin". This autograph is in the archives of the Sisters of Mercy, Dublin.

20 Autograph in the archives of the Sisters of Mercy, Charleville (Rath Luirc).

NOTES TO CHAPTER 2

A General Introduction to the Early Biographical Manuscripts

1 Mary de Pazzi Delany was elected superior of the Baggot Street community on December 2, 1841.

2 The superiors of the foundations made from Baggot Street in the five years immediately following Catherine's death were Mary Francis Creedon, Newfoundland (1842); Mary de Sales White, and later Mary Liguori Gibson, Liverpool (1843); Mary Ursula Frayne, Perth (1846); and Mary Agnes O'Connor, London (1844) and New York (1846). Pittsburgh was founded from Carlow in 1843, with Frances Warde as superior.

3 In his *Tradition and Traditions,* Congar is here interpreting the views of Thomas Aquinas.

4 I have not yet been able to identify the Passionist priest to whom Mary Vincent Harnett refers. Perhaps it is Vincent Grotti who also, on at least one occasion, counseled Mary Vincent Whitty.

5 In volume 1 (lxxxvii–xci) and volume 2 (216–17) of the *Documentary Study,* Mary Angela Bolster compares all these documents to Cork Manuscript 2 (in Clare Moore's handwriting) and Cork Manuscript 3 (transcribed by Mary Vincent Whitty). I believe that the Derry Small, Dundalk, and Liverpool Manuscripts, as well as Cork Manuscript 3, are direct or indirect transcriptions, although somewhat altered, of the biography which appears in the Bermondsey Annals. As I note below in dealing with the Life in the Bermondsey Annals, I believe that the original manuscript from which the Bermondsey Life was copied into the bound Bermondsey Annals was written principally by Clare Moore and that this original manuscript may be Cork Manuscript 2. I have not been able to examine the three Cork manuscripts in great detail. Mary Angela Bolster of the Sisters of Mercy in Cork is assuredly the scholar best placed and equipped to analyze and publish these manuscripts, since they are currently accessible to her and could be further studied as a group. Cork Manuscript 1 is a life of Catherine McAuley attributed to Sister Teresa Wildridge who died in Cork in 1848. Cork Manuscript 3 begins with an original Preface composed by Mary Vincent Whitty in 1860.

6 Stephen Crites's article, "The Narrative Quality of Experience", *Journal of the American Academy of Religion* 10 (1971): 291–311, is a helpful analysis of the relation between experience and story.

7 Someday research might be undertaken and published which could document—if relevant records exist and can be found—the nature of Dr. William Macauley's estate and his bequests, after his death in 1829, as well as the financial transactions of his second son Robert, who died in 1840, and his eldest son James, who died in 1841. See also the notes on William Macauley and the Byrn family in chapter 1.

8 Mary Ursula Frayne had been at Catherine's bedside during her last illness. She went with the founding party to Newfoundland in 1842, and then in 1845 departed from Dublin for Australia. In January 1846 she, five other sisters, and Bishop Brady landed at Freemantle, Western Australia, to found the first community of Sisters of Mercy in Australia, at Perth. In 1857 she founded the community in Melbourne (Carroll, *Leaves* 2:513–26).

9 See James D.G. Dunn, *Unity and Diversity in the New Testament,* for a discussion of the sayings of Jesus, as well as a comprehensive discussion of the traditions about Jesus. While there are, of course, obvious and crucial differences between Jesus and Catherine, Dunn's analysis of the narrative traditions and the traditions of the sayings which were at work in the earliest Christian communities is useful to an analysis of early traditions about Catherine (70–80).

10 Mary Vincent Harnett's published biography, *The Life of Rev. Mother Catherine McAuley* (1864), uses considerable material from these manuscripts, but since the book is based primarily on the Limerick Manuscript which freely incorporates long passages of the Derry Large Manuscript and the Life in the Bermondsey Annals without quotation marks or identification of these sources—except a general reference to "the narrations of others"—one cannot really say that Harnett's published work "quotes" these manuscripts, or the other early manuscripts, such as the Tullamore Annals, whose language also appears in the printed text. However, Harnett does directly quote in full Mary Elizabeth Moore's letter of November 21, 1841 (198–9). An interesting task, but one which lies beyond the intentions of this study, would be to trace the language of Harnett's published biography. Here it is necessary to recall that Harnett's name does not appear on the title page, nor in the "Introduction" to the book. The author of the book is "A Sister of Mercy"; it is "Edited, With an Introduction, by the Venble. Richard Baptist O'Brien D.D."

11 I have quoted extensively from these manuscripts in various chapters of this book, but I would want others to have the same access to the entire manuscripts as I have had, so they may form their own judgments about the material I have quoted, as well as what I have left unquoted, and so they may have these important resources for their own projects.

12 See note 5 above.

NOTES TO CHAPTER 3

Mary Ann (Anna Maria) Doyle, 1809?–1866

1 The Documentary Study gives 1809 as her birth year, as does the Dublin Register. The Tullamore Register which provides the names of her parents does not give the date of her birth. Mary Austin Carroll says that Mary Ann Doyle died "in the fifty-seventh year of her age" (*Life* 293); since the date of her death (September 11, 1866) is generally accepted, it might appear from this that her birth year is 1810, as given in Neumann (396). However, a long biography of Mary Ann Doyle in the Bermondsey Annals (2:[93]–[99]) gives August 6, 1800 as her birth date, and says that she died "in the sixty-seventh year of her age". This may well be the correct birth year; although it is not corroborated by other early documents I have seen, it supports the view that Mary Ann Doyle was considerably older than Catherine Byrn (born in 1812), whom she calls "very young", and than other members of the early Baggot Street community, and that she died at an "advanced age". Despite effort, and considerable help from Mary Paschal Murray and Mary Celestine

Stokes, the archivists in Derry and Tullamore, I have not been able to resolve this matter satisfactorily and so have chosen to use, with a query, the date in the Dublin Register.

2 Catherine McAuley was not resident at Baggot Street until some time later, probably in late May or June 1828, after the death of Edward Armstrong, and then probably not full time. Her sister Mary had died in August 1827 and Catherine occasionally stayed with her brother-in-law Dr. William Macauley, helping to care for his five young children, when she was not at Coolock House, the sale of which was concluded in September 1828. However, she came to Baggot Street almost daily after September 24, 1827.

3 Catherine Byrn, the eldest daughter of Catherine's cousin Anne Conway Byrn, received the habit of the Sisters of Mercy on January 23, 1832. She left to enter the Dominican Sisters on December 1, 1832. Had she remained she probably would have professed her vows as a Sister of Mercy in the first profession ceremony at Baggot Street on January 24, 1833. However, her longstanding desire to be a Dominican is documented in the Dominican records at Drogheda (Degnan 153–56).

4 The Deed of Agreement is dated December 14, 1824. Anna Maria's brother is identified as "Reverend Michael Doyle of Exchange Street Chapel." The Deed looks corrected at this point; perhaps Michael Doyle's name was substituted for that of Joseph Nugent after the latter died on May 30, 1825, at the age of twenty-nine. Joseph Nugent, Catherine's good friend, served as a curate at Sts. Michael and John's in 1824–1825. The Bermondsey biography of Mary Ann Doyle says that the name of her priest-brother who served at Sts. Michael and John's was "James", that he died in 1824, and that her sister Catherine was "a Presentation Nun in James' Street Convent whence she was sent with others to found a house in Killarney" where she died shortly after Anna Maria entered Baggot Street in September 1827. According to Donnelly, a "Michael" Doyle was curate at Sts. Michael and John's in 1824, and he died there in 1844 (98–99, 198). Clearly, further research on Mary Ann Doyle's family needs to be done, though it is beyond the scope of the present study.

5 This undated letter was written before August 21, 1844. The next letter, dated "Aug. 21", clearly is not the first of the sequence, and the third letter, a very short one, is dated "Nov. 17."

6 There is some confusion about whether her name should be spelled "Ann" (Carroll, though rarely; Neumann; and Bolster, *Correspondence*); or "Anne" (Carroll, in *Life*; Burke Savage, Degnan, Regan and Keiss, and Bolster, *Documentary Study*); *or* "Marianne" (Carroll, in *Leaves* 1; and Bourke). Catherine addresses at least two extant letters to her as "Sister Mary Ann" (August 20, 1840 and July 24, 1841). In the third of Catherine's three published letters to her (September 24, 1841), she simply uses the initials "M.A." Clare Moore and Clare Augustine Moore refer to her as "Sister Mary Ann", but Elizabeth Moore addresses her as "Mother Mary Anne". The Tullamore Register also says her name was "Sister Mary Anne Teresa". But when Mary Ann Doyle herself wrote out a copy of her "Act of Profession" she identified herself as "I, Anna Maria Doyle, called in religion Mary Ann Teresa" and signed the "True copy": "Sister Anna Maria Doyle[,] In religion Mary Ann Teresa." This copy, preserved in the archives of the Sisters of Mercy, Derry, is in the same handwriting as Mary Ann Doyle's three autograph letters to Clare Augustine Moore in 1844.

7 See also the letter of Catherine McAuley to Frances Warde, June 30, 1840 (Neumann 219–20). The principal benefactor of the new Tullamore convent, then being completed, was Michael Molloy, Esq., a major distiller.

8 Other letters are quoted in the Tullamore Annals and in Carroll's *Leaves*, vol. 1, or referred to in Catherine's other correspondence.

9 The year of Mary Ann Doyle's death given in Neumann (i.e., 1867) is incorrect (78, 396). Records in the Derry archives and elsewhere say that she died in 1866.

10 I am very grateful to Mary Paschal Murray RSM, the Derry archivist, for her generous help

with the Derry archival materials and for taking me to Mary Ann Doyle's grave and to the first Mercy convent in Derry, on Pump Street.

The Letters of Mary Ann Doyle to Mary Clare Augustine Moore

1 The content and length of this letter suggest that it was probably written sometime before the second letter which is dated "Aug. 21 st." It was presumably written in 1844 sometime after Mary Ann Doyle had founded the Mercy community in Kells on February 9, and about the same time that Clare Moore in Bermondsey began to respond to similar inquiries from Mary Clare Augustine Moore. That this letter and the following two (which are also presumed to have been written in 1844) are addressed to Clare Augustine Moore and that she was then in Dublin may be inferred from the greetings sent to others at Baggot Street with which Mary Ann Doyle concludes these letters. The three autographs are in the archives of the Sisters of Mercy, Dublin. The first letter simply begins with the salutation.

2 It is very difficult to determine the intended punctuation and paragraphing in these autograph letters. I have used the punctuation that seemed appropriate, and have tried to follow the various clues as to Mary Ann Doyle's own paragraphing, except in one instance where the paragraph seemed long and a natural shift in the content seemed to warrant a new paragraph. I have also been somewhat at a loss about whether capital letters are intended for some words, notably some of those beginning with C, N, R, and S; here I have simply tried to be consistent.

3 Quite a few words are misspelled in these letters, including proper names. I have left the misspelled names but have indicated the correct spellings in square brackets. I have used current spellings of "receive", "their", and "occurred".

4 Michael Blake went to Rome in 1824, to re-establish the Irish College.

5 Mary Ann Doyle had an older brother who was a priest, and therefore not living at home: Michael Doyle, curate at Saints Michael and John's. He died in 1844.

6 The words, "on that day", are written after "opened" and then crossed out.

7 Catherine Byrn, then fifteen years old—later, Sister Mary Raymond OP.

8 Edward Armstrong died on May 15, 1828.

9 Mary Macauley—later, Mary Teresa, in religion—was born in 1811.

10 Catherine Macauley was born in 1819.

11 Catherine's three nephews were James, Robert, and William. At the time of their father's death in late January 1829, James and Robert would have been about fourteen and eleven, having been born in 1815 and 1818, respectively (Neumann 54 and Degnan 30). William was just seven when his father died; his birthday was December 9, 1821.

12 The Irish College was re-opened in 1828 and Michael Blake evidently remained in Rome as the rector of the College for some time. Nicholas Donnelly may be correct in saying that Blake returned permanently to Dublin in 1830, if he was merely visiting Dublin in 1829 when he preached at the dedication of the Baggot Street chapel on June 4. See Donnelly 151, 197. However, other early biographical manuscripts about Catherine McAuley seem to imply Blake's presence in Dublin during the critical year (1829–1830) following the dedication of the chapel. Certainly he was in Dublin by August 28, 1830, when Daniel Murray asked him to visit Catherine at Baggot Street prior to her departure to the Presentation Convent, George's Hill (Bolster, *Correspondence* 6–7). The *Documentary Study* says that he left Rome for Ireland on October 9, 1828, and then resumed his work as parish priest of Saints Michael and John's, 1829–1831 (2:193). See also the long biographical account in Mac Suibhne (2:333–53). Mac Suibhne also says "Dr. Blake left Rome on 9 October 1828" (2:352–53).

13 This "jealousy" evidently existed, not among the Sisters of Charity themselves—and certainly not on the part of Mary Aikenhead, their founder—but among their clerical and lay supporters. See Mary Aikenhead's letter of January 25, 1833 (19).

14 Elizabeth Harley, whom Mary Ann Doyle would have known well during their fifteen months' stay at George's Hill.

15 Mary Elizabeth Harley died on April 25, 1832.
16 The word "these" is in the autograph—evidently a reference to the formula for the Act of Profession which was used by the Presentation Sisters, or to the formula in use among the Sisters of Mercy in 1844, after their Rule was confirmed in 1841.
17 The Church of the Immaculate Conception on Marlborough Street was the new Roman Catholic pro-cathedral for the diocese of Dublin, dedicated on November 14, 1825.
18 This salutation does not begin a separate letter, or a separate document. It is simply a greeting that occurs on a separate line in the middle of the ninth page of the twelve-page autograph of Mary Ann Doyle's first letter. This salutation has sometimes led writers to say that Mary Ann wrote four letters about Catherine McAuley, but there are apparently only three extant autograph documents, as presented here. All three are in the Dublin archives.
19 Mary Magdalen de Pazzi (Mary Anne) Delany entered the Baggot Street community on July 12, 1830, at the age of twenty-eight (Burke Savage 118). She remained there, except for a trip to found the Liverpool community in 1843, until her death in January 1872. On December 2, 1841, she was elected superior of the Baggot Street community, succeeding Catherine McAuley. She served three years, but then declined re-election.
20 The word in the autograph is "cholarea".
21 William Callaghan.
22 Mrs. William (Catherine) Callaghan was a Quaker (Burke Savage 30; Degnan 19).
23 Catherine Callaghan died on October 3, 1819.
24 This statement is probably a response to an assertion made in the obituaries on Catherine McAuley which appeared in the Dublin *Morning Register, The Tablet*, and *The Register* (Halifax, Nova Scotia). I have not been able to locate an original of the Halifax *Register* obituary, but an undated, handwritten copy, "From the Halifax Register/Sisters of Mercy", now preserved in the archives of the Sisters of Mercy, Derry, contains the following sentences: "Mrs. McAuley [i.e., Catherine McAuley] was a convert to the Catholic Faith. At a very early age, having been already left an orphan, she became the adopted daughter of a very rich and very conscientious Protestant Lady and Gentleman. The rationally conscientious are always religiously liberal: and Miss McAuley met no opposition to her views when conviction of this truth persuaded her to embrace the doctrines of Catholicity. She not only became a Catholic herself, but lived to behold the venerated Parents of her adoption received into the same faith which had crowned her with happiness." I do not know exactly when the obituary was published in the *The Register* (the Public Archives of Nova Scotia, in Halifax, reports that the 1841–1842 volume of *The Register* is missing from their collection). I also do not know when or by whom the Derry transcript of it was made (the copy is not in Mary Ann Doyle's handwriting). The obituary in *The Register* (Halifax) was written by Richard Baptist O'Brien—later Dean of Limerick, but then President of St. Mary's College, Nova Scotia (Degnan 277, and *Documentary Study* 1:706). In 1864, when O'Brien published his edition of Mary Vincent Harnett's *The Life of Rev. Mother Catherine McAuley,* he acknowledged that he was the author of the obituary and incorporated language from it in the "Introduction" and final chapter of the book; however, no claim that Catherine "was a convert" appears in the book. Presumably after O'Brien returned to Limerick and became acquainted with the thinking of Elizabeth Moore and Mary Vincent Harnett, he altered his interpretation of Catherine's religious development.

Mary Austin Carroll is one of the earliest published researchers to deal explicitly with the Halifax *Register* account, in her first volume of *Leaves from the Annals* (111–15), published in 1881. Carroll does not, however, include the sentences quoted above. Similarly, in her earlier work, *Life of Catherine McAuley*, first published in 1866, Carroll also quotes from the Halifax *Register* obituary, though without explicitly identifying its author (445–47). Here too she does not include the sentences quoted above, even though she gives the following footnote: "In a late memoir of the Foundress, this obituary is not correctly quoted. Through the kindness of Mother Elizabeth S— [Strange?], of Pittsburg, who loaned us the original, we are enabled to give a correct copy. We have made one omission—the reason which delayed Dr. O'Brien in Dublin, 1838—which, of course, would be irrelevant here" (445). In the *Life,* Carroll's text follows the first part of the Derry handwritten copy almost verbatim, except for the sentences noted above. At the present time the archives of the Sisters of Mercy, Pittsburgh, do not contain an original copy of the Halifax *Register* obituary. They do, however, possess a handwritten copy of the obituary which contains the words, "Mrs. McAuley was a convert to the Catholic Faith . . . ." I am grateful to Patricia A. Hodge RSM, the Pittsburgh archivist, for her help in this matter. The quotations from the Halifax *Register* obituary which appear in the *Documentary Study* (1:706–8 and 1:870) are evidently taken from the *Register* text as it appears in Harnett's *Life* (203–6); hence the sentences quoted at the beginning of this note are missing there as well.

However, the actual obituaries that appeared in the Dublin *Morning Register* (December 10, 1841) and the *Tablet* (December 25, 1841) are available in the National Library of Ireland. The *Tablet* article is a shortened version of the earlier article and concludes with the attribution: "Correspondent of the Dublin *Morning Register.*" Both articles contain explicit reference to Catherine's "conversion to the Catholic faith." For further discussion of these obituaries and their author, see note 48 on the text of the Bermondsey Annals in chapter 4.

25 That is, Catherine Byrn.

26 This letter has no closing or signature, even though the autograph is complete and there is room on the last page for a closing. Perhaps Mary Ann Doyle did not think of this document as a "letter", or she may have posted it with a cover letter which is now no longer extant.

27 A "true copy" of Mary Ann Doyle's Act of Profession, in her own handwriting, is preserved in the archives of the Sisters of Mercy, Derry. This may be the copy she enclosed in her August 21, 1844 letter to Clare Augustine Moore, or it may be a copy she made later, in Derry.

28 One can only regret that Mary Ann Doyle made this assessment! Surely her further observations on their experiences at George's Hill would be valuable to biographers of Catherine McAuley.

29 August 28, the feast day of Saint Augustine of Hippo, Clare Augustine Moore's patron saint.

30 Elizabeth Agnew, formerly Sister Mary Clare Agnew, had by then left the Bermondsey community of the Sisters of Mercy; see Degnan 318–20, 378–9. However, the last paragraph of Degnan's note 9 (page 379) is not quite accurate: Mary Ann Doyle is writing from "St. Columbkill's" [*sic*], Kells, founded on February 9, 1844, not from Derry; and Derry was founded in 1848, not 1843.

31 Mary Cecilia Marmion was elected superior of the Baggot Street community on May 23, 1844, succeeding Mary de Pazzi Delany.

32 Mary Vincent Whitty was then mistress of novices at Baggot Street.

33 Mary Ursula (Clara) Frayne received the habit at Baggot Street on January 20, 1835. The specific "appointment" to which Mary Ann Doyle here refers is not clear to me. Catherine McAuley named Mary Ann Doyle her assistant, either on December 13, 1831, when Catherine herself was appointed superior, or shortly thereafter. Perhaps Mary Ann is referring to her appointment to oversee the branch house in Kingstown. The Kingstown convent was opened on March 24, 1835.

34 Mary Gertrude (Mary) Jones professed her vows on February 11, 1834. The "first Chapter" to which Mary Ann Doyle here refers may be a Chapter of the professed members of the Baggot Street community, or a Chapter of Faults. (The relevant sections of the Rule are II.3.8 and II.7.1, 2.) Whereas the Rule indicates that a Chapter of Faults will be held on the last Wednesday of each month, the Bermondsey Annals notes that Catherine

McAuley "could not be prevailed on to hold the prescribed Chapter of Faults for a very long time after being made Superior."

35 Genevieve Jarmy was, in age, the oldest member of the Baggot Street community. She had entered when she was in her sixties and was, according to Degnan, "in her seventy-second year" when Catherine McAuley died (343). She herself died on July 19, 1858 (Harnett 216).

The Derry Large Manuscript

1 There are *two* Derry Manuscripts. Derry "S" (Small) is written on smaller-sized paper and is nearly identical to the Bermondsey, Annals Life of Catherine McAuley. Derry "L" (Large) is written on larger paper, in a copybook. I have called this second manuscript, which is a completely original account, the Derry Large Manuscript, though it should perhaps be called simply the "Derry Manuscript" since it is the only manuscript life of Catherine McAuley in the Derry archives which is distinctive. The practice of distinguishing the two Derry documents dates from the period when it was not realized that the smaller-page document is either a copy of the manuscript (probably Clare Moore's) from which the Bermondsey Annals entry for 1841 was copied or a direct transcription of the Bermondsey Life. The Derry Small Manuscript is not, I believe, in Clare Moore's handwriting.

The Derry Large Manuscript is presently defective: the first page or pages (originally unpaginated) are missing and the narrative begins in mid-sentence. The reference early in the manuscript to "Daniel O'Connell Esq. then Member for Clare, who has ever been a benefactor to our institution" may indicate that the document was partly composed before O'Connell died on May 15, 1847. The handwriting in the manuscript is not Mary Ann Doyle's, but she was presumably the principal source of its content.

An intriguing feature of the Derry Large Manuscript, in terms of its place of composition and perhaps its authorship, is the fact that in the manuscript the word, "here", is used six times in reference to the Baggot Street convent, and that convent is once called "this house". This may indicate that the manuscript was begun at Baggot Street, perhaps before Mary Ann Doyle went to Tullamore in 1836. Since the manuscript does not appear to be in her handwriting—unless her hand changed considerably before or after 1844, when she wrote to Clare Augustine Moore—it is possible that someone at Baggot Street wrote the manuscript under Mary Ann's guidance. The document may have been intended to be the Dublin Annals. Unfortunately I have not so far been able to discover when or how the manuscript got to Derry, unless Mary Ann took it with her to Tullamore and then to Derry. It is also possible that the document was composed in Tullamore, Kells, Derry, or Limerick (where Mary Ann visited for several months in 1846) though the repeated use of "here" in reference to Baggot Street may rule out these possibilities—unless of course the author thought of herself as composing the Dublin Annals for the earliest years. Interestingly, Mary Ann also visited Baggot Street sometime in the mid to late 1840s, according to a comment in an undated letter of Mary Camillus (Teresa) Byrn to Mary Ann Doyle, written sometime during the Irish famine. This letter—dated only, "Feast of the Nativity of B.V." (i.e., September 8)—is preserved in the archives of the Sisters of Mercy, Derry. The fact that the Derry Large Manuscript stops in "1832" may be related to its possible conception as a Dublin Annals (so far as I know there is no other extant Dublin Annals for the earliest years, even though the keeping of Annals must have been valued there since foundations made from Dublin tended to begin their Annals shortly after their founding), or it may simply reflect someone's inability to finish composing or copying the manuscript. Also intriguing is the fact that both Clare Augustine Moore's handwriting (in her Memoir presented later in this volume, and in her July 7, 1875 letter to the Bermondsey community) and Mary de Pazzi Delany's handwriting (in her "Extracts from the Instructions of the Venerated Foundress", now in the Dublin archives) bear a striking, but not perfect, resemblance to the handwriting in the Derry Large Manuscript. Was Clare Augustine or Mary de Pazzi the scribe or the author (using Mary Ann's recollections) of this manuscript?

2 This is the title given to the manuscript in a typescript prepared earlier in the twentieth century. The manuscript itself, as currently extant, has no title; since its first page or pages are missing, it simply begins at the left hand margin with the words "great delight . . . " Each page has a year written at the top in the center of the page; for example, "1823" on the first extant page. These years, in sequence, are also inserted in the middle of the appropriate pages. The typescript of the document which was circulated in the past has a number of inaccuracies in transcription.

3 The words in brackets can be supplied from the Limerick Manuscript, which quotes the Derry Large Manuscript extensively.

4 William Callaghan.

5 On Baggot Street, Dublin.

6 In presenting this manuscript I have changed all ampersands to "and", and inserted an occasional comma or semicolon. I have retained the spellings in the manuscript.

7 Of the House on Baggot Street.

8 This child was probably Ann Rice (Degnan 75).

9 That is, Mary Macauley.

10 John McCormick.

11 The double use of "though" is in the manuscript, at the end of one line and the beginning of the next.

12 Teresa Byrn, and Mary and Catherine Macauley.

13 Sir Patrick Dun's Hospital, founded in 1788 and moved to Grand Canal Street in 1808.

14 Michael Blake.

15 It has not been possible for me to identify this priest, but the author of this manuscript evidently knew his name.

16 This was an establishment under Protestant auspices, situated to the left of Catherine McAuley's House on Baggot Street, as one faces the building.

17 This book is probably *A Journal of Meditations for Every Day of the Year, Gathered out of Divers Authors* (Dublin: Richard Coyne, 1823). Catherine McAuley's own copy is now in the archives of the Sisters of Mercy, Tullamore. It contains the inscription: "This Meditation Book belonged to our Venerated Foundress, who left it after her on one of her visits to Tullamore, about the year 1839 or 1840."

18 The last numeral of this date is unclearly written, or over-written, in the manuscript. It may be a "3" altered to be a "6" or an "8"; it is not a "7". The year 1823 marked the beginning of Catherine McAuley's firm plan to build a House on Baggot Street.

19 This ellipsis is in the manuscript.

20 This may have been Catherine McAuley's one attempt at a pension school (for paying students) in Dublin. The successful schools (i.e., classes) at Baggot Street during her day were for poor children.

21 The "11th of December" date given in this sentence is a strong clue, among others, that this manuscript was not handwritten by Mary Ann Doyle. The date of her reception of the habit was December 9, 1830, as noted in the Dublin Register and elsewhere.

22 The year, "1831", is written for the first time at the top of the manuscript page on which the paragraph which follows is the first full paragraph. Since "1831"is not inserted elsewhere in the text, I have inserted it here.

23 Frances Warde was one of these. See Mary Clare Moore's letter of September 1, 1844.

24 This spelling of her name ("Anne") further suggests that Mary Ann Doyle did not handwrite this manuscript since she always spells her own middle name in religion "Ann".

25 Frances Warde's name in religion is here spelled "Francis". It is spelled with an "e" or with an "i" in different early manuscripts. Catherine McAuley herself uses "Frances" in the salutations of her autograph letters to her; however, in the published editions of these letters "Francis" is used.

26 In the manuscript itself a word is missing; the word "education" is inserted above the line in a different handwriting.

27 Michael Blake.

28 April 25, 1832.

29 The manuscript ends here. On the remaining pages in the notebook poems written by Catherine McAuley are transcribed in a different handwriting.

Excerpts from *The Annals of . . . Sisters of Mercy, Saint Joseph's, Tullamore*

1 The currently extant volume of Tullamore Annals for the first decades of the foundation is not, strictly speaking, the original Tullamore manuscript Annals for those years. In the extant volume, a front page on "The Annalists" explains the origin of the present Annals:

> The Annals of this Convent were kept very faithfully from the beginning in rough copies until the year 1867.
>
> Sr. M. Clare Delamere fulfilled the duty of Annalist in the early days of the Foundation, until she went to Kells in 1844. She was succeeded by Sr. M. Francis Pilsworth who kept a faithful record of passing events until within two months of her happy death in 1867. Unfortunately the notes were discontinued until the year '79.
>
> In 1875, this Book was compiled by M. M. Xavier, who used for the purpose Srs. M. Clare's and Francis's copies, and added many recollections of her own. She wrote the events from '67 to '79 from memory, which accounts for the scantiness of information found in these years. . . . She commenced keeping notes of passing events in 1879 and of transferring them afterwards to this Book.

Evidently the practice of writing notes for the Annals, later transferring them to a bound volume, and then discarding the earlier notes was common in the early foundations. The present Tullamore Annals are preserved in the archives of the Sisters of Mercy, Tullamore. The excerpts presented here, besides contributing knowledge about Catherine McAuley, may serve to illustrate some of the work of the first Sisters of Mercy in foundations outside of Dublin.

2 The first benefactor of the Tullamore foundation was Miss Elizabeth Pentony. Though she died in 1835, seven months before the arrival of the Sisters of Mercy, the Tullamore Annals devotes two full pages to an account of her virtues and good works on behalf of poor youth in Tullamore. In a handwritten document in the archives of the Sisters of Mercy, Derry, Mary Ann Doyle spells this woman's name "Penthany", which is, I believe, incorrect. In his *Tullamore Catholic Parish: A Historical Survey*, Michael Byrne says of her:

> The idea of introducing it [the Sisters of Charity] to Tullamore originated with a certain Miss Elizabeth Pentony, a wealthy Dublin lady who retired to Tullamore in 1823 to work among the poor. Miss Pentony had assistance from some other ladies living in Tullamore, at least three of whom were later to become Mercy nuns. When Miss Pentony died in 1835 her idea of introducing an order of nuns to Tullamore did not die with her. After her death Father O'Rafferty went to Dublin and met Mrs. Aikenhead and requested her to open a convent in Tullamore. However, Mrs. Aikenhead judged that the amount of money left by Miss Pentony under her will was too small to support a foundation and she refused to send nuns to Tullamore. Soon after, Father O'Rafferty introduced himself and his case to Catherine McAuley, the foundress of the Sisters of Mercy (1827) and she agreed to send nuns to Tullamore. . . . Their convent was formally inaugurated in Elizabeth Pentony's old house in Store Street on 23 April. Miss Pentony had purchased two houses on the corner of Store Street and Benburb Street in 1830 from a silk and ribbon manufacturer whose business had failed. (96)

3 Mary Teresa Purcell's *Retreat Instructions of Mother Mary Catherine McAuley*, edited by the Sisters of Mercy, Albany, was published in 1952. Although only her initials, "S.M.B.", appear after the Foreword in this book, Sister Mary Bertrand Degnan RSM is the acknowledged editor of this volume. Mary Teresa Purcell professed her vows in Tullamore on May 27, 1836.

4 The ceremonies of reception of the habit and profession of vows. The names of those who accompanied Catherine on this occasion may be incorrect as listed here. In her correspondence at this time Catherine seems to indicate that her niece Catherine would also be coming from Baggot Street.

5 Mary Clare Delamere went with Mary Ann Doyle to found the community in Kells in 1844. Mary Catherine Locke, accompanied by Mary Ann Doyle, founded the community in Derry in 1848; she founded the community in Dundee, Scotland, in 1859.

6 Two, not four, English women made their novitiate in Cork.

7 A comparable recounting of Myles Gaffney's instruction appears in Catherine McAuley's letter to Frances Warde on May 28, 1841 (341).

8 That is, in Ireland. The Teresa White mentioned in the next sentence is not the same Teresa White who was already superior in Galway.

9 This statement is in a letter to Frances Warde (272).

10 Mary Austin Carroll presents the "letter" quoted here as excerpts from two separate letters: one ("They are a grand tribute . . . centuries.") was written, she says, in 1840 (*Life* 290); and the second ("Notwithstanding . . . I am gray with care . . . vain-glory.") was written, she says, in June 1838 (*Life* 292). In an undated letter to Frances Warde, written probably in early January 1841, Catherine uses comparable language to the first excerpt (285); and in an earlier letter to Frances, written on June 16, 1838, she quotes Mary Ann Doyle as saying, "Notwithstanding this prosperity, I am grey with care" (129). However, the last sentence, about "doing the humble", is not included in the June 16, 1838 autograph. Perhaps Catherine wrote other letters, now not extant, containing all this language. But I suspect that the Tullamore annalist is quoting, not an autograph, but Austin Carroll's *Life*, published just prior to the annalist's re-copying of the Annals (see note 1). Carroll refers to Mary Ann Doyle in the second excerpt as "Sister Marianne" whereas in the autograph Catherine actually writes "Sister M.A." (as in Neumann and Bolster).

Perhaps this situation can be seen to illustrate some of the editorial work which remains to be done on Catherine's correspondence: for example, the search for additional extant autographs and covers, and the correlation of extant but sometimes incomplete autographs with early published and unpublished recordings of Catherine's letters so as to recover, if possible, authentic texts of lost autographs, incomplete autographs, or parts thereof.

11 This information would seem to support the view that Catherine McAuley did not receive her copy of the confirmed Rule before she sailed for England on August 20, 1841.

12 The Tullamore Annals places this "circumstance" in 1841, immediately after a paragraph on the profession of Mary Aloysius (Arabella) Deverell and Mary Agnes (Mary) Murtagh on October 18, 1841. However, Catherine McAuley's letter to Frances Warde, published under the date June 30, 1840, places the situation in 1840 (Neumann 218–20 and Bolster 135–7). Although I have not been able to examine the autograph, the fact that the letter is written from Galway, as well as other internal evidence, suggests that the date of the published letter is correct. The sister re-copying the Tullamore Annals (see note 1) probably places this "circumstance" in the wrong year. Catherine McAuley indicates that the ceremony in question was a reception of the habit, not a profession ceremony (219).

13 Michael Molloy, who had "re-established the Tullamore distillery (Flanagan's) in 1829" (Byrne 36), had laid the foundation stone of the new Tullamore convent and attached poor schools in 1838, and was a principal source of the funds for the construction. The new school rooms were opened in June 1840, but the new convent was still under construction and was not occupied until mid 1841. A Mr. Locke was also an important distiller in Tullamore in 1840 (Byrne 40)—perhaps a relative of Mary Catherine Locke.

14 The autograph of this letter to Mary Ann Doyle, if the letter was in fact addressed to her, is apparently not extant. Comparable wording occurs in Catherine's letter to Frances Warde on June 30, 1840 (Neumann 218–21 and Bolster 135–37). More exact wording is in Carroll's *Life* (293), from which the Tullamore annalist may be copying.

15 This wording is somewhat similar to that in Neumann (219) and Bolster (136). Probably the Tullamore annalist was using an inexact handwritten copy of the original letter.

NOTES TO CHAPTER 4

Mary Clare (Georgiana) Moore, 1814–1874

1 Some biographers, including Carroll, Burke Savage, Degnan, and the artist who lettered her page in the Bermondsey Register, have used "Georgina" as her given name. The Bermondsey Annals entry for 1874, which incorporates a life of Mary Clare Moore, who had died on December 14 of that year, also calls her "Georgina". However, in her "Last Will", dated January 16, 1860, she writes "I, Georgiana Moore . . . ," and signs the will "Georgiana Moore". Moreover, her British passport for service as a nurse in the Crimean War, dated October 16, 1854, designates her as "Miss Georgiana Moore". The will and the passport are preserved in the Bermondsey archives of the Sisters of Mercy. The Derry Large Manuscript also calls her "Georgiana".

2 The Bermondsey Register implies that 1814 is the year of Georgiana Moore's birth when it notes that she received the habit of the Sisters of Mercy in 1832, "being eighteen years of age". Carroll gives the year 1814 (*Leaves* 2:37); Burke Savage, 1814 (80); Neumann, 1810 (396, 400); and Bolster, 1814 (*Documentary Study* 2:198).

3 Several biographers say Georgiana was born in Saint Andrew's parish, Townsend Street. The Saint Anne's Parish referred to in the Bermondsey Register is the Church of Ireland parish on Dawson Street; after their conversion to the Catholic Church the family attended the nearby Saint Andrew's.

4 I have not been able to locate an early source for this information, and Degnan does not indicate her source. Clare Moore would not have mentioned this herself, in her later reminiscences.

5 Mary Clare Augustine Moore's letter to Mary Camillus Dempsey, then superior of the Bermondsey convent, was written on July 7, 1875. The autograph letter is preserved in the archives of the Sisters of Mercy, Bermondsey.

6 The appointment lasted for six years, according to the Bermondsey records, and then was extended for six more months until an election was held on June 8, 1848. The details of Mary Clare Agnew's unfortunate misinterpretation of the priorities of the Sisters of Mercy as set forth in the Rule and Constitutions, and of her subsequent departure from the community are discussed in the Bermondsey Annals (I: [27], [97]–[99]), as well as in Carroll's *Life of Catherine McAuley* (407–22) and her *Leaves from the Annals* (2:84–94).

7 Mary Helen Ellis was elected superior in June 1851 but resigned in September 1852 to become superior of a new foundation made from Bermondsey in Brighton, England. From September 23, 1852 on, Clare Moore was re-elected every three years until she died in office in 1874. Rescripts of dispensation (to permit her to remain superior beyond two consecutive terms) were sought by the Bishop of Southwark and approved in Rome. I am grateful to Mary Hermenia Muldrey for her reflection on Clare's suitability for the London position, where ecumenical sensitivity and intelligent articulation of Catholic beliefs were needed.

8 There is, to date, no full length modern biography of Clare Moore, and no published collection of her letters, although many of her autograph letters are preserved in the archives of the Sisters of Mercy, Bermondsey. Volume 2 of Mary Austin Carroll's *Leaves from the Annals* contains quotations from her letters. The published letters of Catherine McAuley do not contain any letters to Clare Moore. It is not clear whether any are still extant.

9 The date of Clare Moore's death is given in the 1874 entry in the Bermondsey Annals. Mary Austin Carroll also says she died on December 14, 1874 (*Leaves* 1:228).

10 That is, a raincoat.

11 The autographs of these letters are preserved in the archives of the Sisters of Mercy, Dublin. They were written to her sister, Mary Clare Augustine Moore, who was then residing at Baggot Street, Dublin, having returned from Cork sometime after Clare returned to England in December 1841—at least by the summer of 1844. These letters are addressed

to "Sister M. Clare" (or "Sister Mary Clare")—a shortened form of Mary Clare Augustine's name which Catherine McAuley also used.

12 In speaking of the "Bermondsey MS" Life, the *Documentary Study* says that the Bermondsey Annals entry for 1841 (i.e., the handwritten Bermondsey Life) "was destroyed during the German bombing" of Holy Trinity Church and Bermondsey convent on March 2, 1945, during World War II (1:lxxxv). Citing Mary Ignatia Neumann's interview with the superior of Bermondsey on May 28, 1967 (Neumann 184) as verification of "the destruction of Bermondsey", Mary Angela Bolster says that "this MS survives in authenticated typescript, a copy of which is lodged in Mercy General Archives . . . Dublin" (*Documentary Study* 1:xc) and that it does not "exist in original form" (1:lxxxv). Apparently she interprets part of Neumann's account of the interview ("One thing remains belonging to the original community: a metal urn which they carried to and from the Crimea," 184) to mean that little else—at least not the Annals entry in question—remains that belonged to the original community (*Documentary Study* 1:cxv). However, the Bermondsey archives today contains many manuscripts, autographs, and books from the earliest years, including all the early volumes of manuscript Annals, in the first volume of which the handwritten "Bermondsey Life" is contained, under the year 1841.

13 This was the first publication of Catherine McAuley's *Practical Sayings.* The story of its compilation, publication and distribution to other convents of the Sisters of Mercy is contained in the Bermondsey Annals (for the year 1868), volume 2, pages [124]–[130]. See also Muldrey, *Abounding in Mercy*, 170–71, 302–3, 384–5, 423.

14 The original manuscript of Catherine McAuley's untitled essay on the vocation of Sisters of Mercy—now published under the title: "Spirit of the Institute" or "The Mercy Ideal"—is contained in a ruled copybook preserved in the archives of the Sisters of Mercy, Bermondsey. Although this manuscript essay is sometimes referred to as the "Bermondsey Manuscript", this usage is confusing; it would be better to designate it by one of its two published titles, as in Neumann (385–91) and Bolster, *Documentary Study* (1: 660–61) and *Correspondence* (242–46), or in the publication of the Bermondsey Archives. See also Sullivan, "Catherine McAuley's Theological and Literary Debt to Alonso Rodriguez: The 'Spirit of the Institute' Parallels." I am very grateful to Teresa Green, the assistant archivist in Bermondsey, for all her help with the Bermondsey archival materials.

15 I have not been able to study in detail the three Cork MS lives of Catherine McAuley, so I have not thoroughly compared Cork MS. 2 and the Bermondsey Life. However, Cork MS. 3, transcribed by Mary Vincent Whitty in 1860, is apparently a copy of Cork MS. 2 (or of the Bermondsey Life), for in its "Dedication", Mary Vincent says that the text she is copying, as a gift for the superior at Baggot Street, was "compiled by . . . Mother Mary Clare Moore."

16 Much research remains to be done to identify the handwriting of each of the early sisters and to match authentic specimens with the existing manuscripts, although this alone will not resolve the questions of authorship, given the extensive copying and sharing of manuscripts that occurred. While I feel I know the cursive handwriting of a few of the early sisters, further research on the handwriting of others might put new names into the pool of potential authors and transcribers of the early manuscripts. See also, in this regard, notes 5 and 6 in the introduction to Mary Vincent Harnett in this volume.

The Letters of Mary Clare Moore to Mary Clare Augustine Moore

1 Both Catherine McAuley and Mary Clare (Georgiana) Moore refer to Mary Clare's sister, Mary Clare Augustine Moore, the addressee of these letters, as "Sister Mary Clare"; this shortened form of her name in religion can be confusing.

2 Clare Moore's punctuation in these rapidly written autograph letters is often very hard to follow: she uses short and long dashes (and double dashes), as well as commas and periods. I have used commas and semicolons for some of her dashes. Where I am not certain that

a mark of punctuation indicates a full stop, I have generally used a comma or a dash. However, in long passages with numerous dashes I have sometimes placed a period where the sense permitted, though I have not done this where a period would foreclose possible connections between Clare's thoughts. I have followed her capitalizations as carefully as I could: her "C", "R" and "S" capital letters are particularly difficult to discern. I have, however, used "and" for her ampersands, and spelled out some of her abbreviations where her references are obvious—such as, "GH" for George's Hill, "O'H" for O'Hanlon. Where she underlines, I have used italics; and where she refers to titles of books, but does not underline these, I have placed the titles in italics. Finally, some of Clare's paragraphs are extremely long, and some of her long dashes and double dashes evidently indicate new paragraphs (she saves paper by not leaving blank spaces!), so I have occasionally paragraphed in such places.

3 Clare Moore's claim that Catherine "never was a Protestant" is, once again, a response to the obituary in the *Morning Register* (Dublin), *Tablet*, or *Register* (Halifax). See note 24 on the Letters of Mary Ann Doyle, in chapter 3.

Frequently throughout these letters—for example, here—Clare Moore abbreviates "Revd. Mother" to "Revd. M" or "R M". I have changed these abbreviations to "Revd. Mother", which is Clare's form when she does not abbreviate. Where she uses simply "R" for the title of priests, or "M. Revd." or "R. Revd." for bishops, I have used "Revd." or "Most Revd." or "Right Revd." Clare is also sometimes inconsistent in her spelling of certain names—e.g., "Francis" and "Frances", and "McCormack" and "McCormick". I have left these inconsistencies.

4 Sometimes Clare Moore, who is writing these letters under the pressure of time, uses "/28" for the year 1828, and so forth. I have usually used full numerals for the years she so indicates. I have also changed some of her abbreviations of the names of months to the full spelling where her abbreviations may be confusing.

5 The following paragraphs of this letter, to the closing and signature, are a puzzle (presenting two problems). They are written on the front and back of a single sheet of paper of the same size (7 1/2 inches by 9 1/2 inches) as the preceding sheet of the letter (15 inches x 9 1/2 inches) when it is folded, but this half sheet is not folded for mailing in the same way as the preceding sheet. Moreover, the content of the first sentence of the first paragraph seems disjointed from the previous content of the letter, and Clare Moore's claim that "I told you" about the Tullamore foundation seems to imply an earlier letter. For these reasons, I strongly believe that this sheet does *not* belong to this August 23, 1844 letter, even though it has been preserved in the Dublin archives, and transcribed, with the opening sheet of that letter. This second sheet is dated at the end, after the signature, "August 16th [or 26th?: but the first numeral does not look like Clare's usual '2']." The sheet also does not, because of its opening and ending words, appear to belong to the sheets of the August 26, 1845 letter, unless it was a second letter, without salutation, enclosed with that mailing. Possibly there was an August 16th letter, in 1844 or 1845, the opening pages of which have not yet been located, if they are still extant, although 1844 may be ruled out because the opening paragraphs of the August 23, 1844 letter seem to imply that it is the first letter in the series.

Moreover, if this sheet does not belong to the August 23, 1844 letter—which the end date "August 16th [or 26th?]", and the manner of folding seem to rule out—then the original concluding sheet or sheets of the August 23 letter are also missing. Careful archival research in Dublin and Bermondsey has not so far resolved these two problems. Nevertheless, I present the text of this autograph sheet here, despite all the foregoing reasons for not doing so, because the text can stand by itself, and because I hope publication of this fragment may lead to the discovery of both a possible *sixth* letter and the conclusion to the August 23, 1844 letter.

6 This comment would seem to support the hypothesis that this portion of the letter, as described in note 5 above, was written in August 1845.

7 During the period in which Clare Moore wrote all these letters, Mary Cecilia Marmion was superior of the Baggot Street convent where Clare's sister, Mary Clare Augustine Moore, lived.

8 Saint Augustine of Hippo, Clare Augustine Moore's patron saint.

9 What follows in this letter (*if* it is the same letter) is on a separate second sheet of paper folded once; hence there are four sides of script. However, the concluding words of the letter—"You will be shocked at this scribbling . . . ."—and the closing and signature are written sideways in the upper left-hand corner of the first side of the *first* folded sheet—i.e., page one of the letter. It is therefore possible that the following text, which is completely on the second sheet, is not part of this letter but of another letter. One will note that the content of the paragraph preceding this sheet may suggest that that paragraph is a concluding paragraph. The ink at the beginning of the second sheet is lighter than that at the end of the first sheet, though this fact may not be significant. Both sheets (9 1/2 inches x 7 1/2 inches) are folded in the same way, as if for the same mailing. While it is possible that sheets of different autographs have been mismatched, neither of these two sheets is the solution to either of the problems presented in note 5 above. I am more inclined to think that they are the "scraps", as Clare calls them, of the same September 1, 1844 letter.

10 In the manuscript, the words, "brown Carmelite Habit", are crossed out in pencil, in a different handwriting, and "postulant [dress]" is written above the line in pencil. Perhaps this is Mary Clare Augustine Moore's correction.

11 In the manuscript, the words, "While she was dying," are crossed out in pencil, in a different handwriting, and the words, "After she died," are inserted in pencil.

12 "O'Farrell" is written in ink, but then the "O" is crossed out in ink; I have interpreted this as Clare Moore's own revision.

Excerpts from *The Annals of the Convent of Our Lady of Mercy, Bermondsey*

1 This first long excerpt, which constitutes a lengthy biography of Catherine McAuley, begins at the bottom of the fourth page of the 1841 entry in volume 1 of the handwritten Bermondsey Annals; it extends from page [27] to page [85] where the following footnote in Mary Clare Moore's handwriting appears: "The foregoing Memoir of our revered Foundress was written about eight or nine years after her happy and holy death, 1849–1850. What follows was added in the year 1868." The footnote is attached to the last word of a tribute to Catherine McAuley, ascribed to Myles Gaffney, with which the biography concludes. The footnote indicates either that the biography was *composed* in 1849–1850 and inserted in the Annals later, or that it was *inserted* in the Annals in 1849–1850—in the pages saved for it under the year 1841. The biographical entry itself actually begins in Clare Moore's distinctive handwriting, but then, after four lines of script, the handwriting changes, starting with the sentence, "This admirable woman was born . . . ." The new handwriting may still be Clare Moore's—altered over the intervening years since she wrote the letters about Catherine to her sister (1844–1845)—or it may be the hand of another sister living in Bermondsey. If it is the latter, it is interesting to note that Anne Byrn—the second oldest daughter (born in 1817) of Catherine McAuley's cousin, Anne Conway Byrn—entered the Bermondsey community on May 22, 1846 and professed her vows there on December 4, 1848; her name in religion was Mary Margaret Byrn. The available specimens of Mary Margaret Byrn's handwriting (her signatures on her will and Act of Profession) do not rule out the possibility that it was she whom Clare Moore assigned to copy the biography of Catherine McAuley into the Annals. In fact, the two handwritings seem very similar. However, the handwritings of Mary Gonzaga (Georgiana) Barrie, who entered on October 5, 1848, and Mary Stanislaus (Margaret) Jones, who entered on February 12, 1849, are also very similar to that in the biography. While Clare Moore herself appears to have been the regular annalist, copying the biography was a time-consuming task which she could have willingly assigned to someone less busy than herself. This interpretation of course assumes that the biography was *composed* before it was *copied*,

as has been already discussed, and that the scribe who inserted it in the Annals was not Clare Moore, its presumed author, but some other member of the Bermondsey community.

The material "added in the year 1868", which is clearly in Clare Moore's handwriting, deals with Catherine McAuley's burial and with other information related to her. The relatively short excerpts from this section of the 1841 entry presented here are taken from pages [85] to [88], again in volume 1 of the Annals.

2 This biographical account, like the Derry Large Manuscript but unlike the Limerick Manuscript, regards Catherine McAuley as younger than her sister Mary. The inaccurate birth year given here would have somewhat supported this opinion, since otherwise, had Mary been the younger, she would have been no more than seventeen when she married William Macauley in 1804. In the next paragraph of the biography we are told that "on their Mother's death" Catherine's "elder sister and brother . . . were about twelve or thirteen years of age." If Elinor McAuley died in 1798, these ages for Mary and James cannot be accurate, since it is known that their father, James McGauley, died in July 1783, and that James, the youngest child, was born in April 1783.

3 In this sentence, and throughout this biography, exclusive of the opening sentence, Catherine's first name is misspelled "Catharine", as is Catherine Byrn's. In her 1844–1845 letters about Catherine McAuley, Clare Moore never uses Catherine's given name in references to her; but when she uses the same name in references to other persons, she spells it "Catherine"; and when she quotes the rescript of indulgences, she notes that it was " 'for Sr. Catherine McAuley and the other pious women.' " Nonetheless, one suspects that Clare Moore herself was the source of the misspelling in the Bermondsey Annals—either directly, as she herself copied the biography into the Annals, or indirectly, through the original text which she supplied to the one who copied it. In the material that "was added in the year 1868", all of which is clearly in Clare Moore's own handwriting, Clare uses Catherine's first name only once and there spells it "Catharine". The Derry Small Manuscript, which is nearly identical to the Bermondsey Annals biography, spells the name "Catherine". Moreover, Catherine McAuley herself spelled her name "Catherine". While she nearly always signed her correspondence, "M.C. McAuley", or "M.C.M."—so Clare Moore would have rarely seen the name fully spelled out—in two extant documents in which Catherine wrote her name out in full, she wrote "Mary Catherine McAuley": the one, a draft of the petition to Rome in late 1839, and the other, a copy of the letter to Rome on October 14, 1840. Catherine also spelled her niece's name "Catherine". I explain all this in detail, lest readers be confused by the misspelling in this manuscript.

4 Perhaps this was Mary Murphy, whom Clare Augustine Moore identifies as one of her own sources of information.

5 In his July 9, 1884 letter to his cousin Mary Camillus (Teresa) Byrn, who was then serving in the United States, William Armstrong McAuley (Macauley), Catherine McAuley's nephew, who was then living in Tomahawk Creek, Irrewillipe, Victoria, Australia, identified this woman as "Mrs. Harper". A photocopy of his letter is in the Bermondsey archives.

6 This commentary on Teresa Byrn is more extensive than the references to her in other early biographical manuscripts.

7 The awkward word order in this sentence is corrected above the line in the manuscript, but I have chosen to present the original wording, because I cannot tell whether the correction is in the original handwriting. It moves "in Upper Baggot Street" to after "The site".

8 Michael Doyle was curate at Saints Michael and John's, and was Mary Ann (Anna Maria) Doyle's older brother. He died in 1844. In this sentence and the following one, "Byrne", and "Ward" are spelled thus.

9 Carlow College.

10 Catherine McAuley had established the Baggot Street Trust on April 8, 1829, thereby assigning the house to Archbishop Murray should she and the two others named in the Trust (Catherine Byrn and Anna Maria Doyle) cease to fulfill the stated purposes of the house.

11 In the manuscript this sentence does not begin a new paragraph. The reference is to Mary Macauley, later, Mary Teresa Macauley.

12 Mary Francis De Sales Knowd was elected Superior of the Presentation Sisters at George's Hill Convent during Catherine McAuley's novitiate there. The rest of this paragraph is about Mother Francis Knowd—not, I believe, about Catherine McAuley.

13 The view of Catherine McAuley's self-abasement expressed here and in the following sentences is consistent with the opinion Clare Moore expresses in her 1844–1845 letters.

14 Mary Joseph Teresa (Mary) Macauley, whom Catherine generally called Mary Teresa.

15 Myles Gaffney became the Dean of Maynooth College in 1834. He entered the Society of Jesus in 1856, and died in France in 1861.

16 Various sources indicate that the sisters served in the cholera hospital on Townsend Street from April to December 1832.

17 Mary Teresa Macauley professed her vows on November 3, 1833.

18 John Rice, the brother of Edmund Rice.

19 The Presentation Rule and Constitutions was confirmed by Pius VII; the decree of confirmation was promulgated in Rome on April 9, 1805 (Walsh 179).

20 A copy of the Rule and Constitutions with this date and Daniel Murray's seal and signature is in the archives of the Sisters of Mercy, Bermondsey, but since the text is hand-*printed* it is hard to tell whether this is, in fact, the first fair copy of the Rule, as discussed here, which Clare Moore herself is known to have prepared. Significantly, in its discussion of the drafting and approval of the original Rule, the Bermondsey biography of Catherine McAuley makes no mention of Clare Moore who assisted Catherine throughout this process. This may be further evidence that the biography was actually composed by Clare Moore. Another copy of the Rule, signed by Daniel Murray and also dated May 3, 1835, is in the archives of the Sisters of Mercy, Birmingham, England; this copy is in cursive writing, but does not appear to be in Clare Moore's hand.

21 Kingstown, the harbor south of Dublin, was formerly called Dún Leary, but was renamed in honor of George IV in 1821; in 1921 it became Dún Laoghaire.

22 Clare Moore knew Catherine McAuley's travel habits firsthand. She accompanied her on the foundation journeys to Tullamore and Charleville, and traveled with her as the newly designated superior to both Cork and Bermondsey. Clare also knew well Bishop John Murphy of Cork, who died in 1847. The reference to the "late revered Bishop" indicates that this portion of the biography was composed after his death.

23 This sister may have been Clare Moore herself, or Mary de Pazzi Delany—in both of whom Catherine confided. Clare and Mary de Pazzi were friends, and corresponded until the latter's death in 1872. This anecdote appears only in this biographical manuscript (and, of course, in the manuscripts identical to it: see earlier discussions of the relation of these manuscripts).

24 In the Limerick Manuscript, where this passage about Catherine's reading is repeated almost verbatim, "Rodriguez on Christian Perfection" is substituted for Francis Blyth's *Devout Paraphrase on the Seven Penitential Psalms.*

25 This sister may have been Clare Moore's own sister, Clare Augustine Moore, or Mary de Pazzi Delany, both of whom had a temperament different from Catherine McAuley's. The person in question evidently lived at Baggot Street during the period 1837 to 1841.

26 Miss Elizabeth Pentony.

27 The other sister was Mary Teresa (Bridget) Purcell.

28 Miss Mary Clanchy, who subsequently married Arthur French.

29 In the manuscript this sentence does not begin a new paragraph, but the unusual length of the paragraph seems to require a break.

30 Clare Moore is the only available source for this episode since she was the only person traveling with Catherine McAuley on this return trip.

31 Michael Nowlan.

32 Mary Anne Agnes (Catherine) Macauley. A number of early sources spell her name in religion "Ann" (which may be correct), but the Dublin Register has "Anne.".

33 Nowhere in the following discussion of the Cork foundation does the author of this biography indicate that Clare Moore was the first superior of the Cork community. Since the author names the superiors of the other foundations that she discusses in some detail (Tullamore, Charleville, Carlow, and Limerick), the omission of this information in reference to Cork and Bermondsey (where Clare Moore also served in this capacity) is yet another clue to Clare's authorship of this manuscript. The later foundations in Birr, Galway, and Birmingham are mentioned only in passing, without the names of the superiors.

34 Mary Anne Agnes Macauley, whom Catherine McAuley continued to call "our darling Catherine" or "our innocent little Catherine", died of consumption on August 7, 1837 (Neumann 93–4).

35 In the Acts of Profession pronounced in the Baggot Street community on August 19, 1841, before Catherine McAuley received her copy of the confirmed Rule, the added words were included, as evidenced by the written texts of several of these Acts, now preserved in the archives of the Sisters of Mercy, Birmingham, England.

36 In the 1930s, John MacErlean SJ, then Vice Postulator for the cause of canonization of Catherine McAuley, prepared notes on the Derry Small Manuscript, a document which is almost identical to the Bermondsey Annals biography. These notes are now in the Dublin archives. He pointed out that "here" is used twice in this passage in reference to Limerick, and he therefore concluded that the Derry Small Manuscript, which he evidently regarded as original (but one would therefore also have to say, by implication, the Bermondsey Annals biography), "was written it would seem between 1847 and 1856, at Limerick." I do not regard the dual use of "here" as sufficient evidence for MacErlean's conclusion as to the place of composition, especially in view of the numerous other internal signs that Clare Moore was the self-effaced author of this biography. So far as I know Clare did not visit Limerick after August 1839, though she may have done so in Summer or Fall 1841 before she returned permanently to Bermondsey from Cork in early December. If "here" is significant, and not just a substitute for "in Limerick", this would raise the question of Mary Ann Doyle's possible authorship of the original manuscript, to be discussed in the next chapter.

37 The two remaining Poor Clares were Mary Shanahan and Anne Hewitt.

38 As Bishop of Dromore, Michael Blake resided in Violet Hill, Newry.

39 In this remarkably brief discussion of the Bermondsey foundation no mention is made of its first superior, Mary Clare Moore. The two others "destined for Bermondsey" were Mary Clare (Elizabeth) Agnew and Mary Austin (Maria) Taylor, English women who had professed their vows in Cork on August 19, 1839. The two, besides Catherine McAuley, who were to return to Baggot Street were Mary Teresa (Amelia) White, later superior of the Galway foundation (1840), and Mary Cecilia (Mary) Marmion, later superior at Baggot Street (1844–1849).

40 Robert Macauley died on January 4, 1840, at the age of twenty-one (Neumann 194). He was the second of the three nephews, not the eldest.

41 James Macauley, Catherine's eldest nephew, died on April 29, 1841 (Degnan 315–16, and Neumann 337). It was her nephew Robert who died while Catherine was in Bermondsey. The author of this manuscript has these deaths confused.

42 In his October 28, 1903 letter to his daughter, Mary Catherine (Fannie Theresa) McAuley, then a Sister of Mercy in Australia, William Armstrong Macauley, Catherine McAuley's youngest nephew, says that he went to sea twice in the 1830s: the first time, after the death of his sister Catherine, who died on August 7, 1837; the second time, in December 1838. Prior to the first departure he visited his aunt at Baggot Street. He returned to Dublin between the two sailings, but did not visit his aunt prior to his second departure, although he did confer with his uncle, James McAuley, who arranged his second passage.

After William's second departure, Catherine McAuley's contact with him ceased, and he was presumed to have died of consumption or to have been lost at sea. However, he had gone to Australia, and in the mid 1840s, he wrote a letter to Baggot Street, to which Mary Cecilia Marmion and Mary Camillus (Teresa) Byrn responded in 1846, sometime before Mary Camillus' departure for New York on April 13. In this joint letter they told Willie of his Aunt Catherine's death, and of the deaths of his brothers Robert (1840) and James (1841). Writing on September 15, 1885, to his cousin, Mary Margaret (Anne) Byrn, then in Bermondsey, Willie recalls that the letter from Baggot Street affected him grievously, and that it was "many months" before he could get "a mastery over my feelings". In 1862, as he says in his July 9, 1884 letter to his cousin Mary Camillus (Teresa) Byrn, then in Baltimore, he wrote to Mary Xavier Maguire, then superior of the Mercy Convent in Geelong, Australia, to identify himself. It took many years for Sisters of Mercy world-wide to recognize that indeed Willie Macauley was still alive. He died on December 30, 1904 at the home of his son Robert, at Bogan Gate near Parkes in New South Wales. He had lived in Australia sixty-three years, and was eighty-three when he died. He and all the other children of Mary and William Macauley had evidently adopted the spelling of their aunt's surname, "McAuley", as their own, after the death of their father in 1829, but I have here and elsewhere preserved the earlier spelling to avoid confusion. William's 1904 death notice lists him as "McAuley" and his descendants, including his great granddaughter Billee McAuley Morwitch, have continued to use that spelling.

43 This circumstance may refer to Robert Moore Powell, the husband of Mary Anne (or Mary Ann) Powell, cousin of Catherine Callaghan, who would have shared the remainder of the Callaghan estate with Catherine McAuley, as joint residuary legatee, had William Callaghan's codicil not revoked this provision. There is some confusion about Mr. Powell's name. He is listed in William Callaghan's will as both "Richard Moore Powell" and "Robert Moore Powell". Degnan identifies him as Robert Moore Powell (39–40). There is, moreover, according to the *Documentary Study*, a bond preserved in the Dublin archives of the Sisters of Mercy which was drawn up between Catherine McAuley and "Frederick Moore" and dated November 1, 1823. In the bond, according to the *Study*, "Catherine tries to recover outstanding debts on the Callaghan estate, but in her charity toward the debtor, she settles for a smaller sum" (2:8). Frederick Moore may have been a relative of Mr. Powell. However, neither of these situations may in fact be related to the circumstance noted here in the Bermondsey Annals.

44 These decisions and difficulties were initiated by Walter Meyler, parish priest of St. Andrew's Church, Westland Row, Dublin, in whose parish the Baggot Street community was located.

45 This sentence does not begin a new paragraph in the manuscript, but the long paragraph seems to require a break at this point. The "20th of June 1841" reference is incorrect. The approval of the Rule and Constitutions by the Congregation for the Propagation of the Faith occurred on July 20, 1840. Gregory XVI "confirmed" the Rule on June 6, 1841, and the decree to this effect was promulgated on July 5, 1841.

46 Here the Limerick Manuscript has simply "Sister N." Many of the actual names given further on in this text are not given in the Limerick Manuscript's version of this letter.

47 The Bermondsey Annals has three ellipses in its text of this "account"." For the content of these ellipses see Mary Elizabeth Moore's letter of November 21, 1841, presented later in this volume.

48 This tribute to Catherine McAuley, ascribed both here in the Bermondsey Annals and in the Limerick Manuscript to Myles Gaffney, Catherine's close friend, raises a number of questions. Mary Angela Bolster notes that the tribute was "Published in *The Tablet*, 28 December 1841, p. 829," and that "A somewhat similar account was printed in *The Catholic Register*, New York, on 19 February 1842" (*Documentary Study* 2:167). I have not so far been able to find a copy of the *Catholic Register* article to which Angela Bolster refers, but, following her lead, I obtained—through the courtesy of the Librarian of Saint Patrick's College, Maynooth—a photocopy of the *Tablet* article which appeared, actually,

on December 25, 1841 (p. 829). The article is signed: "Correspondent of the Dublin *Morning Register*," and is a slightly shorter version of the obituary which appeared in the *Morning Register* (Dublin) on December 10, 1841. Both articles contain, within the long account of Catherine's life, the letter (but incorrectly dated) of Bishop Michael Blake quoted above in the Bermondsey Annals. Although neither article contains a reference to Myles Gaffney, and the first paragraph recorded in the Bermondsey Annals is in the *Morning Register* article but not in the *Tablet* article, all the remaining paragraphs transcribed in the Annals are in both articles.

However, the articles also contain six paragraphs not transcribed here in the Annals (one is partially presented earlier in the Annals); among the sentences not quoted are these:

> Miss Catherine M'Auley was born in this city, of a respectable Protestant family . . . . God had endowed her with a superior judgment, and this, joined to a very inquisitive turn of mind, led her to examine the grounds on which her faith rested . . . . She read the works of some of the most eminent Protestant divines; but she could not satisfy herself that she was in the true Church of Christ.
>
> . . . To this good and great man [Rev. Dr. Thomas Betagh SJ] the young Miss M'Auley had recourse in her difficulties. She had several conferences with him, which ended in her conversion to the Catholic faith.
>
> Having known and embraced the truth, she was now most anxious that her benefactors, Mr. and Mrs. Callan [*sic*] should enjoy a similar blessing. She never ceased to pray for their conversion . . . . One of her brothers died, and she became a mother to his children . . . . ("A National Loss" 829)

The reference to her brother is inaccurate, unless it means her brother-in-law. The articles also say, inaccurately, that Catherine entered the Presentation Convent on George's Hill in "1828 or 1829".

The *Tablet* article is an identical copy of the obituary in the Dublin *Morning Register*, except that the *Tablet* omits the two opening paragraphs in the *Morning Register* obituary. These paragraphs lament that to date no appropriate panegyric on Catherine McAuley, beyond a mere announcement of her death, has appeared in the Dublin papers. The *Morning Register* article is signed by "M. P." This may be a misprint for "M. G." (Myles Gaffney); if it is not a misprint, I cannot identify the author. The Dublin *Morning Register* is available on microfilm in the National Library of Ireland.

On the basis of the *Morning Register* (and *Tablet*) article, the questions which arise are these: Is Myles Gaffney the author of this whole article, except for Michael Blake's letter? Did he believe that Catherine was a convert to the Catholic Church? Was he, despite his nine or ten years of friendship with her, unclear about specific details of her earlier life? What was the original form of his tribute about Catherine? Was it a shorter letter about her which got expanded for publication by someone else at the *Morning Register*? Is he, or someone else, the "Correspondent of the Dublin *Morning Register*"? I cannot answer any of these questions at this time, except to note, again, that the paragraphs which appear in the Bermondsey Annals and the Limerick Manuscript (and so, also, in Mary Vincent Harnett's published biography) are in each case ascribed to Dean Gaffney. Moreover, when Mary Ann Doyle and Clare Moore take pains to assert that Catherine "never was a Protestant", they may be responding not only to the presumably later Halifax *Register* obituary, as noted elsewhere, but also to the *Morning Register* or *Tablet* article and to any newspaper article with a similar claim about Catherine's "conversion" to the Catholic faith. See also note 24 in the Letters of Mary Ann Doyle in chapter 3 above.

The ellipses in the text presented here are ellipses in the Bermondsey Annals' transcription.

49 The *Morning Register* (and *Tablet)* article lists four objects of the Sisters of Mercy. The "4th" is labeled "third" in the Bermondsey Annals' transcription. The "3d", omitted from the transcription with no ellipsis, is "The care of female orphans."

50 The Limerick Manuscript has the number "fourteen" here, which is, in one sense, correct. However, Myles Gaffney, or the author of the *Morning Register* (and *Tablet*) article, explicitly includes Liverpool, a foundation already planned at the time of Catherine's

death, and for which a novice, Mary Liguori (Frances) Gibson, had already entered the Baggot Street community.

51 The *Morning Register* (and *Tablet)* article has "As long as", not "As much as".

52 This footnote and the paragraphs which follow are clearly in Clare Moore's handwriting.

53 This passage is misleading, as worded. The new cemetery was evidently consecrated on Sunday, November 14, but Catherine McAuley's funeral Mass and burial were on Monday, November 15. See Mary Vincent Whitty's letters of November 13–14 and 16, 1841, which are presented later in this volume.

54 By 1868, when this section of the Bermondsey Annals was written, there were Sisters of Mercy in Newfoundland, the United States, Australia, New Zealand, and South America, as well as in Ireland, England, and Scotland.

55 This birth year is, of course, incorrect.

56 This description of Catherine McAuley's physical appearance, copied into the Annals in 1868, is almost identical to the description of her contained on page 206 in Mary Vincent Harnett's *The Life of Rev. Mother Catherine McAuley,* edited by Richard Baptist O'Brien (Dublin, 1864). The description in the *Life* was presumably written by either Harnett or O'Brien.

57 This silver ring is preserved in the archives of the Sisters of Mercy, Crumlin Road, Belfast. Mary Juliana Delany lived in this Belfast community from 1863 until her death in 1900.

NOTES TO CHAPTER 5

Mary Vincent (Anna Maria) Harnett, 1811–1865

1 No one will be more surprised than I was to discover that Mary Vincent's surname is "Harnett", not "Hartnett". I had used the latter name for years, as had Carroll, Burke Savage, Degnan, Neumann, and Bolster. But I was alerted to the problem in the summer of 1992 by Mary Magdalena Frisby RSM, the Dublin archivist, who sent me information on "Mary Vincent Harnett" from the Dublin Register. In November 1992 I went to the Athlone archives for the first time, and revisited the Limerick archives. In both places I saw more than sufficient evidence to convince me that I had been misspelling Mary Vincent's name: the Limerick Annals, written by her friend Mary de Chantal (Catherine) Meagher, always refers to her as "Harnett"; her page in the Limerick Register gives "Harnett" as her surname; the "Memoir on the Life of Mary Vincent Harnett", a manuscript written by Mary de Chantal Meagher (and preserved in the Limerick archives), uses this name throughout; and in the archives of the Sisters of Mercy, Athlone (where the Roscommon archives are now also housed), there are two legal documents—a Deed of Indemnity (Roscommon) and an Agreement of Lease (Athlone)—on which Mary Vincent herself signed her baptismal and surname, "Anne Harnett", as well as numerous other documents using the name "Harnett". Moreover, in the autograph of Catherine McAuley's letter to Mary Ann Doyle on August 20, 1840, she also spells the name "Harnett". The Dublin and Limerick Registers both give "Anna Maria" as her baptismal name, even though on the legal documents in 1854 and 1858 she signs herself "Anne". I am very grateful to Mary Magdalena Frisby, and to Mary Pierre O'Connor RSM and Mary Laurentia Faherty RSM, the Limerick and Athlone archivists, for helping me with this problem and so many others. Mary Vincent's father, Maurice Harnett, was during her youth, according to Mary de Chantal Meagher's "Memoir", the proprietor of "a large mercantile establishment" in Dublin.

2 According to the Annals (1868) of the Sisters of Mercy in Limerick, Quinn showed the Ardagh treasures to the estate agent who brought them to Bishop George Butler and the sisters. They were examined at the convent by the bishop and Lord Dunraven, a student of archaeology, and then sent to the Royal Irish Academy of Antiquities in Dublin for scrutiny. However, as their value was not immediately recognized, they were in 1871 returned to Limerick where they were kept and admired in Saint Mary's Convent of Mercy

for seven years before they were recalled to Dublin in 1878. In 1871 Bishop Butler, as a Trustee of the Ardagh property for the sisters, purchased the treasures for £50 from the farmer's widowed mother, Mrs. Quinn, who had leased the land from the community; in 1878 the bishop received £100 from the Royal Academy in return for the Ardagh treasures (O'Connor, "Sisters of Mercy and the Ardagh Chalice" 27–28).

3 Bolster, *Documentary Study* 1:xxiv.

4 The fact that references in the Limerick Manuscript to Myles Gaffney note that he became dean at Maynooth in 1834, but do not note that he entered the Society of Jesus in 1856, may indicate that Mary Vincent Harnett completed the original manuscript before 1856. However, since she went to Roscommon in 1853, she may in fact have completed it before that date. For further information on the period of composition, see notes 1, 24, and 48 on the text of the Limerick Manuscript itself, which follows this introduction.

5 The Limerick Annals lists Mary Ann Doyle's visit to Limerick among the entries for 1846, not 1847. Although Mary Ann was superior in Kells from February 9, 1844 on, she was appointed to this office by Bishop John Cantwell of Meath on November 30, 1843. Hence her three-year term of office for Kells would have expired prior to her visit to Limerick in December 1846. However, she may have resigned her office before the end of her term, for reasons of health, and then gone to Limerick before or after her return to Tullamore. She left Tullamore for the Derry foundation in July 1848. I have not so far been able to do research in the Kells archives on the timing of her departure from Kells. Mary Ann also went to Dublin sometime after she left Kells.

6 This sentence is worded and punctuated exactly as it appears in the Limerick Annals (1: 162). The "details" are clearly Mary Ann Doyle's, but "her after Memoir of our Foundress" can be read as referring to Mary Vincent Harnett's or Mary Ann Doyle's. I take "after Memoir" to mean, Memoir written "later" or "afterwards". If it refers to Mary Ann Doyle's, then two questions arise. Did Mary Vincent write down the Derry Large Manuscript or the Derry Small Manuscript for Mary Ann Doyle? Did Mary Vincent commit to writing some other manuscript for Mary Ann? I cannot at present resolve either of these questions, but I do not believe that either of the extant Derry Manuscripts is in Mary Vincent's handwriting, though I may be mistaken in this assessment. If Mary Vincent did, in fact, write down for Mary Ann either the Derry Large Manuscript or the Derry Small Manuscript, as a record of Mary Ann's own recollections, this would explain Mary Vincent's access to these manuscripts and her inclusion of long passages of them in her own Limerick Manuscript. It will be recalled that the Derry Small Manuscript is nearly identical to the Life in the Bermondsey Annals.

7 Mary Vincent Harnett was later also in correspondence with Mary Austin Carroll who had entered the Sisters of Mercy in Cork in December 1853, and had gone to the United States in October 1856. In 1859 Austin Carroll, at Frances Warde's request, also began to collect data for a biography of Catherine McAuley (Muldrey 54–56).

8 The pages of the Derry Large Manuscript were not originally numbered so it is not possible now to ascertain how much of the early part of the manuscript is missing.

9 The Ennis Manuscript contains about two-thirds of the text of the complete copies. It starts at the beginning but stops at events in 1832.

10 This Limerick Manuscript is 104 handwritten pages in length, in a stitched notebook. See note 1 accompanying the Manuscript below, for a detailed evaluation of the two Limerick documents.

11 While she was in Limerick, she had also built an orphanage, Mount St. Vincent's, which was completed in 1850. The proper care of orphaned children was one of Mary Vincent's lifelong concerns, perhaps, in part, because she had lost her own mother when she was only eight or nine years old.

12 Anthrax—the word means "carbuncle"—is an infectious disease caused by the *Bacillus anthracis*; it attacks various species of animals and can be transmitted from them, directly or indirectly, to humans. In Mary Vincent Harnett's case, it took the external form of a

malignant pustule in the neck. The bacteria multiply in the body, invade the blood stream, and cause death by septecemia. Mary Vincent may have contracted anthrax, for example, from a cow, sheep, horse, or mule, or from water, milk, soil, or insects.

The Limerick Manuscript

1 Preserved in the archives of the Sisters of Mercy, Limerick, are two long biographical documents about Catherine McAuley; each one can be regarded as *the* "Limerick Manuscript". The particular Limerick Manuscript presented here is the one contained in a bound notebook with a typed label on the cover: "Life of Mother McAuley. Limerick." The notebook measures 9 3/4 inches by 7 3/4 inches, and the paper inside is 9 1/4 inches by 7 1/2 inches. The decorated title on the cover of the other Limerick Manuscript is "The Life of Our Revered Foundress Mother Mary Catherine McAuley". The two texts have only a few very minor differences in wording, except for the absence in the manuscript presented here of one sentence about Catherine's niece Mary's enjoying "a greater share of her Aunt's confidence", and the different sentence sequences in the section on Dr. William Macauley's anger at his wife Mary's return to the Catholic Church.

I have chosen to present the manuscript labeled "Life of Mother McAuley. Limerick" for two reasons. First, I believe there is a *possibility* that this document is in Mary Vincent Harnett's handwriting. I base my belief only on my own examination of the few specimens of her handwriting which I have so far found: her signature on two legal documents, her inscription in a book, and a letter in the Cork archives which is in her hand, a photocopy of which was kindly given to me by Mary Angela Bolster. Because these specimens are brief, my conjecture rests on matching only a few letters of the alphabet. Until more specimens of her handwriting are verified and compared one cannot be sure.

Secondly, the blank spaces left for future illumination at the top of the first and second sheets of this Limerick Manuscript suggest to me that its author (or scribe) regarded the text of this particular manuscript as in some sense final, that is, satisfactory to the author and ready to be illuminated. Thus, on the opening page of the manuscript, which is unnumbered, only the first two paragraphs of the text appear; they are written in black ink. However, the word, "Introduction", is written in pencil across the blank space which comprises the top third of the page. Similarly, on page one, the words, "Memoirs of the Life of Revd. Mother Mary Catherine McAuley Foundress of the Order of our Lady of Mercy", are written in pencil at the top of the page above the large space which has been saved for illumination of this title. The handwriting in these penciled titles is that of Mary de Chantal (Catherine) Meagher, an early, if not the first, Limerick annalist and Mary Vincent Harnett's close friend.

It is, I believe, impossible to be sure that there is no other extant "Limerick Manuscript" of which one or other of the two I have discussed may be a copy, although a careful search of the Limerick and Athlone archives (the Roscommon archives are now transferred to Athlone) has not yielded any other such manuscript. The Ennis Manuscript, a photocopy of which was kindly given to me by Mary Hermenia Muldrey, is a copy of the other Limerick Manuscript (i.e., the one not presented here); it is incomplete and is not, I believe, in Mary Vincent Harnett's handwriting.

Moreover, I cannot, at this point, be confident that one or other of the two manuscripts in Limerick is the "original" manuscript written by Mary Vincent Harnett—that is, composed as she first composed it. For, to complicate matters further, Mary Vincent herself is said to have written two Memoirs of Catherine McAuley—one, before she left Limerick in August 1853 to found the community in Roscommon; and one, prior to 1864, which was the basis of the 1864 publication of Richard Baptist O'Brien's edition of her *Life of Revd. Mother Catherine McAuley.* Mary de Chantal Meagher—who as a novice went with Mary Vincent from Limerick to Roscommon, was later her Assistant in the branch house founded from Roscommon in Athlone, and some time after Mary Vincent's death in 1865 returned to Limerick and became the Limerick annalist—says in her "Memoir of Mary Vincent Harnett" (now in the Limerick archives):

> On Mother Mary Francis Ward's [*sic*] visit to St. Mary's [Limerick] in 1843, and again on that of Mother M. Anne Doyle in 1846, she procured from them authentic and extensive information of Mother M. C. McAuley's early years, and the establishment of the House and Order in Baggot St., and 'twas a happiness to her indeed when later on Mother M. Elizabeth [Moore, superior of Limerick] wished her to write her (M. McAuley's) Memoir from the notes she had so carefully collected. In 1864 she compiled *another* in Roscommon, without however having the original one to refer to for many circumstances, not in the mere date record within her reach. In her anxiety also to hand down the practices and spirit of the Foundress, for reasons that appeared weighty at the time, she published the book rather too quickly, and without the revisal which would cause her reflecting mind to abridge some parts, or make a few changes in others and that should still leave it most interesting and valuable in the Order, but more suited for seculars in general.

Our problem is not the one Mary de Chantal identifies at the end of this passage, but rather the difficulty of determining whether either of the two extant "Limerick Manuscripts" is the "original one" or the 1864 version. Since the two Limerick Manuscripts are almost identical in wording, it is possible that both are versions of the original and that the 1864 text, which was presumably given to Richard Baptist O'Brien, was not returned to Harnett or to a Mercy archives. However, given the close correspondence between the wording in these two manuscripts and that in certain passages of the published *Life,* it is also possible that one or other of these was the basic text for the 1864 publication, even though the published *Life* has a good deal of the editor's own wording in it.

Despite all these problems, present readers can be assured that of the two extant manuscripts known as the "Limerick Manuscript" and housed in the Limerick archives, one of them is here presented exactly as it is written (except for a few paragraphing and punctuation changes, the conversion of ampersands to "and", and the use of apostrophes to show possessive case); that there are no differences in content between this one and the other and no major differences in wording, except the two instances noted above; and lastly, that this biography of Catherine McAuley was indeed composed by Mary Vincent Harnett, sometime between 1846 and 1864 (see notes 24 and 48 below), using the sources available to her, such as the Derry Large Manuscript, the biography which appears in the Bermondsey Annals, the oral (and written?) recollections of Frances Warde, Mary Ann Doyle, and Mary Elizabeth Moore, and her own personal memories and insights.

2 Sisters of Mercy were in all these places by April 1850. Mary Cecilia Maher and sisters from Carlow founded a community in Auckland, New Zealand in 1850.

3 Perhaps Mary Vincent Harnett composed this paragraph herself, but the somewhat self-congratulatory attitude toward the "exalted virtues" of the Institute makes one suspicious that a non-member of the community suggested or composed this introductory statement. Perhaps it is the work of Richard Baptist O'Brien.

4 As noted earlier, this title is in pencil, in the hand of Mary de Chantal Meagher, an early Limerick annalist.

5 This is the only early manuscript presented in this volume which gives 1778 as Catherine McAuley's birth year, and which explicitly says she was the eldest of her parents' children. However, Mary Vincent Harnett consulted many sources, including Mary Elizabeth Moore and Frances Warde, Catherine's close friends.

6 Catherine's father, James McGauley, was considerably older than her mother. See Degnan 4, 349, and 353, and O'Hara 1.

7 For a comprehensive discussion of the penal laws against Catholics in Ireland from the 1530s onwards, and of the various Catholic Relief Acts beginning in 1778 and leading up to the Catholic Emancipation Act of 1829, see Corish, *Irish Catholic Experience* (63–191).

8 See Catherine McAuley's letter to Mary Elizabeth Moore in Kingstown on August 31, 1837 (Neumann 96).

9 Andrew Lubé was a curate at St. Mary's, Liffey Street, and then parish priest of St. James parish from 1810 until his death in 1831 (Donnelly 88, 231–2).

10 William Armstrong, who lived with his family at 34 Mary Street, Dublin.

11 This sentence does not appear in Harnett's published *Life* as edited by Richard Baptist O'Brien.
12 Apothecaries Hall, with which William Armstrong was affiliated in various official capacities.
13 The content of the two preceding sentences is not included in the published *Life*.
14 This sentence and the following one are, except for one missing clause, identical to the opening sentences of the Derry Large Manuscript in its currently extant form. It will be recalled that the first pages of the Derry Large Manuscript are now lost. Earlier passages in the Limerick Manuscript may also be identical to passages in the once extant pages. Certainly from here on numerous passages in the Limerick Manuscript are identical to passages in the Derry Large Manuscript. These passages are too numerous to note; they stop several pages before the Derry Large Manuscript itself ends.
15 This word is either "unbody" or "imbody"; I think it is the former. I do not think it is "embody".
16 The manuscript does not begin a new paragraph after this sentence, but a break in the long paragraph seems needed.
17 Michael Bernard Keogh, a Capuchin serving as parish priest of Baldoyle (Degnan 35–6).
18 Daniel Murray was consecrated bishop, as coadjutor to Archbishop John Troy, in 1809. He became Archbishop of Dublin in 1823, on the death of Archbishop Troy (Donnelly 147–9).
19 Again, a break in the very long paragraph in the manuscript seems needed here.
20 The word in the manuscript is "flasshed".
21 William Callaghan died on November 10, 1822, according to the death notice which appeared in the *Dublin Evening Post* on November 14, 1822 (Burke Savage 41).
22 The word, "design", is written above the second "destiny" in this sentence and "destiny" is crossed out, but this correction is not in the same handwriting as the rest of the text.
23 Michael Blake became Bishop of Dromore in 1833 and died in 1860.
24 This woman was evidently "Mrs. Harper", according to William Macauley, Catherine's nephew. The close similarity—and in some cases, the identity—between the wording in this paragraph and that in the comparable paragraph in the Bermondsey Annals biography, as well as the many other apparent borrowings from the Life recorded in the Bermondsey Annals, raises the important, but at present not fully resolvable issue of the sharing of manuscripts in the 1840s and 1850s. The close verbal relation between passages in the Limerick and Bermondsey accounts may be explained to some extent by the existence of Cork MS. 2 which, according to Mary Angela Bolster, "is in the handwriting of Sister M. Clare Moore" (*Documentary Study* 1:lxxxvii) and "compiled" by her (*Documentary Study* 2:217), and which, I believe, is probably the original composition which was later copied into the Bermondsey Annals. Certainly a manuscript in Cork would have been at least geographically accessible to Mary Vincent Harnett, and she is known to have corresponded with the Cork superior, Mary Josephine (Sarah) Warde, Frances Warde's sister. In the text which follows, the passages which are similar or identical to passages in the Bermondsey biography are too numerous to cite; they occur intermittently right up to the account of Catherine's death, often alternating with passages from the Derry Large Manuscript.
25 Joseph Nugent died of typhus at the age of twenty-nine (Neumann 53).
26 The sequence of events presented here may be misleading. Catherine's sister Mary Macauley died in August 1827; Catherine completed the sale of Coolock House in September 1828.
27 In this clause "could" may be "would".
28 In the other Limerick Manuscript a sentence not included here appears before this sentence. It reads: "After her mother's death the eldest daughter accompanied her aunt to Catholic places of worship, and being the eldest of the children was honoured with a greater share

of her Aunt's confidence. She was now in her sixteenth year . . . ." This niece was Mary Macauley.

29 From this point in the paragraph and through the next two paragraphs, the sequence of sentences and clauses differs from that in the other Limerick Manuscript, as does the wording occasionally. However, the content is the same in both texts, in the order of events and in the detail. Both Mary Raymond (Catherine) Byrn OP and William Macauley, the youngest son of Dr. William Macauley, later questioned the accuracy of some details in this report, as these appeared publicly in Harnett's *Life* (31–4) and Carroll's *Life of Catherine McAuley* (116–19). For summaries of these disagreements see Degnan (80–1) and Muldrey (79–80, 287–9, and 361–2).

30 That is, during her sister Mary's illness.

31 That is, at Baggot Street.

32 Catherine Byrn, Catherine McAuley's adopted cousin, then about fifteen years old. In this manuscript her name is often spelled "Byrne".

33 The Bermondsey Annals says this permission was given on December 7, 1828.

34 The words, "as the means", are crossed out in the manuscript, but it is not possible to tell whether this was done by the author (or scribe) of the manuscript or by a later hand.

35 According to Mary Bertrand Degnan, Dr. Macauley died on January 25, 1829 (82). In her Memoir, Clare Augustine Moore says Dr. Macauley "took fever in the January of the following year [i.e., in 1829] and died." Mary Ann Doyle also says that he died in January. Only the Limerick Manuscript says that Catherine McAuley moved permanently into Baggot Street after Dr. Macauley's death, that is, after January 1829. The other biographical manuscripts speak of her moving there in late May or June 1828.

36 That is, the prayer known as the "Psalter of Jesus".

37 In the second part of her first letter, Mary Ann Doyle says, "I am not aware of Revd. Mother having any intention of uniting with the Sisters of Charity. Her property was too considerable not to form a new establishment for the poor."

38 The word in the manuscript is actually "dejuné".

39 The Derry Large Manuscript says these two sisters were Anna Maria Doyle and Margaret Dunne. The Bermondsey Annals gives their names in religion: Mary Ann Doyle and Mary Angela Dunne.

40 The manuscript does not begin a new paragraph here, but a break in the long paragraph seems needed.

41 In public or formal situations and on the covers of posted letters during this period in Ireland, the professed members of the community were often designated as "Mrs.", just as priests were given the title "Mr." or "Revd. Mr.".

42 Alonso Rodriguez's particular chapter on obedience referred to here is chapter 10 of the fifth treatise (which is entirely "On Obedience") in volume 3 of his *Practice of Christian and Religious Perfection.* The title of the chapter in the 1806 Kilkenny edition is "The explanation of St. Paul's three arguments for obedience." Apparently Catherine McAuley, like Rodriguez, interpreted "prelates" as "superiors" in this instance, and sought to explain to her new religious community the nature of religious obedience as a mutual interdependence between superiors and members. However, the manuscript in the Dublin archives (it is not in Catherine McAuley's handwriting), on which a later hand has written "On Obedience" and a still later hand has written "Copy of First Lecture given by Mother McAuley", is not a modified transcription of *this* chapter of Rodriguez, but a pastiche of modified transcriptions from earlier chapters in Rodriguez's fifth treatise in volume 3. I think this manuscript was labeled incorrectly earlier in this century.

43 According to other early sources, including the Dublin Register, Mary Aloysius (Anne) O'Grady died on February 8, 1832. The Limerick Manuscript is here following the date given in the Bermondsey Annals biography, although in the list of deaths contained in the material added in 1868 to the Bermondsey Annals for 1841, the date given is February 8. In her letter of September 13, 1844, Clare Moore also says "7th February."

44 In her letter of September 13, 1844, Clare Moore says this lady was Miss Farrell (or O'Farrell).

45 In the manuscript this sentence, written in the same hand, is inserted above the line, and the words "would" and "Mother Superior" are abbreviated.

46 William Kinsella was Bishop of Ossory; the diocesan seat was in Kilkenny. He died in 1845.

47 The Ennis Manuscript, which is an incomplete copy of the other Limerick Manuscript, ends here, in mid sentence. The passage corresponds, though not in exact wording, to the content on page 89 of Harnett's edited *Life.*

48 Myles Gaffney resigned from Maynooth in 1856 to enter the Society of Jesus, and he died in France in 1861. The fact that neither his departure from Maynooth nor his death is noted here may indicate that this manuscript was written before 1856, or at least before 1861. Similarly, in references to Michael Blake elsewhere in this text, his death (in 1860) is not noted, nor are the deaths of Bishop John Murphy of Cork (1847) or Archbishop Murray (1852). These omissions may indicate that this manuscript was composed as early as 1847 or 1852, prior to Mary Vincent Harnett's departure for Roscommon in 1853, or they may be irrelevant to its date of composition and simply reflect the narrative perspective or knowledge of the author or her written sources.

49 In early 1832, Mary Agnes (Anna) Carroll went to the Presentation Sisters, George's Hill, where she became known as Mary Brigid Carroll (Burke Savage 142–3); and in December 1832, Mary Josephine (Catherine) Byrn transferred to the Dominican Sisters, Cabra, where she became known as Mary Raymond Byrn.

50 Dr. James W. McAuley (1783–1873), a military surgeon and Catherine McAuley's brother.

51 The branch house in Kingstown was opened early in 1835, not in 1834.

52 The entire preceding paragraph is an excellent illustration of this manuscript's dependence on the biography of Catherine McAuley in the Bermondsey Annals, or on an earlier manuscript or later copy of it. Every sentence after the first clause is almost identical to the corresponding sentence in the Bermondsey Annals, although one clause and one sentence—referring to Catherine's private repairing of her underclothing, and to her "very scanty" meals as a consequence of her carving for the community—are omitted.

53 The first poem was sent to Mary Teresa Vincent (Ellen) Potter, a novice in Limerick, in late 1838 or early 1839. The autograph is in the Limerick archives and its punctuation and capitalization differ slightly from what is transcribed here. Mary Teresa Potter died of typhus fever on March 20, 1840.

54 This poem was left behind for Mary Elizabeth Moore, superior of the Limerick community, when Catherine departed from Limerick on December 9, 1838. The autograph is in the Limerick archives.

55 The word, "ere", is substituted in this manuscript for "e'er" in Catherine McAuley's autograph.

56 In the autograph "old man" is within quotation marks.

57 Mary Elizabeth Moore. The autograph begins, "My Dearest Sister M.E."

58 In the autograph "all" is underlined.

59 The autograph concludes with the words: "The parting advice of your ever affectionate M. C. M."—that is, Mary Catherine McAuley.

60 Again, this paragraph is almost identical to the comparable passage in the Bermondsey Annals, except for the comment about Jesus' "being neither 'sad nor troublesome,' " the substitution of Rodriguez's work for Blyth's *Devout Paraphrase on the Seven Penitential Psalms,* and the reversed order of two ideas early in the paragraph. From here on, to the account of Catherine's death, this manuscript very closely follows the text of the biography in the Bermondsey Annals.

61 In the manuscript the word is "creared", apparently a slip of the pen.

62 Miss Elizabeth Pentony. Dr. James O'Rafferty was parish priest in Tullamore.

63 Miss Mary Clanchy, afterwards Mrs. Arthur French.

64 This description of Catherine McAuley's younger niece Catherine is peculiar to the Limerick Manuscript, as is the following reflection on the numerous deaths during the first years of the Institute. Since Mary Vincent Harnett entered the Baggot Street community on February 5, 1837—when young Catherine Macauley was just four months professed, and about eighteen years old—she would have known her well and would have been deeply moved by her death six months later.

65 Perhaps more than others, Frances Warde in Carlow and Elizabeth Moore in Limerick would have known of Catherine's acute sorrow at the circumstances of Robert Macauley's death, even though her extant letters to them in January 1840 are laconic, or silent, in reference to it.

66 Miss Helena Heffernan.

67 Mary Teresa (Amelia) White was appointed superior. The appointment was evidently intended to be temporary, but she remained in that role until 1855.

68 Mary Aloysius (Elizabeth) Scott was appointed superior.

69 The Bermondsey Annals biography incorrectly gives the date, "the 20th of June 1841". The date given here in the Limerick Manuscript is the correct one. On *July* 20, 1840, the Congregation for the Propagation of the Faith approved the Rule and Constitutions; it was subsequently forwarded to Gregory XVI for papal confirmation, which occurred on June 6, 1841.

70 The quotation marks in this paragraph are exactly as they appear in the manuscript, even though the opening quotation marks are probably misplaced. The whole prayer is attributed to Catherine McAuley.

71 That is, from eleven o'clock in the morning until ten minutes before eight in the evening. The precise knowledge of the stages of death reflected in Catherine McAuley's letters and in the early annals and biographical manuscripts is remarkable, the more so since none of the early sisters was formally trained as a nurse. It was evidently a consequence of their intimate experience of death, gained in visitation of the sick, in prolonged service in cholera and fever hospitals, and in close attendance on their own dying sisters.

72 The word, "cemetery", is spelled "cemetry" here and below, but in both places an "e" is inserted above the line, apparently by the author (or scribe).

73 This date is incorrect; the Solemn Office and High Mass were on Monday, November 15, 1841.

74 One version of Mary Elizabeth Moore's letters to various Mercy superiors has been presented earlier in this volume—in the conclusion of the life of Catherine McAuley in the Bermondsey Annals—and the autograph of the letter sent to Mary Ann Doyle is presented later in this volume. However, since there are small differences in the wording of the Bermondsey and Limerick transcriptions, perhaps due to differences in the original letters being transcribed, and since the author of the letters was the superior of Limerick, it seems wise to include as well, for the sake of completeness, the version which is recorded here in the Limerick Manuscript. The two ellipses which appear are in the transcription.

75 In the autograph letter which Mary Elizabeth Moore wrote to Mary Ann Doyle on November 21, 1841, the word order is exactly as recorded here: "God may bless you." However, the text transcribed here in the Limerick Manuscript probably is that of a letter to another superior, since it differs slightly from the wording in the letter to Mary Ann Doyle. Elizabeth Moore is known to have written similar letters to the superiors of several, if not all, of the first foundations.

76 For reasons similar to those noted above, the November 13, 1841 letter of Michael Blake to Elizabeth Moore and the statement ascribed to Myles Gaffney are included here, just as they follow in the Limerick Manuscript. Even though both are also part of the Bermondsey Annals biography presented earlier in this volume, repeating them here permits the presentations of both the Bermondsey and the Limerick manuscripts to be complete.

77 See note 48 on the text of the Life in the Bermondsey Annals, presented in the preceding chapter.

78 In the Bermondsey Annals this quotation from Matthew 25 is completely presented.

79 The ellipsis is in the transcription.

NOTES TO CHAPTER 6

Mary Clare Augustine (Mary Clare) Moore, 1808–1880

1 Mary Ignatia Neumann says that "Sister M. Clare Augustine remained in Cork until after the death of Bishop [John] Murphy (April 1, 1847). She returned to Baggot Street March 23, 1848" (182, 316). Neumann undoubtedly found information to support this view. However, Clare Augustine is clearly in Baggot Street in 1844–1845 when she receives the letters of reminiscences about Catherine McAuley from Mary Ann Doyle and Clare Moore, because these correspondents tell her to give their "best love" to Mary de Pazzi Delany, Mary Cecilia Marmion, Mary Vincent Whitty, Magdalen Flynn, Genevieve Jarmy, and Mary Camillus Byrn, all of whom were resident in Baggot Street at the time.

2 For a discussion of the role of several Irish bishops in the November 1854 consistory held in Rome to finalize the text of the papal bull, see Larkin, *The Making of the Roman Catholic Church in Ireland, 1850–1860,* 253–63. While Larkin does not refer to the illuminated memorial, Mary Nathy O'Hara RSM (Dublin) is generally regarded as a reliable source of information. Moreover, Bolster also notes that Clare Augustine "illuminated Canon Ulick Burke's Gaelic version of the Bull of Proclamation of the dogma of the Immaculate Conception. This was presented to Pope Pius IX from Ireland" (*Documentary Study* 2:199).

3 See note 1 above. I regret that I have not been able to ascertain more precisely when Clare Augustine Moore returned to Dublin from Cork.

4 Mary Austin Carroll also notes that after Catherine's death "a sculptor was employed to take a cast of her features, and the Sister frequently mentioned in her letters in connection with the fine arts, painted in oil a life-size portrait, which is tolerably correct, though taken from a corpse." Carroll says that in Clare Augustine Moore's painting, Catherine is "represented in a sitting position, clothed in the costume of her Order, and holding the book of the Rules" and that the "original is in Baggot Street, but several other convents possess copies" (*Life* 439–40). Carroll notes that the likeness in the 1890 edition of her *Life* "is taken from a small portrait executed from memory by one of the Sisters" (440). Considerably more research needs to be done to catalog, and if possible reproduce in a single book, the various portraits of Catherine McAuley which have been made over the years and to record the names and dates of the artists involved. Roland Burke Savage says that the portrait in his book (facing page 364) is "in the Convent of Mercy, Baggot Street," but this portrait does not appear to fit Carroll's description of Clare Augustine Moore's portrait. Burke Savage's frontispiece is a sketch by his contemporary, Seán O'Sullivan RHA. The frontispiece in Degnan's book does appear to fit Carroll's description, though Degnan does not identify the artist. Mary Nathy O'Hara says that some who knew Catherine McAuley, "like Sr. Clare Augustine Moore . . . did make portraits from memory and in 1886 a Sr. Raphael Nelson who, it is said, closely resembled Mother McAuley sat for a portrait. It is in the Mercy convent in Baggot Street and copies can be seen in most Mercy convents" (22–23). The sister who sat for this portrait was Mary Raphael (Annie) Nelson who entered the Baggot Street community in 1881. She professed her vows on November 21, 1883 and died at Baggot Street on April 9, 1889, at the age of twenty-seven. A number of modern artists have also attempted to portray Catherine McAuley, including Marie Henderson RSM (Detroit), who has produced a life-size terra-cotta sculpture of Catherine, a one-third life-size relief of her head and shoulders, and a sketch of the head of the sculpture.

5 This letter of Mary Clare Augustine Moore to Mary Camillus Dempsey, dated July 7, 1875, is preserved in the archives of the Sisters of Mercy, Bermondsey, London.

"A Memoir of the Foundress of the Sisters of Mercy in Ireland"

1 I have put "The Dublin Manuscript" in square brackets to indicate that this is the name by which this manuscript is commonly known, although it is not the title given to it by the author. Mary Clare Augustine Moore is clearly the author of the "Memoir of the Foundress . . . ." The handwriting from beginning to end is identical to the handwriting in her letter about her sister, Mary Clare Moore, written to the superior of Bermondsey on July 7, 1875, seven months after her sister's death. About half of the manuscript is written in ink; where the author begins to write in pencil I note this. The punctuation throughout the manuscript is very sparse and the lack of it is often confusing; I have, therefore, inserted punctuation where this appeared necessary. The words in square brackets are entirely my own additions or corrections, where these seemed necessary for clarity or accuracy. Some corrections are in the notes. The notes are numerous, in part because of the condition of the manuscript, and in part because Clare Augustine's narrative is so detailed.

2 The reference to Michael Blake as the "late Bishop of Dromore" indicates that this paragraph, at least, was written after Blake's death on March 7, 1860. The use of the future tense, in "I shall note my authority", may indicate that the entire Memoir was composed after this date. Reference to Daniel Murray as the "late" Archbishop of Dublin indicates that the Memoir was written after his death in 1852. Clare Augustine Moore actually notes her "authority" only a few times, often by inserting in the left-hand margin of her manuscript the initials of the person or persons from whom she received the information she is reporting. I record these notations, where they occur, in the notes on the text. Sometimes they are illegible, because of the frayed left edges of the manuscript, or are so cryptic as to be now undecipherable. The marginal notation at the beginning of the second paragraph of the manuscript is "M.M./Miss B."; these initials probably refer to "Mary Murphy" and "Miss Byrne" who are listed as sources in the first paragraph. The Byrn family name is spelled "Byrne" throughout the manuscript; I have not corrected this.

3 The birth year given here (1787) is incorrect, and impossible, since Catherine McAuley's father, James McGauley, died in the summer of 1783. His will was made on July 18, 1783 and probated on August 2, 1783 (Degnan 350).

4 There are three lacunae in this autograph Memoir. Here, the words, "greatly by devoting", occur at the end of the second side of the first sheet of the manuscript. At this point *at least* one sheet (two sides) is missing from the manuscript. Consequently, the Memoir leaps forward from Catherine's childhood and her father's devotion to the poor of their neighborhood to her years of residence with William and Catherine Callaghan at Coolock House. It picks up the narration at the point in the story when Mr. Powell (the husband of Catherine Callaghan's young cousin Mary Anne) tried to deflect Mr. Callaghan's reliance on Catherine McAuley in order to secure a greater inheritance for his wife—that is, after the death of Catherine Callaghan on October 3, 1819 and during William Callaghan's decline in health, prior to his death on November 10, 1822. See Degnan 39–40.

5 The will was *altered* by the codicil, not *revoked.* Catherine McAuley and Mary Anne Powell had previously been named "joint residuary legatees", following disbursement of the explicit bequests, but now Catherine was to be "sole residuary legatee". William Callaghan's will, with the codicil added, is in the archives of the Sisters of Mercy, Dublin. In the will proper, the text of which is evidently not in Mr. Callaghan's handwriting, Mr. Powell is called "Richard Moore Powell" near the beginning of the text, and "Robert Moore Powell" near the end. The will is dated January 27, 1822. The codicil incorporates the same date.

6 I have inserted "[and]" for an illegible three-letter word which seems to begin with "a".

7 Again, at least one sheet is missing from the manuscript. The next extant page picks up the narrative in 1823 or 1824, about a year or two before the death of Catherine' s friend,

Rev. Joseph Nugent, who died on May 30, 1825. The "He" of the first full sentence which follows the lacuna, and the "him" whom Joseph Nugent succeeded, may be references to Edward Armstrong who was curate at Liffey Street Chapel until 1823 when he became administrator of St. Andrew's, Townsend Street, upon Daniel Murray's installation as Archbishop of Dublin. The words, "he too was dead", in the second full sentence probably relate Nugent's death back to William Callaghan's in 1822, certainly not to that of Armstrong, who died on May 15, 1828. Or the whole passage may incorrectly name "Liffey St." Chapel, but actually refer to Saints Michael and John's where Joseph Nugent served when Michael Blake went to Rome in 1824. Finding the missing page(s) of the manuscript would obviously be a great help.

8 At least one sheet (two pages) of the manuscript is missing at this point in the Memoir. The "he" referred to in the text which follows is probably Dr. William Macauley, the husband of Catherine's sister Mary. The "incident" referred to may be the already reported incident of their daughter Mary's comment about what she believed, or it may more likely be a subsequent religious "incident", but one which occurred prior to Mary's (i.e., Catherine's sister's) death in August 1827. Throughout this manuscript the name Macauley often appears to be spelled "Macawley", but I have used "Macauley" to avoid further confusion.

9 The "great house" is of course the residence and school rooms Catherine was erecting on Baggot Street, Dublin.

10 In the left-hand margin next to this paragraph Clare Augustine notes her source but her notation is now illegible: "Sr. M—".

11 Here, "a day room" is inserted above the line in pencil. According to the architect's "Deed of Agreement" for the building of the Baggot Street house, dated December 14, 1824, the "Corridor" which came to be known as "St. Anne's Corridor" was evidently across the middle story (i.e., above the street-level story), and that known as "St. Mary's Corridor" was evidently across the upper story (i.e., on the top floor). "Mary Byrne" in this sentence should be Catherine Byrn.

12 This sequence of events is incorrect. Mary Macauley, Catherine's sister, died in August 1827 (Degnan 53). Frances Warde did not participate in the work on Baggot Street until June 1828.

13 Dr. William Macauley's family lived on Military Road, in southwest Dublin below the Liffey River, near to the Royal Hospital Kilmainham where he served as surgeon and apothecary.

14 According to Mary Angela Bolster, the Deed of Sale preserved in the archives of the Sisters of Mercy, Dublin, indicates that Catherine McAuley sold Coolock House on September 15, 1828 (*Documentary Study* 2:15). Burke Savage gives September 18, 1828 as the date of the sale (75). Catherine's elder niece, Mary Macauley, was received into the Catholic Church in the chapel at Baggot Street on November 22, 1828. Her younger niece, Catherine, became a Catholic sometime later.

15 Next to this sentence is the marginal notation of sources: "R.M. & M.M.C." The second set of initials probably refers to Mother Mary Clare Moore or to Mother Mary Cecilia Marmion, but "R.M." is unclear. It may be an abbreviation for "Revd. Mother" and may refer to Catherine McAuley herself. The only Reverend Mothers of Baggot Street, in the period when Clare Augustine was gathering data for her Memoir, who might have known this information firsthand from Catherine McAuley, were Mary de Pazzi Delany, superior from 1841 to 1844, and Mary Cecilia Marmion, superior from 1844 to her death on September 15, 1849.

16 The word, "deal", is written in pencil above the word, "great". The manuscript thus far, and until noted below, is written in ink. Clare Augustine later uses the expression, "a deal of" or "a deal to".

17 This sentence, at the bottom of a page, is incomplete. The next sentence begins at the top of the next page.

18 Some manuscripts say Dr. William Macauley died in February 1829. Clare Augustine Moore seems to imply that he died in late January. January 25, 1829 is the date usually given.
19 "Few" is written in pencil above the line. Since the last part of this manuscript is written in pencil, I think many of the penciled additions in the ink portion of the text may be Clare Augustine Moore's own corrections.
20 At this time Catherine McAuley would have been forty-seven (if born in September 1781) or fifty (if born in September 1778). Clare Augustine Moore assumes that Catherine was born in 1787. See note 3, above.
21 The word "her" is added in pencil before "face".
22 The manuscript definitely says "your" followed by "thought" or "thoughts" (the word is at the right edge of the paper). This passage has sometimes been inaccurately rendered as "reading you through."
23 Marcella (later, Mary Magdalen) Flynn entered the community on July 15, 1829. In the manuscript this sentence and the preceding one have been accurately corrected in pencil by a hand which may or may not be Clare Augustine's. The ink text reads: "She entered in July or September, and another joined them, Margaret Dunne . . . ." Margaret (later, Mary Angela) Dunne entered on September 8, 1829. She died in Charleville on November 12, 1863.
24 "Theresian" is corrected in pencil to "Teresian", but this correction is not in the same handwriting as the ink text.
25 Three and a quarter lines of the manuscript are heavily crossed out here, in ink, and so are illegible.
26 Actually the manuscript has "Gorgiana" here; since she is Clare Augustine Moore's own sister, this must be a slip of the pen.
27 The words, "Doyle" and "I am not sure which", are Clare Augustine's corrections written in pencil above the line. The superior of the Presentation Convent on George's Hill when Catherine McAuley entered was Mother Mary Clare Angela Doyle.
28 The word looks like "spirituals", although the "s" may be crossed out. The term "spirituals" seems to have been frequently used to refer to spiritual activities or duties. Or perhaps Clare Augustine intended parallelism: "household affairs" and "spiritual [affairs]".
29 Seven sisters were received in the ceremony on January 23, 1832, in addition to Mary Aloysius (Anne) O'Grady who, because she was dying, was received privately. Anna Carroll was the "junior Postulant", now a new novice, whose mother removed her to George's Hill.
30 Mary Elizabeth Harley, in fact, died on Easter Wednesday, April 25, 1832.
31 Sir Philip Crampton, an eminent Dublin surgeon, was for about twenty years Surgeon General to the military forces in Ireland, until the office was abolished in 1833. He was then appointed Surgeon-in-Ordinary to the King in Ireland, and in 1839 Queen Victoria made him a Baronet of the United Kingdom. He died on June 10, 1858 (Fitzgerald 1:275–6). Catherine McAuley evidently knew him through the Armstrongs and the Callaghans, or through her brother or brother-in-law. The reference to him as "the late Sir P. Crampton" indicates that this portion of the Memoir was written after June 1858.
32 This sentence appears to be incorrect. Francis L'Estrange ODC, the Carmelite provincial, and presumably also Redmond O'Hanlon ODC were in Rome in early 1830, and may have been instrumental in obtaining, as a response to Catherine's own request for Roman support, the rescript of indulgences which the Baggot Street community received later in 1830, after correspondence between Rome and Archbishop Murray. Five years later, in May 1835, the Sisters of Mercy received word of the praise and papal benediction accorded them as a religious congregation on the basis of Catherine's earlier submission of the two distinctive chapters she wished to add to her revision of the Presentation Rule and Constitutions: "Visitation of the Sick", and "The Admission of Distressed Women". She

had forwarded these two chapters to Rome in December 1833. The praise and benediction were promulgated in a letter addressed to Archbishop Murray and dated March 24, 1835. In 1830 there were, strictly speaking, no "flattering congratulations" addressed to the Archbishop; there was only an inquiry into the status of the Baggot Street community and a request for his "opinion" about what would be "the most suitable graces and faculties" for Rome to grant. The texts of his guarded response and of the 1830 rescript of indulgences are in Bolster, ed., *Correspondence* (4–6). There is no record of Roman action in relation to the community in 1832, although Clare Augustine may be referring to a private and informal communication made through Dr. William J. Whelan ODC.

33 Here, in pencil, "her" before "friend" is crossed out, and "the Revd." and "cousin" are inserted above the line. These appear to be Clare Augustine's own corrections. She is harsher in her treatment of Catherine Byrn than Dominican records justify (see Degnan 153–55).

34 Mary Teresa Macauley professed her vows on November 3, 1833 and died on November 12, 1833.

35 This is an error; the priest was Myles Gaffney.

36 The part of the manuscript written in black ink ends here; the rest of the manuscript is written in pencil, starting with the words "foundation of ours". The part in pencil was evidently begun in 1864, as the parenthetical date in this paragraph implies.

37 The correct name of this priest is John McDonogh. See Degnan 94, 204, 208, and Donnelly 148–9.

38 Michael Blake was assigned as administrator and then parish priest of St. Andrew's in 1831 (Donnelly 151).

39 Michael Blake was consecrated Bishop of Dromore on March 17, 1833 (Neumann 53–4).

40 In the margin next to this paragraph, Clare Augustine notes her "authority": "Mother M. Cecilia" Marmion. Mary Cecilia Marmion died in September 1849. Hence, as is known from other sources, Clare Augustine had indeed begun to collect data for her Memoir in the 1840s.

41 In the sentence: "Many other trials sprang from the same source", the words "Many other trials sprang from the" are written in pencil on top of other now illegible words written in pencil and not fully erased. This revision is in Clare Augustine Moore's handwriting. The topic of the sentence is sensitive and she may have had second thoughts about wording. Dean Walter Meyler was parish priest of St. Andrew's until his death, and vicar general of the diocese until 1852. He died on January 5, 1864.

42 No number or word is visible in the manuscript at this point. Evidently not remembering the exact number, Clare Augustine left a blank space, intending to fill it in later. Mary Elizabeth Harley died on Easter Wednesday (April 25) 1832.

43 The branch house in Kingstown (Dún Laoghaire) was opened on March 24, 1835, not in 1834.

44 Mary de Chantal McCann.

45 Clare Augustine tends to capitalize "Foundress" when she uses the word as a name, but not when it is preceded by "the" or "our". I have followed this pattern.

46 The word, "soon", may, in fact, be crossed out in the manuscript. The word is hard to decipher.

47 Clare Augustine wrote "public", then crossed it out and wrote "general".

48 The word I have rendered as "schouting" is over-written and very unclear in the manuscript. It definitely begins with "sc" and appears to end with "outing". Perhaps "shouting" or "screaming" was intended. Whatever the word is, the women were loud!

49 Clare Augustine Moore describes the behavior of Catherine McAuley's nephews more severely than Catherine would have thought appropriate. Moreover, William Macauley had not died by the time she was writing. He had married Jessie Tompkins in Australia on February 24, 1853, and by 1864, six of their thirteen children had been born. Their first daughter, born on March 21, 1855, was named Mary Catherine. Their tenth child, Fannie

Theresa, born on October 31, 1871, became a Sister of Mercy in Australia, taking the name, Mary Catherine. William died on December 30, 1904, at the age of eighty-three.

50 The correct name is evidently Griffith. Bishop Patrick Raymond Griffith sailed for the Cape of Good Hope on January 20, 1838, taking Daniel Burke with him. Burke died in Grahamstown on April 11, 1839 (Neumann 44, 56, 59).

51 The "lady" referred to in this sentence, and in the following two sentences, is Mary Clare (Elizabeth) Agnew, who was one of the two English novices professed in Cork for the Bermondsey foundation. She served as superior of the Bermondsey foundation for six months in 1841, and then left the Sisters of Mercy in 1842 (see Degnan 318–20, 378–9).

The rest of this paragraph and the following four paragraphs are written in *very* faint pencil on very thin gray paper. The present condition of these pages is one urgent reason for publishing the text of this manuscript.

52 This was perhaps Catherine McAuley's earlier view, or her view in special circumstances. For a different view, see the excerpts from the Tullamore Annals earlier in this volume.

53 See Catherine McAuley's letter of March 14, 1840 to Mary Elizabeth Moore (Neumann 202–3). The appointments occurred on March 6, 1840. Mary Cecilia Marmion was appointed Mistress of Novices, and Mary Aloysius Scott, Bursar.

54 Presumably this incident and the following one refer to Mary Cecilia Marmion.

55 This account of events in Birr does not appear to be accurate. Patrick Kennedy was parish priest of Birr from 1826 until his consecration as coadjutor bishop on January 17, 1836; in June 1836 he succeeded Patrick MacMahon as bishop of Killaloe. In 1826 Michael Crotty, a curate in Birr, objected to Kennedy's appointment as parish priest; from this disagreement as well as Crotty's earlier behavior and subsequent suspension the schism developed. Daniel Vaughan was parish priest in Killaloe from 1827 until he became bishop of the diocese of Killaloe in 1851, succeeding Patrick Kennedy. His curate in Killaloe was William Crotty, a cousin to Michael Crotty in Birr; William was ordained in 1832. I think Clare Augustine Moore means Dr. Kennedy when she writes "Dr. Vaughan". John Spain was appointed parish priest in Birr in 1838. See Murphy, *The Diocese of Killaloe* 2:100–33.

56 The correct name is Theobald Mathew. He was a Capuchin priest and the leader of a temperance movement in Ireland at this time.

57 I have not been able to discover the particulars of this incident, or to identify the "school Sister", who apparently left the community. The Kingstown (Dún Laoghaire) branch house, which Catherine closed in 1838, was re-opened in April 1840, and then closed again in 1842.

58 This story is probably about Mary de Pazzi Delany, who evidently suffered from spells "identified with epilepsy" (Degnan 229).

59 Because Catherine remained in a sitting room on the street-level of the house during evening recreation, she also answered the doorbell. At the beginning of this sentence the words "Sr. M. de Sales and" are crossed out.

60 Above the word "back", the words, "the lower part", are inserted in pencil.

61 Dr. James McAuley.

62 Presumably this was Dr. William Stokes MD (1804–1878) and not his father, Dr. Whitley Stokes MD (1763–1845). Both were eminent Dublin surgeons.

63 The author seems to be placing in the night of November 9–10, 1841, events which occurred during the night of November 10–11, 1841. She was not in Baggot Street at the time. See, later in this volume, the letters of Mary Vincent Whitty and Mary Elizabeth Moore, who were present.

64 Vincent Grotti.

65 The words, "and presided at the Office and funeral", are added to this sentence in the manuscript, but the handwriting does not appear to be Mary Clare Augustine Moore's. The manuscript ends here.

NOTES TO CHAPTER 7

Mary Frances Xavier (Frances) Warde, 1810–1884

1 January 27, 188[2]. Frances, or a secretary, dated the letter "1881", but this is evidently a mistake, since Frances refers to the fiftieth anniversary, just past, of her reception of the habit at Baggot Street on January 23, 1832. The autograph of this letter was once in Wexford. I have consulted a typescript of it, which is in the archives of the Sisters of Mercy, Dublin.

2 According to Kathleen Healy, her modern biographer, "Frances Warde's birth and baptismal certificates are not available" (*Warde* 487). Yet presumably on the basis of the tradition which associates Frances's birth with this year, she says that Frances was born "about 1810" (5). Healy also points out that Frances's mother was Mary Maher (487), not Jane Maher, as given in some early biographies. The Carlow Register agrees.

3 Healy says that it was Frances's brother John who died at this time (16). However, Mary Austin Carroll says that it was an older brother, and that John died later in England in 1839, "leaving a widow and four children" (*Leaves* 1:255). According to Healy (488), a "John Ward" matriculated at Maynooth in humanities on February 15, 1819; she says that in the Maynooth register, in the place for recording his date of ordination, the words, "*Non aliud*" appear. This notation need not imply the death of this "John Ward", nor that he was in fact Frances's brother. Carroll says that her father's "second son [Daniel or William?], a youth of extraordinary promise, died, at Maynooth, I think, on the very day appointed for his ordination" (*Leaves* 1:255). Carroll, it will be recalled, got her information from Frances Warde herself.

4 The illuminated Carlow Register is inaccurate when it states that Frances Warde "entered the Convent of Baggot Street Dublin on the twenty second of June one thousand eight hundred and twenty nine." The Dublin Register says she entered on June 22, 1828.

5 Mary Clare Moore's letter of August 26, 1845.

6 Mary Catherine Garety RSM used this name as the title of the first published biography of Frances: *Rev. Mother M. Xavier Warde* (Boston: Marlier and Co., 1902).

7 See Kathleen Healy's discussion of Frances's name and her various signatures (40–41, 489), and Mary Austin Carroll's discussion of Catherine's preference for feminine names and for the use of "Mary" in each sister's name: "She preferred female Saints as patrons for the Sisters; but if they were particularly devoted to the others, she conceded to their wishes. Afterwards, however, she would playfully revenge herself by styling them, 'My fine boys.' She would, if possible, induce them to be satisfied with the feminine of the names they wanted, as Josephine for Joseph, Aloysia for Aloysius .... In addressing each other, she wished them always to prefix *Mary* to the patronal name. . . . She was very particular about this" (*Life* 453–54). Mary Ignatia Neumann and Mary Angela Bolster both use "Francis" in the salutations of the published letters to Frances Warde, but an examination of photocopies of ten of these autographs reveals that in these letters Catherine wrote "Frances" in the salutation. Since the combination, "Frances Xavier", is an odd one—mixing the feminine with a male saint's name—it is easy to see how "Francis" came to be used in Carlow and elsewhere. Frances herself may have occasionally used "Francis Xavier" in Ireland and in the United States, although Kathleen Healy says she did not. Preserved in the archives of the Sisters of Mercy, Limerick, is the feast day greeting which Frances sent to Catherine McAuley on April 30, 1841 (see Neumann 338). It is a picture of Catherine of Siena, on the back of which is printed: "From Sister Mary Francis Warde/to her beloved Spiritual Mother/Mary Catherine McAuley/Convent of our Lady of Mercy—Carlow/April 30th 1841. Feast of St. Catherine of Sienna." Leaf drawings surround the inscription. If this is Frances's own printing, and not that of someone whom she asked to print and decorate the card, she is here calling herself "Francis". However, in the Carlow

archives there is a manuscript of "Spiritual Maxims" which may be in Frances's own handwriting and which has "Mary Frances Warde" printed on the title page, with the date, "February 2d 1839."

Perhaps this long note presents the matter sufficiently and illustrates why I use the name, "Frances".

8 Kathleen Healy offers a list of autonomous Mercy communities founded, directly or indirectly, by Frances Warde (*Warde* 506).

9 Healy compiles a list of the institutions, as well as the convents, Frances was directly or indirectly involved in founding (*Warde* 518–22). Frances, of course, did not directly establish most of the institutions which these convents subsequently created.

10 The affirmative rescript of dispensation (from the relevant prescription of the Rule) did not arrive from Rome in time to permit her to be re-elected on August 18, 1880 (Healy 433–4).

11 Letter of Mary Ursula Frayne, November 10, 1841. Autographs of this letter sent to all the early foundations are in various archives of the Sisters of Mercy.

12 Catherine McAuley's October 12, 1841 letter to Frances Warde, which is published in both the Neumann (381–2) and Bolster (266) editions, with a few variations, may have been a longer letter than the published versions indicate. Carroll's version of the letter (*Life* 427) may inadvertently involve a transposed portion of another letter, if, for example, she relied on a transcription of it sent to her by one of her sources; *or,* and this is an even stronger possibility, Carroll may have seen the complete autograph or a complete copy of it, all the autograph pages of which are now not together. The photocopy in the archives of the Sisters of Mercy of the Americas (Silver Spring, Maryland) is now incomplete, having no cover. Moreover, the autograph is apparently not there. The addition to the letter which is given by Carroll (427), Burke Savage (370–71), and Healy (135–36) may have been written on the cover (the sheet of paper used as the envelope); I do not know the whereabouts of this piece of the autograph, if it is, in fact, an authentic part of *this* letter. This problem illustrates some of the research that remains to be done, if possible, on Catherine McAuley's letters. Yet, had it not been for Frances Warde and others who have through the years preserved her letters from Catherine McAuley, the published letters of Catherine to Sisters of Mercy would be reduced by forty-five percent: Frances received seventy-two of the 159 published letters to sisters. There are, by contrast, no published letters of Catherine McAuley to Clare Moore. Some letters certainly were written to her and may still be extant somewhere; although it is conceivable that Clare destroyed her letters from Catherine, perhaps because of their references to particular persons, she preserved many such letters from other correspondents.

13 See Mary Clare Augustine Moore, "Memoir", in the preceding chapter.

14 I tend to share Mary Hermenia Muldrey's assessment, expressed in a letter to me on August 27, 1992, that there was probably nothing deliberate on the part of any sister at Baggot Street which specifically prevented Frances Warde's coming to see Catherine in the weeks prior to her death. It is interesting, in this respect, to note that the Baggot Street confessor, Redmond O'Hanlon ODC, who had such close contact with Catherine after her return from Birmingham, may also have had direct contact with Frances Warde in early October 1841, possibly on his return from taking the dying Mary Justina Fleming to Tullamore. On October 12, Catherine wrote to Frances: "Father O'H brought your affectionate note" (382). If Redmond O'Hanlon saw Frances face to face in Carlow, he may have given her a report on Catherine's condition, as he then knew it. According to Catherine's letter, to Mary Aloysius Scott on September 26 (September 20, in the published editions), Catherine and Mary de Pazzi Delany had already heard Dr. William Stokes's diagnosis (that her right lung was diseased), and certainly Redmond O'Hanlon would have been told this as well.

15 Mary Camillus's wording is a little confusing. Frances served as superior in Pittsburgh from December 1843 to May 1850. Therefore in March 1851 she would have been "not in"—that is, out of—office for about a year.

16 Mary Josephine (Ellen) Cullen had come from Carlow in 1843. She had been, according to the Carlow Annals, initially chosen in Carlow to be the superior of the new foundation in Pittsburgh, but then Dr. Francis Haly, Bishop of Kildare and Leighlin, Bishop Michael O'Connor of Pittsburgh, and James Maher, parish priest of Carlow-Graigue and a very close friend of the Carlow community, decided that Frances Warde, because of her greater experience, should go to Pittsburgh as superior. Mary Josephine was appointed superior in Pittsburgh, as Frances's successor, in May 1850. She accompanied Frances to Providence in 1851, and then returned to Pittsburgh, where she died of consumption on April 21, 1852, while still in office. For a discussion of Josephine's relationship with Frances and of the 1850 election, see Healy (213–24). Josephine was not the sister, but the cousin of Paul Cullen, who was named Archbishop of Armagh in 1849 and of Dublin in 1852.

17 The autograph of Mary Camillus Byrn's letter to Mary Ann Doyle, dated "Feast of the Resurrection 1851", is preserved in the archives of the Sisters of Mercy, Derry.

18 Mary Austin Carroll provides an extensive account of the foundation and early activities of the Sisters of Mercy in Pittsburgh (*Leaves* 3:43–141), as does, of course, Kathleen Healy, a member of the Pittsburgh community (*Warde* 148–224).

19 After its first publication in 1866, Carroll's biography was, with some revisions, reprinted eight times by Sadlier: in 1868, 1871, 1874, 1877, 1882, 1884, 1887, and 1890; twice by Kennedy, once with no date, and in 1896; and, after Carroll's death, in an edition by Vincentian Press in 1927 (Muldrey 441). I have used the 1890 Sadlier printing in this study.

20 The archives of the Sisters of Mercy of the Americas (Silver Spring, Maryland) contains, according to Muldrey, a notarized statement verifying "the burning [of] the trunk with all its contents" (433).

Excerpts from *The Annals of Saint Leo's Convent of Mercy, Carlow*

1 The first Carlow annalist was apparently a novice and possibly Mary Elizabeth Strange, or Mary Catherine (Kate) Maher herself, Frances Warde's cousin, who was the Carlow annalist for many years and is said to have recopied the first sheets of the Carlow Annals into a bound red leather volume. The first Annals—according to a later annalist, Mary Imelda O'Reilly (1892–1979)—consisted of loose sheets of paper, covering the years 1837 to 1848, which were left out for the sisters' reading, and in due course "disappeared and may have been lent". Mary Imelda O'Reilly appended a note to the first extant page of a copy "similar to" the older Annals, which says that the "Annals were started by M. Elizabeth Strange." Mary Elizabeth (Hester) Strange entered the Carlow community on December 21, 1839. The first extant page of this copy (the one "similar to" the first Annals) begins with the year 1840, the previous pages having been lost. Fortunately, Mary Catherine Maher, who entered the Carlow community on June 6, 1839, had already copied the Annals into the sturdier volume. Some biographers of Catherine McAuley, notably Carroll and Degnan, quote a slightly different version of the Carlow Annals which I have not been able to locate in Carlow. It is entirely possible that Degnan (245–6) is quoting from Carroll's *Leaves* (1:207–208)—her excerpted text is almost identical to Carroll's—and that Carroll had access to a copy of the original Annals, the now missing "loose sheets", since she was in frequent correspondence with Mary Catherine Maher in Carlow until the latter's death on January 14, 1895.

The text of the Carlow Annals presented here is taken from the two extant copies of the Annals. For the years 1837 through 1839, it is taken from the bound "red leather volume" into which Mary Catherine Maher copied the earlier text of the Annals "started" by Mary Elizabeth (Hester) Strange. For the years 1840 through 1843, the text is taken from the copy said to be "similar to" the earlier text. This copy now has many missing pages; its first extant page begins with "1840". However, pages are also missing for part of the year "1842", so for that period one needs to use Catherine Maher's copy. The differences between the two extant versions are very minor, but there are small copying errors in the "red leather volume". I am grateful to Nessa Cullen RSM, the Carlow archivist, for helping me to understand these documents and Mary Imelda O'Reilly's explanations appended to them.

2 In the Carlow Annals Frances Warde's name is always spelled "Francis".

3 This list may not be completely clear. In addition to Catherine McAuley and her travelling companion, Mary Cecilia Marmion, the two founding members of the group were Frances Warde and Mary Josephine Trennor; evidently the two sisters loaned for a "limited time" were Mary Ursula Frayne and Mary Teresa White, not Mary Cecilia Marmion. See Neumann 85, Degnan 198, Healy 57, and Carroll, *Leaves* 1: 182.

4 The correct name of this Carlow benefactor may be Nowlan. Edward Nolan was Bishop of Kildare and Leighlin at the time of the Carlow founding. He had succeeded Bishop James Doyle in 1834. Throughout these excerpts I have retained most of the many commas in the Annals.

5 "C.C." means "Catholic Curate". Father Daniel Nolan was the younger brother of Bishop Nolan and a great favorite of Catherine McAuley. She liked to tease him, and he, her. She once wrote of him: "It is no wonder I should take a fancy to my adopted son, for he is a real rogue, according to my own taste" (Neumann 111). He was about thirty-one in 1837 (Neumann 397).

6 Mary Anne Agnes (Catherine) Macauley. The manuscript has been corrected, but in another hand, to read "Sr. Mary Agnes McAuley".

7 Again, the name is presumably Nowlan.

8 Actually Catherine McAuley came to Carlow from Limerick, not Dublin. Mary Clare (Eliza) Maher, a half-sister to Mary Cecilia (Ellen) Maher, eventually left the Carlow community because of poor health. Francis Haly had been consecrated Bishop of Kildare and Leighlin on March 25, 1838. Cecilia Maher founded the Auckland community in 1850.

9 Evidently a copyist's error occurs in this line: "as a mark of special attention" is written a second time, after "was". I have omitted the repetition.

10 The humor of this paragraph is all the greater when one realizes that the "young sister of small dimensions" is probably the Carlow annalist herself, Mary Catherine (Kate) Maher. She entered the Carlow community on June 6, 1839 and had to wear the "grotesque" postulant's cap for seven months, until she received the habit on January 8, 1840.

11 The "pensions" were the dowries of the sisters who entered. The amount of the dowry given to the convent often varied from person to person, and city to city. However, John Murphy, Bishop of Cork, insisted that the Cork community require a substantial dowry in all cases.

12 Gerald (i.e., Garrett) Cullen of Craan was the brother-in-law of James Maher and the uncle of Paul Cullen, future Archbishop of Dublin (1852–1878). His three daughters entered the Carlow community: Mary Paul or Paula (Anne) Cullen, founding superior of Westport; Mary Josephine (Ellen) Cullen, one of the founders of the community in Pittsburgh, Pennsylvania; and Mary Juliana (Kate) Cullen, who, after her sister went to Pittsburgh, took the name, Mary Josephine. Their mother was Judith Maher Cullen, sister to James Maher (Mac Suibhne 1:2, 66, 345).

13 The extant copy of the older version of the Carlow Annals begins with this sentence. The rest of the text presented here corresponds to this older version, unless otherwise noted.

14 The retreat director was Rev. Jerome Keogh.

15 See chapter 20 of the First Part of the text of the Rule.

16 See Catherine's letters to Frances Warde on November 24, 1840 and June 3, 1841 on the "thick veil" she gave to the Carlow community (256–57 and 343–44). Evidently Catherine did not like the more expensive gossamer veils used in Carlow and once used at Baggot Street. However, see also Clare Augustine Moore's comment on her reluctance to change the gossamer veils for woolen ones: she believed "that if once changes began no one knew where they would stop."

17 The date here is incorrect, since this statement is given in the Annals for the year 1841.

On July 20, 1840 the Congregation for the Propagation of the Faith approved the Rule and Constitutions. Papal confirmation occurred on June 6, 1841.

18 At least two sheets of the copy of the older version of the Carlow Annals are missing here. Consequently, the text presented here now follows that in the red leather volume.

19 According to the Carlow Annals, Mary Xavier Peppard died in Westport on December 28, 1842, of "an attack of inflammation". The Annals notes that "She had not completed her 21st year."

20 The text presented here follows, once again, the copy of the older version of the Carlow Annals.

21 The reference to Mary Vincent Harnett's published biography indicates that at least this section of the two extant copies of the Carlow Annals was composed after 1864.

NOTES TO CHAPTER 8

Mary Vincent (Ellen) Whitty, 1819–1892

1 This information is contained in the Dublin Register and in O'Donoghue (5).

2 In the autograph of this letter, which I follow here and which is undated but was presumably written on September 26, 1841 (the Sunday after Catherine returned from Birmingham), Catherine says, "Sr L Vincent is head cook making nice rennet whey . . . ." Just prior to August 20, 1841, there had been two sisters with the name "Mary Vincent" in the Baggot Street community: Mary Vincent Whitty and Mary Vincent (Lucy) Bond. Mary Vincent Bond professed her vows on August 19, with Mary Vincent Whitty, and then left the next day for Birmingham, as a member of the founding party. She too was evidently a good cook, having made "raspberry vinegar" for Catherine in July 1841 (Neumann 350). To distinguish the two "Vincents", Catherine evidently called the sister from Birmingham, informally, "Lucy Vincent". However, her writing "Sr L Vincent" in this letter is apparently a slip of the pen, since "Lucy Vincent" was then in Birmingham. She undoubtedly meant Mary Vincent Whitty.

3 Mary Justina Fleming died on December 10, 1841, a month after Catherine's own death. There is irony, therefore, in Catherine's fear, expressed in July 1841, that Baggot Street would experience "a great trial" were Mary Justina to die.

4 Mary Cecilia Marmion's two sisters, who had also joined the community, had died during Catherine's lifetime: Mary Agnes Marmion on February 10, 1836, and Mary Frances Marmion on March 10, 1840.

5 A separate group of five Sisters of Mercy had left earlier from Bermondsey (London), under Clare Moore's leadership, to nurse in the Crimea under the general superintendence of Florence Nightingale. These were later joined by three more from Bermondsey, bringing, with the fifteen in the Irish contingent, the total number of Sisters of Mercy nursing the wounded in the Crimea to twenty-three. Mary Angela Bolster, in *The Sisters of Mercy in the Crimean War*, gives a well documented and detailed account of their nursing service in the desolate conditions of the war zone, particularly of the sisters working under Mary Francis Bridgeman's leadership. Although all the sisters had urgently requested that they receive no remuneration, except their passage and maintenance, the British government eventually offered their respective communities portions of a £230 gift from the Sultan for their services. Two Sisters of Mercy from Liverpool, who were part of the Irish contingent, died in the Crimea and are still buried there: Mary Winifred Sprey, of cholera on October 20, 1855; and Mary Elizabeth Butler, of typhus on February 23, 1856. Mary Elizabeth (Clare) Butler had entered Baggot Street in 1838 and gone to Liverpool in 1845 (Carroll, *Leaves* 2:384).

6 Archbishop Cullen's letter is preserved in the archives of the Sisters of Mercy, Brisbane. It is quoted in O'Donoghue (28).

7 I regret that in this short introduction to Mary Vincent Whitty and her letters about Catherine McAuley I have not been able to make more extensive reference to Frances

(formerly, Mary Xaverius) O'Donoghue's biography, *Mother Vincent Whitty*, published by Melbourne University Press in 1972. I discovered much too late that I needed to search more widely for a copy of the book, and I had for my use only a photocopy of the Introduction and Chapter 1. For the Brisbane years, readers are certainly urged to consult O'Donoghue's account.

8 Carroll's source for this comment may have been Mary Francis Bridgeman. See *Leaves* 2:540–72, for Carroll's extensive account of the Brisbane foundation.

9 An offprint of this newspaper article is preserved in the archives of the Sisters of Mercy, Birmingham, England. The name of the sister who wrote to the *Brisbane Australian* is not given, although the article evidently quotes her verbatim. The offprint is a single sheet with no page number.

10 Katherine O'Brien wrote these comments for the sesquicentennial of the founding of the Institute (1831–1981), when this occasion was celebrated in Brisbane. A typescript of her paper, entitled "Letters written 140 years ago by Mother Mary Vincent Whitty", was sent to me by the Brisbane archivist, Norah Boland RSM.

11 In a written statement signed on January 20, 1911 (and preserved in the Dublin archives), Mary Liguori Keenan—who entered Baggot Street in 1856, whose mistress of novices was Mary Vincent Whitty, and who later served for many years as superior of the Baggot Street community—claims that the following account "was related to me by Mother M. Vincent's own lips":

> The night before our Foundress died she said to Mother M. Vincent, "You are to stay with me tonight." She did so, and when all the Sisters had retired to rest she gave her several instruments of penance to burn, as well as her shoes, which were studded with sharp nails; at the same time charging her not to speak of what she did that night to a human being.
>
> Mother M. Vincent kept the secret for many years, but when making a retreat under Father Vincent [Grotti], Passionist, he said he had been longing to meet someone who knew Mother McAuley well, as he had heard she was an unusually holy woman.
>
> Mother M. Vincent told him about the burning of the instruments of penance. He replied, "You should have spoken of this before." She replied, "I was told not to do so." He then said, "Our Lord told the Apostles 'Tell the vision to no man till the Son of Man is risen from the dead.' "

Clare Augustine Moore knew of this information as she completed her Memoir in 1864 or shortly thereafter. The other documents presented in this volume do not refer to the matter. If they quote Elizabeth Moore's letter they, interestingly, omit her reference to the burning of the shoes.

12 Mary Vincent Whitty's eyewitness account is the primary source of the "good cup of tea" tradition, which Mary Austin Carroll, in her *Life of Catherine McAuley*, later records as a "comfortable cup of tea" (437). Carroll's *Life* was first published in 1866. The offering of hospitable tea to guests is a longstanding, worldwide tradition of Sisters of Mercy.

13 This transcription is designated "Cork MS. 3" in Mary Angela Bolster, *Documentary Study,* vols. 1 and 2. The *Documentary Study* says that "This MS is a first-hand account of the utmost significance" (1:lxxxviii). The prefatory note written by Mary Vincent Whitty in 1860 is her own original composition and is, therefore, of great importance as an eyewitness perspective on Catherine McAuley. The transcription itself is based closely—as Mary Vincent says in her preface—on the text of, or the original of, the earlier Life of Catherine McAuley written by Clare Moore and later copied into the Bermondsey Annals. She would have been dependent on other early sisters for firsthand knowledge of Catherine McAuley in the period 1827 to 1839, and she may have been copying the text of Cork MS. 2, which is said to be in Clare Moore's handwriting (*Documentary Study* 1:lxxxvii). However, her prefatory note movingly reflects her own experience of Catherine in the years 1839 to 1841. In it she claims that the author of the *Dublin Review* article (1847)—which she also transcribes—"rather exaggerates the encouragement given to our Foundress by the late Archbishop, the Right Revd. Dr. Murray—his Lordship did not appear what might be called '*kind*' to our Foundress, but of course he valued the works of

the Institute." She also regrets that Clare Moore did not say more about the difficulties of the Birr foundation.

The Letters of Mary Vincent Whitty to Mary Cecilia Marmion

1 Mary Cecilia Marmion, the mistress of novices at Baggot Street, was in Birmingham temporarily, at Catherine McAuley's request, to assist the new foundation and its young superior, Mary Juliana Hardman. She had last seen Catherine McAuley on September 20, 1841, when Catherine left Birmingham. Mary Vincent Whitty, just professed on August 19, was looking after the novices in Mary Cecilia's absence. Her letters to Mary Cecilia were written under enormous pressures of time, fatigue, and emotion. I have tried to present them exactly as they are written. However, Mary Vincent's nearly constant use of dashes as punctuation and her general lack of paragraphing seem to me to require some minimal alteration for the sake of clarity. Therefore, I have inserted some periods and paragraphing, while attempting to retain the spontaneous character of the letters.

The autographs of these letters are preserved in the archives of the Sisters of Mercy, Brisbane, Queensland, Australia. Norah Boland RSM, the Brisbane archivist, has sent me excellent photocopies of these autographs as well as copies of meticulous typescripts prepared by the former archivist, Katherine O'Brien. I have prepared my texts of these letters from these photocopies and typescripts, and I wish here to express my deep gratitude to Norah Boland, without whose repeated and generous help I would never have been able to include these letters in this volume.

2 Mary de Sales (Jane) White was the sister of Mary Teresa (Amelia) White, superior in Galway. She had been on loan to the Bermondsey community for a year. When Catherine went to Birmingham in August 1841 she intended also to go to Bermondsey to pick up Mary de Sales White and Mary Xavier O'Connell, also on loan, so they could return to Dublin with her from Birmingham. However, she was so ill in Birmingham that Redmond O'Hanlon made the round trip to London for her. Thus, Mary de Sales would have been in Birmingham in September and would now have been anxious to correspond with the sisters there about Catherine's condition. Writing to Teresa White on October 7, 1841, Catherine says of de Sales: "she is my constant affectionate nurse" (Manuscript copy, not in Catherine McAuley's handwriting, Archives of the Sisters of Mercy, Dublin).

3 Dr. Stokes attended Catherine in her last illness: presumably this was William Stokes MD (1804–1878), and not his father Whitley Stokes MD (1763–1845). Both were eminent Dublin physicians. The name is Stokes, not "Stoaks" (Neumann 375).

4 Mary Ursula Frayne, Mary de Sales White, Mary Xavier O'Connell, and, presumably, Mary Catherine Gogarty are the sisters mentioned.

5 Teresa Carton, to whom Catherine wrote a letter from Birmingham on September 6, 1841, giving instructions about how to prepare the infirmary for her. Teresa's health had often been poorly, and Catherine did much to encourage and support her. She was a lay sister until the Chapter on August 31, 1844, in which she was voted a choir sister.

6 Catherine's godchild, Teresa Byrn—in religion, Mary Camillus. In reading the preceding sentences in the letter it is helpful to recall that Mary de Pazzi Delany had a fragile makeup and apparently suffered from spells that "were finally identified with epilepsy" (Degnan 229).

7 Mary Cecilia Marmion was scheduled to return to Baggot Street some time after the profession ceremony of Mary Angela Borini and Mary Magdalen Polding, held in St. Chad's Cathedral, Birmingham, on December 6, 1841.

8 These convents were branch houses of Baggot Street, not autonomous foundations; hence those who lived in them were members of the Baggot Street community.

9 Genevieve Jarmy, an elderly member of the Baggot Street community.

10 Catherine's brother, Dr. James William McAuley, and his wife, Frances Ridgeway McAuley.

11 Evidently James McAuley wished to be alone with his sister for a while before her death.

12 The manuscript has "Mrs." here: this must have been intended as a plural abbreviation for "Mr." because Dr. Andrew Quinn and Dr. W. O'Grady were then curates at St. Andrew's, Westland Row, where Walter Meyler was parish priest. Myles Gaffney was at Maynooth. At this time in Ireland priests were generally given the title "Mr." or "Dr." See Donnelly 153.

13 Mary Vincent Whitty was thus available during the night when Catherine asked her to burn the wrapped parcel containing her shoes and instrument(s) of penance.

14 "September" is obviously an error, written under the distracting emotion Mary Vincent felt as Catherine was dying.

15 This autograph is the most difficult of the five autographs to read. It is one folded sheet of paper with writing on the four sides. However, on three of the four sides there is crosswise writing—i.e., the horizontal writing is overwritten vertically to complete the letter. This method of using stationery was evidently commonly employed to save paper.

16 Mary Magdalen Flynn, Mary de Sales White, and Martha Walplate. I have not been able to identify "Lucy". Possibly this is a familiar name for someone whose baptismal name or name in religion is something else.

17 This request to Teresa Carton, which Catherine makes as she is dying, is the source of the "good cup of tea" tradition among Sisters of Mercy. Mary Austin Carroll calls it "a comfortable cup of tea" (*Life* 436). When the traveling party returned from Birmingham to Ireland in September 1841, Catherine says that they had "comfortable tea" in Kingstown (Neumann 377).

18 Mary Juliana Hardman, superior in Birmingham.

19 Thomas O'Carroll, curate at St. Andrew's; Myles Gaffney, then dean at Maynooth; and George J. P. Browne, Bishop of Galway.

20 John Smyth, curate at Saints Michael and John's.

21 Daniel Murray was ill at the time, and did not officiate at Catherine's Funeral Mass and burial. The meeting on November 6, 1841, was apparently their last visit.

22 John Ryan, Bishop of Limerick.

23 Mary Austin Carroll quotes a letter from Mary Teresa White, written forty years after Catherine's death, which says: "I saw her in death, and was one of those who placed her in her coffin. I was mother-superior in Galway at the time, and came to Dublin hoping to see and speak to her for the last time; but she had departed four hours before I arrived, and I never felt such grief before or since. I cried for many hours without ceasing" (*Leaves* 1:49–50). This would imply that Teresa arrived at Baggot Street about midnight, Thursday, November 11. Perhaps Mary Vincent Whitty, a younger member of the community, did not see her until Saturday morning. Elizabeth Moore, in a letter written to Charleville after Catherine's death, says, "Sr. M. Teresa, Galway, arrived the morning after she expired" (see the next chapter). Teresa White died in Clifden on October 10, 1888.

24 Frances Warde, superior in Carlow.

25 The ground to be used as the cemetery, in the garden at Baggot Street, was consecrated on Sunday, November 14, by William Kinsella, Bishop of Ossory. Dr. Kinsella had been Catherine's friend at least as early as 1831 when he gave the Charity Sermon at Baggot Street.

26 See note 7 above.

27 See note 25 above.

28 November 22.

29 Mary Angela Dunne, superior of Charleville (Rath Luirc).

30 This word in the autograph is, unfortunately, impossible to read. Norah Boland, the Brisbane archivist, agrees, and says that Katherine O'Brien, the former archivist, also could not decipher it. The word is part of a phrase inserted above the line in smaller handwriting, and the first letter of the word is a tall letter. I am not completely confident that it is "bane", but it is the best possibility I can identify, and the meaning of the actual word would be close to this if Catherine, as recorded by Mary Vincent Whitty, was referring to "preference

for one more than another"; if she was referring back to "universal charity" and to "avoid[ing] all appearance at least of preference" the word may be close to the meaning of "essence", although that does not appear to be the actual word in the autograph. I very much regret that our repeated efforts to decipher this word, in so important a context, have all so far failed.

31 Mary de Sales White had probably written frequent letters about Catherine's condition to her sister in Galway. Catherine had originally intended Teresa's appointment as superior in Galway in May 1840 to be temporary; as Catherine's health declined, Teresa may have been uncertain about Catherine's final intention: should she return to the Baggot Street community, or remain in Galway? See the postscript of Catherine McAuley's letter to Elizabeth Moore, March 14, 1840: "Sister M. Teresa for Galway 6 months. Sister [M. Catherine] Leahy to remain—3 postulants" (Neumann 203).

32 Michael Blake, Bishop of Dromore, wrote from Newry to Elizabeth Moore on November 13, 1841.

33 Mary Vincent is probably referring to Bishop George J. P. Browne of Galway and Bishop Francis Haly of Kildare and Leighlin, in whose diocese Carlow was located.

34 Catherine McAuley had adopted the white cloaks worn by the Carmelites as "church cloaks" to be worn by the Sisters of Mercy on major feast days and at ceremonies.

35 Redmond J. O'Hanlon ODC, confessor at Baggot Street and Catherine's faithful guide and friend. Bishop William Kinsella presided and preached.

36 The word, "walk", is crossed out after "hear her" and "in" is inserted above it, by Mary Vincent, I presume.

37 John Ryan, Bishop of Limerick. The word may be "Riun".

38 The word is definitely "her" but "here" may have been intended.

39 Teresa Carton, of whom Catherine was so solicitous, remained in the community until 1865, when she became, according to notes in the oldest Dublin Register, "weak minded". Although she then left the Baggot Street community "under very painful circumstances", she was thereafter financially cared for by the community, until her death in December 1890. The community also paid for her funeral expenses.

40 That is, on October 16, 1841, if by "month" Mary Vincent means the same date in the previous month.

41 This wording is written vertically, across the horizontal wording, and the writing immediately after "6" is not decipherable.

42 That is, October 29, 1841—three weeks prior to the coming Thursday, November 18.

NOTES TO CHAPTER 9

Mary Elizabeth (Anne) Moore, 1806–1868

1 According to the Register of the Sisters of Mercy, Dublin, Anne Moore, the daughter of James and Catherine Moore, was born on June 10, 1806 in the parish of St. James, Dublin. Mary Austin Carroll says that she was the only one of her parents' children to survive infancy, that her father died when she was seven, and that she spent "much of her early life" with her maternal grandmother (*Leaves* 1:322–23).

2 For a discussion of the Kingstown controversy, see Catherine McAuley's letters on the subject (Neumann 86–7, 116, 143–5, 160) and Neumann's own discussion of it (71–3).

3 The autograph of this poem is preserved in the archives of the Sisters of Mercy, Limerick. Various transcribed and printed versions of the poem differ slightly from the autograph. Catherine uses no end punctuation, and she is, if I read her handwriting correctly, inconsistent in her use of capital letters.

4 The Limerick Annals for 1840 says: "Our Foundress fulfilled her promise, and to the great joy of the Community spent nearly a week here in November—but her old children had little idea that it would be the last time they should have the happiness of seeing her amongst

them." I do not see how "November" can be correct: on October 9, Catherine writes from Galway to Teresa Carton in Baggot Street (235); on October 12, she writes from Baggot Street to Frances Warde in Carlow: "We left Galway with a determination to go to you, but a letter was sent after us to Limerick, pressing a speedy return. . . . Sister Teresa Mary we left in Limerick, almost native air" (236–37); on October 18, she writes from Baggot Street to Elizabeth Moore: "I have been speaking so romantically of Limerick that the English Sisters [destined for Birmingham] asked would it be possible for them to see it after their Profession" (240); and in this same letter, she suggests improvements that could be made in the Limerick refectory and kitchen (241). Moreover, all of Catherine's November 1840 letters are written from Baggot Street. It will be recalled that the Limerick Annals, like several of the other early Annals, were written some time after the events occurred, so the possibility of timing errors exists.

5 In June 1840, at the end of Catherine's first trip to Galway, Redmond O'Hanlon, the confessor at Baggot Street—at the apparent insistence of Mary de Pazzi Delany, Catherine's assistant (who could not bear much responsibility), and because Peter Daly, the parish priest in Galway, wanted Catherine to remain there indefinitely—had written to Daly asking that Catherine "return immediately" to Baggot Street (Neumann 218, 221).

6 In late 1988—to celebrate the sesquicentennial of the Sisters of Mercy in Limerick—Marie Therese Courtney RSM published in the *Limerick Leader,* under the general title, "The Nuns of St. Mary's", a series of newspaper articles on the early years of the Limerick foundation. I am indebted to her for information contained in her *Leader* articles: "Fearless Mother Elizabeth Moore" and "Cholera ravages Limerick" (October 15, 1988), and "Mission of Mercy to the poor of Limerick" (September 3, 1988). In another article in this series, " 'The careful instruction of women' " (September 10, 1988), Courtney gives a detailed account of the important role of the Poor Clares who preceded the Sisters of Mercy in Limerick—in particular, of the three who remained when the other Poor Clares withdrew after the death of their abbess, Mother Baptist Clancy, on December 19, 1830: Catherine Shanahan, who died of cholera on April 30, 1834, Mary Shanahan, and Anne Hewitt. All these articles, as well as two by Mary Loreto O'Connor RSM, are republished in a booklet prepared by the Limerick community: *Sisters of Mercy in Limerick,* 1988. My page references are to the articles in this booklet.

7 Mary Bertrand Degnan, in quoting this prayer (339–40), identifies the Birr Annals as her source (381). I have not been able to find any reference to or quotation of the "Suscipe" in any of the currently extant copies of the Birr Annals. From internal evidence it seems clear that the Birr Annals in their present form were begun about twenty years after Birr was founded in late 1840. Perhaps, if the prayer ever was in some version of the Birr Annals, a Birr annalist copied it as she found it in a copy of the Limerick Manuscript or in some other source. However, in Degnan's text of the prayer, in contrast to that in the Limerick Manuscript, "unbounded" is substituted for "unlimited", and in the last phrase, "Thine" replaces "Thy". The wording in the 1868 London publication of the *Practical Sayings* (32–3) is identical to Degnan's text, which may suggest that Bermondsey, not Birr, was her source. Dolores Nieratka RSM (Detroit) has composed a hymn, entitled "Suscipe of C. McAuley", based on the concepts and wording in Catherine's prayer. A Cebuano lyric and music adaptation of Dolores Nieratka's song has been composed for the Sisters of Mercy in the Philippines. Elaine Deasy RSM (Connecticut) and Erica Marshall RSM (Rockhampton, Australia) have also each composed a "Suscipe of Catherine McAuley"; Mary Regina Werntz RSM (Dallas, Pennsylvania) has composed "Catherine McAuley's Prayer"; and Gisela Palacios and Dina Altamiranda RSM, Panama (Brooklyn), have composed "*Suscipe de Catalina*". There may be other such compositions.

8 In the *Documentary Study,* Mary Angela Bolster says that Bishop Blake's letter is addressed to Mary Ann Doyle in Tullamore (1:702), and that "This letter is not extant, though a search has been made in the Dromore Diocesan Archives" (1:703). Perhaps Dr. Blake also wrote to Mary Ann Doyle in Tullamore. However, in Mary Vincent Whitty's

letter to Mary Cecilia Marmion on Tuesday, November 16, 1841, she says: "I send you the coppy [*sic*] of a letter Mother Elizabeth received from Doctor Blake—I think it is so consoling." As Elizabeth Moore says in her own letter to Mary Ann Doyle, she had informed Dr. Blake the day after Catherine's death, and he responded to her on November 13, in the letter which is so frequently copied and quoted. I have not been able to locate the autograph of this letter. I assume that the transcription of it in the Derry archives is the copy Elizabeth Moore sent to Mary Ann Doyle on November 21, 1841.

9 The Dublin *Morning Register* (December 10, 1841) and the *Tablet* (December 25, 1841).

10 The transcription in the Cork archives is not in Elizabeth Moore's handwriting. It is addressed to "My dearest Sister" and is almost, but not perfectly, identical to the autograph letter sent to Mary Angela Dunne in Charleville. It may be an imperfect copy of that letter, or an exact copy of the autograph sent to someone else.

11 I have not so far succeeded in locating comparable autograph letters in Bermondsey, Birmingham, or Birr, if in fact such letters were sent to the superiors there and are still extant. I am assuming that Frances Warde brought the letter she received in Carlow to the United States. Teresa White of Galway was at Baggot Street a few hours after Catherine's death so she would not have received a letter of this sort from Elizabeth Moore.

Roland Burke Savage quotes a great deal of the letter to Mary Ann Doyle, including the paragraph on the boots, but he omits the opening paragraph and the last fourth of the letter (376–79). The *Documentary Study* contains the letter sent to Mary Ann Doyle in Tullamore, but with several ellipses (1:700–1). It notes that the autograph is in the Tullamore archives; however, it is currently in the Derry archives. Mary Bertrand Degnan occasionally quotes passages from one of Elizabeth's letters, but she does not cite the particular letter she is using nor where she found this "circular letter" as she calls it (341–45). I think she is quoting Carroll's *Life* (461–63) as her source.

12 When Elizabeth Moore wrote these letters, soon after Catherine McAuley's death, she was probably totally unaware of information which came to light much later: namely, that Catherine's instruments of penance were burned as well. However, if she knew this, she would not, under the circumstances, have mentioned it in her letters. See note 11 in the introduction to Mary Vincent Whitty in the preceding chapter.

13 Several recordings of versions of the letter contain ellipses.

The Letter of Mary Elizabeth Moore to Mary Ann Doyle

1 In this letter, and the following one, Elizabeth Moore appears to use dashes to indicate new paragraphs. She does not use capital letters at the beginning of new sentences; I have supplied these, and some marks of punctuation. I have also used "and" for her ampersands. The autograph of this letter is in the archives of the Sisters of Mercy, Derry.

2 The letter reads "distinguished through Life . . . ." Presumably "her" was intended.

3 Frances Ridgeway McAuley was married to Catherine's brother James. The McAuleys had eventually six sons and two older daughters, who are probably the "nieces" who were present: Eleanor, born in 1822, and Emily, born in 1824. Their third daughter was then a baby—Frances Catherine, born in 1840 ("McAuley Genealogy II", in Bolster, *Documentary Study* 2: [269]. Further research is needed to identify fully the many descendants of James and Frances McAuley—Catherine's great great grandnieces and grandnephews—among them the Grimstons of England.

4 The word order here is exactly that in the autograph: "God may bless you."

5 Mary Justina Fleming, who died on December 10, 1841. She was a member of the Baggot Street community. Catherine McAuley had asked Mary Ann Doyle to care for her in Tullamore, hoping that the change of air would improve her health.

6 Michael Blake's November 13, 1841 letter to Mary Elizabeth Moore is recorded at the end of both the Bermondsey Annals biography and the Limerick Manuscript, presented earlier in this volume. A handwritten copy of his letter is in the archives of the Sisters of Mercy, Derry. This may be the copy which Elizabeth Moore sent to Mary Ann Doyle.

The Letter of Mary Elizabeth Moore to Mary Angela Dunne

1 Elizabeth Moore wrote these words in the top right-hand corner of the first page of this letter, evidently after she completed the letter, presumably on Sunday, December 12, 1841—the tenth anniversary of the founding of the Sisters of Mercy.
2 Only one sheet of this autograph letter (containing writing on both sides) is now extant. It is preserved in the archives of the Sisters of Mercy, Rath Luirc (Charleville). This fragment, though it contains no signature, is clearly in Elizabeth Moore's handwriting.
3 Agatha Brennan, a lay sister, died December 27, 1841.
4 Mary Justina Fleming died December 10, 1841. She is undoubtedly the sister to whom Elizabeth refers in her closing note at the beginning of the letter.

NOTES TO CHAPTER 10

An Introduction to Catherine McAuley's Manuscript of the Rule and Constitutions of the Sisters of Mercy

1 Mary Hermenia Muldrey RSM has demonstrated in her *Abounding in Mercy* (56–7, 348–9, and 356–7) that Myles Gaffney, not Dominick Murphy of Cork, is the author of the anonymous biographical sketch of Catherine McAuley—under the title, "*La Regola e le Costituzioni delle Religiose nominate Sorelle della Misericordia. Roma*: 1846"—in the *Dublin Review* 22 (March 1847): 1–25. The title of his article is the title of the approved Italian text of the Rule and Constitutions of the Sisters of Mercy which was confirmed in Rome in 1841.
2 The full title of the document is "*Rules and Constitutions of the Institute of the Religious Sisterhood of the Presentation of the Ever Blessed Virgin Mary*, Established in the City of Cork, for the Charitable Instruction of Poor Girls, Conformably to the Rules of the late Pope, Pius VI of Happy Memory, and to the Subsequent Decree of the Sacred Congregation, Approved of by His Present Holiness, Pius VII, Now Happily Reigning." This document, here referred to as the "Presentation Rule", was prepared in 1793 (some years after the death of Nano Nagle); confirmed in an Apostolical Brief of Pius VII on April 9, 1805; translated from the Italian into English, and approved as a translation "literally conformable to the Italian" by Florence McCarthy, Bishop of Antinoe, in Cork on December 26, 1805; signed by John Thomas Troy, Archbishop of Dublin, on February 21, 1806; and printed in English in 1809 by James Haly, Bookseller and Stationer, Cork. This 1809 edition of the Presentation Rule, the first in English, is the document consulted in this study.
3 Perhaps Mary Austin Carroll is correct in saying that "the Rule and Constitutions of the Institute were not completed till 1834" (*Life* 239), if she means Catherine's original manuscript, but she is not correct in quoting "January 23, 1834" as the date of Dr. Murray's approval (*Life* 242), if she means, as she implies, his approval of a complete fair copy of an entire Rule and Constitutions incorporating all his previous revisions. On the basis of my reading of the early manuscript biographies of Catherine McAuley, I am not confident of an "1834" date for Dr. Murray's approval of any complete and revised fair copy. Moreover, the early manuscripts say that Rev. John Rice offered his services in 1833, not in 1834 as Carroll indicates (*Life* 241). See also Degnan 163.
4 In 1859, when Mary Ann Doyle was in the community founded in Derry in 1848, sisters were sent from Derry to found a community in Dundee, Scotland. Mary Ann may have had in the Derry community, and then given to the Dundee founders, the handwritten copy of the Rule which Daniel Murray had dated "23d January 1837". However, the "Dundee Manuscript", as it is now called, is now preserved in the archives of the Sisters of Mercy, Dublin. I have located two fair copies which Daniel Murray dated "3d May 1835": one which is preserved in the archives of the Sisters of Mercy, Birmingham; and the one used in this study, which is preserved in the archives of the Sisters of Mercy, Bermondsey.

5 The first three autonomous foundations of Sisters of Mercy to go out from Baggot Street went to Tullamore (April 21, 1836), Charleville (October 29, 1836), and Carlow (April 11, 1837). In late August 1837 Catherine wrote to Frances Warde in Carlow: "The Rule is ready for you, but we wait, hoping to get his Grace to affix his approbation" (95). Presumably, handwritten copies of the Rule, with Daniel Murray's dated signature, had already been sent to Tullamore and Charleville, and would be sent later to the other foundations made in Catherine's lifetime, prior to the approved translations of the confirmed Italian Rule. It is possible, given the evident delay in getting copies ready, that the Dundee Manuscript, dated January 23, 1837, is the copy that was sent to Tullamore where Mary Ann Doyle was superior; she went to Kells in 1844, and from Tullamore to Derry in 1848. See note 4 above.

6 This section of the chapter is an expansion of a portion of a lecture entitled " 'Songs Prepared for the Journey': The Reading, Writings, and Prayers of Catherine McAuley", given in Windham, New Hampshire, to the Governing Board of the Federation of the Sisters of Mercy of the Americas on June 24, 1989. On the occasion I distributed a typed transcription of the First Part of Catherine's manuscript, and the notes which accompany that part. I am glad to publish this material now because other writers have wished to use it in their own research.

7 Unless otherwise indicated, when the text of Catherine's manuscript of the Rule and Constitutions is cited, the chapter and article (paragraph) numbers are given in parentheses and are separated by a period—if the reference is to the First Part of the Rule. Thus, for example, (3. 1) indicates chapter 3, article 1, in the First Part. References to the Second Part of the Rule include the roman numeral II in the parentheses. Thus (II.2.1), for example, indicates chapter 2, article 1, in the Second Part. The same method is used in citing the Presentation Rule, where this is necessary, but "PR" is also included in the parentheses. Technically, the First Part of Catherine McAuley's document is the "Rule" and the Second Part is the "Constitutions", but Catherine did not make this distinction explicit, nor did Daniel Murray. In citing Catherine's chapters I follow her numbering and sequence as slightly revised by Daniel Murray, not Clare Moore's.

8 Three minor differences in spelling, capitalization, and punctuation appear in the "23d January 1837" fair copy.

9 The "3d May 1835" fair copy in the Birmingham archives is in cursive writing, but it is not, I believe, Clare Moore's handwriting, nor is it identical to that in the "23d January 1837" fair copy. However, two nagging thoughts hover in the background of these analyses of handwriting: first, Clare Moore's own handwriting may have changed over the years, say, from 1835 to 1844; and, second, she may have used a different style of writing in preparing a fair copy of this importance, from what she used in her hurried letters of 1844–1845. We know that Catherine McAuley wrote of Clare to Frances Warde on November 9, 1840, after receiving a letter from Clare telling of a second sister's death from typhus in Bermondsey: "My poor Sister Mary Clare almost exhausted. You would not know her writing" (250). There remains also the possibility, noted above, that the "3d May 1835" hand-printed copy of the Rule now in Bermondsey is, in fact, Clare Moore's hand-printing.

10 See Catherine McAuley's letter to Bishop John Murphy of Cork in November 1839 (Bolster, ed. 103–4). (Catherine's dating of the autograph of this letter is very difficult to read, but, in view of the content of the letter, I think the date she wrote is the "10th" or "13th". It cannot be November 18, the day on which she sailed to England, because she refers to "Monday next" as the day of departure.)

11 The text of this letter as it appears in Neumann's edition has been corrected by reference to the photocopy (of the autograph) in the archives of the Institute of the Sisters of Mercy of the Americas, Silver Spring, Maryland: the word is "we", not "he", in the last clause quoted.

12 In the two preceding paragraphs, I have relied on the translations of the documents of the

Congregation for the Propagation of the Faith which were prepared by John MacErlean SJ earlier in the present century. Handwritten and typed copies of the relevant Latin documents in the Archives of Propaganda Fide, and in the Dublin Diocesan Archives, as well as MacErlean's handwritten and typed translations are preserved in the archives of the Sisters of Mercy, Dublin. All the quotations I use above are taken from these translations. I wish to express my gratitude for them, and to acknowledge more broadly the debt which the Sisters of Mercy owe to the late John MacErlean SJ for his extensive research on the early days of the Institute.

In her 1991 doctoral dissertation, entitled, "The Institute of the Sisters of Mercy of the Americas: The Canonical Development of the *Proposed Governance Model*" (St. Paul University, Ottawa), Catherine C. Darcy RSM provides detailed references to these Roman documents, and discusses the process of confirmation of the first Rule and Constitutions of the Sisters of Mercy (1840–1841). According to Darcy, in his *votum* Paul Gavino Secchi-Murro "deemed the Sisters of Mercy worthy of supreme approval because of their 'solid piety' and 'perfect charity' ", but he also "noted that while the rule is quite adequate, the constitutions did not give the needed specificity. He listed areas in the constitutions which were in further need of development. These areas included the subjects to be taught in the schools, a norm regarding the entrance of externs into a religious house, and a system of penances" (30). See also Degnan, where parts of Secchi-Murro's long *votum* are presented in translation (278–79), and the two important chapters on the Rule and Constitutions in Bolster, *Documentary Study* 1: 190-294.

13 This letter, of course, made no mention of recommended modifications of the Rule and Constitutions, since the final Italian text was now confirmed and published.

14 A copy of this Italian text (1841) of the Rule and Constitutions of the Sisters of Mercy is in the archives of the Sisters of Mercy, Dublin. The bound copy which was sent to Dr. Thomas Griffiths, Vicar Apostolic of the London District, is now preserved in the archives of the Sisters of Mercy, Bermondsey (London). This copy has Dr. Griffiths' name written in pencil, and only partially erased, on the title page. His copy may have been one of the ten copies originally sent to Archbishop Murray, or it may have been sent directly to Dr. Griffiths from Rome. I have not sought to locate other copies of this text.

15 Clare Moore was now back in Cork as superior, having returned from Bermondsey to Dublin on June 14, 1841. She was to have been only the temporary superior in London, until that foundation was firmly established, but as it subsequently turned out, she was recalled to London on December 10, 1841, to resume the role of superior there.

16 In a letter on October 20, 1992, Mary Hermenia Muldrey alerted me to the existence of this letter to Mary Angela Dunne. The autograph is preserved in the archives of the Sisters of Mercy, Charleville (Rath Luirc).

17 Mary Angela Bolster says that "the original English copy, with Italian and Latin translations," was given to Paul Gavino Secchi-Murro in Rome on February 20, 1840. After "translations", she provides this endnote: "The translation was done by Father Redmond O'Hanlon ODC" (*Documentary Study* 1:284 and 2:53). Since a source for the endnote is not given, I have not been able to ascertain which "translation" is intended. If the endnote refers to a Latin translation, this implies that a Latin translation was prepared in and sent from Dublin, where Redmond O'Hanlon was located, even though the Congregation for the Propagation of the Faith seems to have treated the Italian translation as its official, working text of the Rule.

18 Laurence Forde was an alumnus of the Irish College, Rome, and a frequent aide to Archbishop Paul Cullen. He served as master of ceremonies for the Synod of Thurles (1850); as curate of Blackrock; as senior curate of Saint Andrew's Church; as parish priest of Booterstown; as professor of canon law at the Catholic University in Dublin; and as one of Archbishop Cullen's vicars general. I am indebted to Emmet Larkin's published volumes on the history of the Catholic Church in Ireland during the period, 1850–1870, for this information. Two of Canon Forde's sisters, Mary Agnes (Ellen) Forde and Mary

Evangelist (Mary Jane) Forde, were members of the Dublin community of the Sisters of Mercy. Mary Agnes died in 1864 and Mary Evangelist was superior of the Dublin community from 1870 to 1876 and from 1882 to 1888. See also Mac Suibhne 2:295 and Donnelly 155.

19 An edition of the *Rule and Constitutions of the Religious Sisters of Mercy* was printed by William Stone and published in Birmingham in 1844. Its title page contains the words, "Permissu Superiorum", presumably indicating that the translation was approved by Dr. Thomas Walsh, Vicar Apostolic of the Midland District in England from 1826 to 1849. Copies of this volume are in the archives of the Sisters of Mercy, Birmingham, and the Sisters of Mercy, Athlone, Ireland. The *Rule and Constitutions of the Religious Sisters of Our Blessed Lady of Mercy* was published in London in 1856, seven years prior to the printed publication in Dublin. A copy of the London volume, which was "Printed for the Sisters by T. Jones, Paternoster Row", is in the archives of the Sisters of Mercy, Dublin. This English translation was approved by Thomas Grant, Bishop of Southwark. Although his approval is not mentioned in the volume, Clare Moore's letters to him in 1856, and his to her, as well as the Bermondsey Annals (1: [309]), indicate that his approval of the publication was sought and received. In fact, on September 3, 1856, he wrote to Clare Moore: "I have gone over the Rule with the original Italian, trying to correct it according to the latter [letter?]. If any of your Sisters who know Italian, have time to compare my work with the original I shall be very grateful as I fear I may not have fully succeeded." Both of these editions preceded the 1863 Dublin publication.

20 The page references given in parentheses are to *The Rule and Constitutions of the Religious Called Sisters of Mercy, in Italian and English* (Dublin: James Duffy, 1863). I use this approved English translation for comparison, because it was published in Dublin, and because I will later comment on the problems associated with the fact that it was made directly from the Italian text, apparently without reference to Catherine's English text, even though her text was presumably available in Dublin.

21 The Bermondsey Annals reports on the use of the words, "and the service of the Poor, Sick, and Ignorant": Bishop John Murphy of Cork expressed a wish, on October 25, 1837, that

> an alteration . . . be made in the formula of the Act of Profession; . . . he proved to our Foundress the necessity of declaring the special object of the Institute distinct from others, and therefore the following words were introduced, "and the service of the poor, sick, and ignorant." But this was not generally adopted until after the Confirmation of our Holy Rule in 1841.

However, see Catherine McAuley's letter to Angela Dunne on January 20, 1841 (296–7). See also the monograph of M. Michael [Joanne] Lappetito, "Toward an Apostolic Spirituality: Thesis on the Fourth Vow". Mary Camillus (Teresa) Byrn's Act of Profession, made in Dublin, in the presence of Catherine McAuley on May 4, 1841, does not contain the words, "and the service of the Poor, Sick, and Ignorant." The original parchment is in the Archives of the Institute of the Sisters of Mercy of the Americas, Silver Spring, Maryland. However, those who professed their vows at Baggot Street on August 19, 1841, did use this wording, as is evident in the original Acts of Profession preserved in the archives of the Sisters of Mercy, Birmingham.

22 This quotation has been corrected by reference to the autograph, as noted earlier.

23 I have not been able to examine the papers in the Archives of the Congregation for the Propagation of the Faith in Rome. I have relied on the work of Mary Bertrand Degnan, Mary Angela Bolster, and Catherine Darcy, none of whom has reported that she reviewed correspondence to or from Rome about correcting passages in the confirmed Italian text of the Rule and Constitutions. Mary Angela Bolster provides the following endnote (21) to chapter 10 in the *Documentary Study*:

> Judging from a note written to Sister M. F. Warde, Carlow, on 12 October 1841 . . . , Mother Catherine was aware that inaccuracies in the translation had been discussed. She asked Sister to look into the matter for her and, if necessary, to consult with Archbishop Murray and to forward any corrections to Dr. Kirby, Vice-President of the Irish College, Rome. There is no further

evidence to corroborate that any errors were detected or that any negotiations took place between Sister M. F. Warde and the ecclesiastics mentioned by Mother Catherine. (*Fondi* in APF [Archives of Propaganda Fide] have been examined for the years 1841–1851 in pursuit of this investigation). (*Documentary Study* 2:54).

Angela Bolster is here referring to Catherine's letter to Frances (Neumann 381–82) which has been quoted above. She interprets the letter as asking Frances "to look into the matter", and if necessary to act upon it. I am not able to give it that interpretation.

24 By 1866 Mary Austin Carroll had seen the English translation published in Dublin in 1863; on pages 427–8 of the 1890 edition of her *Life* she has a long footnote about it, in which she discusses the usefulness of printing, as it does, parallel texts in Italian and English.

25 T. J. Walsh's *Nano Nagle and the Presentation Sisters* provides an excellent history of the composition of the Presentation Rule and Constitutions, and a thoughtful analysis of its spirit. See especially 130–39, 161–81.

26 "Augustine, Rule of St.," *New Catholic Encyclopedia,* 1967 ed.

27 The 1863 translation published in Dublin was until the 1950s the basic text for many printings of the Rule used in certain parts of the world where communities of the Sisters of Mercy were founded from communities in Ireland. For example, when a woman entered the Sisters of Mercy in Rochester, New York in 1950—a community founded in 1857 and descended from Carlow through Pittsburgh and Providence, Rhode Island—she received a copy of *The Rule and Constitutions of The Religious, called Sisters of Mercy* (Dublin: Browne & Nolan, n.d.) which, except for canonical changes made by the Sacred Congregation of Religious in 1913 and inserted in 1926, is identical to the 1863 Dublin translation.

NOTES TO EPILOGUE

1 The complete text of this prayer, which Catherine is known to have prayed often, is in William A. Gahan's *Catholic Piety* (263–64). This prayer book was used by the Baggot Street community at least as early as 1828.

2 The complete text of this prayer is in *The Golden Manual: or, Guide to Catholic Devotion* (438–40). Catherine also prayed the "Thirty Days Prayer To the Blessed Virgin Mary, In Honour of the Sacred Passion of our Lord Jesus Christ" which is also in the *Golden Manual* (441–44) and in the Supplement in William A. Gahan's *Catholic Piety* (127–31).

NOTES TO APPENDIX 1

1 Mary Bertrand Degnan calls him "Father Raymund O'Hanlon", using his name in religion. Although Catherine McAuley does not use his first name in her letters, in her Last Will and Testament, dated August 20, 1841, she names him, "the Very Reverend Redmond O'Hanlon". The will and its November 11, 1841 codicil are in the archives of the Sisters of Mercy, Dublin. See also Bolster, *Documentary Study* 1:662–63. While O'Hanlon's name in religion clearly was "Father Raymund of the Virgin of Carmel," as Phelim Monahan OCD has confirmed, I have used his baptismal name, as in Catherine's will, even though I recognize that, for legal purposes, all the names in the will are baptismal names, not names in religion. Burke Savage, Neumann, and Bolster also use "Redmond".

2 Further research in the Dublin diocesan archives and in the Carmelite archives in Dublin may one day resolve this question more precisely.

3 I am indebted to Mary Dominick Foster's list of dates for Redmond O'Hanlon, as presented in Neumann's *Letters* (56); to Degnan's summary of O'Hanlon's life (359); and especially to Rev. Phelim Monahan OCD for his informative conversation and correspondence, and for sharing his extensive research on the "Discalced Carmelites in Ireland". This research, available in typescript, gives detailed information on several Discalced Carmelites in Dublin who were Catherine's friends and supporters: for example, William Whelan, Francis L'Estrange, and Redmond O'Hanlon. See his chapters 5 (pp. 24–33) and 6 (especially pp. 34–35).

4 See Mary Hermenia Muldrey, "Mother McAuley and the Carmelites".

5 I have examined this letter as printed in Neumann's edition against the autograph in the archives of the Sisters of Mercy, Birr, and have made a few corrections. The letter was written, I believe, on Sunday, September 26, 1841.

6 The physicians who came to Baggot Street in Catherine's lifetime were distinguished Irish practitioners. Valuable information about William Stokes, as well as Philip Crampton and Dominic Corrigan, can be found in *The Oxford Companion to Medicine* and in John Talbott's *A Biographical History of Medicine.*

NOTES TO APPENDIX 2

1 This appendix is a revision of material which appears on pages 129–30 of my article, "Catherine McAuley's Spiritual Reading and Prayers." I include it here because of its close relation to the biographical manuscripts presented in this volume.

2 I am grateful to Séamus Enright CSsR (Marianella, Dublin) for his telling me that the author of this book is Ursula Young (1783–1830), of the Ursuline community in Cork, who also published a book with the title, *The Ardent Lover of Jesus; or, The Soul Elevated to Jesus in the Adorable Sacrament* (London: Keating and Brown, 1820). James Duffy, the Dublin publisher of the *Standard Library of Catholic Divinity* (1883), containing *The Soul United to Jesus,* probably also published the edition of *The Soul United to Jesus* which Catherine McAuley read, since the *Standard Library* is a collection of the firm's earlier publications. Clare Augustine Moore's comment about this book suggests that Catherine McAuley valued it and read it often.

3 Mary Austin Carroll lists some publications of the Sisters of Mercy prior to 1881 (*Leaves* 1:240–42). It is possible that Abbé Asselin's book, *Exhortations on the Vows* (written in French), was the source for the transcription, *On the Three Vows* (I have not been able to study this transcription in detail). Mary Vincent Deasy of Cork, formerly of Baggot Street, published a translation of Asselin's book (London: Simms and McIntyre, 1843), entitled, *A Series of Exhortations on the Nature and Duties of the Religious State,* as well as a translation of a book entitled *The Perfect Religious*, which may be that written by Marin. Further work on the transcription, *Spiritual Maxims,* is needed to ascertain whether the *Spiritual Maxims* of John Grou SJ is the source for this transcription. Grou's work was published in French in 1789. Again, I am grateful to Séamus Enright for information about Deasy's translation of Asselin's book.

Works Cited

PRINCIPAL MANUSCRIPTS

Doyle, Mary Ann, RSM, "Letters of Mary Ann Doyle to Mary Clare Augustine Moore, Dublin." 1844. Three autograph letters. Archives, Sisters of Mercy, Baggot Street, Dublin, Ireland.

"The Derry Large Manuscript." Archives, Sisters of Mercy, Thornhill, Culmore Road, Derry, Northern Ireland.

Harnett, Mary Vincent, RSM, "The Limerick Manuscript." Archives, Sisters of Mercy, St. Mary's Convent, Bishop Street, Limerick, Ireland.

McAuley, Catherine. "Rule and Constitutions of the Religious Sisters of Mercy." Autograph manuscript, with Archbishop Daniel Murray's penciled revisions. Archives, Sisters of Mercy, Baggot Street, Dublin, Ireland.

— "Rule and Constitutions of the Religious Sisters of Mercy." Fair copy of Catherine McAuley's original manuscript, with Archbishop Daniel Murray's revisions incorporated. [Compiled by Mary Clare Moore]. Approved by Archbishop Murray, and dated May 3, 1835. Two manuscript copies: Archives, Sisters of Mercy, Parker's Row, Bermondsey, London, England; and Archives, Sisters of Mercy, Hunter's Road, Handsworth, Birmingham, England.

— "Rule and Constitutions of the Religious Sisters of Mercy." [The Dundee Manuscript]. Fair copy of Catherine McAuley's original manuscript, with Archbishop Daniel Murray's revisions incorporated. [Compiled by Mary Clare Moore]. Approved by Archbishop Murray, and dated January 23, 1837. Archives, Sisters of Mercy, Baggot Street, Dublin, Ireland.

Moore, Mary Clare, RSM, "Letters of Mary Clare Moore to Mary Clare Augustine Moore, Dublin." 1844–1845. Five autograph letters. Archives, Sisters of Mercy, Baggot Street, Dublin, Ireland.

Moore, Mary Clare Augustine, RSM, "A Memoir of the Foundress of the Sisters of Mercy in Ireland." [The Dublin Manuscript]. Autograph manuscript. Archives, Sisters of Mercy, Baggot Street, Dublin, Ireland.

Moore, Mary Elizabeth, RSM, "Letter of Mary Elizabeth Moore to Mary Angela Dunne, Charleville." December 10, 1841. Autograph fragment. Archives, Sisters of Mercy, Rath Luirc (Charleville), Ireland.

— "Letter of Mary Elizabeth Moore to Mary Ann Doyle, Tullamore." November 21, 1841. Autograph letter. Archives, Sisters of Mercy, Thornhill, Culmore Road, Derry, Northern Ireland.

Sisters of Mercy, Bermondsey. "Annals of the Convent of Our Lady of Mercy, Bermondsey." Archives, Sisters of Mercy, Parker's Row, Bermondsey, London, England.

Sisters of Mercy, Carlow. "Annals of Saint Leo's Convent of Mercy, Carlow." Archives, Saint Leo's Convent of Mercy, Carlow, Ireland.

Sisters of Mercy, Tullamore. "Annals of the Sisters of Mercy, St. Joseph's Convent, Tullamore." Archives, Sisters of Mercy, Tullamore, Ireland.

Whitty, Mary Vincent, RSM, "Letters of Mary Vincent Whitty to Mary Cecilia Marmion, Birmingham." November 7–November 16, 1841. Five autograph letters. Archives, Sisters of Mercy, Brisbane Congregation, Simpson's Road, Bardon, Queensland, Australia.

PUBLISHED WORKS BY CATHERINE McAULEY

McAuley, Catherine. *The Correspondence of Catherine McAuley, 1827–1841.* Ed. Mary Angela Bolster, RSM. Cork: Congregation of the Sisters of Mercy, Dioceses of Cork and Ross, 1989. Contains the "Spirit of the Institute" essay and "Personal Act of Consecration".

— *The Letters of Catherine McAuley, 1827–1841.* Ed. Mary Ignatia Neumann, RSM. Baltimore: Helicon, 1969. Contains the "Spirit of the Institute" essay and "Personal Act of Consecration". Excerpts from Catherine McAuley's letters quoted in this volume are generally from this edition, unless otherwise noted, and usually only page numbers are given in parentheses.

— *A Little Book of Practical Sayings, Advices and Prayers of our Revered Foundress Mother Mary Catharine* [*sic*] *McAuley.* Ed. [Mary Clare Moore, RSM]. London: Burns, Oates and Co., 1868.

— *Retreat Instructions of Mother Mary Catherine McAuley.* Comp. Mary Teresa Purcell, RSM. Ed. [Mary Bertrand Degnan, RSM]. Westminster, Maryland: Newman Press, 1952.

PUBLICATIONS OF THE RULE AND CONSTITUTIONS

La Regola e Le Costituzioni delle Religiose nominate Sorelle della Misericordia. [Rome]: [S. Congregationis Generalis de Propaganda Fide], [1841]. Copies in Archives, Sisters of Mercy, Baggot Street, Dublin, and Archives, Sisters of Mercy, Parker's Row, Bermondsey, London.

Rule and Constitutions of the Religious Sisters of Mercy. Birmingham, England: William Stone, 1844. Copies in Archives, Sisters of Mercy, Hunter's Road, Handsworth, Birmingham, England, and Archives, Sisters of Mercy, Athlone, Ireland.

Rule and Constitutions of the Religious Sisters of Our Blessed Lady of Mercy. London: Printed for the Sisters by T. Jones, 1856. Copy in Archives, Sisters of Mercy, Baggot Street, Dublin.

The Rule and Constitutions of the Religious called Sisters of Mercy. In Italian and English. [Afterword] by L[aurence] Can[on] Forde. Dublin: James Duffy, 1863. Copy in Archives, Sisters of Mercy, Baggot Street, Dublin.

THE PRESENTATION RULES AND CONSTITUTIONS

Rules and Constitutions of the Institute of the Religious Sisterhood of the Presentation of the Ever Blessed Virgin Mary . . . for the Charitable Instruction of Poor Girls . . . . Cork: James Haly, 1809.

OTHER WORKS

Aikenhead, Mary. *Letters of Mary Aikenhead.* Dublin: M. H. Gill and Son, 1914.

Augustine, Saint. *Confessions.* Trans. Vernon J. Bourke. The Fathers of the Church. Vol. 21. New York: Fathers of the Church, Inc., 1953.

— *The Rule of Saint Augustine.* Trans. Raymond Canning OSA. Introd. and commentary. Tarsicius J. Van Bavel OSA. London: Darton, Longman and Todd, 1984.

Bolster, Evelyn [Mary Angela, RSM]. *The Sisters of Mercy in the Crimean War.* Cork: Mercier Press, 1964.

Bolster, Mary Angela, RSM. *Catherine McAuley: Venerable for Mercy.* Dublin: Dominican Publications, 1990.

— *Catherine McAuley: In Her Own Words.* Dublin: Dublin Diocesan Office for Causes, 1978.

[Bolster, Mary Angela, RSM]. *Documentary Study for the Canonization Process of the Servant of God Catherine McAuley, Founder of the Congregation of Sisters of Mercy, 1778–1841: Positio Super Virtutibus.* 2 vols. Rome: Sacred Congregation for the Causes of Saints (Prot. N. 1296), 1985.

Bourke, Mary Carmel, RSM. A *Woman Sings of Mercy.* Sydney: E. J. Dwyer, 1987.

Burke Savage, Roland, SJ. *Catherine McAuley: The First Sister of Mercy.* Dublin: M. H. Gill and Son, 1949.

Byrne, Michael. *Tullamore Catholic Parish: A Historical Survey.* Tullamore: Tullamore Parish Committee, 1987.

[Carroll, Mary Austin, RSM]. *Leaves from the Annals of the Sisters of Mercy.* 4 vols. Vol. 1. Ireland. New York: Catholic Publication Society, 1881; Vol. 2. England, Crimea, Scotland, Australia, and New Zealand. New York: Catholic Publication Society, 1883; Vol. 3. Newfoundland and the United States. New York: Catholic Publication Society, 1889; Vol. 4. South America, Central America, and the United States. New York: P. O'Shea, 1895.

— *Life of Catherine McAuley.* 1866. New York: D. & J. Sadlier, 1890.

[Coleridge, Henry J., SJ]. "The First Sister of Mercy." *The Month* 4 (February 1866): 111–127.

Congar, Yves M.-J., OP. *Tradition and Traditions.* Trans. Michael Naseby and Thomas Rainborough. New York: Macmillan, 1967.

Congregatio de Causis Sanctorum. "*Decretum Dublinen. Canonizationis Servae Dei Catharinae McAuley Fundatricis Congregationis Sororum a Misericordia (1778–1841).*" [Rome]: Congregatio de Causis Sanctorum, April 9, 1990.

Corish, Patrick J. *The Irish Catholic Experience: A Historical Survey.* Dublin: Gill and Macmillan, 1985.

Courtney, Marie Therese, RSM. " 'The Careful Instruction of Women.' " *Sisters of Mercy in Limerick.* Limerick: n.p., 1988. 14–22. This article was first published in the *Limerick Leader* (September 10, 1988).

— "Fearless Mother Elizabeth Moore." *Sisters of Mercy in Limerick.* Limerick: n.p., 1988. 31–37. This article was first published in the *Limerick Leader* (October 15, 1988).

— "Mission of Mercy to the Poor of Limerick." *Sisters of Mercy in Limerick.* Limerick: n.p., 1988. 9–12. This article was first published in the *Limerick Leader* (September 3, 1988).

Crites, Stephen. "The Narrative Quality of Experience." *Journal of the American Academy of Religion* 10 (1971): 291–311.

Darcy, Catherine C., RSM. "The Institute of the Sisters of Mercy of the Americas: The Canonical Development of the *Proposed Governance Model.*" Diss. Saint Paul University, 1991.

Dean, Joseph Joy, ed. *Devotions to the Sacred Heart of Jesus: Exercises for the Holy Sacrifice of the Mass, Confession and Communion; Visits to the Blessed Sacrament . . . .* Trans. from the French. Dublin: Chambers and Hallagan, 1820.

Degnan, Mary Bertrand, RSM. *Mercy Unto Thousands: Life of Mother Mary Catherine McAuley, Foundress of the Sisters of Mercy.* Westminster, Maryland: Newman Press, 1957.

Donnelly, N[icholas]. "A Short History of Some Dublin Parishes" and "Short Histories of Dublin Parishes." Vol. 2, Parts 7 and 8, of *History of Dublin Parishes.* Dublin: Catholic Truth Society of Ireland, [1909, 1910]. 3 vols. 1905–1913.

Dunn, James D. G. *Unity and Diversity in the New Testament.* London: SCM Press, 1977.

Edel, Leon. *Writing Lives: Principia Biographica.* 1959. New York and London: W. W. Norton, 1984.

Fitzgerald, Thomas W. H. *Ireland and Her People: A Library of Irish Biography.* Vols. I and 2. Second edition. Chicago: Fitzgerald Book Co., 1909. "Daniel O'Connell," 1:85–96; "William Stokes," 1:268–70; "Philip Crampton," 1:275–76; "Theobald Mathew," 2:1–7. 5 vols. 1909–191 1.

[Gaffney, Myles]. "*La Regola e le Costituzioni delle Religiose nominate Sorelle della Misericordia.*" *The Dublin Review* 22 (March 1847): 1–25.

Gahan, William A., OSA. *The Christian's Guide to Heaven: Or, A Complete Manual of Catholic Piety.* Fourteenth edition, including Supplement. Dublin: Reynolds, 1804.

Garety, Mary Catherine, RSM. *Rev. Mother M. Xavier Warde.* Boston: Marlier and Co., 1902.

Gavigan, J. J. "Augustine, Rule of St." *New Catholic Encyclopedia.* 1967 ed. 1059–60.

The Golden Manual: Or, Guide to Catholic Devotion, Public and Private. London: Burns and Lambert, [1850].

[Harnett, Mary Vincent, RSM]. A *Catechism of Scripture History Compiled by The Sisters of Mercy, for the Use of the Children Attending Their Schools.* Revised by Rev. Dr. [Edmund] O'Reilly. London: Charles Dolman, 1852.

— *The Life of Rev. Mother Catherine McAuley, Foundress of the Order of Mercy.* Ed. Richard Baptist O'Brien. Dublin: John Fowler, 1864.

Healy, Kathleen, RSM. *Frances Warde: American Founder of the Sisters of Mercy.* New York: Seabury Press, 1973.

Lappetito, M. Michael [Joanne], RSM. "Our Life Together in Mercy: Toward an

Apostolic Spirituality." [Rochester, New York]: The Federation of the Sisters of Mercy of the Americas, 1980.

Larkin, Emmet. *The Consolidation of the Roman Catholic Church in Ireland, 1860–1870.* Chapel Hill and London: University of North Carolina Press, 1987.

— *The Making of the Roman Catholic Church in Ireland, 1850-1860.* Chapel Hill: University of North Carolina Press, 1980.

"The Late Mother Vincent." *Brisbane Australian.* 19 March 1892.

Lawless, George OSA. *Augustine of Hippo and his Monastic Rule.* Oxford: Clarendon Press, 1987.

Mac Suibhne, Peader. *Paul Cullen and his Contemporaries, with their Letters.* 3 vols. Naas, Ireland: Leinster Leader, 1961–1965.

Meagher, Mary de Chantal. "Memoir on Mother Mary Vincent Harnett". Autograph manuscript. Archives, Sisters of Mercy, St Mary's Convent, Bishop Street, Limerick, Ireland.

Moltmann, Jürgen. *The Church in the Power of the Spirit.* Trans. Margaret Kohl. London: SCM Press, 1977.

Monahan, Phelim, OCD. "Discalced Carmelites in Ireland." Unpublished typescript. Discalced Carmelites, 55 Marlborough Road, Dublin.

Muldrey, Mary Hermenia, RSM. *Abounding in Mercy: Mother Austin Carroll.* New Orleans: Habersham, 1988.

— "Mother McAuley and the Carmelites." *Carmel* (November-December 1984): 21–24.

Murphy, Dominick. *Sketches of Irish Nunneries.* Dublin: James Duffy, 1865.

Murphy, Ignatius. *The Diocese of Killaloe: 1800-1850.* Vol. 2 of *The Diocese of Killaloe.* Dublin: Four Courts Press, 1992. 3 vols. 1991, 1992, 1995.

"A National Loss—Death of Mrs. Catherine M'Auley, Foundress of the Order of the Sisters of Mercy in Ireland." *Morning Register* [Dublin]. 10 December 1841: 3–4.

"A National Loss—Death of Mrs. Catherine M'Auley, Foundress of the Order of the Sisters of Mercy in Ireland." *Tablet.* 25 December 1841: 829.

Nightingale, Florence. *Florence Nightingale's Letters to Revd. Mother Clare Moore, 1855–1874.* London: Institute of Our Lady of Mercy, Bermondsey, n.d.

O'Brien, Katherine, RSM. "Letters written 140 years ago by Mother Mary Vincent Whitty." Unpublished typescript. Archives of the Sisters of Mercy, Brisbane Congregation, Simpson's Road, Bardon, Queensland, Australia.

O'Brien, Richard Baptist. *An Eight-Day Retreat, Intended Principally for The Sisters of Mercy and The Active Orders.* Second edition. Revised. Dublin: James Duffy, [1868].

O'Connor, M. Loreto, RSM. "Sisters of Mercy and the Ardagh Chalice." *Sisters of Mercy in Limerick.* Limerick: n.p., 1988. 27–30. This article was first published in the *Limerick Leader* (1 October 1988).

O'Donoghue, Mary Xaverius [Frances], RSM. *Mother Vincent Whitty.* Carlton, Victoria, Australia: Melbourne University Press, 1972.

O'Hara, Mary Nathy, RSM. *Catherine McAuley, Mercy Foundress.* Dublin:Veritas, 1979.

Regan, Joanna, RSM, and Isabelle Keiss, RSM. *Tender Courage.* Chicago: Franciscan Herald Press, 1988.

Rodriguez, Alonsus, SJ. The *Practice of Christian and Religious Perfection.* Trans. from the French copy of M. l'Abbé Regnier des Marais. 3 vols. Kilkenny: John Reynolds, 1806.

Sheldrake, Philip, SJ. *Spirituality and History.* New York, Crossroad: 1992.

Southern, R. S. *Western Society and the Church in the Middle Ages.* 1970. Middlesex, England: Penguin Books, 1978.

Sullivan, Mary C., RSM. "Catherine McAuley's Spiritual Reading and Prayers." *Irish Theological Quarterly* 57 (1991): 124–46.

— "Catherine McAuley's Theological and Literary Debt to Alonso Rodriguez: The 'Spirit of the Institute' Parallels." *Recusant History* 20 (May 1990): 81–105.

Talbott, John H. A *Biographical History of Medicine.* New York and London: Grune and Stratton, 1970. "Abraham Colles (1773–1843)", 337–339; "Sir Dominic John Corrigan (1802–1880)", 1058–1060; "William Stokes (1804–1878)", 1060–1063.

Teresa of Avila. *The Letters of St. Teresa of Jesus.* 1951. Trans. E. Allison Peers. 2 vols. London: Sheed and Ward, 1980.

Walsh, T. J. *Nano Nagle and the Presentation Sisters.* Dublin: M. H. Gill and Son, 1959.

Walton, John, Paul B. Beeson, and Ronald Bodley Scott, eds. *The Oxford Companion to Medicine.* 2 vols. Oxford and New York: Oxford University Press, 1986.

Index